Walt Disney's

Donald Duck

by Carl Barks

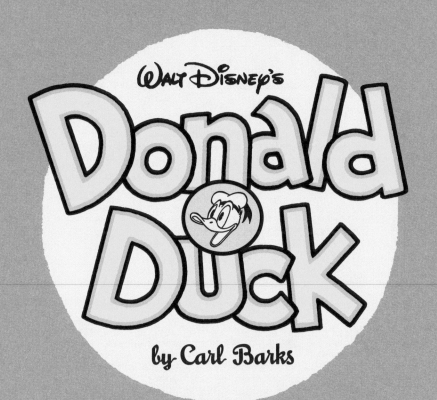

Editor: GARY GROTH
Associate Editor: J. MICHAEL CATRON
Cover Designer: JACOB COVEY
Layout Designer: TONY ONG
Colorist: RICH TOMMASO
Production: PAUL BARESH and PRESTON WHITE
Associate Publisher: ERIC REYNOLDS
Publishers: GARY GROTH and KIM THOMPSON

Fantagraphics Books, Inc.
7563 Lake City Way NE
Seattle WA 98115

To receive a free catalogue of more books like this, as well as an amazing variety of
cutting-edge graphic novels, classic comic book and newspaper strip collections, eclectic
prose novels, uniquely insightful cultural criticism, and other fine works of artistry, call
(800) 657-1100 or visit Fantagraphics.com. Follow us on Twitter at @fantagraphics and on
Facebook at facebook.com/fantagraphics.

Special thanks to: Jason T. Miles, Thomas Jensen, Kim Thompson, and Susan Daigle-Leach.

ISBN 978-1-60699-653-9

Printed in Singapore

Also available in this series:
Walt Disney's Donald Duck: *"Lost In The Andes"* (Vol. 7)
Walt Disney's Donald Duck: *"A Christmas For Shacktown"* (Vol. 11)
Walt Disney's Uncle Scrooge: *"Only A Poor Old Man"* (Vol. 12)

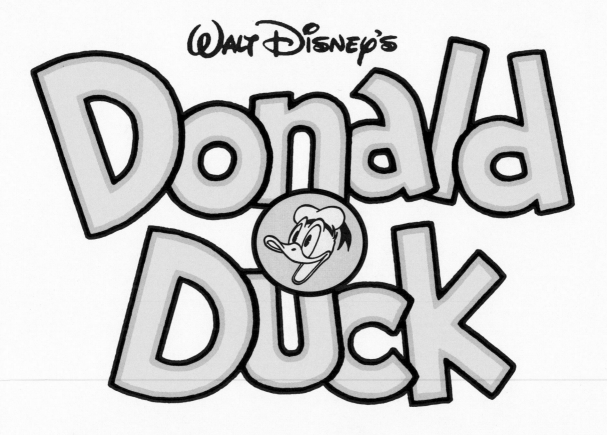

Walt Disney's

Donald Duck

"The Old Castle's Secret"

by Carl Barks

FANTAGRAPHICS BOOKS

Contents

The Old Castle's Secret 1

Bird Watching 33

Horseshoe Luck 34

Wintertime Wager 35

Watching the Watchman 45

Wired 55

Going Ape 65

Darkest Africa 75

Bean Taken 97

Sorry to Be Safe 98

Spoil the Rod 99

Rocket Race to the Moon 109

Donald of the Coast Patrol 119

Gladstone Returns 129

Sheriff of Bullet Valley 139

Best Laid Plans 171

The Genuine Article 172

Links Hijinks 173

Pearls of Wisdom 183

Foxy Relations 193

Story Notes 203

Carl Barks: Life Among the Ducks by Donald Ault 223

Biographies 225

Where Did These Stories First Appear? 226

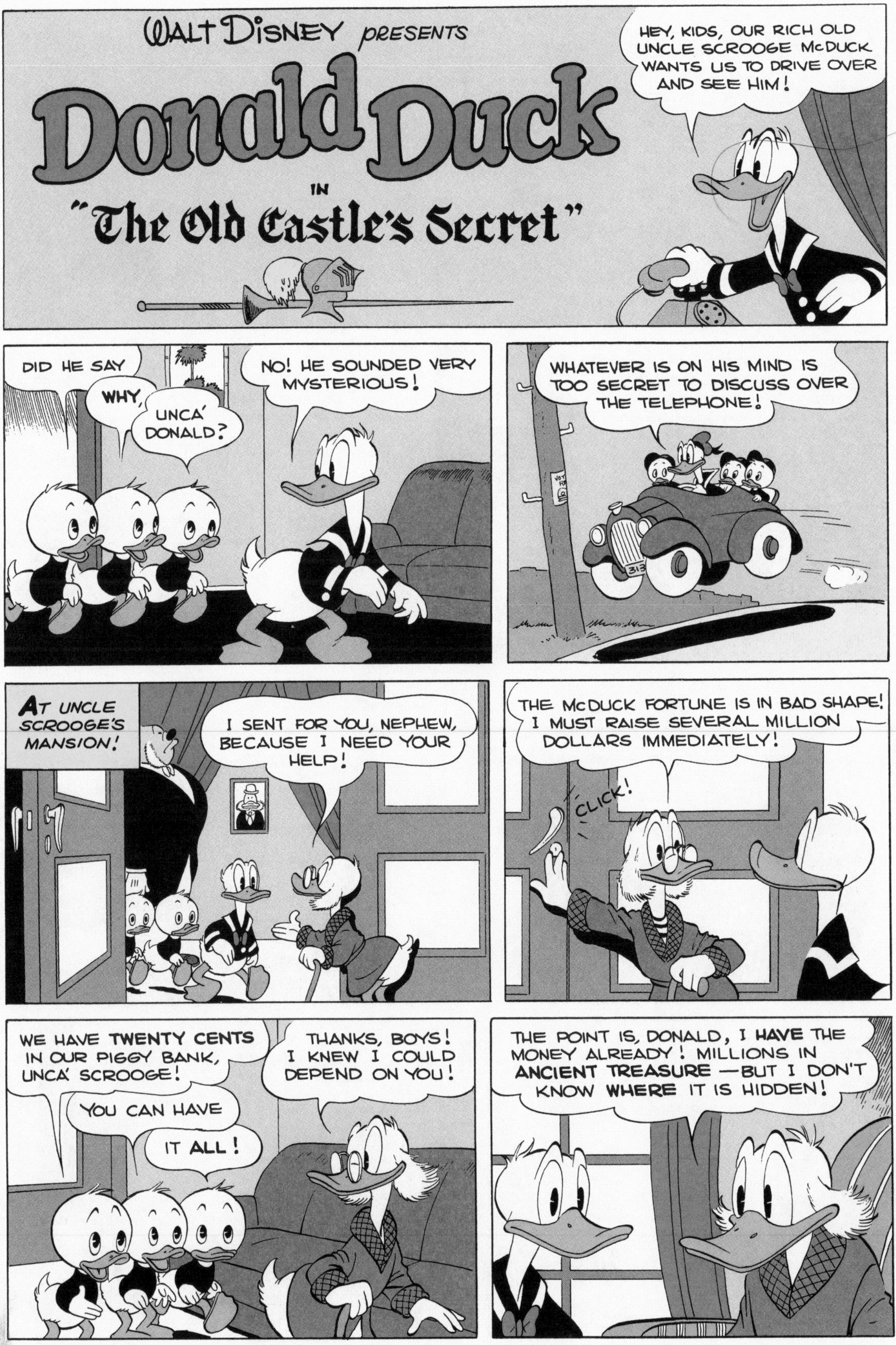
WALT DISNEY PRESENTS
Donald Duck
IN
"The Old Castle's Secret"
HEY, KIDS, OUR RICH OLD UNCLE SCROOGE McDUCK WANTS US TO DRIVE OVER AND SEE HIM!
DID HE SAY
WHY,
UNCA' DONALD?
NO! HE SOUNDED VERY MYSTERIOUS!
WHATEVER IS ON HIS MIND IS TOO SECRET TO DISCUSS OVER THE TELEPHONE!
313
AT UNCLE SCROOGE'S MANSION!
I SENT FOR YOU, NEPHEW, BECAUSE I NEED YOUR HELP!
THE McDUCK FORTUNE IS IN BAD SHAPE! I MUST RAISE SEVERAL MILLION DOLLARS IMMEDIATELY!
CLICK!
WE HAVE TWENTY CENTS IN OUR PIGGY BANK, UNCA' SCROOGE!
YOU CAN HAVE
IT ALL!
THANKS, BOYS! I KNEW I COULD DEPEND ON YOU!
THE POINT IS, DONALD, I HAVE THE MONEY ALREADY! MILLIONS IN ANCIENT TREASURE—BUT I DON'T KNOW WHERE IT IS HIDDEN!

ANCIENT TREASURE?

IS IT ON A DESERT ISLAND?

PIRATE GOLD?

SHH! WE MUST SPEAK IN LOW VOICES! NO ONE KNOWS OF THE TREASURE BUT US FIVE! THE SECRET HAS BEEN KEPT IN MY FAMILY FOR **NINE HUNDRED YEARS**!

THE TREASURE IS IN SCOTLAND! I ONLY KNOW IT IS **SOMEWHERE** IN THE HUGE OLD CASTLE OF DISMAL DOWNS, WHICH I OWN, AS THE LAST OF THE CLAN McDUCK!

YOU LADS COME WITH ME TO SCOTLAND, AND I'M SURE WE CAN FIND THE HOARD!

IN AN OLD GLOOMY CASTLE!

FULL OF **GHOSTS**, MAYBE!

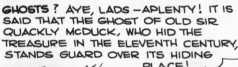

GHOSTS? AYE, LADS —APLENTY! IT IS SAID THAT THE GHOST OF OLD SIR QUACKLY McDUCK, WHO HID THE TREASURE IN THE ELEVENTH CENTURY, STANDS GUARD OVER ITS HIDING PLACE!

THEN IT SHOULD BE EASY TO FIND THE GOLD! FIND THE GHOST, AND **THERE** IT IS!

AYE! BUT TO **FIND** THE GHOST! HE IS INVISIBLE!

GENERATIONS OF McDUCKS HAVE SEARCHED FOR THE TREASURE! BUT I BELIEVE THAT I, THE LAST OF THE CLAN, HAVE THE MEANS OF FINDING IT!

HOW?

WITH THIS **X-RAY** MACHINE! THE OTHERS MERELY TAPPED THE WALLS —I WILL LOOK THROUGH THE WALLS!

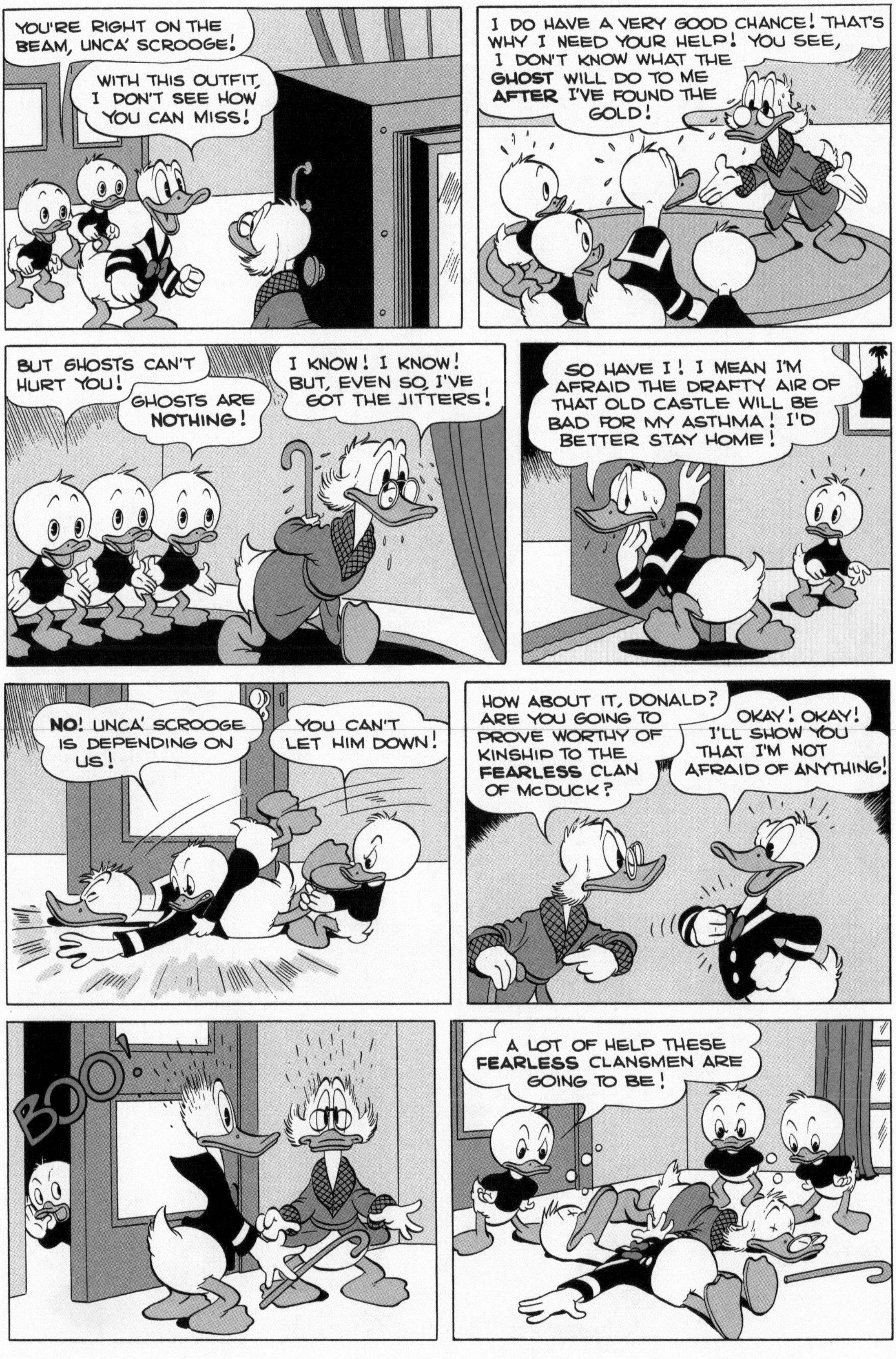
YOU'RE RIGHT ON THE BEAM, UNCA' SCROOGE!
WITH THIS OUTFIT, I DON'T SEE HOW YOU CAN MISS!
I DO HAVE A VERY GOOD CHANCE! THAT'S WHY I NEED YOUR HELP! YOU SEE, I DON'T KNOW WHAT THE GHOST WILL DO TO ME AFTER I'VE FOUND THE GOLD!
BUT GHOSTS CAN'T HURT YOU!
GHOSTS ARE NOTHING!
I KNOW! I KNOW! BUT, EVEN SO, I'VE GOT THE JITTERS!
SO HAVE I! I MEAN I'M AFRAID THE DRAFTY AIR OF THAT OLD CASTLE WILL BE BAD FOR MY ASTHMA! I'D BETTER STAY HOME!
NO! UNCA' SCROOGE IS DEPENDING ON US!
YOU CAN'T LET HIM DOWN!
HOW ABOUT IT, DONALD? ARE YOU GOING TO PROVE WORTHY OF KINSHIP TO THE FEARLESS CLAN OF McDUCK?
OKAY! OKAY! I'LL SHOW YOU THAT I'M NOT AFRAID OF ANYTHING!
BOO!
A LOT OF HELP THESE FEARLESS CLANSMEN ARE GOING TO BE!

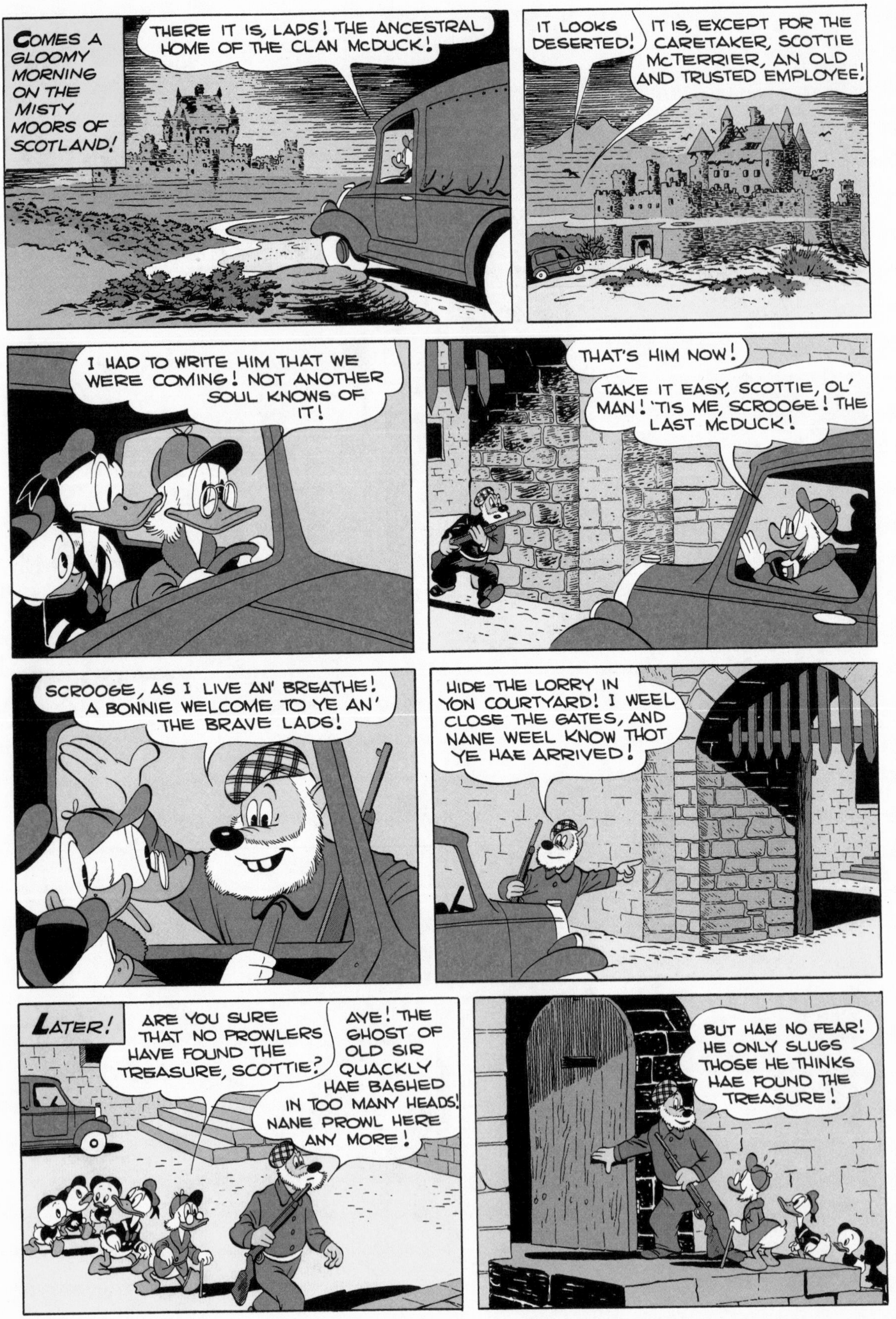
COMES A GLOOMY MORNING ON THE MISTY MOORS OF SCOTLAND!
THERE IT IS, LADS! THE ANCESTRAL HOME OF THE CLAN McDUCK!
IT LOOKS DESERTED!
IT IS, EXCEPT FOR THE CARETAKER, SCOTTIE McTERRIER, AN OLD AND TRUSTED EMPLOYEE!
I HAD TO WRITE HIM THAT WE WERE COMING! NOT ANOTHER SOUL KNOWS OF IT!
THAT'S HIM NOW!
TAKE IT EASY, SCOTTIE, OL' MAN! 'TIS ME, SCROOGE! THE LAST McDUCK!
SCROOGE, AS I LIVE AN' BREATHE! A BONNIE WELCOME TO YE AN' THE BRAVE LADS!
HIDE THE LORRY IN YON COURTYARD! I WEEL CLOSE THE GATES, AND NANE WEEL KNOW THOT YE HAE ARRIVED!
LATER!
ARE YOU SURE THAT NO PROWLERS HAVE FOUND THE TREASURE, SCOTTIE?
AYE! THE GHOST OF OLD SIR QUACKLY HAE BASHED IN TOO MANY HEADS! NANE PROWL HERE ANY MORE!
BUT HAE NO FEAR! HE ONLY SLUGS THOSE HE THINKS HAE FOUND THE TREASURE!

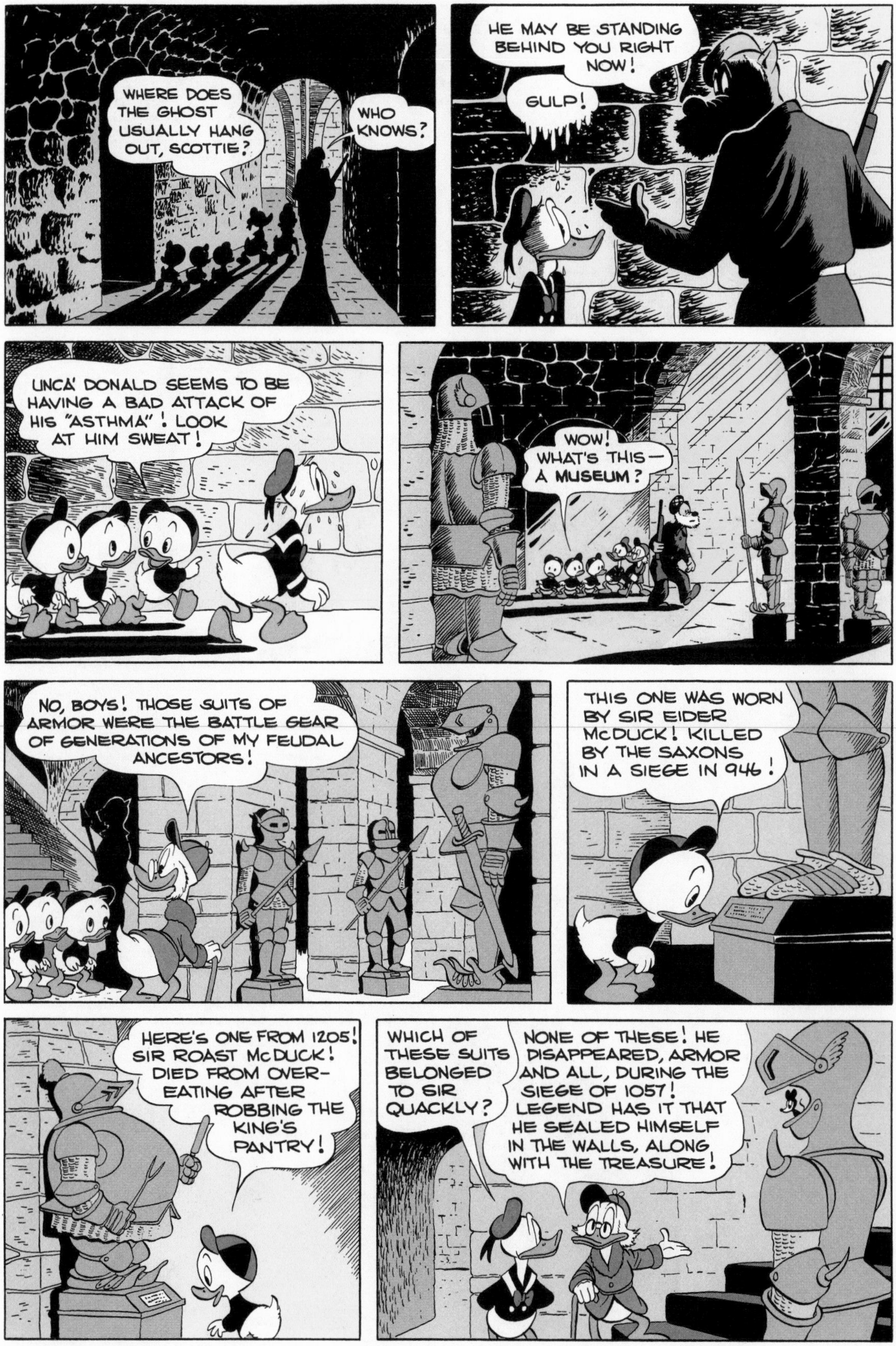
WHERE DOES THE GHOST USUALLY HANG OUT, SCOTTIE?
WHO KNOWS?
HE MAY BE STANDING BEHIND YOU RIGHT NOW!
GULP!
UNCA' DONALD SEEMS TO BE HAVING A BAD ATTACK OF HIS "ASTHMA"! LOOK AT HIM SWEAT!
WOW! WHAT'S THIS— A MUSEUM?
NO, BOYS! THOSE SUITS OF ARMOR WERE THE BATTLE GEAR OF GENERATIONS OF MY FEUDAL ANCESTORS!
THIS ONE WAS WORN BY SIR EIDER McDUCK! KILLED BY THE SAXONS IN A SIEGE IN 946!
HERE'S ONE FROM 1205! SIR ROAST McDUCK! DIED FROM OVER-EATING AFTER ROBBING THE KING'S PANTRY!
WHICH OF THESE SUITS BELONGED TO SIR QUACKLY?
NONE OF THESE! HE DISAPPEARED, ARMOR AND ALL, DURING THE SIEGE OF 1057! LEGEND HAS IT THAT HE SEALED HIMSELF IN THE WALLS, ALONG WITH THE TREASURE!

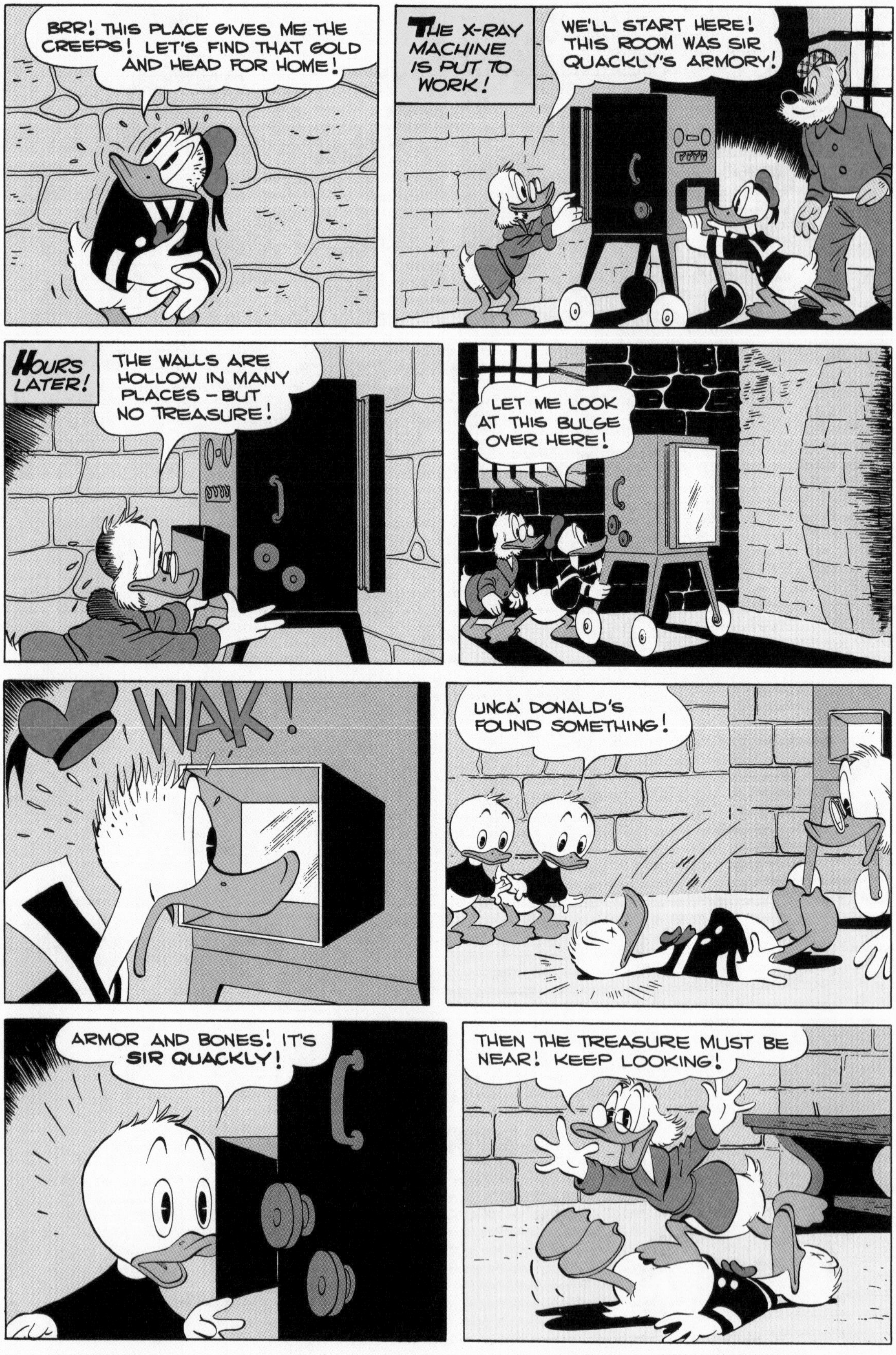

BRR! THIS PLACE GIVES ME THE CREEPS! LET'S FIND THAT GOLD AND HEAD FOR HOME!
THE X-RAY MACHINE IS PUT TO WORK!
WE'LL START HERE! THIS ROOM WAS SIR QUACKLY'S ARMORY!
HOURS LATER!
THE WALLS ARE HOLLOW IN MANY PLACES – BUT NO TREASURE!
LET ME LOOK AT THIS BULGE OVER HERE!
WAK!
UNCA' DONALD'S FOUND SOMETHING!
ARMOR AND BONES! IT'S SIR QUACKLY!
THEN THE TREASURE MUST BE NEAR! KEEP LOOKING!

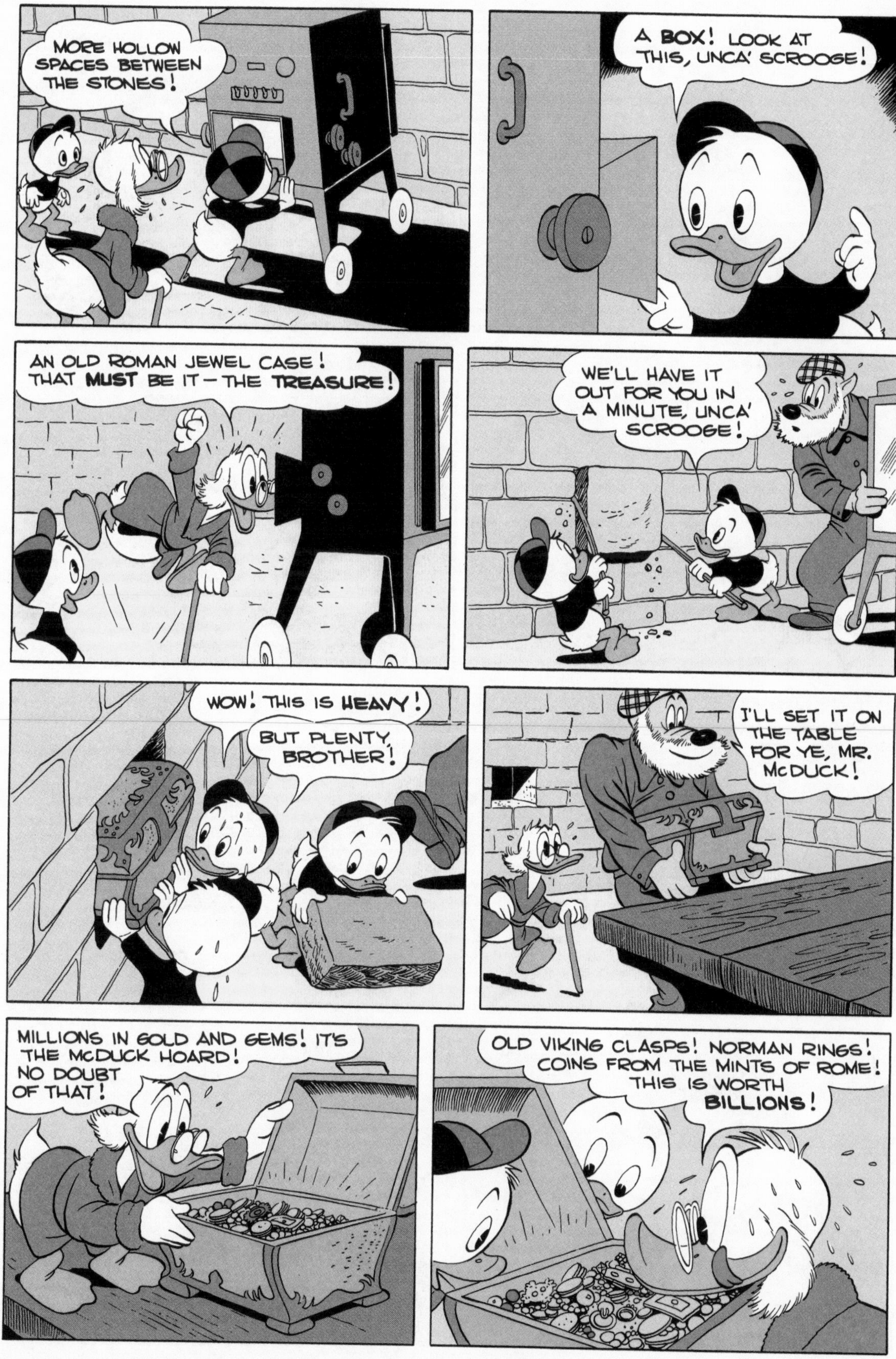
MORE HOLLOW SPACES BETWEEN THE STONES!
A BOX! LOOK AT THIS, UNCA' SCROOGE!
AN OLD ROMAN JEWEL CASE! THAT MUST BE IT—THE TREASURE!
WE'LL HAVE IT OUT FOR YOU IN A MINUTE, UNCA' SCROOGE!
WOW! THIS IS HEAVY!
BUT PLENTY, BROTHER!
I'LL SET IT ON THE TABLE FOR YE, MR. McDUCK!
MILLIONS IN GOLD AND GEMS! IT'S THE McDUCK HOARD! NO DOUBT OF THAT!
OLD VIKING CLASPS! NORMAN RINGS! COINS FROM THE MINTS OF ROME! THIS IS WORTH BILLIONS!

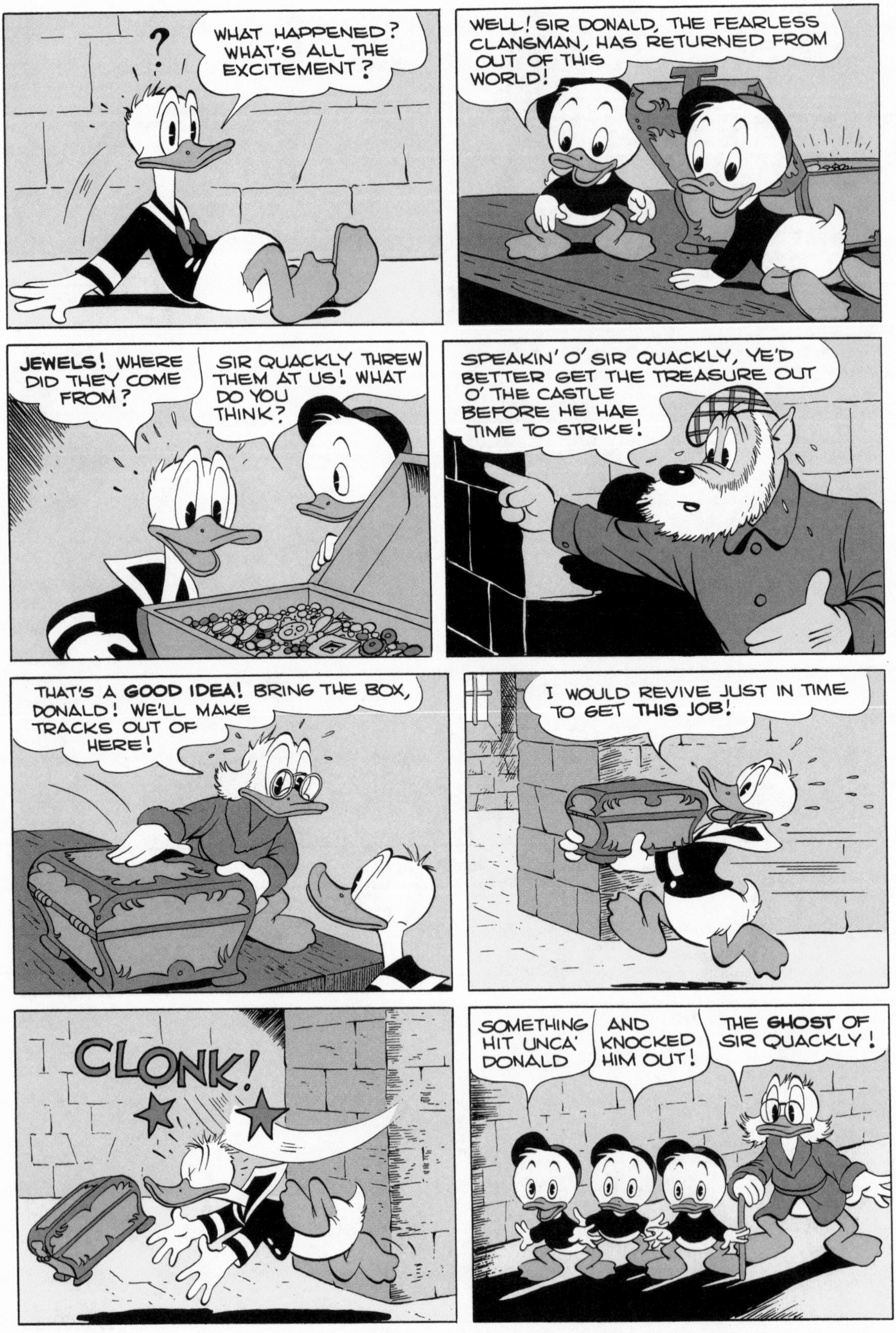
?
WHAT HAPPENED? WHAT'S ALL THE EXCITEMENT?
WELL! SIR DONALD, THE FEARLESS CLANSMAN, HAS RETURNED FROM OUT OF THIS WORLD!
JEWELS! WHERE DID THEY COME FROM?
SIR QUACKLY THREW THEM AT US! WHAT DO YOU THINK?
SPEAKIN' O' SIR QUACKLY, YE'D BETTER GET THE TREASURE OUT O' THE CASTLE BEFORE HE HAE TIME TO STRIKE!
THAT'S A GOOD IDEA! BRING THE BOX, DONALD! WE'LL MAKE TRACKS OUT OF HERE!
I WOULD REVIVE JUST IN TIME TO GET THIS JOB!
CLONK!
SOMETHING HIT UNCA' DONALD
AND KNOCKED HIM OUT!
THE GHOST OF SIR QUACKLY!

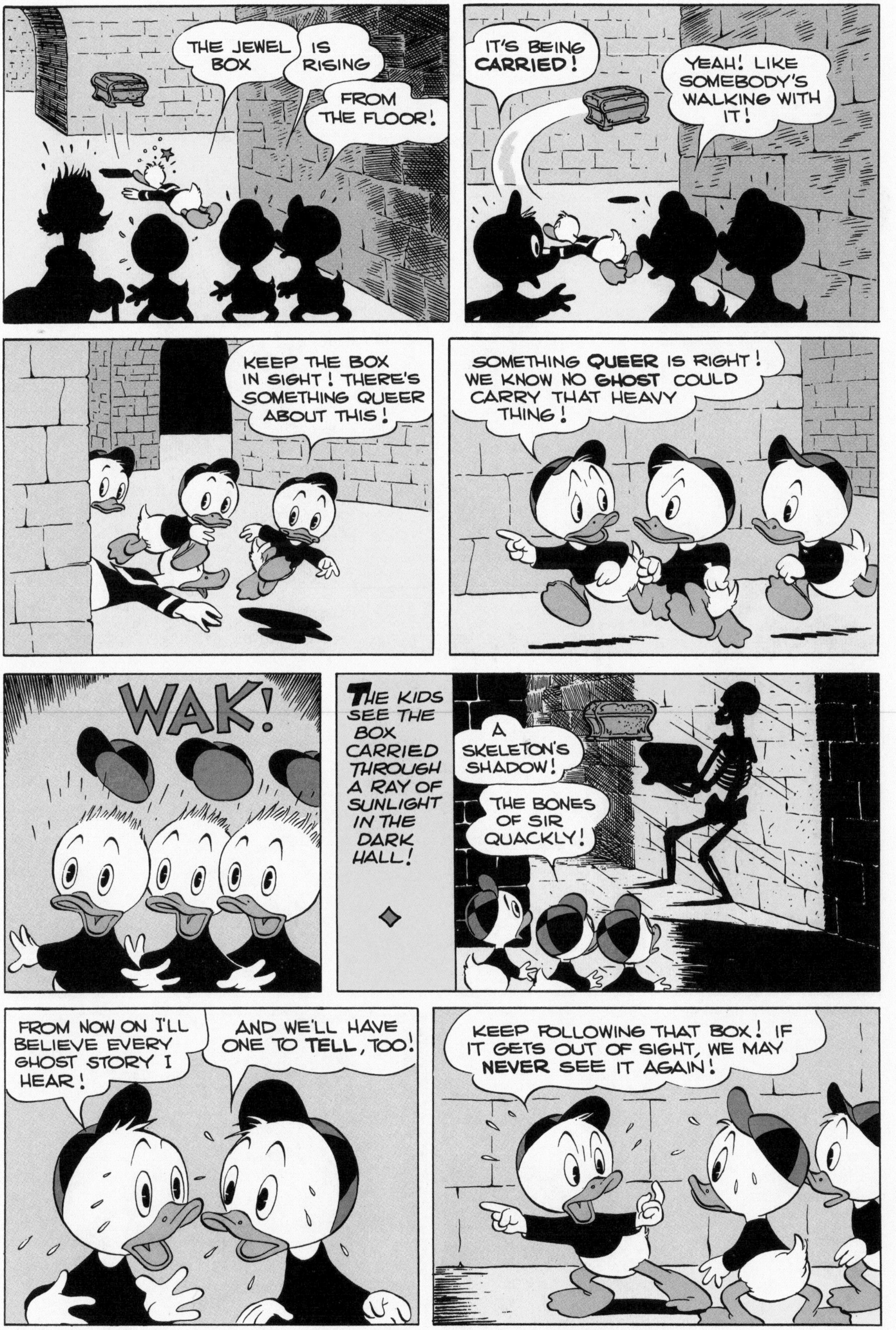
THE JEWEL BOX
IS RISING
FROM THE FLOOR!
IT'S BEING CARRIED!
YEAH! LIKE SOMEBODY'S WALKING WITH IT!
KEEP THE BOX IN SIGHT! THERE'S SOMETHING QUEER ABOUT THIS!
SOMETHING QUEER IS RIGHT! WE KNOW NO GHOST COULD CARRY THAT HEAVY THING!
WAK!
THE KIDS SEE THE BOX CARRIED THROUGH A RAY OF SUNLIGHT IN THE DARK HALL!
A SKELETON'S SHADOW!
THE BONES OF SIR QUACKLY!
FROM NOW ON I'LL BELIEVE EVERY GHOST STORY I HEAR!
AND WE'LL HAVE ONE TO TELL, TOO!
KEEP FOLLOWING THAT BOX! IF IT GETS OUT OF SIGHT, WE MAY NEVER SEE IT AGAIN!

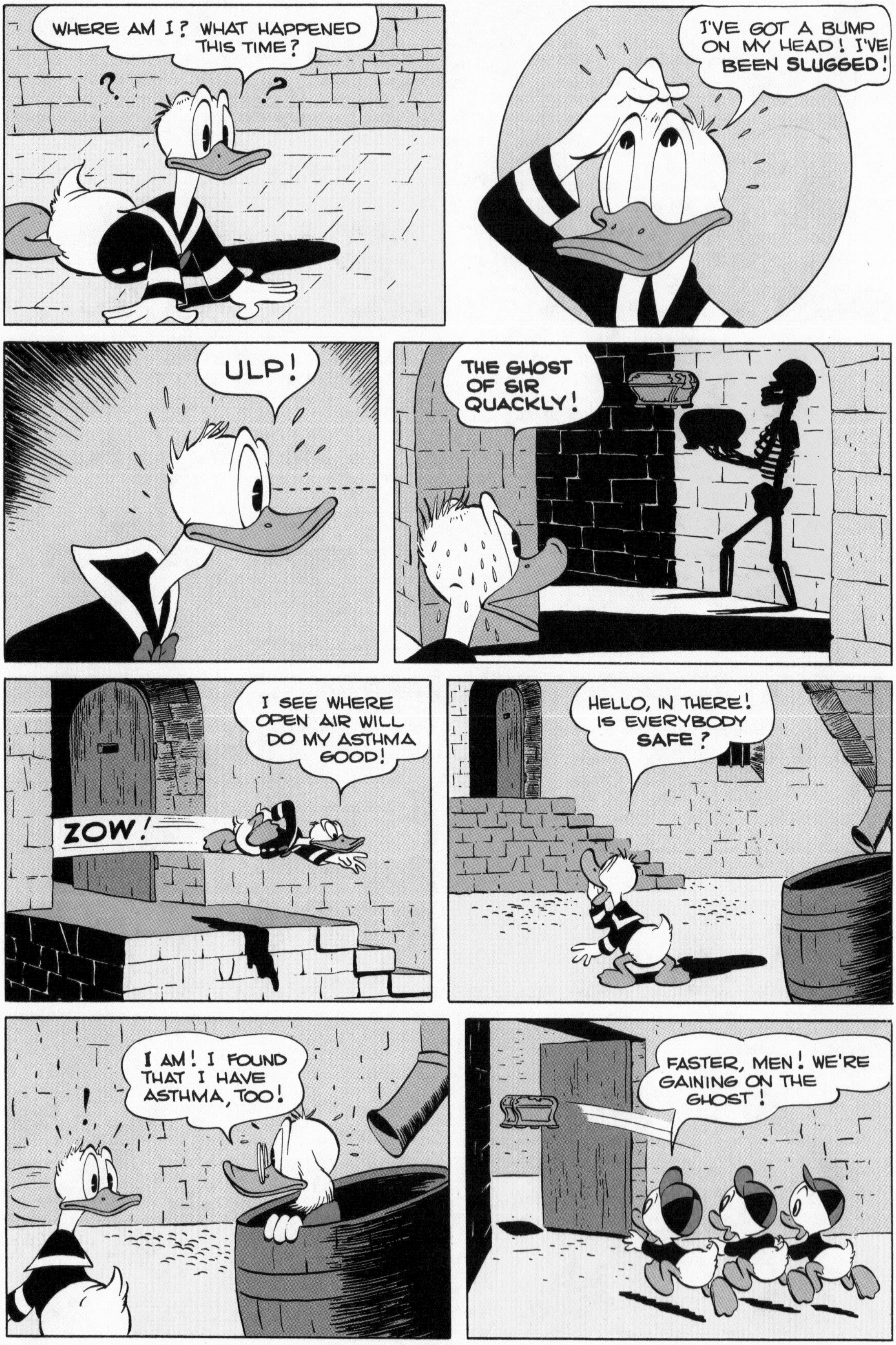

WHERE AM I? WHAT HAPPENED THIS TIME?
I'VE GOT A BUMP ON MY HEAD! I'VE BEEN SLUGGED!
ULP!
THE GHOST OF SIR QUACKLY!
I SEE WHERE OPEN AIR WILL DO MY ASTHMA GOOD!
ZOW!
HELLO, IN THERE! IS EVERYBODY SAFE?
I AM! I FOUND THAT I HAVE ASTHMA, TOO!
FASTER, MEN! WE'RE GAINING ON THE GHOST!

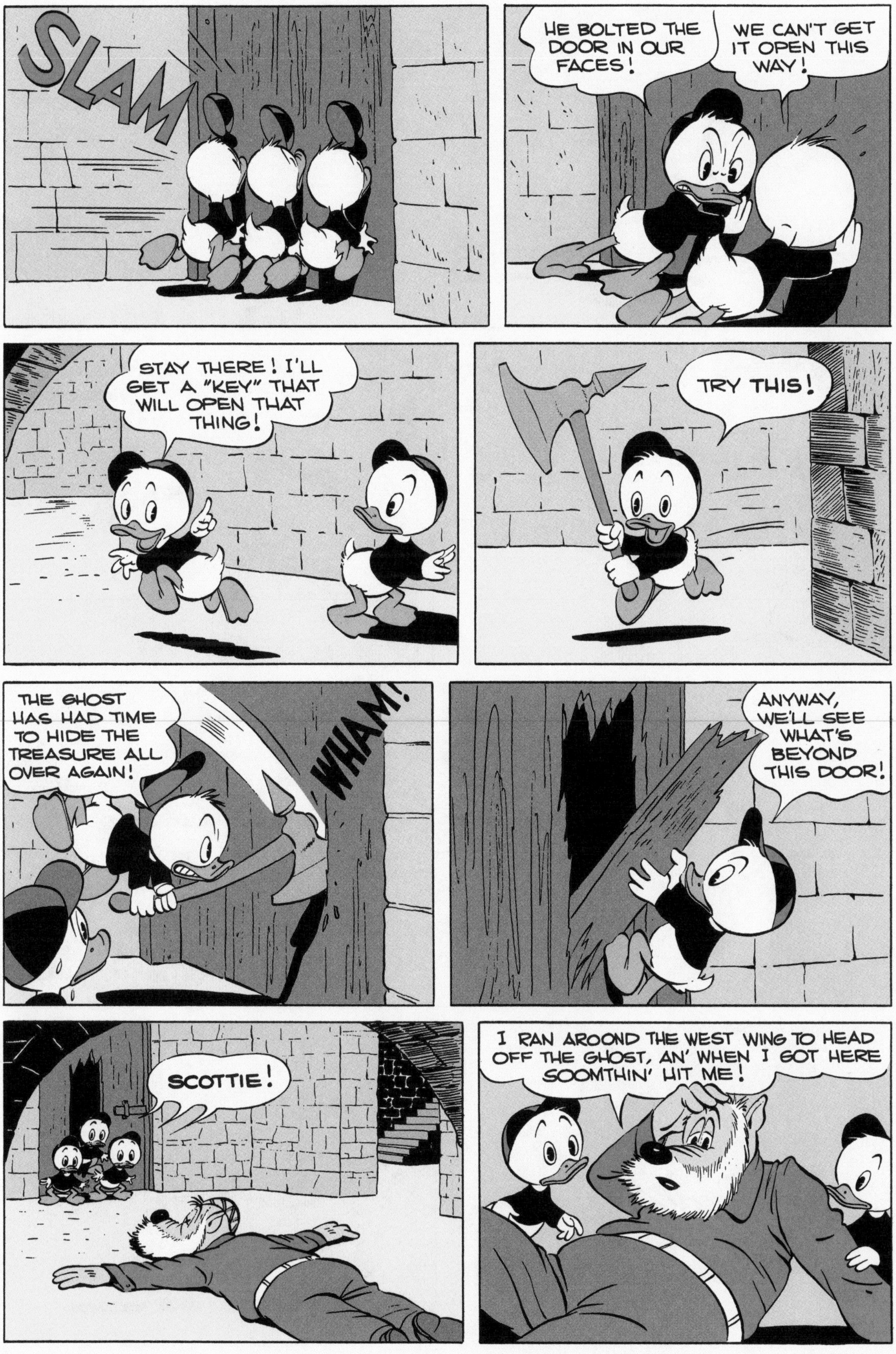
SLAM
HE BOLTED THE DOOR IN OUR FACES!
WE CAN'T GET IT OPEN THIS WAY!
STAY THERE! I'LL GET A "KEY" THAT WILL OPEN THAT THING!
TRY THIS!
THE GHOST HAS HAD TIME TO HIDE THE TREASURE ALL OVER AGAIN!
WHAM!
ANYWAY, WE'LL SEE WHAT'S BEYOND THIS DOOR!
SCOTTIE!
I RAN AROOND THE WEST WING TO HEAD OFF THE GHOST, AN' WHEN I GOT HERE SOOMTHIN' HIT ME!

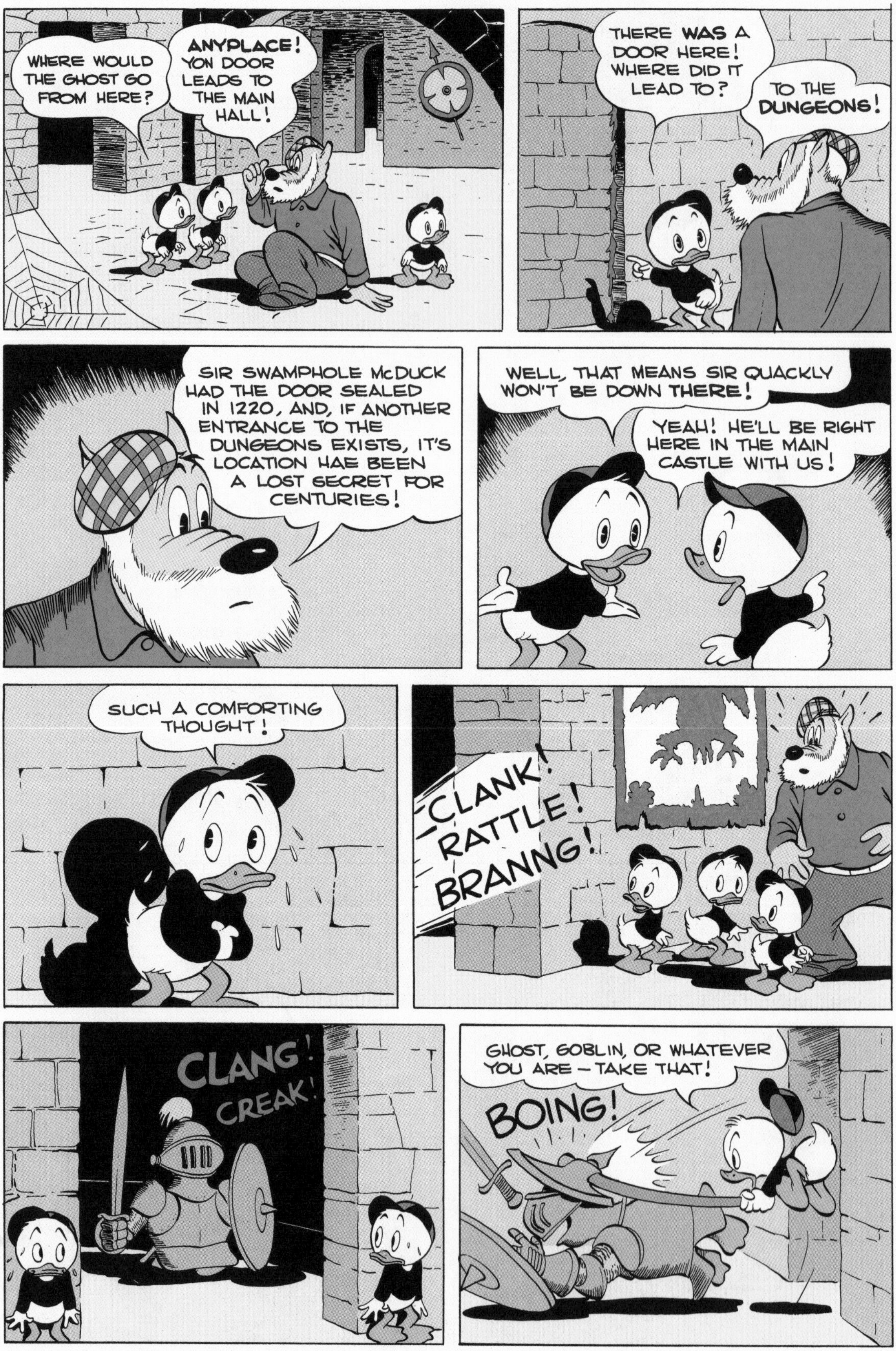
WHERE WOULD THE GHOST GO FROM HERE?
ANYPLACE! YON DOOR LEADS TO THE MAIN HALL!
THERE WAS A DOOR HERE! WHERE DID IT LEAD TO?
TO THE DUNGEONS!
SIR SWAMPHOLE McDUCK HAD THE DOOR SEALED IN 1220, AND, IF ANOTHER ENTRANCE TO THE DUNGEONS EXISTS, IT'S LOCATION HAE BEEN A LOST SECRET FOR CENTURIES!
WELL, THAT MEANS SIR QUACKLY WON'T BE DOWN THERE!
YEAH! HE'LL BE RIGHT HERE IN THE MAIN CASTLE WITH US!
SUCH A COMFORTING THOUGHT!
CLANK! RATTLE! BRANNG!
CLANG! CREAK!
GHOST, GOBLIN, OR WHATEVER YOU ARE—TAKE THAT!
BOING!

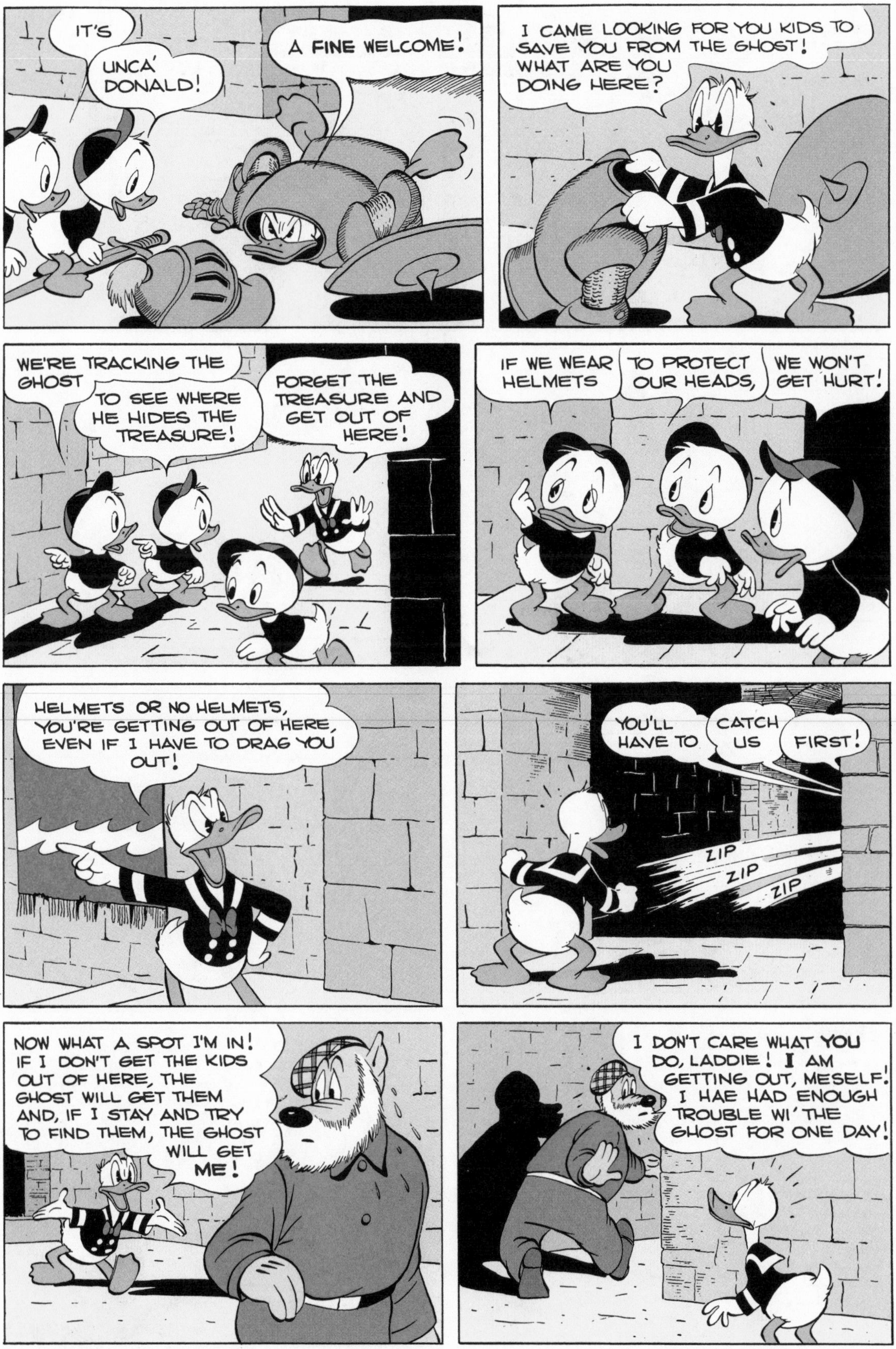
IT'S
UNCA' DONALD!
A FINE WELCOME!
I CAME LOOKING FOR YOU KIDS TO SAVE YOU FROM THE GHOST! WHAT ARE YOU DOING HERE?
WE'RE TRACKING THE GHOST
TO SEE WHERE HE HIDES THE TREASURE!
FORGET THE TREASURE AND GET OUT OF HERE!
IF WE WEAR HELMETS
TO PROTECT OUR HEADS,
WE WON'T GET HURT!
HELMETS OR NO HELMETS, YOU'RE GETTING OUT OF HERE, EVEN IF I HAVE TO DRAG YOU OUT!
YOU'LL HAVE TO
CATCH US
FIRST!
ZIP
ZIP
ZIP
NOW WHAT A SPOT I'M IN! IF I DON'T GET THE KIDS OUT OF HERE, THE GHOST WILL GET THEM AND, IF I STAY AND TRY TO FIND THEM, THE GHOST WILL GET ME!
I DON'T CARE WHAT YOU DO, LADDIE! I AM GETTING OUT, MESELF! I HAE HAD ENOUGH TROUBLE WI' THE GHOST FOR ONE DAY!

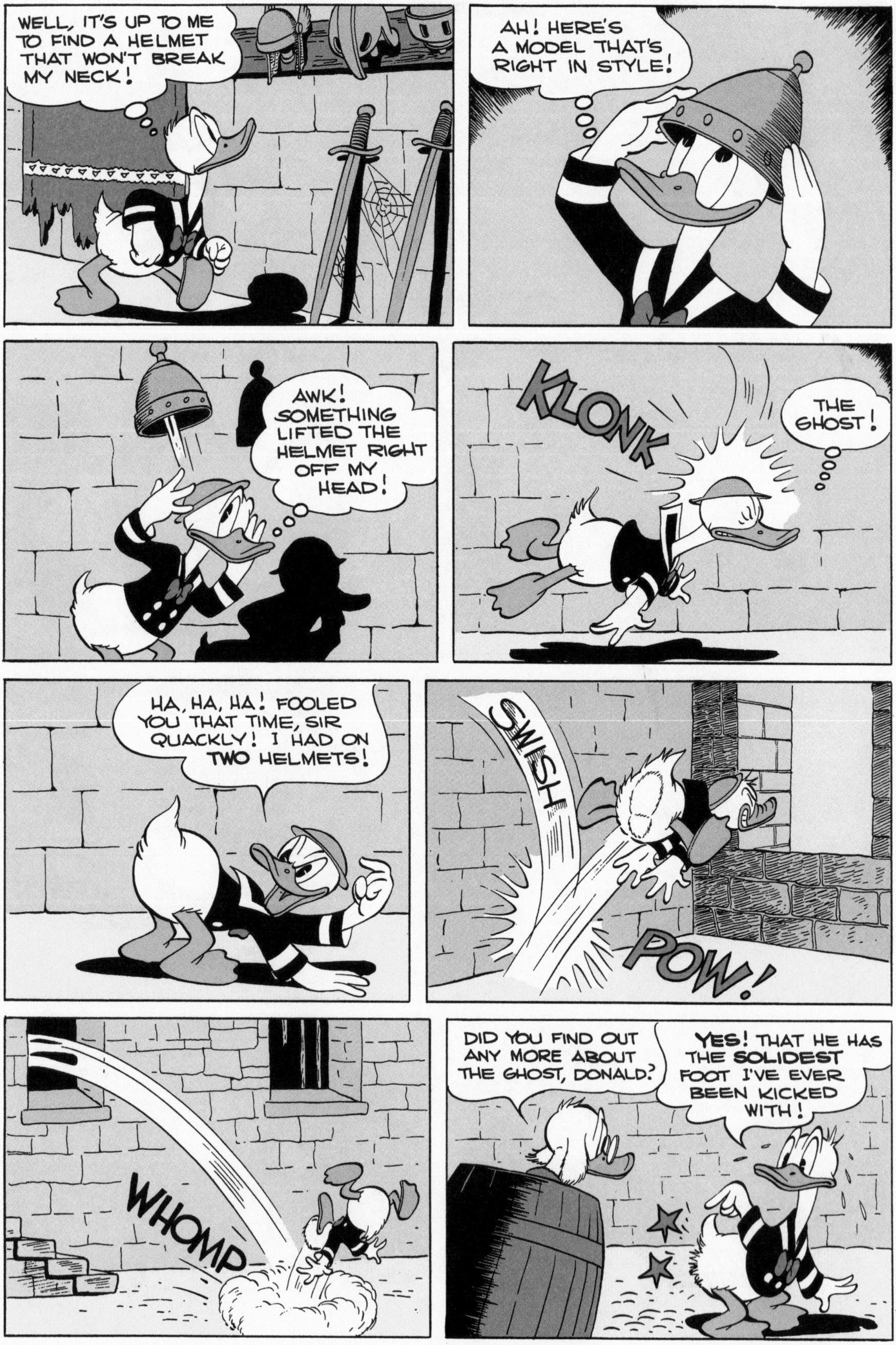
WELL, IT'S UP TO ME TO FIND A HELMET THAT WON'T BREAK MY NECK!
AH! HERE'S A MODEL THAT'S RIGHT IN STYLE!
AWK! SOMETHING LIFTED THE HELMET RIGHT OFF MY HEAD!
KLONK
THE GHOST!
HA, HA, HA! FOOLED YOU THAT TIME, SIR QUACKLY! I HAD ON TWO HELMETS!
SWISH
POW!
WHOMP
DID YOU FIND OUT ANY MORE ABOUT THE GHOST, DONALD?
YES! THAT HE HAS THE SOLIDEST FOOT I'VE EVER BEEN KICKED WITH!

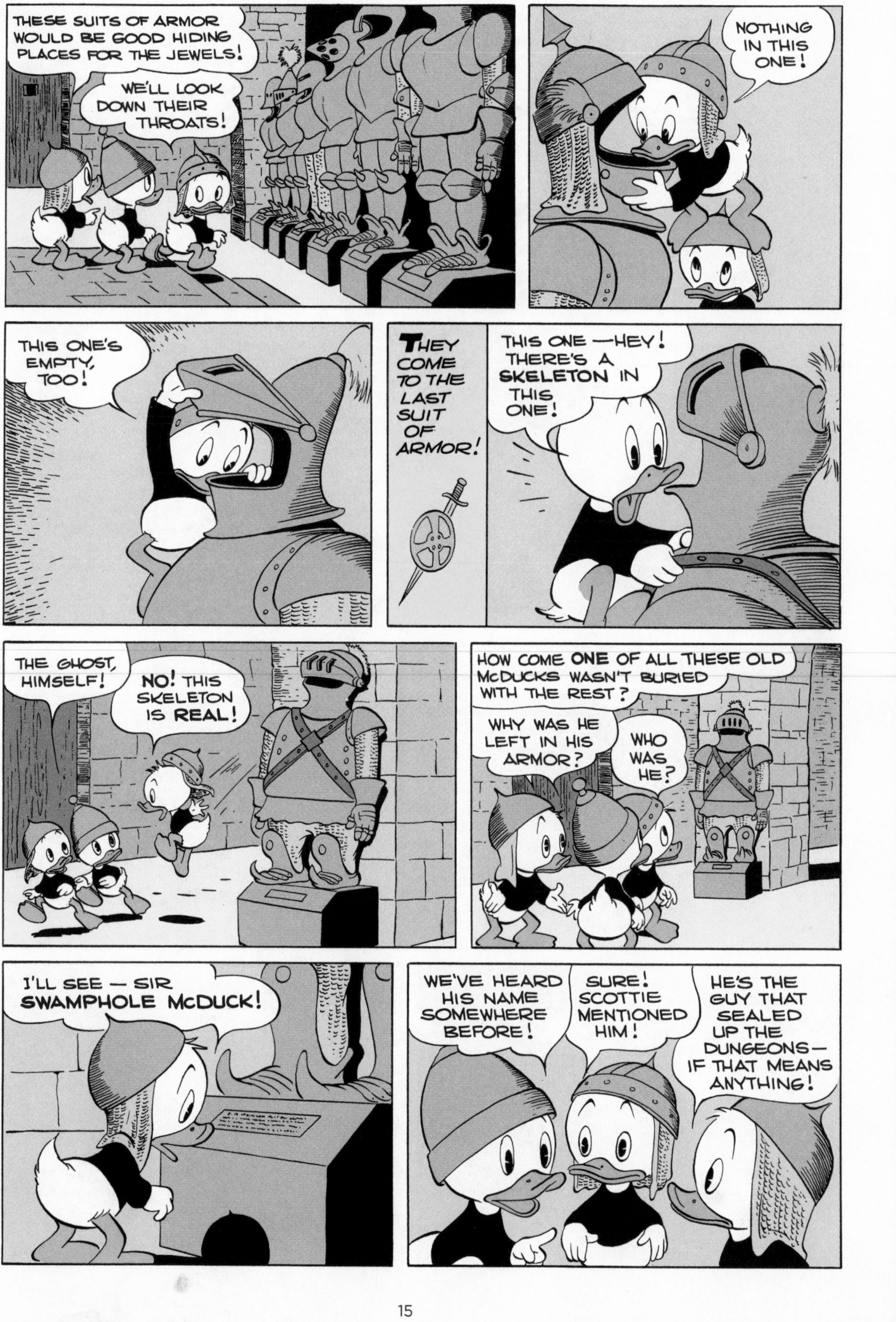
THESE SUITS OF ARMOR WOULD BE GOOD HIDING PLACES FOR THE JEWELS!
WE'LL LOOK DOWN THEIR THROATS!
NOTHING IN THIS ONE!
THIS ONE'S EMPTY, TOO!
THEY COME TO THE LAST SUIT OF ARMOR!
THIS ONE —HEY! THERE'S A SKELETON IN THIS ONE!
THE GHOST, HIMSELF!
NO! THIS SKELETON IS REAL!
HOW COME ONE OF ALL THESE OLD McDUCKS WASN'T BURIED WITH THE REST?
WHY WAS HE LEFT IN HIS ARMOR?
WHO WAS HE?
I'LL SEE — SIR SWAMPHOLE McDUCK!
WE'VE HEARD HIS NAME SOMEWHERE BEFORE!
SURE! SCOTTIE MENTIONED HIM!
HE'S THE GUY THAT SEALED UP THE DUNGEONS— IF THAT MEANS ANYTHING!

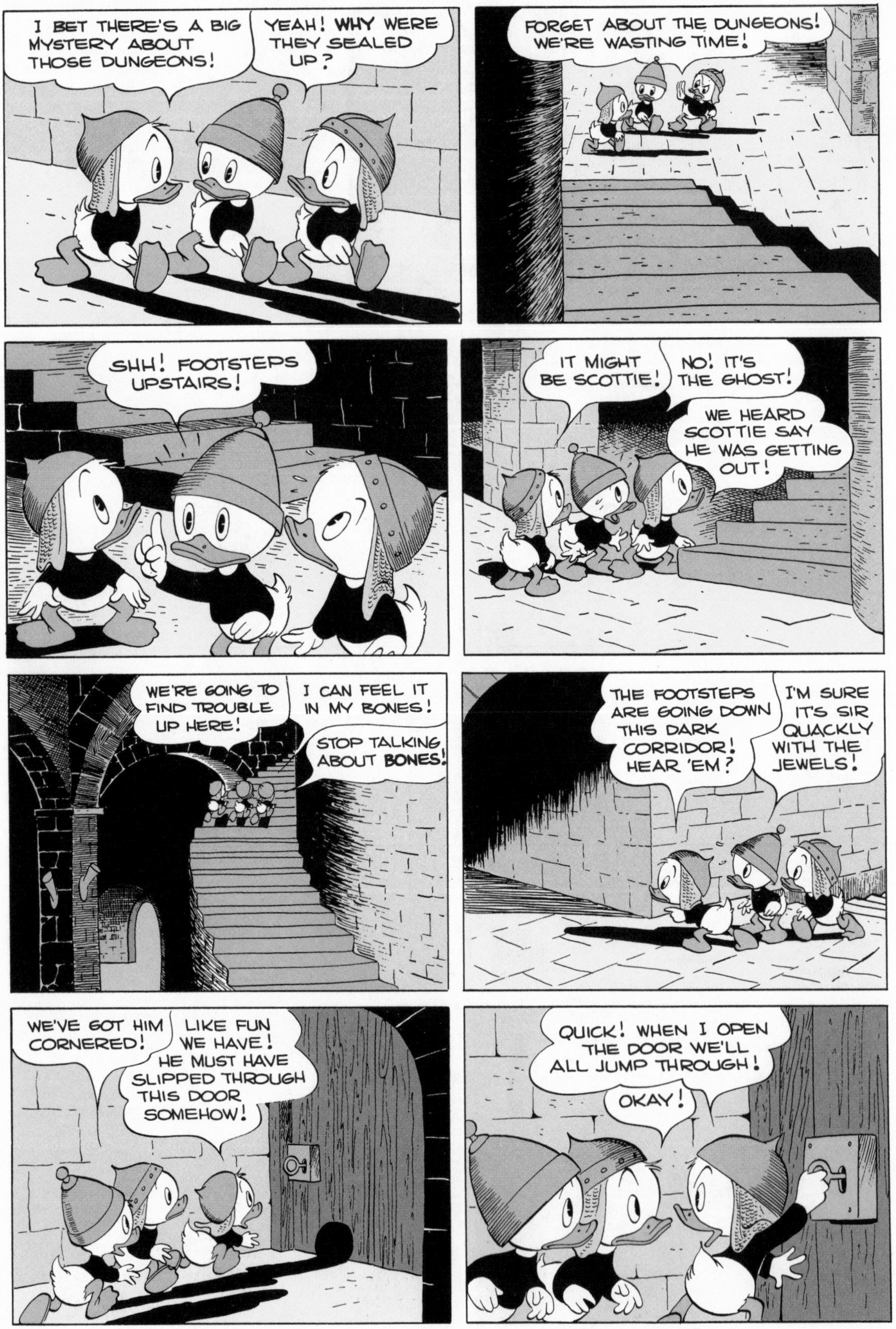
I BET THERE'S A BIG MYSTERY ABOUT THOSE DUNGEONS!
YEAH! WHY WERE THEY SEALED UP?
FORGET ABOUT THE DUNGEONS! WE'RE WASTING TIME!
SHH! FOOTSTEPS UPSTAIRS!
IT MIGHT BE SCOTTIE!
NO! IT'S THE GHOST!
WE HEARD SCOTTIE SAY HE WAS GETTING OUT!
WE'RE GOING TO FIND TROUBLE UP HERE!
I CAN FEEL IT IN MY BONES!
STOP TALKING ABOUT BONES!
THE FOOTSTEPS ARE GOING DOWN THIS DARK CORRIDOR! HEAR 'EM?
I'M SURE IT'S SIR QUACKLY WITH THE JEWELS!
WE'VE GOT HIM CORNERED!
LIKE FUN WE HAVE! HE MUST HAVE SLIPPED THROUGH THIS DOOR SOMEHOW!
QUICK! WHEN I OPEN THE DOOR WE'LL ALL JUMP THROUGH!
OKAY!

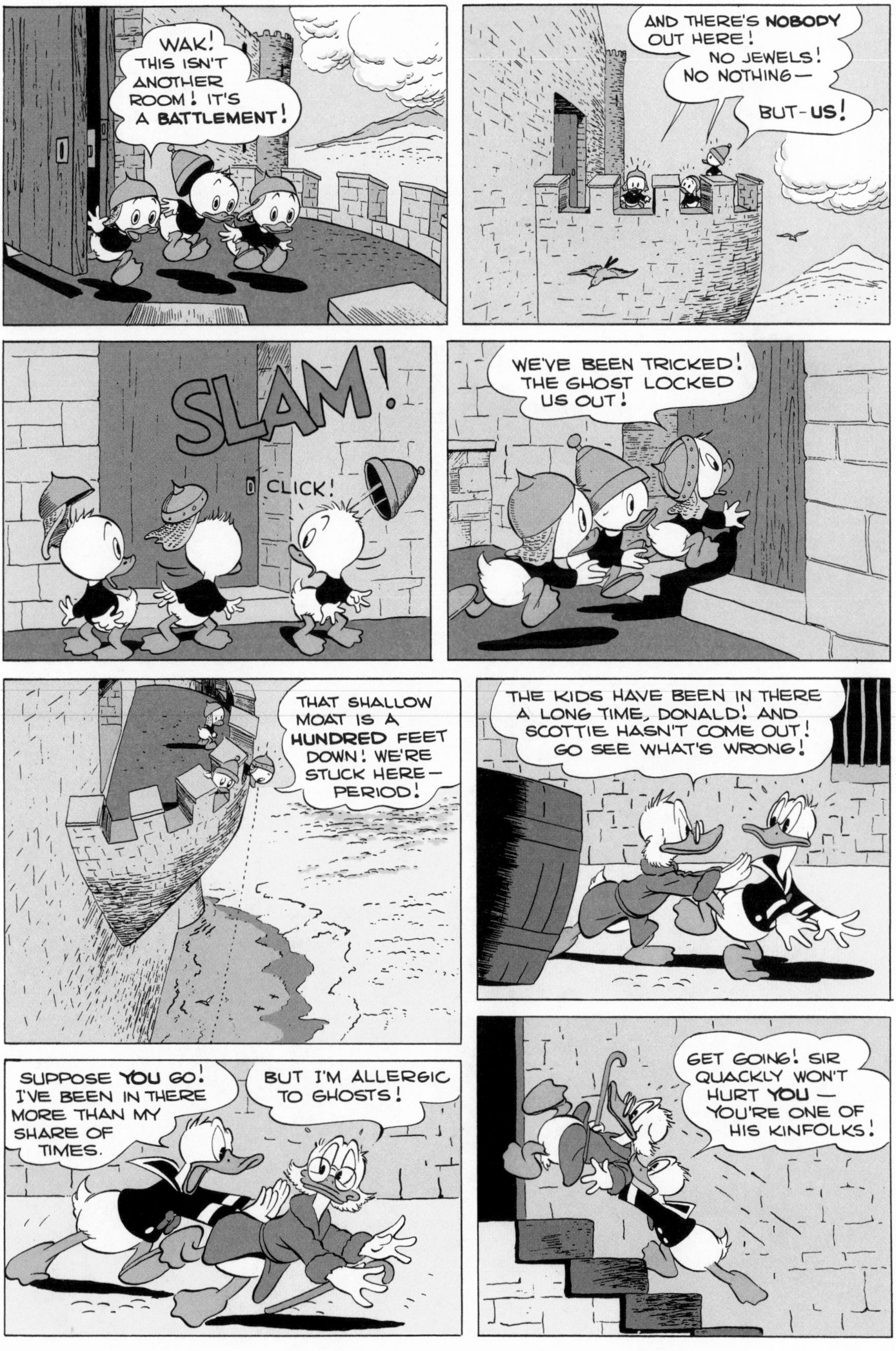
WAK! THIS ISN'T ANOTHER ROOM! IT'S A BATTLEMENT!
AND THERE'S NOBODY OUT HERE!
NO JEWELS! NO NOTHING—
BUT-US!
SLAM!
CLICK!
WE'VE BEEN TRICKED! THE GHOST LOCKED US OUT!
THAT SHALLOW MOAT IS A HUNDRED FEET DOWN! WE'RE STUCK HERE— PERIOD!
THE KIDS HAVE BEEN IN THERE A LONG TIME, DONALD! AND SCOTTIE HASN'T COME OUT! GO SEE WHAT'S WRONG!
SUPPOSE YOU GO! I'VE BEEN IN THERE MORE THAN MY SHARE OF TIMES.
BUT I'M ALLERGIC TO GHOSTS!
GET GOING! SIR QUACKLY WON'T HURT YOU— YOU'RE ONE OF HIS KINFOLKS!

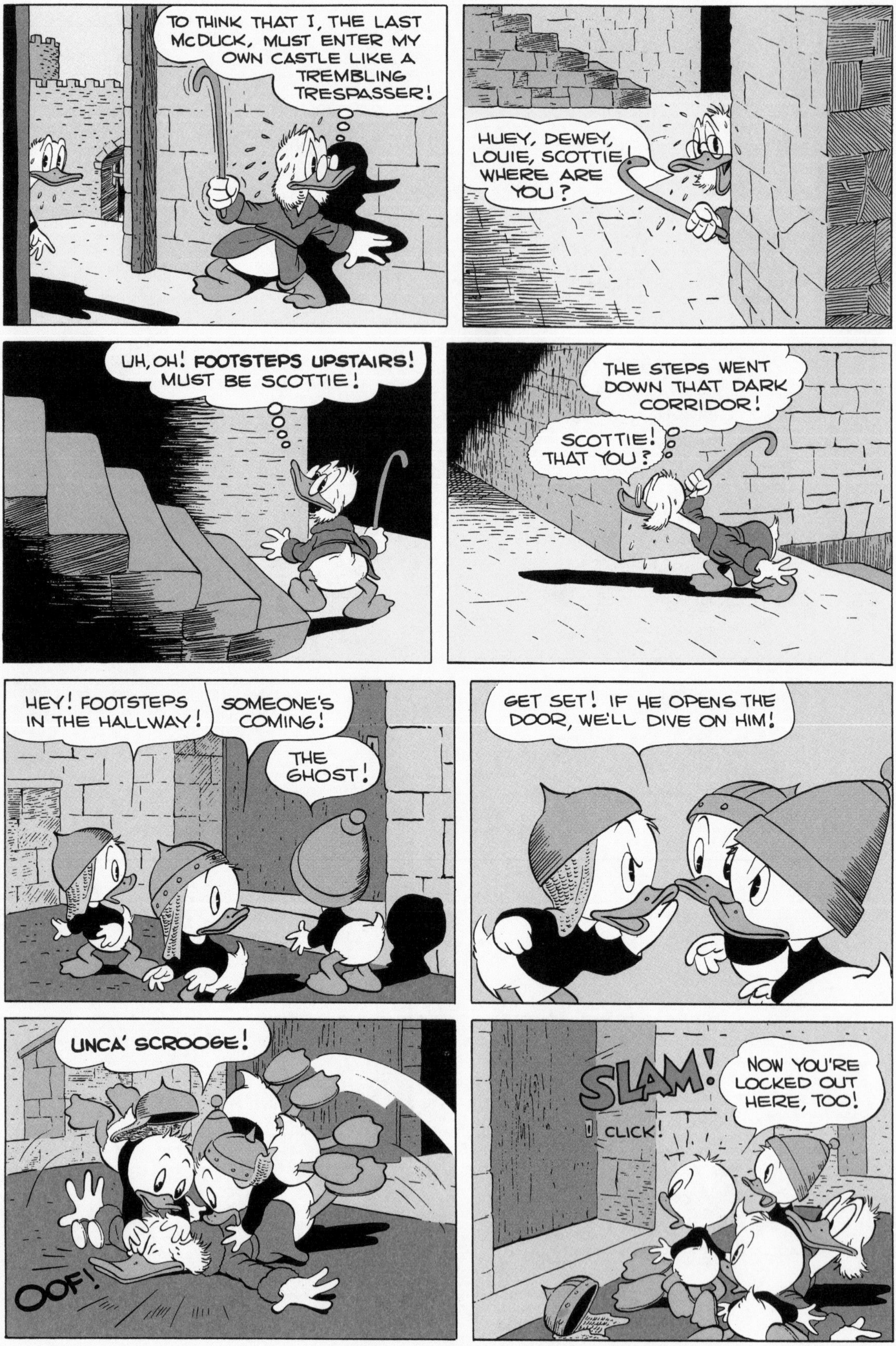
TO THINK THAT I, THE LAST McDUCK, MUST ENTER MY OWN CASTLE LIKE A TREMBLING TRESPASSER!
HUEY, DEWEY, LOUIE, SCOTTIE! WHERE ARE YOU?
UH, OH! FOOTSTEPS UPSTAIRS! MUST BE SCOTTIE!
THE STEPS WENT DOWN THAT DARK CORRIDOR!
SCOTTIE! THAT YOU?
HEY! FOOTSTEPS IN THE HALLWAY!
SOMEONE'S COMING!
THE GHOST!
GET SET! IF HE OPENS THE DOOR, WE'LL DIVE ON HIM!
UNCA' SCROOGE!
OOF!
SLAM!
CLICK!
NOW YOU'RE LOCKED OUT HERE, TOO!

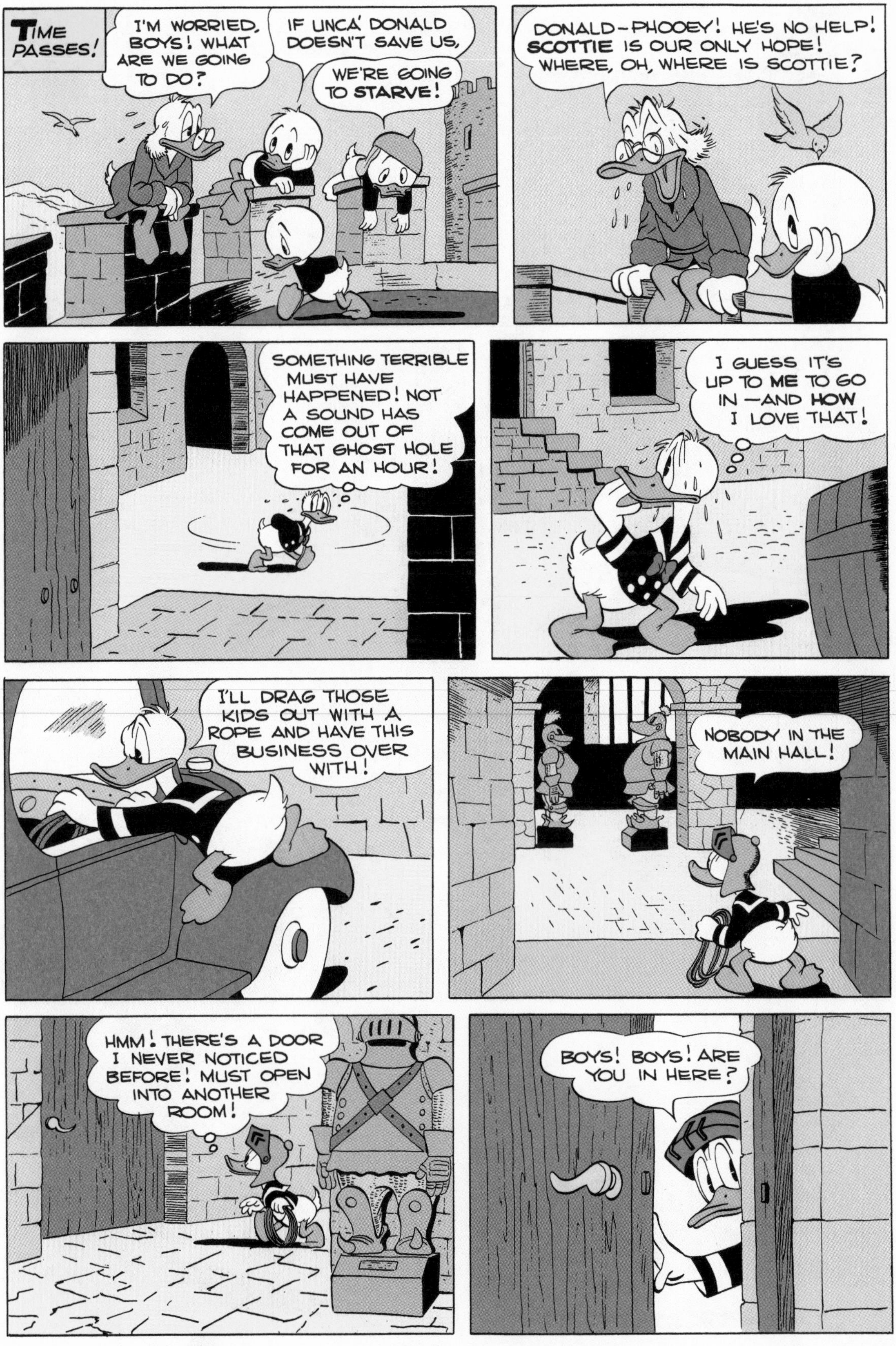
TIME PASSES!
I'M WORRIED, BOYS! WHAT ARE WE GOING TO DO?
IF UNCA' DONALD DOESN'T SAVE US,
WE'RE GOING TO STARVE!
DONALD-PHOOEY! HE'S NO HELP! SCOTTIE IS OUR ONLY HOPE! WHERE, OH, WHERE IS SCOTTIE?
SOMETHING TERRIBLE MUST HAVE HAPPENED! NOT A SOUND HAS COME OUT OF THAT GHOST HOLE FOR AN HOUR!
I GUESS IT'S UP TO ME TO GO IN —AND HOW I LOVE THAT!
I'LL DRAG THOSE KIDS OUT WITH A ROPE AND HAVE THIS BUSINESS OVER WITH!
NOBODY IN THE MAIN HALL!
HMM! THERE'S A DOOR I NEVER NOTICED BEFORE! MUST OPEN INTO ANOTHER ROOM!
BOYS! BOYS! ARE YOU IN HERE?

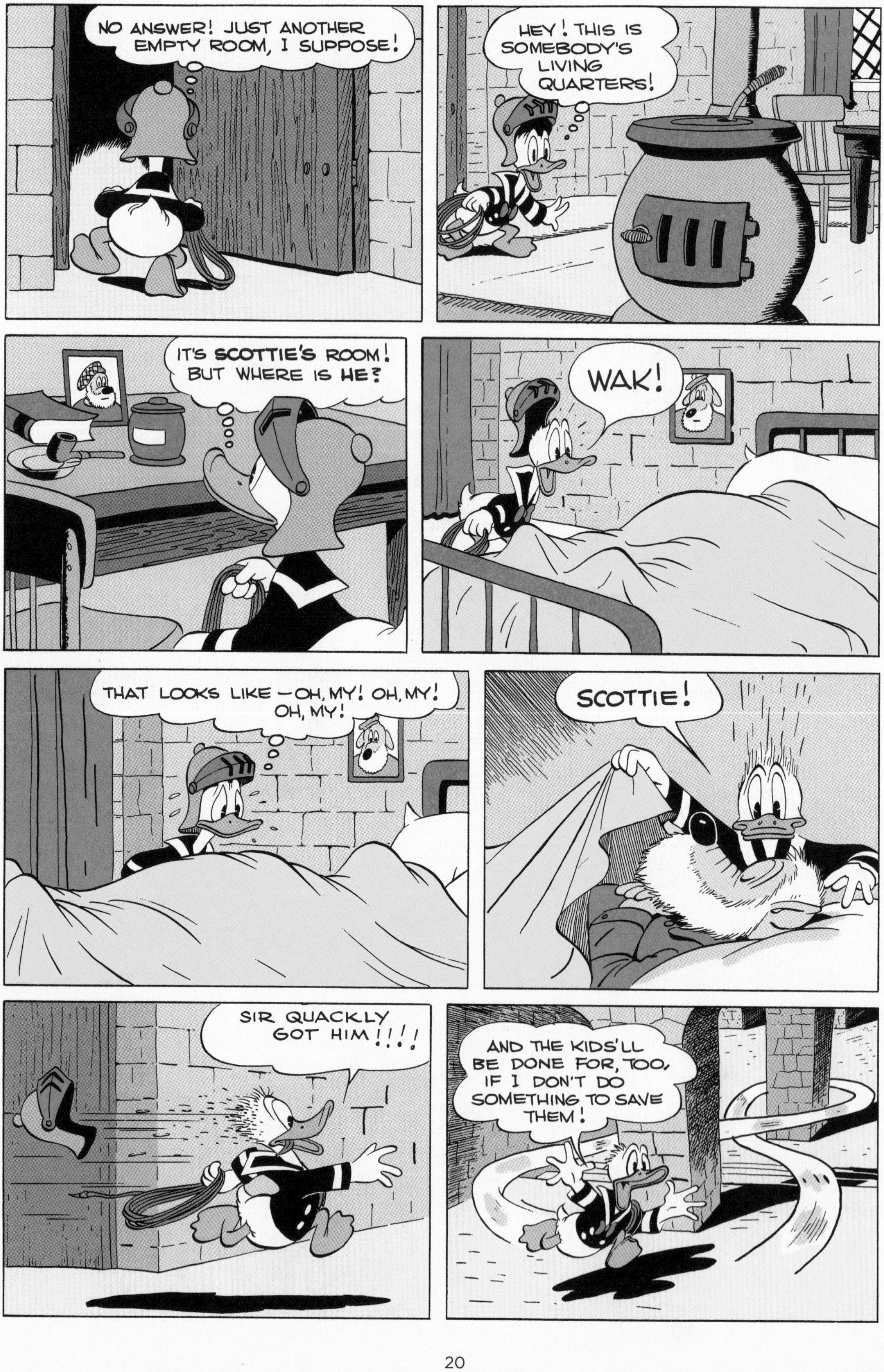
NO ANSWER! JUST ANOTHER EMPTY ROOM, I SUPPOSE!
HEY! THIS IS SOMEBODY'S LIVING QUARTERS!
IT'S SCOTTIE'S ROOM! BUT WHERE IS HE?
WAK!
THAT LOOKS LIKE—OH, MY! OH, MY! OH, MY!
SCOTTIE!
SIR QUACKLY GOT HIM!!!!
AND THE KIDS'LL BE DONE FOR, TOO, IF I DON'T DO SOMETHING TO SAVE THEM!

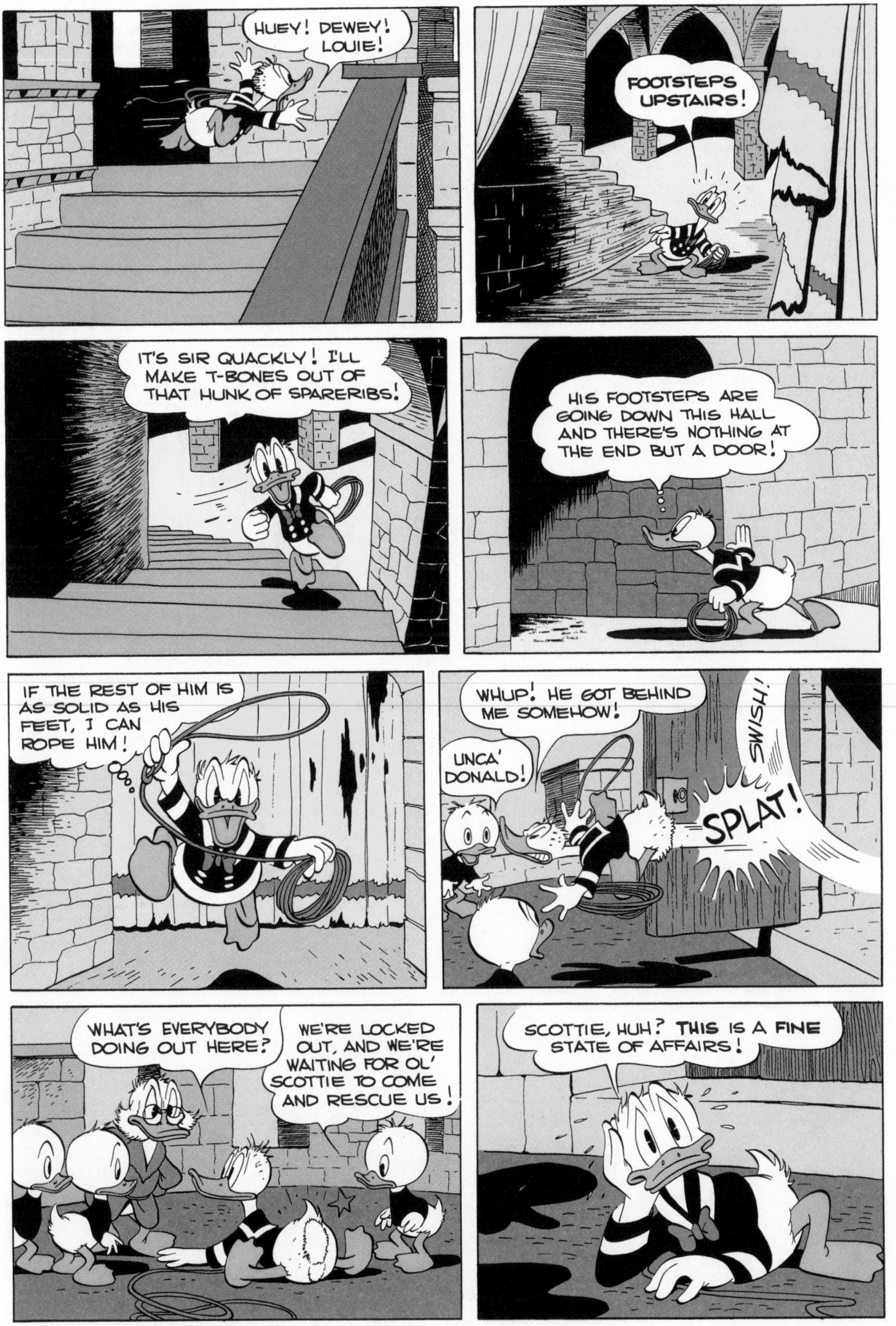
HUEY! DEWEY! LOUIE!
FOOTSTEPS UPSTAIRS!
IT'S SIR QUACKLY! I'LL MAKE T-BONES OUT OF THAT HUNK OF SPARERIBS!
HIS FOOTSTEPS ARE GOING DOWN THIS HALL AND THERE'S NOTHING AT THE END BUT A DOOR!
IF THE REST OF HIM IS AS SOLID AS HIS FEET, I CAN ROPE HIM!
WHUP! HE GOT BEHIND ME SOMEHOW!
UNCA' DONALD!
SWISH!
SPLAT!
WHAT'S EVERYBODY DOING OUT HERE?
WE'RE LOCKED OUT, AND WE'RE WAITING FOR OL' SCOTTIE TO COME AND RESCUE US!
SCOTTIE, HUH? **THIS** IS A **FINE** STATE OF AFFAIRS!

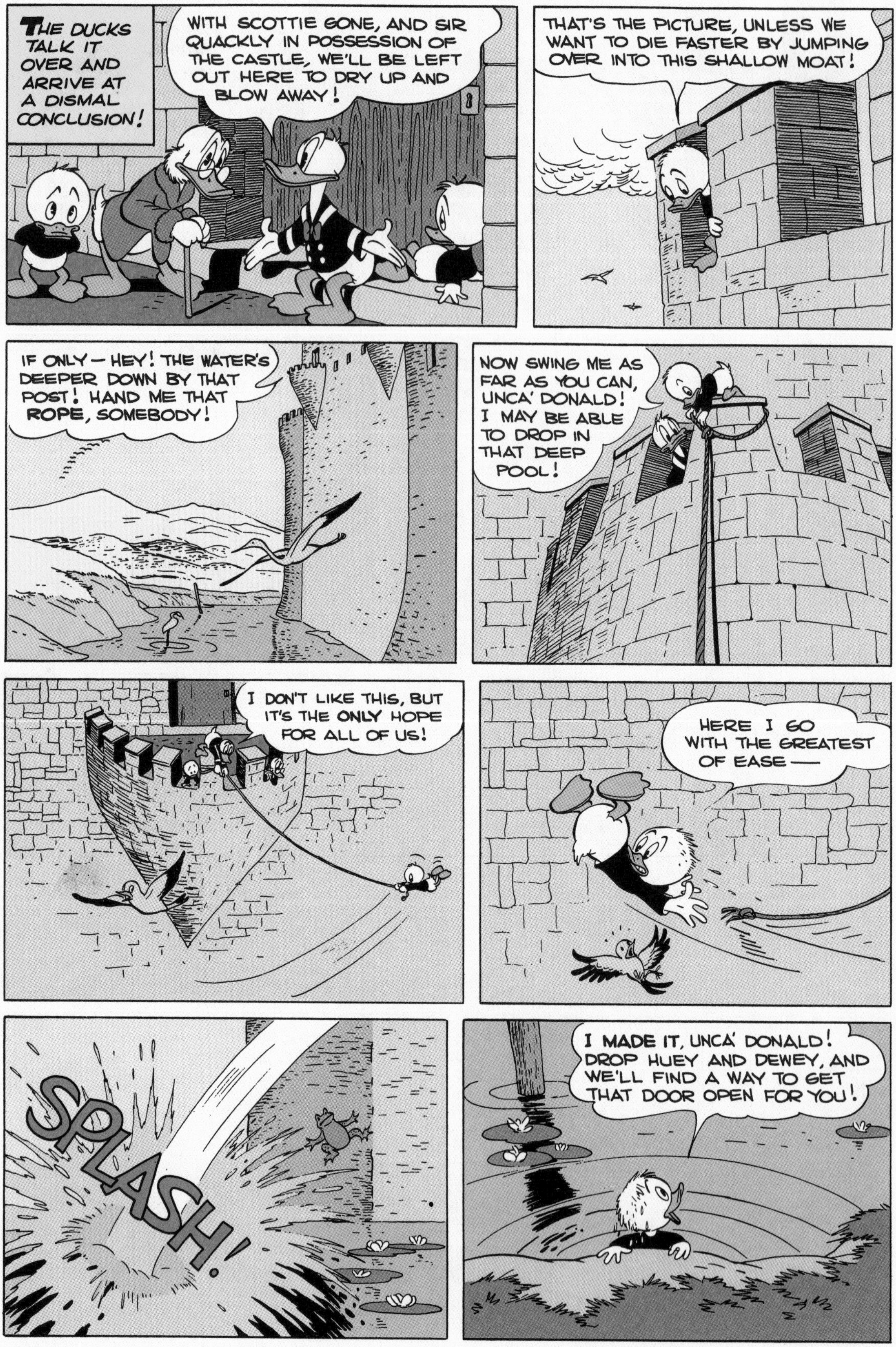

THE DUCKS TALK IT OVER AND ARRIVE AT A DISMAL CONCLUSION!
WITH SCOTTIE GONE, AND SIR QUACKLY IN POSSESSION OF THE CASTLE, WE'LL BE LEFT OUT HERE TO DRY UP AND BLOW AWAY!
THAT'S THE PICTURE, UNLESS WE WANT TO DIE FASTER BY JUMPING OVER INTO THIS SHALLOW MOAT!
IF ONLY — HEY! THE WATER'S DEEPER DOWN BY THAT POST! HAND ME THAT ROPE, SOMEBODY!
NOW SWING ME AS FAR AS YOU CAN, UNCA' DONALD! I MAY BE ABLE TO DROP IN THAT DEEP POOL!
I DON'T LIKE THIS, BUT IT'S THE ONLY HOPE FOR ALL OF US!
HERE I GO WITH THE GREATEST OF EASE —
SPLASH!
I MADE IT, UNCA' DONALD! DROP HUEY AND DEWEY, AND WE'LL FIND A WAY TO GET THAT DOOR OPEN FOR YOU!

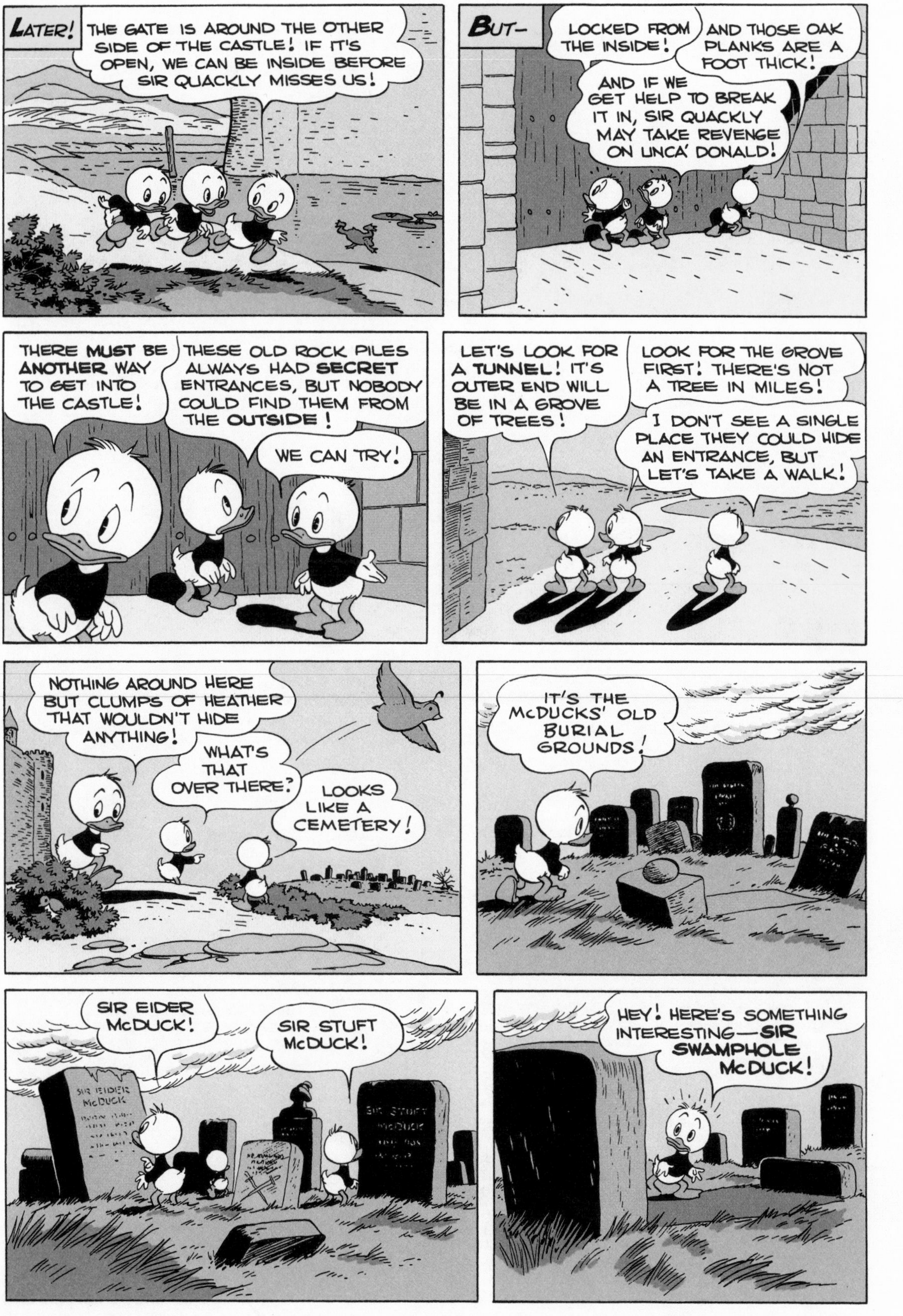
LATER!
THE GATE IS AROUND THE OTHER SIDE OF THE CASTLE! IF IT'S OPEN, WE CAN BE INSIDE BEFORE SIR QUACKLY MISSES US!
BUT-
LOCKED FROM THE INSIDE!
AND THOSE OAK PLANKS ARE A FOOT THICK!
AND IF WE GET HELP TO BREAK IT IN, SIR QUACKLY MAY TAKE REVENGE ON UNCA' DONALD!
THERE **MUST** BE **ANOTHER** WAY TO GET INTO THE CASTLE!
THESE OLD ROCK PILES ALWAYS HAD **SECRET** ENTRANCES, BUT NOBODY COULD FIND THEM FROM THE **OUTSIDE**!
WE CAN TRY!
LET'S LOOK FOR A **TUNNEL**! IT'S OUTER END WILL BE IN A GROVE OF TREES!
LOOK FOR THE GROVE FIRST! THERE'S NOT A TREE IN MILES!
I DON'T SEE A SINGLE PLACE THEY COULD HIDE AN ENTRANCE, BUT LET'S TAKE A WALK!
NOTHING AROUND HERE BUT CLUMPS OF HEATHER THAT WOULDN'T HIDE ANYTHING!
WHAT'S THAT OVER THERE?
LOOKS LIKE A CEMETERY!
IT'S THE McDUCKS' OLD BURIAL GROUNDS!
SIR EIDER McDUCK!
SIR STUFT McDUCK!
SIR EIDER McDUCK
SIR STUFT McDUCK
HEY! HERE'S SOMETHING INTERESTING—**SIR SWAMPHOLE McDUCK!**

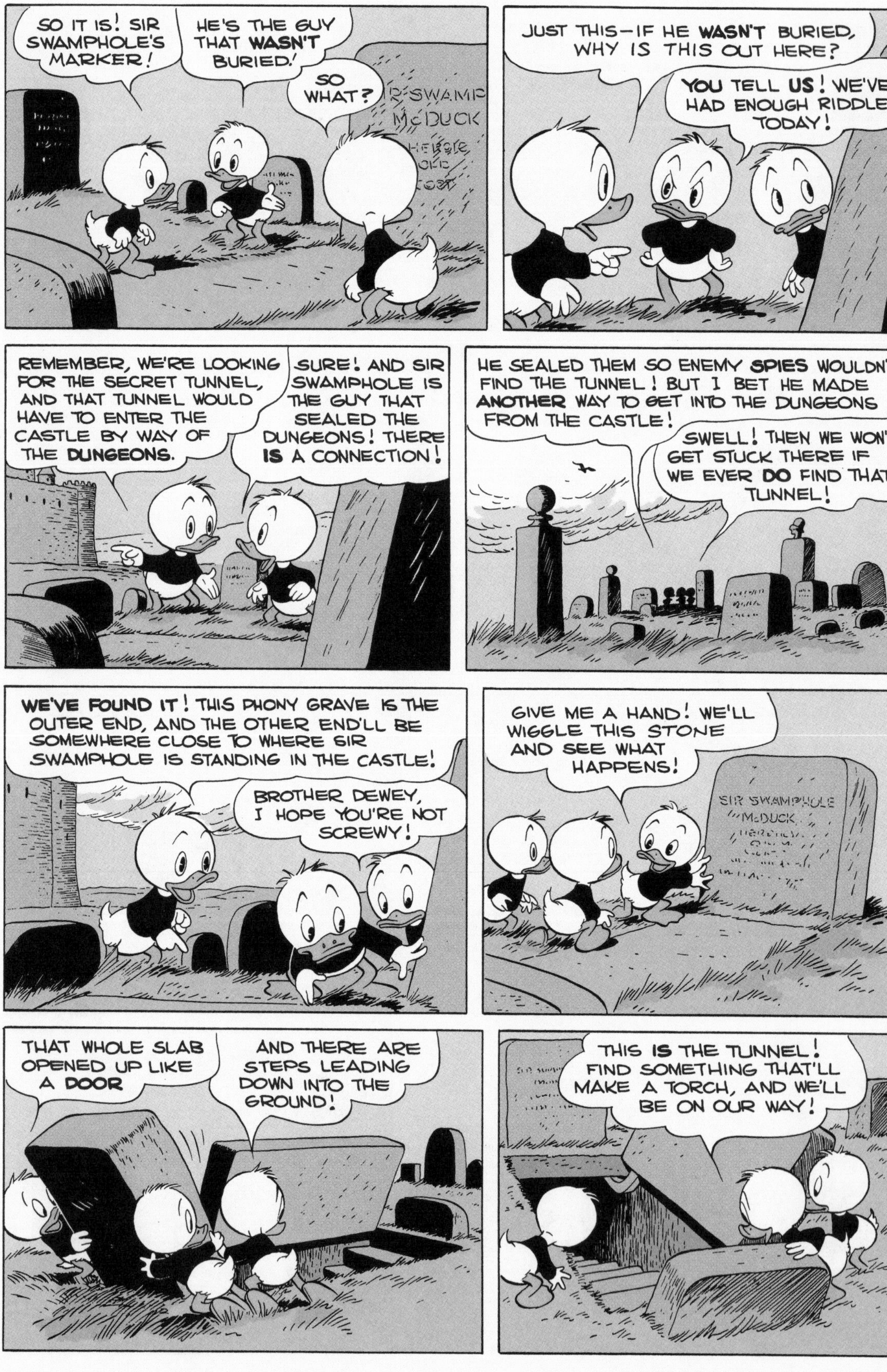

SO IT IS! SIR SWAMPHOLE'S MARKER!
HE'S THE GUY THAT **WASN'T** BURIED!
SO WHAT?
JUST THIS—IF HE **WASN'T** BURIED, WHY IS THIS OUT HERE?
YOU TELL **US**! WE'VE HAD ENOUGH RIDDLES TODAY!
REMEMBER, WE'RE LOOKING FOR THE SECRET TUNNEL, AND THAT TUNNEL WOULD HAVE TO ENTER THE CASTLE BY WAY OF THE **DUNGEONS**.
SURE! AND SIR SWAMPHOLE IS THE GUY THAT SEALED THE DUNGEONS! THERE **IS** A CONNECTION!
HE SEALED THEM SO ENEMY **SPIES** WOULDN'T FIND THE TUNNEL! BUT I BET HE MADE **ANOTHER** WAY TO GET INTO THE DUNGEONS FROM THE CASTLE!
SWELL! THEN WE WON'T GET STUCK THERE IF WE EVER **DO** FIND THAT TUNNEL!
WE'VE FOUND IT! THIS PHONY GRAVE IS THE OUTER END, AND THE OTHER END'LL BE SOMEWHERE CLOSE TO WHERE SIR SWAMPHOLE IS STANDING IN THE CASTLE!
BROTHER DEWEY, I HOPE YOU'RE NOT SCREWY!
GIVE ME A HAND! WE'LL WIGGLE THIS STONE AND SEE WHAT HAPPENS!
SIR SWAMPHOLE McDUCK
THAT WHOLE SLAB OPENED UP LIKE A **DOOR**
AND THERE ARE STEPS LEADING DOWN INTO THE GROUND!
THIS **IS** THE TUNNEL! FIND SOMETHING THAT'LL MAKE A TORCH, AND WE'LL BE ON OUR WAY!

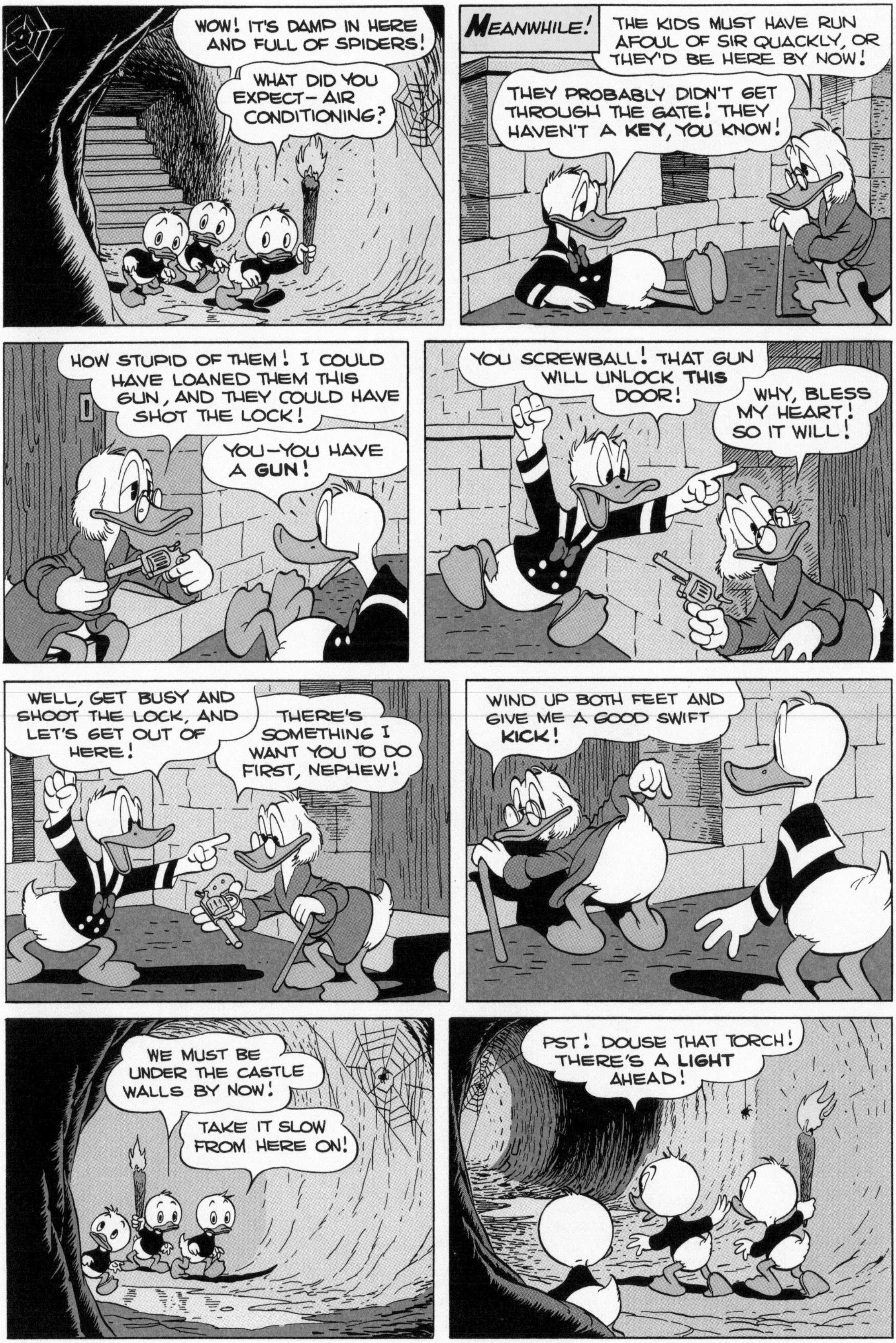
WOW! IT'S DAMP IN HERE AND FULL OF SPIDERS!
WHAT DID YOU EXPECT– AIR CONDITIONING?
MEANWHILE!
THE KIDS MUST HAVE RUN AFOUL OF SIR QUACKLY, OR THEY'D BE HERE BY NOW!
THEY PROBABLY DIDN'T GET THROUGH THE GATE! THEY HAVEN'T A KEY, YOU KNOW!
HOW STUPID OF THEM! I COULD HAVE LOANED THEM THIS GUN, AND THEY COULD HAVE SHOT THE LOCK!
YOU–YOU HAVE A GUN!
YOU SCREWBALL! THAT GUN WILL UNLOCK THIS DOOR!
WHY, BLESS MY HEART! SO IT WILL!
WELL, GET BUSY AND SHOOT THE LOCK, AND LET'S GET OUT OF HERE!
THERE'S SOMETHING I WANT YOU TO DO FIRST, NEPHEW!
WIND UP BOTH FEET AND GIVE ME A GOOD SWIFT KICK!
WE MUST BE UNDER THE CASTLE WALLS BY NOW!
TAKE IT SLOW FROM HERE ON!
PST! DOUSE THAT TORCH! THERE'S A LIGHT AHEAD!

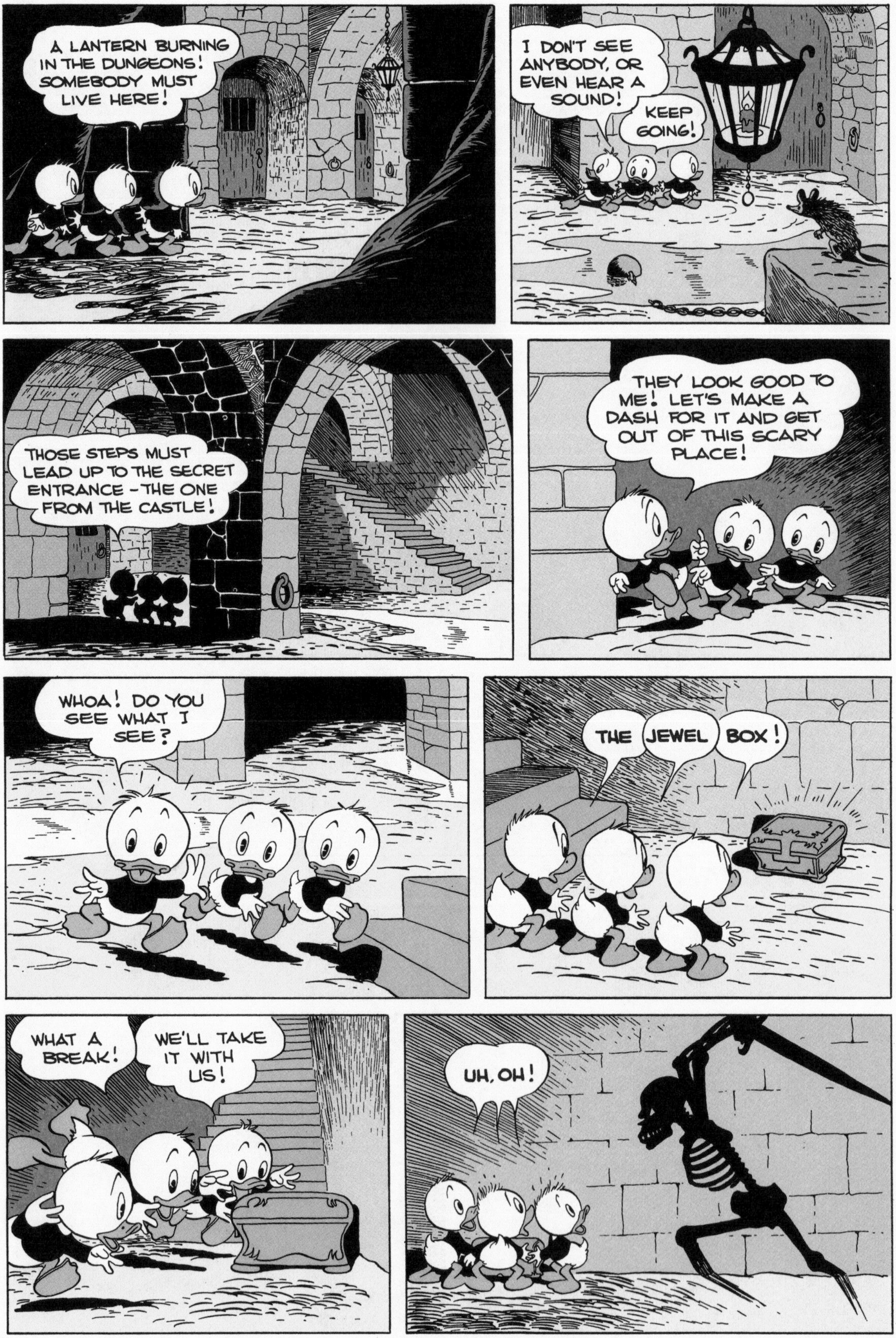
A LANTERN BURNING IN THE DUNGEONS! SOMEBODY MUST LIVE HERE!
I DON'T SEE ANYBODY, OR EVEN HEAR A SOUND!
KEEP GOING!
THOSE STEPS MUST LEAD UP TO THE SECRET ENTRANCE - THE ONE FROM THE CASTLE!
THEY LOOK GOOD TO ME! LET'S MAKE A DASH FOR IT AND GET OUT OF THIS SCARY PLACE!
WHOA! DO YOU SEE WHAT I SEE?
THE
JEWEL
BOX!
WHAT A BREAK!
WE'LL TAKE IT WITH US!
UH, OH!

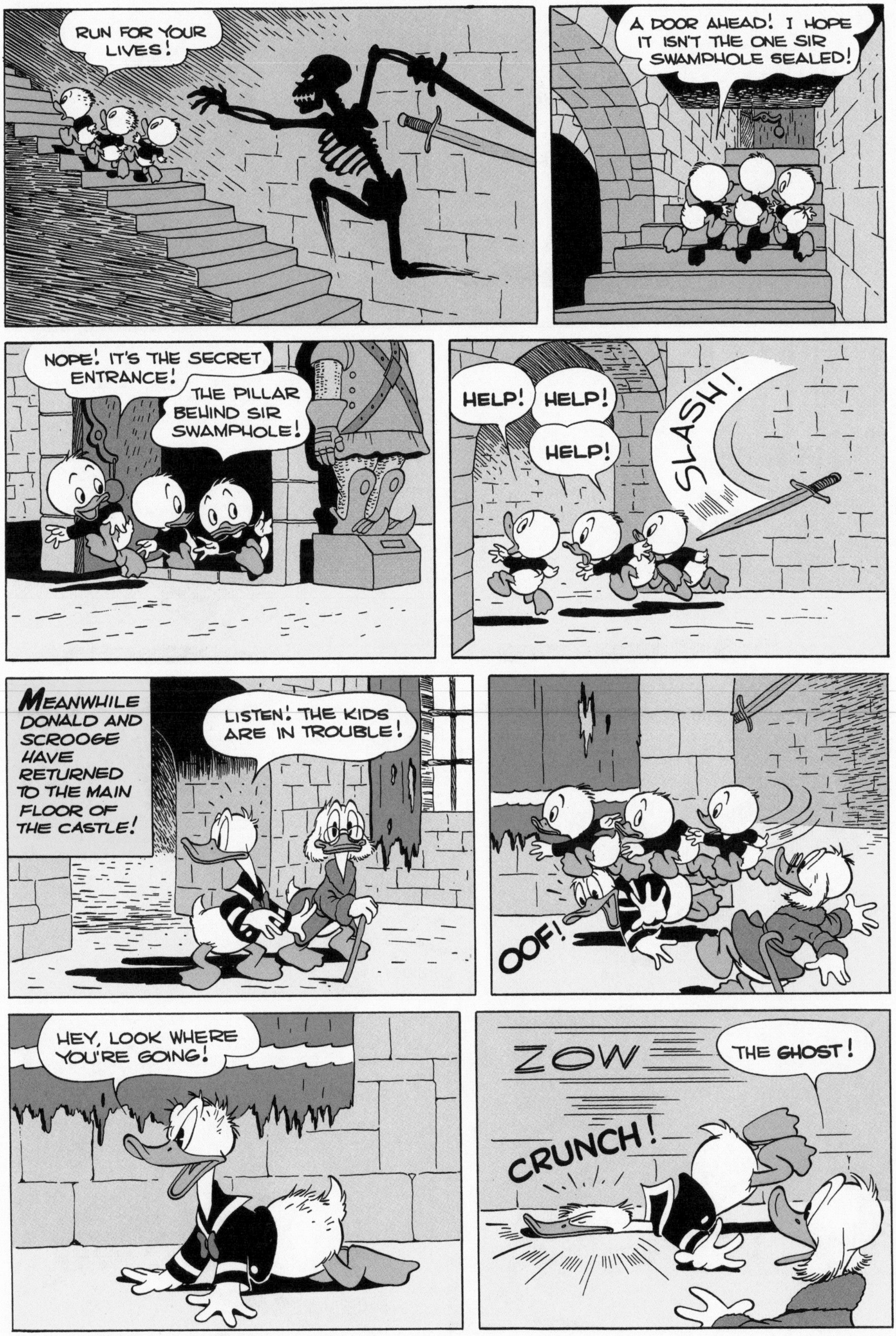
RUN FOR YOUR LIVES!
A DOOR AHEAD! I HOPE IT ISN'T THE ONE SIR SWAMPHOLE SEALED!
NOPE! IT'S THE SECRET ENTRANCE!
THE PILLAR BEHIND SIR SWAMPHOLE!
HELP!
HELP!
HELP!
SLASH!
MEANWHILE DONALD AND SCROOGE HAVE RETURNED TO THE MAIN FLOOR OF THE CASTLE!
LISTEN! THE KIDS ARE IN TROUBLE!
OOF!
HEY, LOOK WHERE YOU'RE GOING!
ZOW
THE GHOST!
CRUNCH!

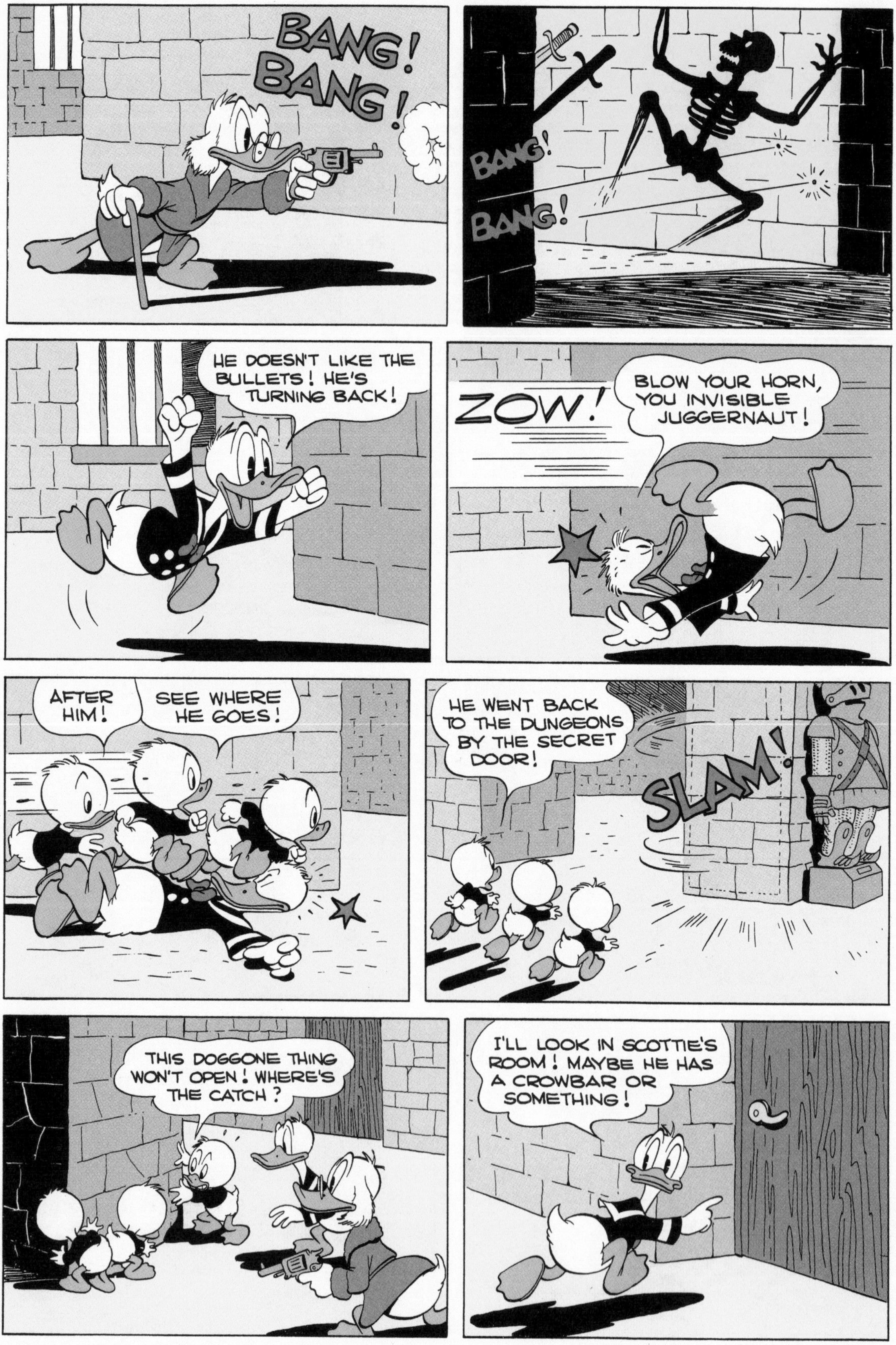
BANG! BANG!
BANG! BANG!
HE DOESN'T LIKE THE BULLETS! HE'S TURNING BACK!
ZOW!
BLOW YOUR HORN, YOU INVISIBLE JUGGERNAUT!
AFTER HIM!
SEE WHERE HE GOES!
HE WENT BACK TO THE DUNGEONS BY THE SECRET DOOR!
SLAM!
THIS DOGGONE THING WON'T OPEN! WHERE'S THE CATCH?
I'LL LOOK IN SCOTTIE'S ROOM! MAYBE HE HAS A CROWBAR OR SOMETHING!

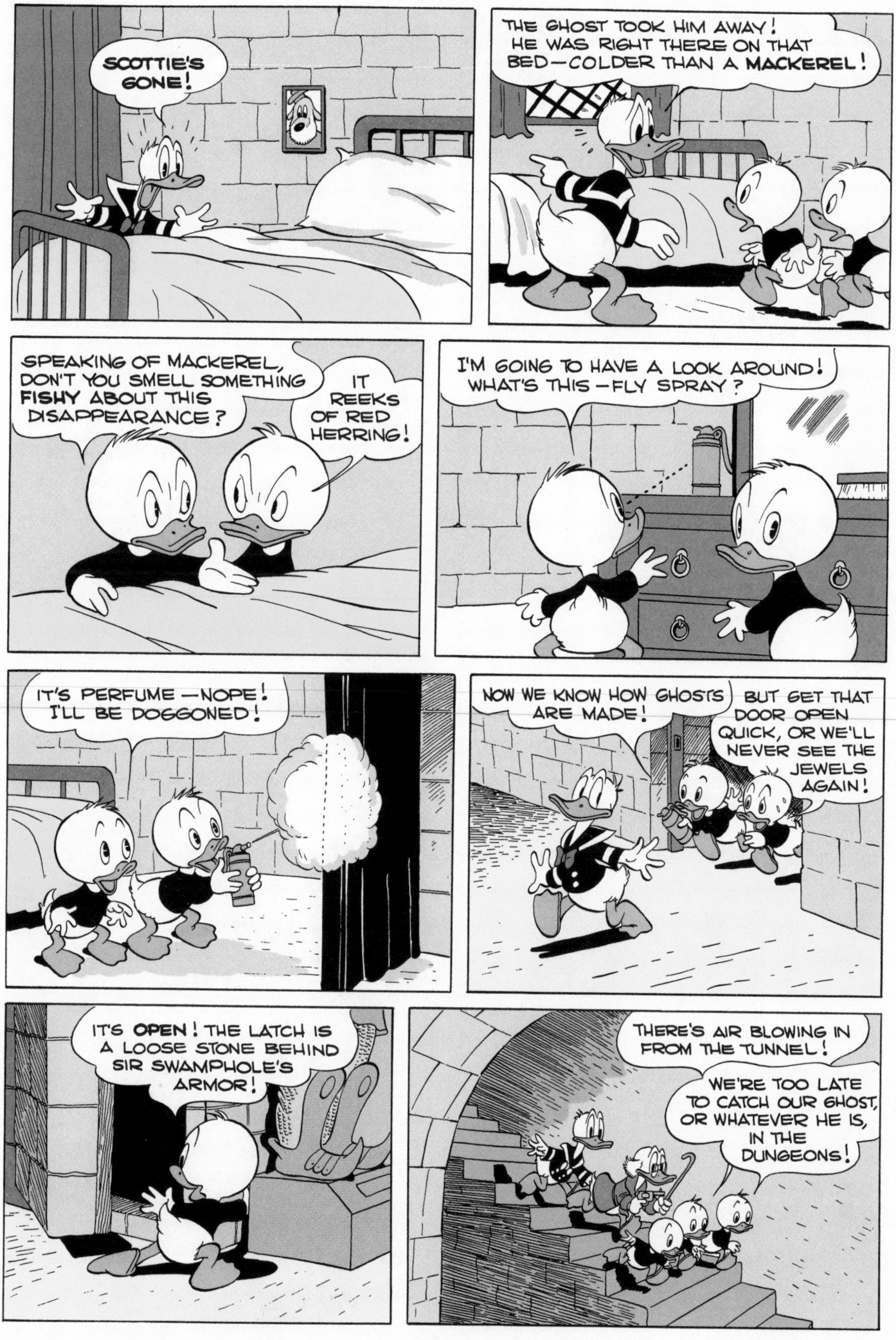

SCOTTIE'S GONE!
THE GHOST TOOK HIM AWAY! HE WAS RIGHT THERE ON THAT BED—COLDER THAN A MACKEREL!
SPEAKING OF MACKEREL, DON'T YOU SMELL SOMETHING FISHY ABOUT THIS DISAPPEARANCE?
IT REEKS OF RED HERRING!
I'M GOING TO HAVE A LOOK AROUND! WHAT'S THIS—FLY SPRAY?
IT'S PERFUME—NOPE! I'LL BE DOGGONED!
NOW WE KNOW HOW GHOSTS ARE MADE!
BUT GET THAT DOOR OPEN QUICK, OR WE'LL NEVER SEE THE JEWELS AGAIN!
IT'S OPEN! THE LATCH IS A LOOSE STONE BEHIND SIR SWAMPHOLE'S ARMOR!
THERE'S AIR BLOWING IN FROM THE TUNNEL!
WE'RE TOO LATE TO CATCH OUR GHOST, OR WHATEVER HE IS, IN THE DUNGEONS!

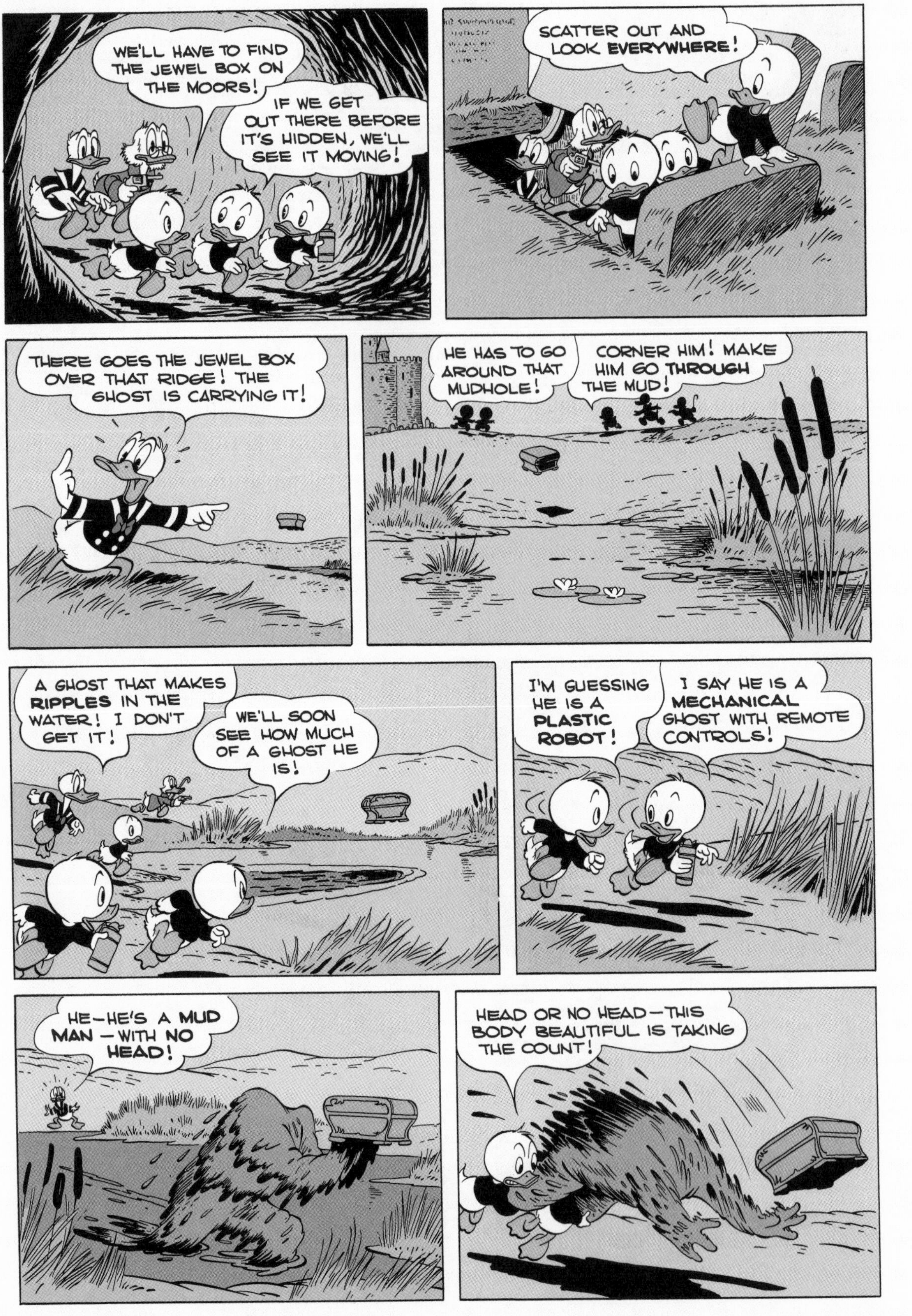
WE'LL HAVE TO FIND THE JEWEL BOX ON THE MOORS!
IF WE GET OUT THERE BEFORE IT'S HIDDEN, WE'LL SEE IT MOVING!
SCATTER OUT AND LOOK EVERYWHERE!
THERE GOES THE JEWEL BOX OVER THAT RIDGE! THE GHOST IS CARRYING IT!
HE HAS TO GO AROUND THAT MUDHOLE!
CORNER HIM! MAKE HIM GO THROUGH THE MUD!
A GHOST THAT MAKES RIPPLES IN THE WATER! I DON'T GET IT!
WE'LL SOON SEE HOW MUCH OF A GHOST HE IS!
I'M GUESSING HE IS A PLASTIC ROBOT!
I SAY HE IS A MECHANICAL GHOST WITH REMOTE CONTROLS!
HE—HE'S A MUD MAN—WITH NO HEAD!
HEAD OR NO HEAD—THIS BODY BEAUTIFUL IS TAKING THE COUNT!

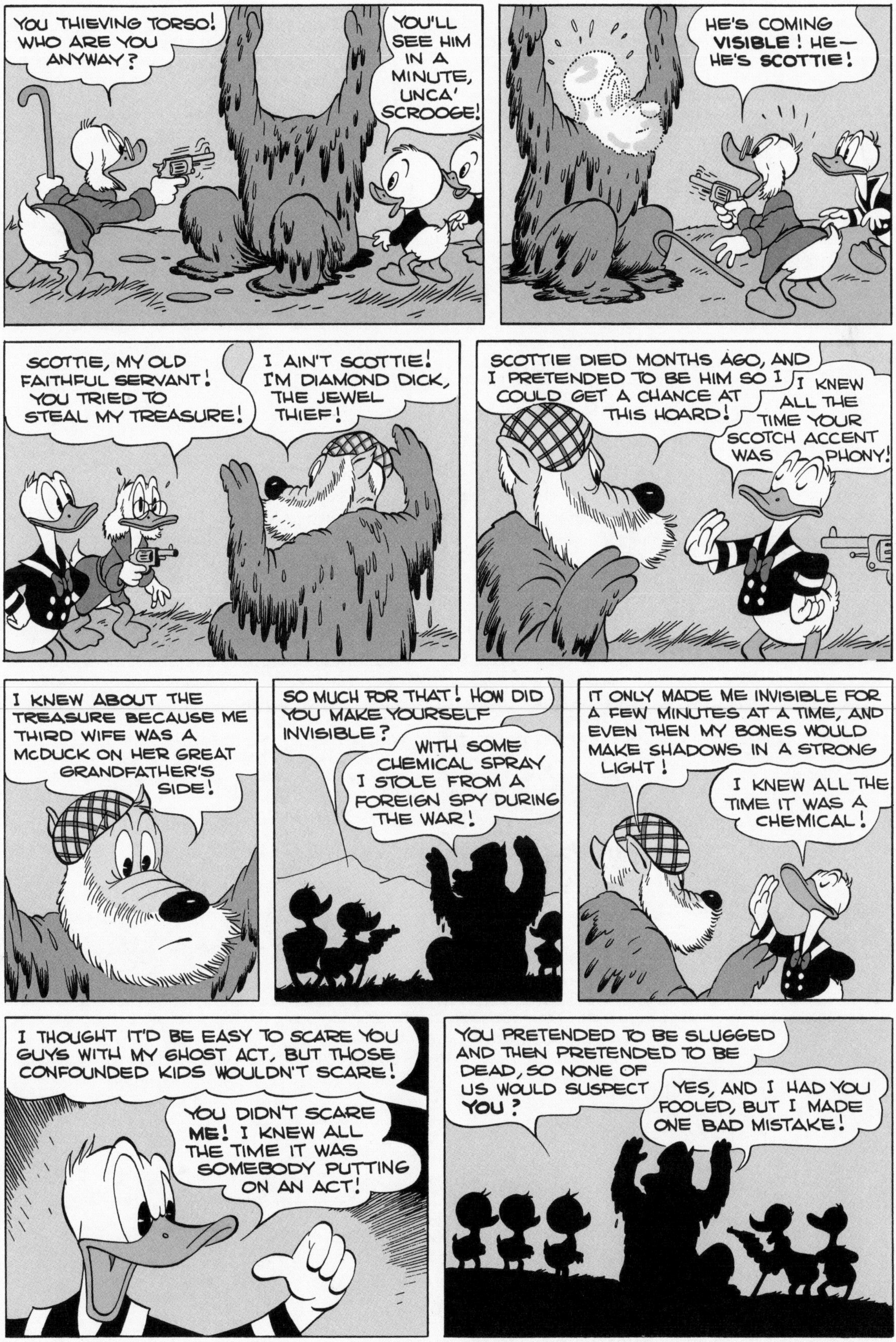
YOU THIEVING TORSO! WHO ARE YOU ANYWAY?
YOU'LL SEE HIM IN A MINUTE, UNCA' SCROOGE!
HE'S COMING VISIBLE! HE— HE'S SCOTTIE!
SCOTTIE, MY OLD FAITHFUL SERVANT! YOU TRIED TO STEAL MY TREASURE!
I AIN'T SCOTTIE! I'M DIAMOND DICK, THE JEWEL THIEF!
SCOTTIE DIED MONTHS AGO, AND I PRETENDED TO BE HIM SO I COULD GET A CHANCE AT THIS HOARD!
I KNEW ALL THE TIME YOUR SCOTCH ACCENT WAS PHONY!
I KNEW ABOUT THE TREASURE BECAUSE ME THIRD WIFE WAS A McDUCK ON HER GREAT GRANDFATHER'S SIDE!
SO MUCH FOR THAT! HOW DID YOU MAKE YOURSELF INVISIBLE?
WITH SOME CHEMICAL SPRAY I STOLE FROM A FOREIGN SPY DURING THE WAR!
IT ONLY MADE ME INVISIBLE FOR A FEW MINUTES AT A TIME, AND EVEN THEN MY BONES WOULD MAKE SHADOWS IN A STRONG LIGHT!
I KNEW ALL THE TIME IT WAS A CHEMICAL!
I THOUGHT IT'D BE EASY TO SCARE YOU GUYS WITH MY GHOST ACT, BUT THOSE CONFOUNDED KIDS WOULDN'T SCARE!
YOU DIDN'T SCARE ME! I KNEW ALL THE TIME IT WAS SOMEBODY PUTTING ON AN ACT!
YOU PRETENDED TO BE SLUGGED AND THEN PRETENDED TO BE DEAD, SO NONE OF US WOULD SUSPECT YOU?
YES, AND I HAD YOU FOOLED, BUT I MADE ONE BAD MISTAKE!

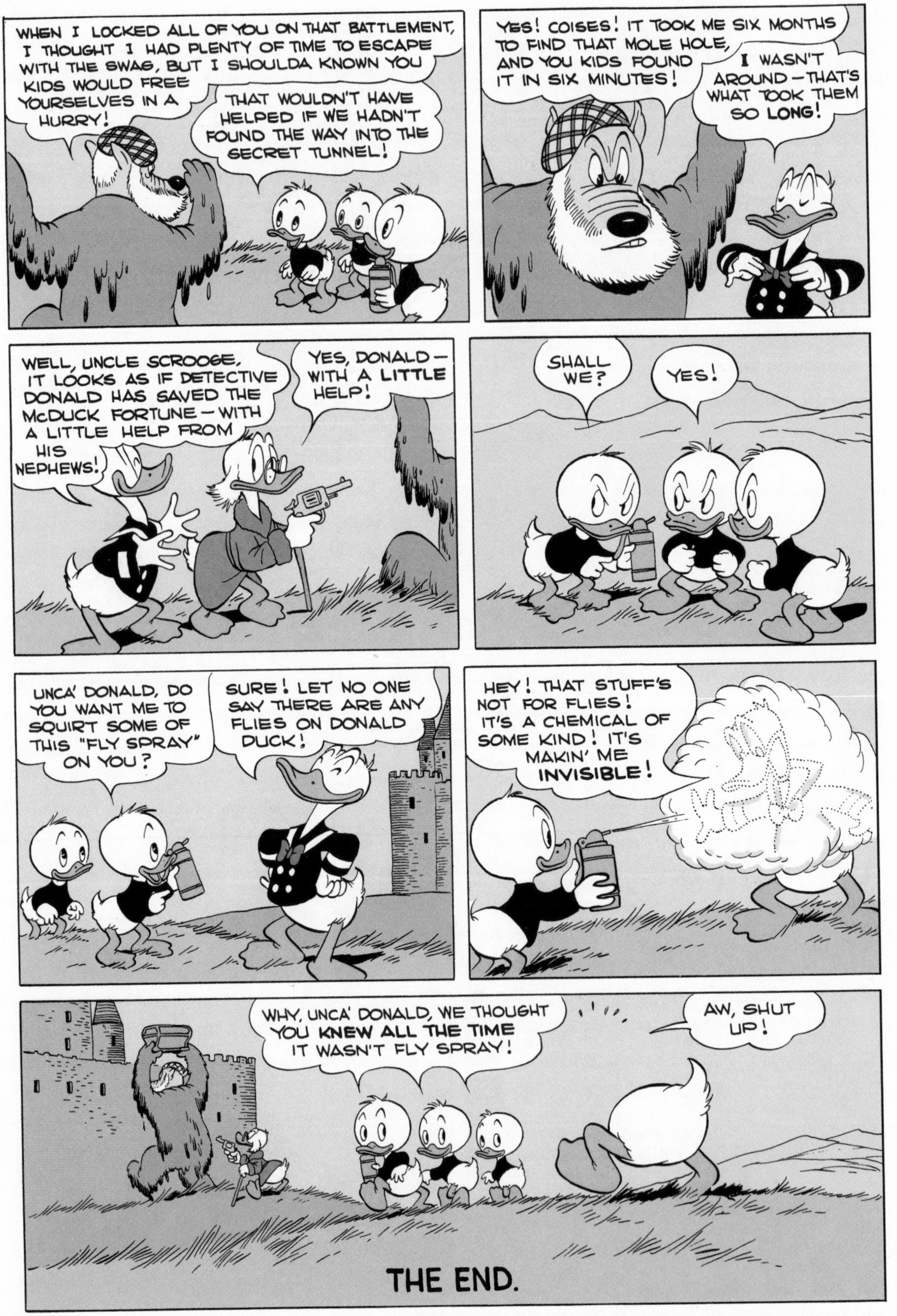
WHEN I LOCKED ALL OF YOU ON THAT BATTLEMENT, I THOUGHT I HAD PLENTY OF TIME TO ESCAPE WITH THE SWAG, BUT I SHOULDA KNOWN YOU KIDS WOULD FREE YOURSELVES IN A HURRY!
THAT WOULDN'T HAVE HELPED IF WE HADN'T FOUND THE WAY INTO THE SECRET TUNNEL!
YES! COISES! IT TOOK ME SIX MONTHS TO FIND THAT MOLE HOLE, AND YOU KIDS FOUND IT IN SIX MINUTES!
I WASN'T AROUND—THAT'S WHAT TOOK THEM SO LONG!
WELL, UNCLE SCROOGE, IT LOOKS AS IF DETECTIVE DONALD HAS SAVED THE McDUCK FORTUNE—WITH A LITTLE HELP FROM HIS NEPHEWS!
YES, DONALD—WITH A LITTLE HELP!
SHALL WE?
YES!
UNCA' DONALD, DO YOU WANT ME TO SQUIRT SOME OF THIS "FLY SPRAY" ON YOU?
SURE! LET NO ONE SAY THERE ARE ANY FLIES ON DONALD DUCK!
HEY! THAT STUFF'S NOT FOR FLIES! IT'S A CHEMICAL OF SOME KIND! IT'S MAKIN' ME INVISIBLE!
WHY, UNCA' DONALD, WE THOUGHT YOU KNEW ALL THE TIME IT WASN'T FLY SPRAY!
AW, SHUT UP!
THE END.

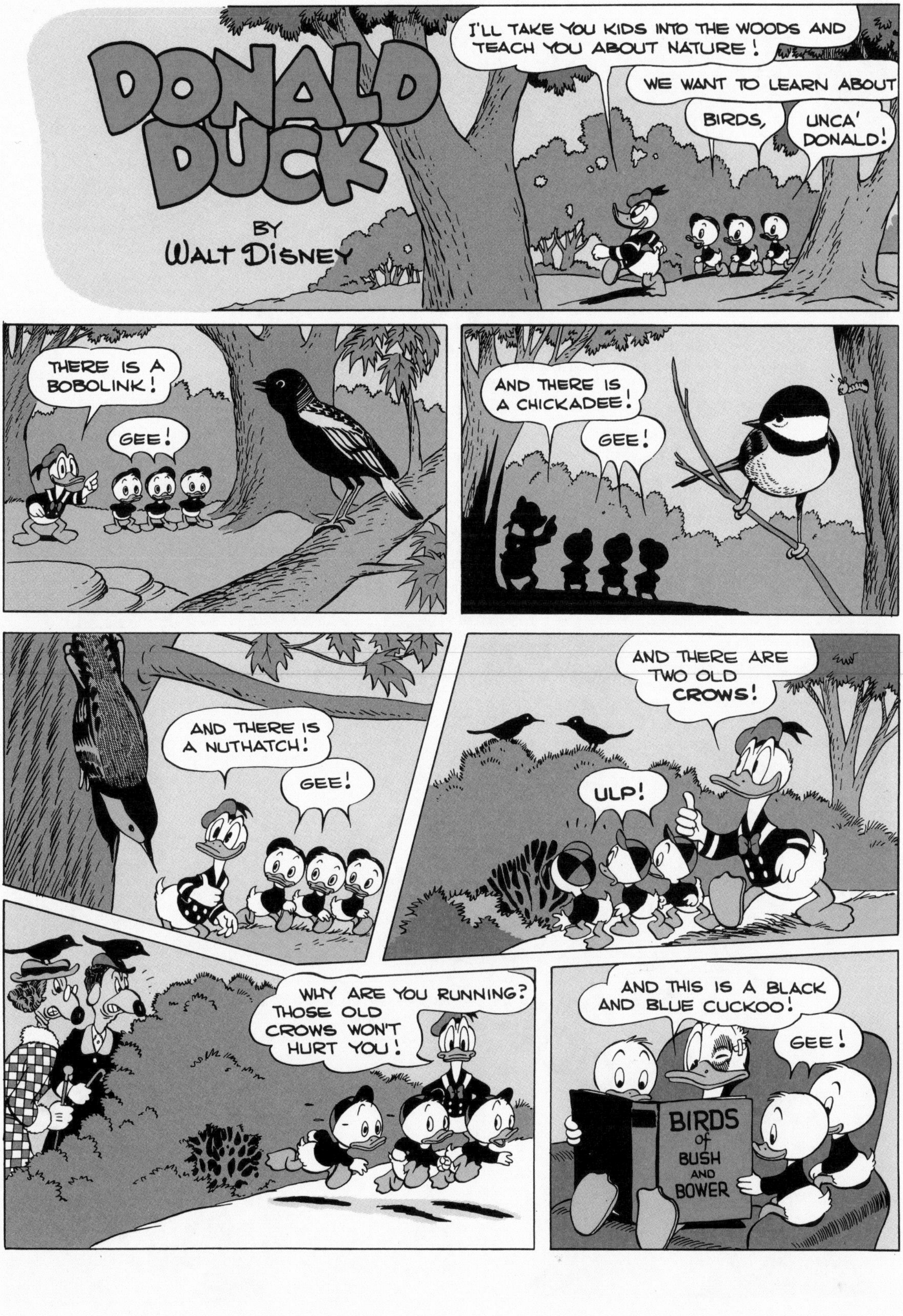
DONALD DUCK
BY WALT DISNEY
I'LL TAKE YOU KIDS INTO THE WOODS AND TEACH YOU ABOUT NATURE!
WE WANT TO LEARN ABOUT
BIRDS,
UNCA' DONALD!
THERE IS A BOBOLINK!
GEE!
AND THERE IS A CHICKADEE!
GEE!
AND THERE IS A NUTHATCH!
GEE!
AND THERE ARE TWO OLD CROWS!
ULP!
WHY ARE YOU RUNNING? THOSE OLD CROWS WON'T HURT YOU!
AND THIS IS A BLACK AND BLUE CUCKOO!
GEE!
BIRDS of BUSH AND BOWER

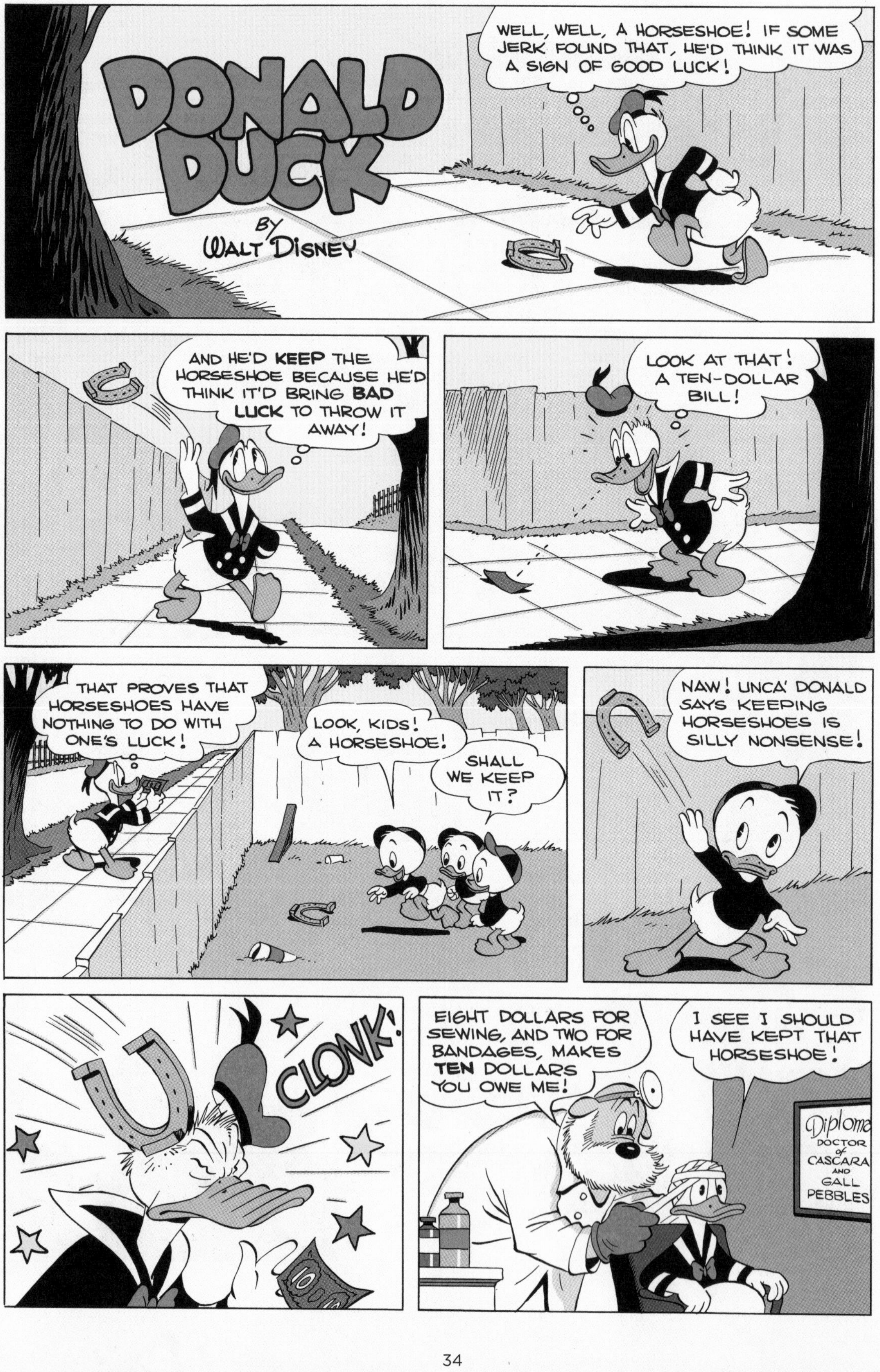
DONALD DUCK
BY WALT DISNEY
WELL, WELL, A HORSESHOE! IF SOME JERK FOUND THAT, HE'D THINK IT WAS A SIGN OF GOOD LUCK!
AND HE'D KEEP THE HORSESHOE BECAUSE HE'D THINK IT'D BRING BAD LUCK TO THROW IT AWAY!
LOOK AT THAT! A TEN-DOLLAR BILL!
THAT PROVES THAT HORSESHOES HAVE NOTHING TO DO WITH ONE'S LUCK!
LOOK, KIDS! A HORSESHOE!
SHALL WE KEEP IT?
NAW! UNCA' DONALD SAYS KEEPING HORSESHOES IS SILLY NONSENSE!
CLONK!
EIGHT DOLLARS FOR SEWING, AND TWO FOR BANDAGES, MAKES TEN DOLLARS YOU OWE ME!
I SEE I SHOULD HAVE KEPT THAT HORSESHOE!
Diploma DOCTOR of CASCARA AND GALL PEBBLES

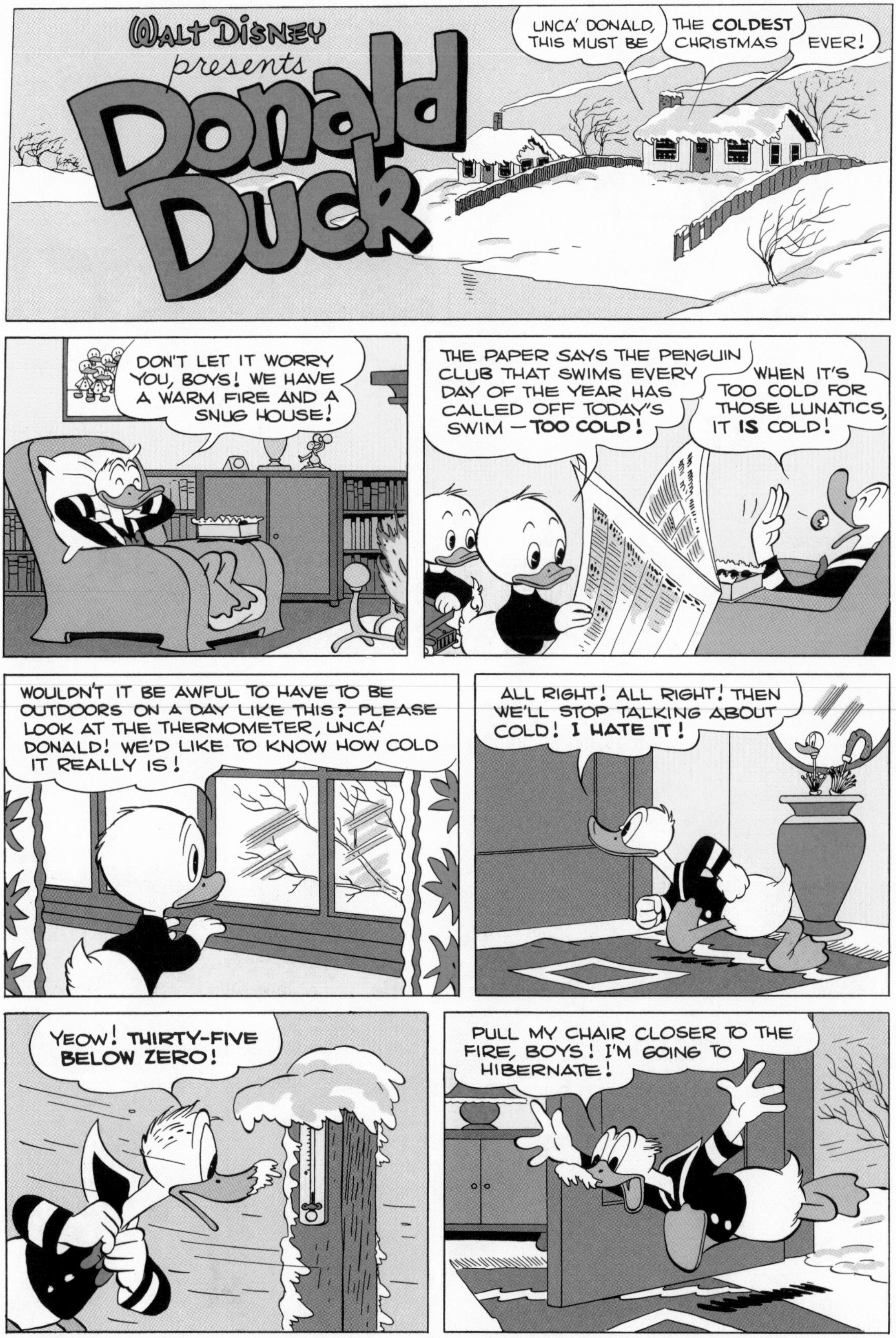
WALT DISNEY
presents
Donald Duck
UNCA' DONALD, THIS MUST BE
THE COLDEST CHRISTMAS
EVER!
DON'T LET IT WORRY YOU, BOYS! WE HAVE A WARM FIRE AND A SNUG HOUSE!
THE PAPER SAYS THE PENGUIN CLUB THAT SWIMS EVERY DAY OF THE YEAR HAS CALLED OFF TODAY'S SWIM — TOO COLD!
WHEN IT'S TOO COLD FOR THOSE LUNATICS, IT IS COLD!
WOULDN'T IT BE AWFUL TO HAVE TO BE OUTDOORS ON A DAY LIKE THIS? PLEASE LOOK AT THE THERMOMETER, UNCA' DONALD! WE'D LIKE TO KNOW HOW COLD IT REALLY IS!
ALL RIGHT! ALL RIGHT! THEN WE'LL STOP TALKING ABOUT COLD! I HATE IT!
YEOW! THIRTY-FIVE BELOW ZERO!
PULL MY CHAIR CLOSER TO THE FIRE, BOYS! I'M GOING TO HIBERNATE!

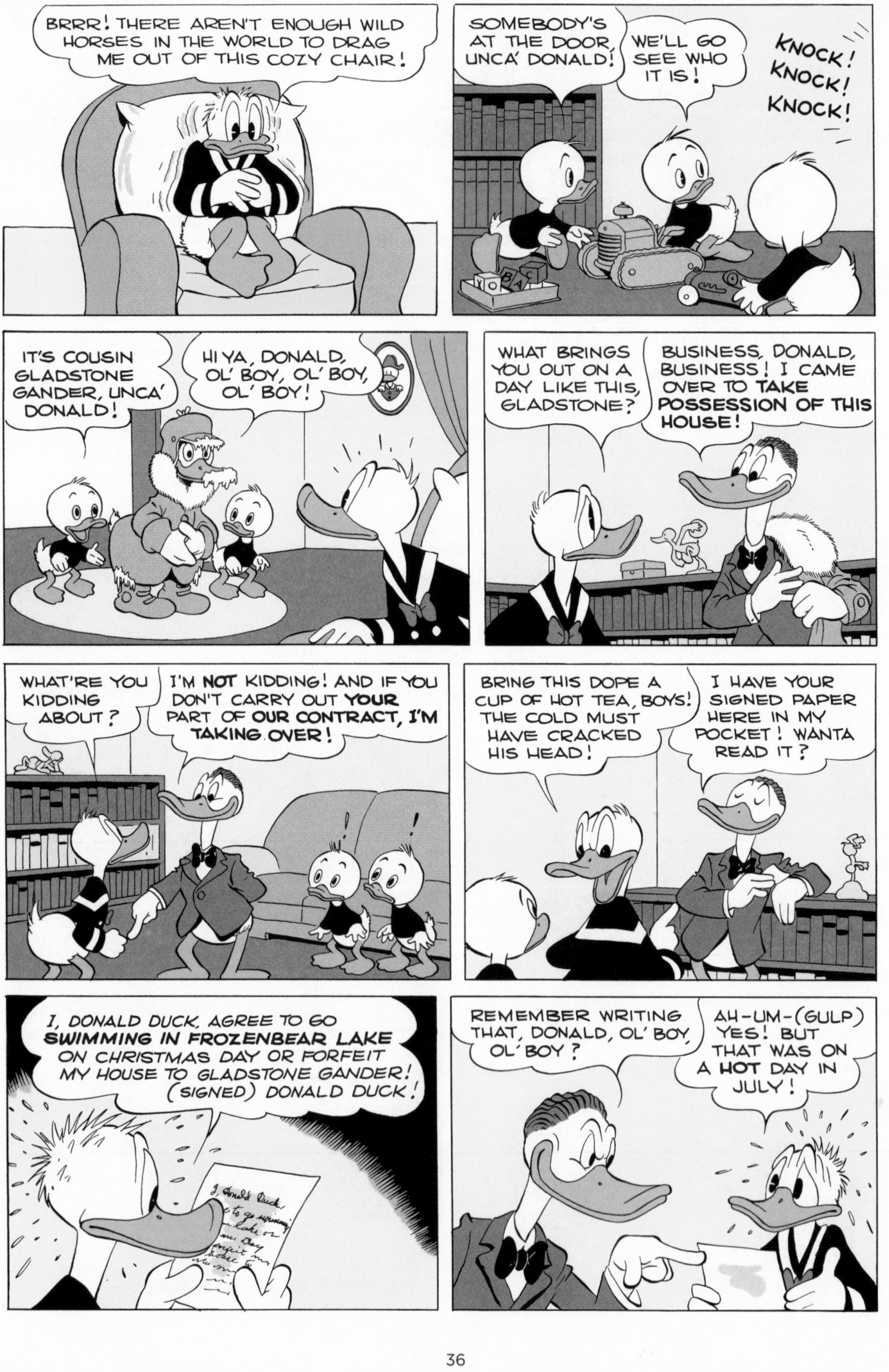
BRRR! THERE AREN'T ENOUGH WILD HORSES IN THE WORLD TO DRAG ME OUT OF THIS COZY CHAIR!
SOMEBODY'S AT THE DOOR, UNCA' DONALD!
WE'LL GO SEE WHO IT IS!
KNOCK! KNOCK! KNOCK!
IT'S COUSIN GLADSTONE GANDER, UNCA' DONALD!
HI YA, DONALD, OL' BOY, OL' BOY, OL' BOY!
WHAT BRINGS YOU OUT ON A DAY LIKE THIS, GLADSTONE?
BUSINESS, DONALD, BUSINESS! I CAME OVER TO **TAKE POSSESSION OF THIS HOUSE!**
WHAT'RE YOU KIDDING ABOUT?
I'M **NOT** KIDDING! AND IF YOU DON'T CARRY OUT **YOUR** PART OF **OUR CONTRACT, I'M TAKING OVER!**
BRING THIS DOPE A CUP OF HOT TEA, BOYS! THE COLD MUST HAVE CRACKED HIS HEAD!
I HAVE YOUR SIGNED PAPER HERE IN MY POCKET! WANTA READ IT?
I, DONALD DUCK, AGREE TO GO **SWIMMING IN FROZENBEAR LAKE** *ON CHRISTMAS DAY OR FORFEIT MY HOUSE TO GLADSTONE GANDER! (SIGNED) DONALD DUCK!*
REMEMBER WRITING THAT, DONALD, OL' BOY, OL' BOY?
AH-UM-(GULP) YES! BUT THAT WAS ON A **HOT** DAY IN JULY!

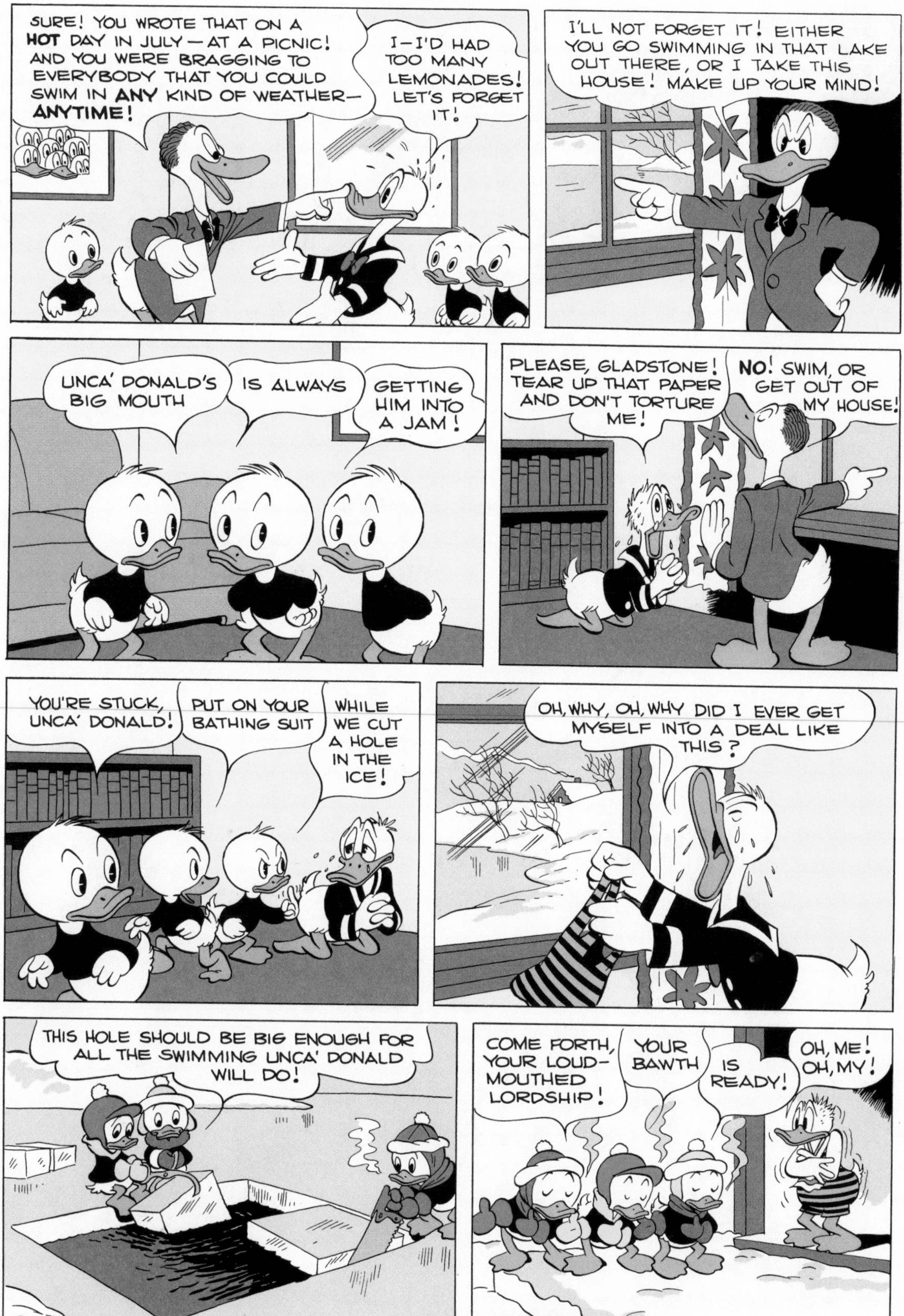
SURE! YOU WROTE THAT ON A HOT DAY IN JULY—AT A PICNIC! AND YOU WERE BRAGGING TO EVERYBODY THAT YOU COULD SWIM IN ANY KIND OF WEATHER— ANYTIME!
I—I'D HAD TOO MANY LEMONADES! LET'S FORGET IT!
I'LL NOT FORGET IT! EITHER YOU GO SWIMMING IN THAT LAKE OUT THERE, OR I TAKE THIS HOUSE! MAKE UP YOUR MIND!
UNCA' DONALD'S BIG MOUTH
IS ALWAYS
GETTING HIM INTO A JAM!
PLEASE, GLADSTONE! TEAR UP THAT PAPER AND DON'T TORTURE ME!
NO! SWIM, OR GET OUT OF MY HOUSE!
YOU'RE STUCK, UNCA' DONALD!
PUT ON YOUR BATHING SUIT
WHILE WE CUT A HOLE IN THE ICE!
OH, WHY, OH, WHY DID I EVER GET MYSELF INTO A DEAL LIKE THIS?
THIS HOLE SHOULD BE BIG ENOUGH FOR ALL THE SWIMMING UNCA' DONALD WILL DO!
COME FORTH, YOUR LOUD-MOUTHED LORDSHIP!
YOUR BAWTH
IS READY!
OH, ME! OH, MY!

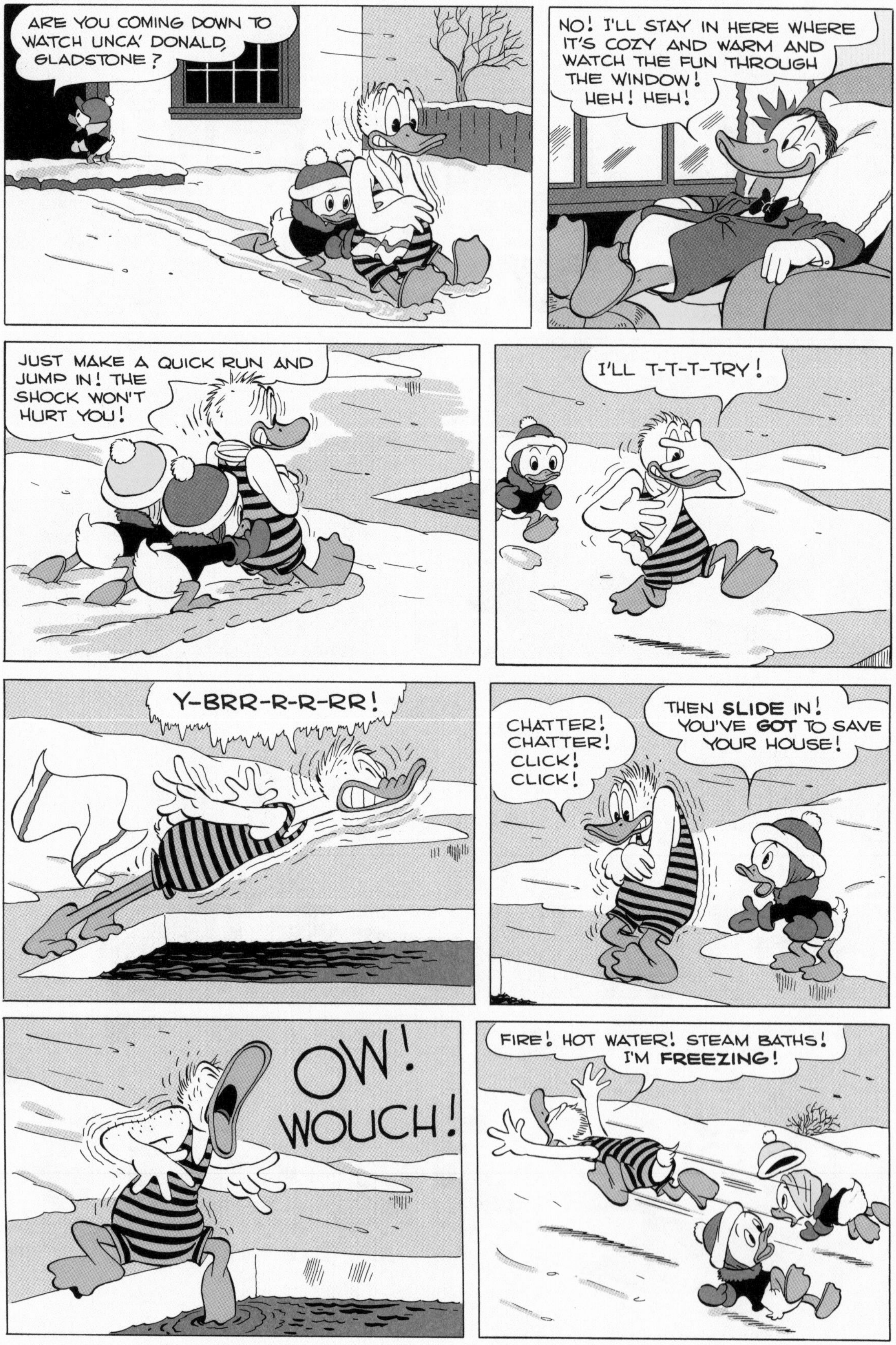
ARE YOU COMING DOWN TO WATCH UNCA' DONALD, GLADSTONE?
NO! I'LL STAY IN HERE WHERE IT'S COZY AND WARM AND WATCH THE FUN THROUGH THE WINDOW! HEH! HEH!
JUST MAKE A QUICK RUN AND JUMP IN! THE SHOCK WON'T HURT YOU!
I'LL T-T-T-TRY!
Y-BRR-R-R-RR!
CHATTER! CHATTER! CLICK! CLICK!
THEN **SLIDE** IN! YOU'VE **GOT** TO SAVE YOUR HOUSE!
OW! WOUCH!
FIRE! HOT WATER! STEAM BATHS! I'M **FREEZING**!

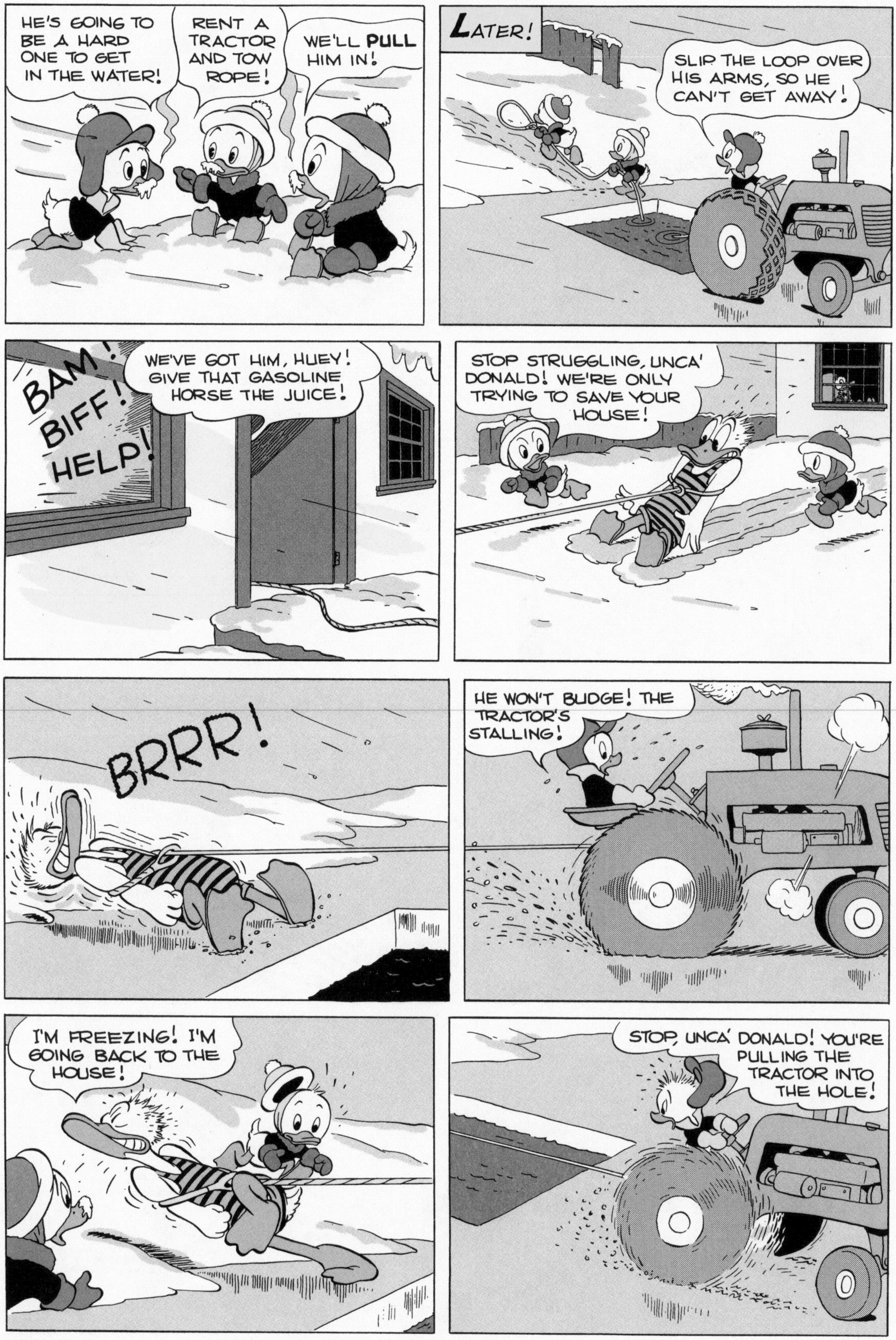
HE'S GOING TO BE A HARD ONE TO GET IN THE WATER!
RENT A TRACTOR AND TOW ROPE!
WE'LL **PULL** HIM IN!
LATER!
SLIP THE LOOP OVER HIS ARMS, SO HE CAN'T GET AWAY!
BAM! BIFF! HELP!
WE'VE GOT HIM, HUEY! GIVE THAT GASOLINE HORSE THE JUICE!
STOP STRUGGLING, UNCA' DONALD! WE'RE ONLY TRYING TO SAVE YOUR HOUSE!
BRRR!
HE WON'T BUDGE! THE TRACTOR'S STALLING!
I'M FREEZING! I'M GOING BACK TO THE HOUSE!
STOP, UNCA' DONALD! YOU'RE PULLING THE TRACTOR INTO THE HOLE!

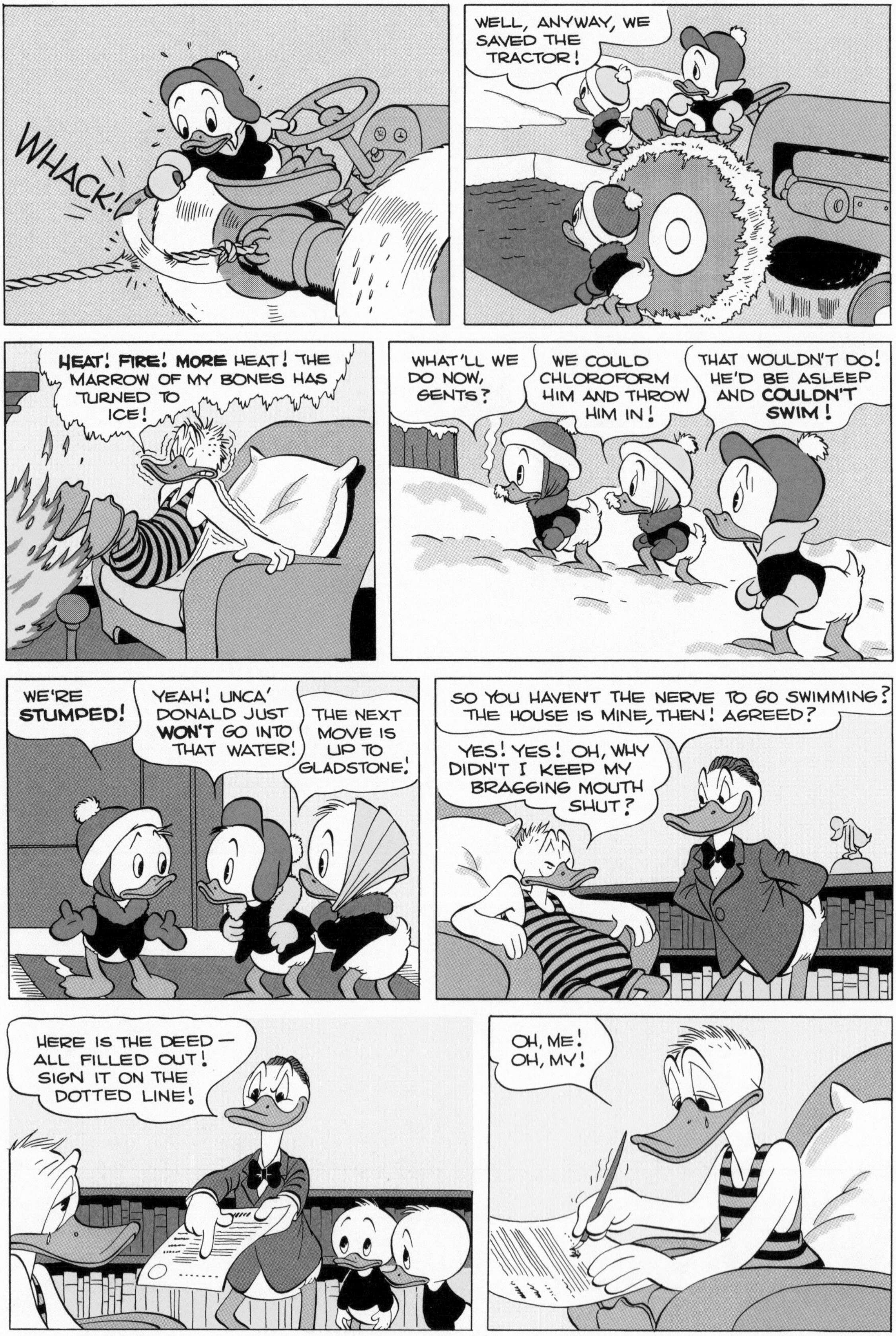
WHACK!
WELL, ANYWAY, WE SAVED THE TRACTOR!
HEAT! FIRE! MORE HEAT! THE MARROW OF MY BONES HAS TURNED TO ICE!
WHAT'LL WE DO NOW, GENTS?
WE COULD CHLOROFORM HIM AND THROW HIM IN!
THAT WOULDN'T DO! HE'D BE ASLEEP AND COULDN'T SWIM!
WE'RE STUMPED!
YEAH! UNCA' DONALD JUST WON'T GO INTO THAT WATER!
THE NEXT MOVE IS UP TO GLADSTONE!
SO YOU HAVEN'T THE NERVE TO GO SWIMMING? THE HOUSE IS MINE, THEN! AGREED?
YES! YES! OH, WHY DIDN'T I KEEP MY BRAGGING MOUTH SHUT?
HERE IS THE DEED— ALL FILLED OUT! SIGN IT ON THE DOTTED LINE!
OH, ME! OH, MY!

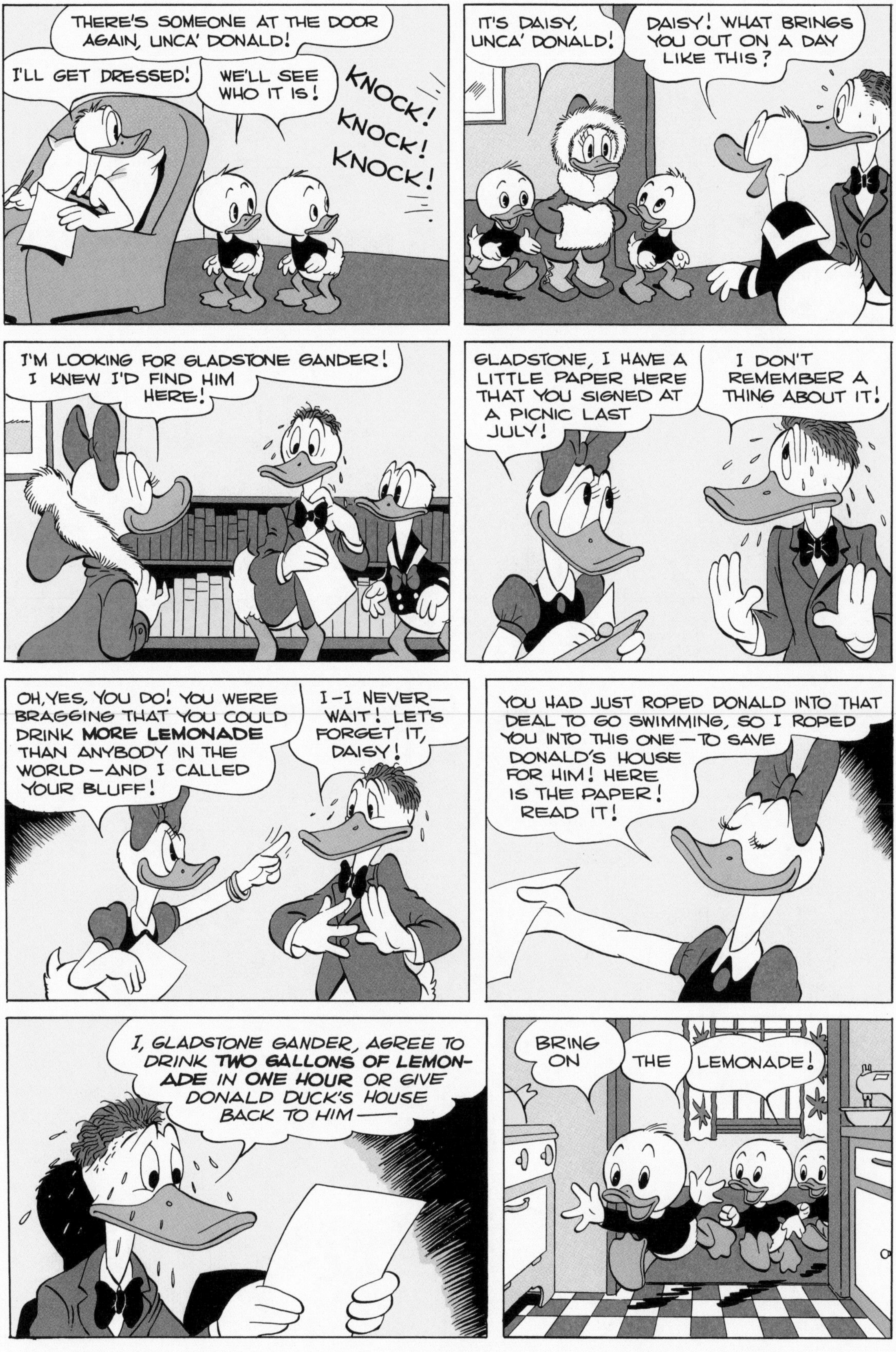
THERE'S SOMEONE AT THE DOOR AGAIN, UNCA' DONALD!
I'LL GET DRESSED!
WE'LL SEE WHO IT IS!
KNOCK! KNOCK! KNOCK!
IT'S DAISY, UNCA' DONALD!
DAISY! WHAT BRINGS YOU OUT ON A DAY LIKE THIS?
I'M LOOKING FOR GLADSTONE GANDER! I KNEW I'D FIND HIM HERE!
GLADSTONE, I HAVE A LITTLE PAPER HERE THAT YOU SIGNED AT A PICNIC LAST JULY!
I DON'T REMEMBER A THING ABOUT IT!
OH, YES, YOU DO! YOU WERE BRAGGING THAT YOU COULD DRINK **MORE LEMONADE** THAN ANYBODY IN THE WORLD—AND I CALLED YOUR BLUFF!
I—I NEVER— WAIT! LET'S FORGET IT, DAISY!
YOU HAD JUST ROPED DONALD INTO THAT DEAL TO GO SWIMMING, SO I ROPED YOU INTO THIS ONE—TO SAVE DONALD'S HOUSE FOR HIM! HERE IS THE PAPER! READ IT!
I, GLADSTONE GANDER, AGREE TO DRINK ***TWO GALLONS OF LEMONADE IN ONE HOUR*** *OR GIVE DONALD DUCK'S HOUSE BACK TO HIM——*
BRING ON
THE
LEMONADE!

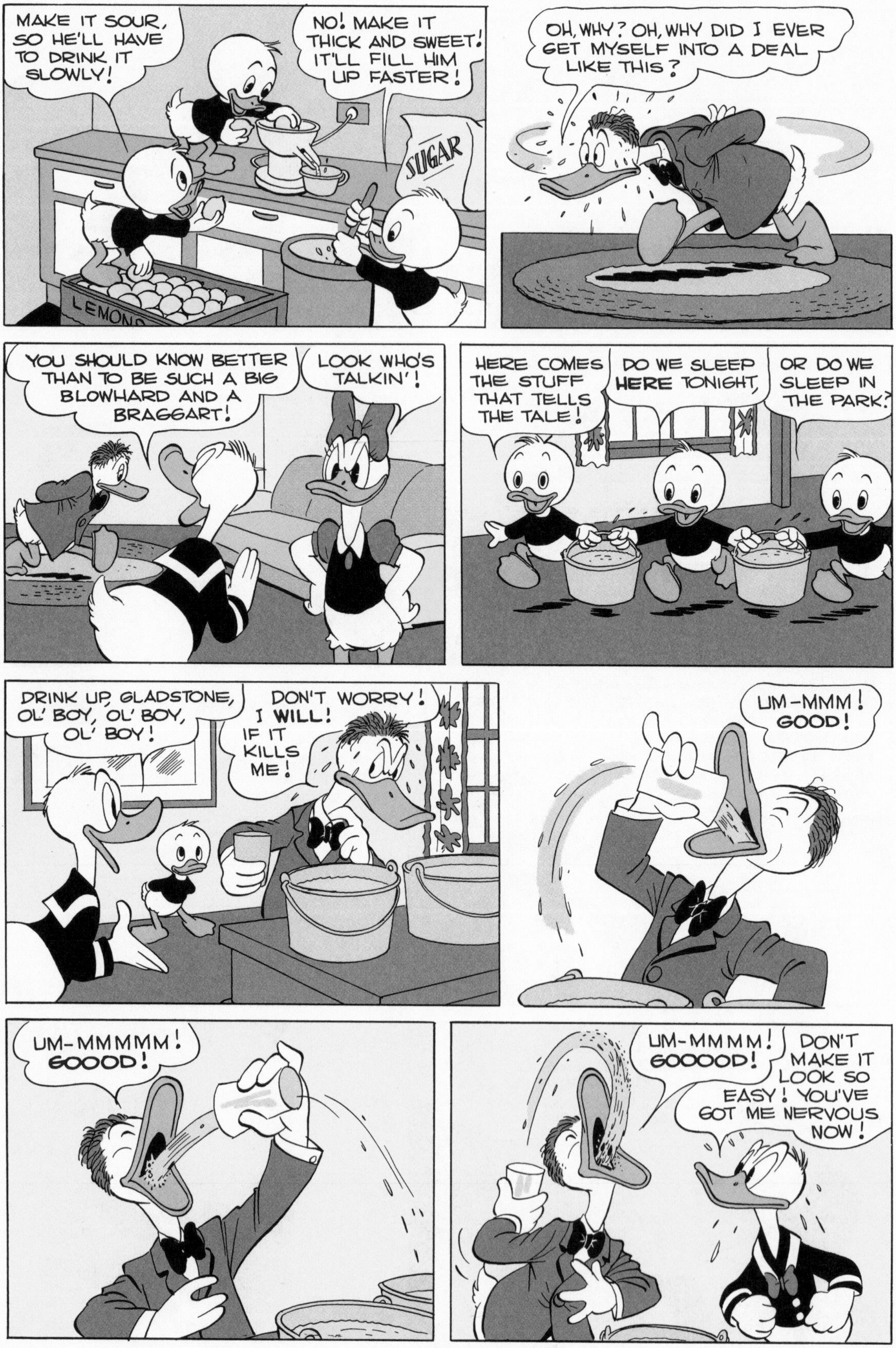
MAKE IT SOUR, SO HE'LL HAVE TO DRINK IT SLOWLY!
NO! MAKE IT THICK AND SWEET! IT'LL FILL HIM UP FASTER!
SUGAR
LEMONS
OH, WHY? OH, WHY DID I EVER GET MYSELF INTO A DEAL LIKE THIS?
YOU SHOULD KNOW BETTER THAN TO BE SUCH A BIG BLOWHARD AND A BRAGGART!
LOOK WHO'S TALKIN'!
HERE COMES THE STUFF THAT TELLS THE TALE!
DO WE SLEEP **HERE** TONIGHT,
OR DO WE SLEEP IN THE PARK?
DRINK UP, GLADSTONE, OL' BOY, OL' BOY, OL' BOY!
DON'T WORRY! I **WILL**! IF IT KILLS ME!
UM-MMM! **GOOD**!
UM-MMMMM! **GOOOD**!
UM-MMMM! **GOOOOD**!
DON'T MAKE IT LOOK SO EASY! YOU'VE GOT ME NERVOUS NOW!

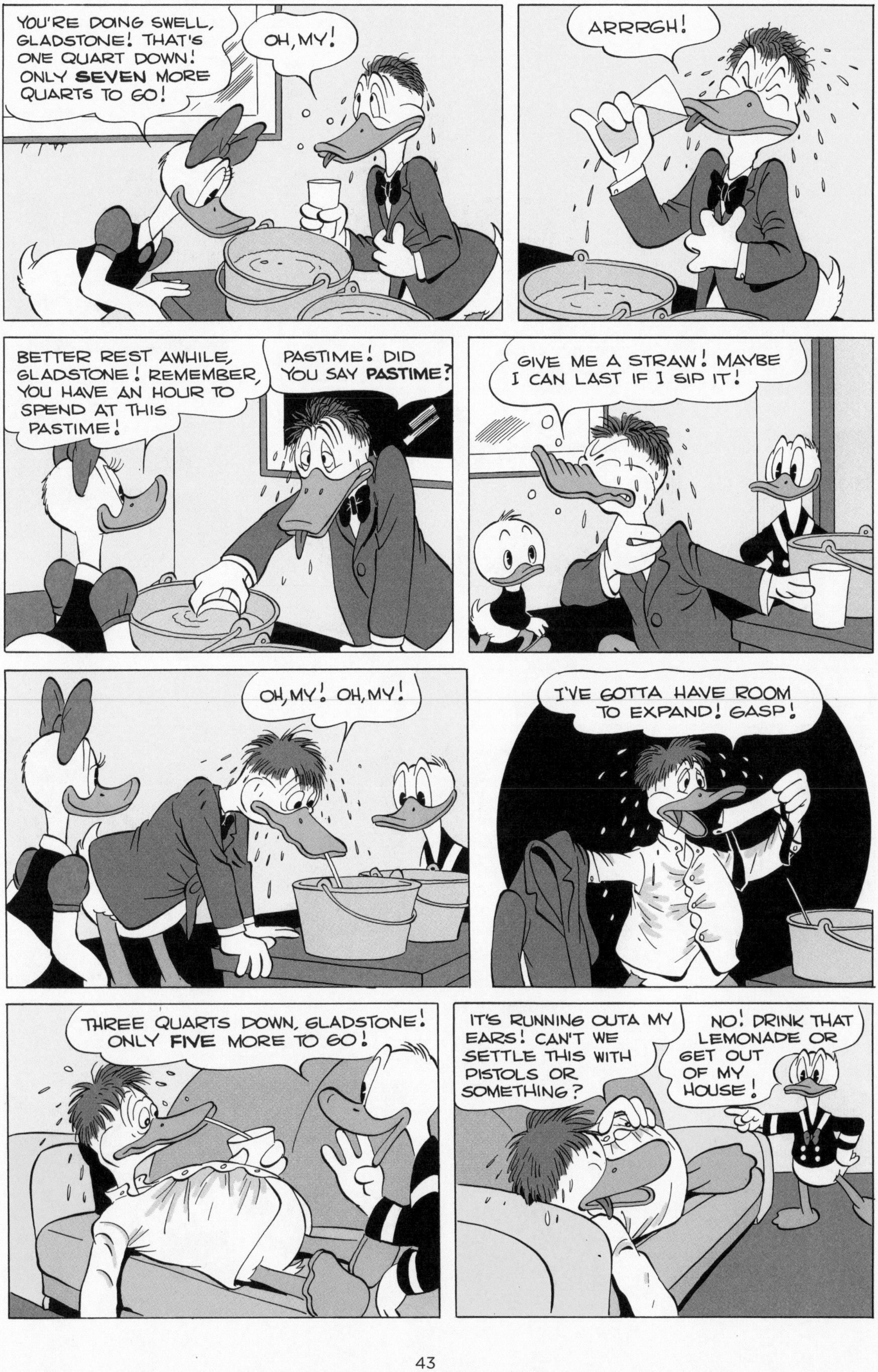
YOU'RE DOING SWELL, GLADSTONE! THAT'S ONE QUART DOWN! ONLY SEVEN MORE QUARTS TO GO!
OH, MY!
ARRRGH!
BETTER REST AWHILE, GLADSTONE! REMEMBER, YOU HAVE AN HOUR TO SPEND AT THIS PASTIME!
PASTIME! DID YOU SAY PASTIME?
GIVE ME A STRAW! MAYBE I CAN LAST IF I SIP IT!
OH, MY! OH, MY!
I'VE GOTTA HAVE ROOM TO EXPAND! GASP!
THREE QUARTS DOWN, GLADSTONE! ONLY FIVE MORE TO GO!
IT'S RUNNING OUTA MY EARS! CAN'T WE SETTLE THIS WITH PISTOLS OR SOMETHING?
NO! DRINK THAT LEMONADE OR GET OUT OF MY HOUSE!

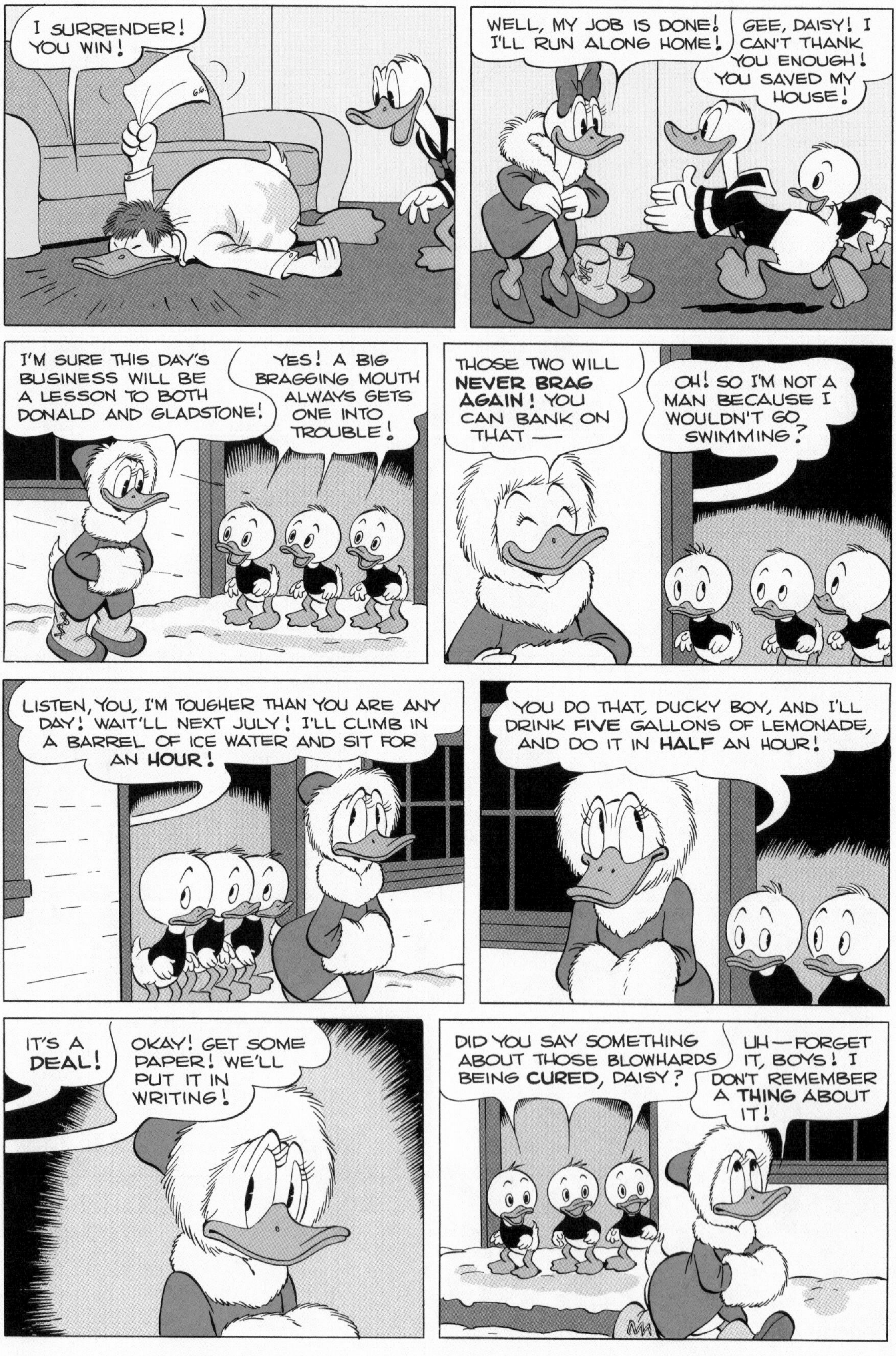
I SURRENDER! YOU WIN!
G.G.
WELL, MY JOB IS DONE! I'LL RUN ALONG HOME!
GEE, DAISY! I CAN'T THANK YOU ENOUGH! YOU SAVED MY HOUSE!
I'M SURE THIS DAY'S BUSINESS WILL BE A LESSON TO BOTH DONALD AND GLADSTONE!
YES! A BIG BRAGGING MOUTH ALWAYS GETS ONE INTO TROUBLE!
THOSE TWO WILL NEVER BRAG AGAIN! YOU CAN BANK ON THAT —
OH! SO I'M NOT A MAN BECAUSE I WOULDN'T GO SWIMMING?
LISTEN, YOU, I'M TOUGHER THAN YOU ARE ANY DAY! WAIT'LL NEXT JULY! I'LL CLIMB IN A BARREL OF ICE WATER AND SIT FOR AN HOUR!
YOU DO THAT, DUCKY BOY, AND I'LL DRINK FIVE GALLONS OF LEMONADE, AND DO IT IN HALF AN HOUR!
IT'S A DEAL!
OKAY! GET SOME PAPER! WE'LL PUT IT IN WRITING!
DID YOU SAY SOMETHING ABOUT THOSE BLOWHARDS BEING CURED, DAISY?
UH—FORGET IT, BOYS! I DON'T REMEMBER A THING ABOUT IT!

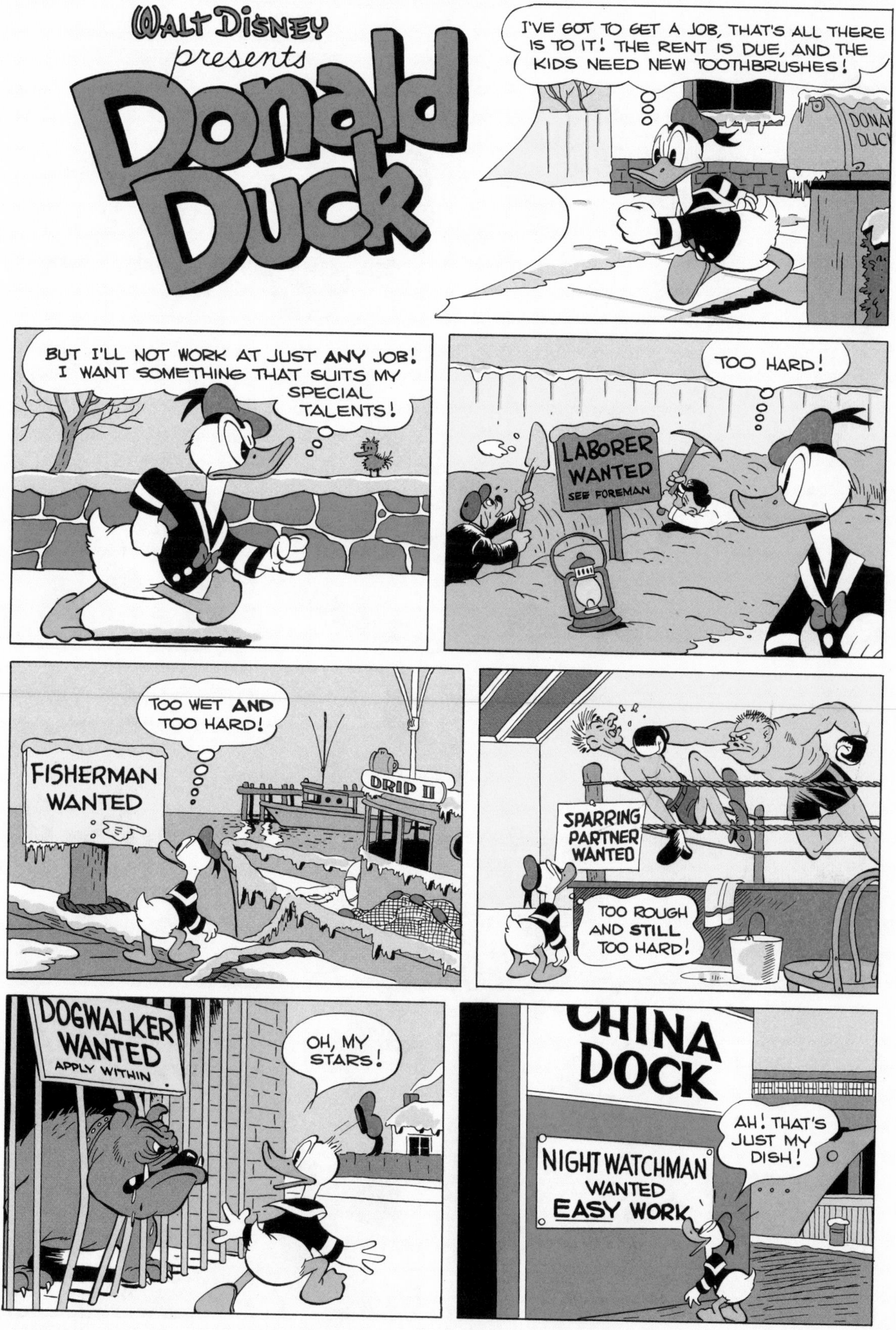
WALT DISNEY
presents
Donald Duck
I'VE GOT TO GET A JOB, THAT'S ALL THERE IS TO IT! THE RENT IS DUE, AND THE KIDS NEED NEW TOOTHBRUSHES!
BUT I'LL NOT WORK AT JUST ANY JOB! I WANT SOMETHING THAT SUITS MY SPECIAL TALENTS!
LABORER WANTED SEE FOREMAN
TOO HARD!
FISHERMAN WANTED
DRIP II
TOO WET AND TOO HARD!
SPARRING PARTNER WANTED
TOO ROUGH AND STILL TOO HARD!
DOGWALKER WANTED APPLY WITHIN
OH, MY STARS!
CHINA DOCK
NIGHT WATCHMAN WANTED EASY WORK
AH! THAT'S JUST MY DISH!

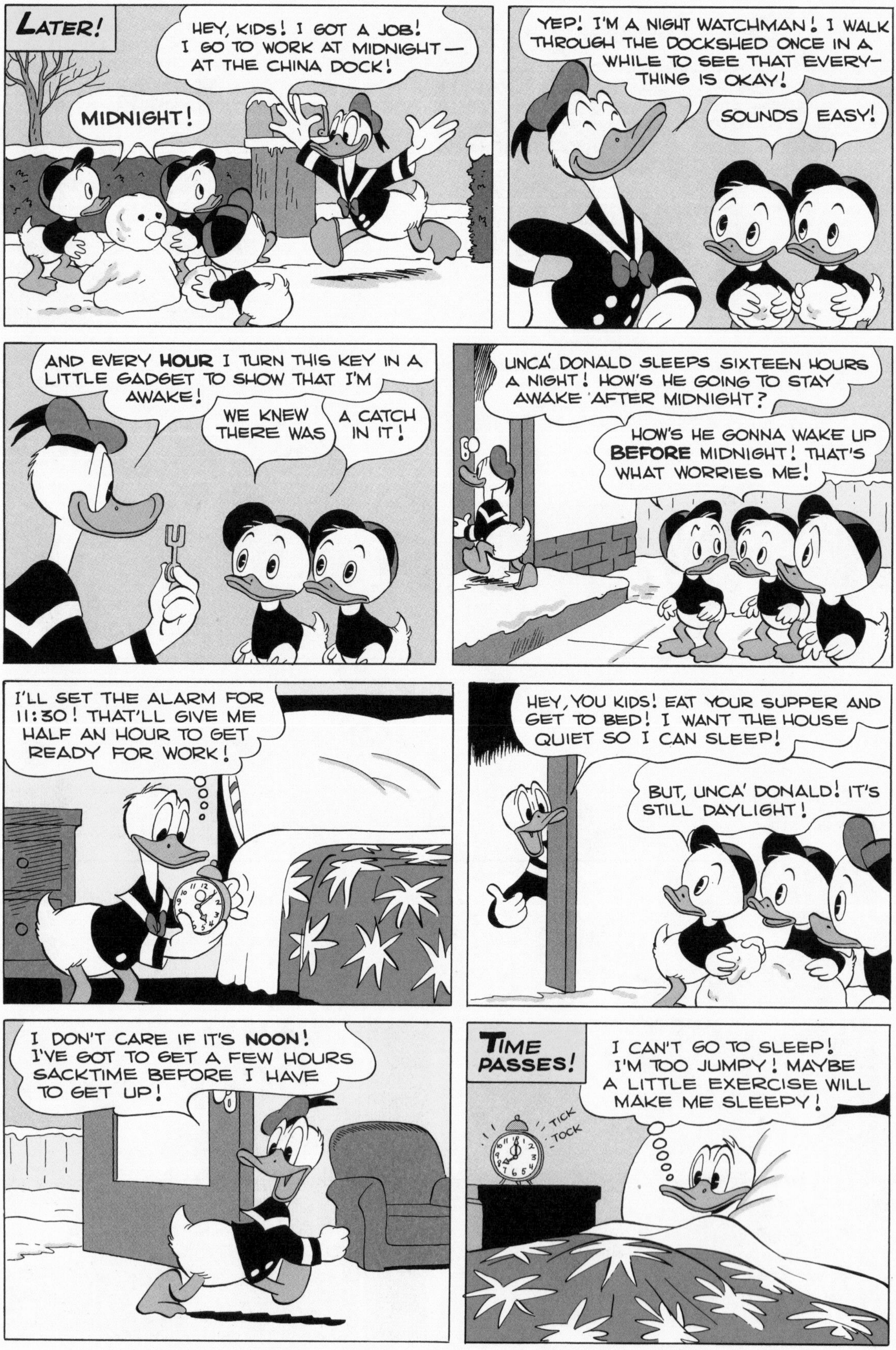
LATER!
HEY, KIDS! I GOT A JOB! I GO TO WORK AT MIDNIGHT— AT THE CHINA DOCK!
MIDNIGHT!
YEP! I'M A NIGHT WATCHMAN! I WALK THROUGH THE DOCKSHED ONCE IN A WHILE TO SEE THAT EVERY-THING IS OKAY!
SOUNDS
EASY!
AND EVERY HOUR I TURN THIS KEY IN A LITTLE GADGET TO SHOW THAT I'M AWAKE!
WE KNEW THERE WAS
A CATCH IN IT!
UNCA' DONALD SLEEPS SIXTEEN HOURS A NIGHT! HOW'S HE GOING TO STAY AWAKE AFTER MIDNIGHT?
HOW'S HE GONNA WAKE UP BEFORE MIDNIGHT! THAT'S WHAT WORRIES ME!
I'LL SET THE ALARM FOR 11:30! THAT'LL GIVE ME HALF AN HOUR TO GET READY FOR WORK!
HEY, YOU KIDS! EAT YOUR SUPPER AND GET TO BED! I WANT THE HOUSE QUIET SO I CAN SLEEP!
BUT, UNCA' DONALD! IT'S STILL DAYLIGHT!
I DON'T CARE IF IT'S NOON! I'VE GOT TO GET A FEW HOURS SACKTIME BEFORE I HAVE TO GET UP!
TIME PASSES!
I CAN'T GO TO SLEEP! I'M TOO JUMPY! MAYBE A LITTLE EXERCISE WILL MAKE ME SLEEPY!
TICK
TOCK

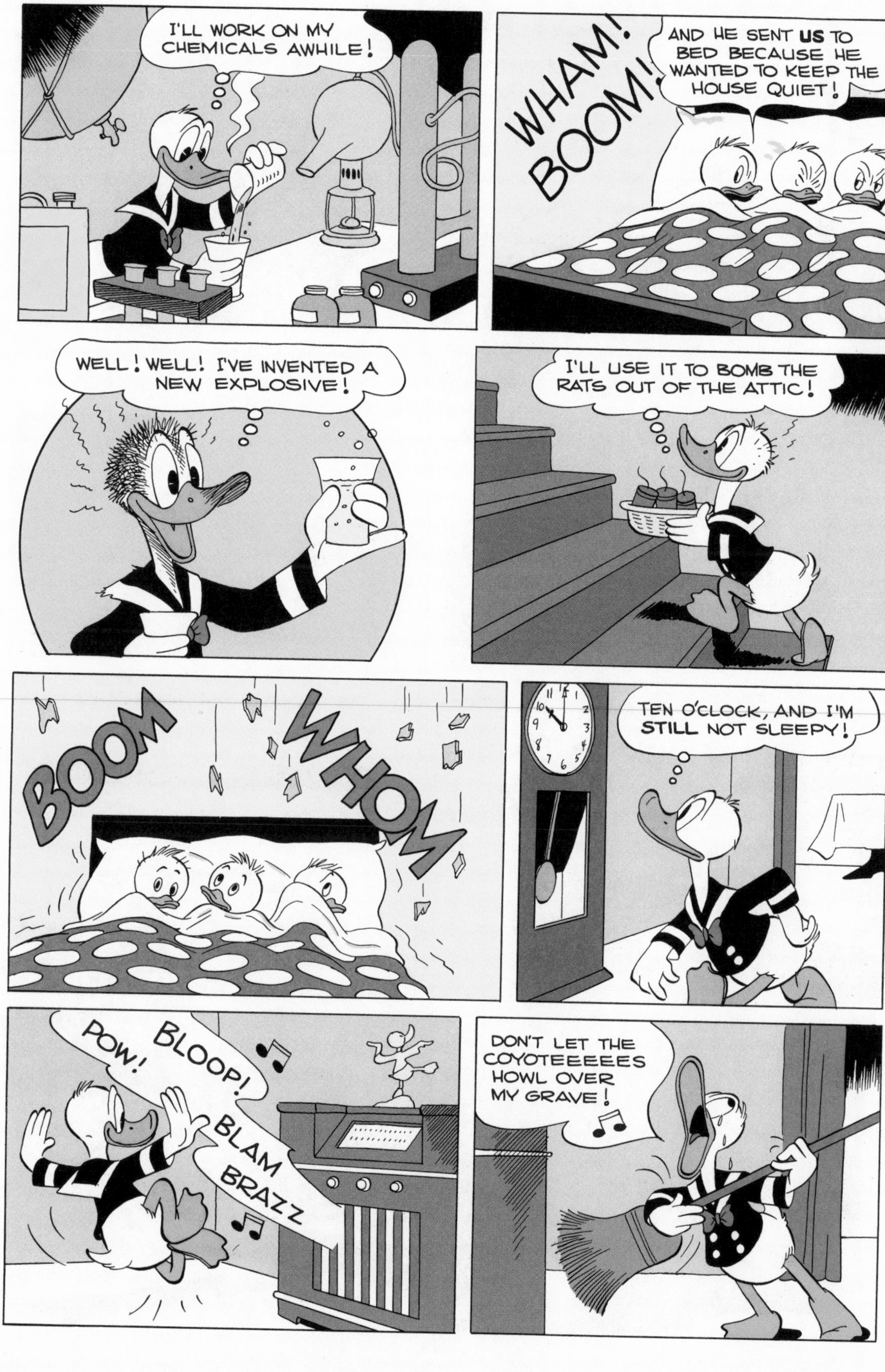

I'LL WORK ON MY CHEMICALS AWHILE!
WHAM! BOOM!
AND HE SENT US TO BED BECAUSE HE WANTED TO KEEP THE HOUSE QUIET!
WELL! WELL! I'VE INVENTED A NEW EXPLOSIVE!
I'LL USE IT TO BOMB THE RATS OUT OF THE ATTIC!
BOOM
WHOM
TEN O'CLOCK, AND I'M STILL NOT SLEEPY!
POW!
BLOOP!
BLAM
BRAZZ
DON'T LET THE COYOTEEEEES HOWL OVER MY GRAVE!

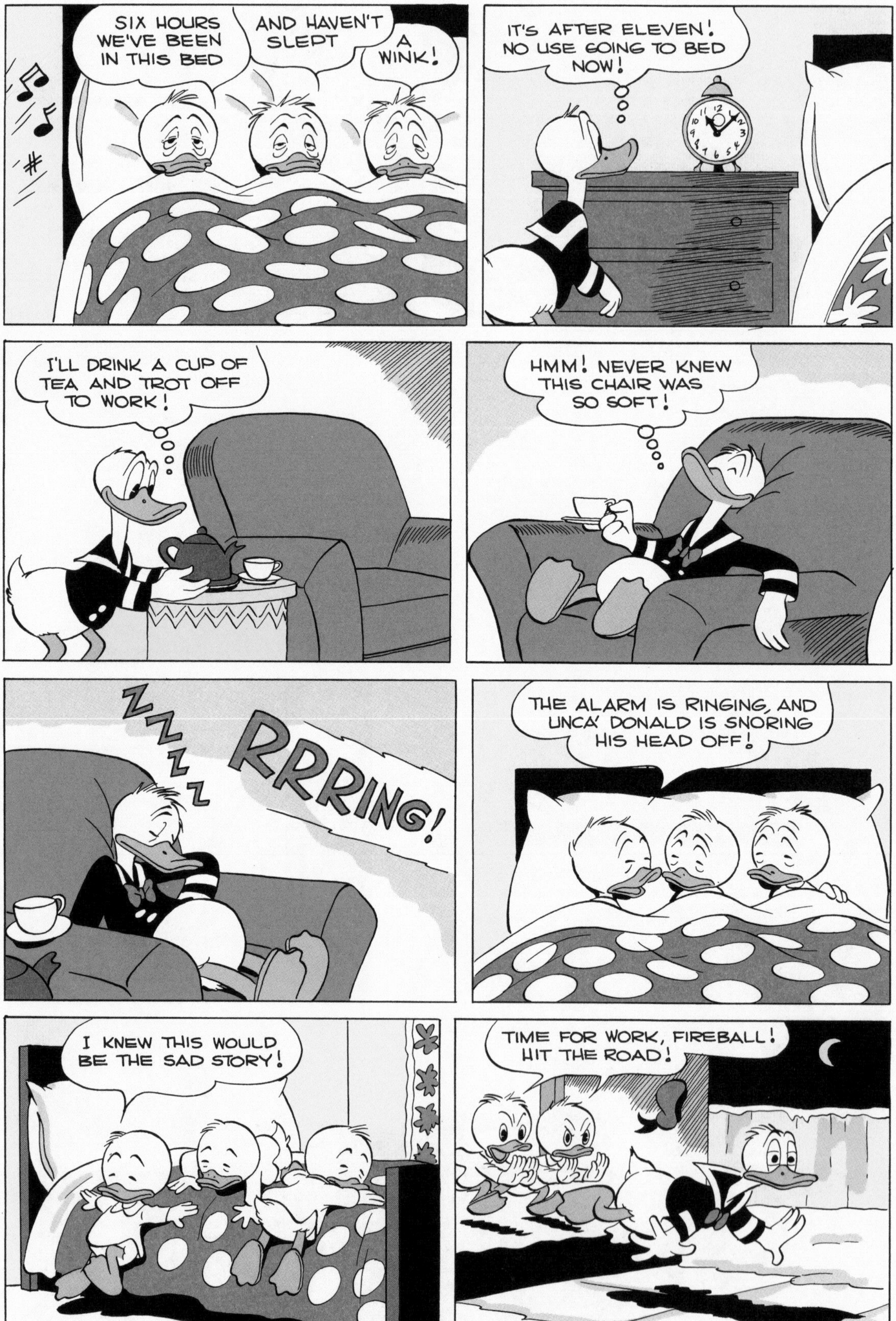

SIX HOURS WE'VE BEEN IN THIS BED
AND HAVEN'T SLEPT
A WINK!
IT'S AFTER ELEVEN! NO USE GOING TO BED NOW!
I'LL DRINK A CUP OF TEA AND TROT OFF TO WORK!
HMM! NEVER KNEW THIS CHAIR WAS SO SOFT!
ZZZZZ
RRRING!
THE ALARM IS RINGING, AND UNCA' DONALD IS SNORING HIS HEAD OFF!
I KNEW THIS WOULD BE THE SAD STORY!
TIME FOR WORK, FIREBALL! HIT THE ROAD!

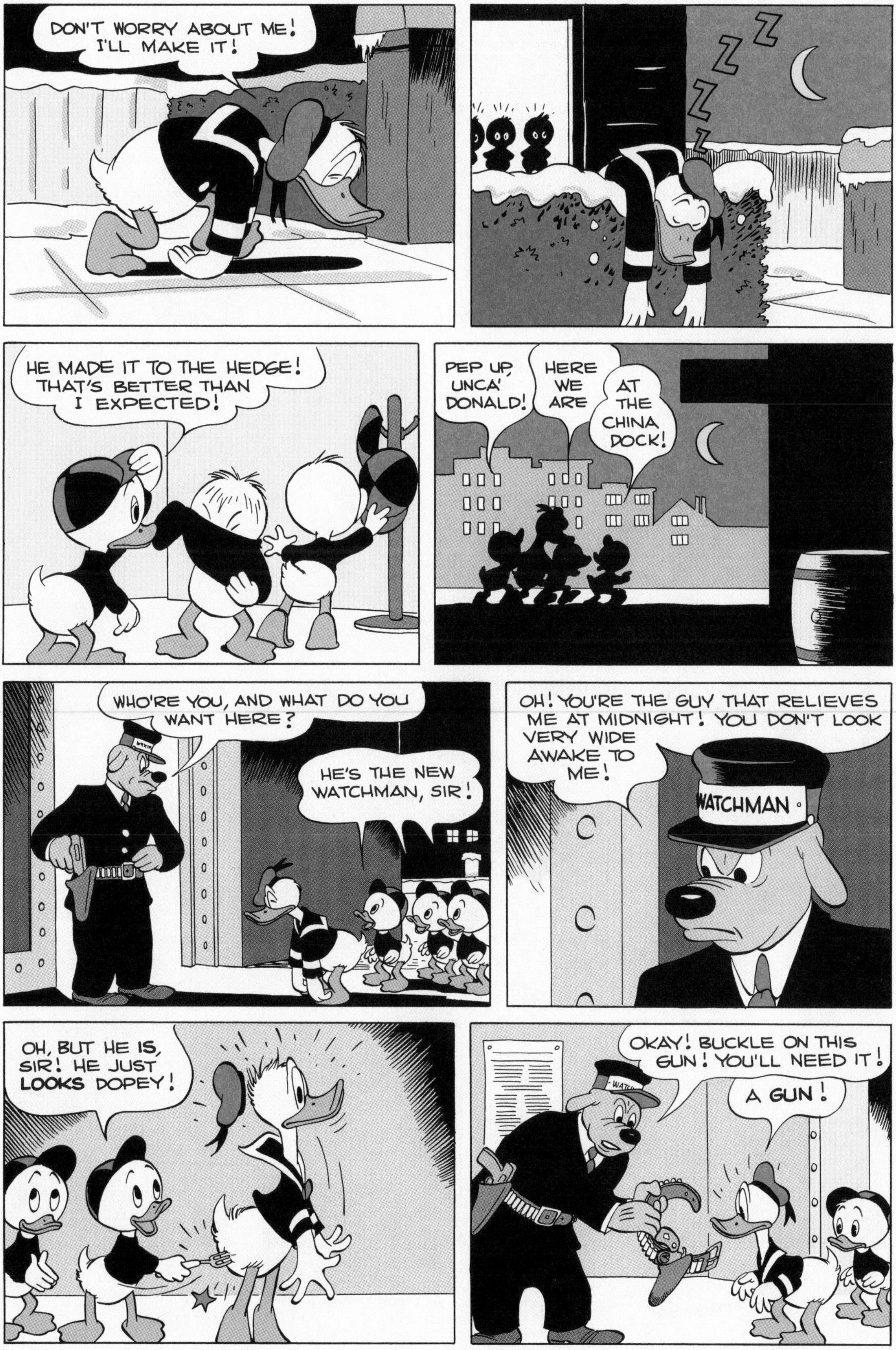
DON'T WORRY ABOUT ME! I'LL MAKE IT!
HE MADE IT TO THE HEDGE! THAT'S BETTER THAN I EXPECTED!
PEP UP, UNCA' DONALD!
HERE WE ARE
AT THE CHINA DOCK!
WHO'RE YOU, AND WHAT DO YOU WANT HERE?
HE'S THE NEW WATCHMAN, SIR!
OH! YOU'RE THE GUY THAT RELIEVES ME AT MIDNIGHT! YOU DON'T LOOK VERY WIDE AWAKE TO ME!
WATCHMAN
OH, BUT HE **IS**, SIR! HE JUST **LOOKS** DOPEY!
OKAY! BUCKLE ON THIS GUN! YOU'LL NEED IT!
A **GUN**!

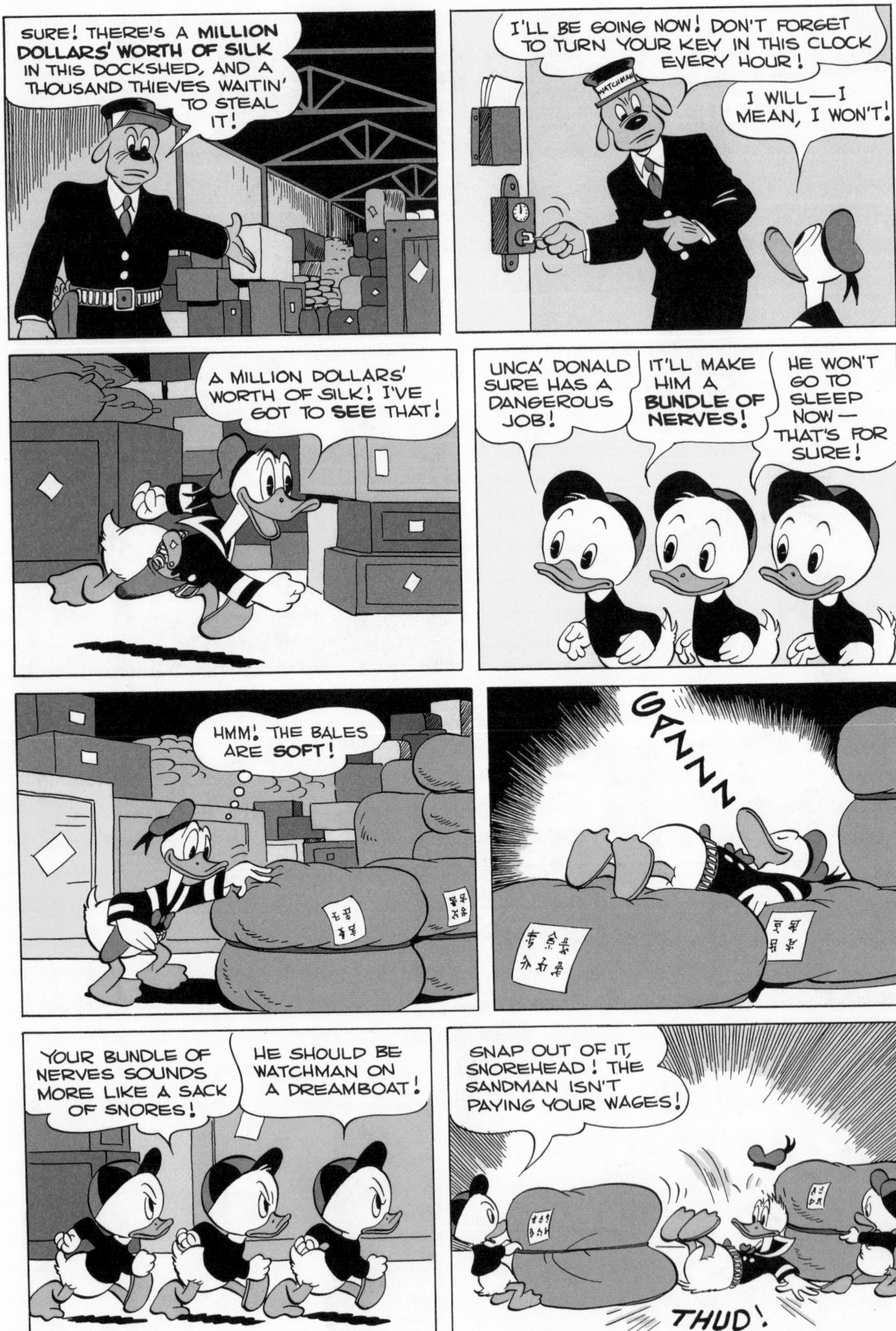
SURE! THERE'S A MILLION DOLLARS' WORTH OF SILK IN THIS DOCKSHED, AND A THOUSAND THIEVES WAITIN' TO STEAL IT!
I'LL BE GOING NOW! DON'T FORGET TO TURN YOUR KEY IN THIS CLOCK EVERY HOUR!
WATCHMAN
I WILL—I MEAN, I WON'T!
A MILLION DOLLARS' WORTH OF SILK! I'VE GOT TO SEE THAT!
UNCA' DONALD SURE HAS A DANGEROUS JOB!
IT'LL MAKE HIM A BUNDLE OF NERVES!
HE WON'T GO TO SLEEP NOW—THAT'S FOR SURE!
HMM! THE BALES ARE SOFT!
GANNNN
YOUR BUNDLE OF NERVES SOUNDS MORE LIKE A SACK OF SNORES!
HE SHOULD BE WATCHMAN ON A DREAMBOAT!
SNAP OUT OF IT, SNOREHEAD! THE SANDMAN ISN'T PAYING YOUR WAGES!
THUD!

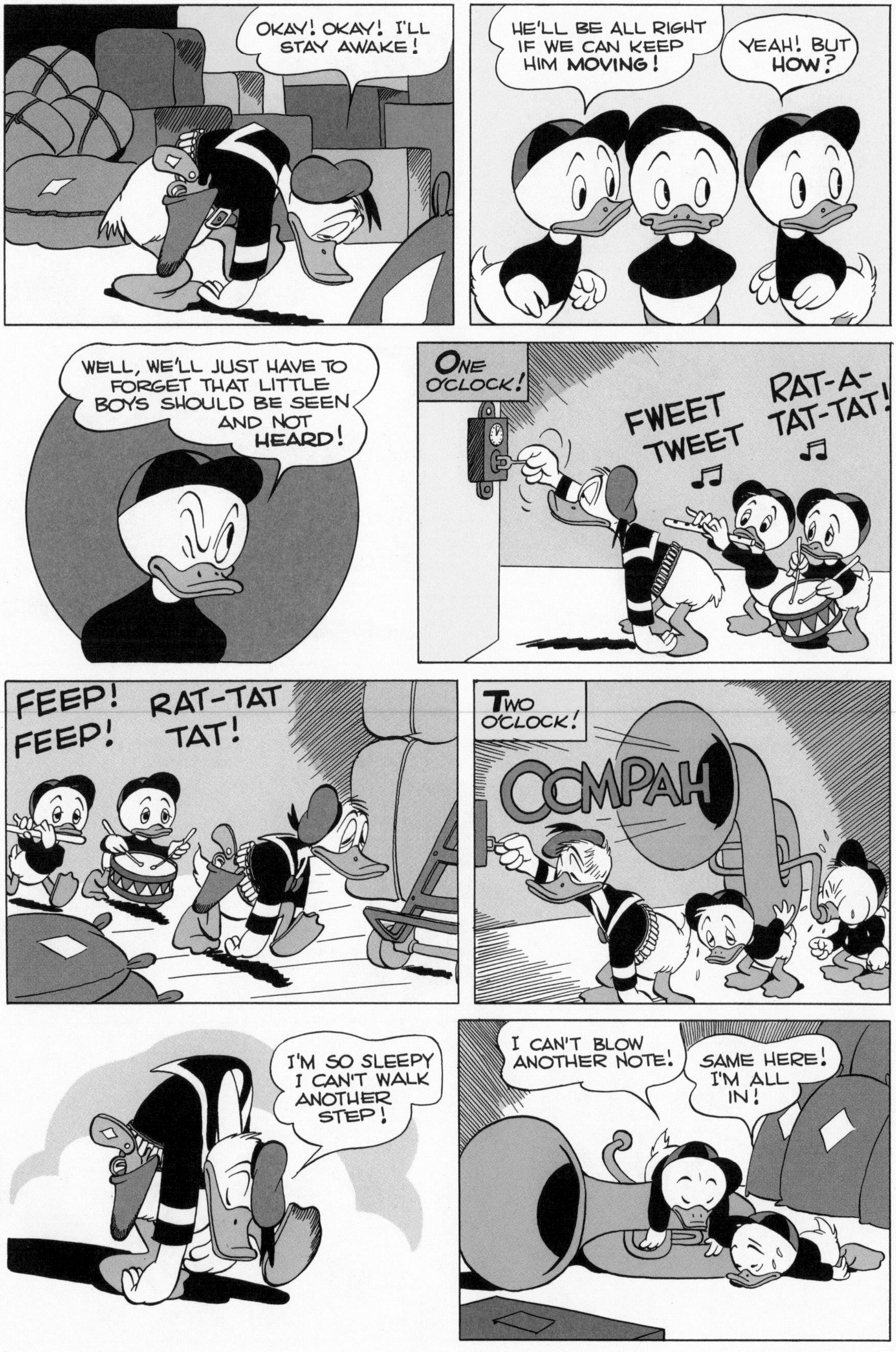
OKAY! OKAY! I'LL STAY AWAKE!
HE'LL BE ALL RIGHT IF WE CAN KEEP HIM MOVING!
YEAH! BUT HOW?
WELL, WE'LL JUST HAVE TO FORGET THAT LITTLE BOYS SHOULD BE SEEN AND NOT HEARD!
ONE O'CLOCK!
FWEET TWEET
RAT-A-TAT-TAT!
FEEP! FEEP!
RAT-TAT TAT!
TWO O'CLOCK!
OOMPAH
I'M SO SLEEPY I CAN'T WALK ANOTHER STEP!
I CAN'T BLOW ANOTHER NOTE!
SAME HERE! I'M ALL IN!

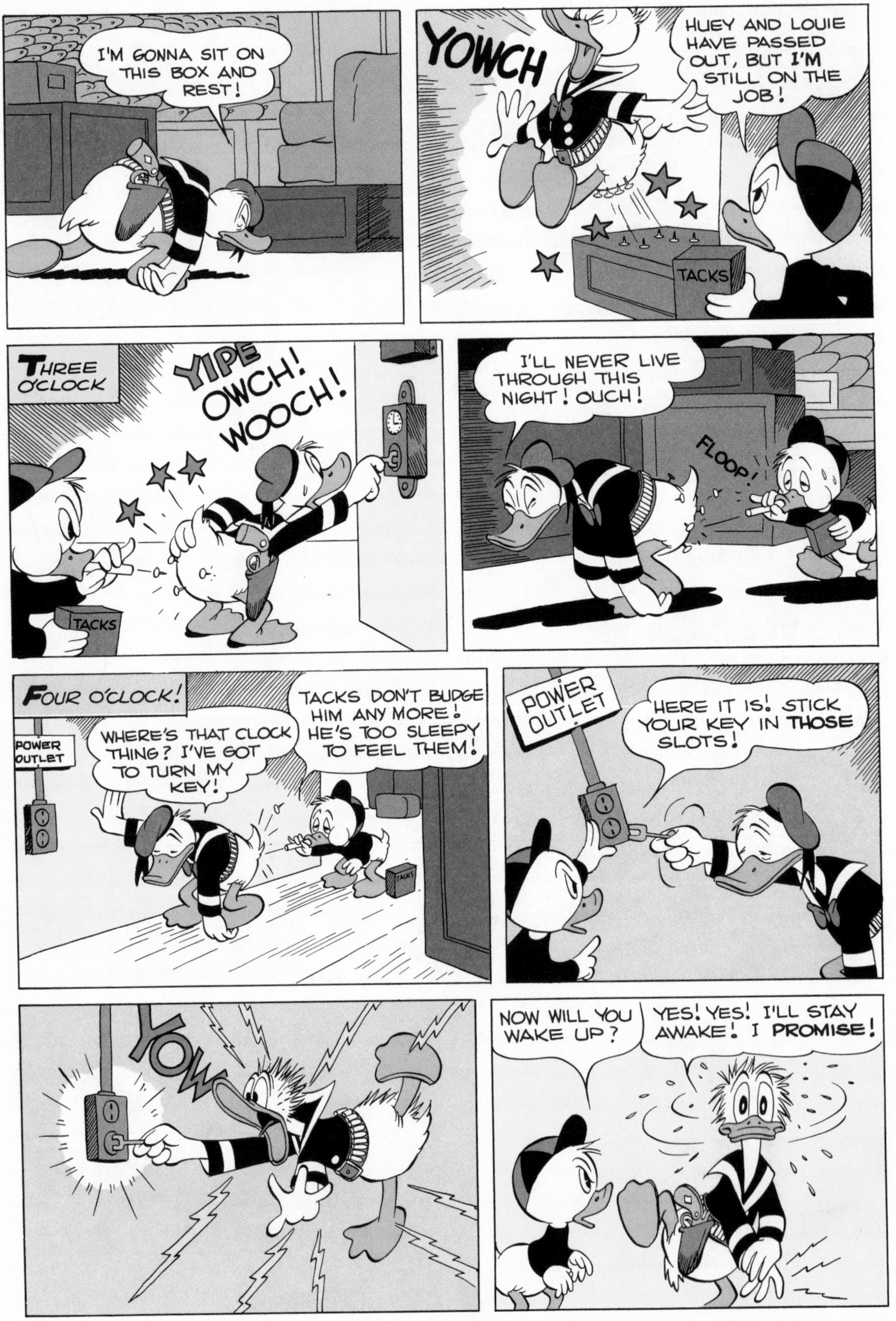

I'M GONNA SIT ON THIS BOX AND REST!
YOWCH
HUEY AND LOUIE HAVE PASSED OUT, BUT I'M STILL ON THE JOB!
TACKS
THREE O'CLOCK
YIPE
OWCH! WOOCH!
TACKS
I'LL NEVER LIVE THROUGH THIS NIGHT! OUCH!
FLOOP!
FOUR O'CLOCK!
POWER OUTLET
WHERE'S THAT CLOCK THING? I'VE GOT TO TURN MY KEY!
TACKS DON'T BUDGE HIM ANY MORE! HE'S TOO SLEEPY TO FEEL THEM!
POWER OUTLET
HERE IT IS! STICK YOUR KEY IN THOSE SLOTS!
YOW
NOW WILL YOU WAKE UP?
YES! YES! I'LL STAY AWAKE! I PROMISE!

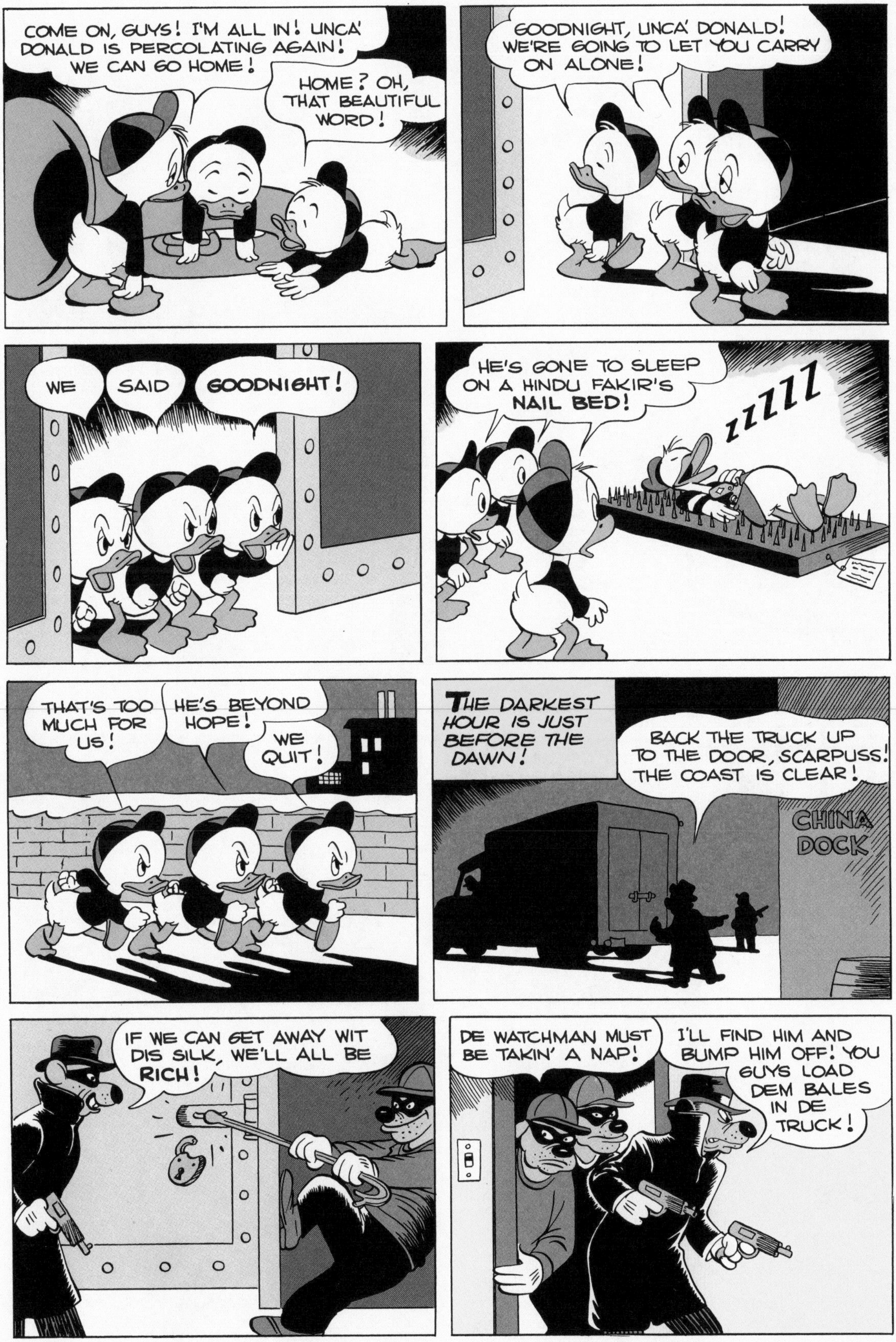
COME ON, GUYS! I'M ALL IN! UNCA' DONALD IS PERCOLATING AGAIN! WE CAN GO HOME!
HOME? OH, THAT BEAUTIFUL WORD!
GOODNIGHT, UNCA' DONALD! WE'RE GOING TO LET YOU CARRY ON ALONE!
WE
SAID
GOODNIGHT!
HE'S GONE TO SLEEP ON A HINDU FAKIR'S NAIL BED!
ZZZZZ
THAT'S TOO MUCH FOR US!
HE'S BEYOND HOPE!
WE QUIT!
THE DARKEST HOUR IS JUST BEFORE THE DAWN!
BACK THE TRUCK UP TO THE DOOR, SCARPUSS! THE COAST IS CLEAR!
CHINA DOCK
IF WE CAN GET AWAY WIT DIS SILK, WE'LL ALL BE RICH!
DE WATCHMAN MUST BE TAKIN' A NAP!
I'LL FIND HIM AND BUMP HIM OFF! YOU GUYS LOAD DEM BALES IN DE TRUCK!

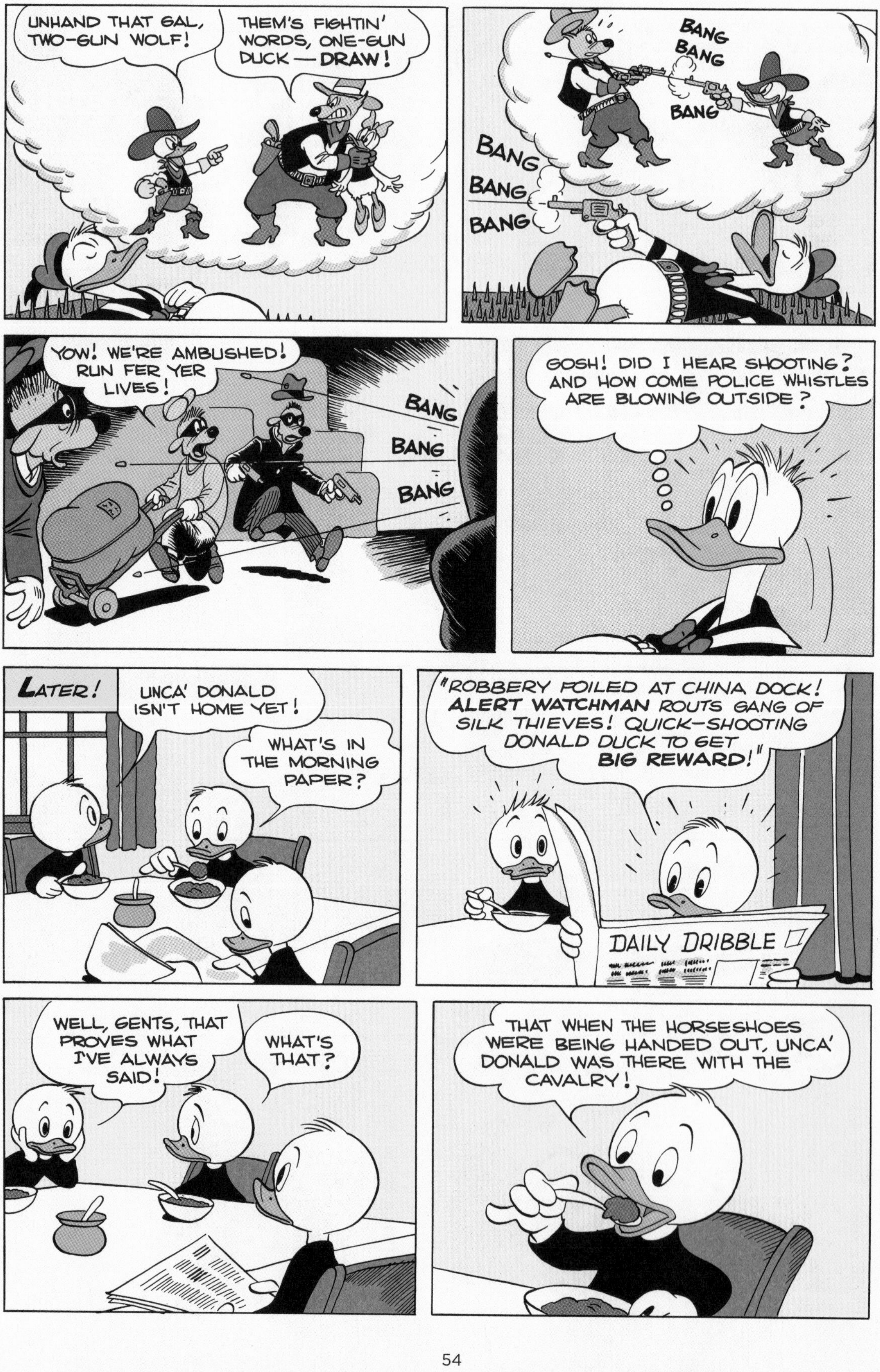
UNHAND THAT GAL, TWO-GUN WOLF!
THEM'S FIGHTIN' WORDS, ONE-GUN DUCK — DRAW!
BANG BANG
BANG
BANG
BANG
BANG
YOW! WE'RE AMBUSHED! RUN FER YER LIVES!
BANG
BANG
BANG
GOSH! DID I HEAR SHOOTING? AND HOW COME POLICE WHISTLES ARE BLOWING OUTSIDE?
LATER!
UNCA' DONALD ISN'T HOME YET!
WHAT'S IN THE MORNING PAPER?
"ROBBERY FOILED AT CHINA DOCK! ALERT WATCHMAN ROUTS GANG OF SILK THIEVES! QUICK-SHOOTING DONALD DUCK TO GET BIG REWARD!"
DAILY DRIBBLE
WELL, GENTS, THAT PROVES WHAT I'VE ALWAYS SAID!
WHAT'S THAT?
THAT WHEN THE HORSESHOES WERE BEING HANDED OUT, UNCA' DONALD WAS THERE WITH THE CAVALRY!

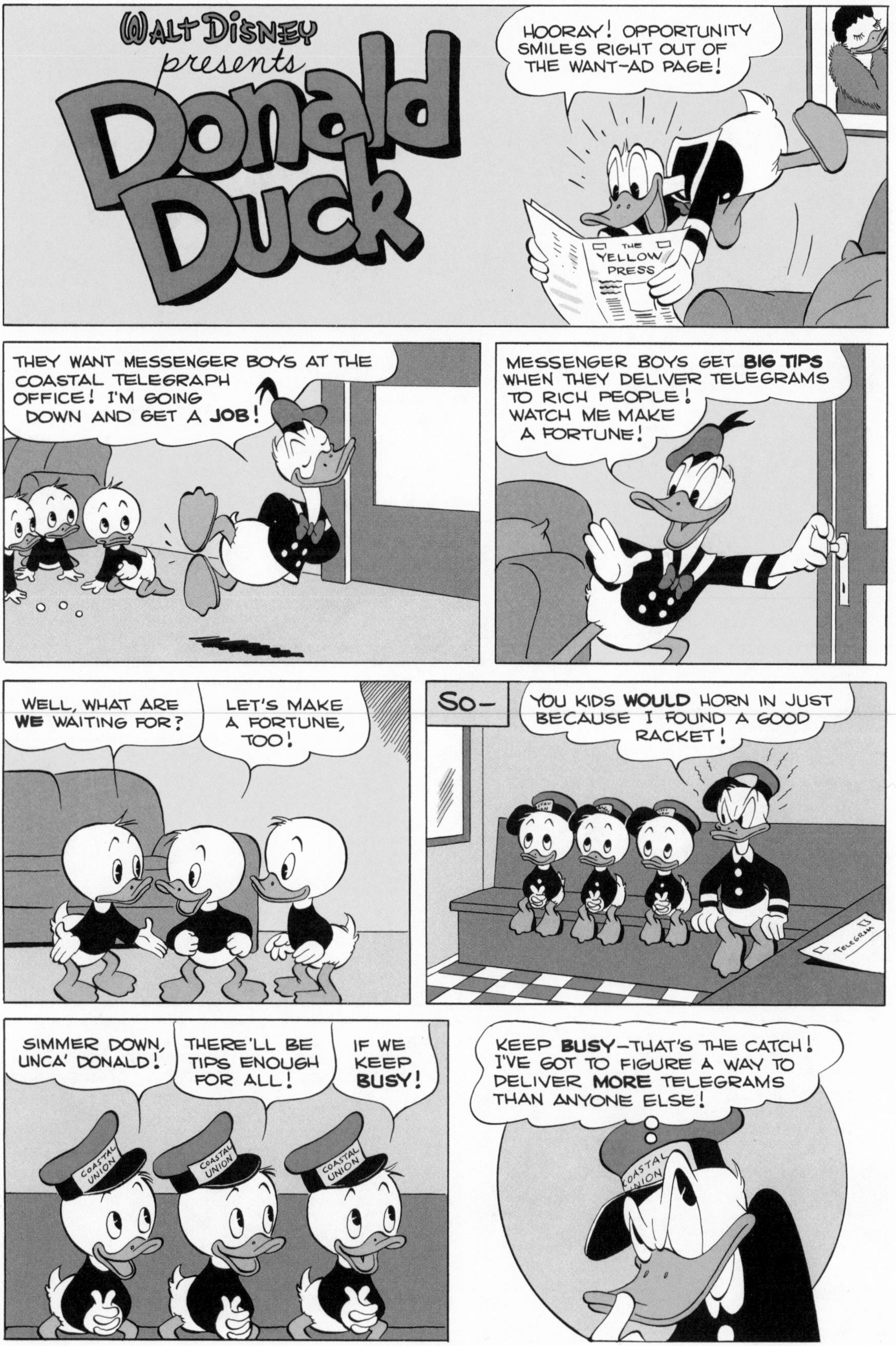
WALT DISNEY
presents
Donald Duck
HOORAY! OPPORTUNITY SMILES RIGHT OUT OF THE WANT-AD PAGE!
THE YELLOW PRESS
THEY WANT MESSENGER BOYS AT THE COASTAL TELEGRAPH OFFICE! I'M GOING DOWN AND GET A JOB!
MESSENGER BOYS GET BIG TIPS WHEN THEY DELIVER TELEGRAMS TO RICH PEOPLE! WATCH ME MAKE A FORTUNE!
WELL, WHAT ARE WE WAITING FOR?
LET'S MAKE A FORTUNE, TOO!
SO—
YOU KIDS WOULD HORN IN JUST BECAUSE I FOUND A GOOD RACKET!
TELEGRAM
SIMMER DOWN, UNCA' DONALD!
THERE'LL BE TIPS ENOUGH FOR ALL!
IF WE KEEP BUSY!
COASTAL UNION
KEEP BUSY—THAT'S THE CATCH! I'VE GOT TO FIGURE A WAY TO DELIVER MORE TELEGRAMS THAN ANYONE ELSE!

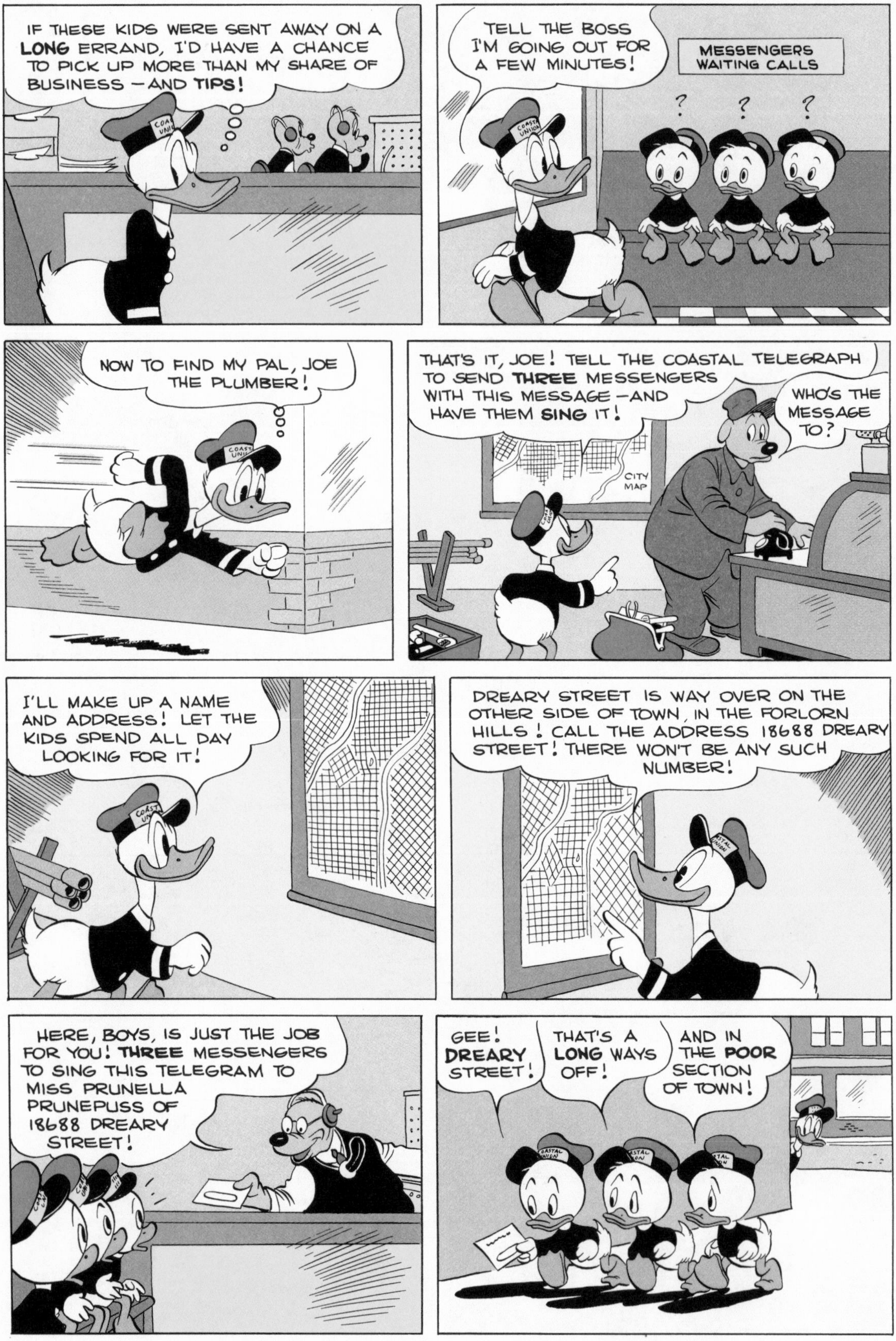
IF THESE KIDS WERE SENT AWAY ON A LONG ERRAND, I'D HAVE A CHANCE TO PICK UP MORE THAN MY SHARE OF BUSINESS —AND TIPS!
TELL THE BOSS I'M GOING OUT FOR A FEW MINUTES!
MESSENGERS WAITING CALLS
? ? ?
NOW TO FIND MY PAL, JOE THE PLUMBER!
THAT'S IT, JOE! TELL THE COASTAL TELEGRAPH TO SEND THREE MESSENGERS WITH THIS MESSAGE —AND HAVE THEM SING IT!
WHO'S THE MESSAGE TO?
CITY MAP
I'LL MAKE UP A NAME AND ADDRESS! LET THE KIDS SPEND ALL DAY LOOKING FOR IT!
DREARY STREET IS WAY OVER ON THE OTHER SIDE OF TOWN, IN THE FORLORN HILLS! CALL THE ADDRESS 18688 DREARY STREET! THERE WON'T BE ANY SUCH NUMBER!
HERE, BOYS, IS JUST THE JOB FOR YOU! THREE MESSENGERS TO SING THIS TELEGRAM TO MISS PRUNELLA PRUNEPUSS OF 18688 DREARY STREET!
GEE! DREARY STREET!
THAT'S A LONG WAYS OFF!
AND IN THE POOR SECTION OF TOWN!

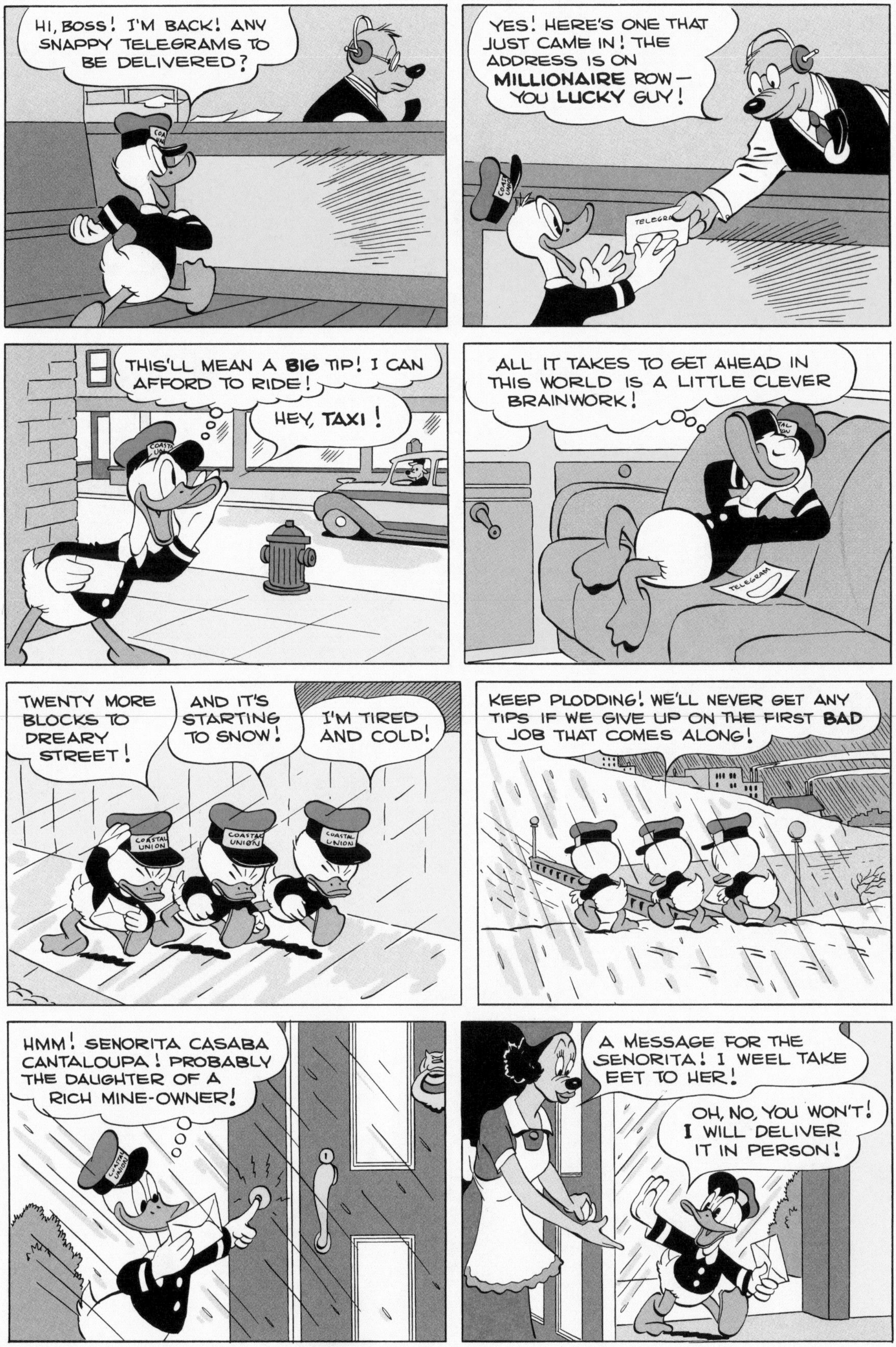
HI, BOSS! I'M BACK! ANY SNAPPY TELEGRAMS TO BE DELIVERED?
COASTAL UNION
YES! HERE'S ONE THAT JUST CAME IN! THE ADDRESS IS ON **MILLIONAIRE** ROW— YOU **LUCKY** GUY!
TELEGRAM
THIS'LL MEAN A **BIG** TIP! I CAN AFFORD TO RIDE!
HEY, **TAXI**!
ALL IT TAKES TO GET AHEAD IN THIS WORLD IS A LITTLE CLEVER BRAINWORK!
TELEGRAM
TWENTY MORE BLOCKS TO DREARY STREET!
AND IT'S STARTING TO SNOW!
I'M TIRED AND COLD!
COASTAL UNION
KEEP PLODDING! WE'LL NEVER GET ANY TIPS IF WE GIVE UP ON THE FIRST **BAD** JOB THAT COMES ALONG!
HMM! SENORITA CASABA CANTALOUPA! PROBABLY THE DAUGHTER OF A RICH MINE-OWNER!
A MESSAGE FOR THE SENORITA! I WEEL TAKE EET TO HER!
OH, NO, YOU WON'T! **I** WILL DELIVER IT IN PERSON!

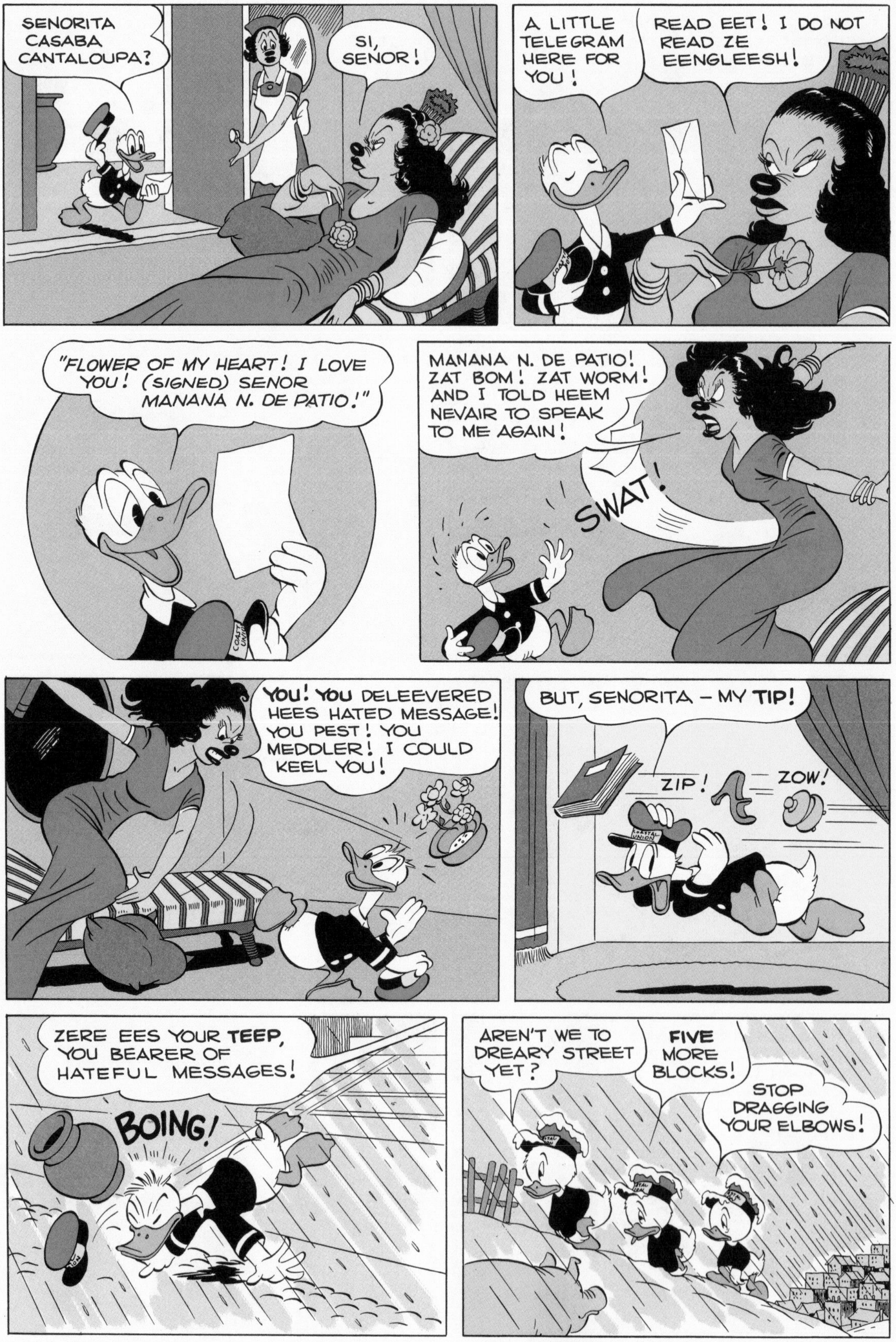
SENORITA CASABA CANTALOUPA?
SI, SENOR!
A LITTLE TELEGRAM HERE FOR YOU!
READ EET! I DO NOT READ ZE EENGLEESH!
"FLOWER OF MY HEART! I LOVE YOU! (SIGNED) SENOR MANANA N. DE PATIO!"
MANANA N. DE PATIO! ZAT BOM! ZAT WORM! AND I TOLD HEEM NEVAIR TO SPEAK TO ME AGAIN!
SWAT!
YOU! YOU DELEEVERED HEES HATED MESSAGE! YOU PEST! YOU MEDDLER! I COULD KEEL YOU!
BUT, SENORITA – MY TIP!
ZIP!
ZOW!
ZERE EES YOUR TEEP, YOU BEARER OF HATEFUL MESSAGES!
BOING!
AREN'T WE TO DREARY STREET YET?
FIVE MORE BLOCKS!
STOP DRAGGING YOUR ELBOWS!

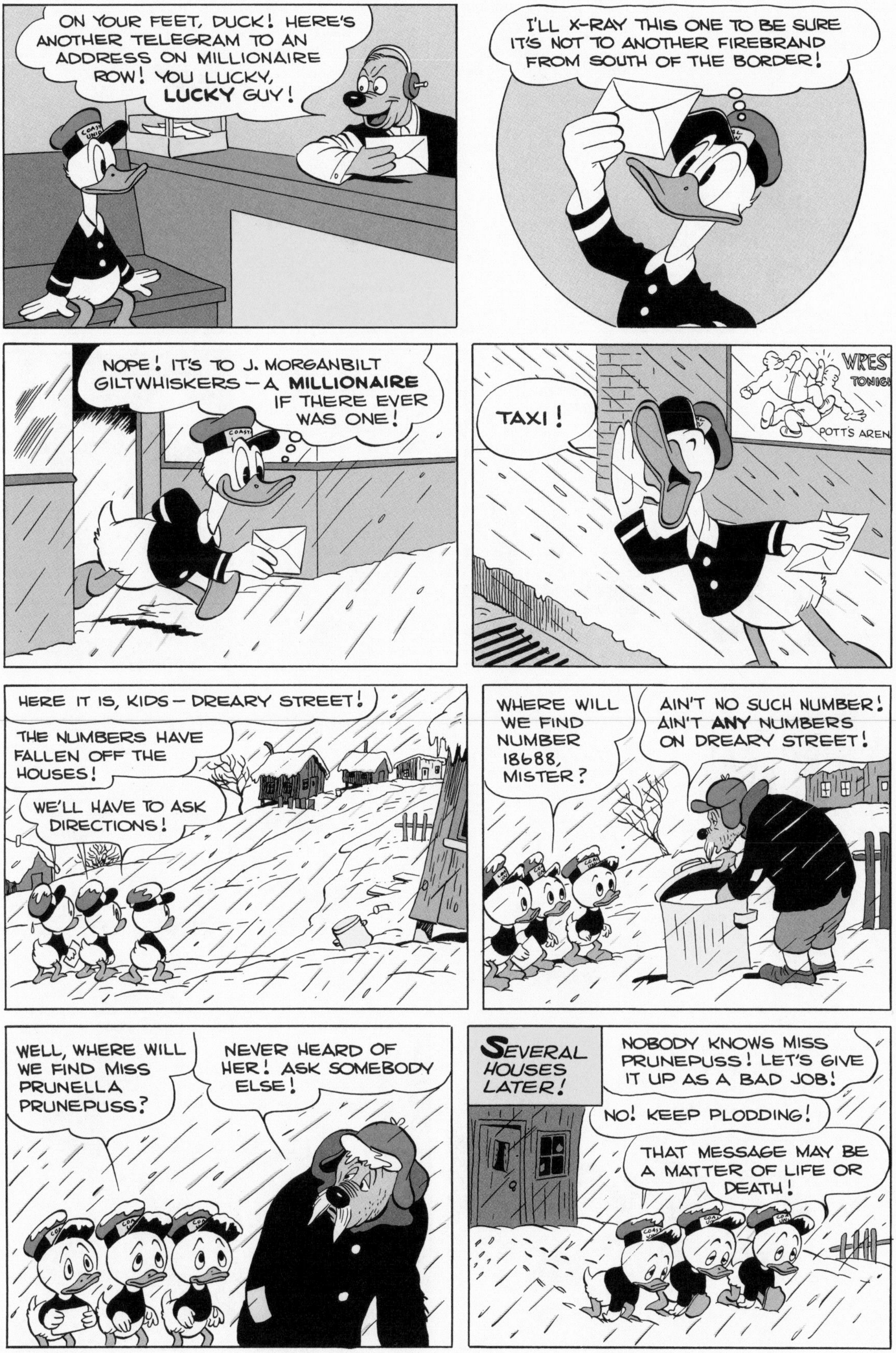
ON YOUR FEET, DUCK! HERE'S ANOTHER TELEGRAM TO AN ADDRESS ON MILLIONAIRE ROW! YOU LUCKY, LUCKY GUY!
I'LL X-RAY THIS ONE TO BE SURE IT'S NOT TO ANOTHER FIREBRAND FROM SOUTH OF THE BORDER!
NOPE! IT'S TO J. MORGANBILT GILTWHISKERS — A MILLIONAIRE IF THERE EVER WAS ONE!
TAXI!
POTT'S AREN
HERE IT IS, KIDS — DREARY STREET!
THE NUMBERS HAVE FALLEN OFF THE HOUSES!
WE'LL HAVE TO ASK DIRECTIONS!
WHERE WILL WE FIND NUMBER 18688, MISTER?
AIN'T NO SUCH NUMBER! AIN'T ANY NUMBERS ON DREARY STREET!
WELL, WHERE WILL WE FIND MISS PRUNELLA PRUNEPUSS?
NEVER HEARD OF HER! ASK SOMEBODY ELSE!
SEVERAL HOUSES LATER!
NOBODY KNOWS MISS PRUNEPUSS! LET'S GIVE IT UP AS A BAD JOB!
NO! KEEP PLODDING!
THAT MESSAGE MAY BE A MATTER OF LIFE OR DEATH!

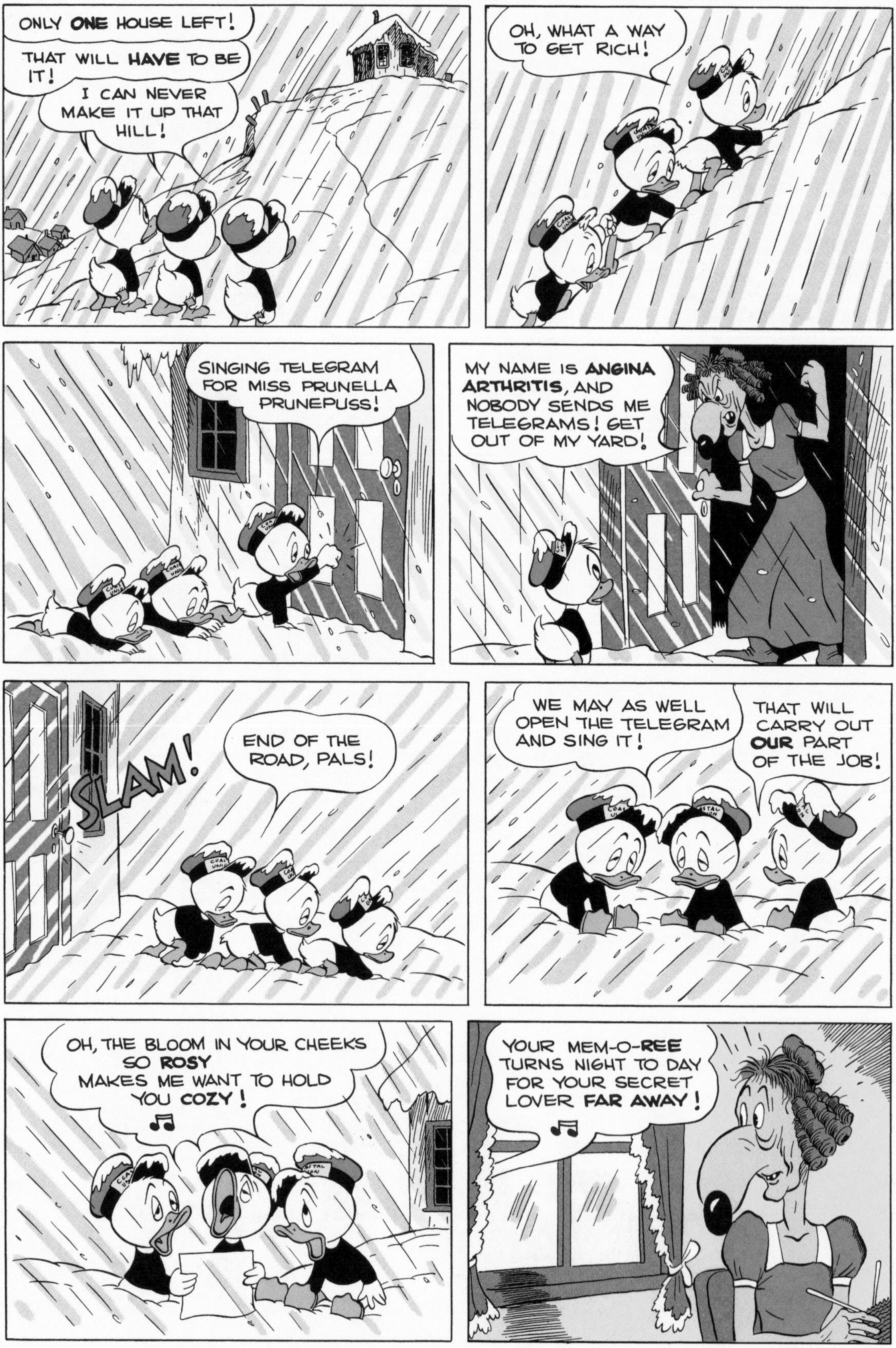
ONLY ONE HOUSE LEFT!
THAT WILL HAVE TO BE IT!
I CAN NEVER MAKE IT UP THAT HILL!
OH, WHAT A WAY TO GET RICH!
SINGING TELEGRAM FOR MISS PRUNELLA PRUNEPUSS!
MY NAME IS ANGINA ARTHRITIS, AND NOBODY SENDS ME TELEGRAMS! GET OUT OF MY YARD!
SLAM!
END OF THE ROAD, PALS!
WE MAY AS WELL OPEN THE TELEGRAM AND SING IT!
THAT WILL CARRY OUT OUR PART OF THE JOB!
OH, THE BLOOM IN YOUR CHEEKS SO ROSY MAKES ME WANT TO HOLD YOU COZY!
YOUR MEM-O-REE TURNS NIGHT TO DAY FOR YOUR SECRET LOVER FAR AWAY!

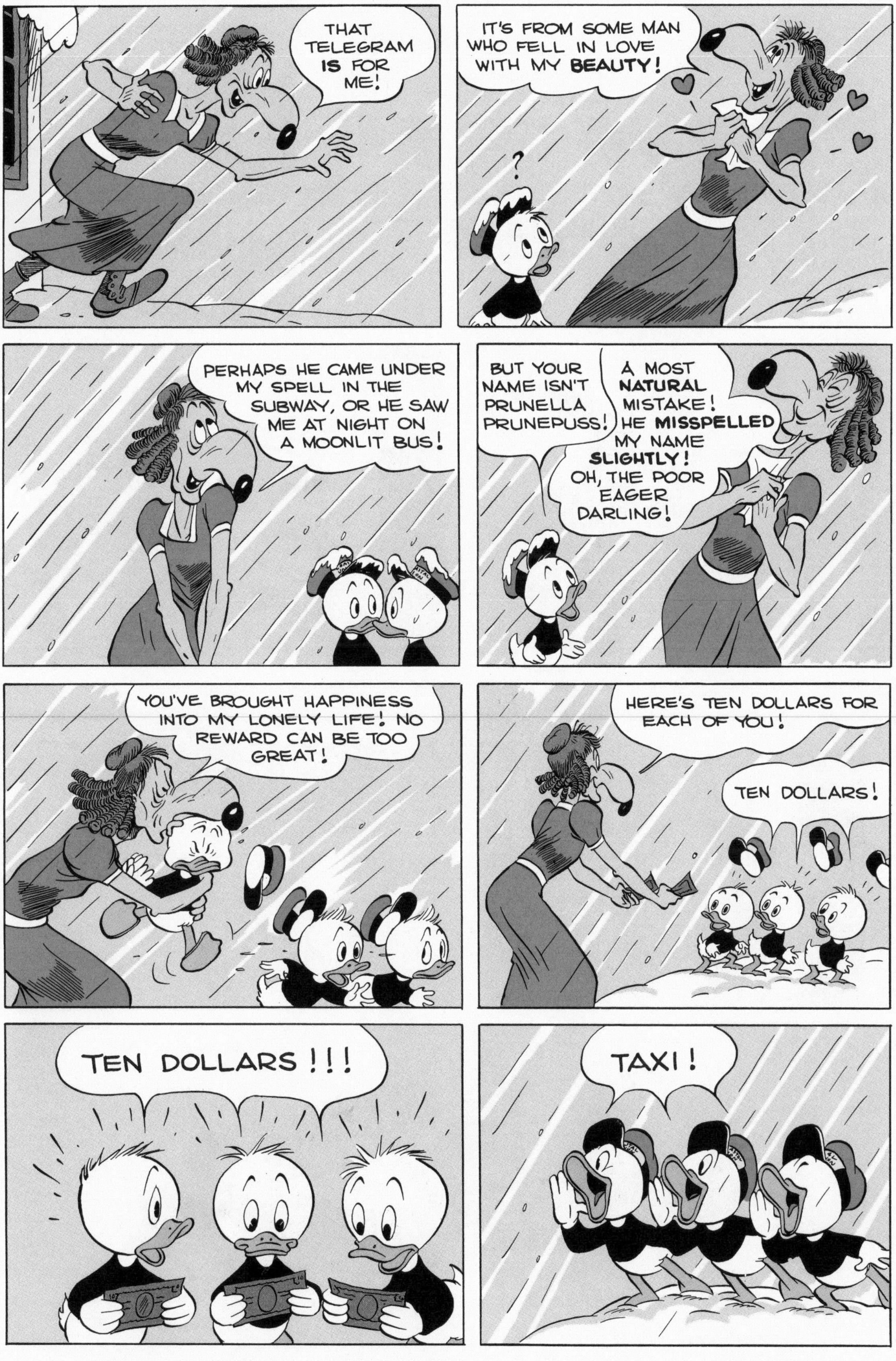
THAT TELEGRAM IS FOR ME!
IT'S FROM SOME MAN WHO FELL IN LOVE WITH MY BEAUTY!
?
PERHAPS HE CAME UNDER MY SPELL IN THE SUBWAY, OR HE SAW ME AT NIGHT ON A MOONLIT BUS!
BUT YOUR NAME ISN'T PRUNELLA PRUNEPUSS!
A MOST NATURAL MISTAKE! HE MISSPELLED MY NAME SLIGHTLY! OH, THE POOR EAGER DARLING!
YOU'VE BROUGHT HAPPINESS INTO MY LONELY LIFE! NO REWARD CAN BE TOO GREAT!
HERE'S TEN DOLLARS FOR EACH OF YOU!
TEN DOLLARS!
TEN DOLLARS!!!
TAXI!

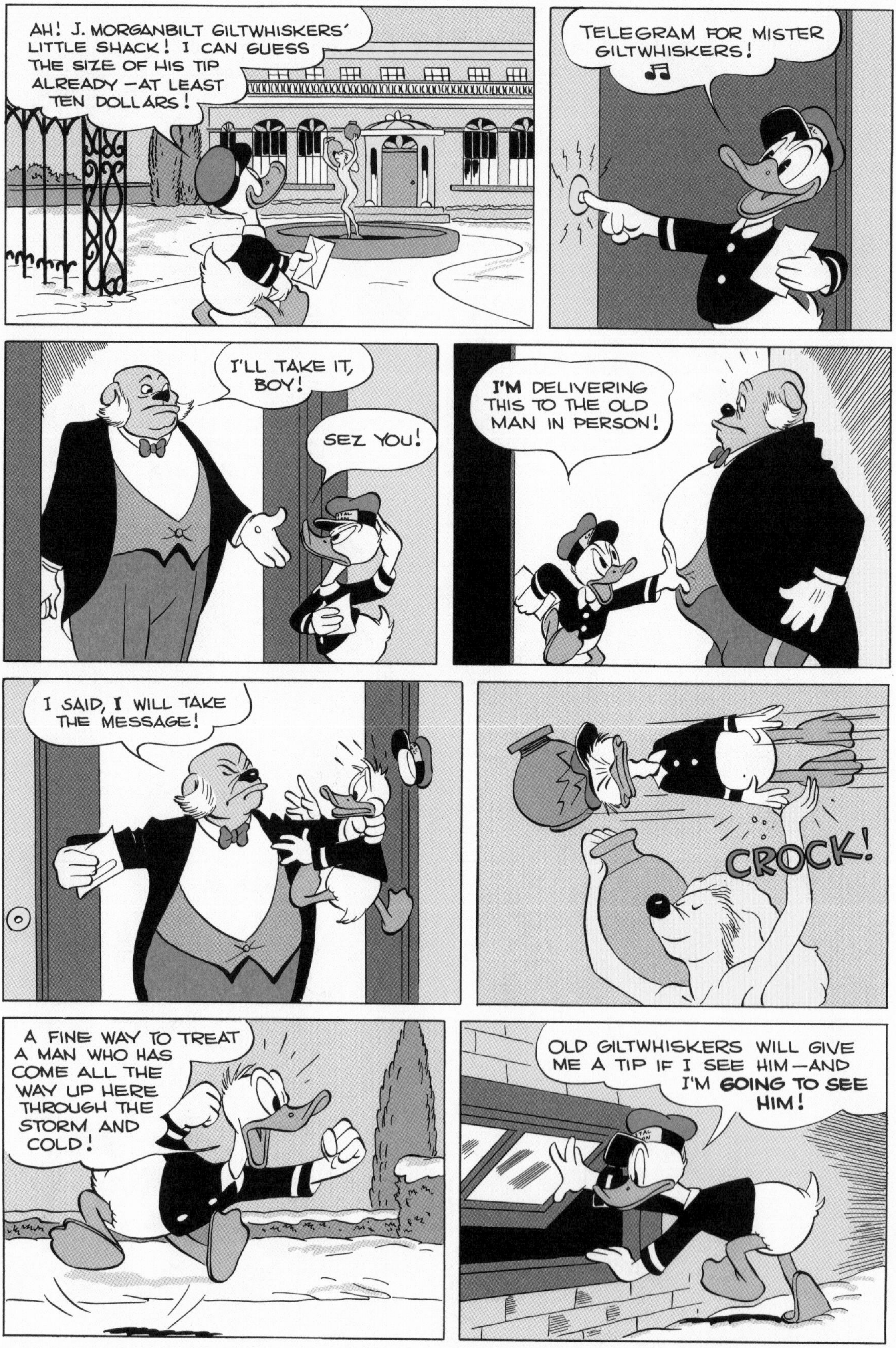
AH! J. MORGANBILT GILTWHISKERS' LITTLE SHACK! I CAN GUESS THE SIZE OF HIS TIP ALREADY —AT LEAST TEN DOLLARS!
TELEGRAM FOR MISTER GILTWHISKERS!
I'LL TAKE IT, BOY!
SEZ YOU!
I'M DELIVERING THIS TO THE OLD MAN IN PERSON!
I SAID, I WILL TAKE THE MESSAGE!
CROCK!
A FINE WAY TO TREAT A MAN WHO HAS COME ALL THE WAY UP HERE THROUGH THE STORM AND COLD!
OLD GILTWHISKERS WILL GIVE ME A TIP IF I SEE HIM—AND I'M GOING TO SEE HIM!

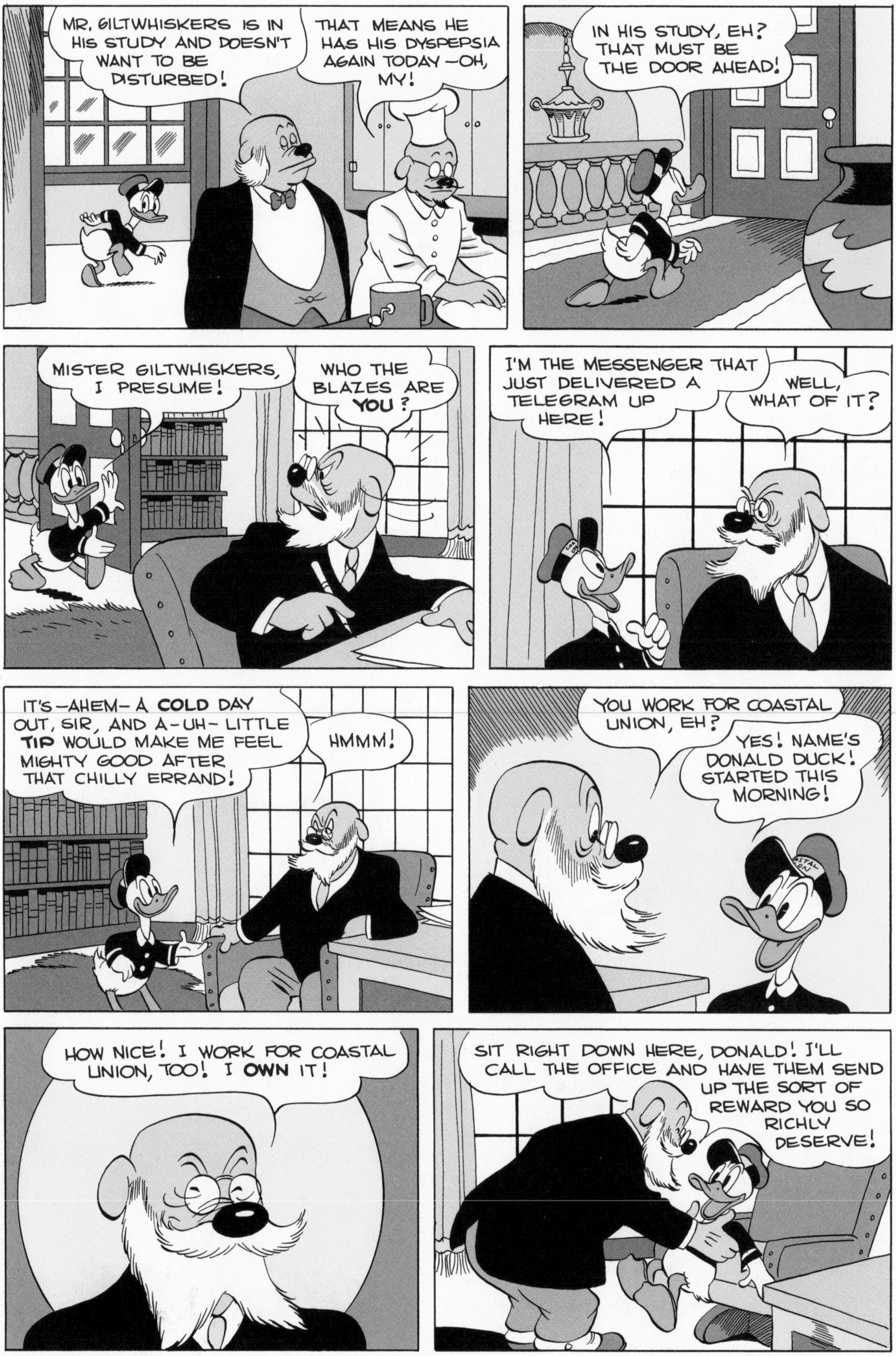
MR. GILTWHISKERS IS IN HIS STUDY AND DOESN'T WANT TO BE DISTURBED!
THAT MEANS HE HAS HIS DYSPEPSIA AGAIN TODAY—OH, MY!
IN HIS STUDY, EH? THAT MUST BE THE DOOR AHEAD!
MISTER GILTWHISKERS, I PRESUME!
WHO THE BLAZES ARE YOU?
I'M THE MESSENGER THAT JUST DELIVERED A TELEGRAM UP HERE!
WELL, WHAT OF IT?
IT'S—AHEM— A COLD DAY OUT, SIR, AND A-UH- LITTLE TIP WOULD MAKE ME FEEL MIGHTY GOOD AFTER THAT CHILLY ERRAND!
HMMM!
YOU WORK FOR COASTAL UNION, EH?
YES! NAME'S DONALD DUCK! STARTED THIS MORNING!
HOW NICE! I WORK FOR COASTAL UNION, TOO! I OWN IT!
SIT RIGHT DOWN HERE, DONALD! I'LL CALL THE OFFICE AND HAVE THEM SEND UP THE SORT OF REWARD YOU SO RICHLY DESERVE!

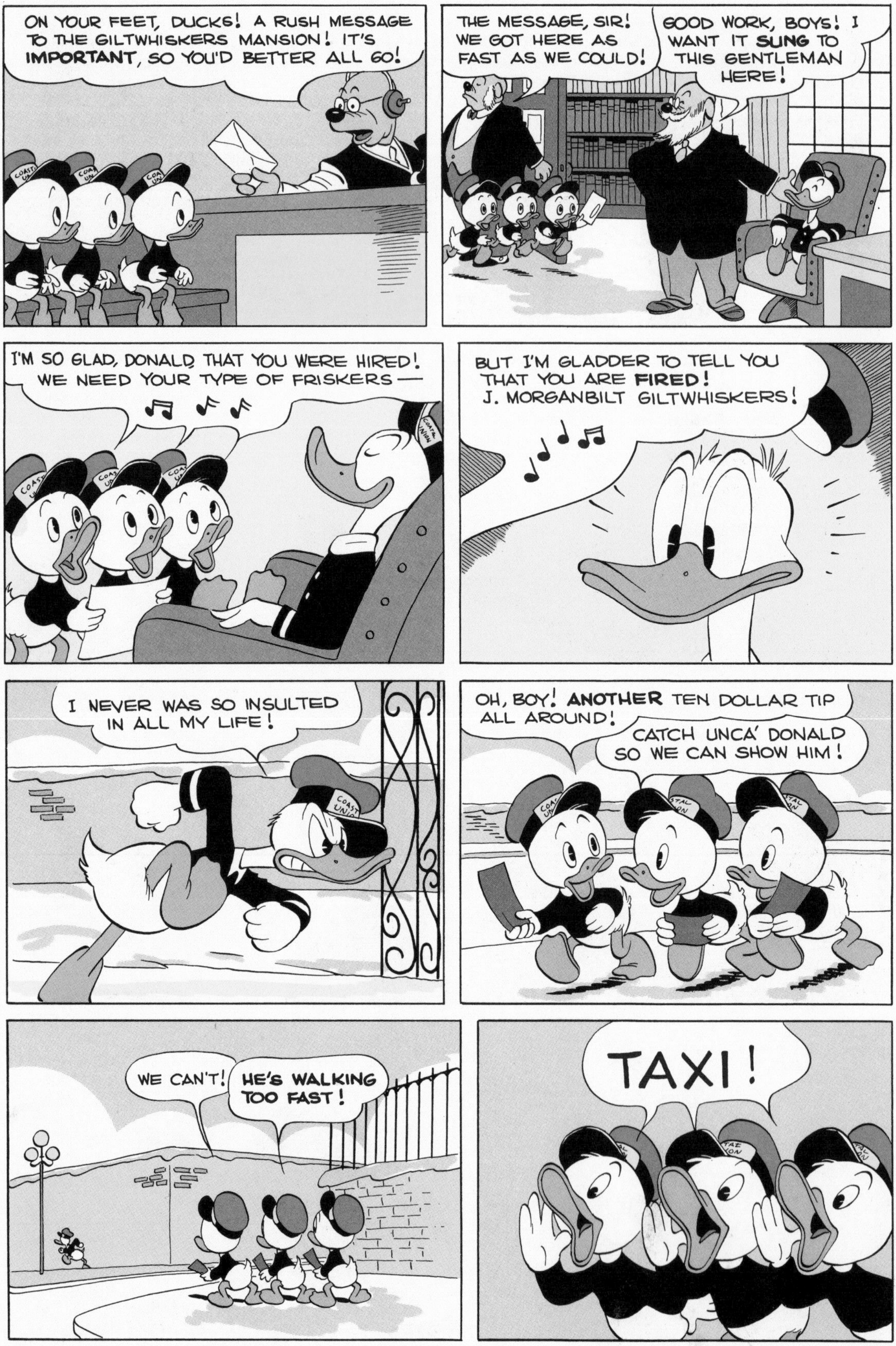
ON YOUR FEET, DUCKS! A RUSH MESSAGE TO THE GILTWHISKERS MANSION! IT'S IMPORTANT, SO YOU'D BETTER ALL GO!
THE MESSAGE, SIR! WE GOT HERE AS FAST AS WE COULD!
GOOD WORK, BOYS! I WANT IT SUNG TO THIS GENTLEMAN HERE!
I'M SO GLAD, DONALD THAT YOU WERE HIRED! WE NEED YOUR TYPE OF FRISKERS —
BUT I'M GLADDER TO TELL YOU THAT YOU ARE FIRED! J. MORGANBILT GILTWHISKERS!
I NEVER WAS SO INSULTED IN ALL MY LIFE!
OH, BOY! ANOTHER TEN DOLLAR TIP ALL AROUND!
CATCH UNCA' DONALD SO WE CAN SHOW HIM!
WE CAN'T!
HE'S WALKING TOO FAST!
TAXI!

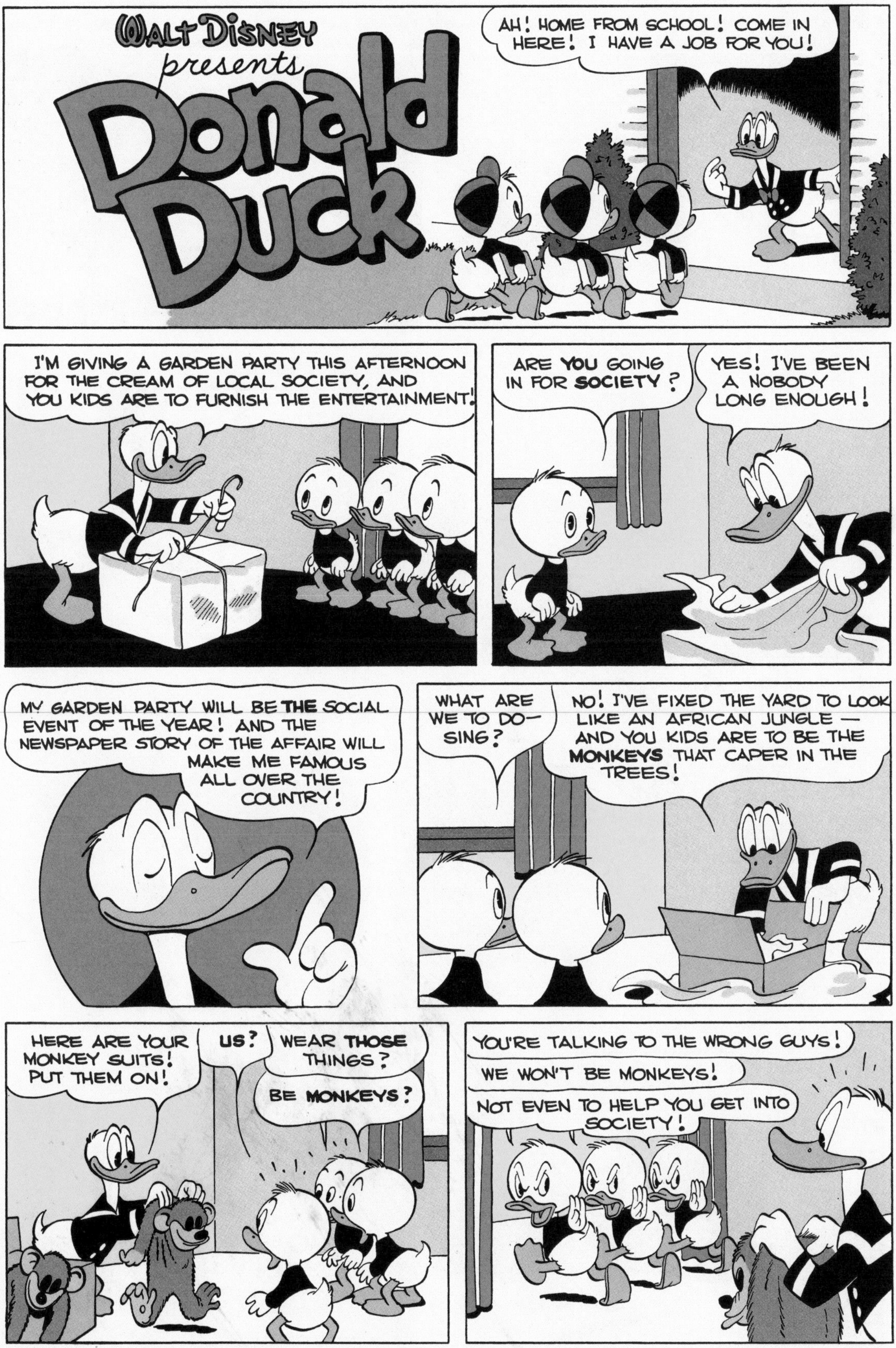
WALT DISNEY
presents
Donald Duck
AH! HOME FROM SCHOOL! COME IN HERE! I HAVE A JOB FOR YOU!
I'M GIVING A GARDEN PARTY THIS AFTERNOON FOR THE CREAM OF LOCAL SOCIETY, AND YOU KIDS ARE TO FURNISH THE ENTERTAINMENT!
ARE YOU GOING IN FOR SOCIETY?
YES! I'VE BEEN A NOBODY LONG ENOUGH!
MY GARDEN PARTY WILL BE THE SOCIAL EVENT OF THE YEAR! AND THE NEWSPAPER STORY OF THE AFFAIR WILL MAKE ME FAMOUS ALL OVER THE COUNTRY!
WHAT ARE WE TO DO-SING?
NO! I'VE FIXED THE YARD TO LOOK LIKE AN AFRICAN JUNGLE — AND YOU KIDS ARE TO BE THE MONKEYS THAT CAPER IN THE TREES!
HERE ARE YOUR MONKEY SUITS! PUT THEM ON!
US?
WEAR THOSE THINGS?
BE MONKEYS?
YOU'RE TALKING TO THE WRONG GUYS!
WE WON'T BE MONKEYS!
NOT EVEN TO HELP YOU GET INTO SOCIETY!

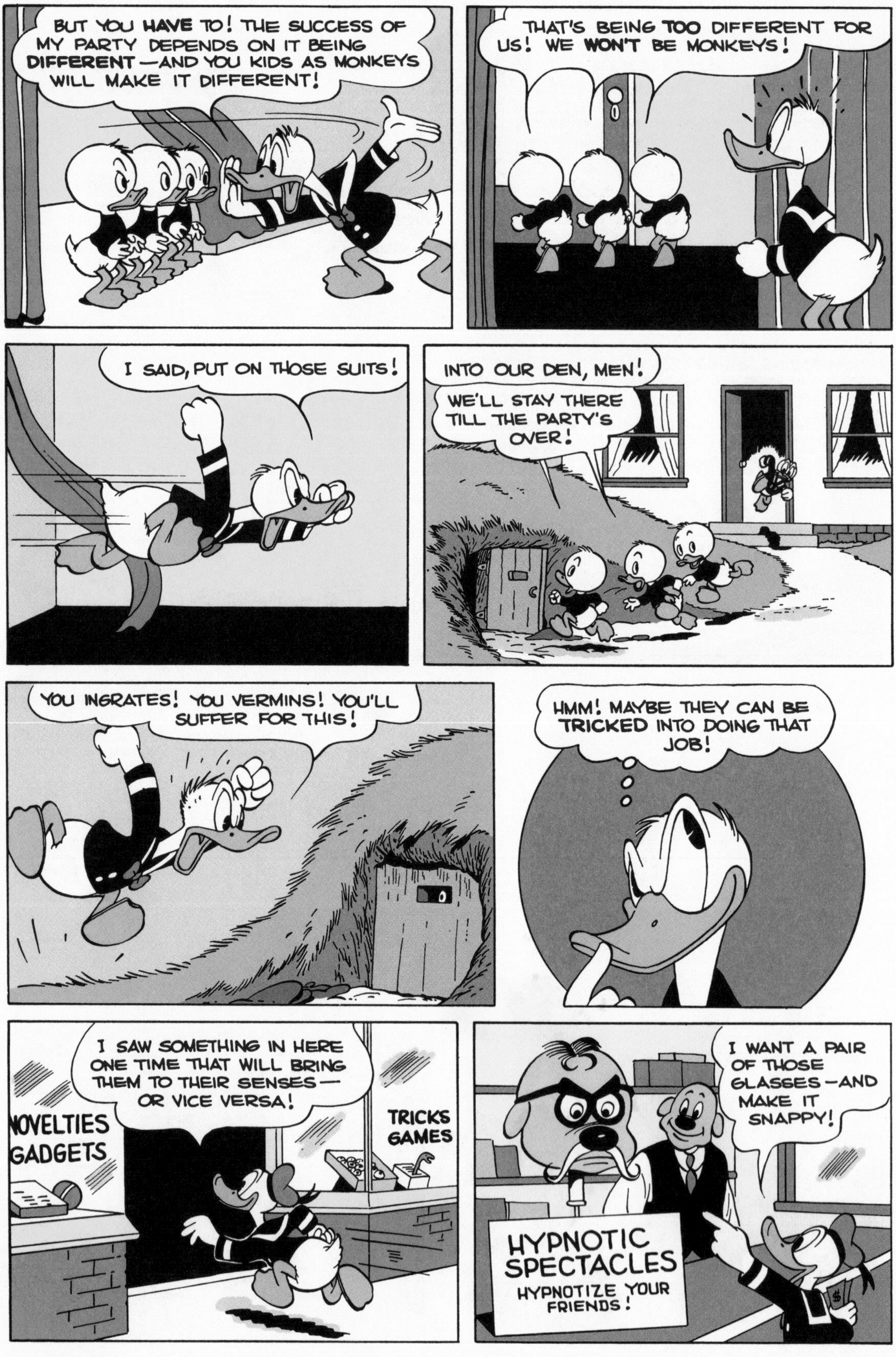
BUT YOU HAVE TO! THE SUCCESS OF MY PARTY DEPENDS ON IT BEING DIFFERENT—AND YOU KIDS AS MONKEYS WILL MAKE IT DIFFERENT!
THAT'S BEING TOO DIFFERENT FOR US! WE WON'T BE MONKEYS!
I SAID, PUT ON THOSE SUITS!
INTO OUR DEN, MEN!
WE'LL STAY THERE TILL THE PARTY'S OVER!
YOU INGRATES! YOU VERMINS! YOU'LL SUFFER FOR THIS!
HMM! MAYBE THEY CAN BE TRICKED INTO DOING THAT JOB!
I SAW SOMETHING IN HERE ONE TIME THAT WILL BRING THEM TO THEIR SENSES—OR VICE VERSA!
NOVELTIES
GADGETS
TRICKS
GAMES
I WANT A PAIR OF THOSE GLASSES—AND MAKE IT SNAPPY!
HYPNOTIC SPECTACLES
HYPNOTIZE YOUR FRIENDS!

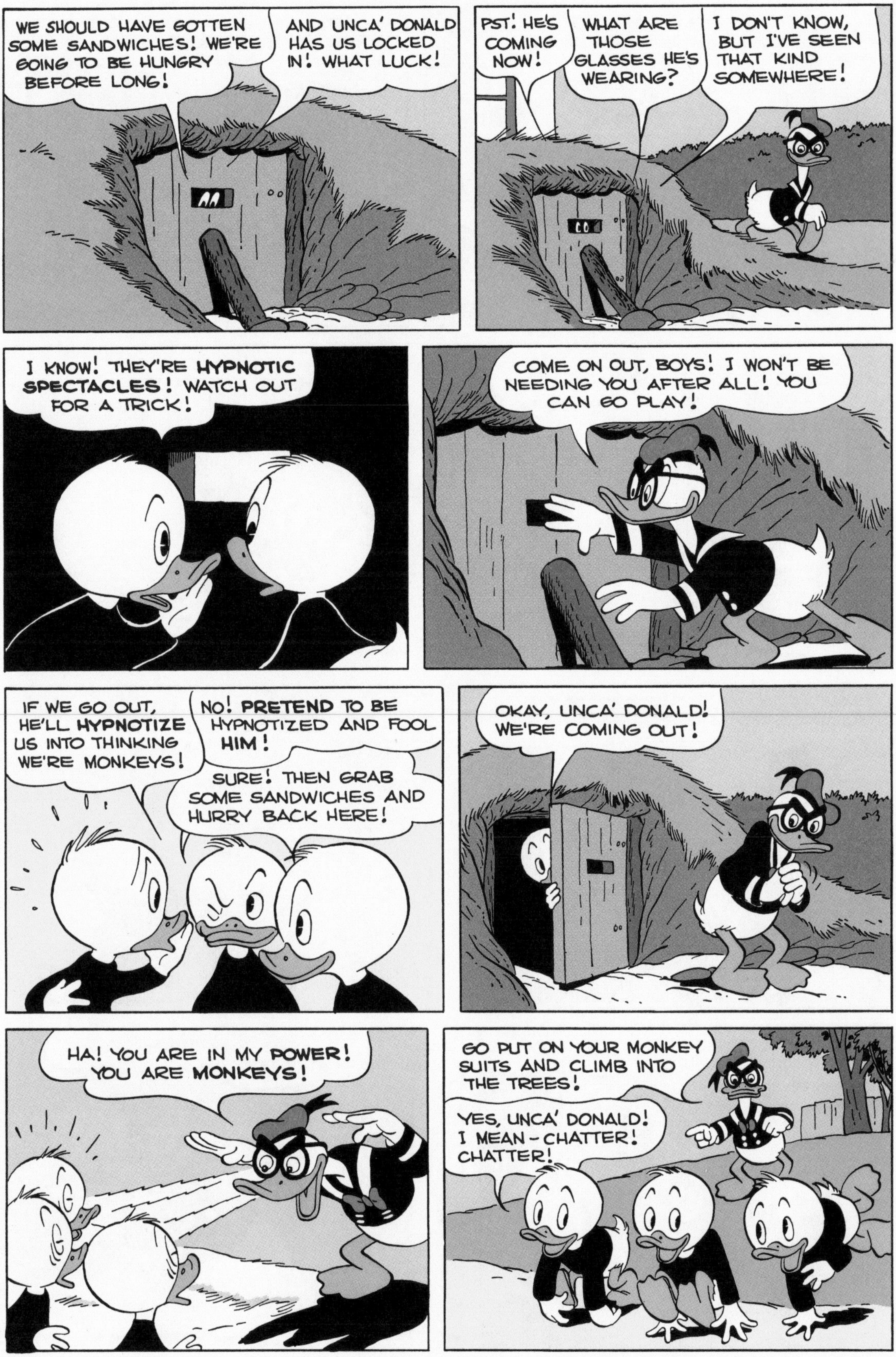
WE SHOULD HAVE GOTTEN SOME SANDWICHES! WE'RE GOING TO BE HUNGRY BEFORE LONG!
AND UNCA' DONALD HAS US LOCKED IN! WHAT LUCK!
PST! HE'S COMING NOW!
WHAT ARE THOSE GLASSES HE'S WEARING?
I DON'T KNOW, BUT I'VE SEEN THAT KIND SOMEWHERE!
I KNOW! THEY'RE HYPNOTIC SPECTACLES! WATCH OUT FOR A TRICK!
COME ON OUT, BOYS! I WON'T BE NEEDING YOU AFTER ALL! YOU CAN GO PLAY!
IF WE GO OUT, HE'LL HYPNOTIZE US INTO THINKING WE'RE MONKEYS!
NO! PRETEND TO BE HYPNOTIZED AND FOOL HIM!
SURE! THEN GRAB SOME SANDWICHES AND HURRY BACK HERE!
OKAY, UNCA' DONALD! WE'RE COMING OUT!
HA! YOU ARE IN MY POWER! YOU ARE MONKEYS!
GO PUT ON YOUR MONKEY SUITS AND CLIMB INTO THE TREES!
YES, UNCA' DONALD! I MEAN—CHATTER! CHATTER!

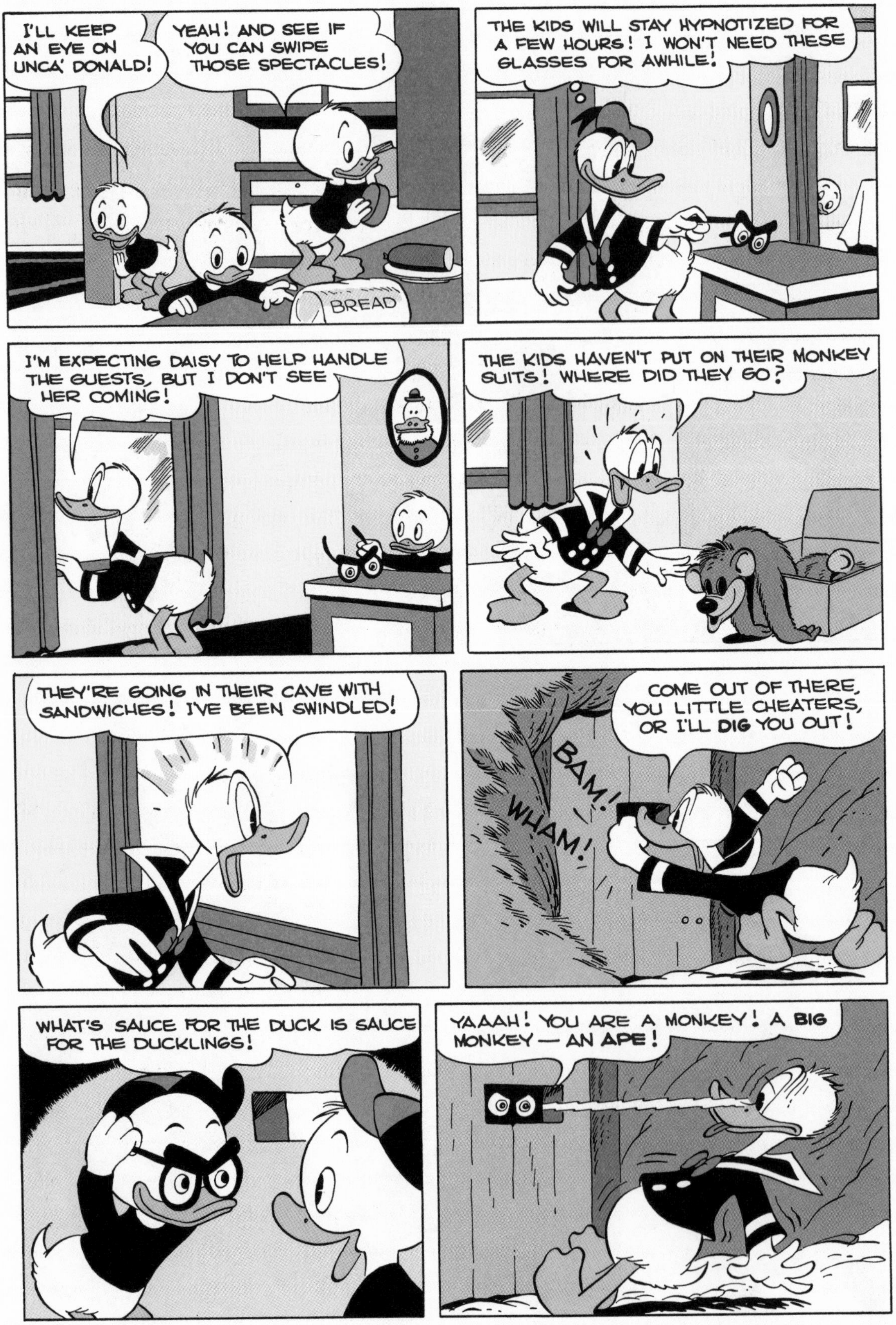
I'LL KEEP AN EYE ON UNCA' DONALD!
YEAH! AND SEE IF YOU CAN SWIPE THOSE SPECTACLES!
BREAD
THE KIDS WILL STAY HYPNOTIZED FOR A FEW HOURS! I WON'T NEED THESE GLASSES FOR AWHILE!
I'M EXPECTING DAISY TO HELP HANDLE THE GUESTS, BUT I DON'T SEE HER COMING!
THE KIDS HAVEN'T PUT ON THEIR MONKEY SUITS! WHERE DID THEY GO?
THEY'RE GOING IN THEIR CAVE WITH SANDWICHES! I'VE BEEN SWINDLED!
BAM!
WHAM!
COME OUT OF THERE, YOU LITTLE CHEATERS, OR I'LL **DIG** YOU OUT!
WHAT'S SAUCE FOR THE DUCK IS SAUCE FOR THE DUCKLINGS!
YAAAH! YOU ARE A MONKEY! A **BIG** MONKEY — AN **APE**!

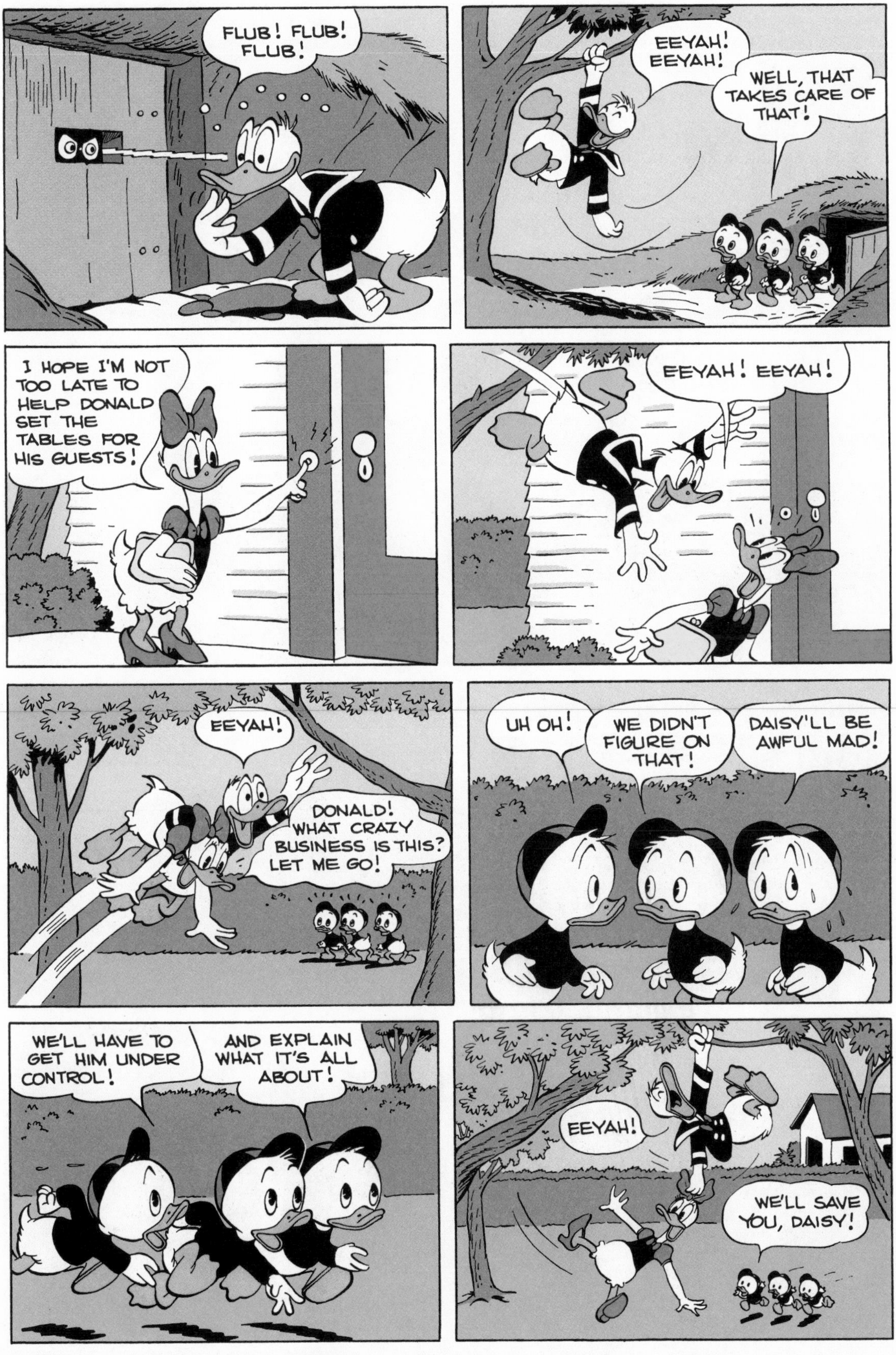
FLUB! FLUB! FLUB!
EEYAH! EEYAH!
WELL, THAT TAKES CARE OF THAT!
I HOPE I'M NOT TOO LATE TO HELP DONALD SET THE TABLES FOR HIS GUESTS!
EEYAH! EEYAH!
EEYAH!
DONALD! WHAT CRAZY BUSINESS IS THIS? LET ME GO!
UH OH!
WE DIDN'T FIGURE ON THAT!
DAISY'LL BE AWFUL MAD!
WE'LL HAVE TO GET HIM UNDER CONTROL!
AND EXPLAIN WHAT IT'S ALL ABOUT!
EEYAH!
WE'LL SAVE YOU, DAISY!

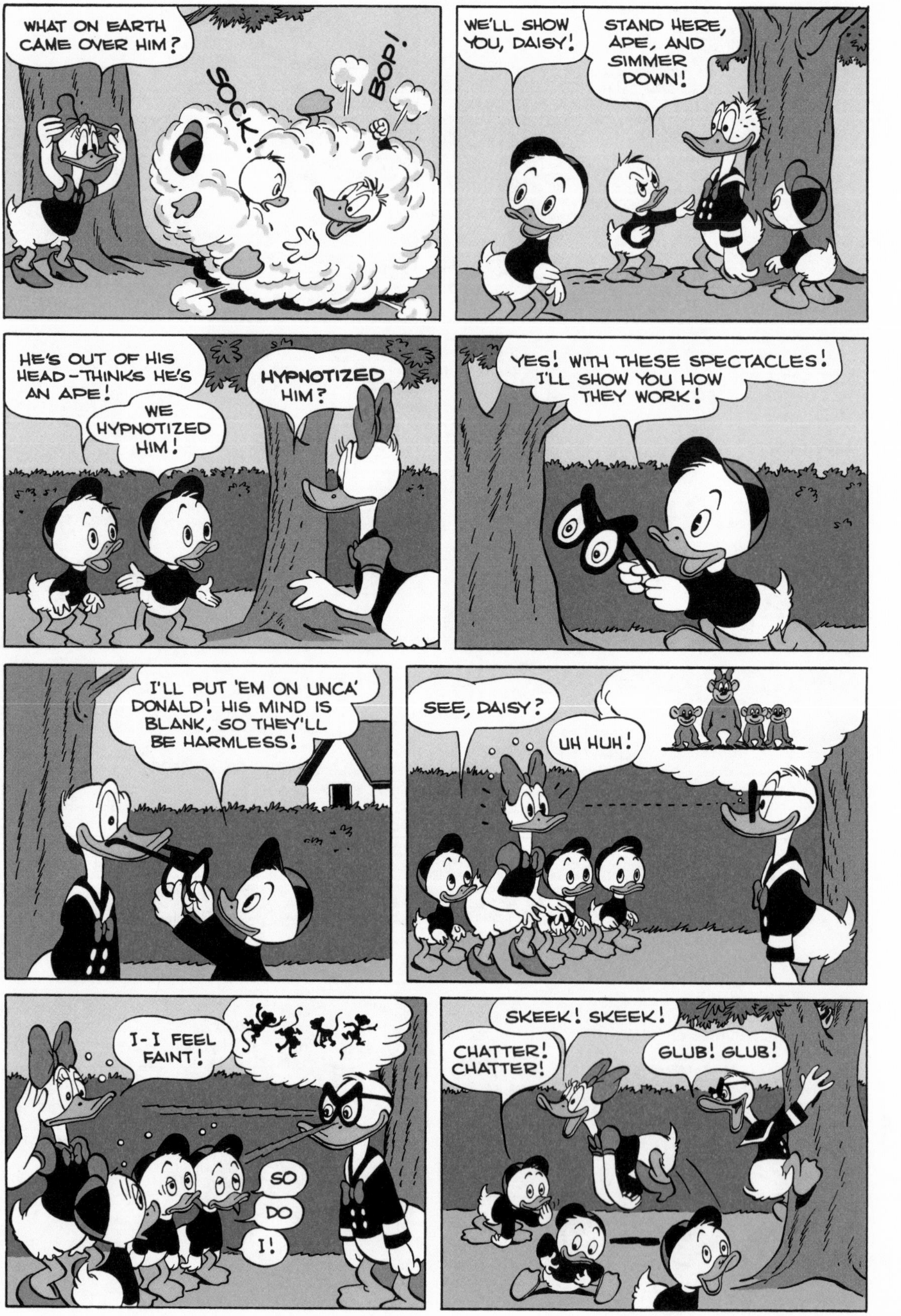
WHAT ON EARTH CAME OVER HIM?
SOCK!
BOP!
WE'LL SHOW YOU, DAISY!
STAND HERE, APE, AND SIMMER DOWN!
HE'S OUT OF HIS HEAD-THINKS HE'S AN APE!
WE HYPNOTIZED HIM!
HYPNOTIZED HIM?
YES! WITH THESE SPECTACLES! I'LL SHOW YOU HOW THEY WORK!
I'LL PUT 'EM ON UNCA' DONALD! HIS MIND IS BLANK, SO THEY'LL BE HARMLESS!
SEE, DAISY?
UH HUH!
I-I FEEL FAINT!
SO
DO
I!
SKEEK! SKEEK!
CHATTER! CHATTER!
GLUB! GLUB!

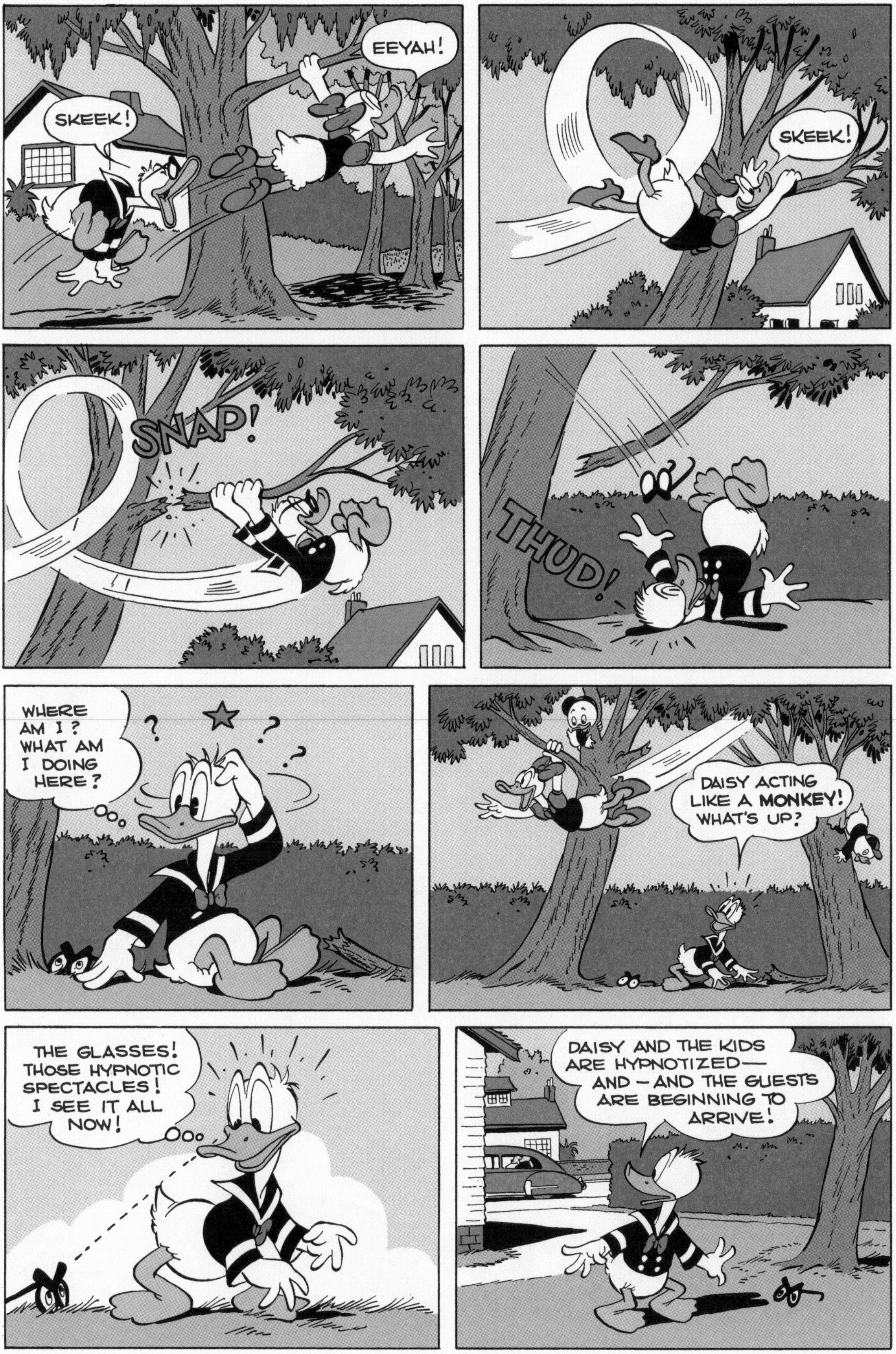
EEYAH!
SKEEK!
SKEEK!
SNAP!
THUD!
WHERE AM I? WHAT AM I DOING HERE?
DAISY ACTING LIKE A MONKEY! WHAT'S UP?
THE GLASSES! THOSE HYPNOTIC SPECTACLES! I SEE IT ALL NOW!
DAISY AND THE KIDS ARE HYPNOTIZED— AND – AND THE GUESTS ARE BEGINNING TO ARRIVE!

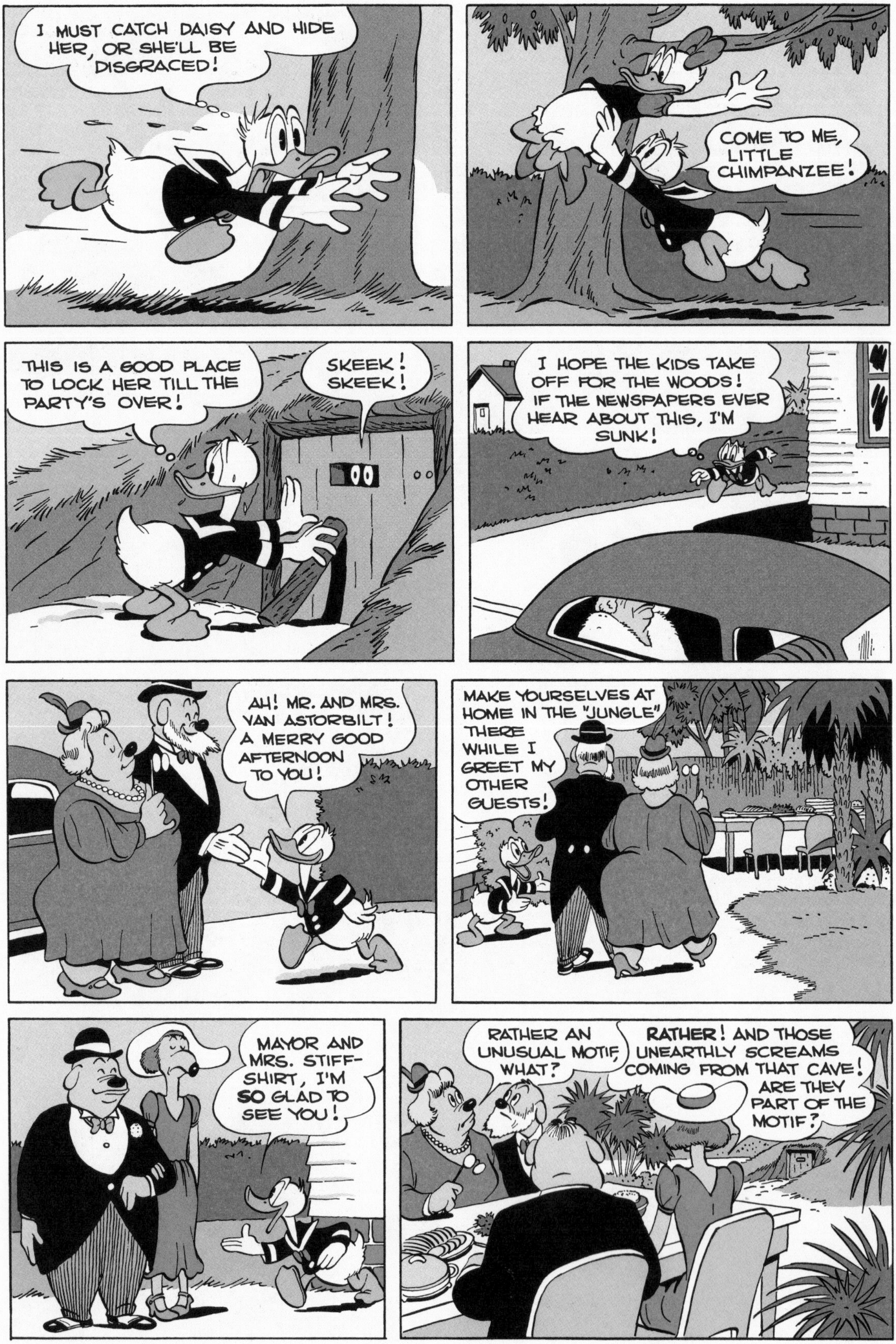

I MUST CATCH DAISY AND HIDE HER, OR SHE'LL BE DISGRACED!
COME TO ME, LITTLE CHIMPANZEE!
THIS IS A GOOD PLACE TO LOCK HER TILL THE PARTY'S OVER!
SKEEK! SKEEK!
I HOPE THE KIDS TAKE OFF FOR THE WOODS! IF THE NEWSPAPERS EVER HEAR ABOUT THIS, I'M SUNK!
AH! MR. AND MRS. VAN ASTORBILT! A MERRY GOOD AFTERNOON TO YOU!
MAKE YOURSELVES AT HOME IN THE "JUNGLE" THERE WHILE I GREET MY OTHER GUESTS!
MAYOR AND MRS. STIFF-SHIRT, I'M SO GLAD TO SEE YOU!
RATHER AN UNUSUAL MOTIF, WHAT?
RATHER! AND THOSE UNEARTHLY SCREAMS COMING FROM THAT CAVE! ARE THEY PART OF THE MOTIF?

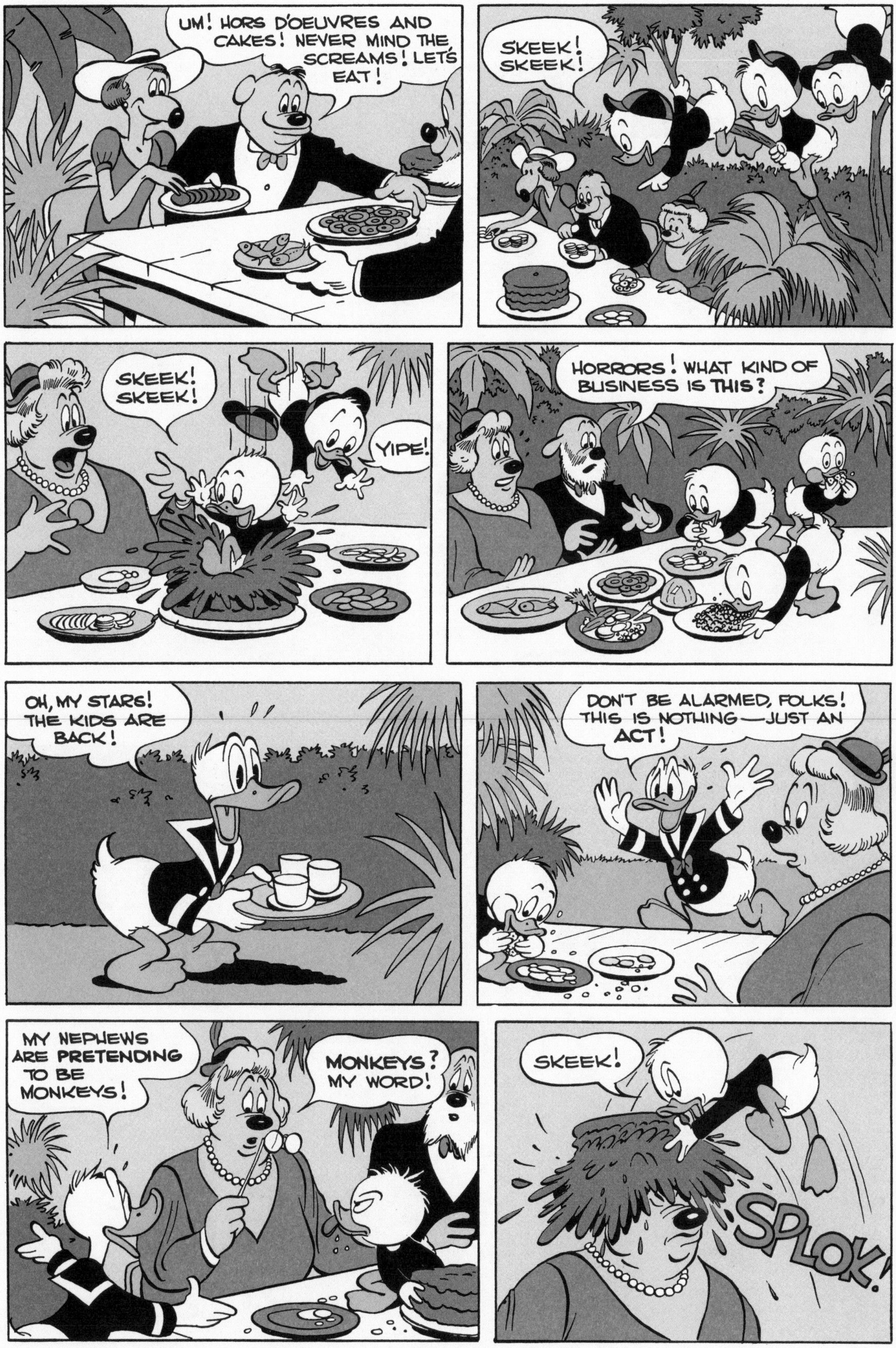
UM! HORS D'OEUVRES AND CAKES! NEVER MIND THE SCREAMS! LET'S EAT!
SKEEK! SKEEK!
SKEEK! SKEEK!
YIPE!
HORRORS! WHAT KIND OF BUSINESS IS THIS?
OH, MY STARS! THE KIDS ARE BACK!
DON'T BE ALARMED, FOLKS! THIS IS NOTHING—JUST AN ACT!
MY NEPHEWS ARE PRETENDING TO BE MONKEYS!
MONKEYS? MY WORD!
SKEEK!
SPLOK!

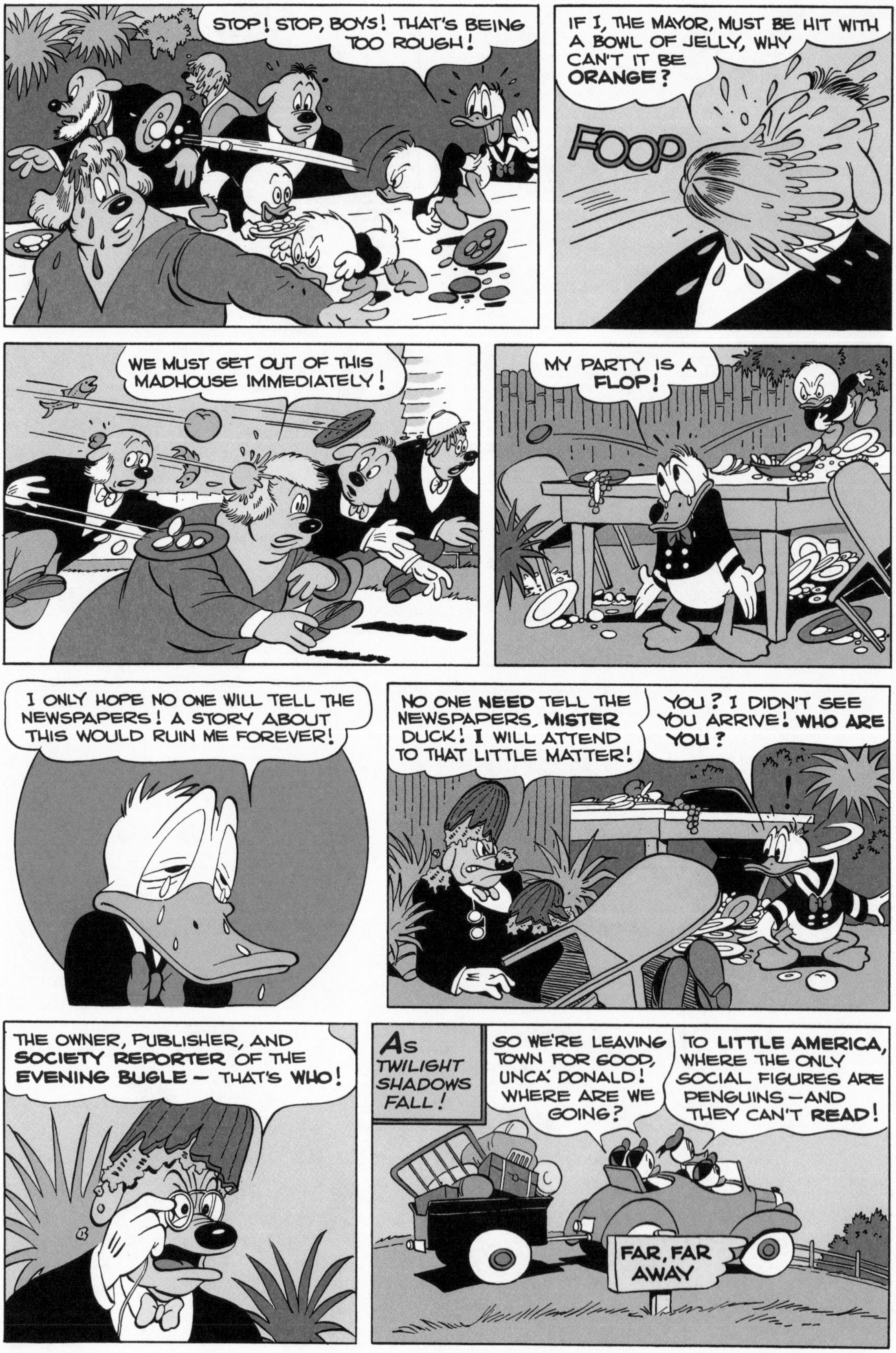

STOP! STOP, BOYS! THAT'S BEING TOO ROUGH!
IF I, THE MAYOR, MUST BE HIT WITH A BOWL OF JELLY, WHY CAN'T IT BE ORANGE?
FOOP
WE MUST GET OUT OF THIS MADHOUSE IMMEDIATELY!
MY PARTY IS A FLOP!
I ONLY HOPE NO ONE WILL TELL THE NEWSPAPERS! A STORY ABOUT THIS WOULD RUIN ME FOREVER!
NO ONE NEED TELL THE NEWSPAPERS, MISTER DUCK! I WILL ATTEND TO THAT LITTLE MATTER!
YOU? I DIDN'T SEE YOU ARRIVE! WHO ARE YOU?
THE OWNER, PUBLISHER, AND SOCIETY REPORTER OF THE EVENING BUGLE — THAT'S WHO!
AS TWILIGHT SHADOWS FALL!
SO WE'RE LEAVING TOWN FOR GOOD, UNCA' DONALD! WHERE ARE WE GOING?
TO LITTLE AMERICA, WHERE THE ONLY SOCIAL FIGURES ARE PENGUINS — AND THEY CAN'T READ!
FAR, FAR AWAY

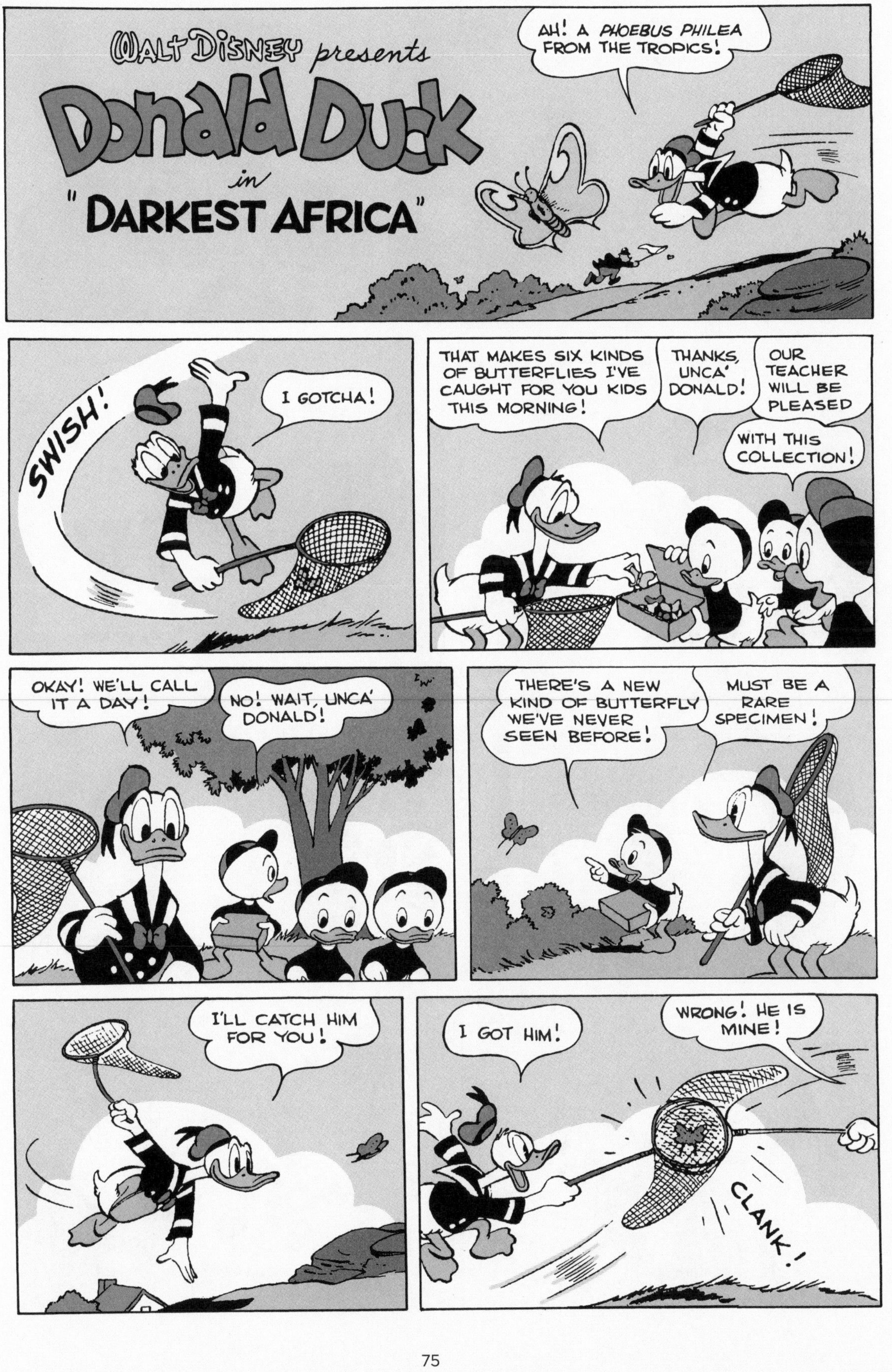

WALT DISNEY presents
Donald Duck
in
"DARKEST AFRICA"
AH! A PHOEBUS PHILEA FROM THE TROPICS!
SWISH!
I GOTCHA!
THAT MAKES SIX KINDS OF BUTTERFLIES I'VE CAUGHT FOR YOU KIDS THIS MORNING!
THANKS, UNCA' DONALD!
OUR TEACHER WILL BE PLEASED
WITH THIS COLLECTION!
OKAY! WE'LL CALL IT A DAY!
NO! WAIT, UNCA' DONALD!
THERE'S A NEW KIND OF BUTTERFLY WE'VE NEVER SEEN BEFORE!
MUST BE A RARE SPECIMEN!
I'LL CATCH HIM FOR YOU!
I GOT HIM!
WRONG! HE IS MINE!
CLANK!

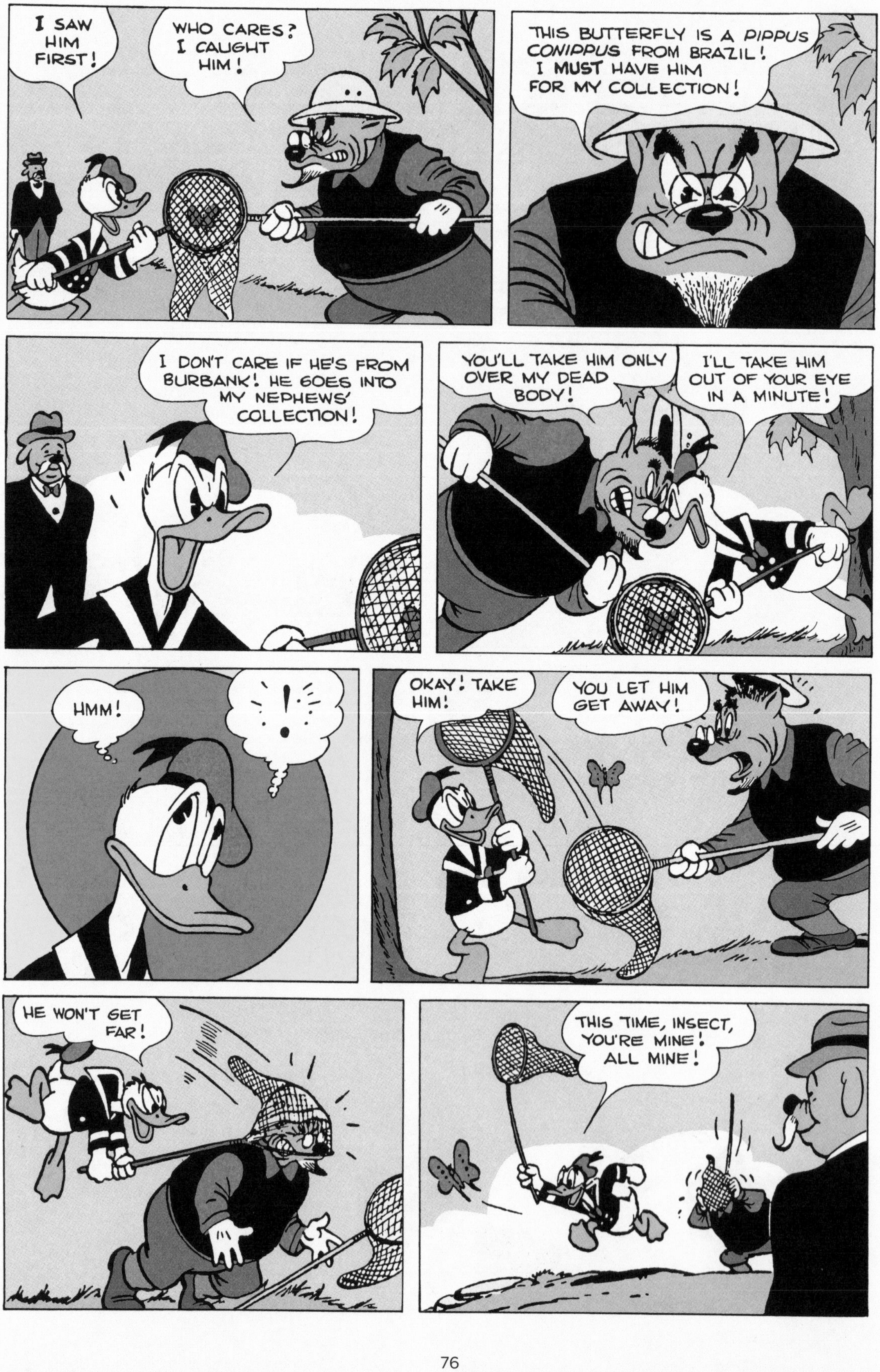
I SAW HIM FIRST!
WHO CARES? I CAUGHT HIM!
THIS BUTTERFLY IS A *PIPPUS CONIPPUS* FROM BRAZIL! I **MUST** HAVE HIM FOR MY COLLECTION!
I DON'T CARE IF HE'S FROM BURBANK! HE GOES INTO MY NEPHEWS' COLLECTION!
YOU'LL TAKE HIM ONLY OVER MY DEAD BODY!
I'LL TAKE HIM OUT OF YOUR EYE IN A MINUTE!
HMM!
!
OKAY! TAKE HIM!
YOU LET HIM GET AWAY!
HE WON'T GET FAR!
THIS TIME, INSECT, YOU'RE MINE! ALL MINE!

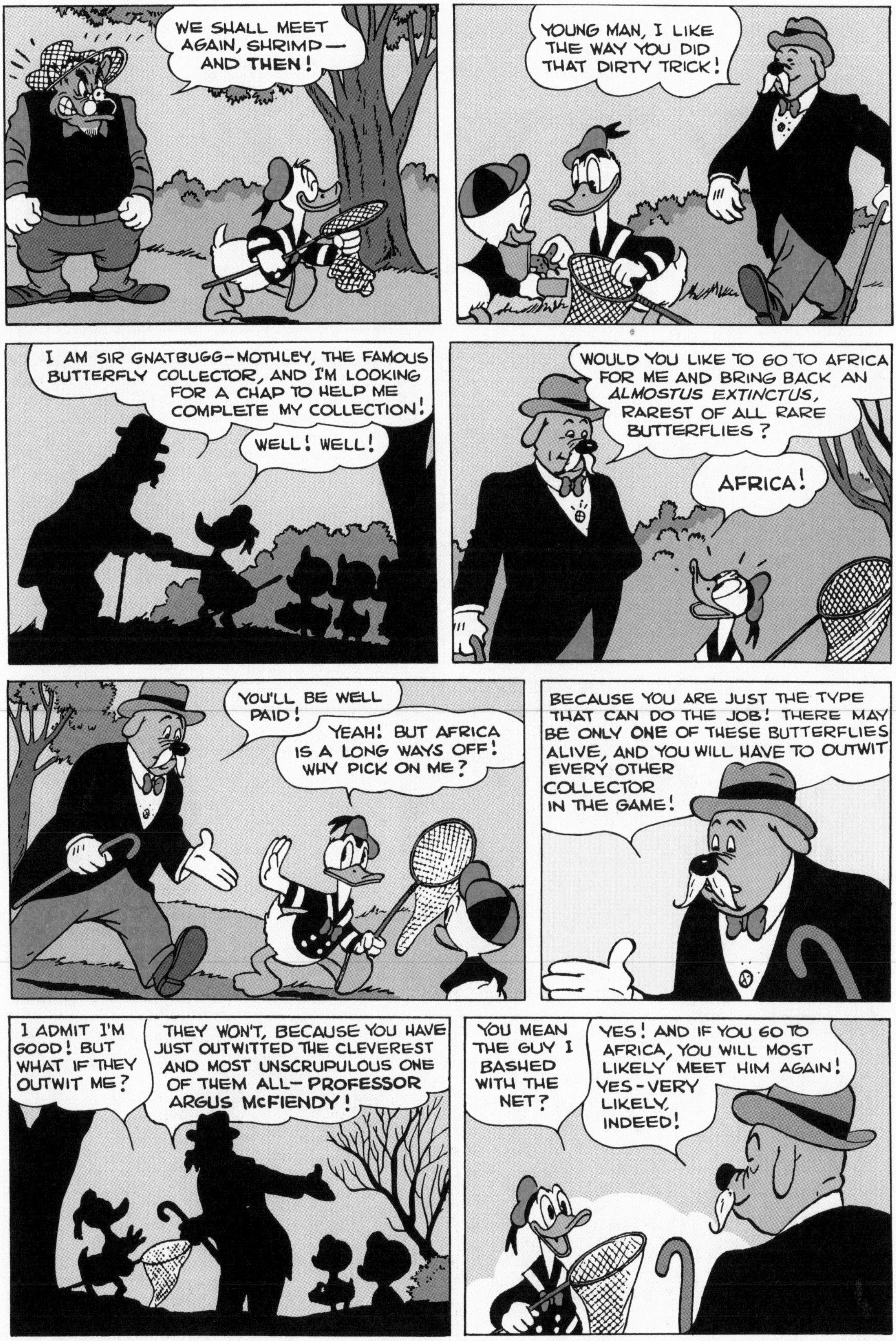
WE SHALL MEET AGAIN, SHRIMP— AND THEN!
YOUNG MAN, I LIKE THE WAY YOU DID THAT DIRTY TRICK!
I AM SIR GNATBUGG-MOTHLEY, THE FAMOUS BUTTERFLY COLLECTOR, AND I'M LOOKING FOR A CHAP TO HELP ME COMPLETE MY COLLECTION!
WELL! WELL!
WOULD YOU LIKE TO GO TO AFRICA FOR ME AND BRING BACK AN *ALMOSTUS EXTINCTUS*, RAREST OF ALL RARE BUTTERFLIES?
AFRICA!
YOU'LL BE WELL PAID!
YEAH! BUT AFRICA IS A LONG WAYS OFF! WHY PICK ON ME?
BECAUSE YOU ARE JUST THE TYPE THAT CAN DO THE JOB! THERE MAY BE ONLY ONE OF THESE BUTTERFLIES ALIVE, AND YOU WILL HAVE TO OUTWIT EVERY OTHER COLLECTOR IN THE GAME!
I ADMIT I'M GOOD! BUT WHAT IF THEY OUTWIT ME?
THEY WON'T, BECAUSE YOU HAVE JUST OUTWITTED THE CLEVEREST AND MOST UNSCRUPULOUS ONE OF THEM ALL—PROFESSOR ARGUS McFIENDY!
YOU MEAN THE GUY I BASHED WITH THE NET?
YES! AND IF YOU GO TO AFRICA, YOU WILL MOST LIKELY MEET HIM AGAIN! YES-VERY LIKELY, INDEED!

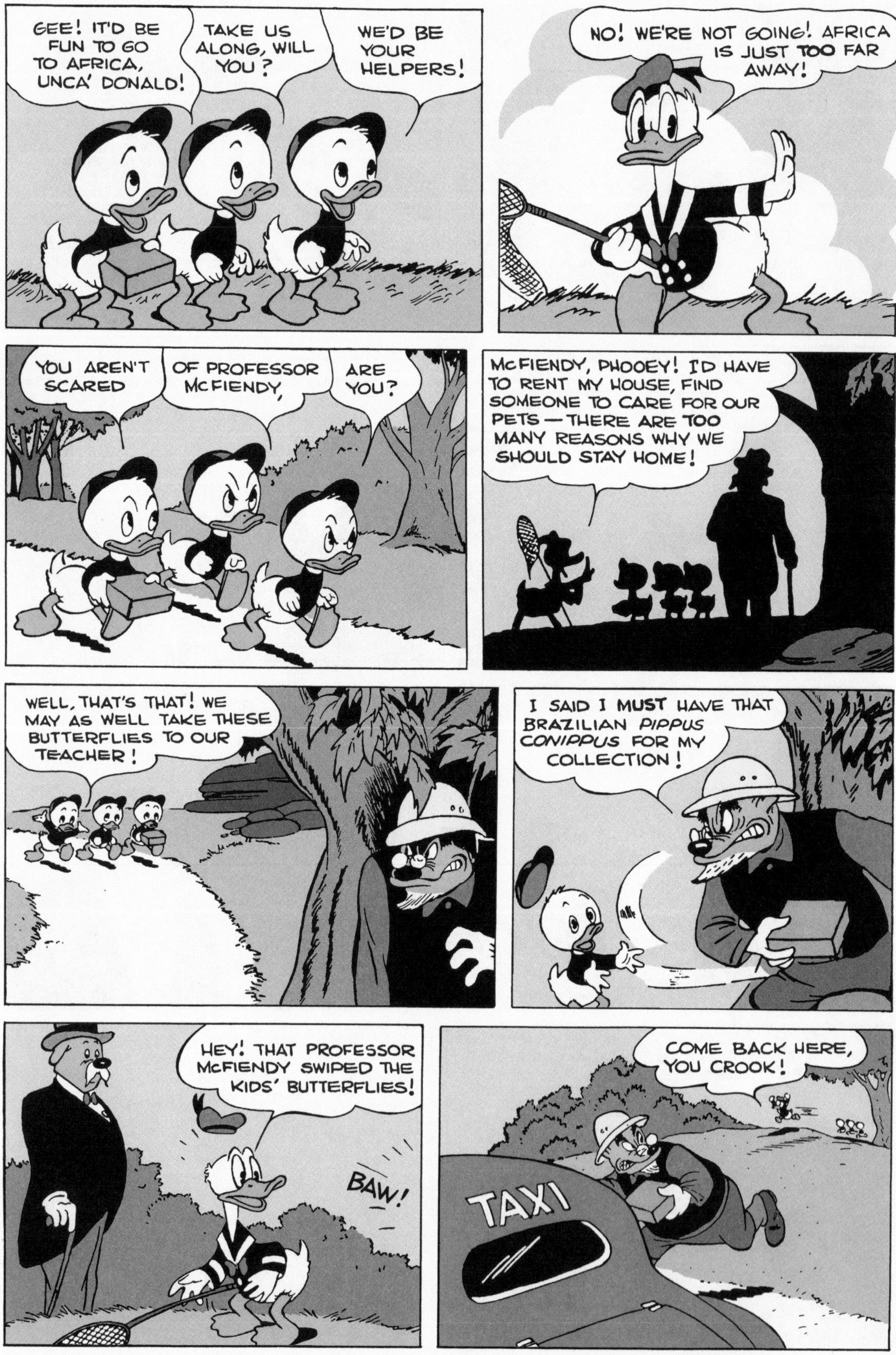
GEE! IT'D BE FUN TO GO TO AFRICA, UNCA' DONALD!
TAKE US ALONG, WILL YOU?
WE'D BE YOUR HELPERS!
NO! WE'RE NOT GOING! AFRICA IS JUST TOO FAR AWAY!
YOU AREN'T SCARED
OF PROFESSOR McFIENDY,
ARE YOU?
McFIENDY, PHOOEY! I'D HAVE TO RENT MY HOUSE, FIND SOMEONE TO CARE FOR OUR PETS — THERE ARE TOO MANY REASONS WHY WE SHOULD STAY HOME!
WELL, THAT'S THAT! WE MAY AS WELL TAKE THESE BUTTERFLIES TO OUR TEACHER!
I SAID I MUST HAVE THAT BRAZILIAN *PIPPUS CONIPPUS* FOR MY COLLECTION!
HEY! THAT PROFESSOR McFIENDY SWIPED THE KIDS' BUTTERFLIES!
BAW!
COME BACK HERE, YOU CROOK!
TAXI

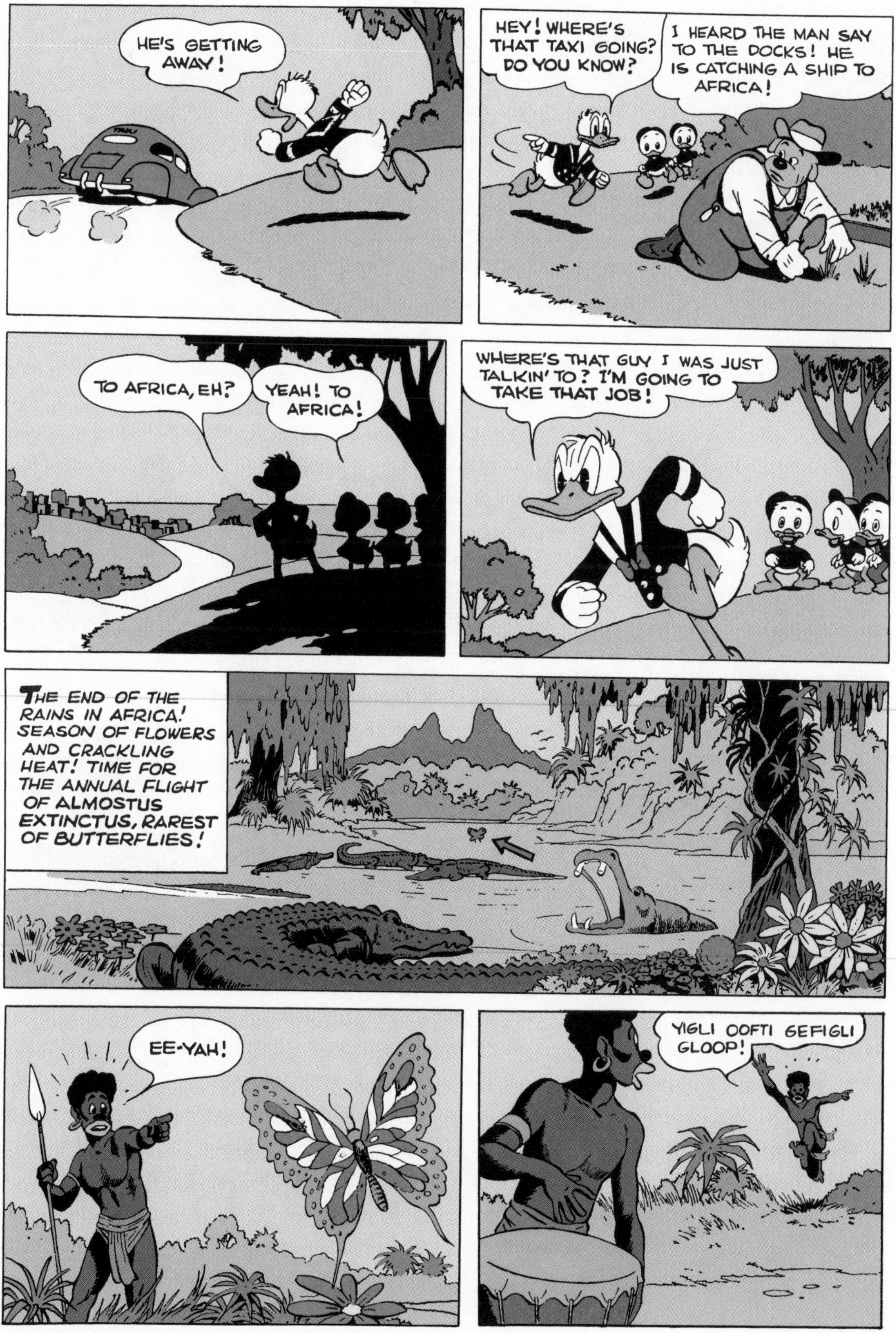
HE'S GETTING AWAY!
HEY! WHERE'S THAT TAXI GOING? DO YOU KNOW?
I HEARD THE MAN SAY TO THE DOCKS! HE IS CATCHING A SHIP TO AFRICA!
TO AFRICA, EH?
YEAH! TO AFRICA!
WHERE'S THAT GUY I WAS JUST TALKIN' TO? I'M GOING TO TAKE THAT JOB!
THE END OF THE RAINS IN AFRICA! SEASON OF FLOWERS AND CRACKLING HEAT! TIME FOR THE ANNUAL FLIGHT OF ALMOSTUS EXTINCTUS, RAREST OF BUTTERFLIES!
EE-YAH!
YIGLI OOFTI GEFIGLI GLOOP!

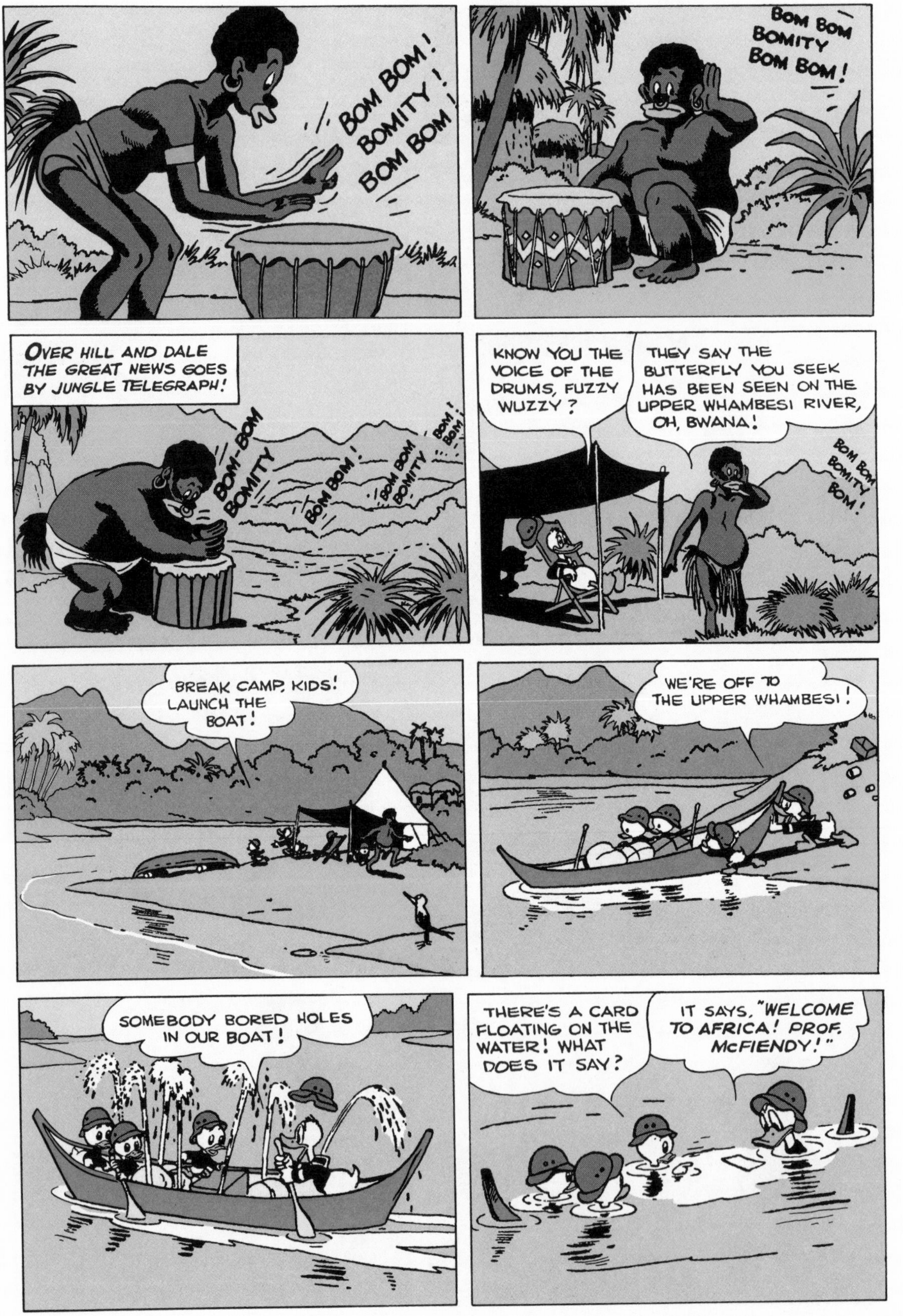
BOM BOM!
BOMITY!
BOM BOM!
BOM BOM
BOMITY
BOM BOM!
OVER HILL AND DALE THE GREAT NEWS GOES BY JUNGLE TELEGRAPH!
BOM-BOM
BOMITY
BOM BOM!
BOM BOM
BOMITY
BOM BOM
KNOW YOU THE VOICE OF THE DRUMS, FUZZY WUZZY?
THEY SAY THE BUTTERFLY YOU SEEK HAS BEEN SEEN ON THE UPPER WHAMBESI RIVER, OH, BWANA!
BOM BOM
BOMITY
BOM!
BREAK CAMP, KIDS! LAUNCH THE BOAT!
WE'RE OFF TO THE UPPER WHAMBESI!
SOMEBODY BORED HOLES IN OUR BOAT!
THERE'S A CARD FLOATING ON THE WATER! WHAT DOES IT SAY?
IT SAYS, "WELCOME TO AFRICA! PROF. McFIENDY!"

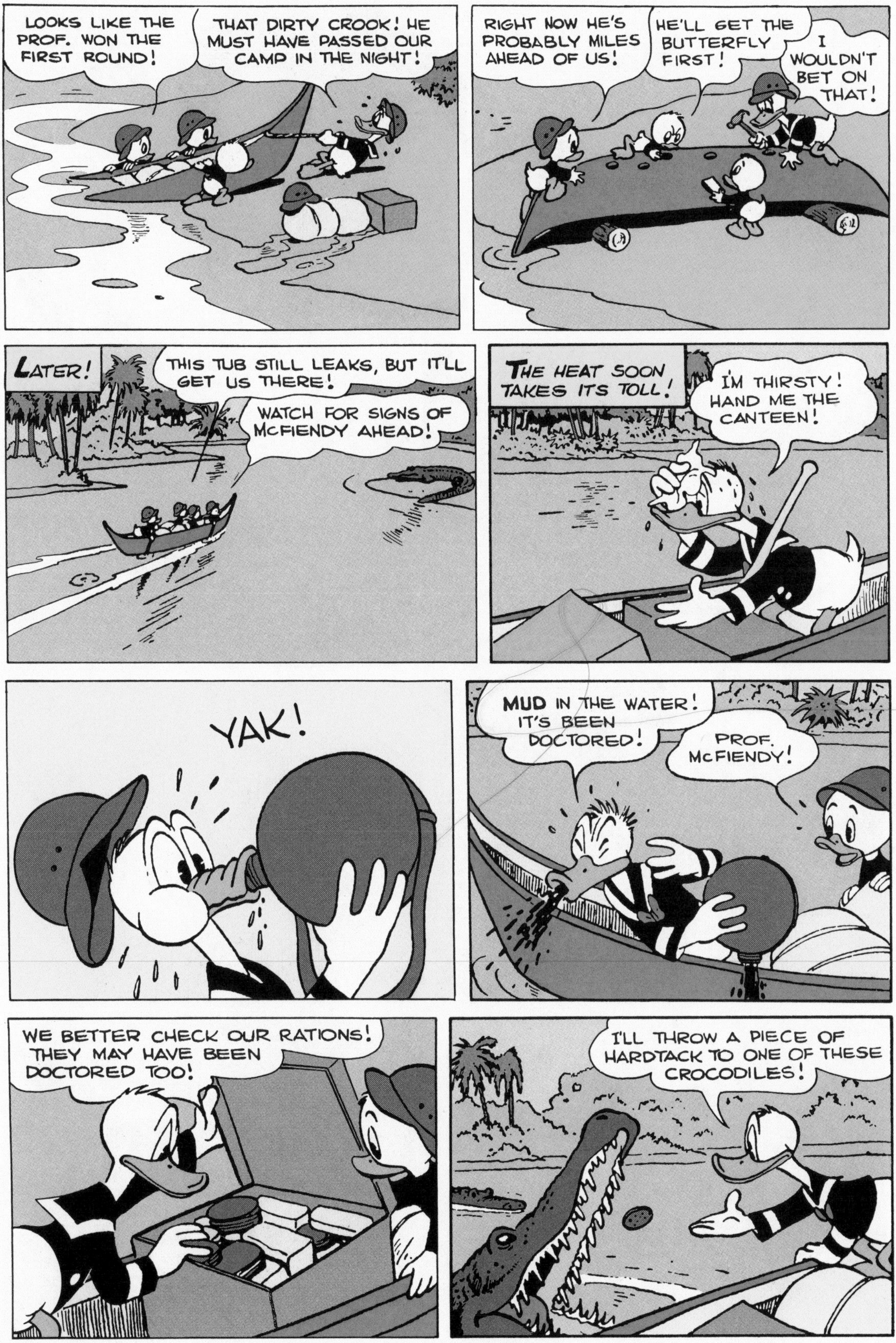
LOOKS LIKE THE PROF. WON THE FIRST ROUND!
THAT DIRTY CROOK! HE MUST HAVE PASSED OUR CAMP IN THE NIGHT!
RIGHT NOW HE'S PROBABLY MILES AHEAD OF US!
HE'LL GET THE BUTTERFLY FIRST!
I WOULDN'T BET ON THAT!
LATER!
THIS TUB STILL LEAKS, BUT IT'LL GET US THERE!
WATCH FOR SIGNS OF McFIENDY AHEAD!
THE HEAT SOON TAKES ITS TOLL!
I'M THIRSTY! HAND ME THE CANTEEN!
YAK!
MUD IN THE WATER! IT'S BEEN DOCTORED!
PROF. McFIENDY!
WE BETTER CHECK OUR RATIONS! THEY MAY HAVE BEEN DOCTORED TOO!
I'LL THROW A PIECE OF HARDTACK TO ONE OF THESE CROCODILES!

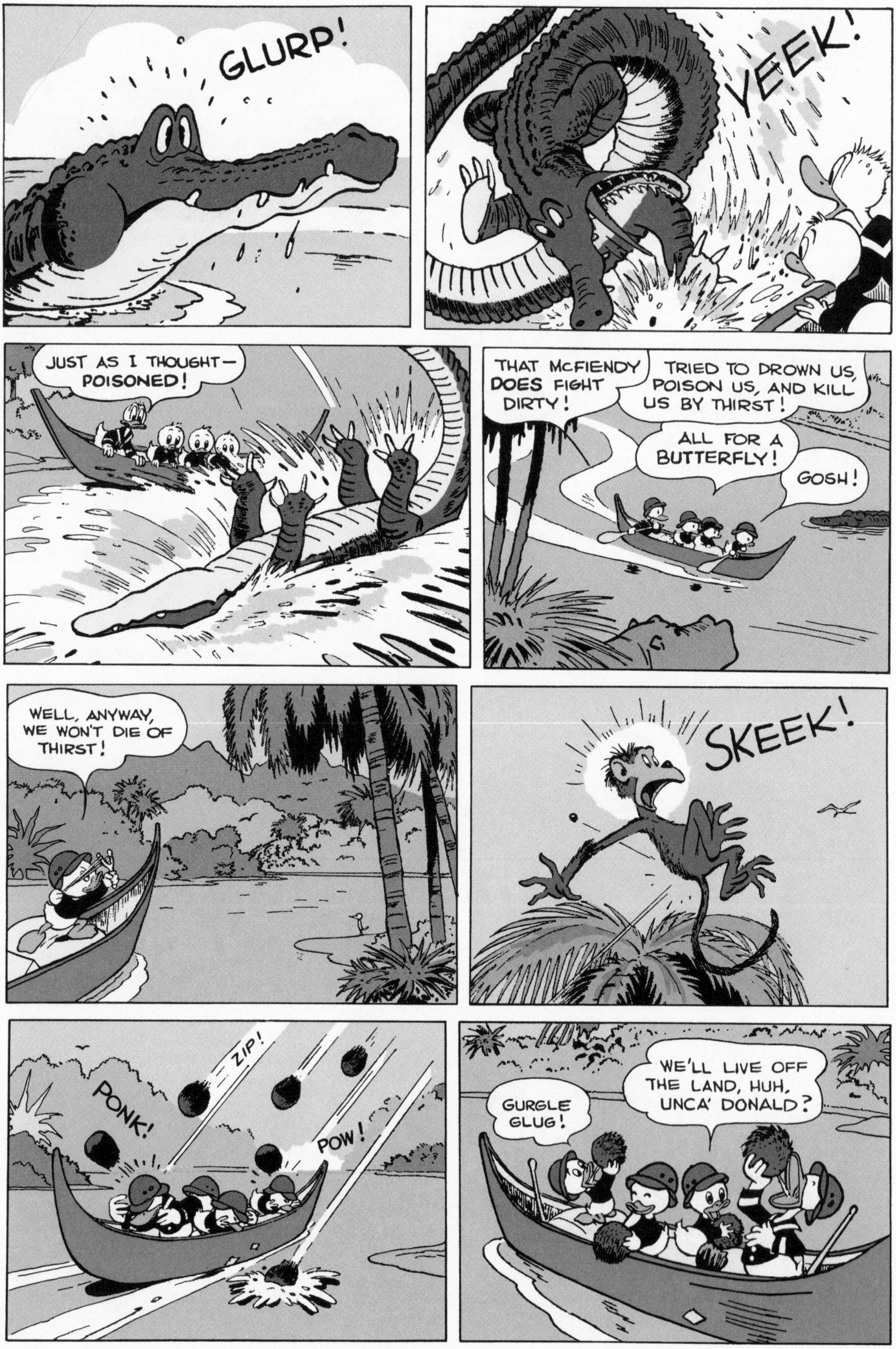
GLURP!
YEEK!
JUST AS I THOUGHT— POISONED!
THAT McFIENDY DOES FIGHT DIRTY!
TRIED TO DROWN US, POISON US, AND KILL US BY THIRST!
ALL FOR A BUTTERFLY!
GOSH!
WELL, ANYWAY, WE WON'T DIE OF THIRST!
SKEEK!
PONK!
ZIP!
POW!
GURGLE GLUG!
WE'LL LIVE OFF THE LAND, HUH, UNCA' DONALD?

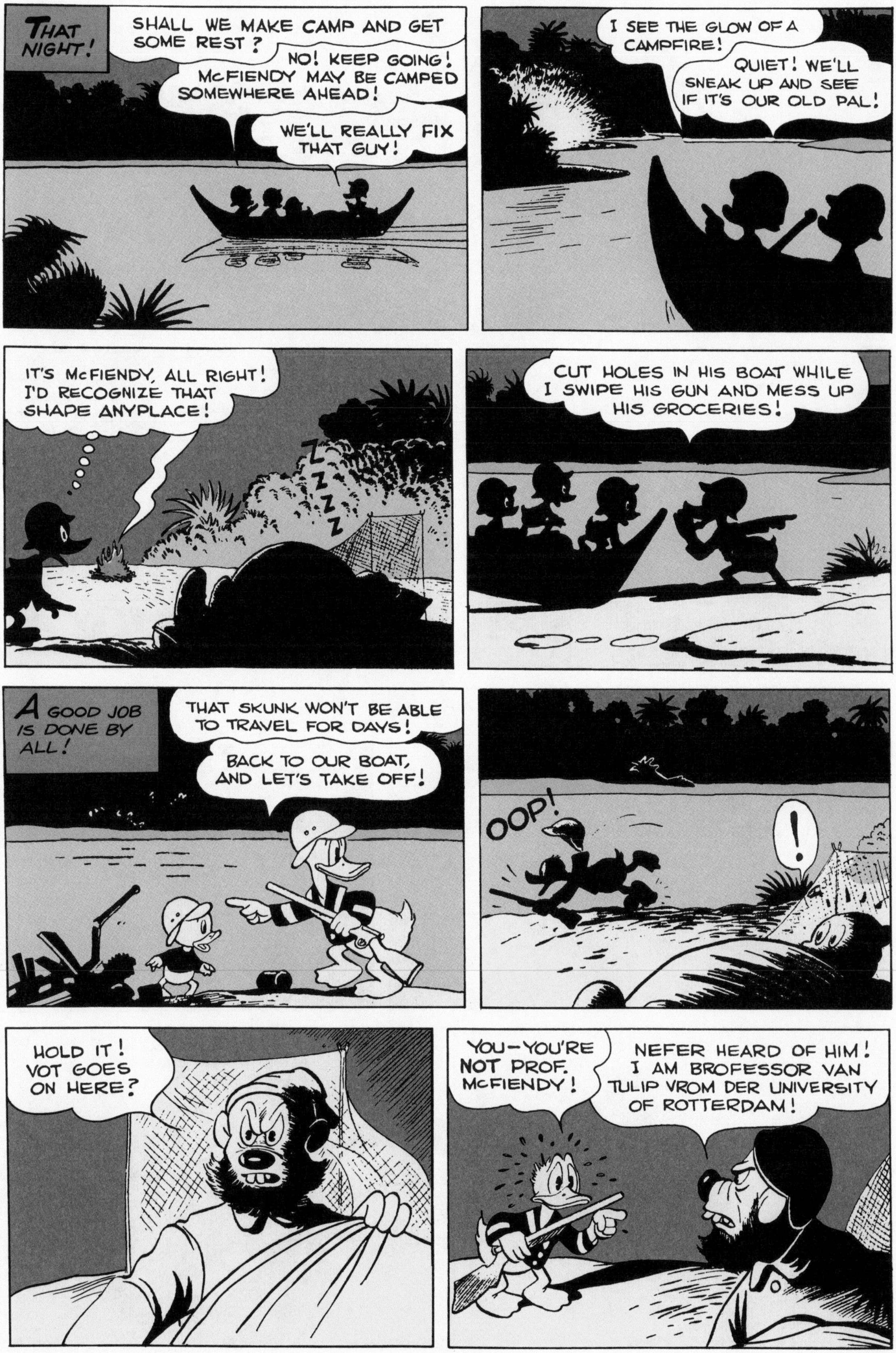

THAT NIGHT!
SHALL WE MAKE CAMP AND GET SOME REST?
NO! KEEP GOING! McFIENDY MAY BE CAMPED SOMEWHERE AHEAD!
WE'LL REALLY FIX THAT GUY!
I SEE THE GLOW OF A CAMPFIRE!
QUIET! WE'LL SNEAK UP AND SEE IF IT'S OUR OLD PAL!
IT'S McFIENDY, ALL RIGHT! I'D RECOGNIZE THAT SHAPE ANYPLACE!
Z Z Z Z
CUT HOLES IN HIS BOAT WHILE I SWIPE HIS GUN AND MESS UP HIS GROCERIES!
A GOOD JOB IS DONE BY ALL!
THAT SKUNK WON'T BE ABLE TO TRAVEL FOR DAYS!
BACK TO OUR BOAT, AND LET'S TAKE OFF!
OOP!
!
HOLD IT! VOT GOES ON HERE?
YOU—YOU'RE NOT PROF. McFIENDY!
NEFER HEARD OF HIM! I AM BROFESSOR VAN TULIP VROM DER UNIVERSITY OF ROTTERDAM!

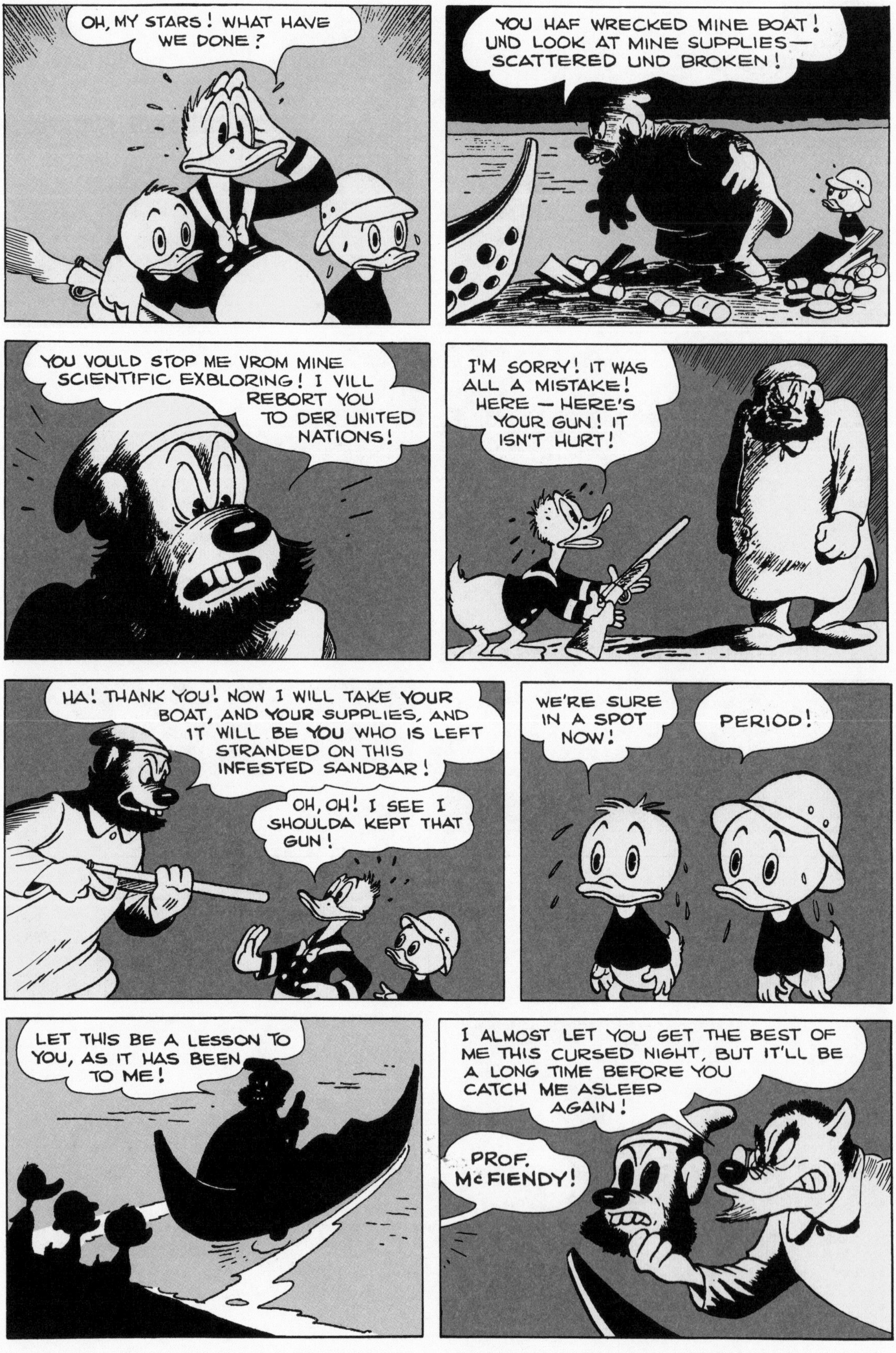
OH, MY STARS! WHAT HAVE WE DONE?
YOU HAF WRECKED MINE BOAT! UND LOOK AT MINE SUPPLIES— SCATTERED UND BROKEN!
YOU VOULD STOP ME VROM MINE SCIENTIFIC EXBLORING! I VILL REBORT YOU TO DER UNITED NATIONS!
I'M SORRY! IT WAS ALL A MISTAKE! HERE — HERE'S YOUR GUN! IT ISN'T HURT!
HA! THANK YOU! NOW I WILL TAKE YOUR BOAT, AND YOUR SUPPLIES, AND IT WILL BE YOU WHO IS LEFT STRANDED ON THIS INFESTED SANDBAR!
OH, OH! I SEE I SHOULDA KEPT THAT GUN!
WE'RE SURE IN A SPOT NOW!
PERIOD!
LET THIS BE A LESSON TO YOU, AS IT HAS BEEN TO ME!
I ALMOST LET YOU GET THE BEST OF ME THIS CURSED NIGHT, BUT IT'LL BE A LONG TIME BEFORE YOU CATCH ME ASLEEP AGAIN!
PROF. McFIENDY!

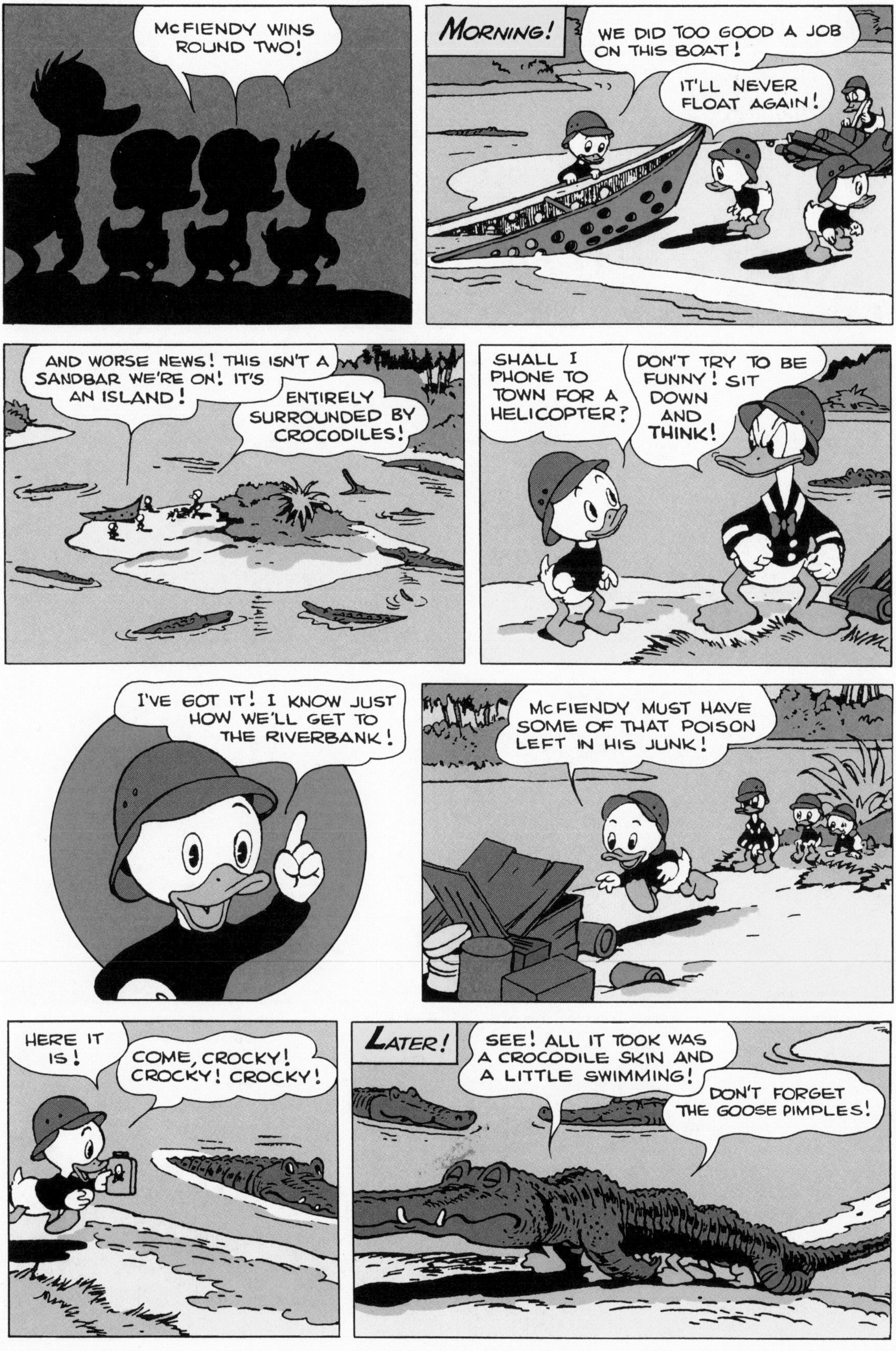
McFIENDY WINS ROUND TWO!
MORNING!
WE DID TOO GOOD A JOB ON THIS BOAT!
IT'LL NEVER FLOAT AGAIN!
AND WORSE NEWS! THIS ISN'T A SANDBAR WE'RE ON! IT'S AN ISLAND!
ENTIRELY SURROUNDED BY CROCODILES!
SHALL I PHONE TO TOWN FOR A HELICOPTER?
DON'T TRY TO BE FUNNY! SIT DOWN AND THINK!
I'VE GOT IT! I KNOW JUST HOW WE'LL GET TO THE RIVERBANK!
McFIENDY MUST HAVE SOME OF THAT POISON LEFT IN HIS JUNK!
HERE IT IS!
COME, CROCKY! CROCKY! CROCKY!
LATER!
SEE! ALL IT TOOK WAS A CROCODILE SKIN AND A LITTLE SWIMMING!
DON'T FORGET THE GOOSE PIMPLES!

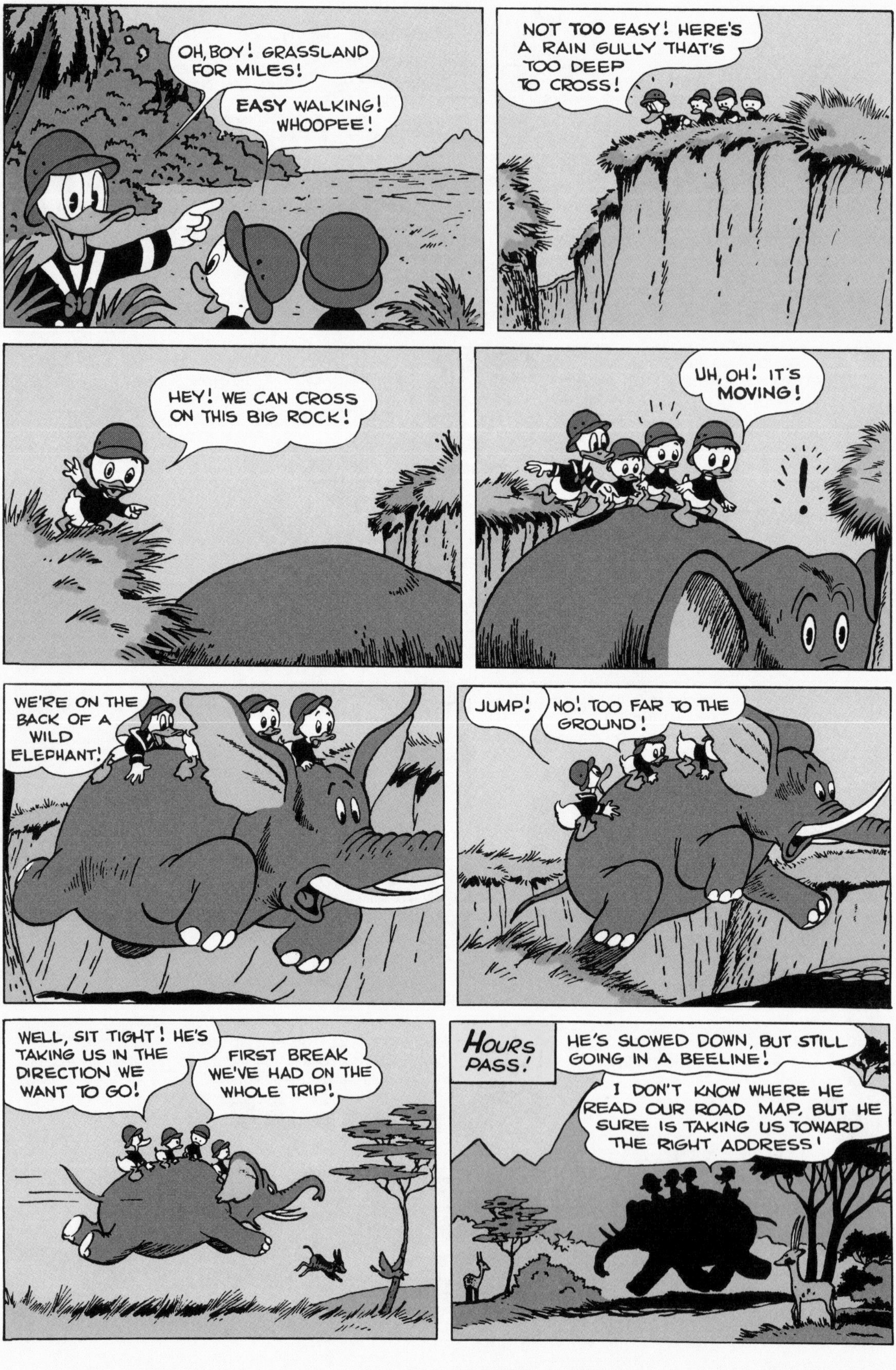
OH, BOY! GRASSLAND FOR MILES!
EASY WALKING! WHOOPEE!
NOT TOO EASY! HERE'S A RAIN GULLY THAT'S TOO DEEP TO CROSS!
HEY! WE CAN CROSS ON THIS BIG ROCK!
UH, OH! IT'S MOVING!
!
WE'RE ON THE BACK OF A WILD ELEPHANT!
JUMP!
NO! TOO FAR TO THE GROUND!
WELL, SIT TIGHT! HE'S TAKING US IN THE DIRECTION WE WANT TO GO!
FIRST BREAK WE'VE HAD ON THE WHOLE TRIP!
HOURS PASS!
HE'S SLOWED DOWN, BUT STILL GOING IN A BEELINE!
I DON'T KNOW WHERE HE READ OUR ROAD MAP, BUT HE SURE IS TAKING US TOWARD THE RIGHT ADDRESS!

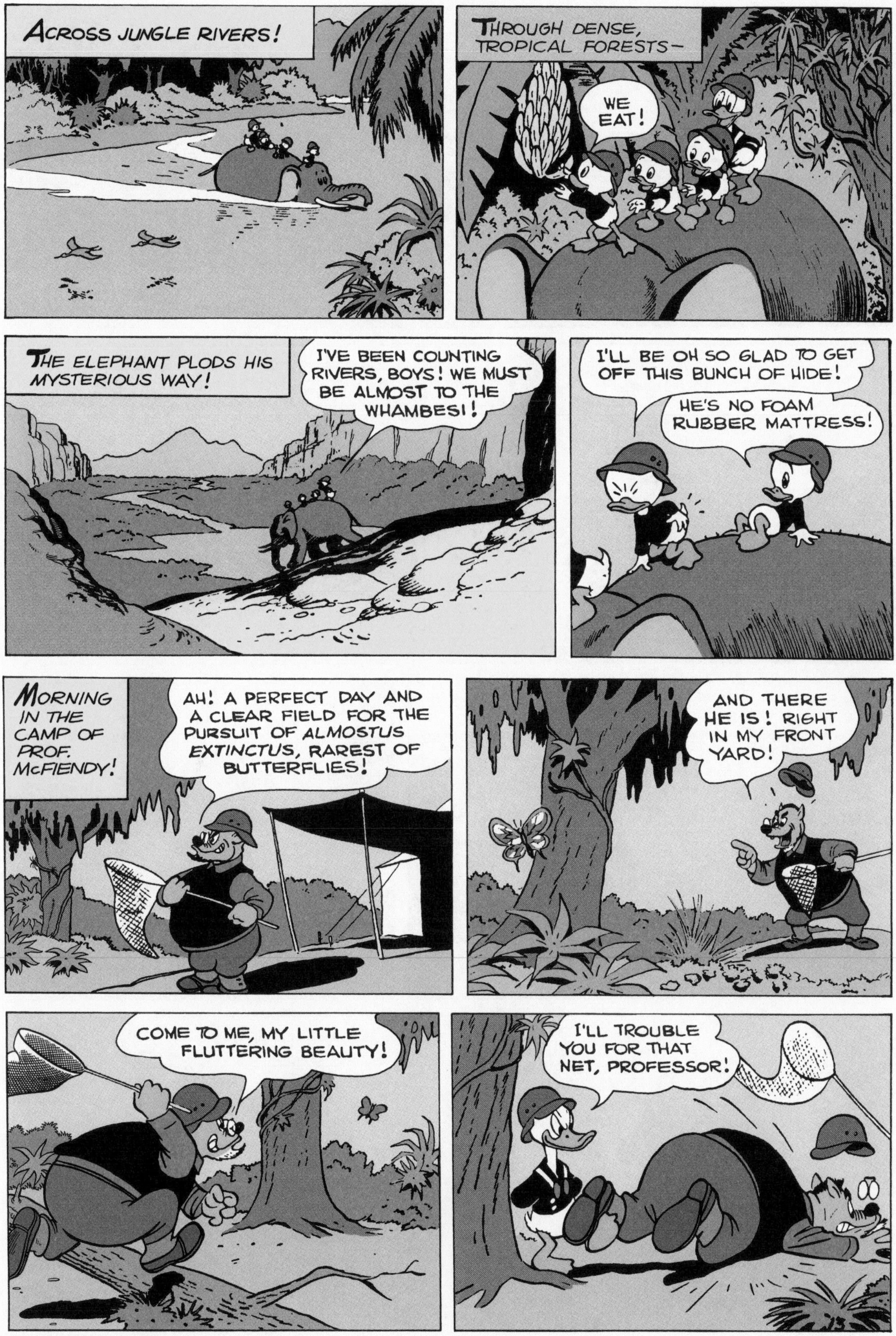
ACROSS JUNGLE RIVERS!
THROUGH DENSE, TROPICAL FORESTS—
WE EAT!
THE ELEPHANT PLODS HIS MYSTERIOUS WAY!
I'VE BEEN COUNTING RIVERS, BOYS! WE MUST BE ALMOST TO THE WHAMBESI!
I'LL BE OH SO GLAD TO GET OFF THIS BUNCH OF HIDE!
HE'S NO FOAM RUBBER MATTRESS!
MORNING IN THE CAMP OF PROF. McFIENDY!
AH! A PERFECT DAY AND A CLEAR FIELD FOR THE PURSUIT OF *ALMOSTUS EXTINCTUS*, RAREST OF BUTTERFLIES!
AND THERE HE IS! RIGHT IN MY FRONT YARD!
COME TO ME, MY LITTLE FLUTTERING BEAUTY!
I'LL TROUBLE YOU FOR THAT NET, PROFESSOR!

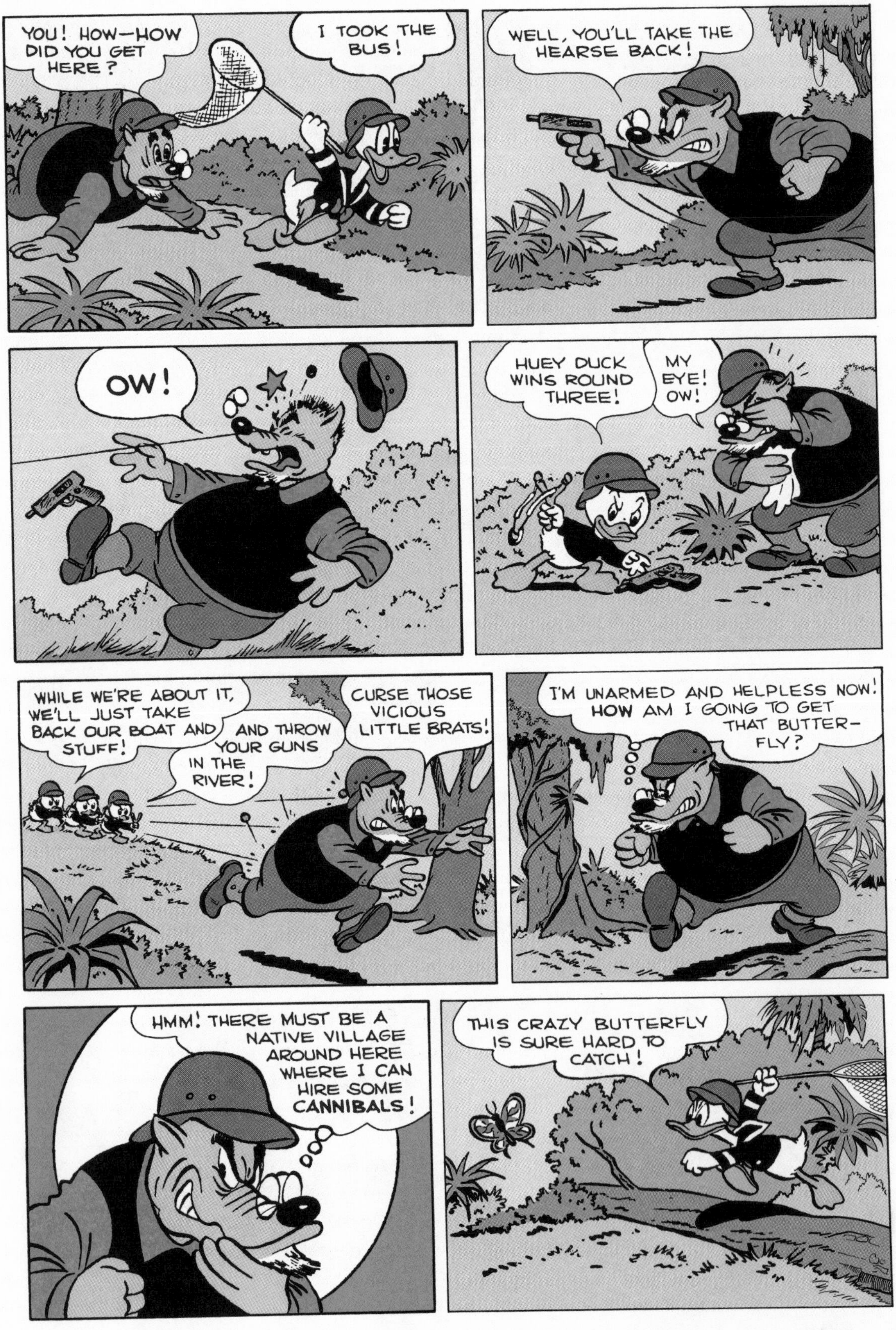
YOU! HOW—HOW DID YOU GET HERE?
I TOOK THE BUS!
WELL, YOU'LL TAKE THE HEARSE BACK!
OW!
HUEY DUCK WINS ROUND THREE!
MY EYE! OW!
WHILE WE'RE ABOUT IT, WE'LL JUST TAKE BACK OUR BOAT AND STUFF!
AND THROW YOUR GUNS IN THE RIVER!
CURSE THOSE VICIOUS LITTLE BRATS!
I'M UNARMED AND HELPLESS NOW! HOW AM I GOING TO GET THAT BUTTER-FLY?
HMM! THERE MUST BE A NATIVE VILLAGE AROUND HERE WHERE I CAN HIRE SOME CANNIBALS!
THIS CRAZY BUTTERFLY IS SURE HARD TO CATCH!

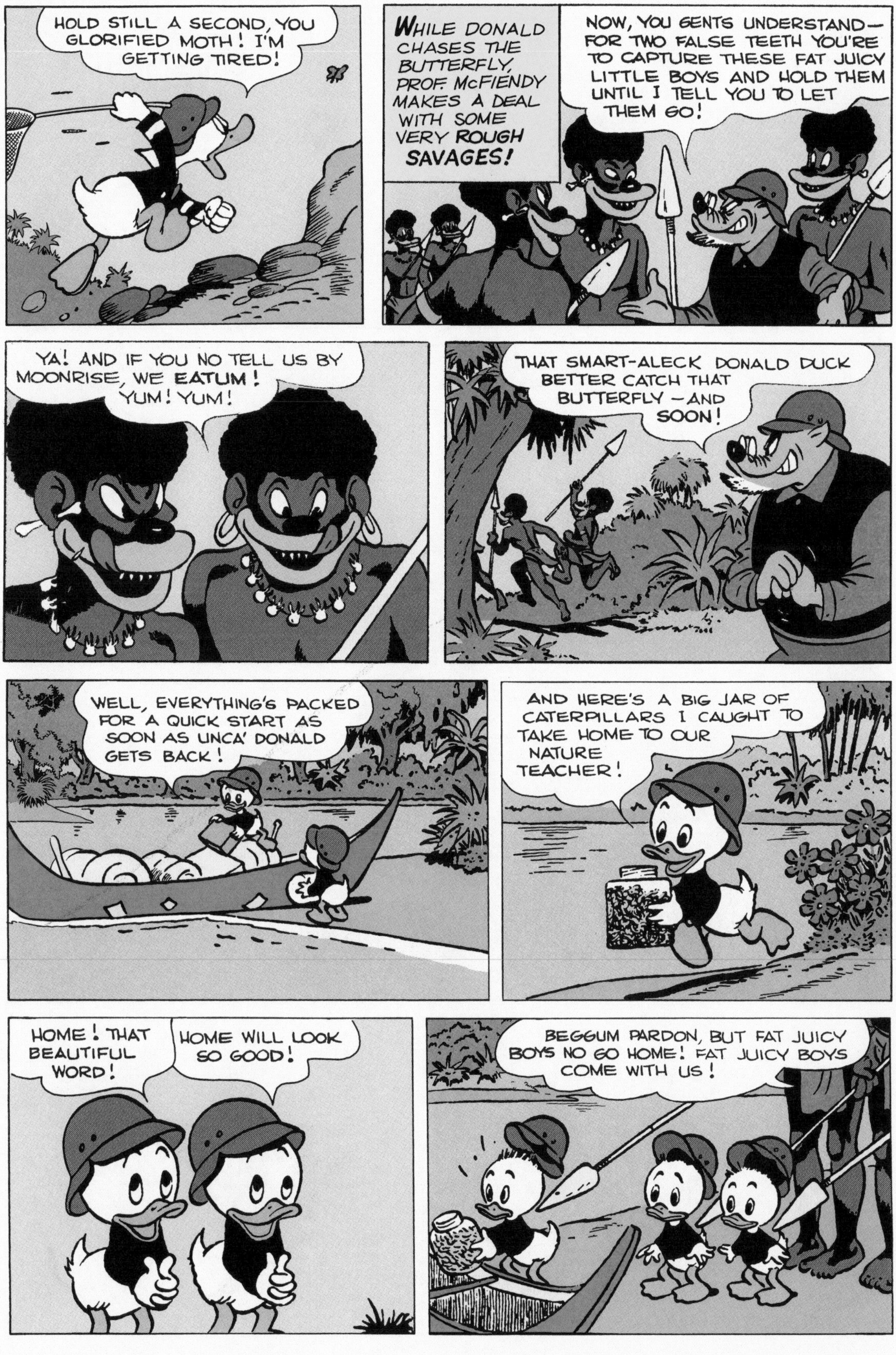
HOLD STILL A SECOND, YOU GLORIFIED MOTH! I'M GETTING TIRED!
WHILE DONALD CHASES THE BUTTERFLY, PROF. McFIENDY MAKES A DEAL WITH SOME VERY ROUGH SAVAGES!
NOW, YOU GENTS UNDERSTAND— FOR TWO FALSE TEETH YOU'RE TO CAPTURE THESE FAT JUICY LITTLE BOYS AND HOLD THEM UNTIL I TELL YOU TO LET THEM GO!
YA! AND IF YOU NO TELL US BY MOONRISE, WE EATUM! YUM! YUM!
THAT SMART-ALECK DONALD DUCK BETTER CATCH THAT BUTTERFLY —AND SOON!
WELL, EVERYTHING'S PACKED FOR A QUICK START AS SOON AS UNCA' DONALD GETS BACK!
AND HERE'S A BIG JAR OF CATERPILLARS I CAUGHT TO TAKE HOME TO OUR NATURE TEACHER!
HOME! THAT BEAUTIFUL WORD!
HOME WILL LOOK SO GOOD!
BEGGUM PARDON, BUT FAT JUICY BOYS NO GO HOME! FAT JUICY BOYS COME WITH US!
!

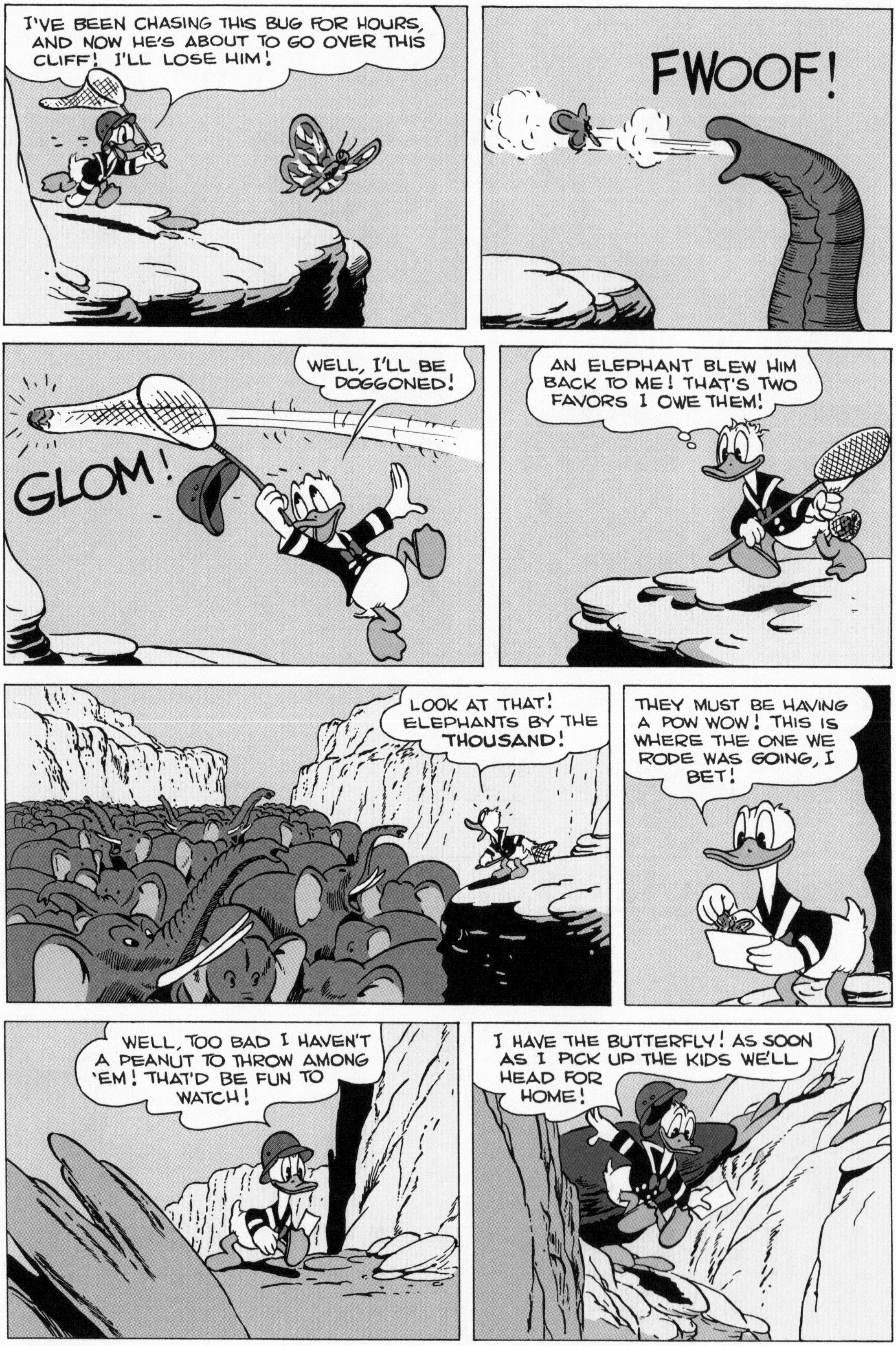
I'VE BEEN CHASING THIS BUG FOR HOURS, AND NOW HE'S ABOUT TO GO OVER THIS CLIFF! I'LL LOSE HIM!
FWOOF!
WELL, I'LL BE DOGGONED!
GLOM!
AN ELEPHANT BLEW HIM BACK TO ME! THAT'S TWO FAVORS I OWE THEM!
LOOK AT THAT! ELEPHANTS BY THE THOUSAND!
THEY MUST BE HAVING A POW WOW! THIS IS WHERE THE ONE WE RODE WAS GOING, I BET!
WELL, TOO BAD I HAVEN'T A PEANUT TO THROW AMONG 'EM! THAT'D BE FUN TO WATCH!
I HAVE THE BUTTERFLY! AS SOON AS I PICK UP THE KIDS WE'LL HEAD FOR HOME!

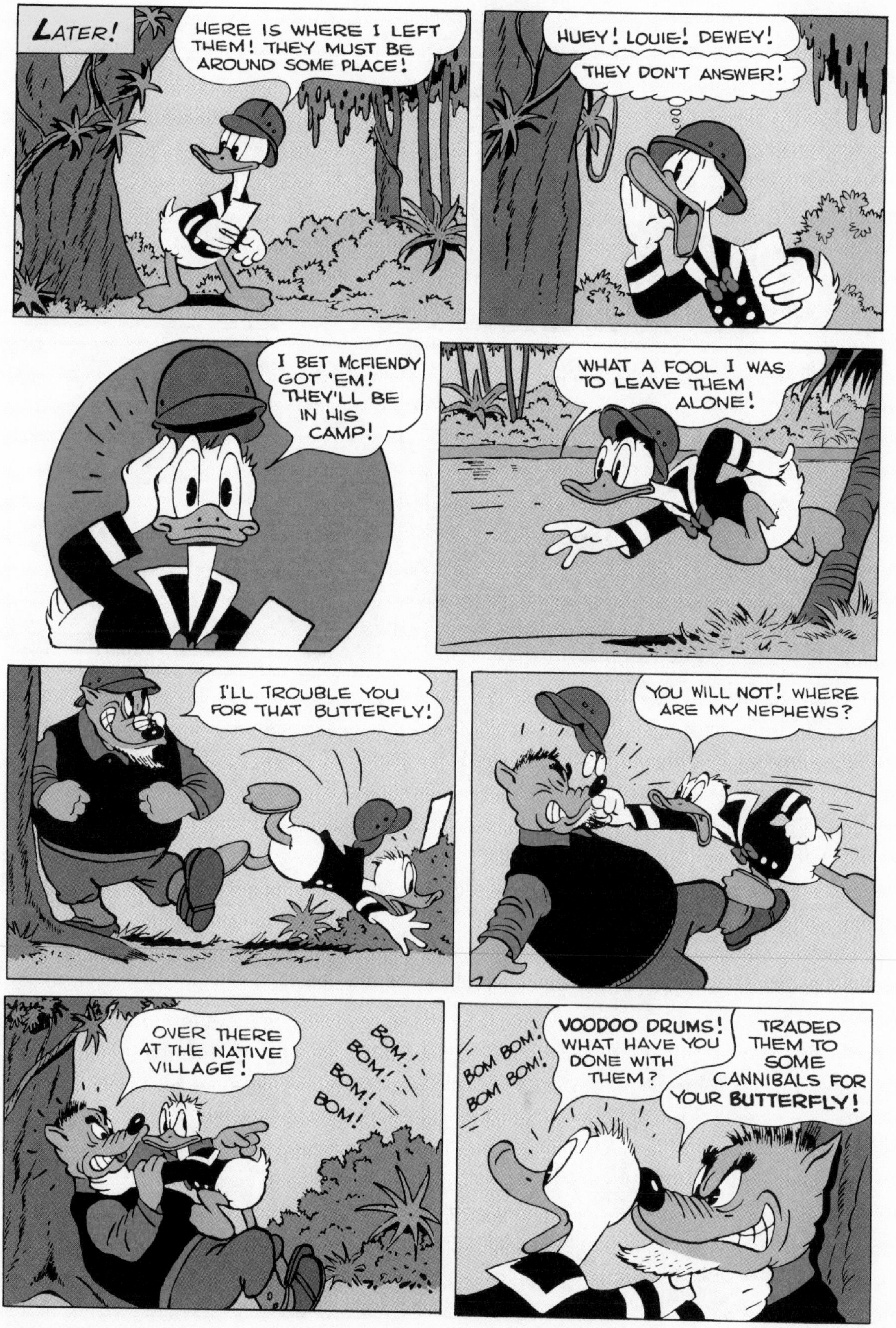
LATER!
HERE IS WHERE I LEFT THEM! THEY MUST BE AROUND SOME PLACE!
HUEY! LOUIE! DEWEY!
THEY DON'T ANSWER!
I BET McFIENDY GOT 'EM! THEY'LL BE IN HIS CAMP!
WHAT A FOOL I WAS TO LEAVE THEM ALONE!
I'LL TROUBLE YOU FOR THAT BUTTERFLY!
YOU WILL NOT! WHERE ARE MY NEPHEWS?
OVER THERE AT THE NATIVE VILLAGE!
BOM! BOM! BOM! BOM!
BOM BOM! BOM BOM!
VOODOO DRUMS! WHAT HAVE YOU DONE WITH THEM?
TRADED THEM TO SOME CANNIBALS FOR YOUR BUTTERFLY!

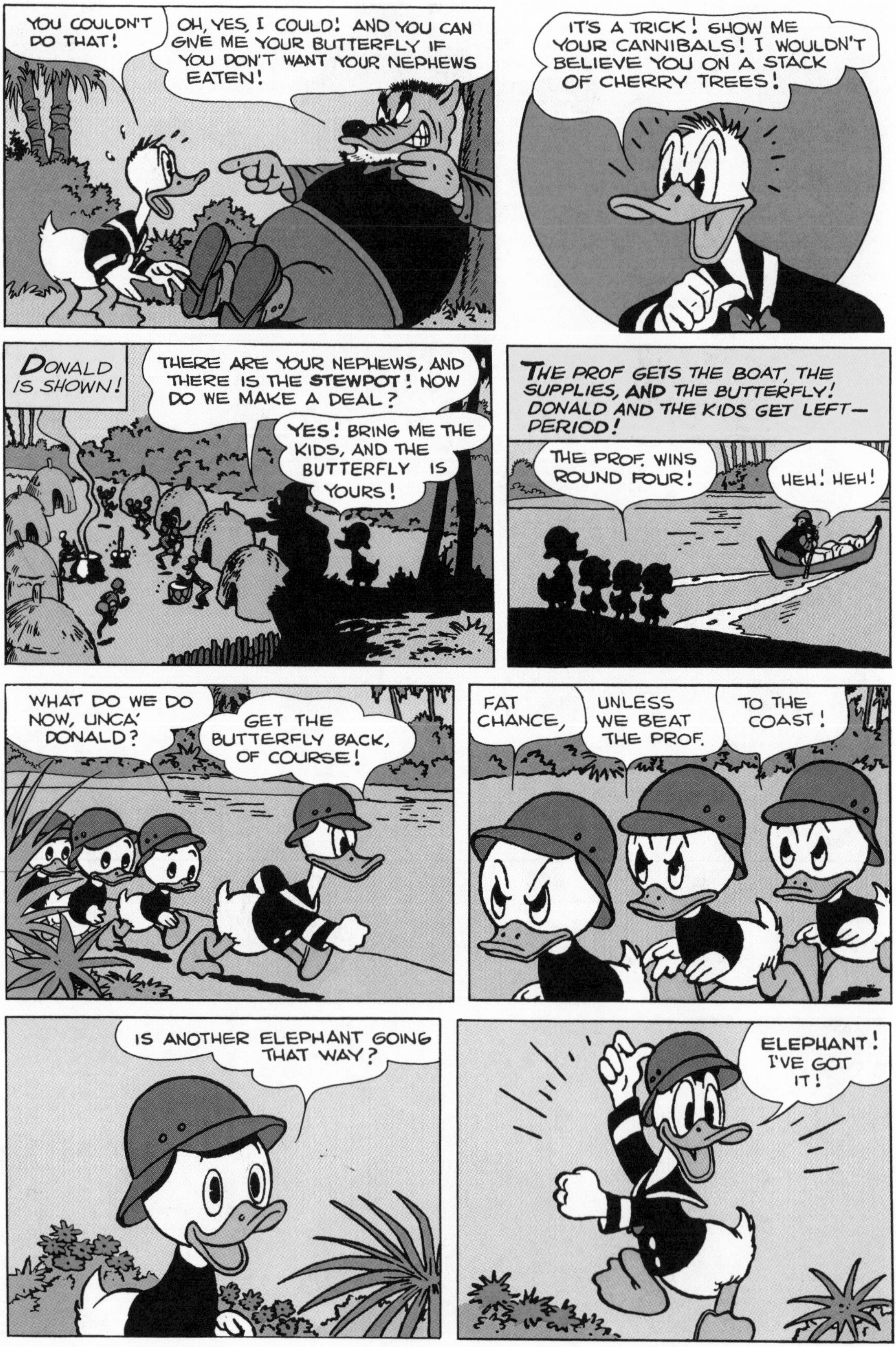
YOU COULDN'T DO THAT!
OH, YES, I COULD! AND YOU CAN GIVE ME YOUR BUTTERFLY IF YOU DON'T WANT YOUR NEPHEWS EATEN!
IT'S A TRICK! SHOW ME YOUR CANNIBALS! I WOULDN'T BELIEVE YOU ON A STACK OF CHERRY TREES!
DONALD IS SHOWN!
THERE ARE YOUR NEPHEWS, AND THERE IS THE STEWPOT! NOW DO WE MAKE A DEAL?
YES! BRING ME THE KIDS, AND THE BUTTERFLY IS YOURS!
THE PROF GETS THE BOAT, THE SUPPLIES, AND THE BUTTERFLY! DONALD AND THE KIDS GET LEFT— PERIOD!
THE PROF. WINS ROUND FOUR!
HEH! HEH!
WHAT DO WE DO NOW, UNCA' DONALD?
GET THE BUTTERFLY BACK, OF COURSE!
FAT CHANCE,
UNLESS WE BEAT THE PROF.
TO THE COAST!
IS ANOTHER ELEPHANT GOING THAT WAY?
ELEPHANT! I'VE GOT IT!

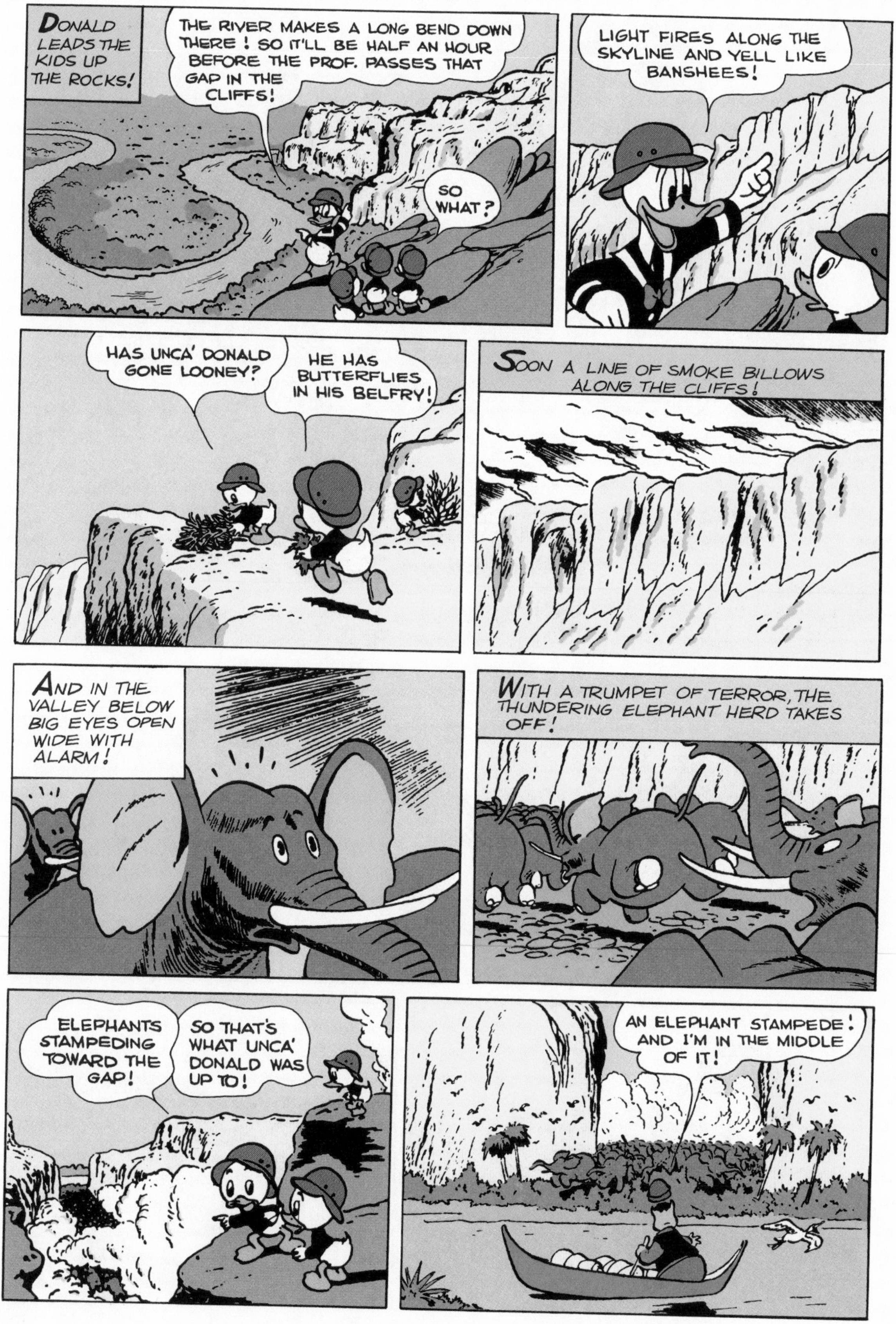
DONALD LEADS THE KIDS UP THE ROCKS!
THE RIVER MAKES A LONG BEND DOWN THERE! SO IT'LL BE HALF AN HOUR BEFORE THE PROF. PASSES THAT GAP IN THE CLIFFS!
SO WHAT?
LIGHT FIRES ALONG THE SKYLINE AND YELL LIKE BANSHEES!
HAS UNCA' DONALD GONE LOONEY?
HE HAS BUTTERFLIES IN HIS BELFRY!
SOON A LINE OF SMOKE BILLOWS ALONG THE CLIFFS!
AND IN THE VALLEY BELOW BIG EYES OPEN WIDE WITH ALARM!
WITH A TRUMPET OF TERROR, THE THUNDERING ELEPHANT HERD TAKES OFF!
ELEPHANTS STAMPEDING TOWARD THE GAP!
SO THAT'S WHAT UNCA' DONALD WAS UP TO!
AN ELEPHANT STAMPEDE! AND I'M IN THE MIDDLE OF IT!

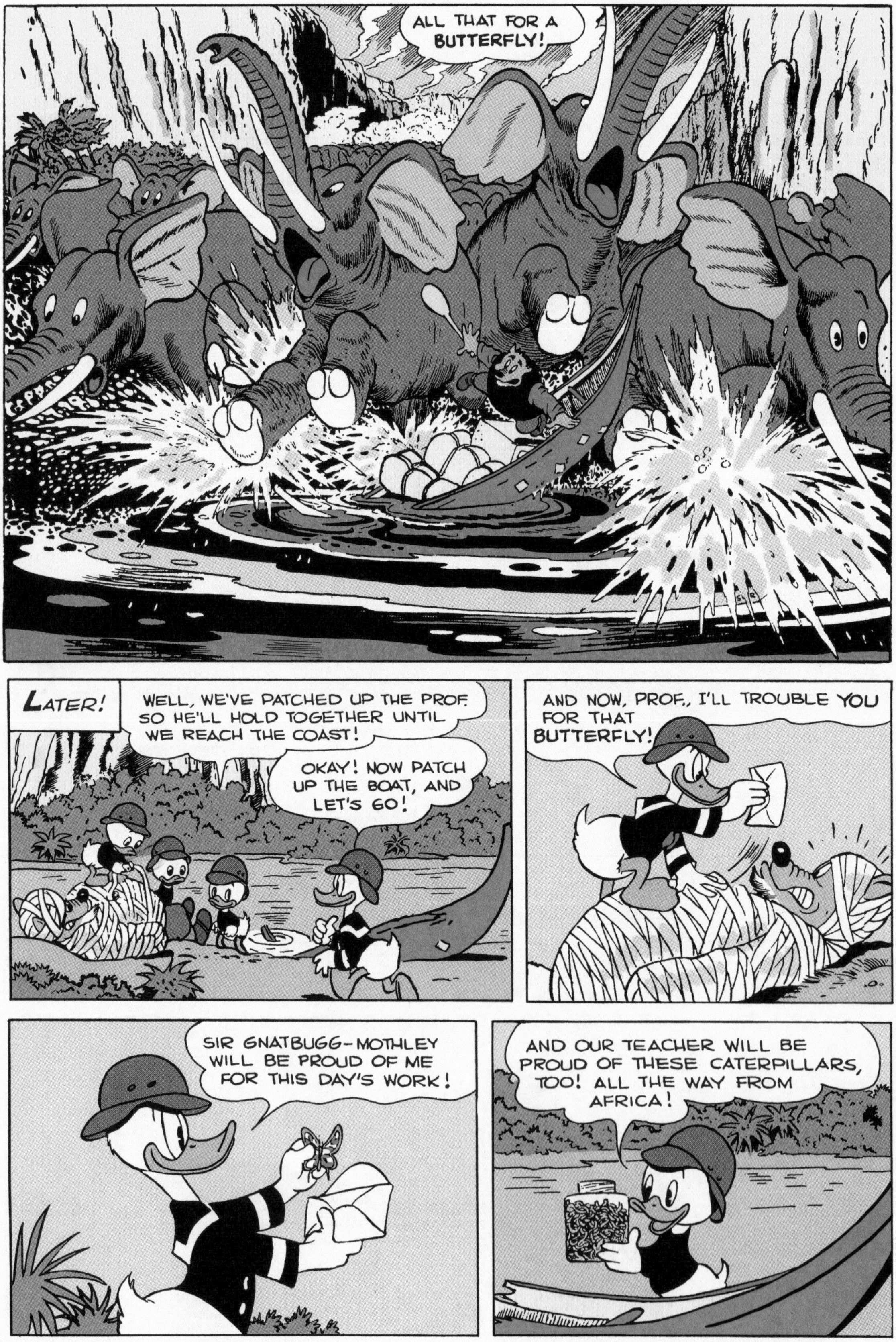
ALL THAT FOR A BUTTERFLY!
LATER!
WELL, WE'VE PATCHED UP THE PROF. SO HE'LL HOLD TOGETHER UNTIL WE REACH THE COAST!
OKAY! NOW PATCH UP THE BOAT, AND LET'S GO!
AND NOW, PROF., I'LL TROUBLE YOU FOR THAT BUTTERFLY!
SIR GNATBUGG-MOTHLEY WILL BE PROUD OF ME FOR THIS DAY'S WORK!
AND OUR TEACHER WILL BE PROUD OF THESE CATERPILLARS, TOO! ALL THE WAY FROM AFRICA!

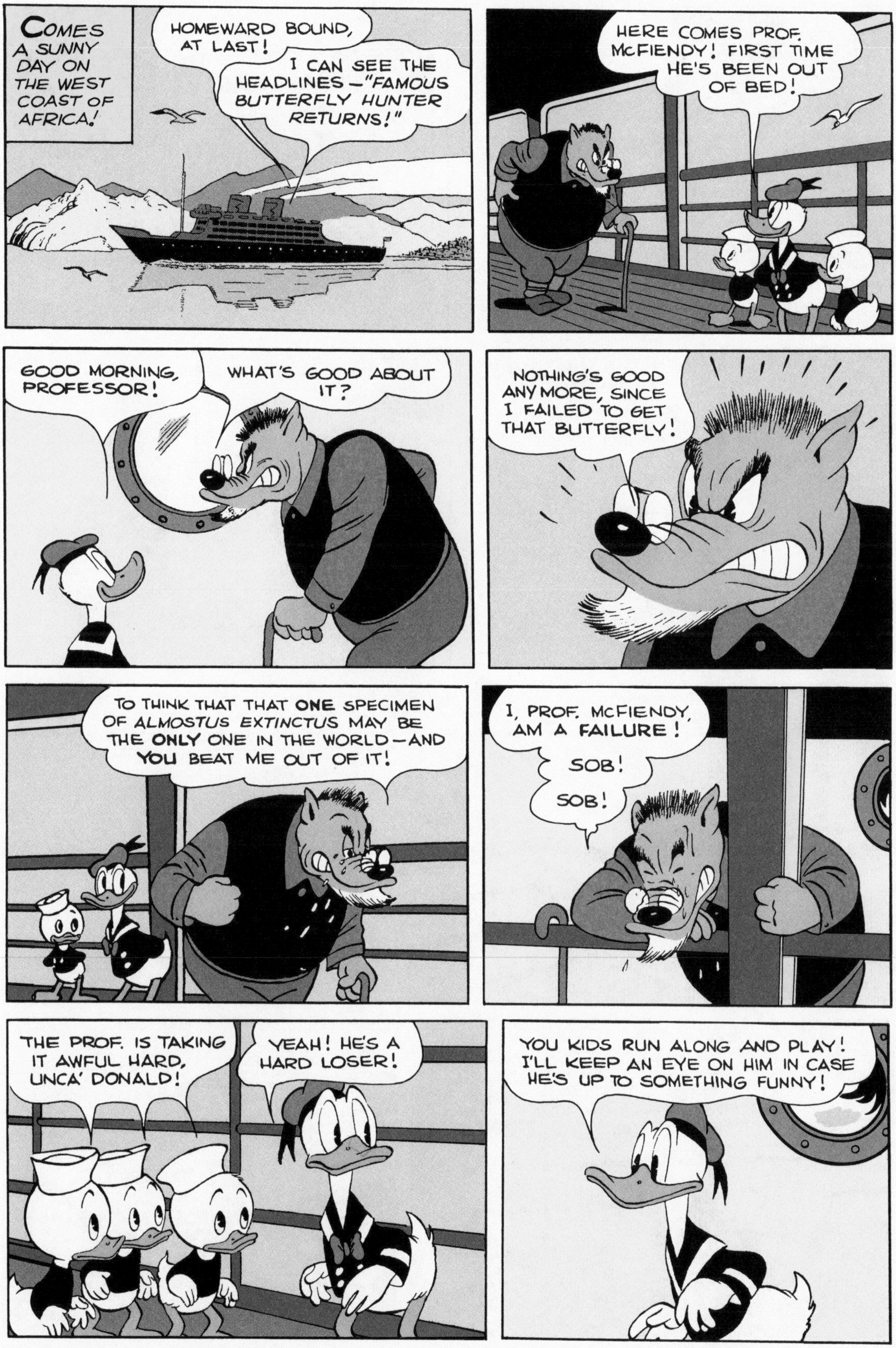
COMES A SUNNY DAY ON THE WEST COAST OF AFRICA!
HOMEWARD BOUND, AT LAST!
I CAN SEE THE HEADLINES—"FAMOUS BUTTERFLY HUNTER RETURNS!"
HERE COMES PROF. McFIENDY! FIRST TIME HE'S BEEN OUT OF BED!
GOOD MORNING, PROFESSOR!
WHAT'S GOOD ABOUT IT?
NOTHING'S GOOD ANY MORE, SINCE I FAILED TO GET THAT BUTTERFLY!
TO THINK THAT THAT ONE SPECIMEN OF ALMOSTUS EXTINCTUS MAY BE THE ONLY ONE IN THE WORLD—AND YOU BEAT ME OUT OF IT!
I, PROF. McFIENDY, AM A FAILURE!
SOB!
SOB!
THE PROF. IS TAKING IT AWFUL HARD, UNCA' DONALD!
YEAH! HE'S A HARD LOSER!
YOU KIDS RUN ALONG AND PLAY! I'LL KEEP AN EYE ON HIM IN CASE HE'S UP TO SOMETHING FUNNY!

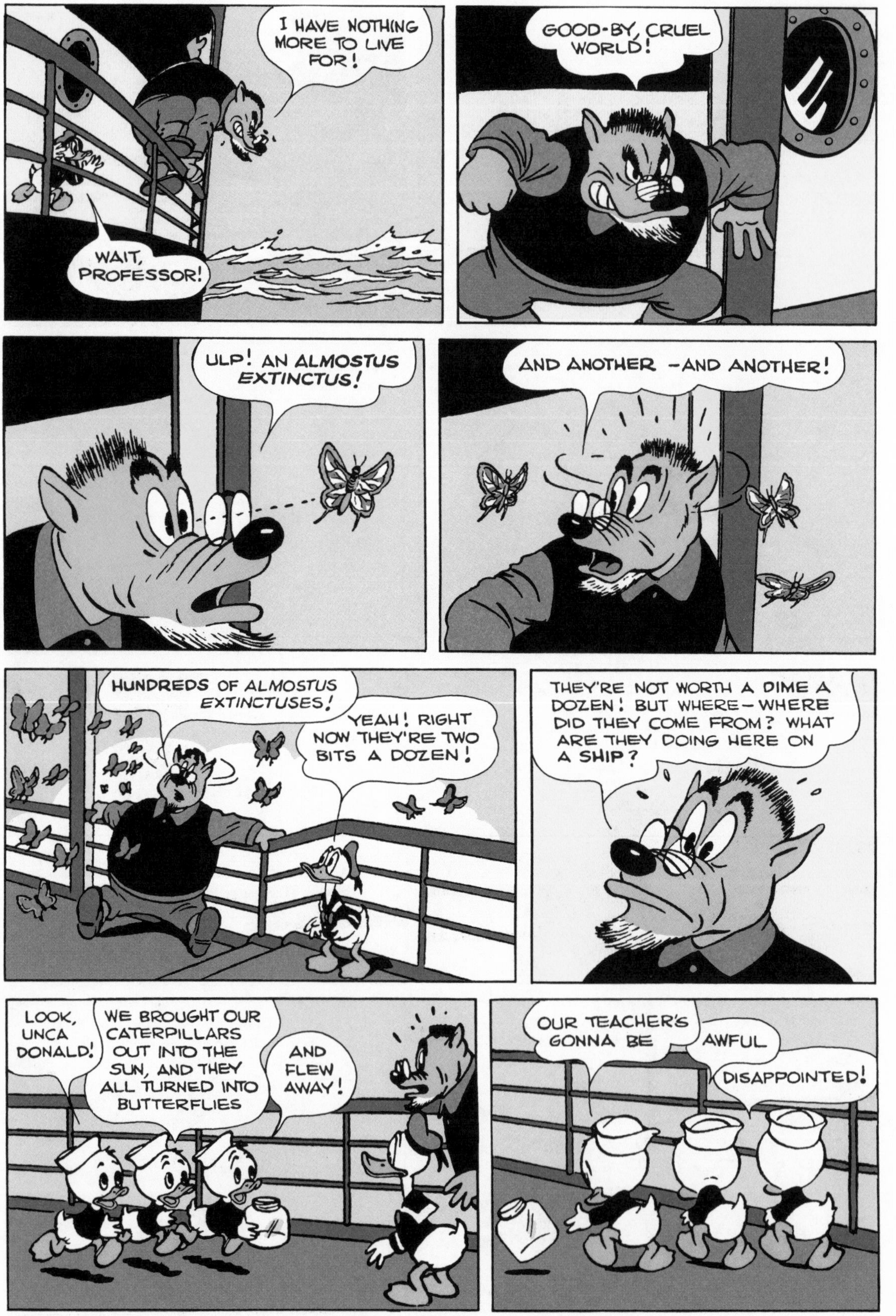
I HAVE NOTHING MORE TO LIVE FOR!
WAIT, PROFESSOR!
GOOD-BY, CRUEL WORLD!
ULP! AN ALMOSTUS EXTINCTUS!
AND ANOTHER —AND ANOTHER!
HUNDREDS OF ALMOSTUS EXTINCTUSES!
YEAH! RIGHT NOW THEY'RE TWO BITS A DOZEN!
THEY'RE NOT WORTH A DIME A DOZEN! BUT WHERE—WHERE DID THEY COME FROM? WHAT ARE THEY DOING HERE ON A SHIP?
LOOK, UNCA DONALD!
WE BROUGHT OUR CATERPILLARS OUT INTO THE SUN, AND THEY ALL TURNED INTO BUTTERFLIES
AND FLEW AWAY!
OUR TEACHER'S GONNA BE
AWFUL
DISAPPOINTED!

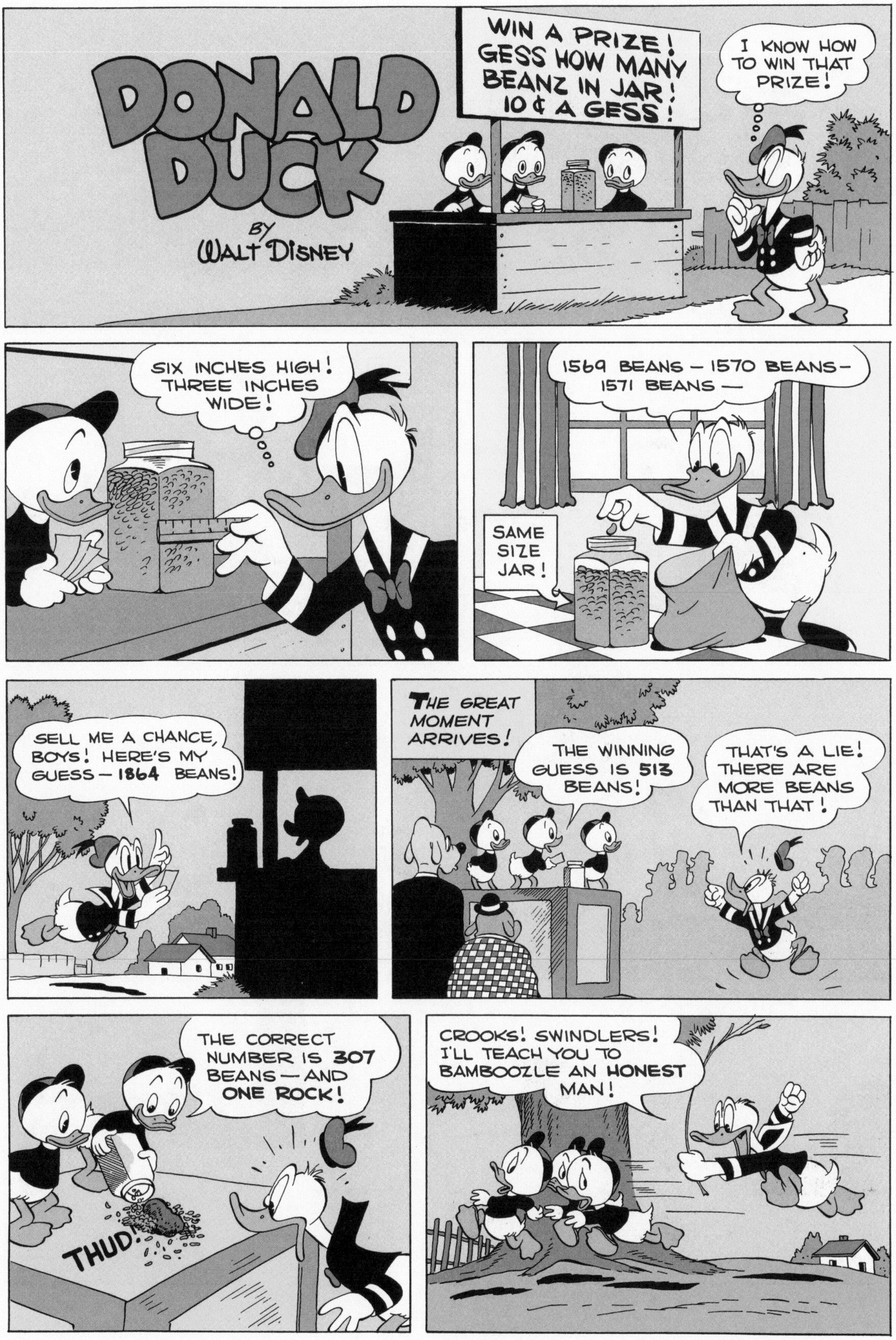
DONALD DUCK
BY WALT DISNEY
WIN A PRIZE! GESS HOW MANY BEANZ IN JAR! 10¢ A GESS!
I KNOW HOW TO WIN THAT PRIZE!
SIX INCHES HIGH! THREE INCHES WIDE!
1569 BEANS — 1570 BEANS — 1571 BEANS —
SAME SIZE JAR!
SELL ME A CHANCE, BOYS! HERE'S MY GUESS — 1864 BEANS!
THE GREAT MOMENT ARRIVES!
THE WINNING GUESS IS 513 BEANS!
THAT'S A LIE! THERE ARE MORE BEANS THAN THAT!
THE CORRECT NUMBER IS 307 BEANS — AND ONE ROCK!
THUD!
CROOKS! SWINDLERS! I'LL TEACH YOU TO BAMBOOZLE AN HONEST MAN!

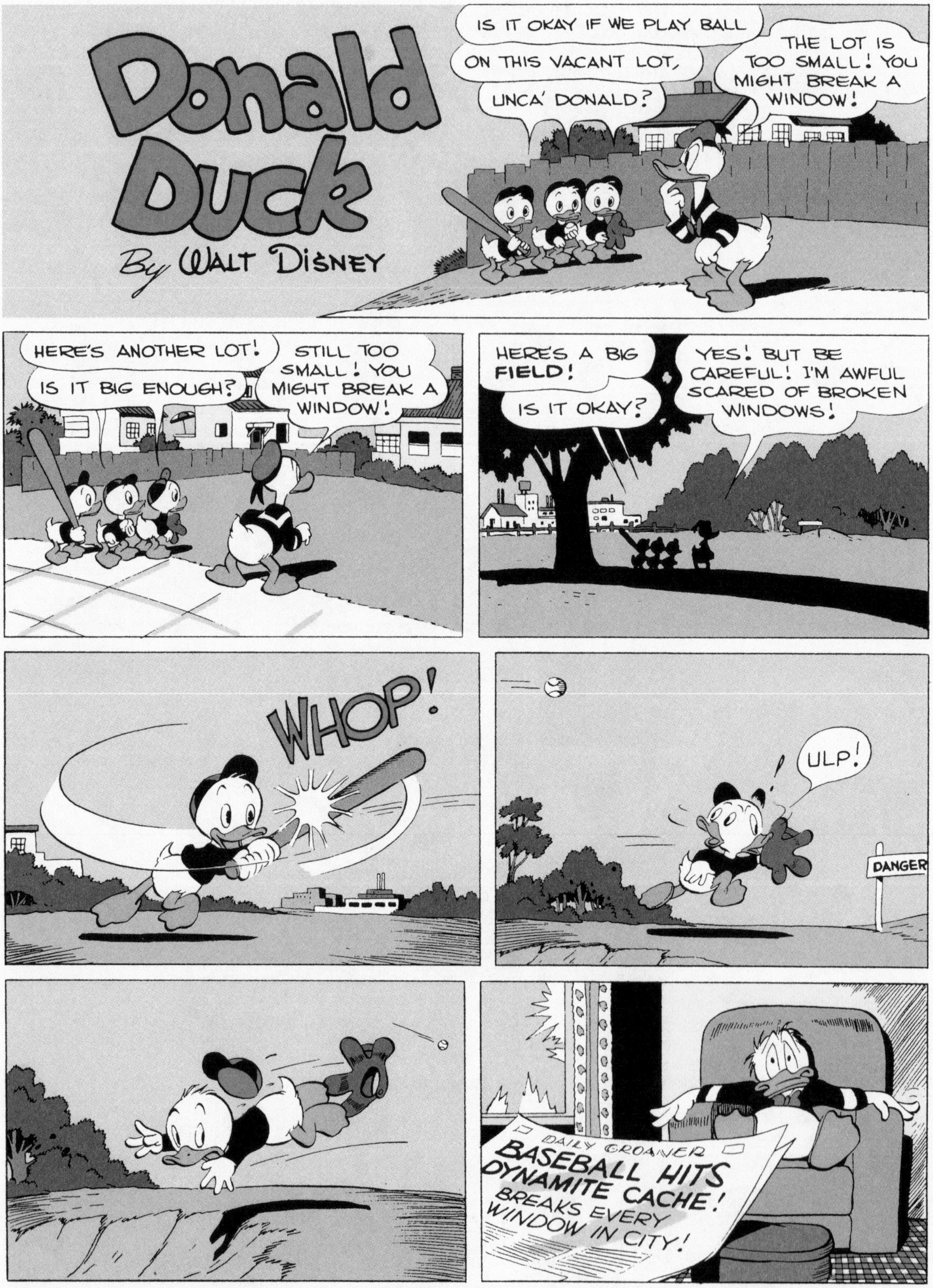

Donald Duck
By Walt Disney
IS IT OKAY IF WE PLAY BALL
ON THIS VACANT LOT,
UNCA' DONALD?
THE LOT IS TOO SMALL! YOU MIGHT BREAK A WINDOW!
HERE'S ANOTHER LOT!
IS IT BIG ENOUGH?
STILL TOO SMALL! YOU MIGHT BREAK A WINDOW!
HERE'S A BIG **FIELD**!
IS IT OKAY?
YES! BUT BE CAREFUL! I'M AWFUL SCARED OF BROKEN WINDOWS!
WHOP!
ULP!
DANGER
DAILY GROANER
BASEBALL HITS DYNAMITE CACHE!
BREAKS EVERY WINDOW IN CITY!

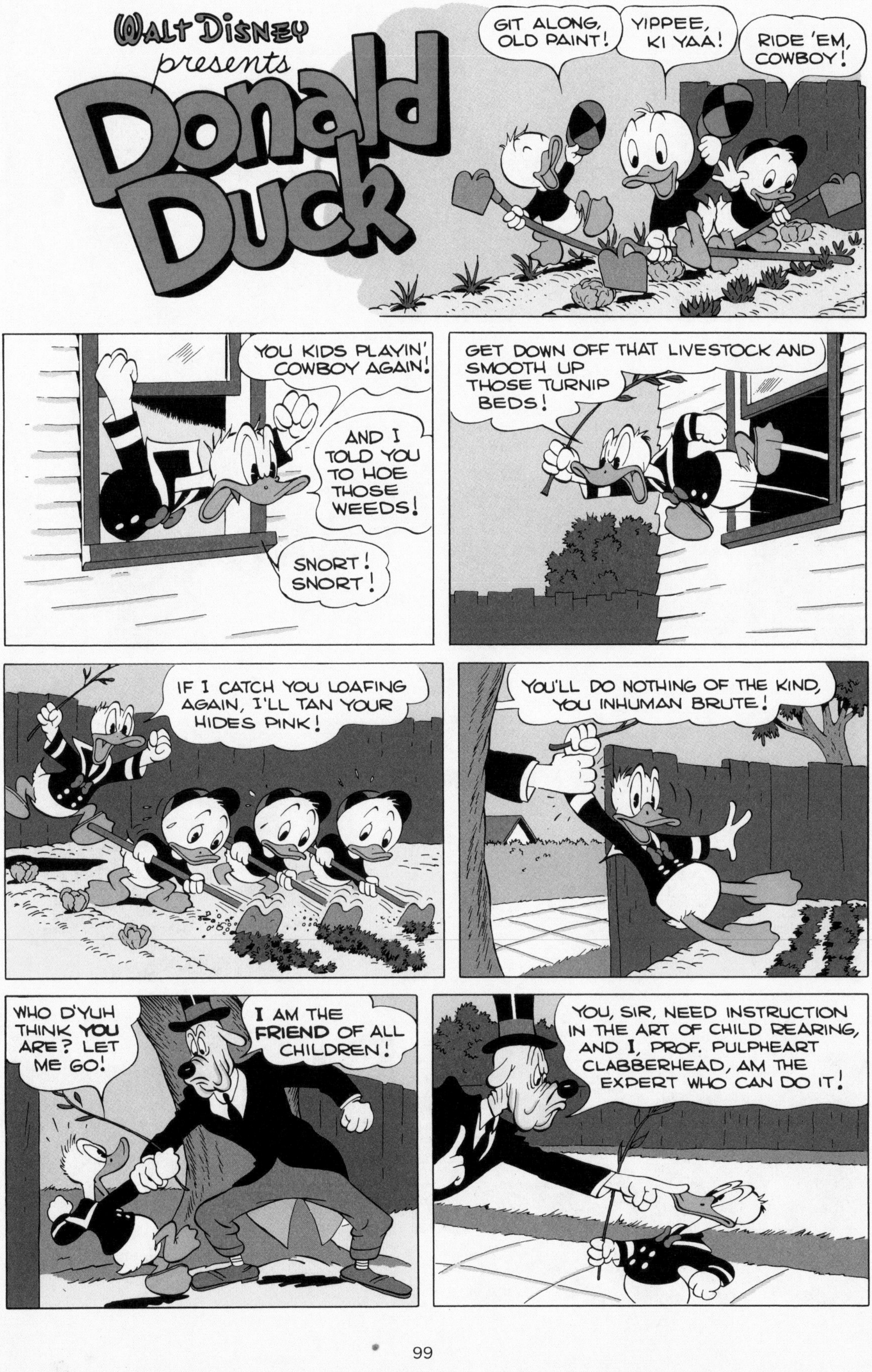
WALT DISNEY
presents
Donald Duck
GIT ALONG, OLD PAINT!
YIPPEE, KI YAA!
RIDE 'EM, COWBOY!
YOU KIDS PLAYIN' COWBOY AGAIN!
AND I TOLD YOU TO HOE THOSE WEEDS!
SNORT! SNORT!
GET DOWN OFF THAT LIVESTOCK AND SMOOTH UP THOSE TURNIP BEDS!
IF I CATCH YOU LOAFING AGAIN, I'LL TAN YOUR HIDES PINK!
YOU'LL DO NOTHING OF THE KIND, YOU INHUMAN BRUTE!
WHO D'YUH THINK YOU ARE? LET ME GO!
I AM THE FRIEND OF ALL CHILDREN!
YOU, SIR, NEED INSTRUCTION IN THE ART OF CHILD REARING, AND I, PROF. PULPHEART CLABBERHEAD, AM THE EXPERT WHO CAN DO IT!

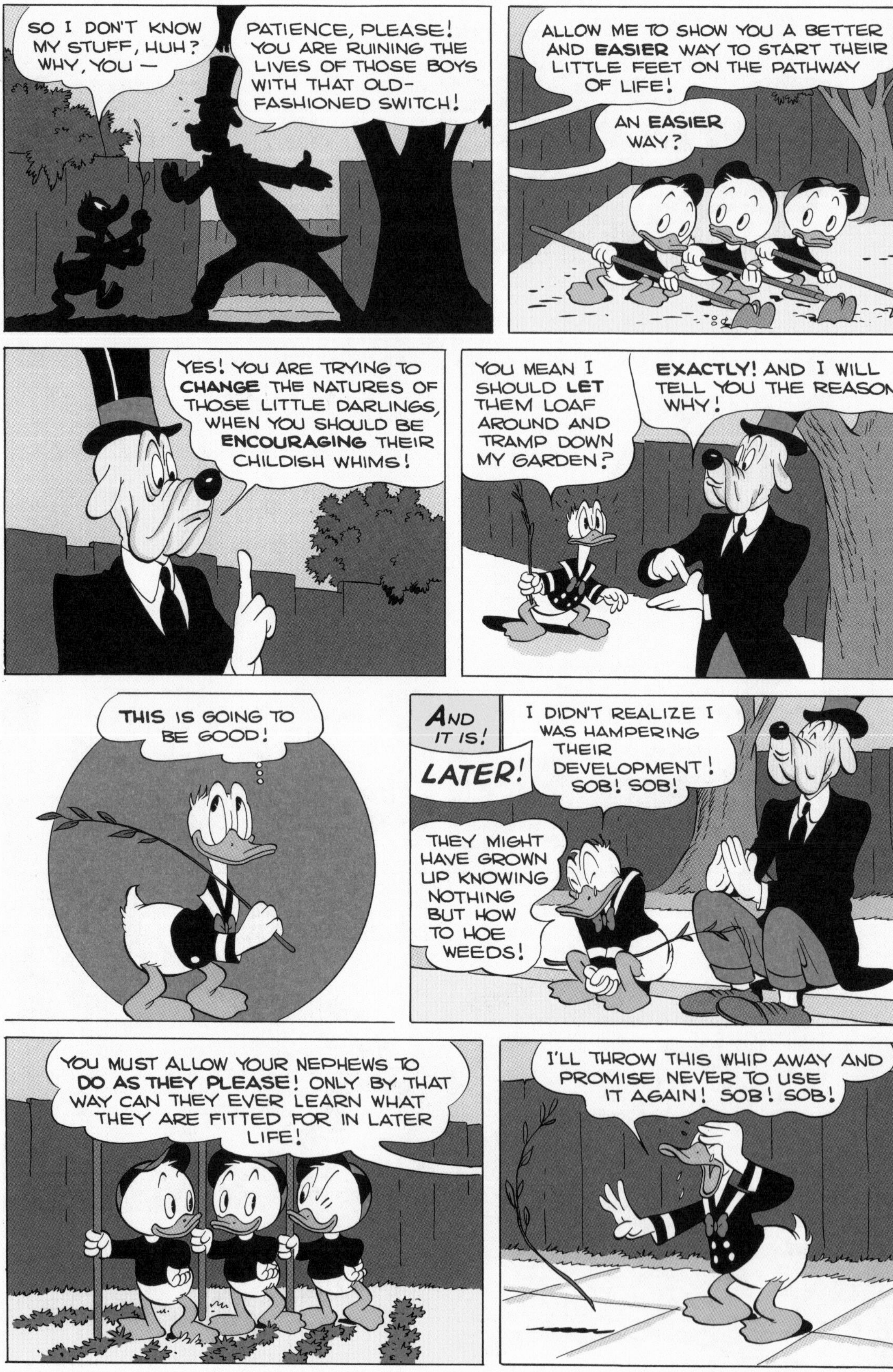

SO I DON'T KNOW MY STUFF, HUH? WHY, YOU —
PATIENCE, PLEASE! YOU ARE RUINING THE LIVES OF THOSE BOYS WITH THAT OLD-FASHIONED SWITCH!
ALLOW ME TO SHOW YOU A BETTER AND EASIER WAY TO START THEIR LITTLE FEET ON THE PATHWAY OF LIFE!
AN EASIER WAY?
YES! YOU ARE TRYING TO CHANGE THE NATURES OF THOSE LITTLE DARLINGS, WHEN YOU SHOULD BE ENCOURAGING THEIR CHILDISH WHIMS!
YOU MEAN I SHOULD LET THEM LOAF AROUND AND TRAMP DOWN MY GARDEN?
EXACTLY! AND I WILL TELL YOU THE REASON WHY!
THIS IS GOING TO BE GOOD!
AND IT IS!
LATER!
I DIDN'T REALIZE I WAS HAMPERING THEIR DEVELOPMENT! SOB! SOB!
THEY MIGHT HAVE GROWN UP KNOWING NOTHING BUT HOW TO HOE WEEDS!
YOU MUST ALLOW YOUR NEPHEWS TO DO AS THEY PLEASE! ONLY BY THAT WAY CAN THEY EVER LEARN WHAT THEY ARE FITTED FOR IN LATER LIFE!
I'LL THROW THIS WHIP AWAY AND PROMISE NEVER TO USE IT AGAIN! SOB! SOB!

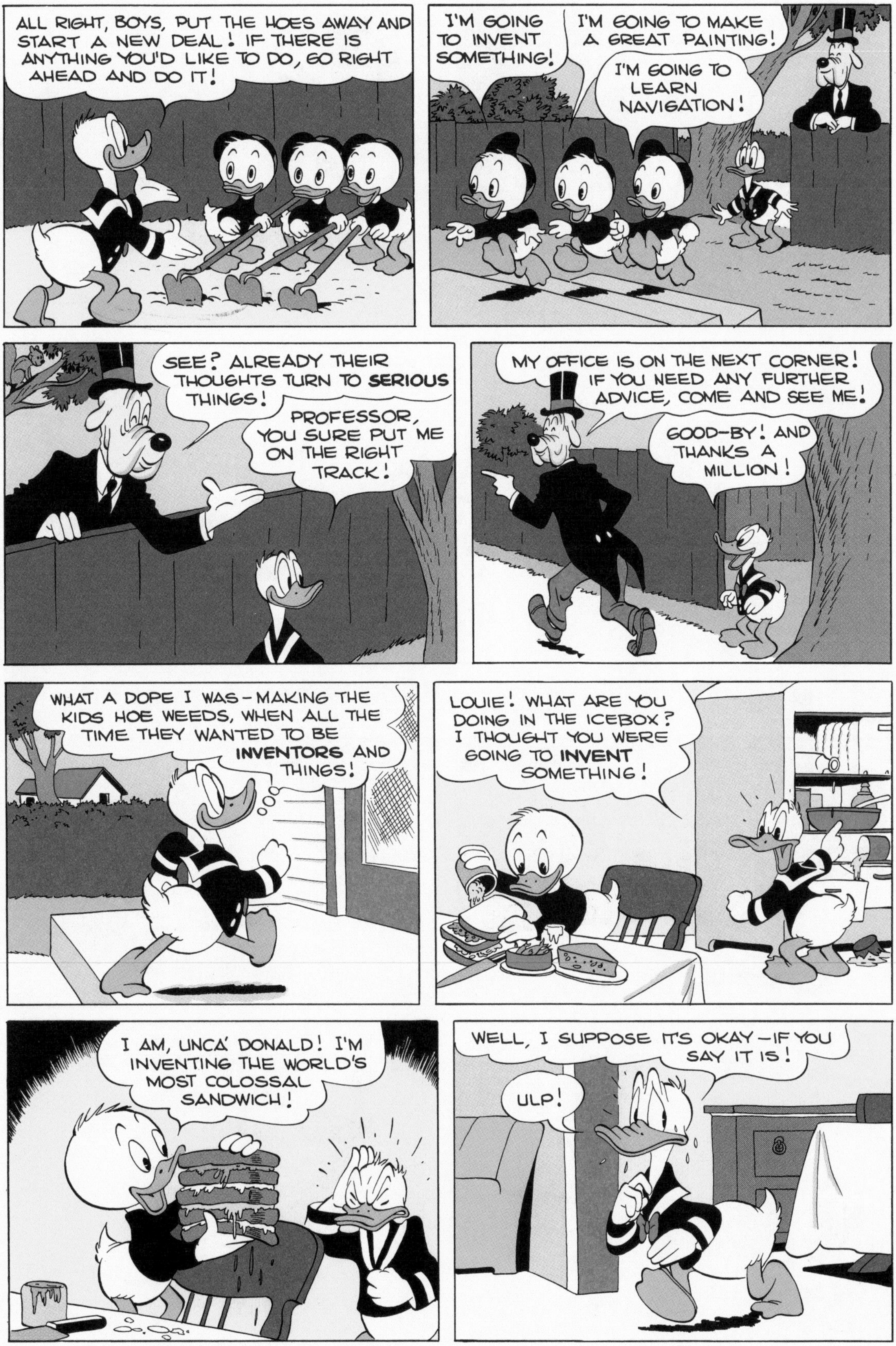
ALL RIGHT, BOYS, PUT THE HOES AWAY AND START A NEW DEAL! IF THERE IS ANYTHING YOU'D LIKE TO DO, GO RIGHT AHEAD AND DO IT!
I'M GOING TO INVENT SOMETHING!
I'M GOING TO MAKE A GREAT PAINTING!
I'M GOING TO LEARN NAVIGATION!
SEE? ALREADY THEIR THOUGHTS TURN TO **SERIOUS** THINGS!
PROFESSOR, YOU SURE PUT ME ON THE RIGHT TRACK!
MY OFFICE IS ON THE NEXT CORNER! IF YOU NEED ANY FURTHER ADVICE, COME AND SEE ME!
GOOD-BY! AND THANKS A MILLION!
WHAT A DOPE I WAS-MAKING THE KIDS HOE WEEDS, WHEN ALL THE TIME THEY WANTED TO BE **INVENTORS** AND THINGS!
LOUIE! WHAT ARE YOU DOING IN THE ICEBOX? I THOUGHT YOU WERE GOING TO **INVENT** SOMETHING!
I AM, UNCA' DONALD! I'M INVENTING THE WORLD'S MOST COLOSSAL SANDWICH!
WELL, I SUPPOSE IT'S OKAY-IF YOU SAY IT IS!
ULP!

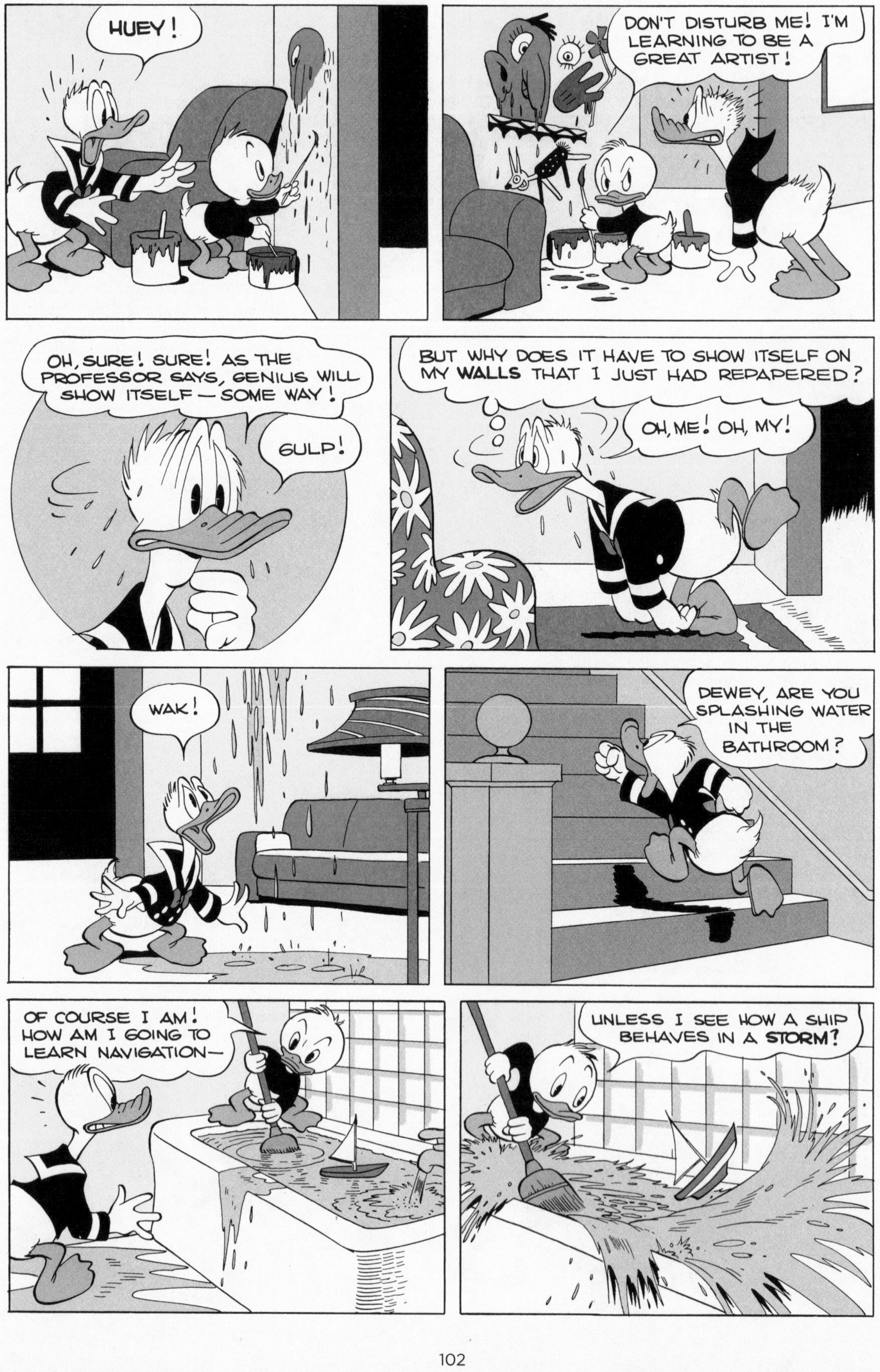
HUEY!
DON'T DISTURB ME! I'M LEARNING TO BE A GREAT ARTIST!
OH, SURE! SURE! AS THE PROFESSOR SAYS, GENIUS WILL SHOW ITSELF—SOME WAY!
GULP!
BUT WHY DOES IT HAVE TO SHOW ITSELF ON MY WALLS THAT I JUST HAD REPAPERED?
OH, ME! OH, MY!
WAK!
DEWEY, ARE YOU SPLASHING WATER IN THE BATHROOM?
OF COURSE I AM! HOW AM I GOING TO LEARN NAVIGATION—
UNLESS I SEE HOW A SHIP BEHAVES IN A STORM?

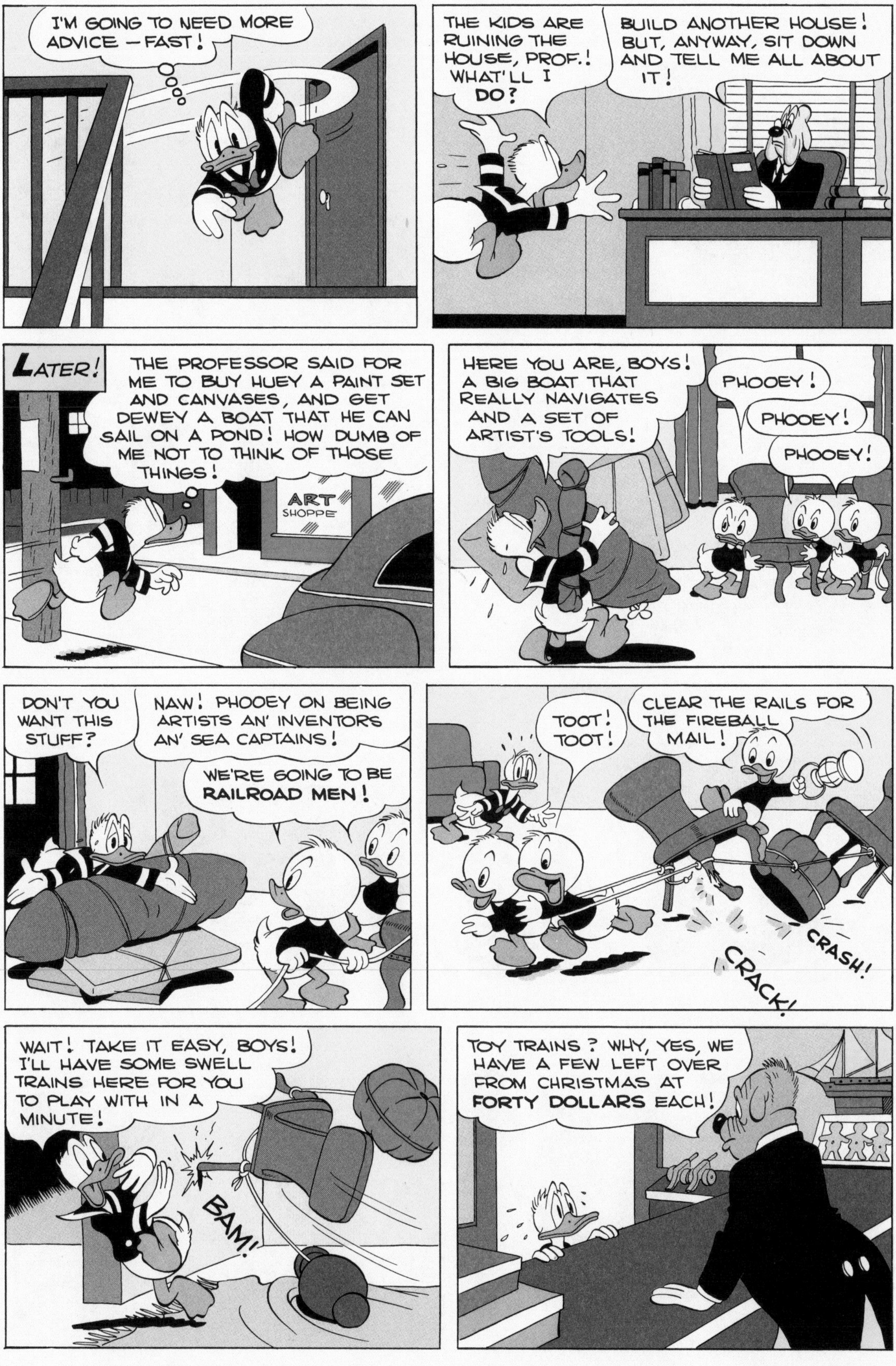
I'M GOING TO NEED MORE ADVICE — FAST!
THE KIDS ARE RUINING THE HOUSE, PROF.! WHAT'LL I DO?
BUILD ANOTHER HOUSE! BUT, ANYWAY, SIT DOWN AND TELL ME ALL ABOUT IT!
LATER!
THE PROFESSOR SAID FOR ME TO BUY HUEY A PAINT SET AND CANVASES, AND GET DEWEY A BOAT THAT HE CAN SAIL ON A POND! HOW DUMB OF ME NOT TO THINK OF THOSE THINGS!
ART SHOPPE
HERE YOU ARE, BOYS! A BIG BOAT THAT REALLY NAVIGATES AND A SET OF ARTIST'S TOOLS!
PHOOEY!
PHOOEY!
PHOOEY!
DON'T YOU WANT THIS STUFF?
NAW! PHOOEY ON BEING ARTISTS AN' INVENTORS AN' SEA CAPTAINS!
WE'RE GOING TO BE RAILROAD MEN!
TOOT! TOOT!
CLEAR THE RAILS FOR THE FIREBALL MAIL!
CRASH!
CRACK!
WAIT! TAKE IT EASY, BOYS! I'LL HAVE SOME SWELL TRAINS HERE FOR YOU TO PLAY WITH IN A MINUTE!
BAM!
TOY TRAINS? WHY, YES, WE HAVE A FEW LEFT OVER FROM CHRISTMAS AT FORTY DOLLARS EACH!

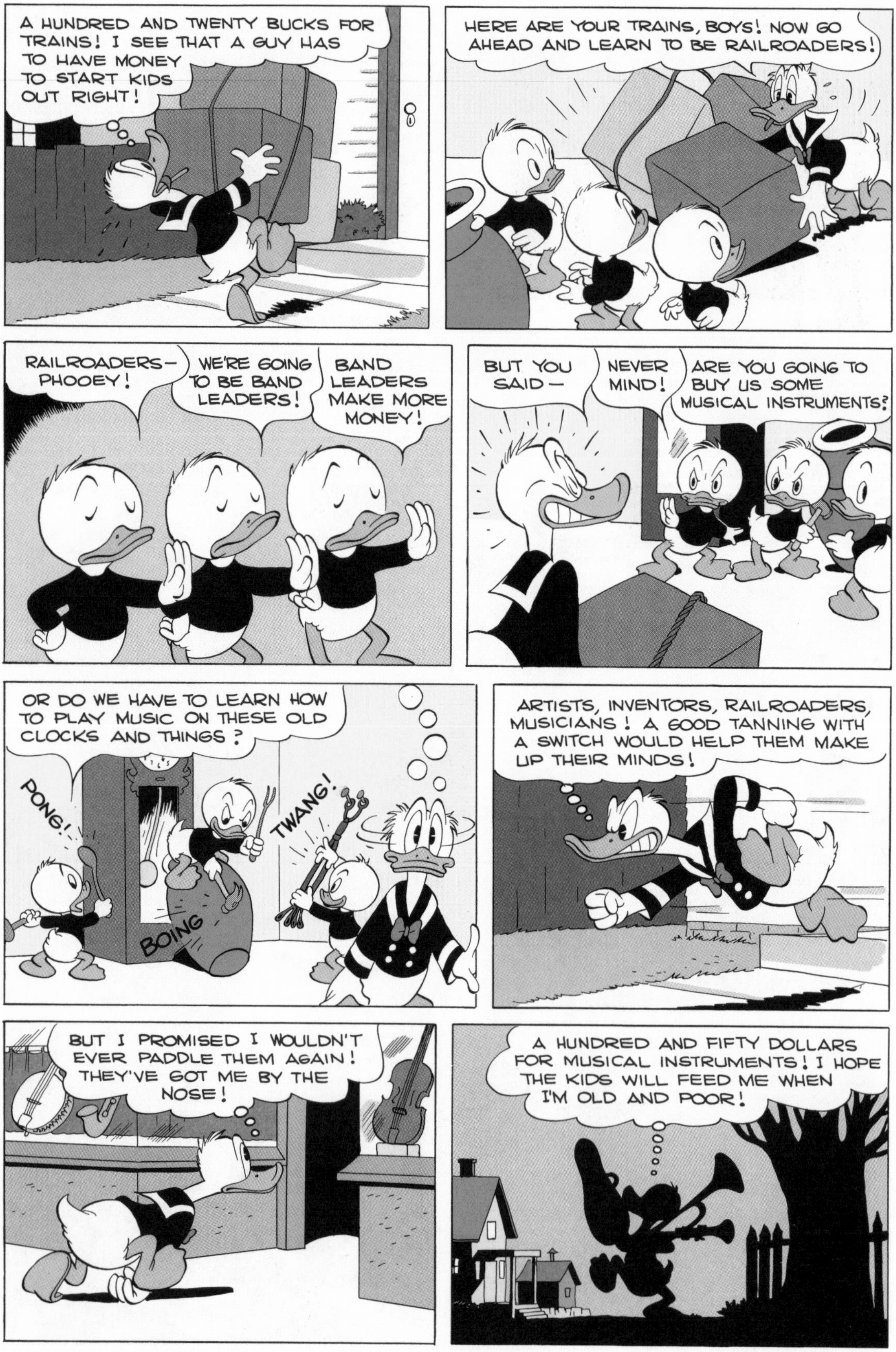
A HUNDRED AND TWENTY BUCKS FOR TRAINS! I SEE THAT A GUY HAS TO HAVE MONEY TO START KIDS OUT RIGHT!
HERE ARE YOUR TRAINS, BOYS! NOW GO AHEAD AND LEARN TO BE RAILROADERS!
RAILROADERS— PHOOEY!
WE'RE GOING TO BE BAND LEADERS!
BAND LEADERS MAKE MORE MONEY!
BUT YOU SAID—
NEVER MIND!
ARE YOU GOING TO BUY US SOME MUSICAL INSTRUMENTS?
OR DO WE HAVE TO LEARN HOW TO PLAY MUSIC ON THESE OLD CLOCKS AND THINGS?
PONG!
TWANG!
BOING
ARTISTS, INVENTORS, RAILROADERS, MUSICIANS! A GOOD TANNING WITH A SWITCH WOULD HELP THEM MAKE UP THEIR MINDS!
BUT I PROMISED I WOULDN'T EVER PADDLE THEM AGAIN! THEY'VE GOT ME BY THE NOSE!
A HUNDRED AND FIFTY DOLLARS FOR MUSICAL INSTRUMENTS! I HOPE THE KIDS WILL FEED ME WHEN I'M OLD AND POOR!

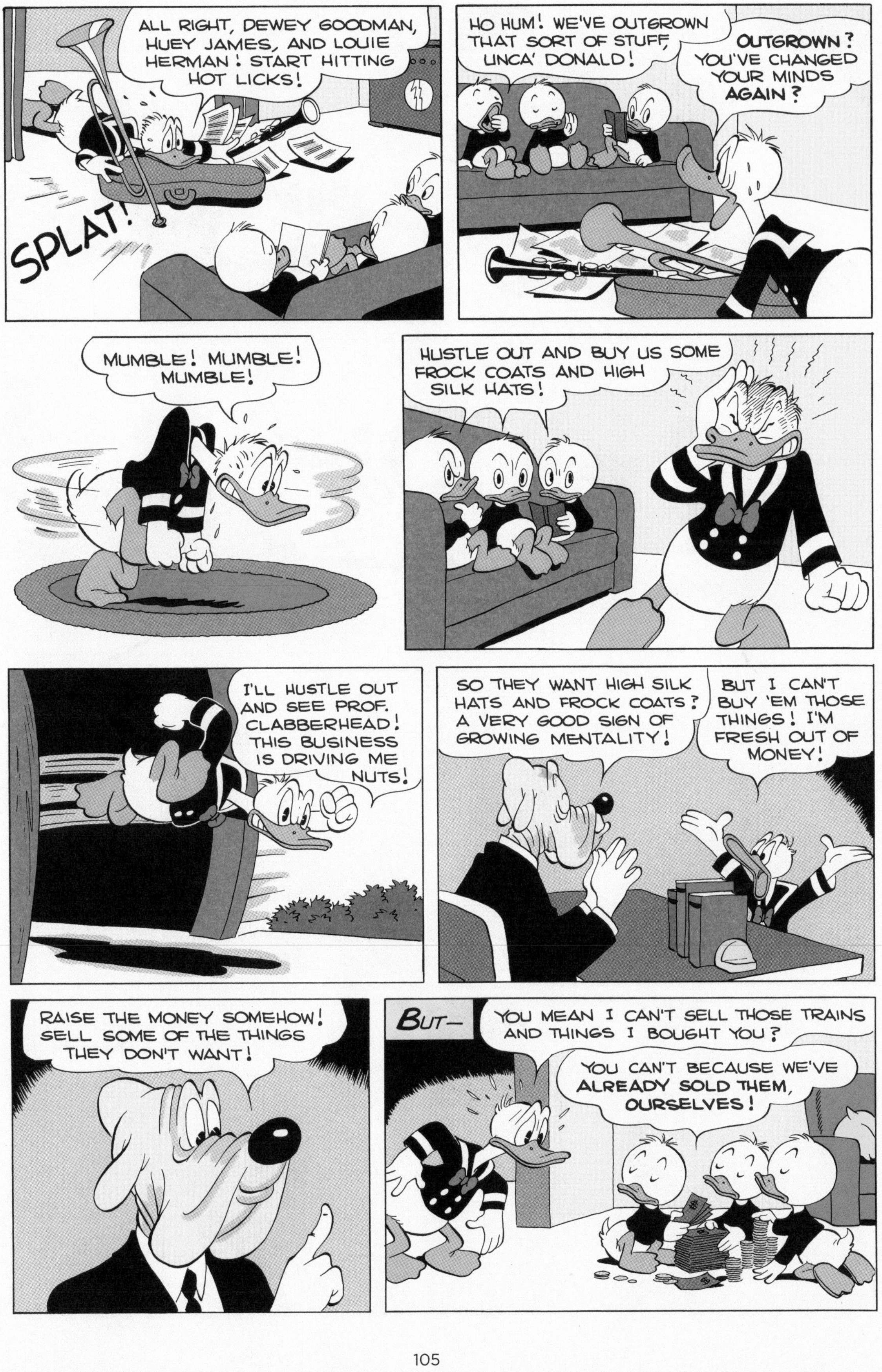
ALL RIGHT, DEWEY GOODMAN, HUEY JAMES, AND LOUIE HERMAN! START HITTING HOT LICKS!
SPLAT!
HO HUM! WE'VE OUTGROWN THAT SORT OF STUFF, UNCA' DONALD!
OUTGROWN? YOU'VE CHANGED YOUR MINDS AGAIN?
MUMBLE! MUMBLE! MUMBLE!
HUSTLE OUT AND BUY US SOME FROCK COATS AND HIGH SILK HATS!
I'LL HUSTLE OUT AND SEE PROF. CLABBERHEAD! THIS BUSINESS IS DRIVING ME NUTS!
SO THEY WANT HIGH SILK HATS AND FROCK COATS? A VERY GOOD SIGN OF GROWING MENTALITY!
BUT I CAN'T BUY 'EM THOSE THINGS! I'M FRESH OUT OF MONEY!
RAISE THE MONEY SOMEHOW! SELL SOME OF THE THINGS THEY DON'T WANT!
BUT—
YOU MEAN I CAN'T SELL THOSE TRAINS AND THINGS I BOUGHT YOU?
YOU CAN'T BECAUSE WE'VE ALREADY SOLD THEM, OURSELVES!

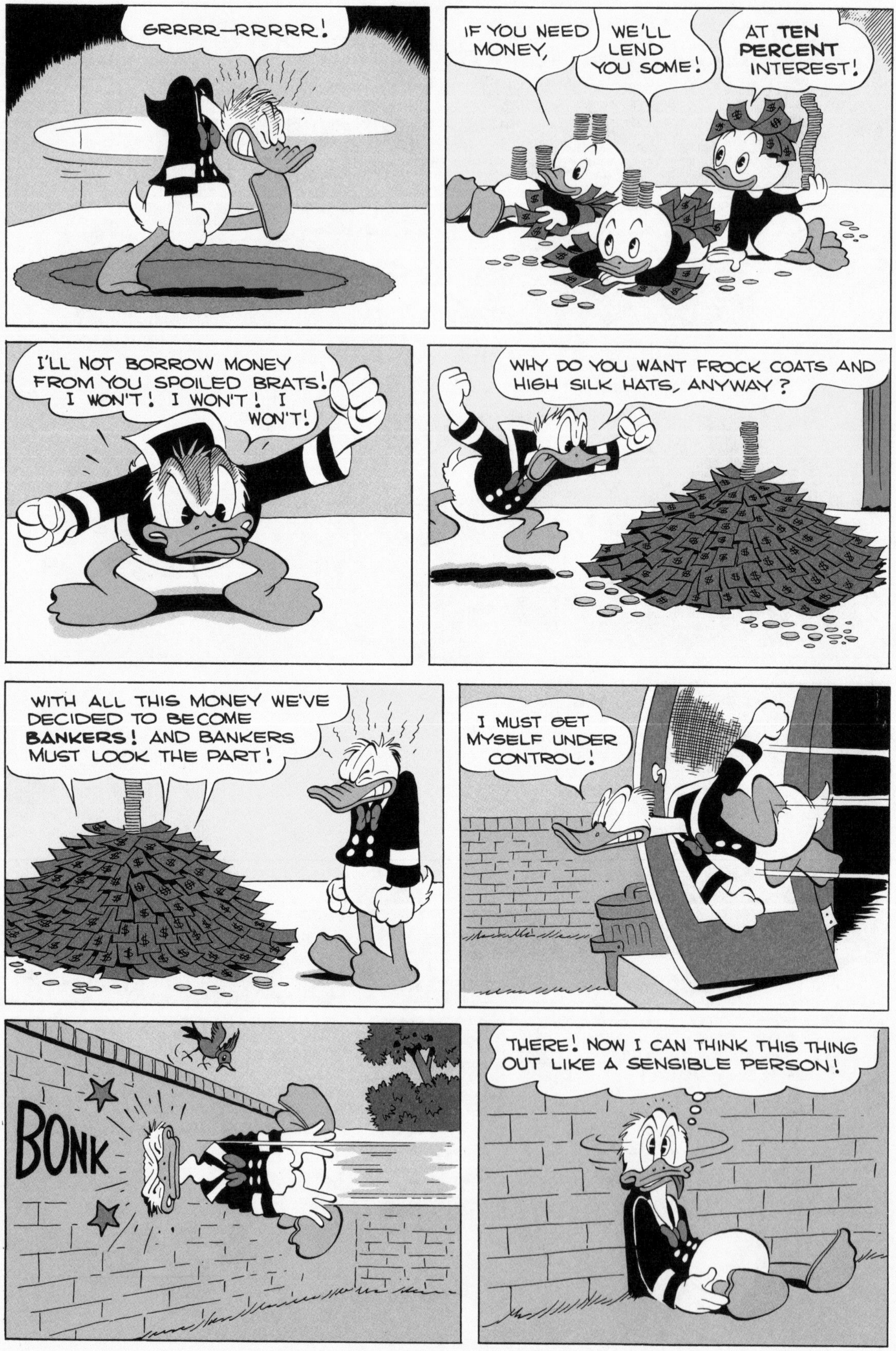
GRRRR—RRRRR!
IF YOU NEED MONEY,
WE'LL LEND YOU SOME!
AT TEN PERCENT INTEREST!
I'LL NOT BORROW MONEY FROM YOU SPOILED BRATS! I WON'T! I WON'T! I WON'T!
WHY DO YOU WANT FROCK COATS AND HIGH SILK HATS, ANYWAY?
WITH ALL THIS MONEY WE'VE DECIDED TO BECOME BANKERS! AND BANKERS MUST LOOK THE PART!
I MUST GET MYSELF UNDER CONTROL!
BONK
THERE! NOW I CAN THINK THIS THING OUT LIKE A SENSIBLE PERSON!

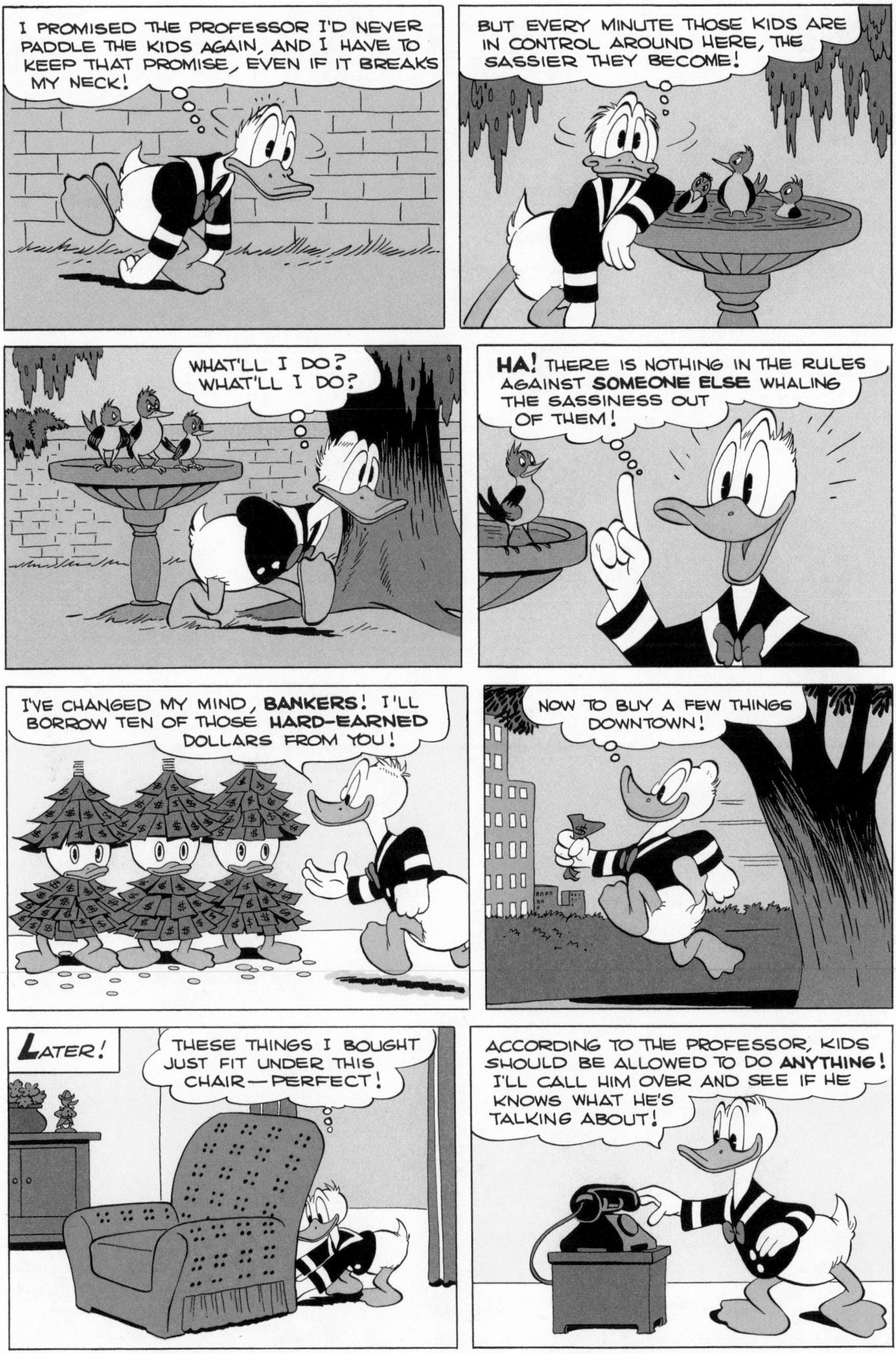
I PROMISED THE PROFESSOR I'D NEVER PADDLE THE KIDS AGAIN, AND I HAVE TO KEEP THAT PROMISE, EVEN IF IT BREAKS MY NECK!
BUT EVERY MINUTE THOSE KIDS ARE IN CONTROL AROUND HERE, THE SASSIER THEY BECOME!
WHAT'LL I DO? WHAT'LL I DO?
HA! THERE IS NOTHING IN THE RULES AGAINST SOMEONE ELSE WHALING THE SASSINESS OUT OF THEM!
I'VE CHANGED MY MIND, BANKERS! I'LL BORROW TEN OF THOSE HARD-EARNED DOLLARS FROM YOU!
NOW TO BUY A FEW THINGS DOWNTOWN!
LATER!
THESE THINGS I BOUGHT JUST FIT UNDER THIS CHAIR—PERFECT!
ACCORDING TO THE PROFESSOR, KIDS SHOULD BE ALLOWED TO DO ANYTHING! I'LL CALL HIM OVER AND SEE IF HE KNOWS WHAT HE'S TALKING ABOUT!

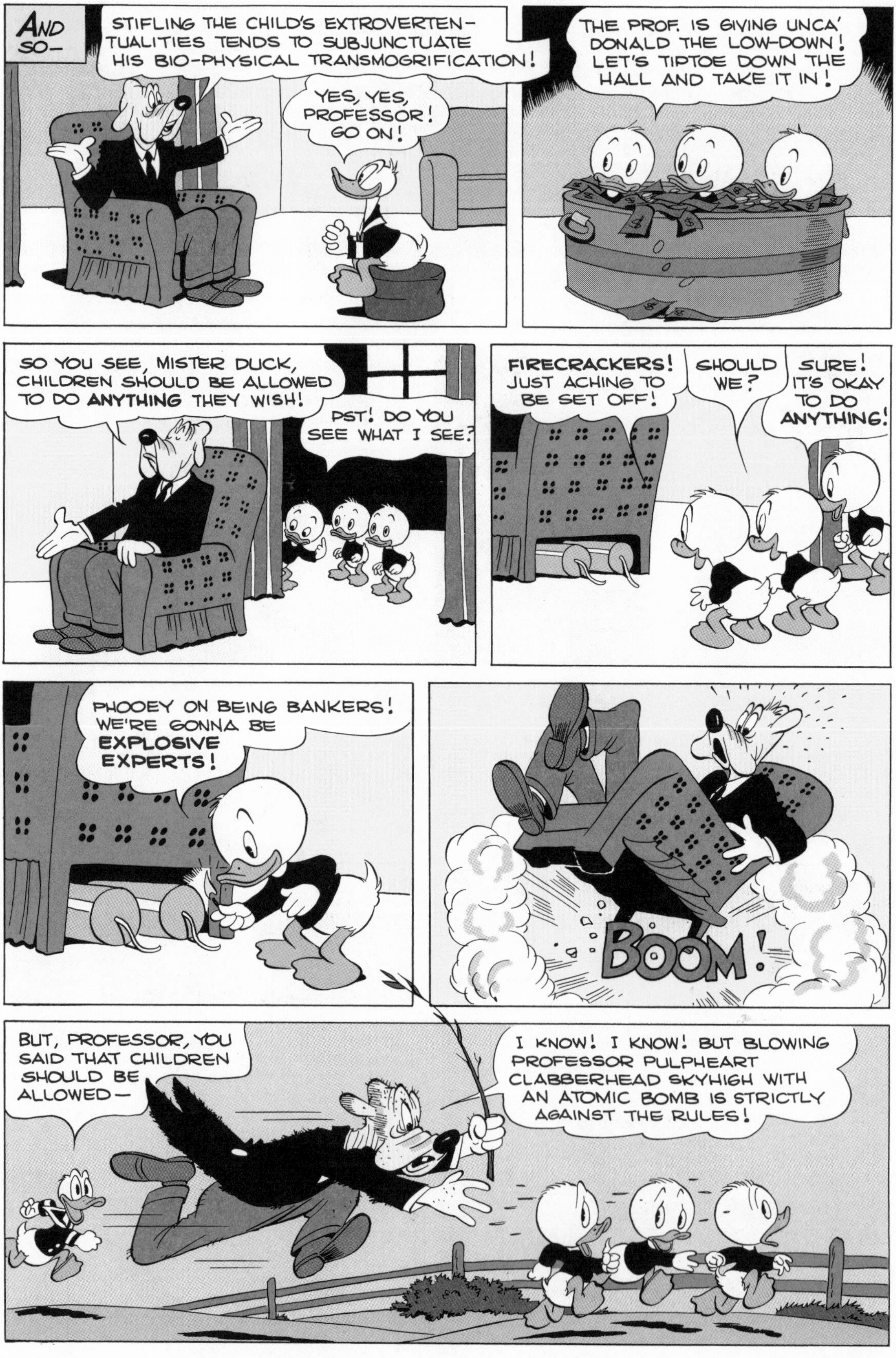
AND SO—
STIFLING THE CHILD'S EXTROVERTEN-TUALITIES TENDS TO SUBJUNCTUATE HIS BIO-PHYSICAL TRANSMOGRIFICATION!
YES, YES, PROFESSOR! GO ON!
THE PROF. IS GIVING UNCA' DONALD THE LOW-DOWN! LET'S TIPTOE DOWN THE HALL AND TAKE IT IN!
SO YOU SEE, MISTER DUCK, CHILDREN SHOULD BE ALLOWED TO DO ANYTHING THEY WISH!
PST! DO YOU SEE WHAT I SEE?
FIRECRACKERS! JUST ACHING TO BE SET OFF!
SHOULD WE?
SURE! IT'S OKAY TO DO ANYTHING!
PHOOEY ON BEING BANKERS! WE'RE GONNA BE EXPLOSIVE EXPERTS!
BOOM!
BUT, PROFESSOR, YOU SAID THAT CHILDREN SHOULD BE ALLOWED—
I KNOW! I KNOW! BUT BLOWING PROFESSOR PULPHEART CLABBERHEAD SKYHIGH WITH AN ATOMIC BOMB IS STRICTLY AGAINST THE RULES!

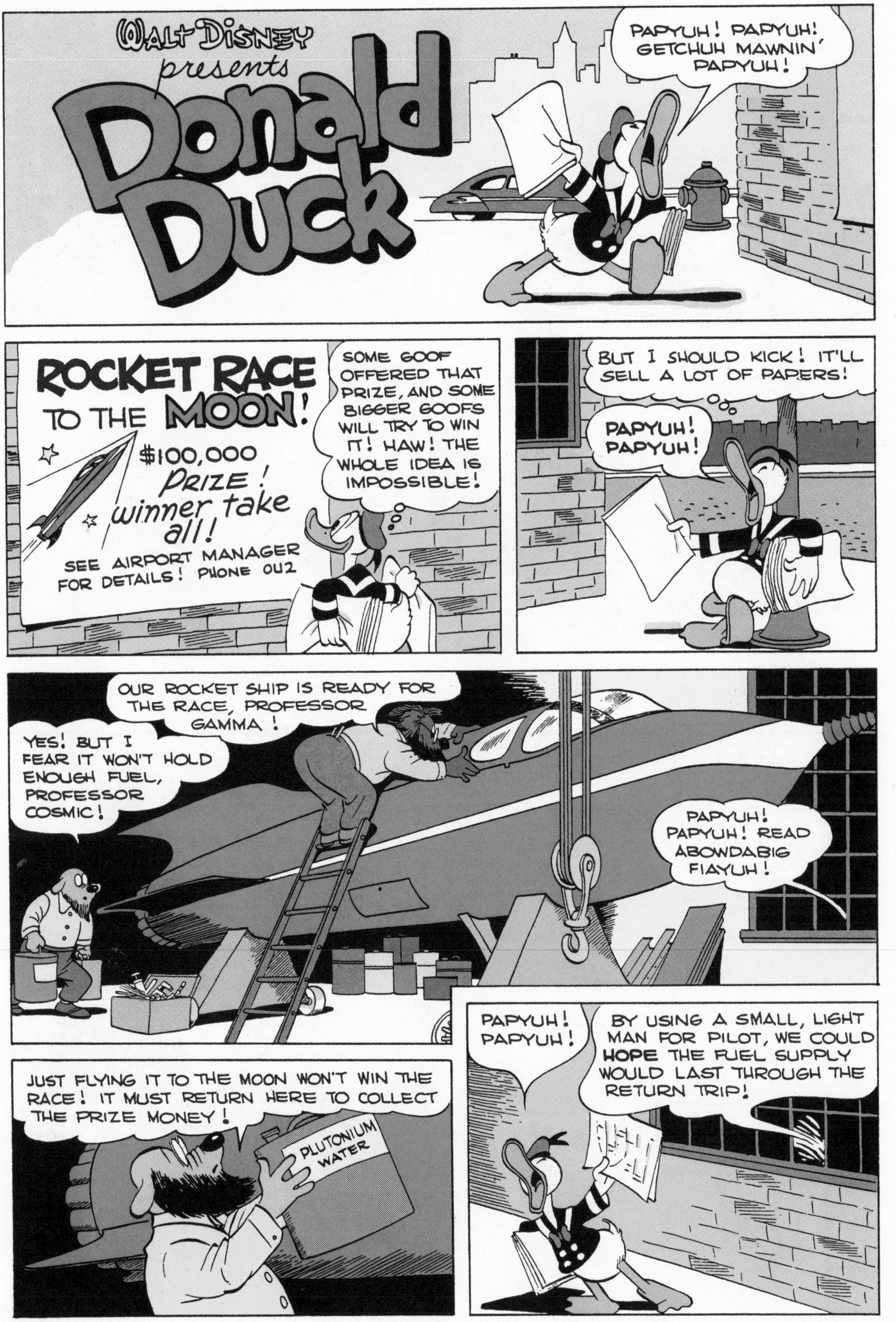
Walt Disney presents
Donald Duck
PAPYUH! PAPYUH! GETCHUH MAWNIN' PAPYUH!
ROCKET RACE TO THE MOON!
$100,000 PRIZE! winner take all!
SEE AIRPORT MANAGER FOR DETAILS! PHONE 0U2
SOME GOOF OFFERED THAT PRIZE, AND SOME BIGGER GOOFS WILL TRY TO WIN IT! HAW! THE WHOLE IDEA IS IMPOSSIBLE!
BUT I SHOULD KICK! IT'LL SELL A LOT OF PAPERS!
PAPYUH! PAPYUH!
OUR ROCKET SHIP IS READY FOR THE RACE, PROFESSOR GAMMA!
YES! BUT I FEAR IT WON'T HOLD ENOUGH FUEL, PROFESSOR COSMIC!
PAPYUH! PAPYUH! READ ABOWDABIG FIAYUH!
JUST FLYING IT TO THE MOON WON'T WIN THE RACE! IT MUST RETURN HERE TO COLLECT THE PRIZE MONEY!
PLUTONIUM WATER
PAPYUH! PAPYUH!
BY USING A SMALL, LIGHT MAN FOR PILOT, WE COULD HOPE THE FUEL SUPPLY WOULD LAST THROUGH THE RETURN TRIP!

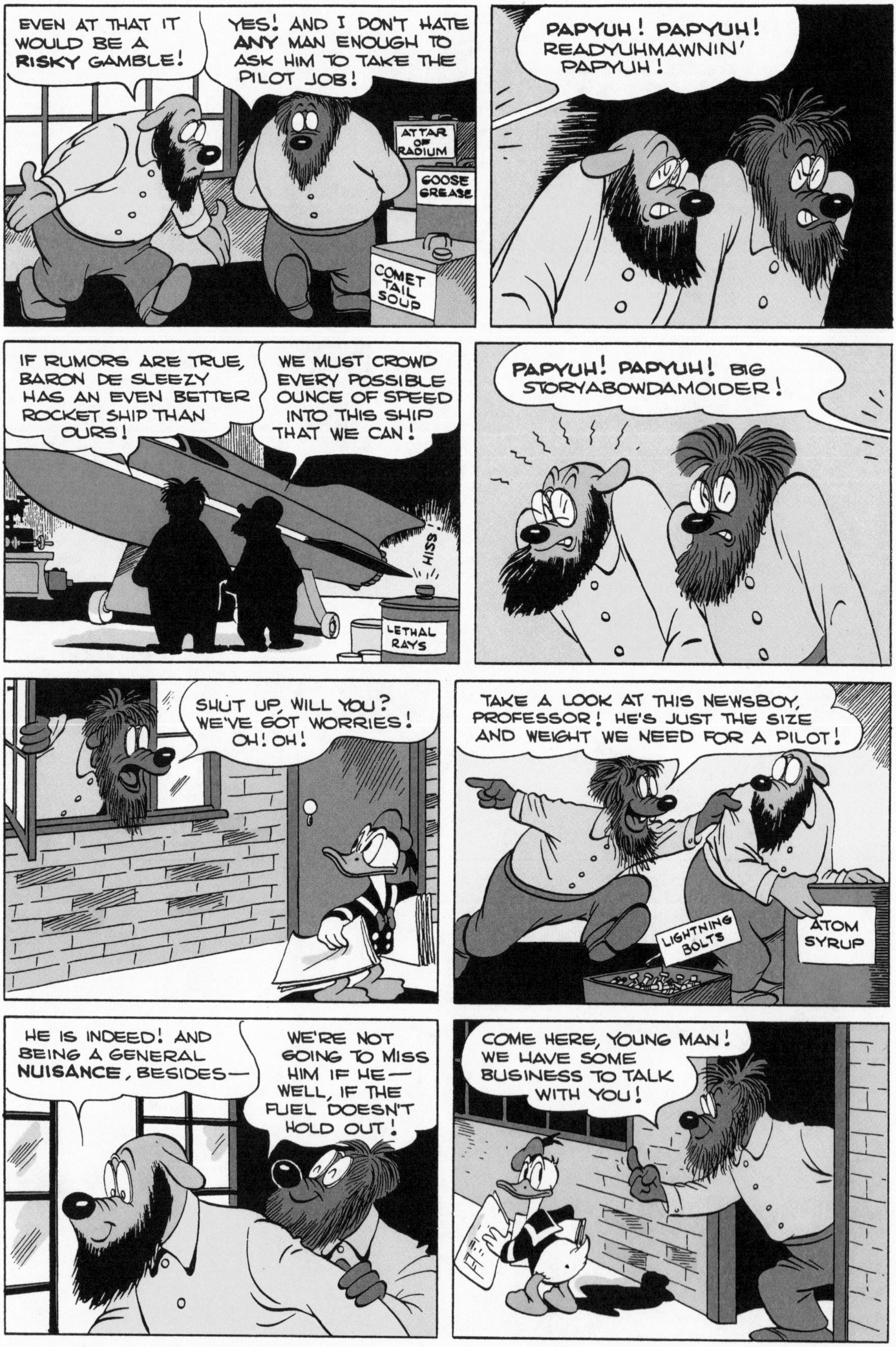
EVEN AT THAT IT WOULD BE A RISKY GAMBLE!
YES! AND I DON'T HATE ANY MAN ENOUGH TO ASK HIM TO TAKE THE PILOT JOB!
ATTAR OF RADIUM
GOOSE GREASE
COMET TAIL SOUP
PAPYUH! PAPYUH! READYUHMAWNIN' PAPYUH!
IF RUMORS ARE TRUE, BARON DE SLEEZY HAS AN EVEN BETTER ROCKET SHIP THAN OURS!
WE MUST CROWD EVERY POSSIBLE OUNCE OF SPEED INTO THIS SHIP THAT WE CAN!
HISS!
LETHAL RAYS
PAPYUH! PAPYUH! BIG STORYABOWDAMOIDER!
SHUT UP, WILL YOU? WE'VE GOT WORRIES! OH! OH!
TAKE A LOOK AT THIS NEWSBOY, PROFESSOR! HE'S JUST THE SIZE AND WEIGHT WE NEED FOR A PILOT!
LIGHTNING BOLTS
ATOM SYRUP
HE IS INDEED! AND BEING A GENERAL NUISANCE, BESIDES—
WE'RE NOT GOING TO MISS HIM IF HE— WELL, IF THE FUEL DOESN'T HOLD OUT!
COME HERE, YOUNG MAN! WE HAVE SOME BUSINESS TO TALK WITH YOU!

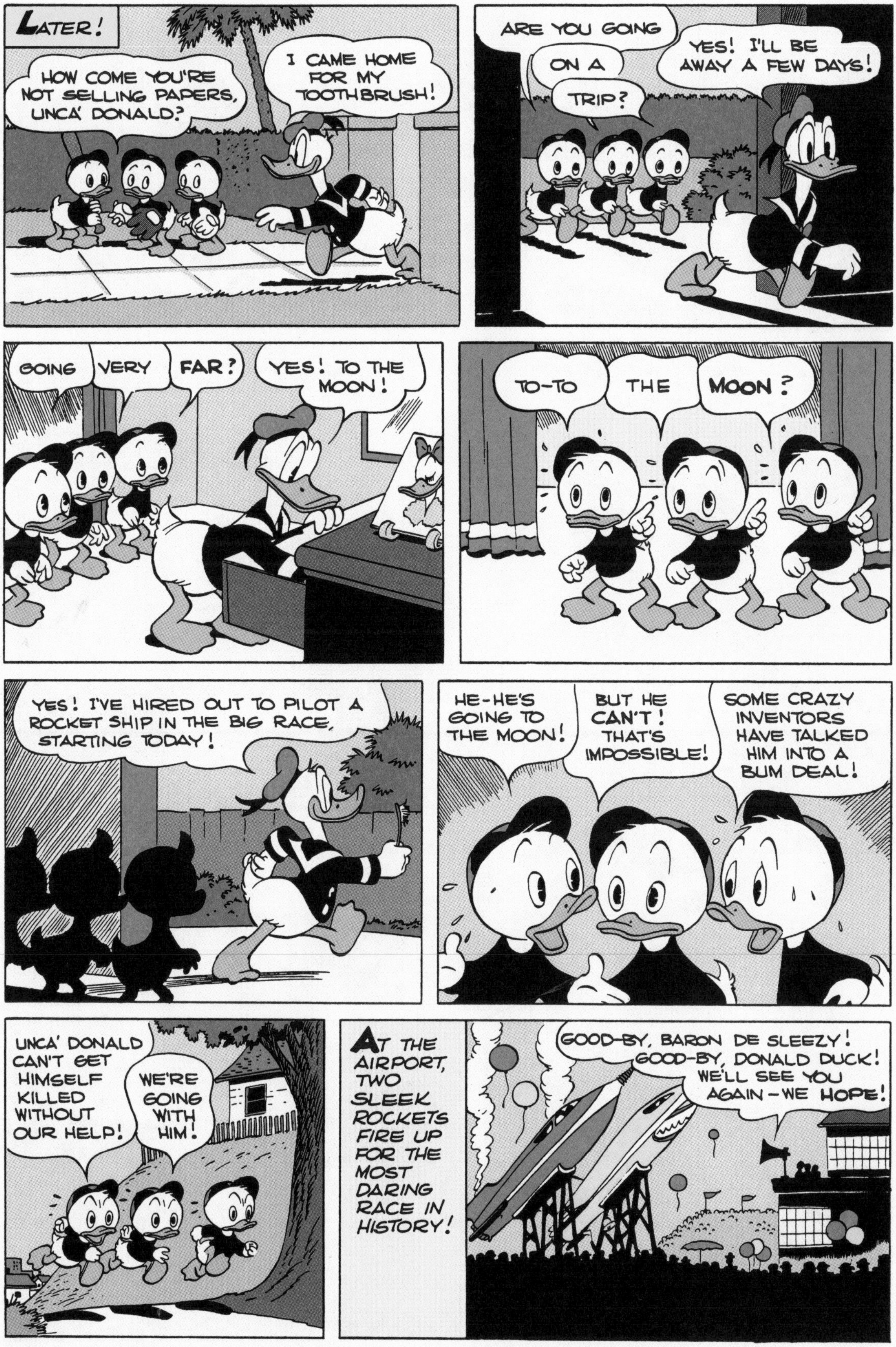
LATER!
HOW COME YOU'RE NOT SELLING PAPERS, UNCA' DONALD?
I CAME HOME FOR MY TOOTHBRUSH!
ARE YOU GOING
ON A
TRIP?
YES! I'LL BE AWAY A FEW DAYS!
GOING
VERY
FAR?
YES! TO THE MOON!
TO-TO
THE
MOON?
YES! I'VE HIRED OUT TO PILOT A ROCKET SHIP IN THE BIG RACE, STARTING TODAY!
HE-HE'S GOING TO THE MOON!
BUT HE CAN'T! THAT'S IMPOSSIBLE!
SOME CRAZY INVENTORS HAVE TALKED HIM INTO A BUM DEAL!
UNCA' DONALD CAN'T GET HIMSELF KILLED WITHOUT OUR HELP!
WE'RE GOING WITH HIM!
AT THE AIRPORT, TWO SLEEK ROCKETS FIRE UP FOR THE MOST DARING RACE IN HISTORY!
GOOD-BY, BARON DE SLEEZY! GOOD-BY, DONALD DUCK! WE'LL SEE YOU AGAIN—WE HOPE!

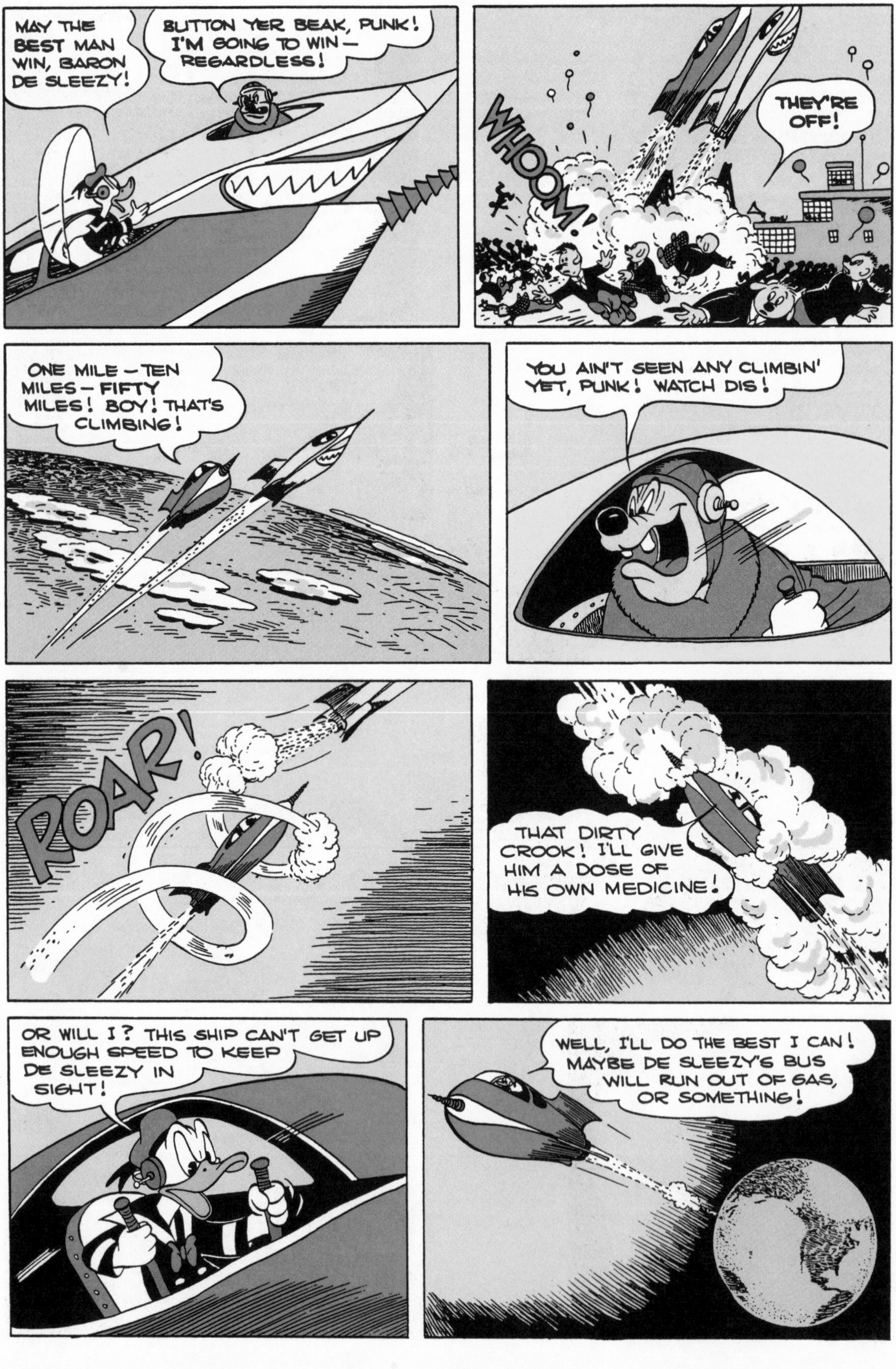
MAY THE BEST MAN WIN, BARON DE SLEEZY!
BUTTON YER BEAK, PUNK! I'M GOING TO WIN — REGARDLESS!
WHOOM!
THEY'RE OFF!
ONE MILE — TEN MILES — FIFTY MILES! BOY! THAT'S CLIMBING!
YOU AIN'T SEEN ANY CLIMBIN' YET, PUNK! WATCH DIS!
ROAR!
THAT DIRTY CROOK! I'LL GIVE HIM A DOSE OF HIS OWN MEDICINE!
OR WILL I? THIS SHIP CAN'T GET UP ENOUGH SPEED TO KEEP DE SLEEZY IN SIGHT!
WELL, I'LL DO THE BEST I CAN! MAYBE DE SLEEZY'S BUS WILL RUN OUT OF GAS, OR SOMETHING!

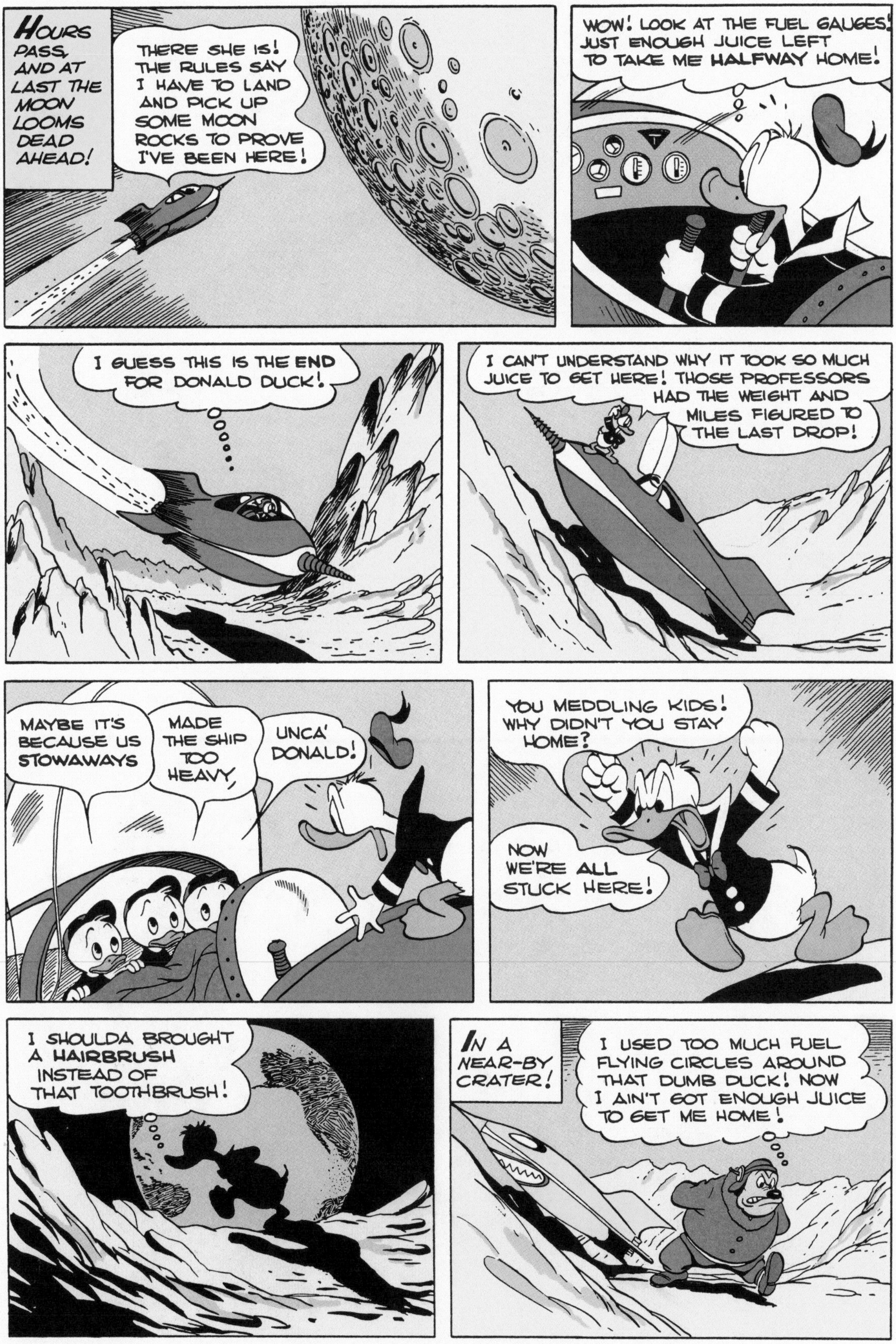
HOURS PASS, AND AT LAST THE MOON LOOMS DEAD AHEAD!
THERE SHE IS! THE RULES SAY I HAVE TO LAND AND PICK UP SOME MOON ROCKS TO PROVE I'VE BEEN HERE!
WOW! LOOK AT THE FUEL GAUGES! JUST ENOUGH JUICE LEFT TO TAKE ME HALFWAY HOME!
I GUESS THIS IS THE END FOR DONALD DUCK!
I CAN'T UNDERSTAND WHY IT TOOK SO MUCH JUICE TO GET HERE! THOSE PROFESSORS HAD THE WEIGHT AND MILES FIGURED TO THE LAST DROP!
MAYBE IT'S BECAUSE US STOWAWAYS
MADE THE SHIP TOO HEAVY,
UNCA' DONALD!
YOU MEDDLING KIDS! WHY DIDN'T YOU STAY HOME?
NOW WE'RE ALL STUCK HERE!
I SHOULDA BROUGHT A HAIRBRUSH INSTEAD OF THAT TOOTHBRUSH!
IN A NEAR-BY CRATER!
I USED TOO MUCH FUEL FLYING CIRCLES AROUND THAT DUMB DUCK! NOW I AIN'T GOT ENOUGH JUICE TO GET ME HOME!

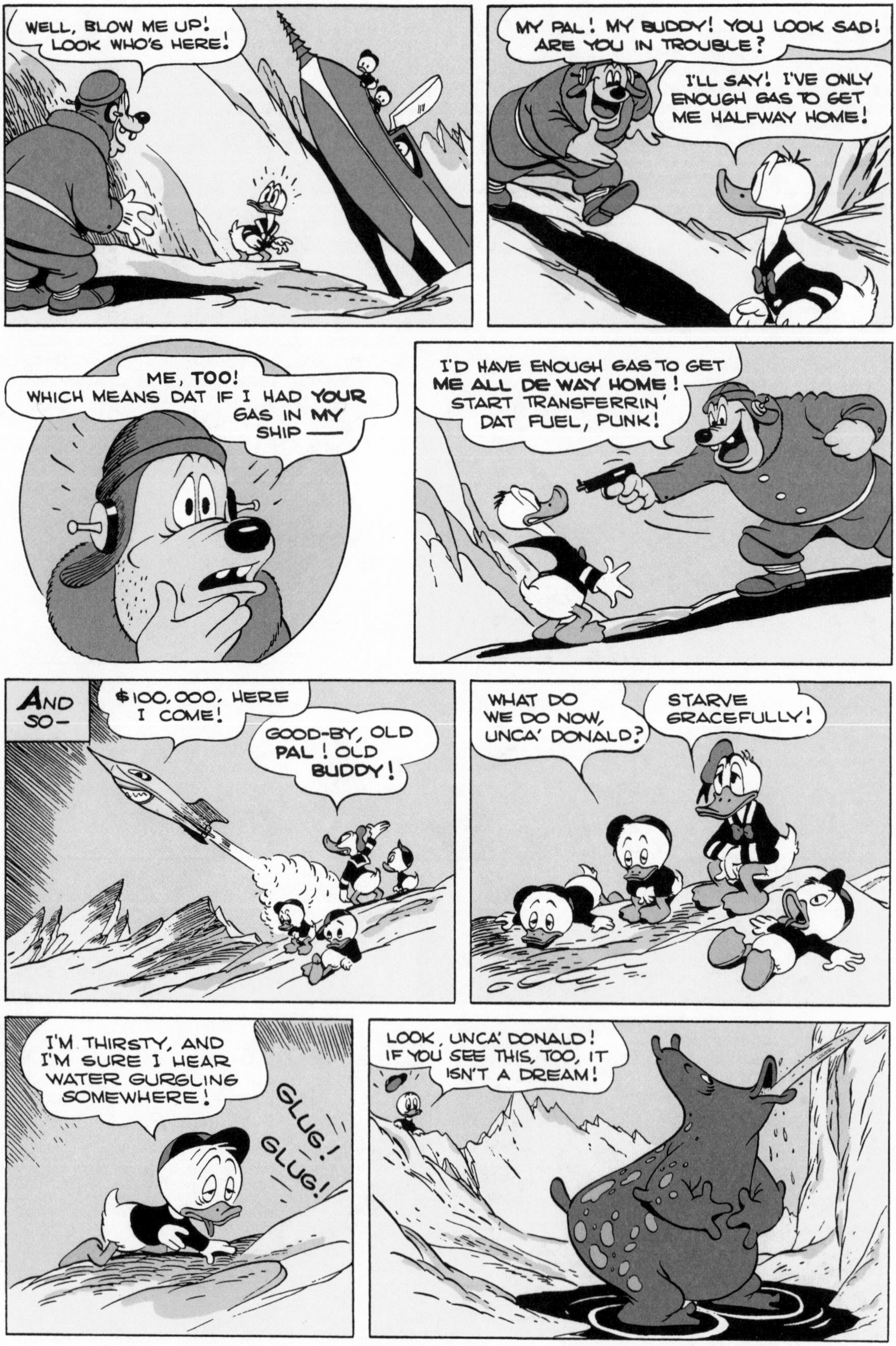
WELL, BLOW ME UP! LOOK WHO'S HERE!
MY PAL! MY BUDDY! YOU LOOK SAD! ARE YOU IN TROUBLE?
I'LL SAY! I'VE ONLY ENOUGH GAS TO GET ME HALFWAY HOME!
ME, TOO! WHICH MEANS DAT IF I HAD YOUR GAS IN MY SHIP ——
I'D HAVE ENOUGH GAS TO GET ME ALL DE WAY HOME! START TRANSFERRIN' DAT FUEL, PUNK!
AND SO—
$100,000, HERE I COME!
GOOD-BY, OLD PAL! OLD BUDDY!
WHAT DO WE DO NOW, UNCA' DONALD?
STARVE GRACEFULLY!
I'M THIRSTY, AND I'M SURE I HEAR WATER GURGLING SOMEWHERE!
GLUG! GLUG!
LOOK, UNCA' DONALD! IF YOU SEE THIS, TOO, IT ISN'T A DREAM!

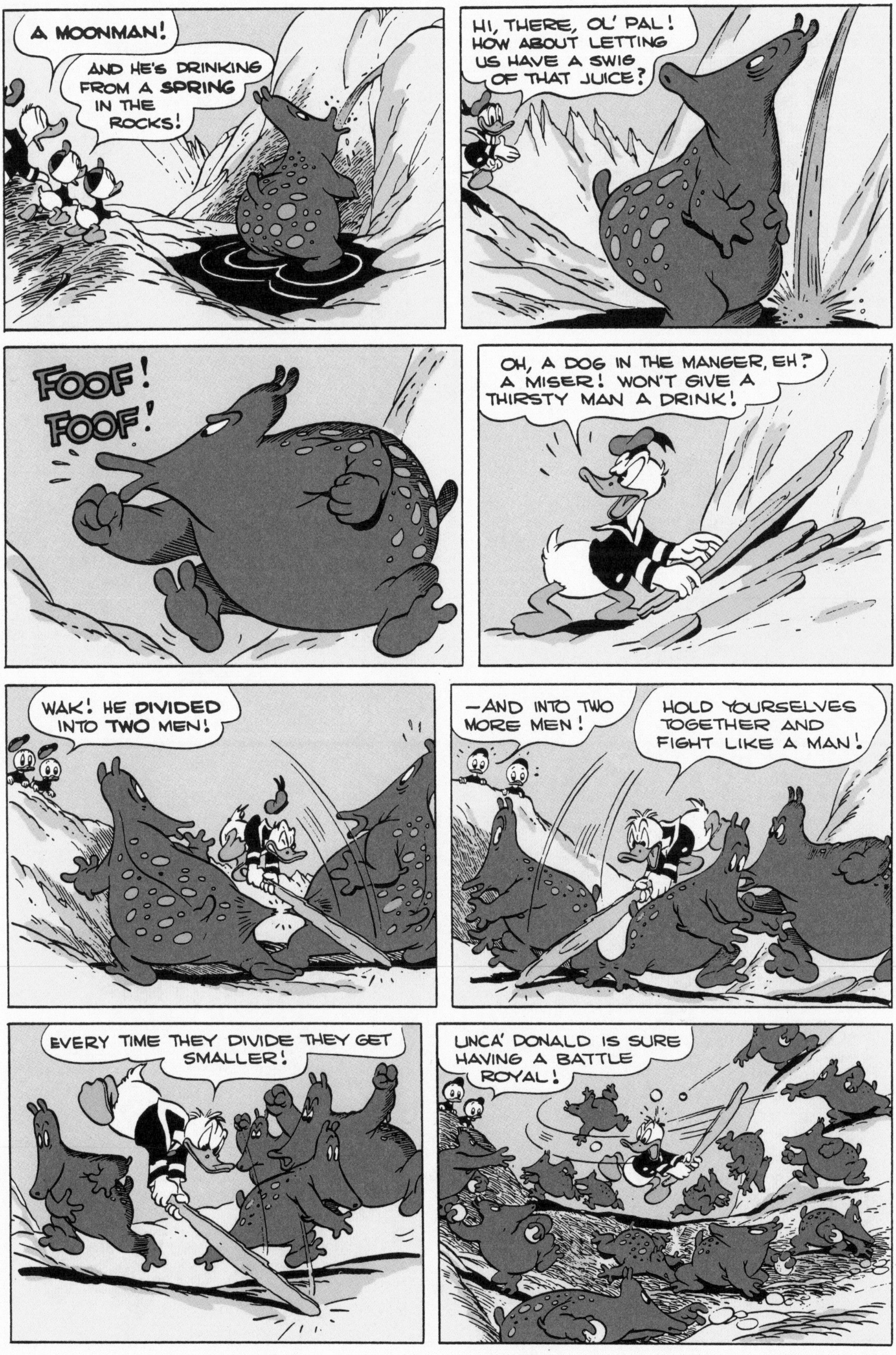
A MOONMAN!
AND HE'S DRINKING FROM A SPRING IN THE ROCKS!
HI, THERE, OL' PAL! HOW ABOUT LETTING US HAVE A SWIG OF THAT JUICE?
FOOF! FOOF!
OH, A DOG IN THE MANGER, EH? A MISER! WON'T GIVE A THIRSTY MAN A DRINK!
WAK! HE DIVIDED INTO TWO MEN!
—AND INTO TWO MORE MEN!
HOLD YOURSELVES TOGETHER AND FIGHT LIKE A MAN!
EVERY TIME THEY DIVIDE THEY GET SMALLER!
UNCA' DONALD IS SURE HAVING A BATTLE ROYAL!

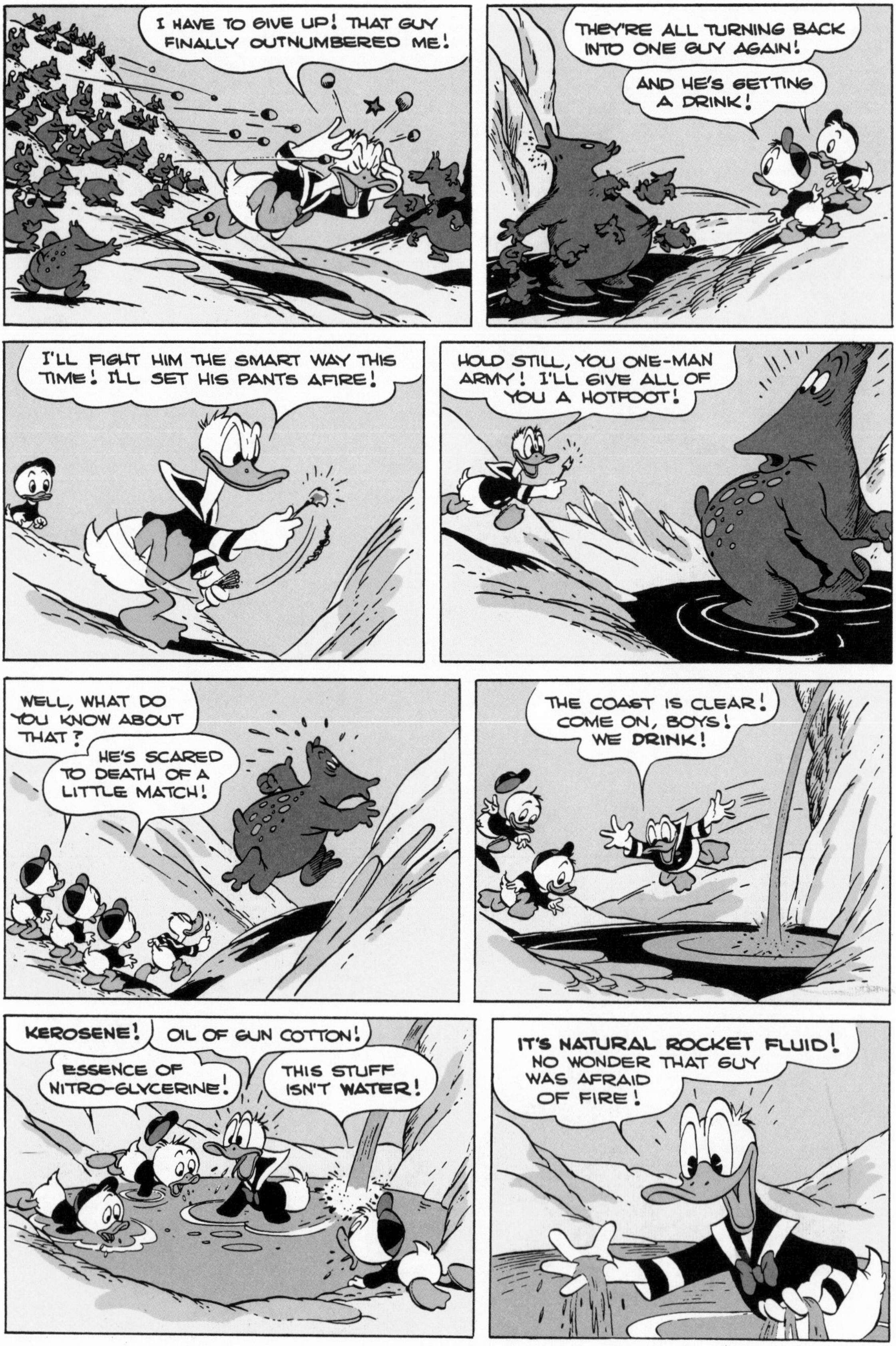

I HAVE TO GIVE UP! THAT GUY FINALLY OUTNUMBERED ME!
THEY'RE ALL TURNING BACK INTO ONE GUY AGAIN!
AND HE'S GETTING A DRINK!
I'LL FIGHT HIM THE SMART WAY THIS TIME! I'LL SET HIS PANTS AFIRE!
HOLD STILL, YOU ONE-MAN ARMY! I'LL GIVE ALL OF YOU A HOTFOOT!
WELL, WHAT DO YOU KNOW ABOUT THAT?
HE'S SCARED TO DEATH OF A LITTLE MATCH!
THE COAST IS CLEAR! COME ON, BOYS! WE DRINK!
KEROSENE!
OIL OF GUN COTTON!
ESSENCE OF NITRO-GLYCERINE!
THIS STUFF ISN'T WATER!
IT'S NATURAL ROCKET FLUID! NO WONDER THAT GUY WAS AFRAID OF FIRE!

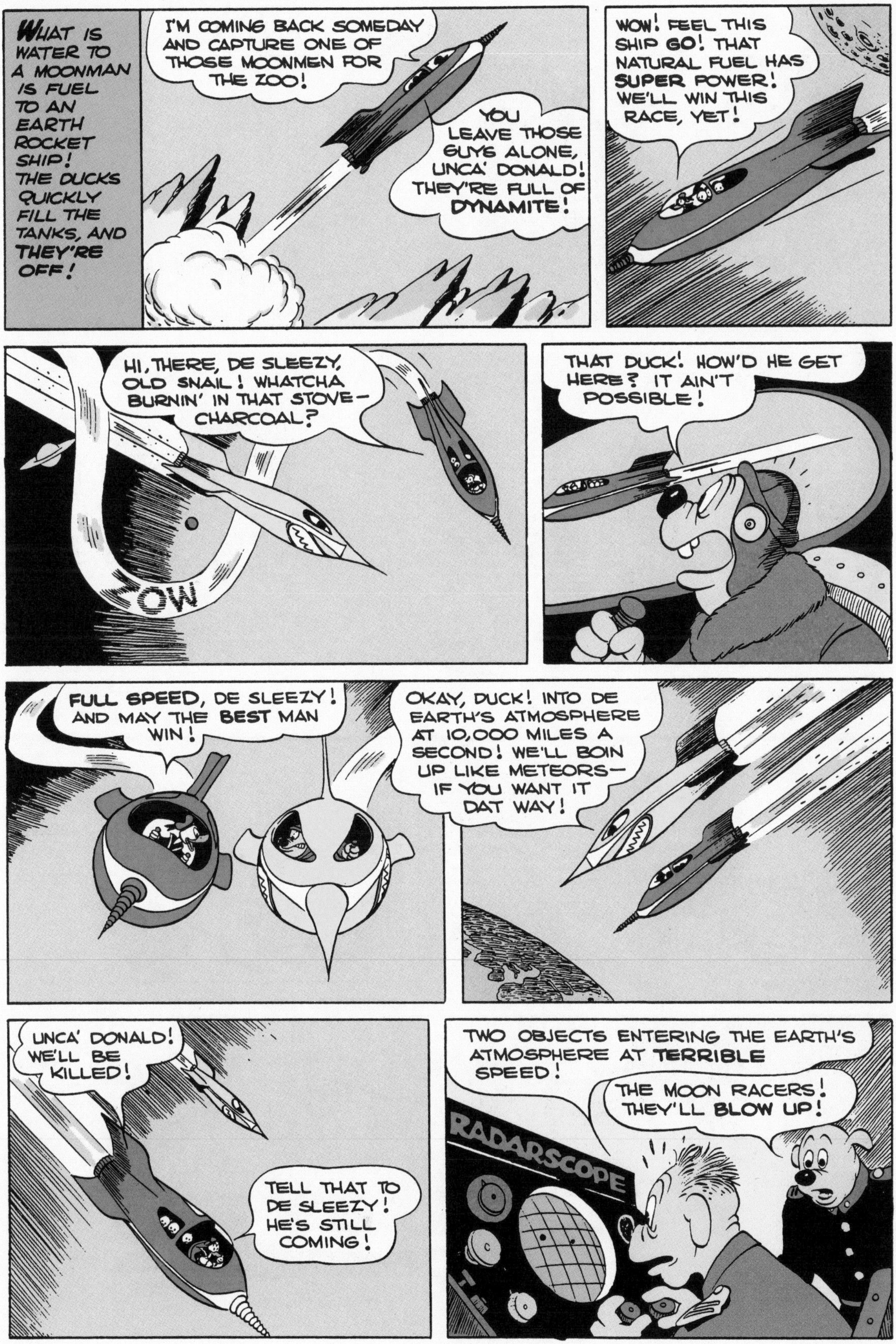
WHAT IS WATER TO A MOONMAN IS FUEL TO AN EARTH ROCKET SHIP! THE DUCKS QUICKLY FILL THE TANKS, AND THEY'RE OFF!
I'M COMING BACK SOMEDAY AND CAPTURE ONE OF THOSE MOONMEN FOR THE ZOO!
YOU LEAVE THOSE GUYS ALONE, UNCA' DONALD! THEY'RE FULL OF DYNAMITE!
WOW! FEEL THIS SHIP GO! THAT NATURAL FUEL HAS SUPER POWER! WE'LL WIN THIS RACE, YET!
HI, THERE, DE SLEEZY, OLD SNAIL! WHATCHA BURNIN' IN THAT STOVE— CHARCOAL?
ZOW
THAT DUCK! HOW'D HE GET HERE? IT AIN'T POSSIBLE!
FULL SPEED, DE SLEEZY! AND MAY THE BEST MAN WIN!
OKAY, DUCK! INTO DE EARTH'S ATMOSPHERE AT 10,000 MILES A SECOND! WE'LL BOIN UP LIKE METEORS— IF YOU WANT IT DAT WAY!
UNCA' DONALD! WE'LL BE KILLED!
TELL THAT TO DE SLEEZY! HE'S STILL COMING!
TWO OBJECTS ENTERING THE EARTH'S ATMOSPHERE AT TERRIBLE SPEED!
THE MOON RACERS! THEY'LL BLOW UP!
RADARSCOPE

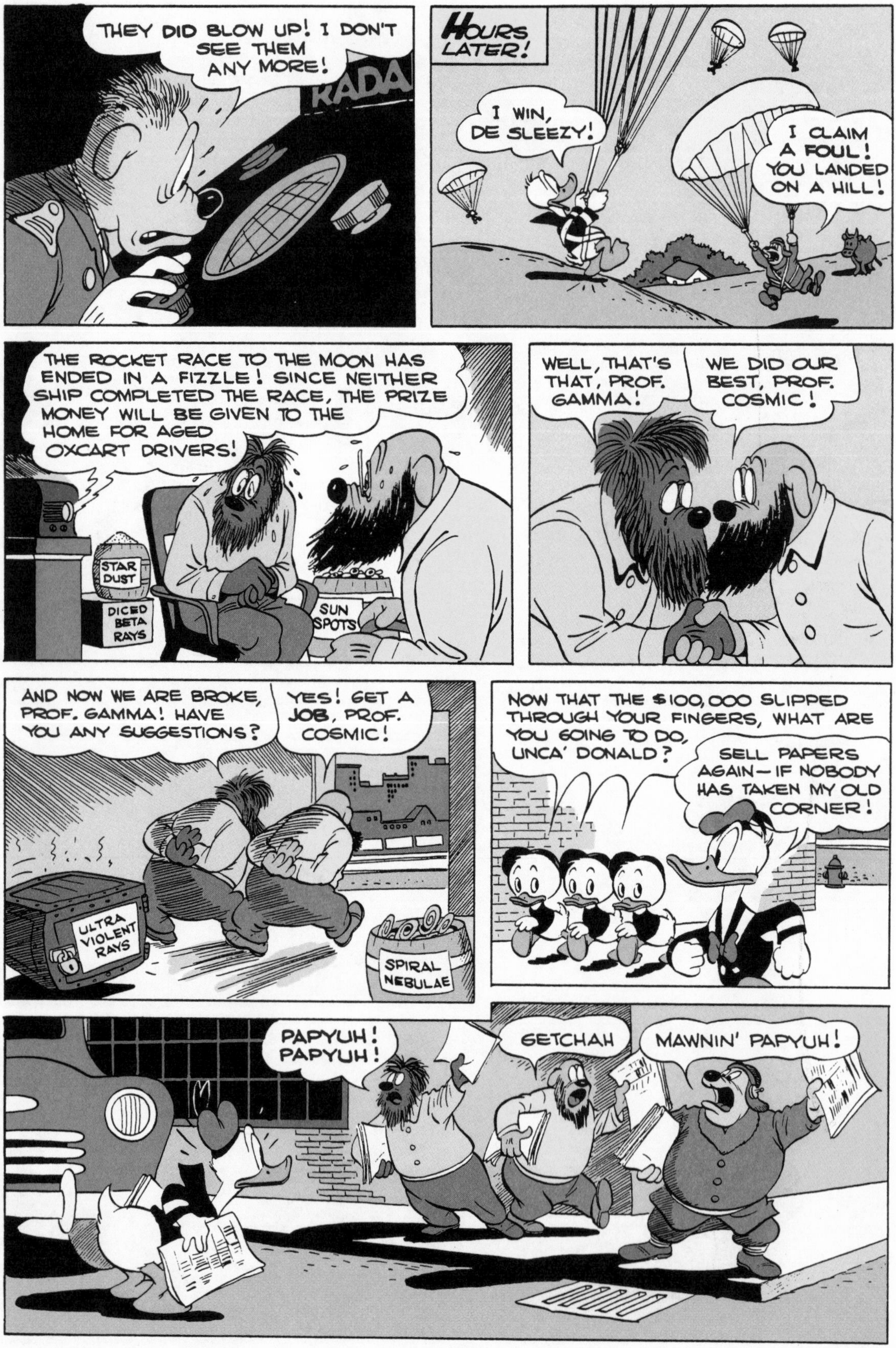
THEY DID BLOW UP! I DON'T SEE THEM ANY MORE!
RADA
HOURS LATER!
I WIN, DE SLEEZY!
I CLAIM A FOUL! YOU LANDED ON A HILL!
THE ROCKET RACE TO THE MOON HAS ENDED IN A FIZZLE! SINCE NEITHER SHIP COMPLETED THE RACE, THE PRIZE MONEY WILL BE GIVEN TO THE HOME FOR AGED OXCART DRIVERS!
STAR DUST
DICED BETA RAYS
SUN SPOTS
WELL, THAT'S THAT, PROF. GAMMA!
WE DID OUR BEST, PROF. COSMIC!
AND NOW WE ARE BROKE, PROF. GAMMA! HAVE YOU ANY SUGGESTIONS?
YES! GET A JOB, PROF. COSMIC!
ULTRA VIOLENT RAYS
SPIRAL NEBULAE
NOW THAT THE $100,000 SLIPPED THROUGH YOUR FINGERS, WHAT ARE YOU GOING TO DO, UNCA' DONALD?
SELL PAPERS AGAIN—IF NOBODY HAS TAKEN MY OLD CORNER!
PAPYUH! PAPYUH!
GETCHAH
MAWNIN' PAPYUH!

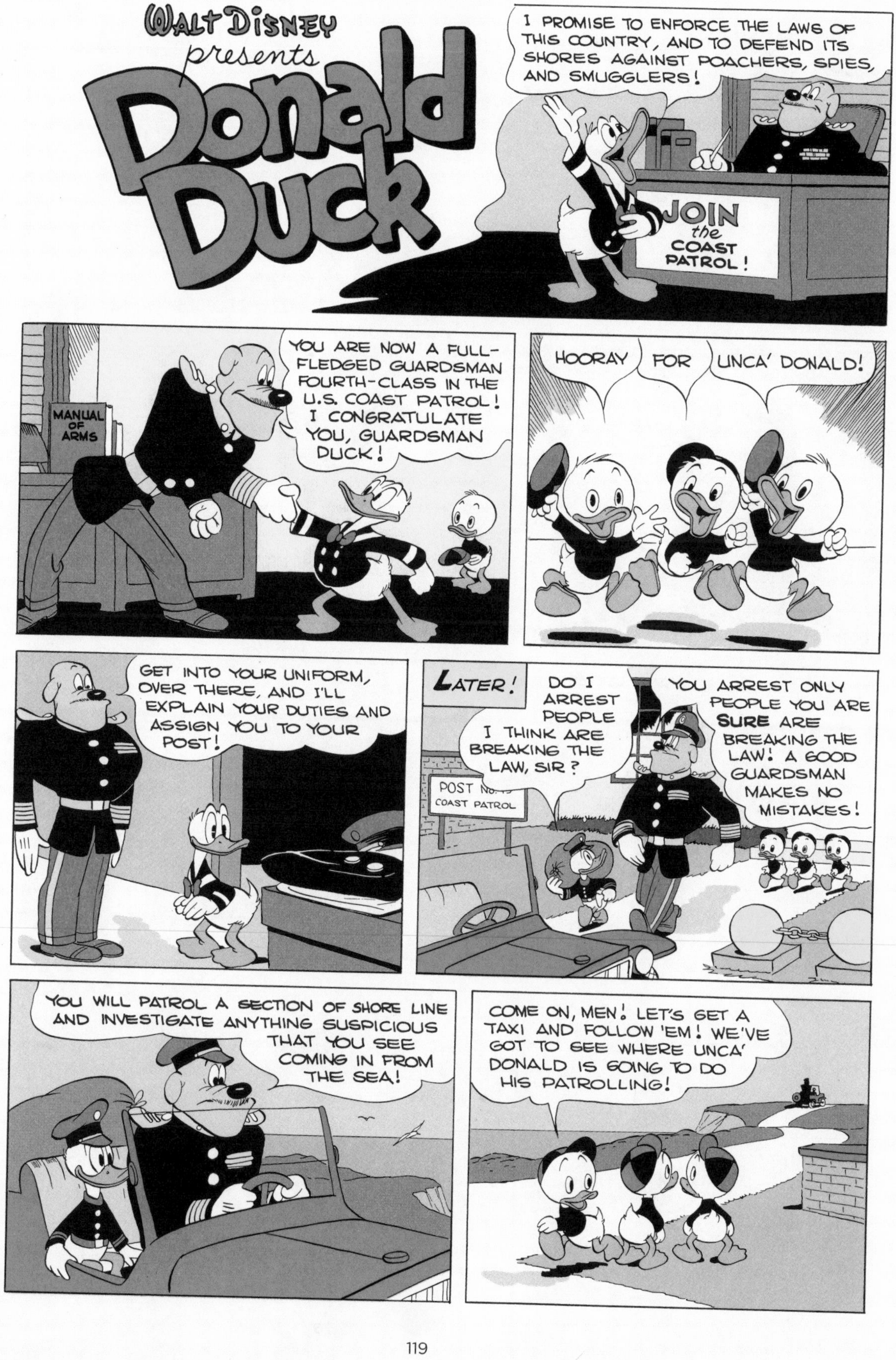
WALT DISNEY presents
Donald Duck
I PROMISE TO ENFORCE THE LAWS OF THIS COUNTRY, AND TO DEFEND ITS SHORES AGAINST POACHERS, SPIES, AND SMUGGLERS!
JOIN the COAST PATROL!
MANUAL OF ARMS
YOU ARE NOW A FULL-FLEDGED GUARDSMAN FOURTH-CLASS IN THE U.S. COAST PATROL! I CONGRATULATE YOU, GUARDSMAN DUCK!
HOORAY
FOR
UNCA' DONALD!
GET INTO YOUR UNIFORM, OVER THERE, AND I'LL EXPLAIN YOUR DUTIES AND ASSIGN YOU TO YOUR POST!
LATER!
DO I ARREST PEOPLE I THINK ARE BREAKING THE LAW, SIR?
YOU ARREST ONLY PEOPLE YOU ARE SURE ARE BREAKING THE LAW! A GOOD GUARDSMAN MAKES NO MISTAKES!
POST
COAST PATROL
YOU WILL PATROL A SECTION OF SHORE LINE AND INVESTIGATE ANYTHING SUSPICIOUS THAT YOU SEE COMING IN FROM THE SEA!
COME ON, MEN! LET'S GET A TAXI AND FOLLOW 'EM! WE'VE GOT TO SEE WHERE UNCA' DONALD IS GOING TO DO HIS PATROLLING!

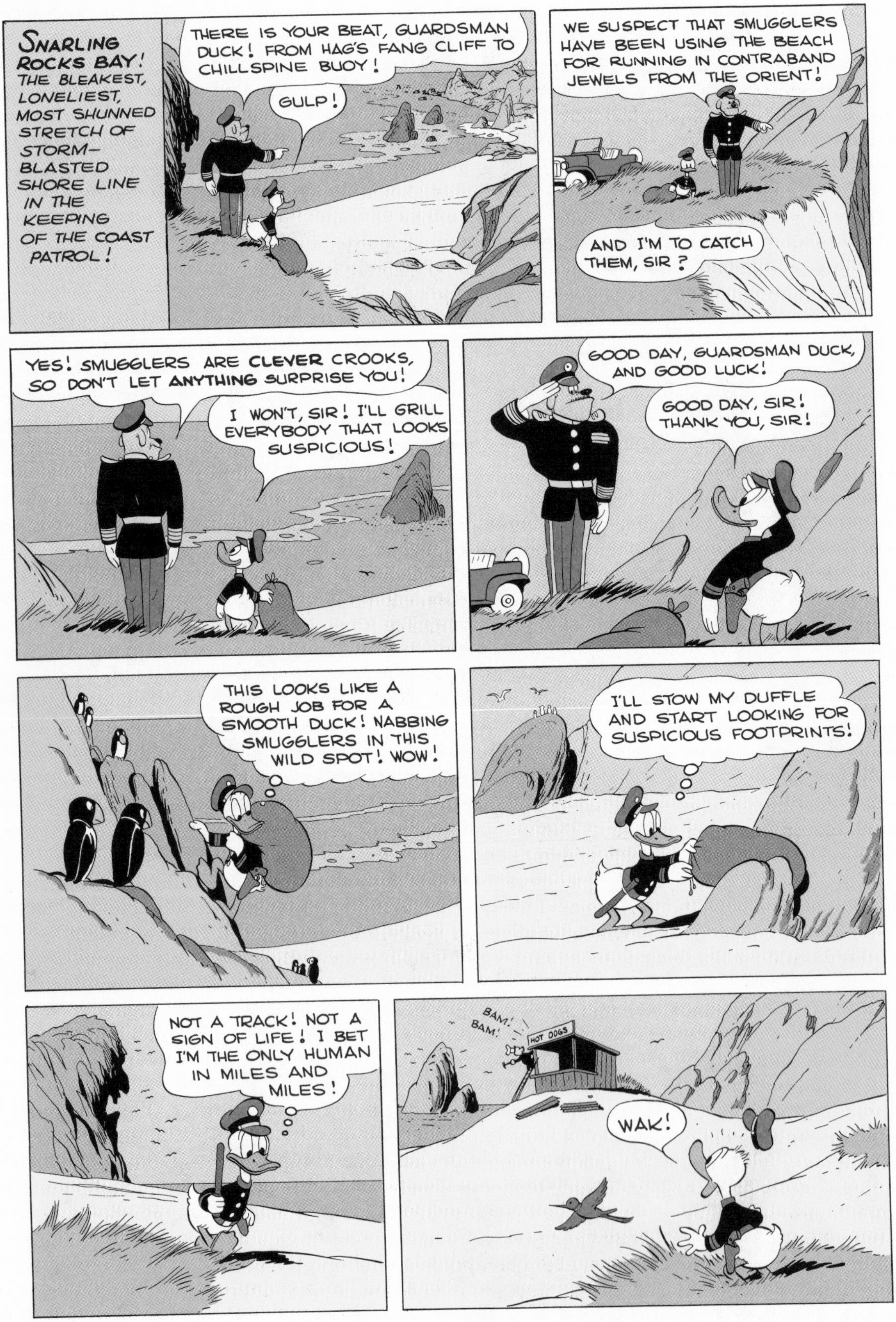
SNARLING ROCKS BAY! THE BLEAKEST, LONELIEST, MOST SHUNNED STRETCH OF STORM-BLASTED SHORE LINE IN THE KEEPING OF THE COAST PATROL!
THERE IS YOUR BEAT, GUARDSMAN DUCK! FROM HAG'S FANG CLIFF TO CHILLSPINE BUOY!
GULP!
WE SUSPECT THAT SMUGGLERS HAVE BEEN USING THE BEACH FOR RUNNING IN CONTRABAND JEWELS FROM THE ORIENT!
AND I'M TO CATCH THEM, SIR?
YES! SMUGGLERS ARE CLEVER CROOKS, SO DON'T LET ANYTHING SURPRISE YOU!
I WON'T, SIR! I'LL GRILL EVERYBODY THAT LOOKS SUSPICIOUS!
GOOD DAY, GUARDSMAN DUCK, AND GOOD LUCK!
GOOD DAY, SIR! THANK YOU, SIR!
THIS LOOKS LIKE A ROUGH JOB FOR A SMOOTH DUCK! NABBING SMUGGLERS IN THIS WILD SPOT! WOW!
I'LL STOW MY DUFFLE AND START LOOKING FOR SUSPICIOUS FOOTPRINTS!
NOT A TRACK! NOT A SIGN OF LIFE! I BET I'M THE ONLY HUMAN IN MILES AND MILES!
BAM! BAM!
HOT DOGS
WAK!

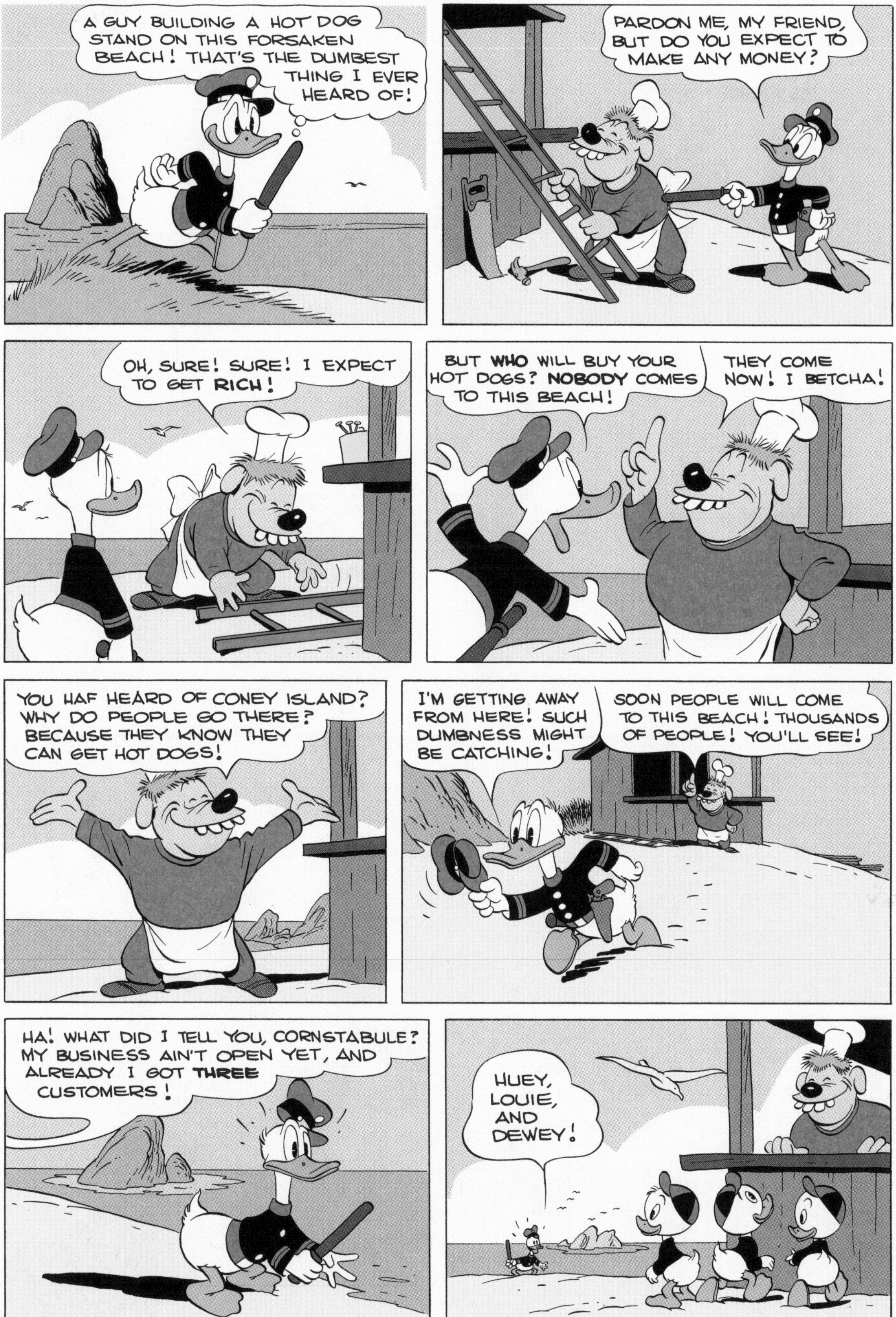
A GUY BUILDING A HOT DOG STAND ON THIS FORSAKEN BEACH! THAT'S THE DUMBEST THING I EVER HEARD OF!
PARDON ME, MY FRIEND, BUT DO YOU EXPECT TO MAKE ANY MONEY?
OH, SURE! SURE! I EXPECT TO GET RICH!
BUT WHO WILL BUY YOUR HOT DOGS? NOBODY COMES TO THIS BEACH!
THEY COME NOW! I BETCHA!
YOU HAF HEARD OF CONEY ISLAND? WHY DO PEOPLE GO THERE? BECAUSE THEY KNOW THEY CAN GET HOT DOGS!
I'M GETTING AWAY FROM HERE! SUCH DUMBNESS MIGHT BE CATCHING!
SOON PEOPLE WILL COME TO THIS BEACH! THOUSANDS OF PEOPLE! YOU'LL SEE!
HA! WHAT DID I TELL YOU, CORNSTABULE? MY BUSINESS AIN'T OPEN YET, AND ALREADY I GOT THREE CUSTOMERS!
HUEY, LOUIE, AND DEWEY!

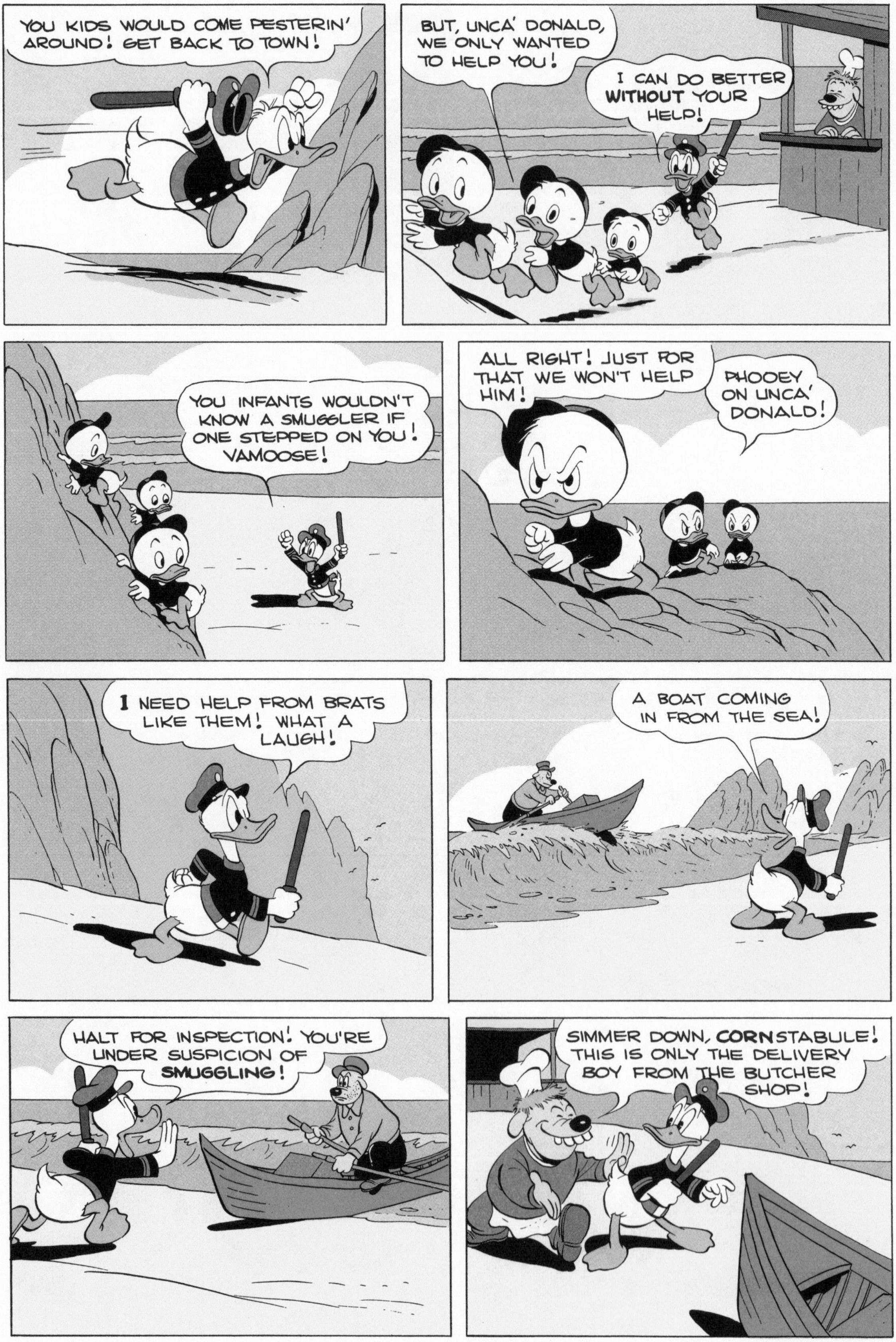
YOU KIDS WOULD COME PESTERIN' AROUND! GET BACK TO TOWN!
BUT, UNCA' DONALD, WE ONLY WANTED TO HELP YOU!
I CAN DO BETTER WITHOUT YOUR HELP!
YOU INFANTS WOULDN'T KNOW A SMUGGLER IF ONE STEPPED ON YOU! VAMOOSE!
ALL RIGHT! JUST FOR THAT WE WON'T HELP HIM!
PHOOEY ON UNCA' DONALD!
I NEED HELP FROM BRATS LIKE THEM! WHAT A LAUGH!
A BOAT COMING IN FROM THE SEA!
HALT FOR INSPECTION! YOU'RE UNDER SUSPICION OF SMUGGLING!
SIMMER DOWN, CORNSTABULE! THIS IS ONLY THE DELIVERY BOY FROM THE BUTCHER SHOP!

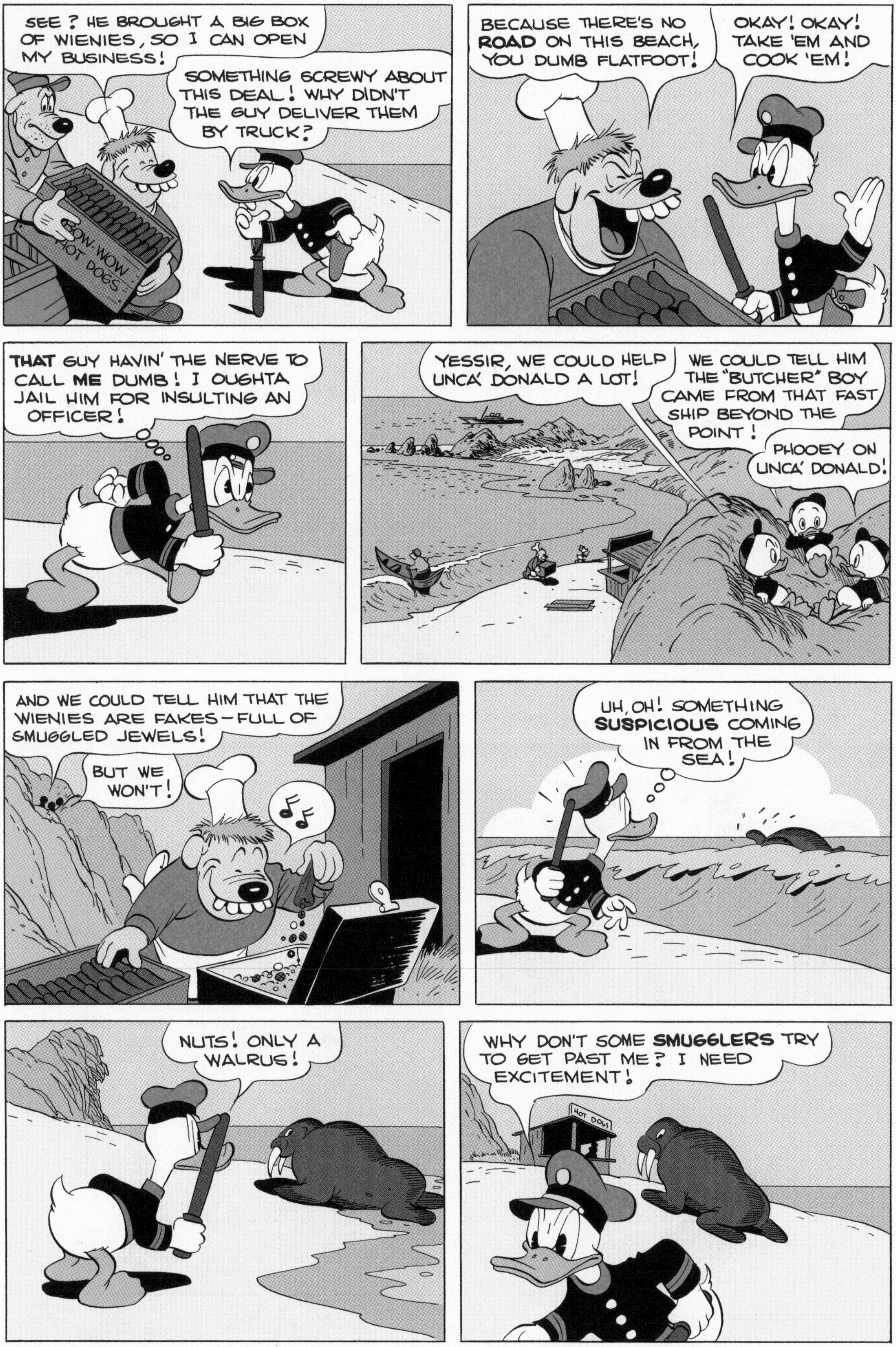

SEE? HE BROUGHT A BIG BOX OF WIENIES, SO I CAN OPEN MY BUSINESS!
SOMETHING SCREWY ABOUT THIS DEAL! WHY DIDN'T THE GUY DELIVER THEM BY TRUCK?
BOW-WOW HOT DOGS
BECAUSE THERE'S NO ROAD ON THIS BEACH, YOU DUMB FLATFOOT!
OKAY! OKAY! TAKE 'EM AND COOK 'EM!
THAT GUY HAVIN' THE NERVE TO CALL ME DUMB! I OUGHTA JAIL HIM FOR INSULTING AN OFFICER!
YESSIR, WE COULD HELP UNCA' DONALD A LOT!
WE COULD TELL HIM THE "BUTCHER" BOY CAME FROM THAT FAST SHIP BEYOND THE POINT!
PHOOEY ON UNCA' DONALD!
AND WE COULD TELL HIM THAT THE WIENIES ARE FAKES—FULL OF SMUGGLED JEWELS!
BUT WE WON'T!
UH, OH! SOMETHING SUSPICIOUS COMING IN FROM THE SEA!
NUTS! ONLY A WALRUS!
WHY DON'T SOME SMUGGLERS TRY TO GET PAST ME? I NEED EXCITEMENT!
HOT DOGS

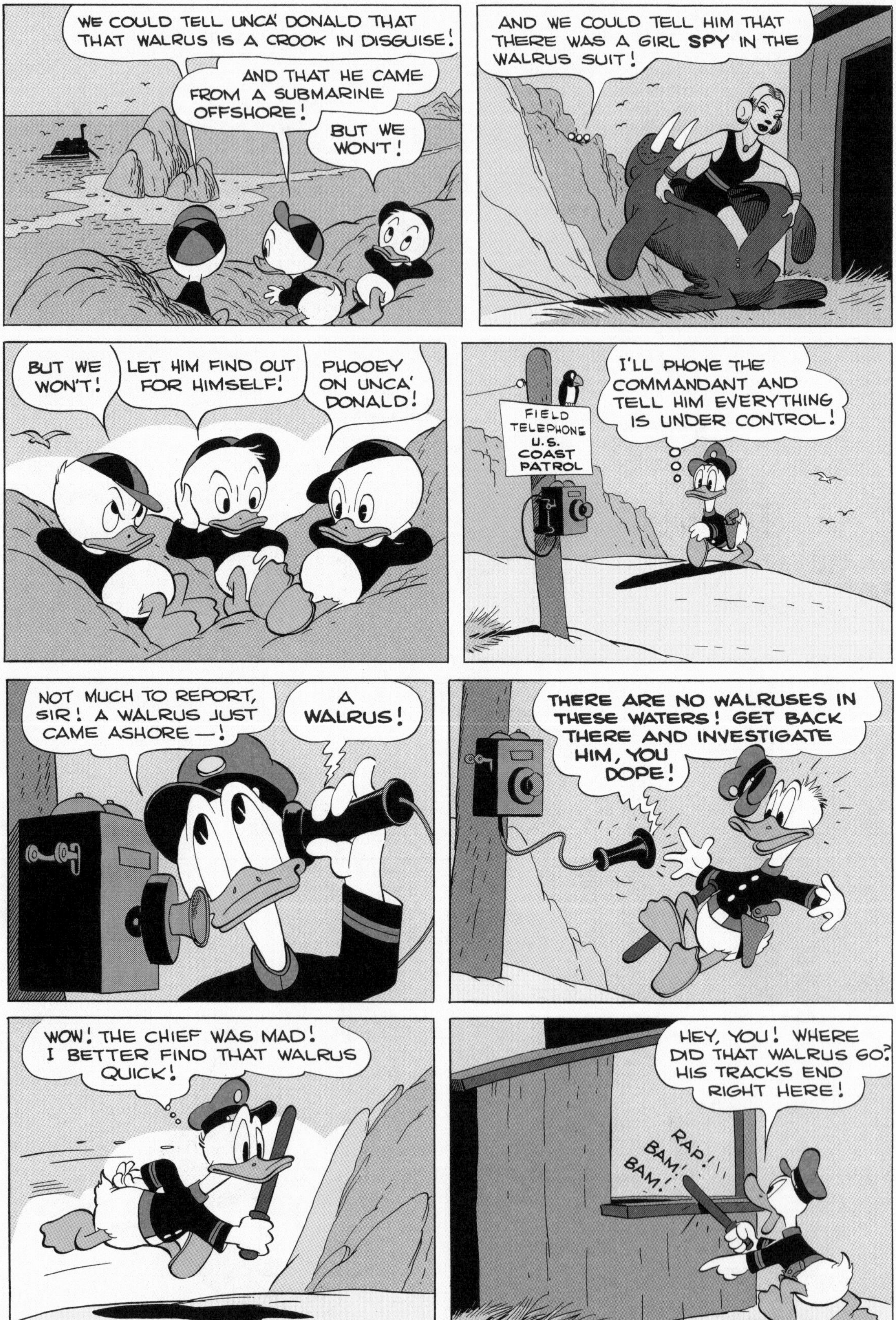
WE COULD TELL UNCA' DONALD THAT THAT WALRUS IS A CROOK IN DISGUISE!
AND THAT HE CAME FROM A SUBMARINE OFFSHORE!
BUT WE WON'T!
AND WE COULD TELL HIM THAT THERE WAS A GIRL SPY IN THE WALRUS SUIT!
BUT WE WON'T!
LET HIM FIND OUT FOR HIMSELF!
PHOOEY ON UNCA' DONALD!
FIELD TELEPHONE U.S. COAST PATROL
I'LL PHONE THE COMMANDANT AND TELL HIM EVERYTHING IS UNDER CONTROL!
NOT MUCH TO REPORT, SIR! A WALRUS JUST CAME ASHORE—!
A WALRUS!
THERE ARE NO WALRUSES IN THESE WATERS! GET BACK THERE AND INVESTIGATE HIM, YOU DOPE!
WOW! THE CHIEF WAS MAD! I BETTER FIND THAT WALRUS QUICK!
HEY, YOU! WHERE DID THAT WALRUS GO? HIS TRACKS END RIGHT HERE!
RAP! BAM! BAM!

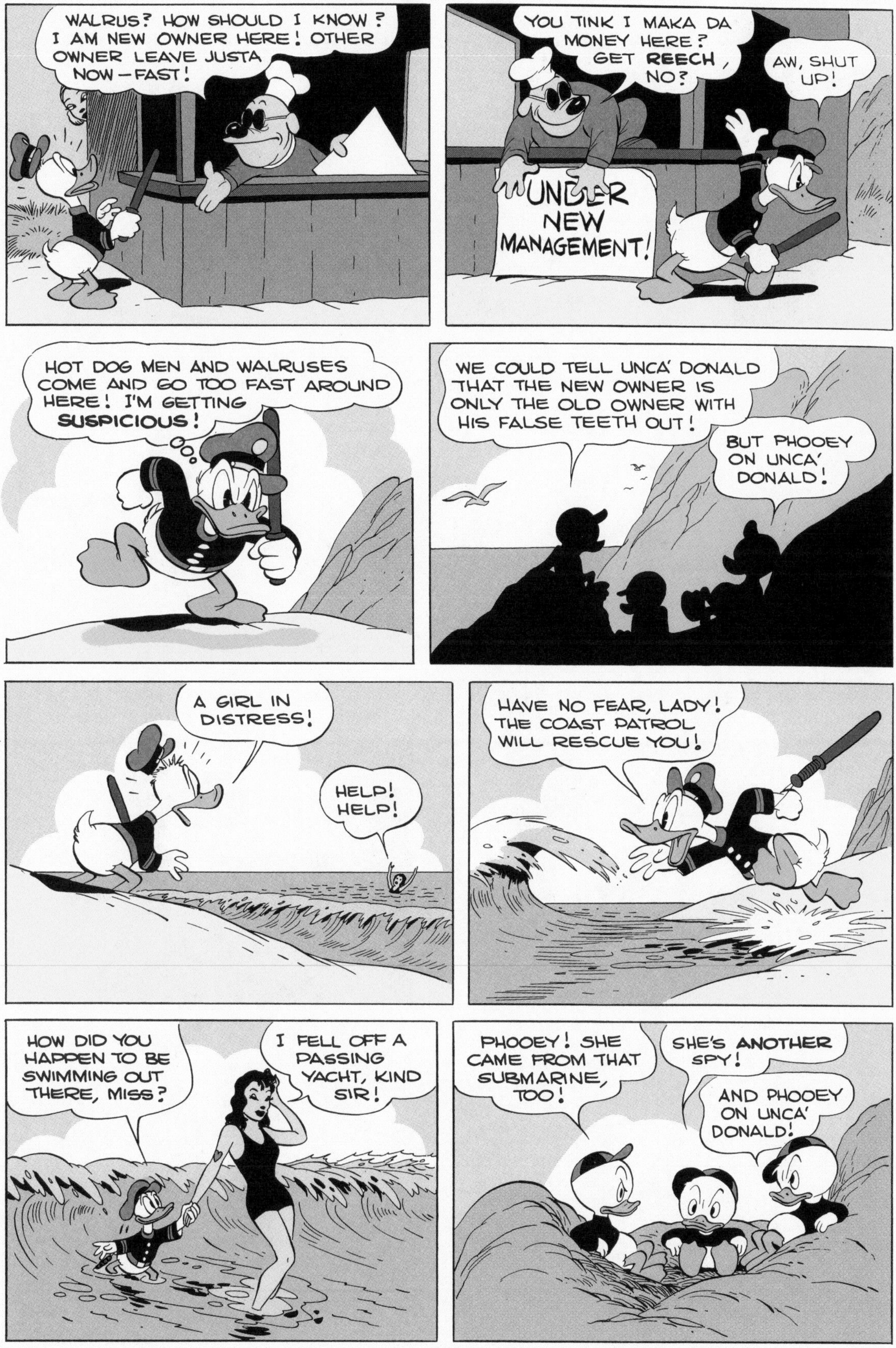
WALRUS? HOW SHOULD I KNOW? I AM NEW OWNER HERE! OTHER OWNER LEAVE JUSTA NOW—FAST!
YOU TINK I MAKA DA MONEY HERE? GET REECH, NO?
AW, SHUT UP!
UNDER NEW MANAGEMENT!
HOT DOG MEN AND WALRUSES COME AND GO TOO FAST AROUND HERE! I'M GETTING SUSPICIOUS!
WE COULD TELL UNCA' DONALD THAT THE NEW OWNER IS ONLY THE OLD OWNER WITH HIS FALSE TEETH OUT!
BUT PHOOEY ON UNCA' DONALD!
A GIRL IN DISTRESS!
HELP! HELP!
HAVE NO FEAR, LADY! THE COAST PATROL WILL RESCUE YOU!
HOW DID YOU HAPPEN TO BE SWIMMING OUT THERE, MISS?
I FELL OFF A PASSING YACHT, KIND SIR!
PHOOEY! SHE CAME FROM THAT SUBMARINE, TOO!
SHE'S ANOTHER SPY!
AND PHOOEY ON UNCA' DONALD!

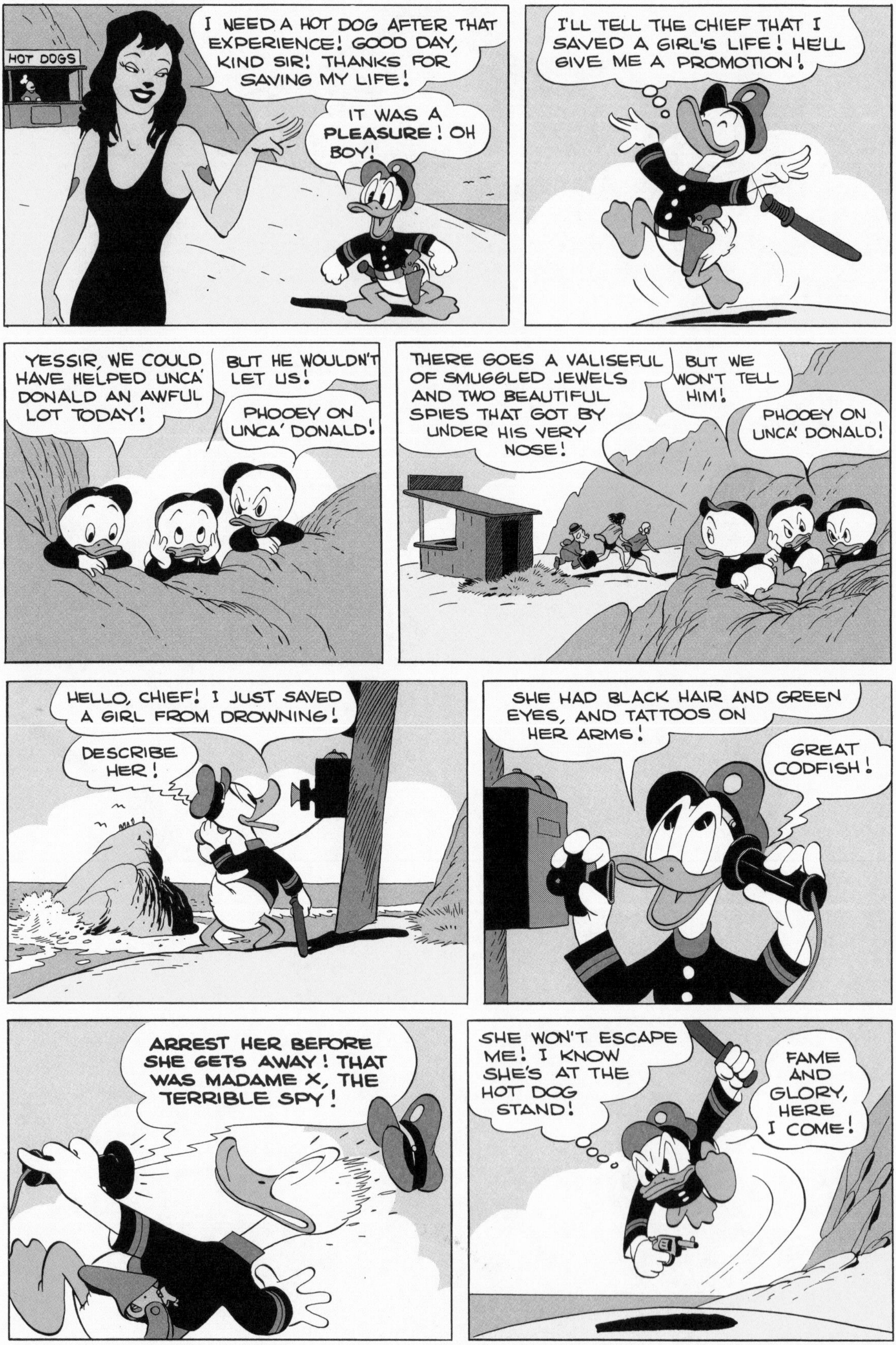
HOT DOGS
I NEED A HOT DOG AFTER THAT EXPERIENCE! GOOD DAY, KIND SIR! THANKS FOR SAVING MY LIFE!
IT WAS A PLEASURE! OH BOY!
I'LL TELL THE CHIEF THAT I SAVED A GIRL'S LIFE! HE'LL GIVE ME A PROMOTION!
YESSIR, WE COULD HAVE HELPED UNCA' DONALD AN AWFUL LOT TODAY!
BUT HE WOULDN'T LET US!
PHOOEY ON UNCA' DONALD!
THERE GOES A VALISEFUL OF SMUGGLED JEWELS AND TWO BEAUTIFUL SPIES THAT GOT BY UNDER HIS VERY NOSE!
BUT WE WON'T TELL HIM!
PHOOEY ON UNCA' DONALD!
HELLO, CHIEF! I JUST SAVED A GIRL FROM DROWNING!
DESCRIBE HER!
SHE HAD BLACK HAIR AND GREEN EYES, AND TATTOOS ON HER ARMS!
GREAT CODFISH!
ARREST HER BEFORE SHE GETS AWAY! THAT WAS MADAME X, THE TERRIBLE SPY!
SHE WON'T ESCAPE ME! I KNOW SHE'S AT THE HOT DOG STAND!
FAME AND GLORY, HERE I COME!

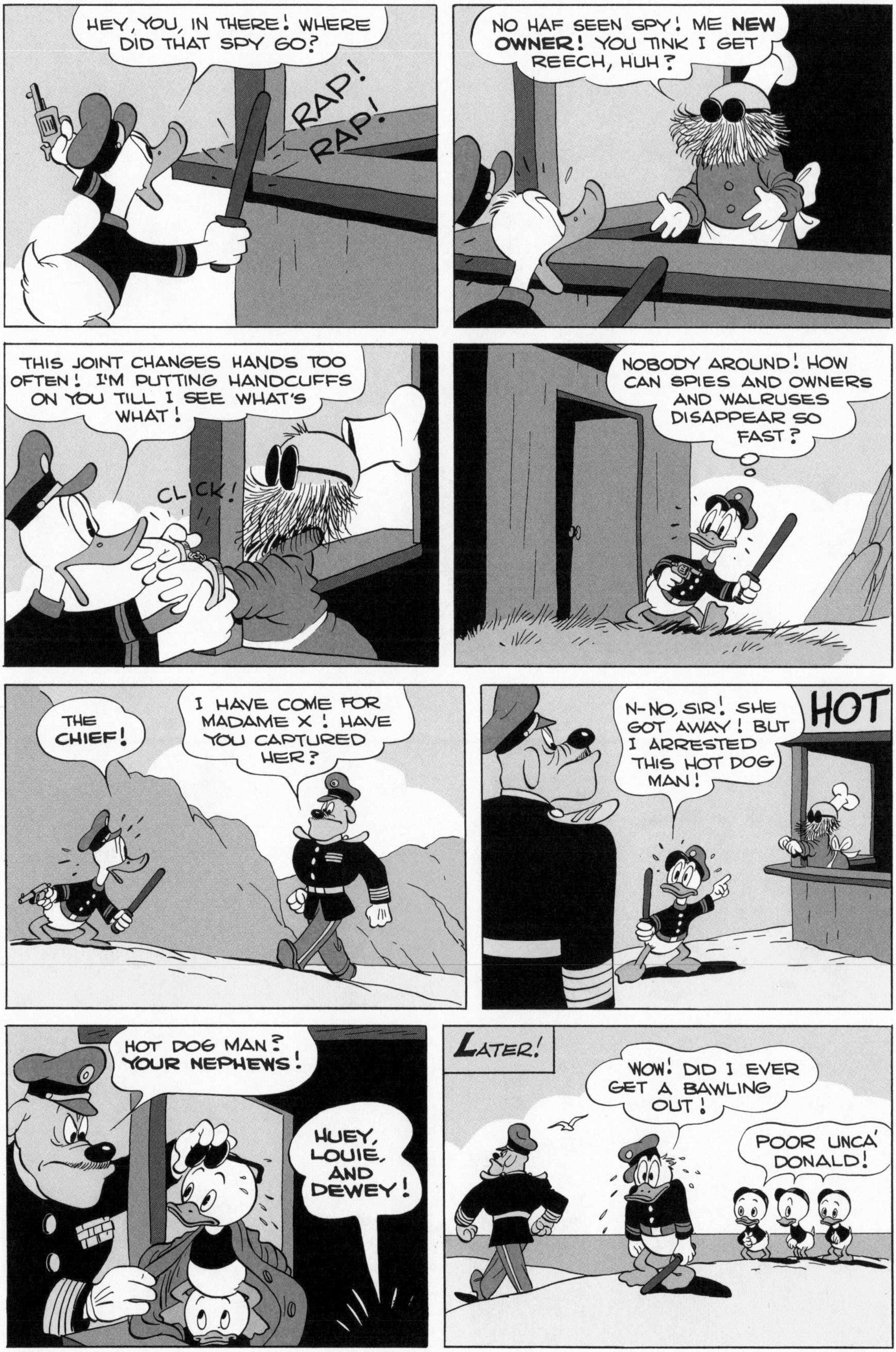
HEY, YOU, IN THERE! WHERE DID THAT SPY GO?
RAP! RAP!
NO HAF SEEN SPY! ME NEW OWNER! YOU TINK I GET REECH, HUH?
THIS JOINT CHANGES HANDS TOO OFTEN! I'M PUTTING HANDCUFFS ON YOU TILL I SEE WHAT'S WHAT!
CLICK!
NOBODY AROUND! HOW CAN SPIES AND OWNERS AND WALRUSES DISAPPEAR SO FAST?
THE CHIEF!
I HAVE COME FOR MADAME X! HAVE YOU CAPTURED HER?
N-NO, SIR! SHE GOT AWAY! BUT I ARRESTED THIS HOT DOG MAN!
HOT
HOT DOG MAN? YOUR NEPHEWS!
HUEY, LOUIE, AND DEWEY!
LATER!
WOW! DID I EVER GET A BAWLING OUT!
POOR UNCA' DONALD!

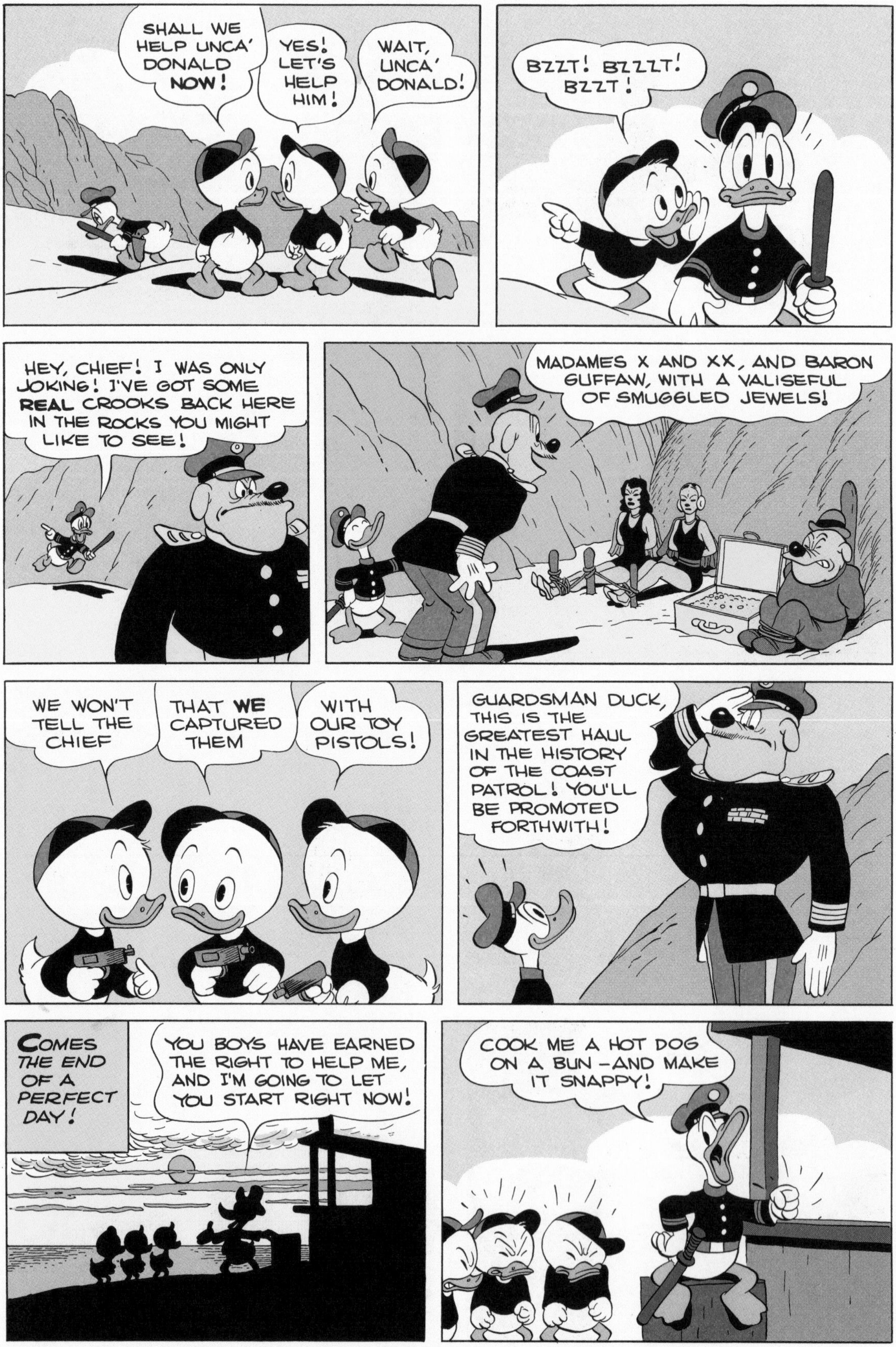
SHALL WE HELP UNCA' DONALD NOW!
YES! LET'S HELP HIM!
WAIT, UNCA' DONALD!
BZZT! BZZZT! BZZT!
HEY, CHIEF! I WAS ONLY JOKING! I'VE GOT SOME REAL CROOKS BACK HERE IN THE ROCKS YOU MIGHT LIKE TO SEE!
MADAMES X AND XX, AND BARON GUFFAW, WITH A VALISEFUL OF SMUGGLED JEWELS!
WE WON'T TELL THE CHIEF
THAT WE CAPTURED THEM
WITH OUR TOY PISTOLS!
GUARDSMAN DUCK, THIS IS THE GREATEST HAUL IN THE HISTORY OF THE COAST PATROL! YOU'LL BE PROMOTED FORTHWITH!
COMES THE END OF A PERFECT DAY!
YOU BOYS HAVE EARNED THE RIGHT TO HELP ME, AND I'M GOING TO LET YOU START RIGHT NOW!
COOK ME A HOT DOG ON A BUN—AND MAKE IT SNAPPY!

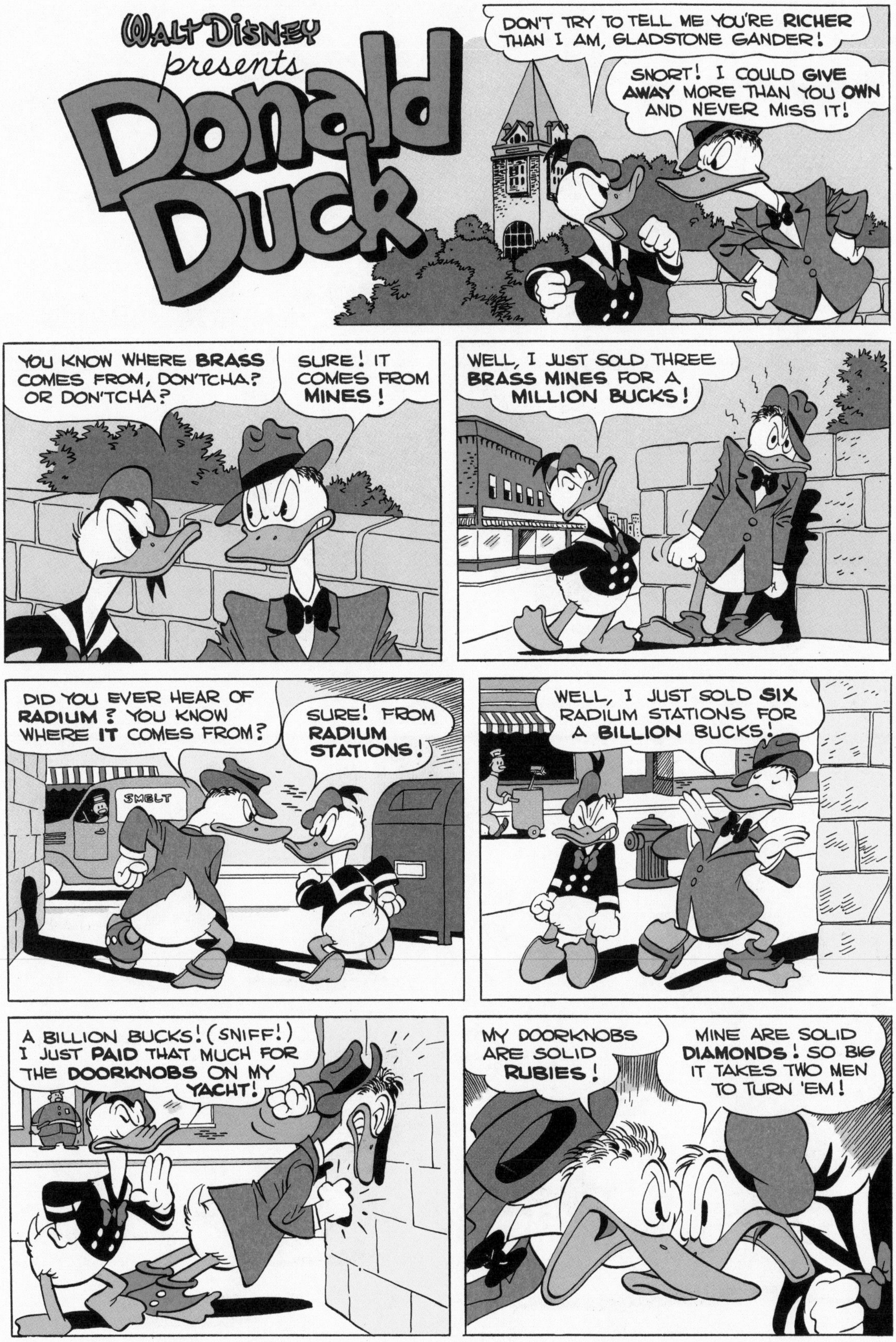
WALT DISNEY
presents
Donald Duck
DON'T TRY TO TELL ME YOU'RE RICHER THAN I AM, GLADSTONE GANDER!
SNORT! I COULD GIVE AWAY MORE THAN YOU OWN AND NEVER MISS IT!
YOU KNOW WHERE BRASS COMES FROM, DON'TCHA? OR DON'TCHA?
SURE! IT COMES FROM MINES!
WELL, I JUST SOLD THREE BRASS MINES FOR A MILLION BUCKS!
DID YOU EVER HEAR OF RADIUM? YOU KNOW WHERE IT COMES FROM?
SURE! FROM RADIUM STATIONS!
SMELT
WELL, I JUST SOLD SIX RADIUM STATIONS FOR A BILLION BUCKS!
A BILLION BUCKS! (SNIFF!) I JUST PAID THAT MUCH FOR THE DOORKNOBS ON MY YACHT!
MY DOORKNOBS ARE SOLID RUBIES!
MINE ARE SOLID DIAMONDS! SO BIG IT TAKES TWO MEN TO TURN 'EM!

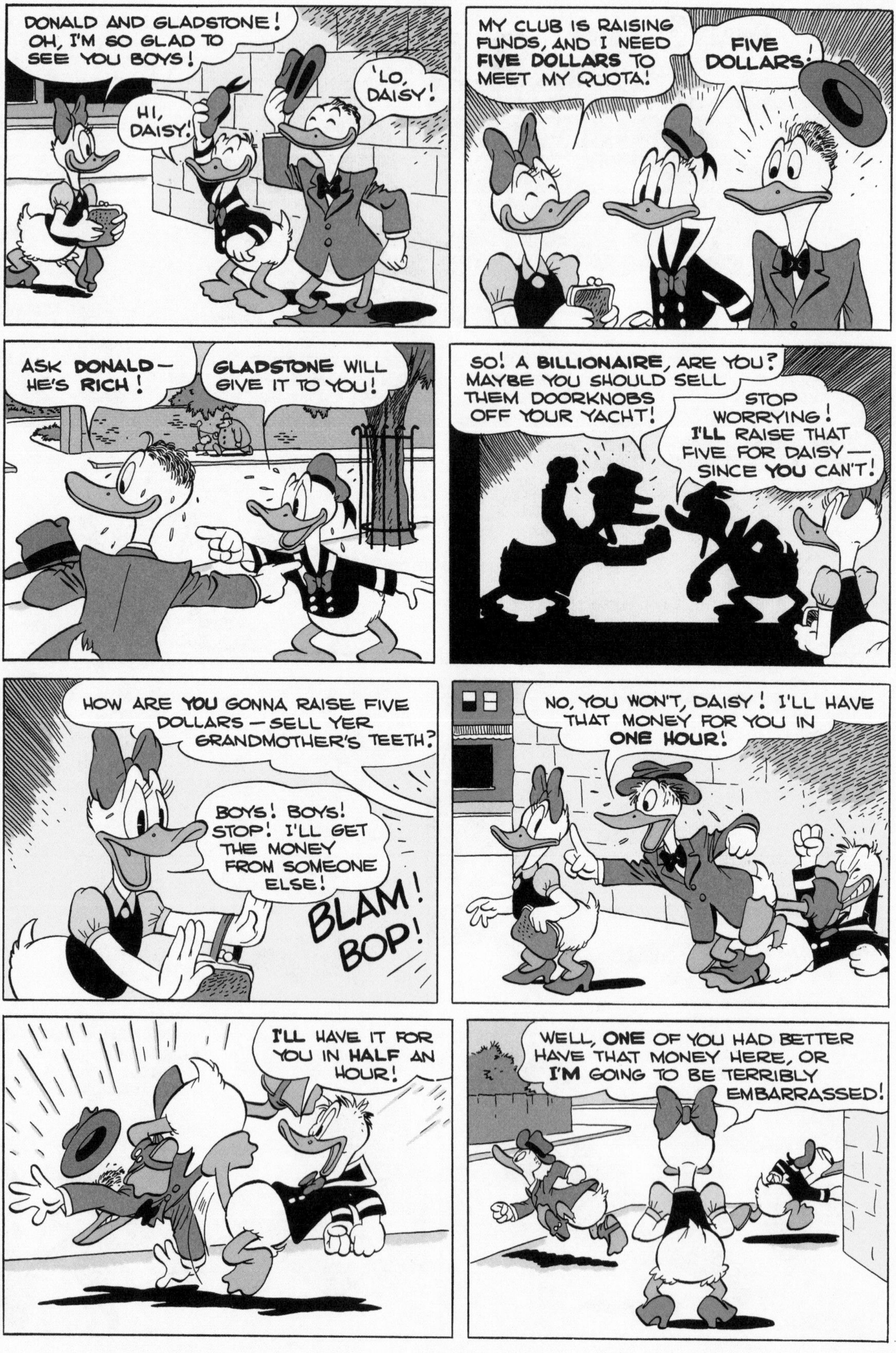
DONALD AND GLADSTONE! OH, I'M SO GLAD TO SEE YOU BOYS!
HI, DAISY!
'LO, DAISY!
MY CLUB IS RAISING FUNDS, AND I NEED **FIVE DOLLARS** TO MEET MY QUOTA!
FIVE DOLLARS!
ASK **DONALD**— HE'S **RICH**!
GLADSTONE WILL GIVE IT TO YOU!
SO! A **BILLIONAIRE**, ARE YOU? MAYBE YOU SHOULD SELL THEM DOORKNOBS OFF YOUR YACHT!
STOP WORRYING! **I'LL** RAISE THAT FIVE FOR DAISY— SINCE **YOU** CAN'T!
HOW ARE **YOU** GONNA RAISE FIVE DOLLARS—SELL YER GRANDMOTHER'S TEETH?
BOYS! BOYS! STOP! I'LL GET THE MONEY FROM SOMEONE ELSE!
BLAM! BOP!
NO, YOU WON'T, DAISY! I'LL HAVE THAT MONEY FOR YOU IN **ONE HOUR**!
I'LL HAVE IT FOR YOU IN **HALF** AN HOUR!
WELL, **ONE** OF YOU HAD BETTER HAVE THAT MONEY HERE, OR **I'M** GOING TO BE TERRIBLY EMBARRASSED!

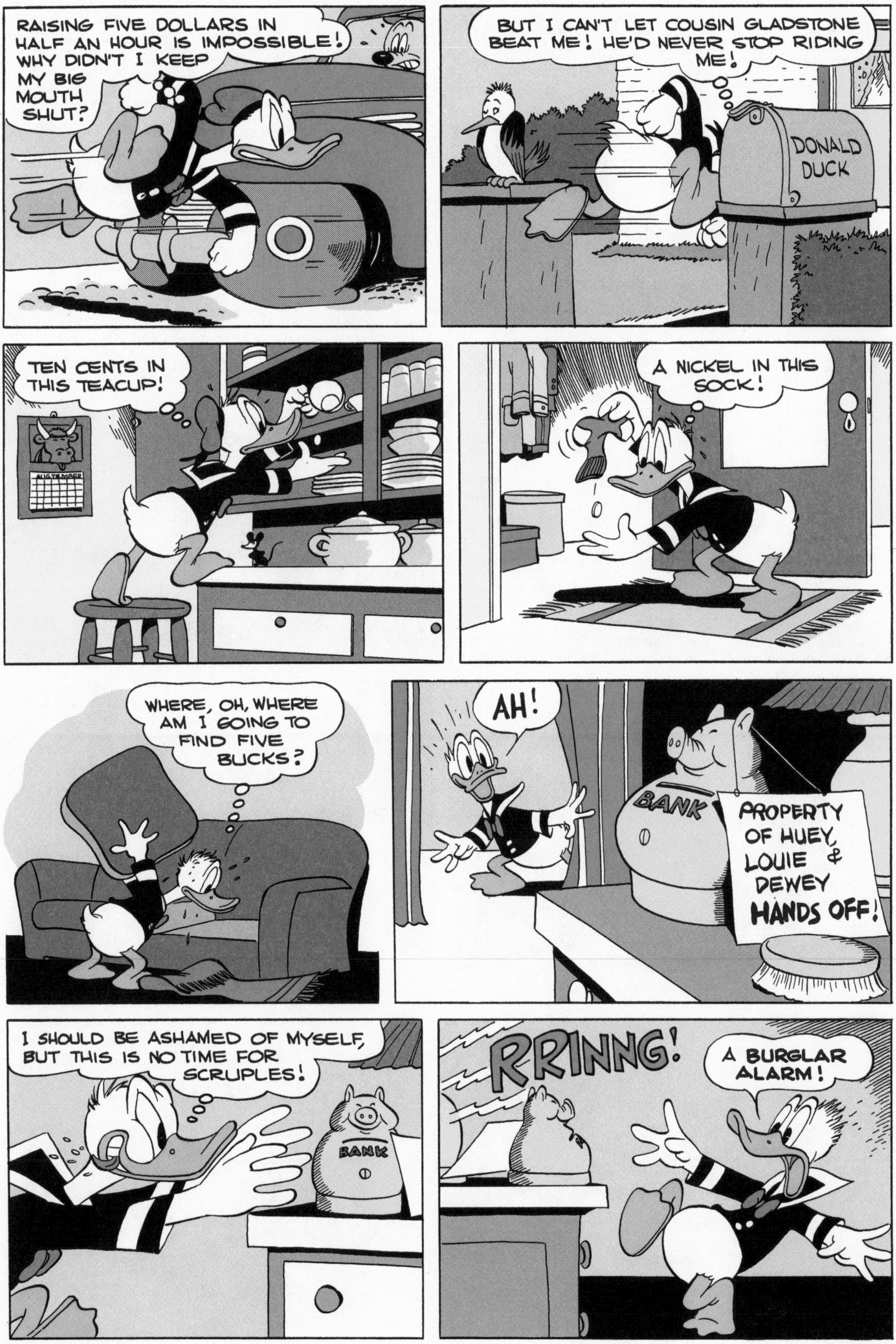
RAISING FIVE DOLLARS IN HALF AN HOUR IS IMPOSSIBLE! WHY DIDN'T I KEEP MY BIG MOUTH SHUT?
BUT I CAN'T LET COUSIN GLADSTONE BEAT ME! HE'D NEVER STOP RIDING ME!
DONALD DUCK
TEN CENTS IN THIS TEACUP!
A NICKEL IN THIS SOCK!
WHERE, OH, WHERE AM I GOING TO FIND FIVE BUCKS?
AH!
BANK
PROPERTY OF HUEY, LOUIE & DEWEY HANDS OFF!
I SHOULD BE ASHAMED OF MYSELF, BUT THIS IS NO TIME FOR SCRUPLES!
BANK
RRINNG!
A BURGLAR ALARM!

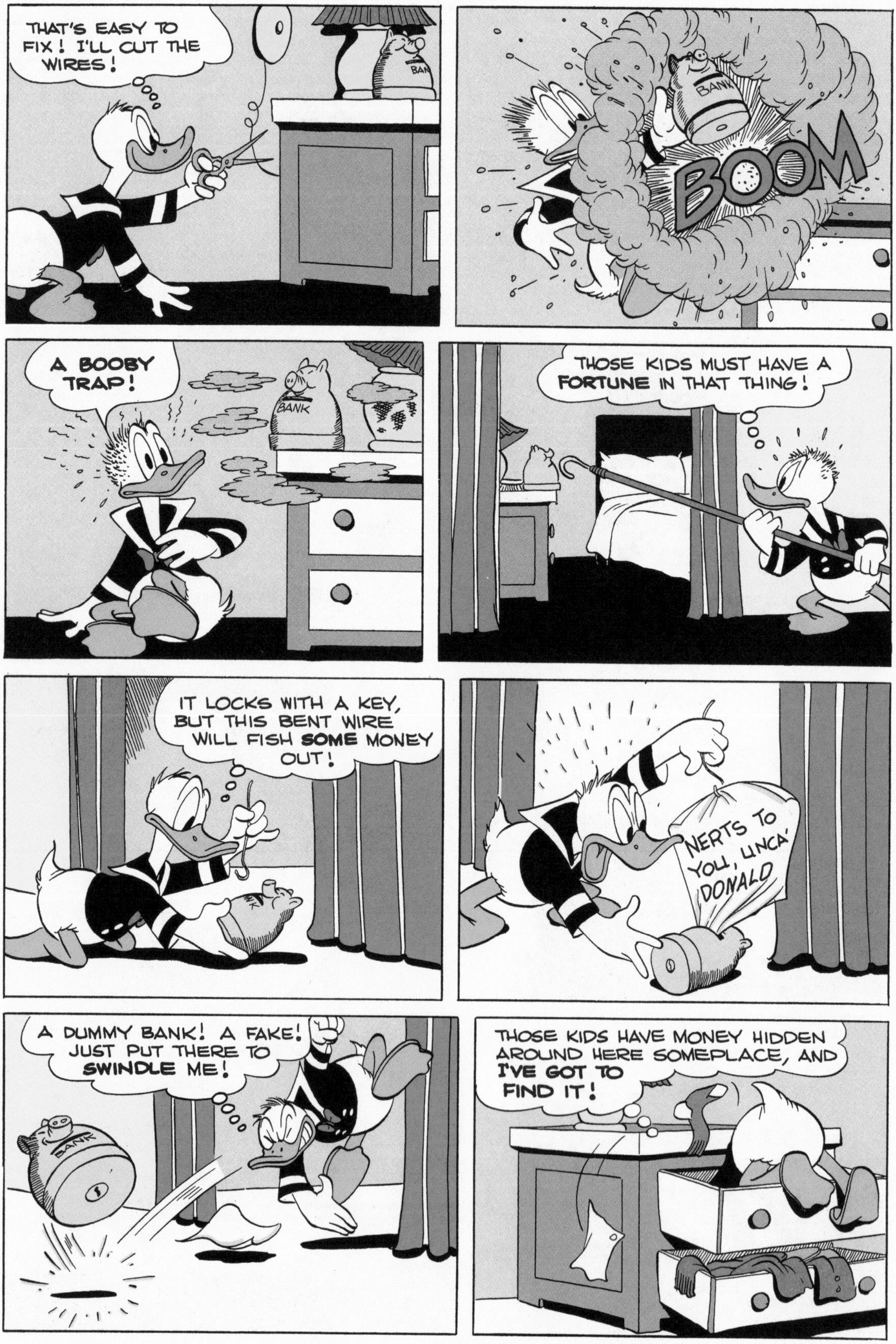
THAT'S EASY TO FIX! I'LL CUT THE WIRES!
BANK
BANK
BOOM
A BOOBY TRAP!
BANK
THOSE KIDS MUST HAVE A FORTUNE IN THAT THING!
IT LOCKS WITH A KEY, BUT THIS BENT WIRE WILL FISH SOME MONEY OUT!
NERTS TO YOU, UNCA' DONALD
A DUMMY BANK! A FAKE! JUST PUT THERE TO SWINDLE ME!
BANK
THOSE KIDS HAVE MONEY HIDDEN AROUND HERE SOMEPLACE, AND I'VE GOT TO FIND IT!

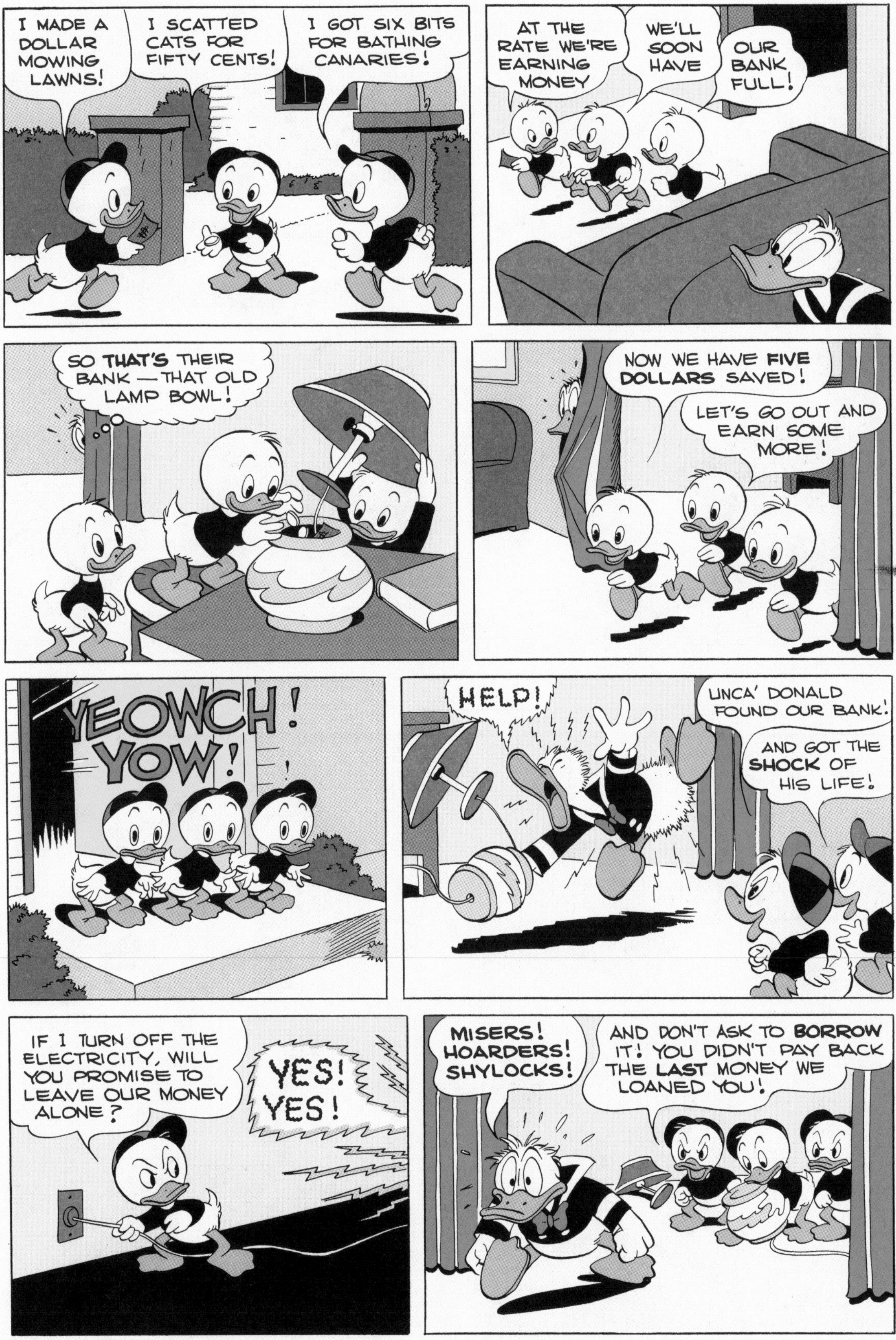
I MADE A DOLLAR MOWING LAWNS!
I SCATTED CATS FOR FIFTY CENTS!
I GOT SIX BITS FOR BATHING CANARIES!
AT THE RATE WE'RE EARNING MONEY
WE'LL SOON HAVE
OUR BANK FULL!
SO THAT'S THEIR BANK — THAT OLD LAMP BOWL!
NOW WE HAVE FIVE DOLLARS SAVED!
LET'S GO OUT AND EARN SOME MORE!
YEOWCH! YOW!
HELP!
UNCA' DONALD FOUND OUR BANK!
AND GOT THE SHOCK OF HIS LIFE!
IF I TURN OFF THE ELECTRICITY, WILL YOU PROMISE TO LEAVE OUR MONEY ALONE?
YES! YES!
MISERS! HOARDERS! SHYLOCKS!
AND DON'T ASK TO BORROW IT! YOU DIDN'T PAY BACK THE LAST MONEY WE LOANED YOU!

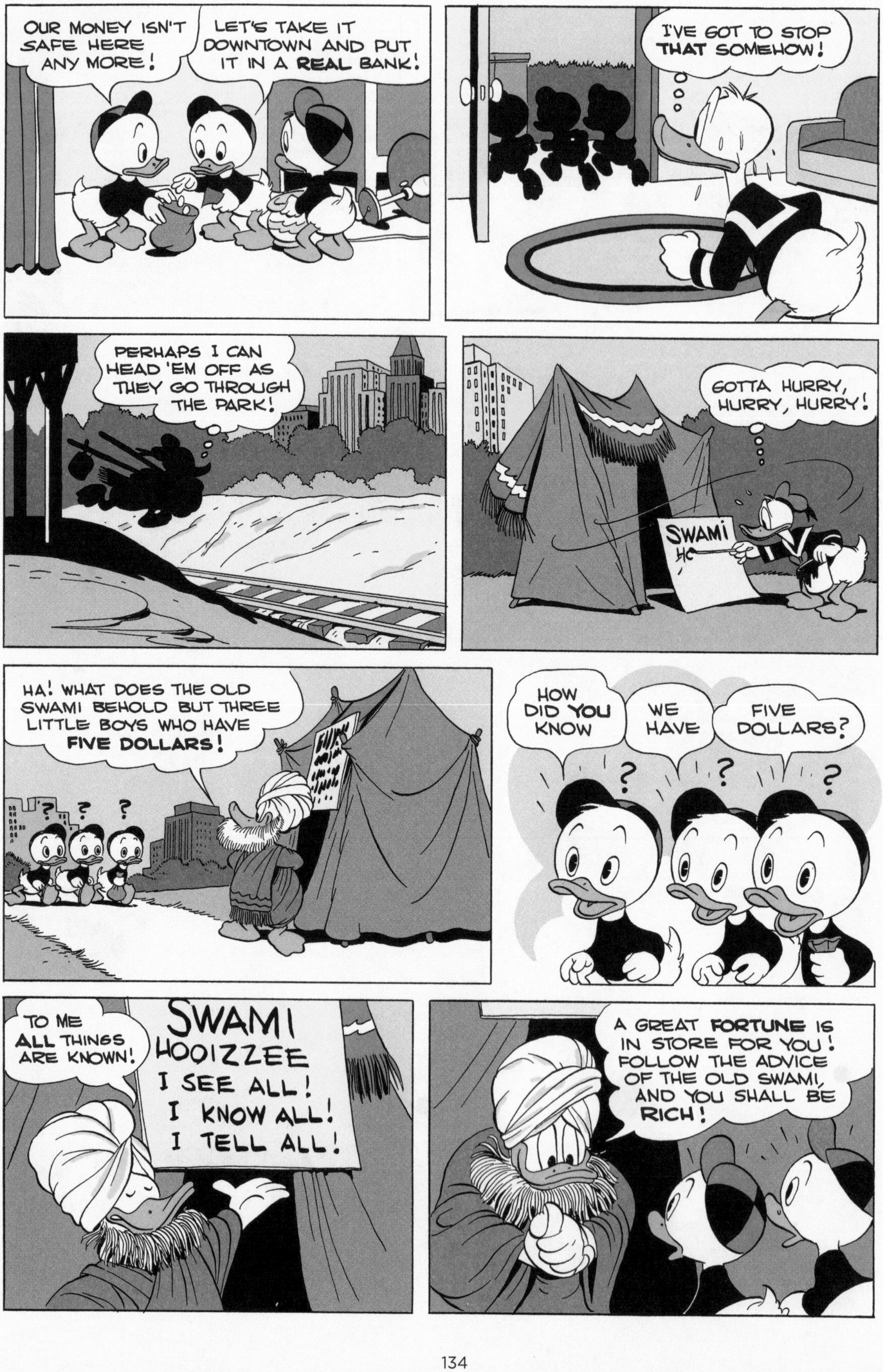
OUR MONEY ISN'T SAFE HERE ANY MORE!
LET'S TAKE IT DOWNTOWN AND PUT IT IN A **REAL** BANK!
I'VE GOT TO STOP **THAT** SOMEHOW!
PERHAPS I CAN HEAD 'EM OFF AS THEY GO THROUGH THE PARK!
GOTTA HURRY, HURRY, HURRY!
SWAMI
HA! WHAT DOES THE OLD SWAMI BEHOLD BUT THREE LITTLE BOYS WHO HAVE **FIVE DOLLARS**!
HOW DID **YOU** KNOW
WE HAVE
FIVE DOLLARS?
TO ME **ALL** THINGS ARE KNOWN!
SWAMI HOOIZZEE
I SEE ALL!
I KNOW ALL!
I TELL ALL!
A GREAT **FORTUNE** IS IN STORE FOR YOU! FOLLOW THE ADVICE OF THE OLD SWAMI, AND YOU SHALL BE **RICH**!

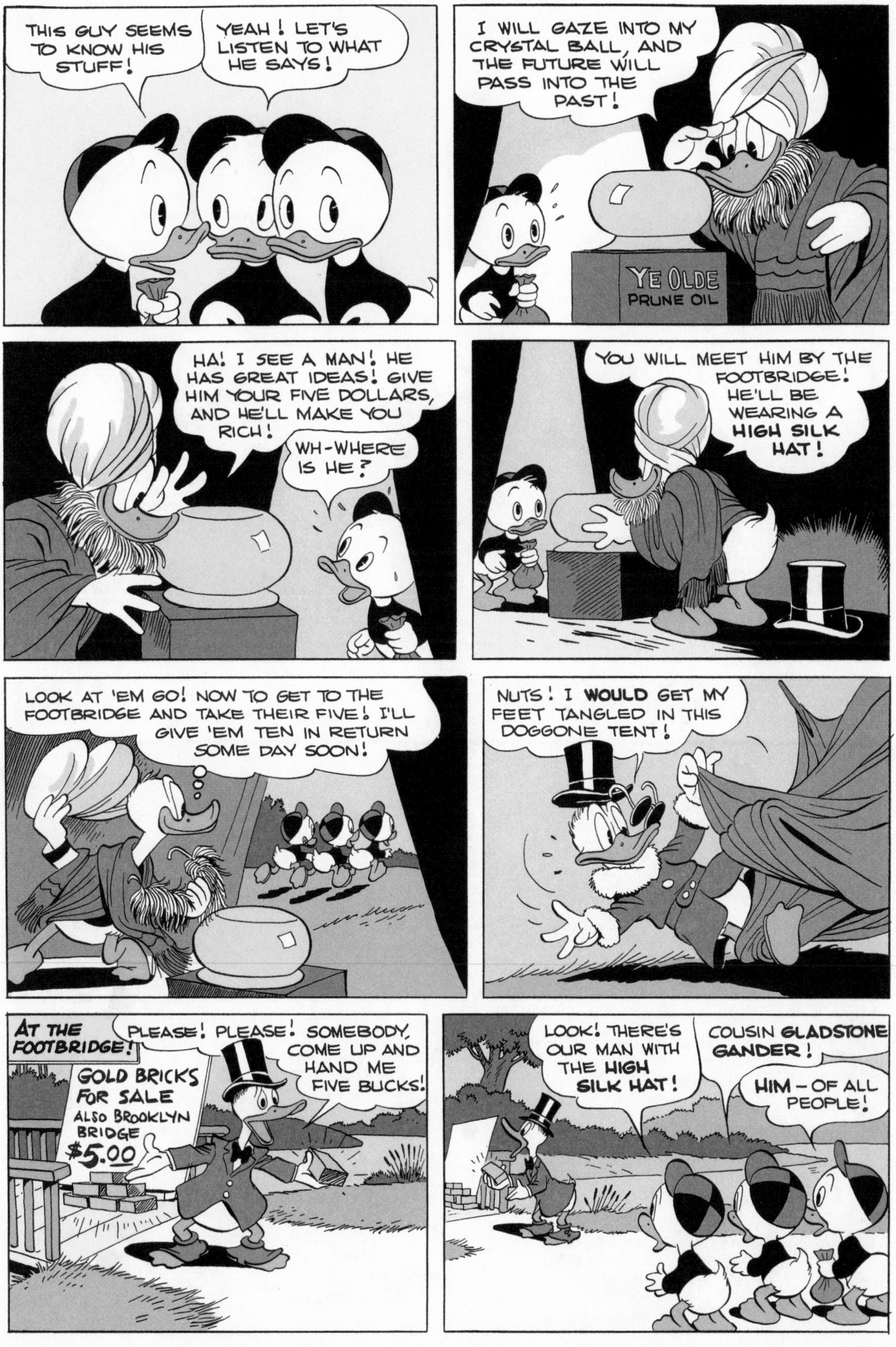
THIS GUY SEEMS TO KNOW HIS STUFF!
YEAH! LET'S LISTEN TO WHAT HE SAYS!
I WILL GAZE INTO MY CRYSTAL BALL, AND THE FUTURE WILL PASS INTO THE PAST!
YE OLDE PRUNE OIL
HA! I SEE A MAN! HE HAS GREAT IDEAS! GIVE HIM YOUR FIVE DOLLARS, AND HE'LL MAKE YOU RICH!
WH-WHERE IS HE?
YOU WILL MEET HIM BY THE FOOTBRIDGE! HE'LL BE WEARING A **HIGH SILK HAT**!
LOOK AT 'EM GO! NOW TO GET TO THE FOOTBRIDGE AND TAKE THEIR FIVE! I'LL GIVE 'EM TEN IN RETURN SOME DAY SOON!
NUTS! I **WOULD** GET MY FEET TANGLED IN THIS DOGGONE TENT!
AT THE FOOTBRIDGE!
PLEASE! PLEASE! SOMEBODY, COME UP AND HAND ME FIVE BUCKS!
GOLD BRICKS FOR SALE ALSO BROOKLYN BRIDGE $5.00
LOOK! THERE'S OUR MAN WITH THE **HIGH SILK HAT**!
COUSIN **GLADSTONE GANDER**!
HIM – OF ALL PEOPLE!

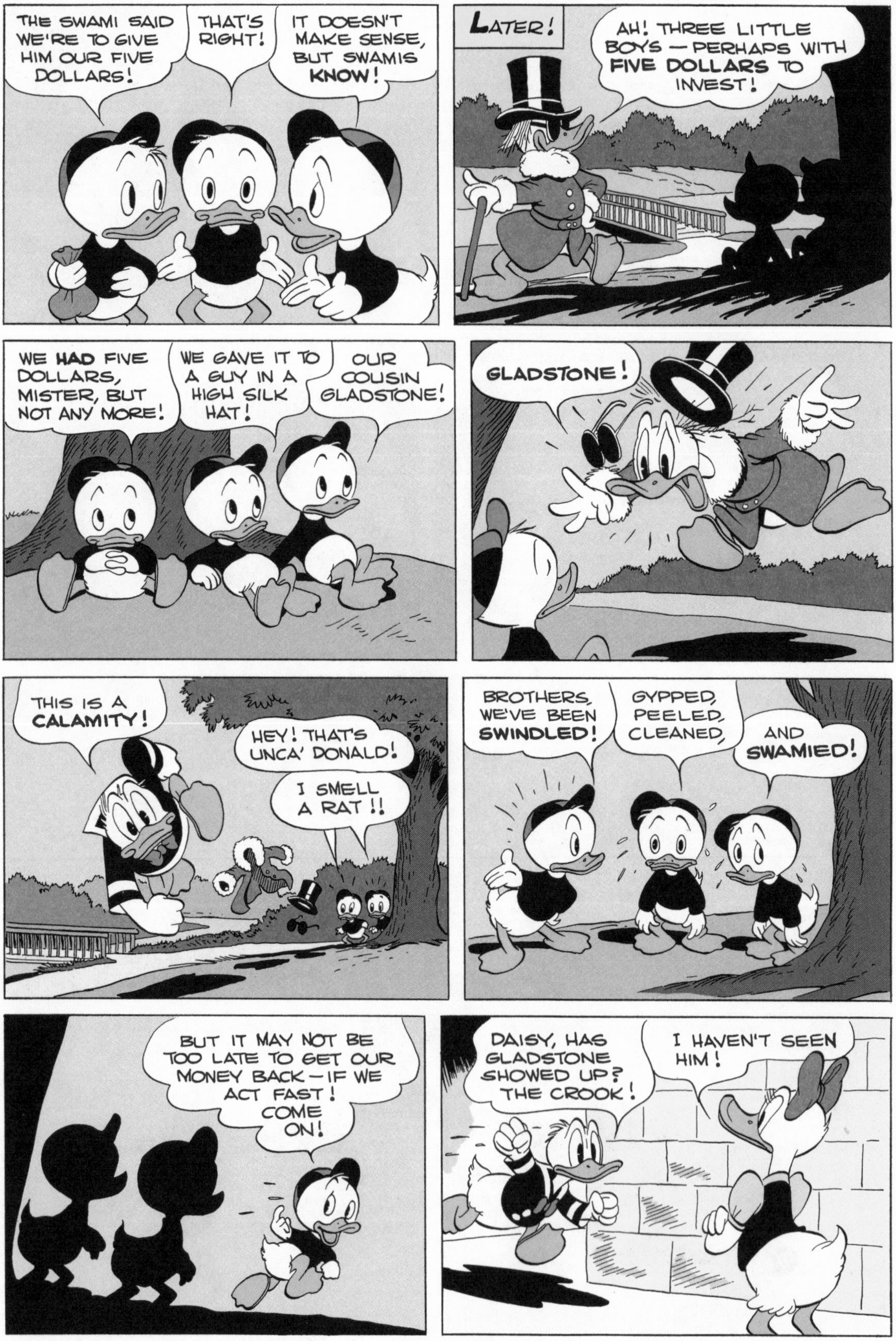
THE SWAMI SAID WE'RE TO GIVE HIM OUR FIVE DOLLARS!
THAT'S RIGHT!
IT DOESN'T MAKE SENSE, BUT SWAMIS KNOW!
LATER!
AH! THREE LITTLE BOYS — PERHAPS WITH FIVE DOLLARS TO INVEST!
WE HAD FIVE DOLLARS, MISTER, BUT NOT ANY MORE!
WE GAVE IT TO A GUY IN A HIGH SILK HAT!
OUR COUSIN GLADSTONE!
GLADSTONE!
THIS IS A CALAMITY!
HEY! THAT'S UNCA' DONALD!
I SMELL A RAT!!
BROTHERS, WE'VE BEEN SWINDLED!
GYPPED, PEELED, CLEANED,
AND SWAMIED!
BUT IT MAY NOT BE TOO LATE TO GET OUR MONEY BACK—IF WE ACT FAST! COME ON!
DAISY, HAS GLADSTONE SHOWED UP? THE CROOK!
I HAVEN'T SEEN HIM!

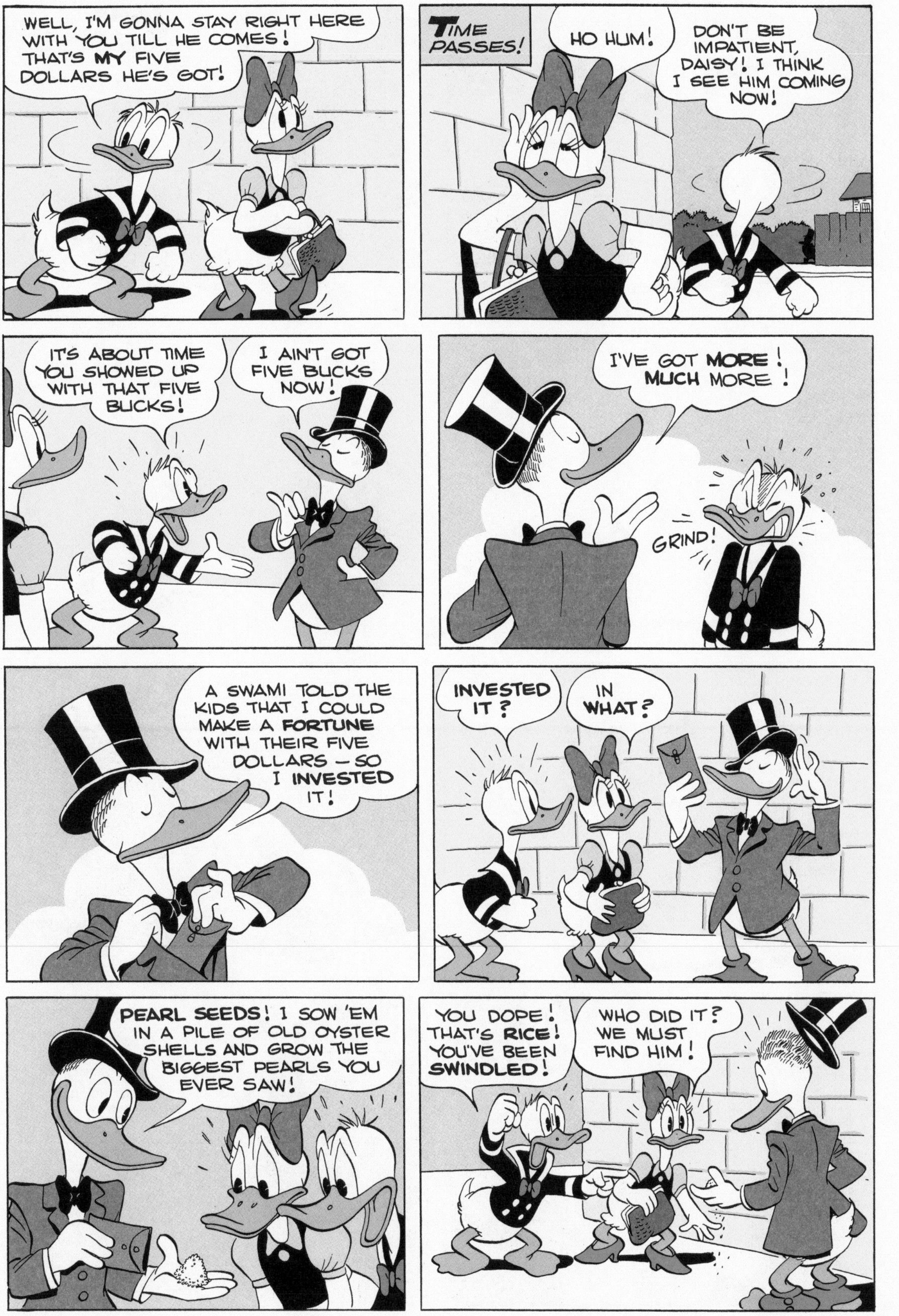
WELL, I'M GONNA STAY RIGHT HERE WITH YOU TILL HE COMES! THAT'S **MY** FIVE DOLLARS HE'S GOT!
TIME PASSES!
HO HUM!
DON'T BE IMPATIENT, DAISY! I THINK I SEE HIM COMING NOW!
IT'S ABOUT TIME YOU SHOWED UP WITH THAT FIVE BUCKS!
I AIN'T GOT FIVE BUCKS NOW!
I'VE GOT **MORE**! **MUCH** MORE!
GRIND!
A SWAMI TOLD THE KIDS THAT I COULD MAKE A **FORTUNE** WITH THEIR FIVE DOLLARS — SO I **INVESTED** IT!
INVESTED IT?
IN **WHAT**?
PEARL SEEDS! I SOW 'EM IN A PILE OF OLD OYSTER SHELLS AND GROW THE BIGGEST PEARLS YOU EVER SAW!
YOU DOPE! THAT'S **RICE**! YOU'VE BEEN **SWINDLED**!
WHO DID IT? WE MUST FIND HIM!

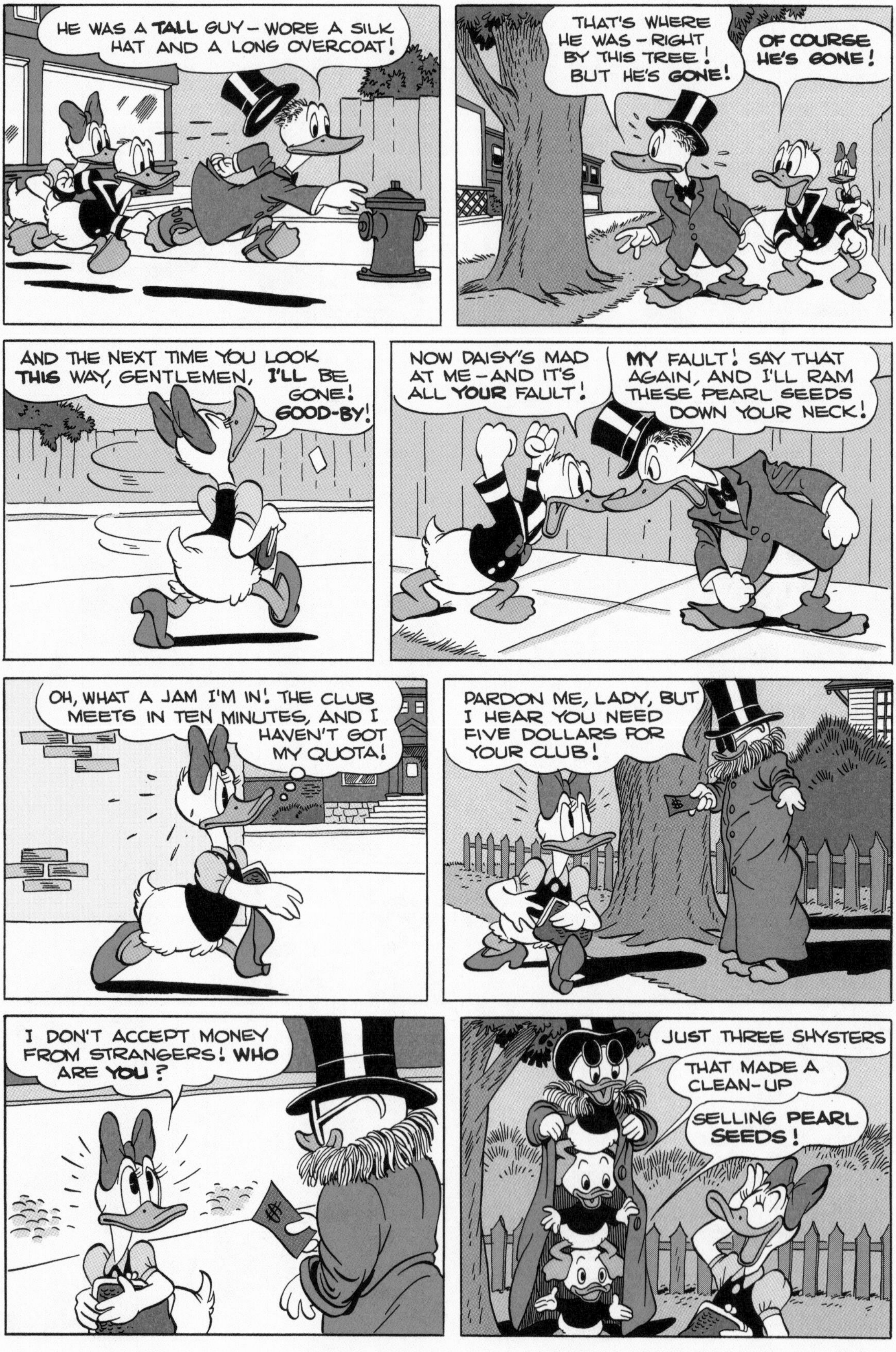
HE WAS A TALL GUY—WORE A SILK HAT AND A LONG OVERCOAT!
THAT'S WHERE HE WAS—RIGHT BY THIS TREE! BUT HE'S GONE!
OF COURSE HE'S GONE!
AND THE NEXT TIME YOU LOOK THIS WAY, GENTLEMEN, I'LL BE GONE! GOOD-BY!
NOW DAISY'S MAD AT ME—AND IT'S ALL YOUR FAULT!
MY FAULT! SAY THAT AGAIN, AND I'LL RAM THESE PEARL SEEDS DOWN YOUR NECK!
OH, WHAT A JAM I'M IN! THE CLUB MEETS IN TEN MINUTES, AND I HAVEN'T GOT MY QUOTA!
PARDON ME, LADY, BUT I HEAR YOU NEED FIVE DOLLARS FOR YOUR CLUB!
I DON'T ACCEPT MONEY FROM STRANGERS! WHO ARE YOU?
JUST THREE SHYSTERS
THAT MADE A CLEAN-UP
SELLING PEARL SEEDS!

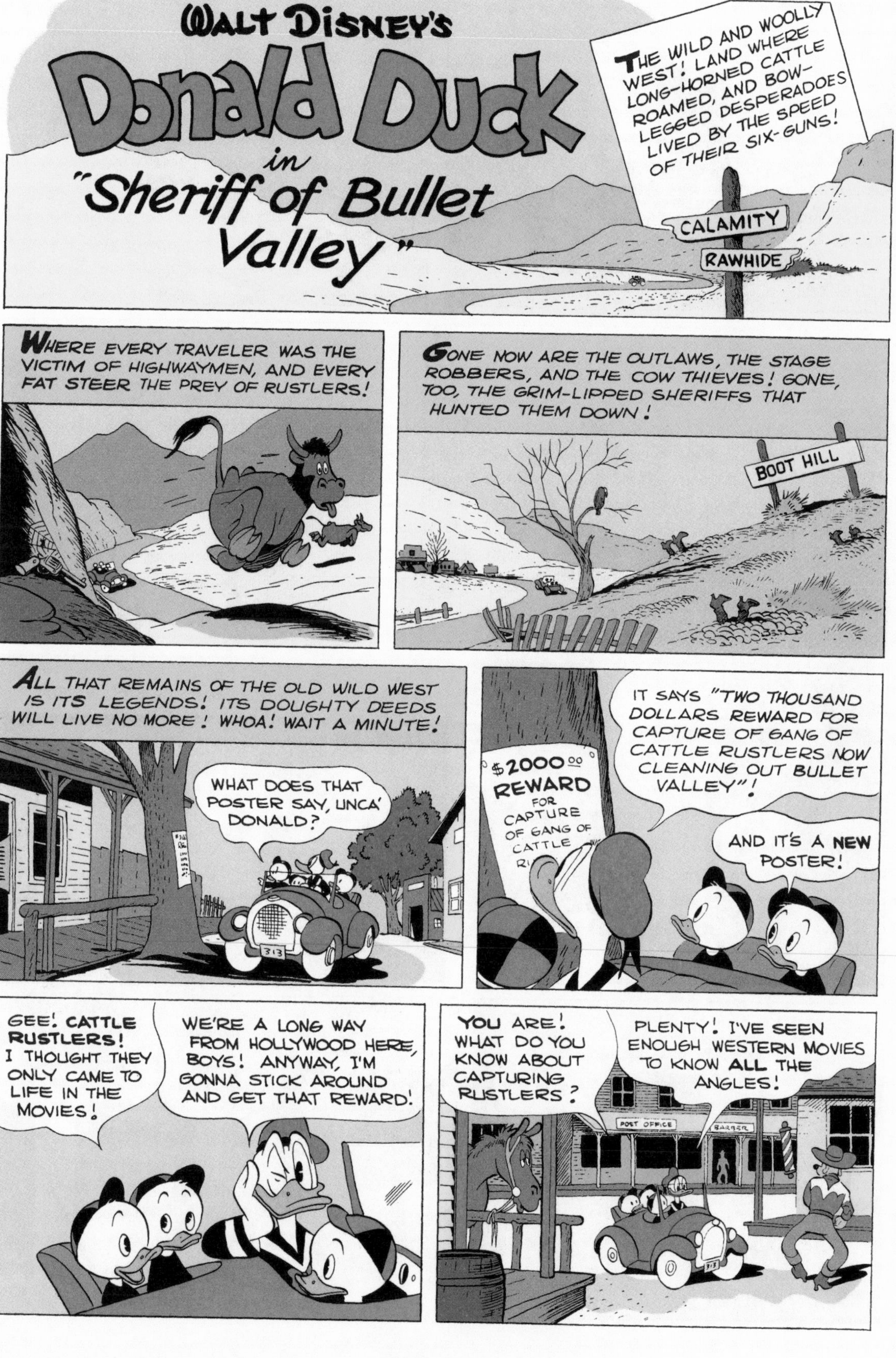

WALT DISNEY'S
Donald Duck
in
"Sheriff of Bullet Valley"
THE WILD AND WOOLLY WEST! LAND WHERE LONG-HORNED CATTLE ROAMED, AND BOW-LEGGED DESPERADOES LIVED BY THE SPEED OF THEIR SIX-GUNS!
CALAMITY
RAWHIDE
WHERE EVERY TRAVELER WAS THE VICTIM OF HIGHWAYMEN, AND EVERY FAT STEER THE PREY OF RUSTLERS!
GONE NOW ARE THE OUTLAWS, THE STAGE ROBBERS, AND THE COW THIEVES! GONE, TOO, THE GRIM-LIPPED SHERIFFS THAT HUNTED THEM DOWN!
BOOT HILL
ALL THAT REMAINS OF THE OLD WILD WEST IS ITS LEGENDS! ITS DOUGHTY DEEDS WILL LIVE NO MORE! WHOA! WAIT A MINUTE!
WHAT DOES THAT POSTER SAY, UNCA' DONALD?
313
$2000.00 REWARD FOR CAPTURE OF GANG OF CATTLE
IT SAYS "TWO THOUSAND DOLLARS REWARD FOR CAPTURE OF GANG OF CATTLE RUSTLERS NOW CLEANING OUT BULLET VALLEY"!
AND IT'S A NEW POSTER!
GEE! CATTLE RUSTLERS! I THOUGHT THEY ONLY CAME TO LIFE IN THE MOVIES!
WE'RE A LONG WAY FROM HOLLYWOOD HERE, BOYS! ANYWAY, I'M GONNA STICK AROUND AND GET THAT REWARD!
YOU ARE! WHAT DO YOU KNOW ABOUT CAPTURING RUSTLERS?
PLENTY! I'VE SEEN ENOUGH WESTERN MOVIES TO KNOW ALL THE ANGLES!
POST OFFICE
BARBER

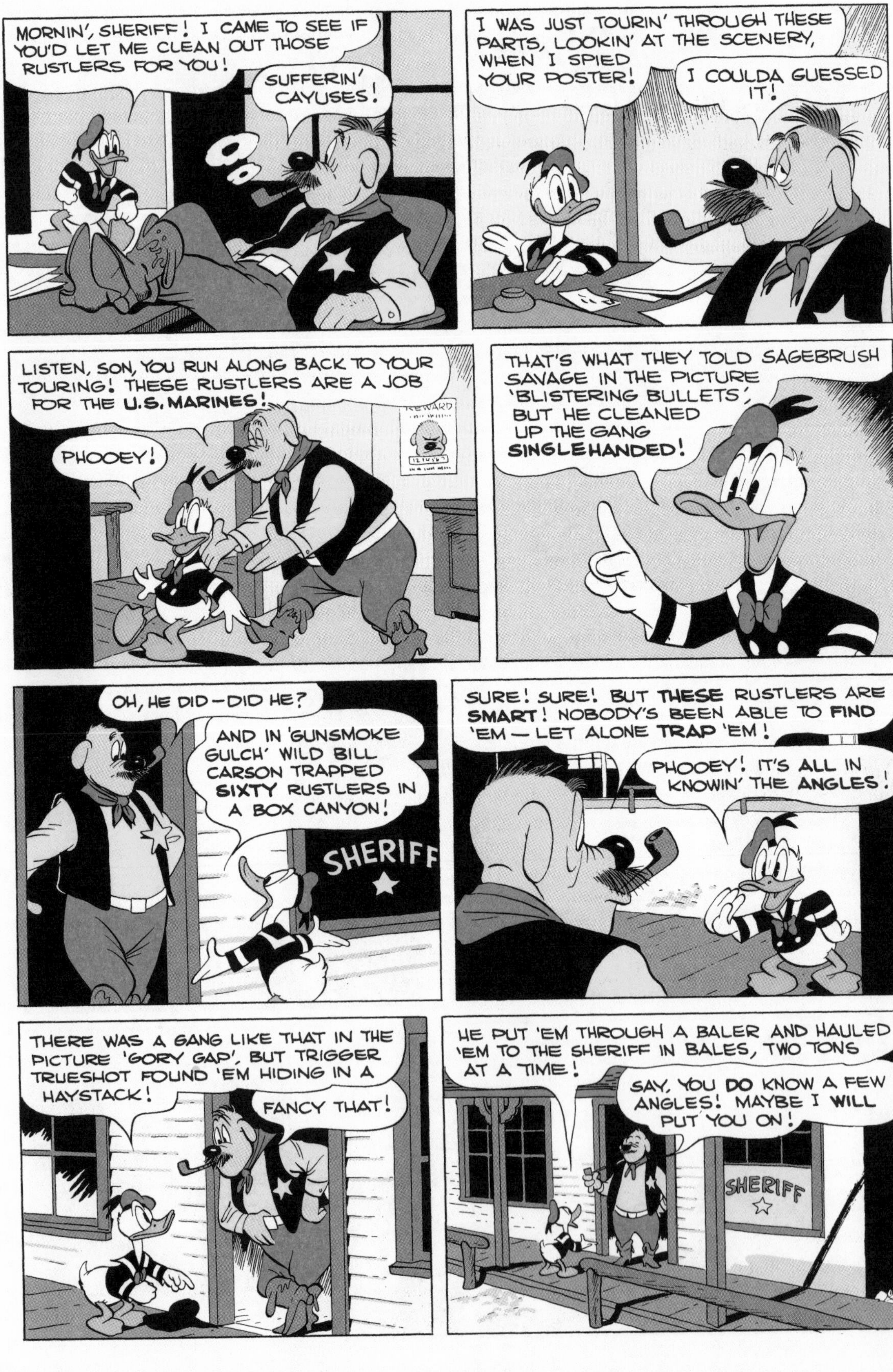
MORNIN', SHERIFF! I CAME TO SEE IF YOU'D LET ME CLEAN OUT THOSE RUSTLERS FOR YOU!
SUFFERIN' CAYUSES!
I WAS JUST TOURIN' THROUGH THESE PARTS, LOOKIN' AT THE SCENERY, WHEN I SPIED YOUR POSTER!
I COULDA GUESSED IT!
LISTEN, SON, YOU RUN ALONG BACK TO YOUR TOURING! THESE RUSTLERS ARE A JOB FOR THE U.S. MARINES!
REWARD
PHOOEY!
THAT'S WHAT THEY TOLD SAGEBRUSH SAVAGE IN THE PICTURE 'BLISTERING BULLETS', BUT HE CLEANED UP THE GANG SINGLEHANDED!
OH, HE DID—DID HE?
AND IN 'GUNSMOKE GULCH' WILD BILL CARSON TRAPPED SIXTY RUSTLERS IN A BOX CANYON!
SHERIFF
SURE! SURE! BUT THESE RUSTLERS ARE SMART! NOBODY'S BEEN ABLE TO FIND 'EM—LET ALONE TRAP 'EM!
PHOOEY! IT'S ALL IN KNOWIN' THE ANGLES!
THERE WAS A GANG LIKE THAT IN THE PICTURE 'GORY GAP', BUT TRIGGER TRUESHOT FOUND 'EM HIDING IN A HAYSTACK!
FANCY THAT!
HE PUT 'EM THROUGH A BALER AND HAULED 'EM TO THE SHERIFF IN BALES, TWO TONS AT A TIME!
SAY, YOU DO KNOW A FEW ANGLES! MAYBE I WILL PUT YOU ON!
SHERIFF

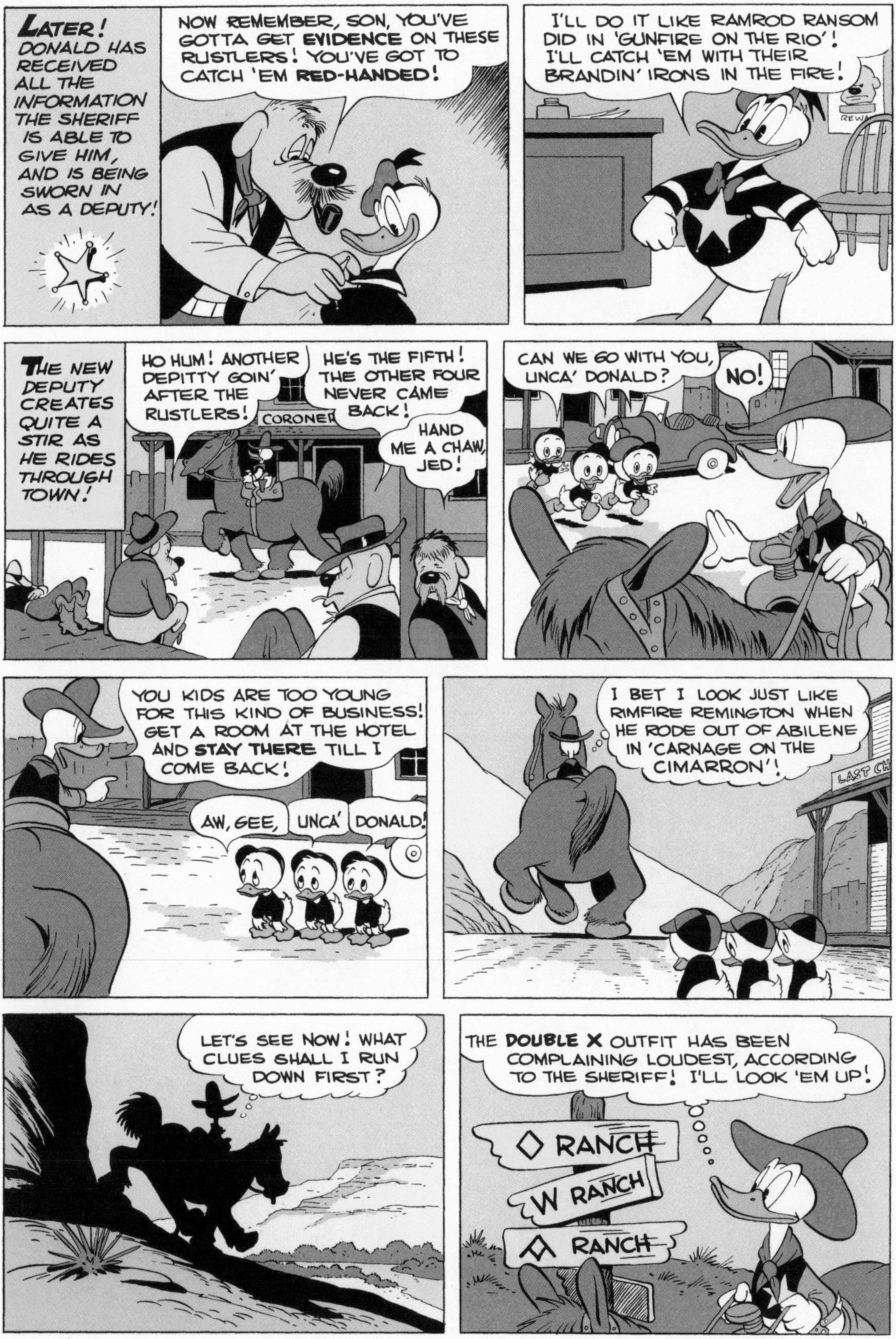
LATER! DONALD HAS RECEIVED ALL THE INFORMATION THE SHERIFF IS ABLE TO GIVE HIM, AND IS BEING SWORN IN AS A DEPUTY!
NOW REMEMBER, SON, YOU'VE GOTTA GET **EVIDENCE** ON THESE RUSTLERS! YOU'VE GOT TO CATCH 'EM **RED-HANDED**!
I'LL DO IT LIKE RAMROD RANSOM DID IN 'GUNFIRE ON THE RIO'! I'LL CATCH 'EM WITH THEIR BRANDIN' IRONS IN THE FIRE!
THE NEW DEPUTY CREATES QUITE A STIR AS HE RIDES THROUGH TOWN!
HO HUM! ANOTHER DEPITTY GOIN' AFTER THE RUSTLERS!
HE'S THE FIFTH! THE OTHER FOUR NEVER CAME BACK!
CORONER
HAND ME A CHAW, JED!
CAN WE GO WITH YOU, UNCA' DONALD?
NO!
YOU KIDS ARE TOO YOUNG FOR THIS KIND OF BUSINESS! GET A ROOM AT THE HOTEL AND **STAY THERE** TILL I COME BACK!
AW, GEE,
UNCA'
DONALD!
I BET I LOOK JUST LIKE RIMFIRE REMINGTON WHEN HE RODE OUT OF ABILENE IN 'CARNAGE ON THE CIMARRON'!
LET'S SEE NOW! WHAT CLUES SHALL I RUN DOWN FIRST?
THE **DOUBLE X** OUTFIT HAS BEEN COMPLAINING LOUDEST, ACCORDING TO THE SHERIFF! I'LL LOOK 'EM UP!
RANCH
W RANCH
RANCH

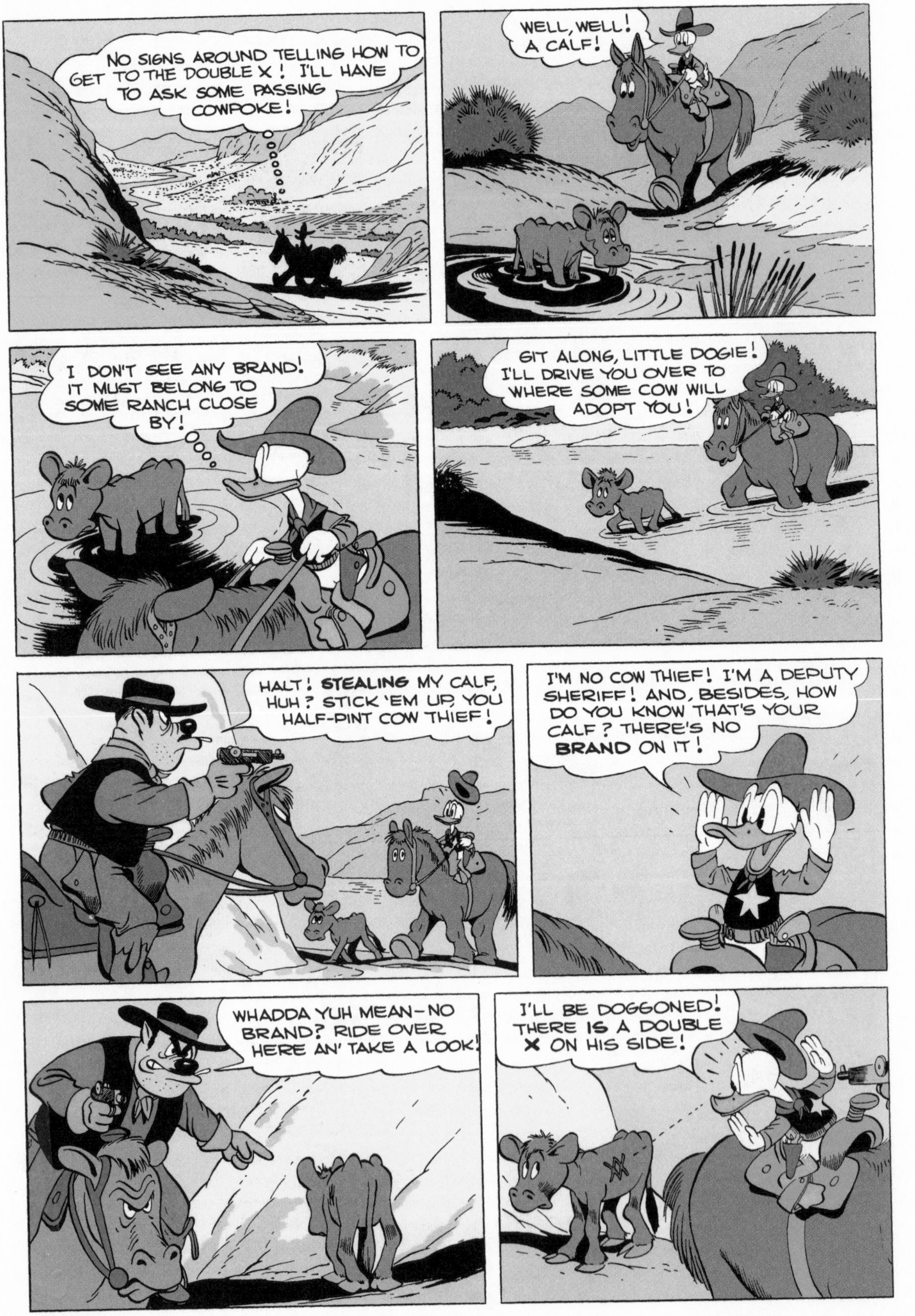
NO SIGNS AROUND TELLING HOW TO GET TO THE DOUBLE X! I'LL HAVE TO ASK SOME PASSING COWPOKE!
WELL, WELL! A CALF!
I DON'T SEE ANY BRAND! IT MUST BELONG TO SOME RANCH CLOSE BY!
GIT ALONG, LITTLE DOGIE! I'LL DRIVE YOU OVER TO WHERE SOME COW WILL ADOPT YOU!
HALT! STEALING MY CALF, HUH? STICK 'EM UP, YOU HALF-PINT COW THIEF!
I'M NO COW THIEF! I'M A DEPUTY SHERIFF! AND, BESIDES, HOW DO YOU KNOW THAT'S YOUR CALF? THERE'S NO BRAND ON IT!
WHADDA YUH MEAN—NO BRAND? RIDE OVER HERE AN' TAKE A LOOK!
I'LL BE DOGGONED! THERE IS A DOUBLE X ON HIS SIDE!

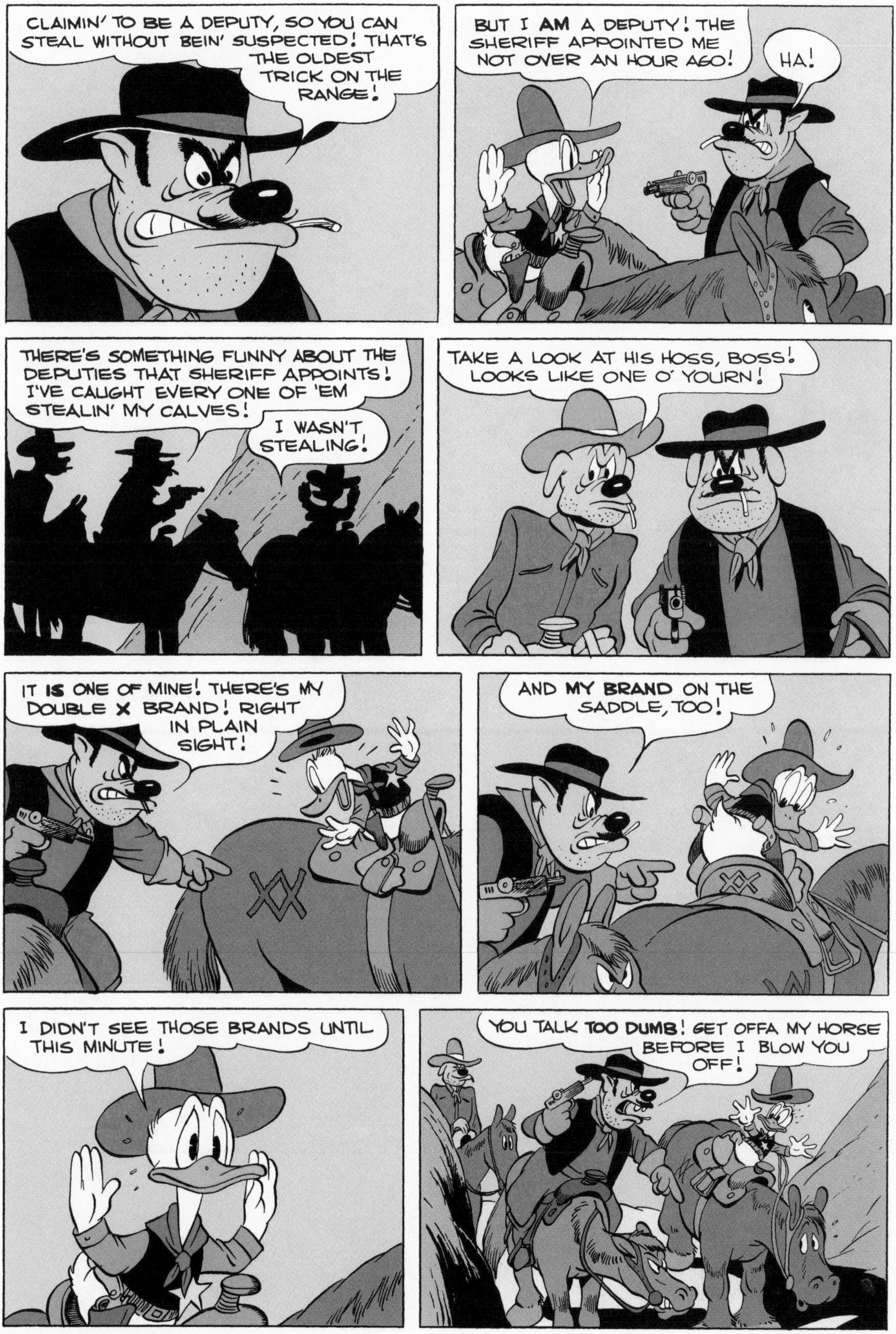
CLAIMIN' TO BE A DEPUTY, SO YOU CAN STEAL WITHOUT BEIN' SUSPECTED! THAT'S THE OLDEST TRICK ON THE RANGE!
BUT I **AM** A DEPUTY! THE SHERIFF APPOINTED ME NOT OVER AN HOUR AGO!
HA!
THERE'S SOMETHING FUNNY ABOUT THE DEPUTIES THAT SHERIFF APPOINTS! I'VE CAUGHT EVERY ONE OF 'EM STEALIN' MY CALVES!
I WASN'T STEALING!
TAKE A LOOK AT HIS HOSS, BOSS! LOOKS LIKE ONE O' YOURN!
IT **IS** ONE OF MINE! THERE'S MY DOUBLE **X** BRAND! RIGHT IN PLAIN SIGHT!
AND **MY BRAND** ON THE SADDLE, TOO!
I DIDN'T SEE THOSE BRANDS UNTIL THIS MINUTE!
YOU TALK **TOO DUMB**! GET OFFA MY HORSE BEFORE I BLOW YOU OFF!

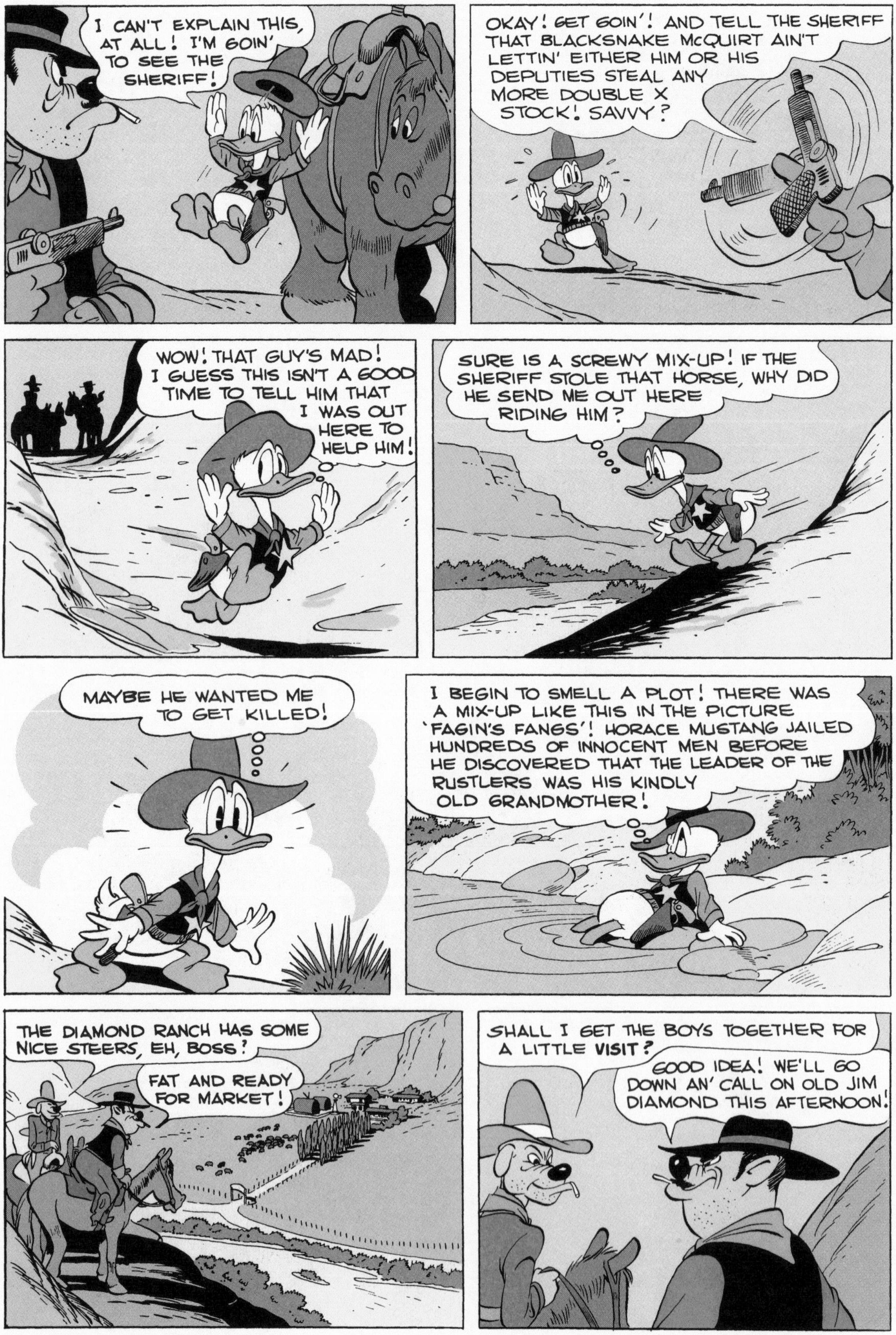
I CAN'T EXPLAIN THIS, AT ALL! I'M GOIN' TO SEE THE SHERIFF!
OKAY! GET GOIN'! AND TELL THE SHERIFF THAT BLACKSNAKE McQUIRT AIN'T LETTIN' EITHER HIM OR HIS DEPUTIES STEAL ANY MORE DOUBLE X STOCK! SAVVY?
WOW! THAT GUY'S MAD! I GUESS THIS ISN'T A GOOD TIME TO TELL HIM THAT I WAS OUT HERE TO HELP HIM!
SURE IS A SCREWY MIX-UP! IF THE SHERIFF STOLE THAT HORSE, WHY DID HE SEND ME OUT HERE RIDING HIM?
MAYBE HE WANTED ME TO GET KILLED!
I BEGIN TO SMELL A PLOT! THERE WAS A MIX-UP LIKE THIS IN THE PICTURE 'FAGIN'S FANGS'! HORACE MUSTANG JAILED HUNDREDS OF INNOCENT MEN BEFORE HE DISCOVERED THAT THE LEADER OF THE RUSTLERS WAS HIS KINDLY OLD GRANDMOTHER!
THE DIAMOND RANCH HAS SOME NICE STEERS, EH, BOSS?
FAT AND READY FOR MARKET!
SHALL I GET THE BOYS TOGETHER FOR A LITTLE VISIT?
GOOD IDEA! WE'LL GO DOWN AN' CALL ON OLD JIM DIAMOND THIS AFTERNOON!

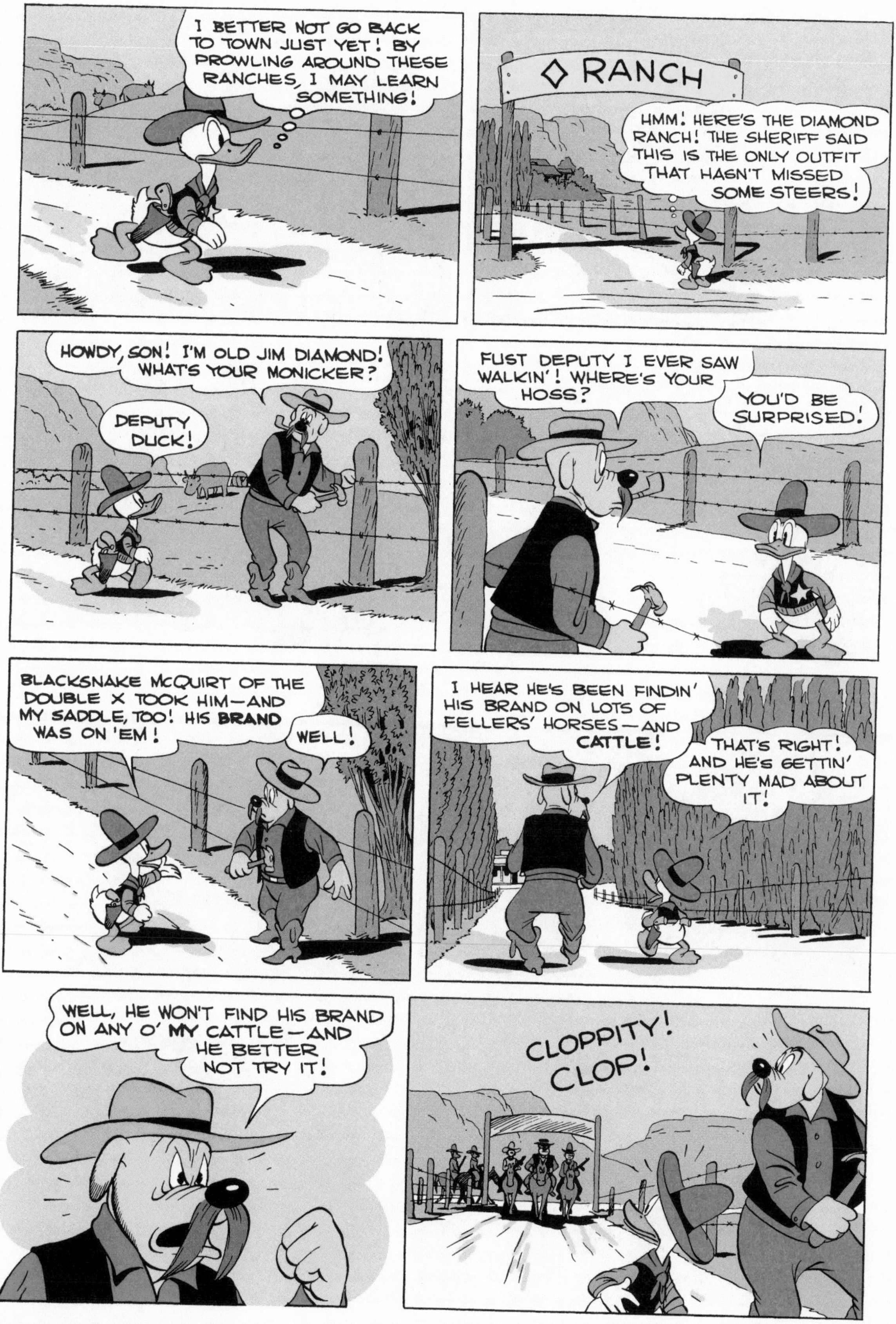
I BETTER NOT GO BACK TO TOWN JUST YET! BY PROWLING AROUND THESE RANCHES, I MAY LEARN SOMETHING!
◊ RANCH
HMM! HERE'S THE DIAMOND RANCH! THE SHERIFF SAID THIS IS THE ONLY OUTFIT THAT HASN'T MISSED SOME STEERS!
HOWDY, SON! I'M OLD JIM DIAMOND! WHAT'S YOUR MONICKER?
DEPUTY DUCK!
FUST DEPUTY I EVER SAW WALKIN'! WHERE'S YOUR HOSS?
YOU'D BE SURPRISED!
BLACKSNAKE McQUIRT OF THE DOUBLE X TOOK HIM—AND MY SADDLE, TOO! HIS BRAND WAS ON 'EM!
WELL!
I HEAR HE'S BEEN FINDIN' HIS BRAND ON LOTS OF FELLERS' HORSES—AND CATTLE!
THAT'S RIGHT! AND HE'S GETTIN' PLENTY MAD ABOUT IT!
WELL, HE WON'T FIND HIS BRAND ON ANY O' MY CATTLE—AND HE BETTER NOT TRY IT!
CLOPPITY! CLOP!

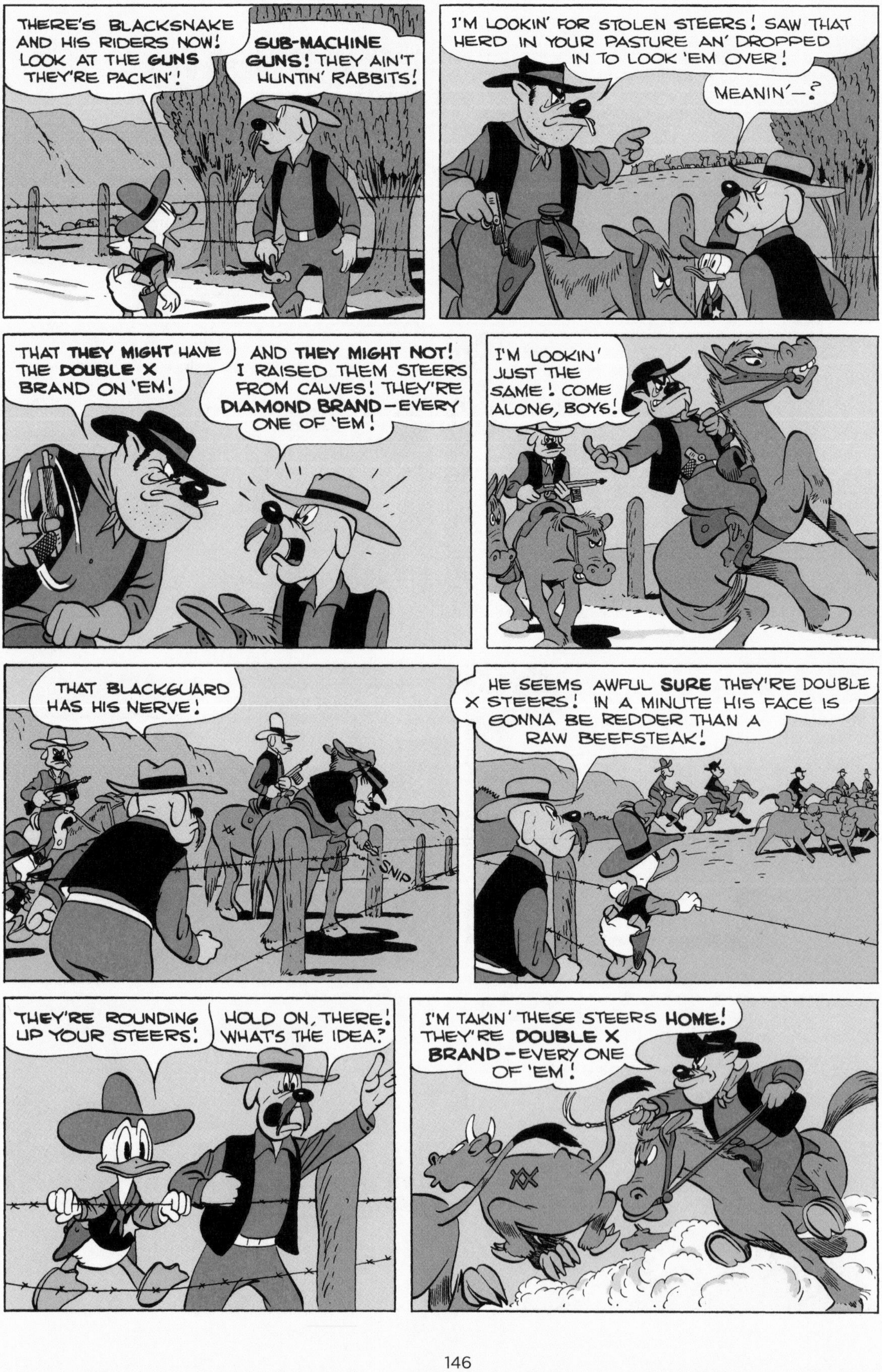
THERE'S BLACKSNAKE AND HIS RIDERS NOW! LOOK AT THE **GUNS** THEY'RE PACKIN'!
SUB-MACHINE GUNS! THEY AIN'T HUNTIN' RABBITS!
I'M LOOKIN' FOR STOLEN STEERS! SAW THAT HERD IN YOUR PASTURE AN' DROPPED IN TO LOOK 'EM OVER!
MEANIN'—?
THAT **THEY MIGHT** HAVE THE **DOUBLE X** BRAND ON 'EM!
AND **THEY MIGHT NOT**! I RAISED THEM STEERS FROM CALVES! THEY'RE **DIAMOND BRAND**—EVERY ONE OF 'EM!
I'M LOOKIN' JUST THE SAME! COME ALONG, BOYS!
THAT BLACKGUARD HAS HIS NERVE!
SNIP
HE SEEMS AWFUL **SURE** THEY'RE DOUBLE X STEERS! IN A MINUTE HIS FACE IS GONNA BE REDDER THAN A RAW BEEFSTEAK!
THEY'RE ROUNDING UP YOUR STEERS!
HOLD ON, THERE! WHAT'S THE IDEA?
I'M TAKIN' THESE STEERS **HOME**! THEY'RE **DOUBLE X BRAND**—EVERY ONE OF 'EM!

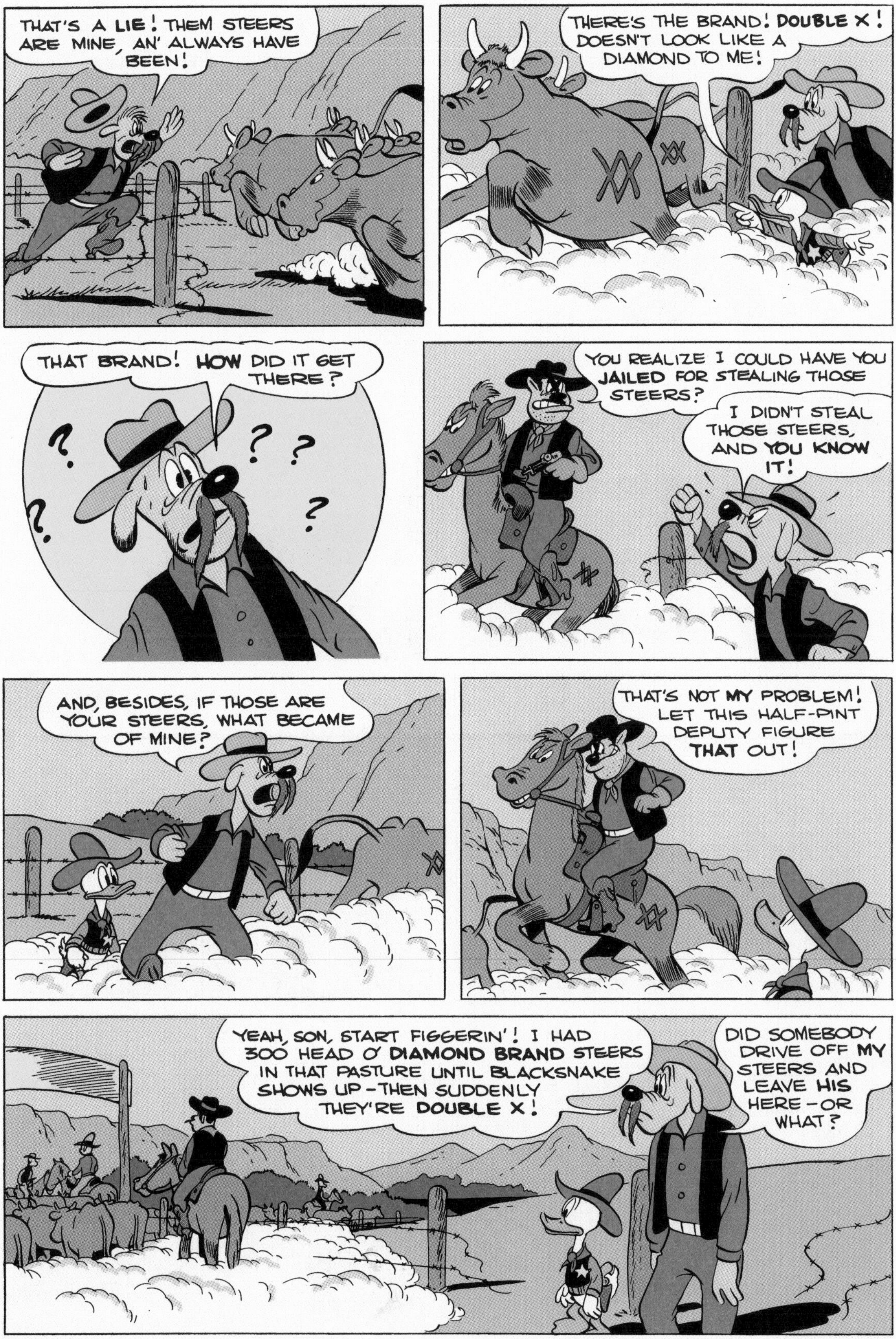
THAT'S A LIE! THEM STEERS ARE MINE, AN' ALWAYS HAVE BEEN!
THERE'S THE BRAND! DOUBLE X! DOESN'T LOOK LIKE A DIAMOND TO ME!
THAT BRAND! HOW DID IT GET THERE?
YOU REALIZE I COULD HAVE YOU JAILED FOR STEALING THOSE STEERS?
I DIDN'T STEAL THOSE STEERS, AND YOU KNOW IT!
AND, BESIDES, IF THOSE ARE YOUR STEERS, WHAT BECAME OF MINE?
THAT'S NOT MY PROBLEM! LET THIS HALF-PINT DEPUTY FIGURE THAT OUT!
YEAH, SON, START FIGGERIN'! I HAD 300 HEAD O' DIAMOND BRAND STEERS IN THAT PASTURE UNTIL BLACKSNAKE SHOWS UP—THEN SUDDENLY THEY'RE DOUBLE X!
DID SOMEBODY DRIVE OFF MY STEERS AND LEAVE HIS HERE—OR WHAT?

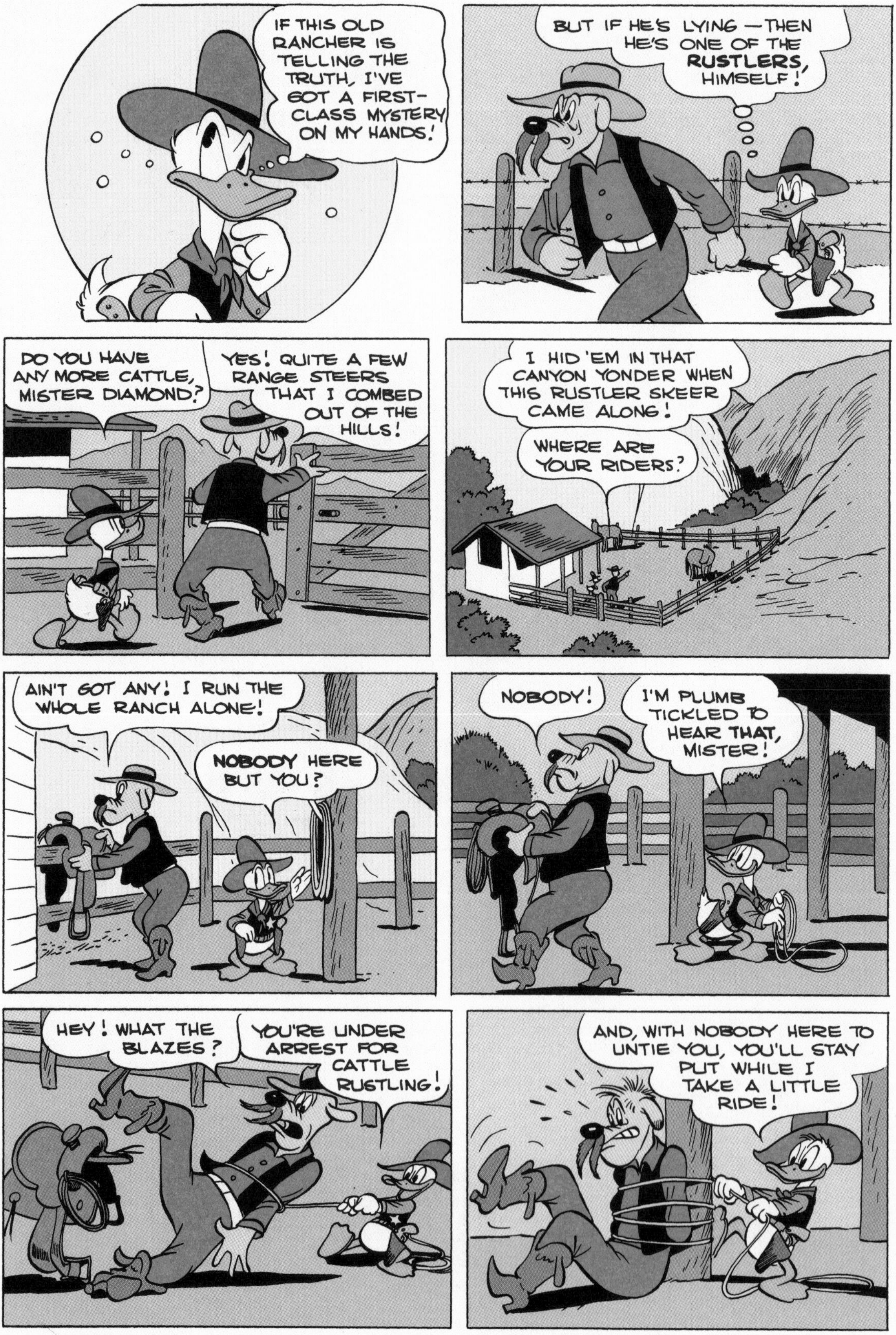
IF THIS OLD RANCHER IS TELLING THE TRUTH, I'VE GOT A FIRST-CLASS MYSTERY ON MY HANDS!
BUT IF HE'S LYING — THEN HE'S ONE OF THE RUSTLERS, HIMSELF!
DO YOU HAVE ANY MORE CATTLE, MISTER DIAMOND?
YES! QUITE A FEW RANGE STEERS THAT I COMBED OUT OF THE HILLS!
I HID 'EM IN THAT CANYON YONDER WHEN THIS RUSTLER SKEER CAME ALONG!
WHERE ARE YOUR RIDERS?
AIN'T GOT ANY! I RUN THE WHOLE RANCH ALONE!
NOBODY HERE BUT YOU?
NOBODY!
I'M PLUMB TICKLED TO HEAR THAT, MISTER!
HEY! WHAT THE BLAZES?
YOU'RE UNDER ARREST FOR CATTLE RUSTLING!
AND, WITH NOBODY HERE TO UNTIE YOU, YOU'LL STAY PUT WHILE I TAKE A LITTLE RIDE!

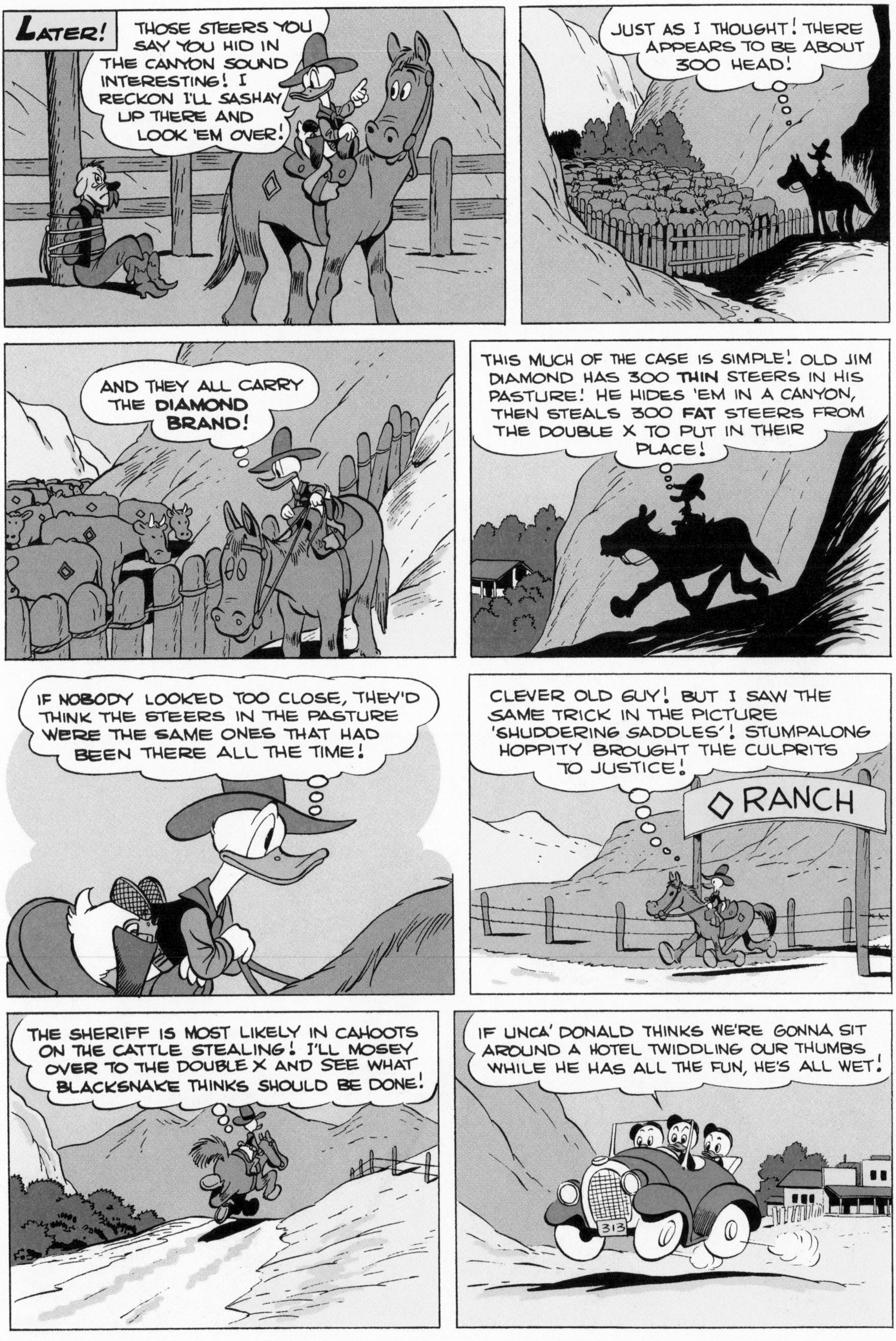
LATER!
THOSE STEERS YOU SAY YOU HID IN THE CANYON SOUND INTERESTING! I RECKON I'LL SASHAY UP THERE AND LOOK 'EM OVER!
JUST AS I THOUGHT! THERE APPEARS TO BE ABOUT 300 HEAD!
AND THEY ALL CARRY THE **DIAMOND BRAND**!
THIS MUCH OF THE CASE IS SIMPLE! OLD JIM DIAMOND HAS 300 **THIN** STEERS IN HIS PASTURE! HE HIDES 'EM IN A CANYON, THEN STEALS 300 **FAT** STEERS FROM THE DOUBLE X TO PUT IN THEIR PLACE!
IF NOBODY LOOKED TOO CLOSE, THEY'D THINK THE STEERS IN THE PASTURE WERE THE SAME ONES THAT HAD BEEN THERE ALL THE TIME!
CLEVER OLD GUY! BUT I SAW THE SAME TRICK IN THE PICTURE 'SHUDDERING SADDLES'! STUMPALONG HOPPITY BROUGHT THE CULPRITS TO JUSTICE!
◇ RANCH
THE SHERIFF IS MOST LIKELY IN CAHOOTS ON THE CATTLE STEALING! I'LL MOSEY OVER TO THE DOUBLE X AND SEE WHAT BLACKSNAKE THINKS SHOULD BE DONE!
IF UNCA' DONALD THINKS WE'RE GONNA SIT AROUND A HOTEL TWIDDLING OUR THUMBS WHILE HE HAS ALL THE FUN, HE'S ALL WET!
313

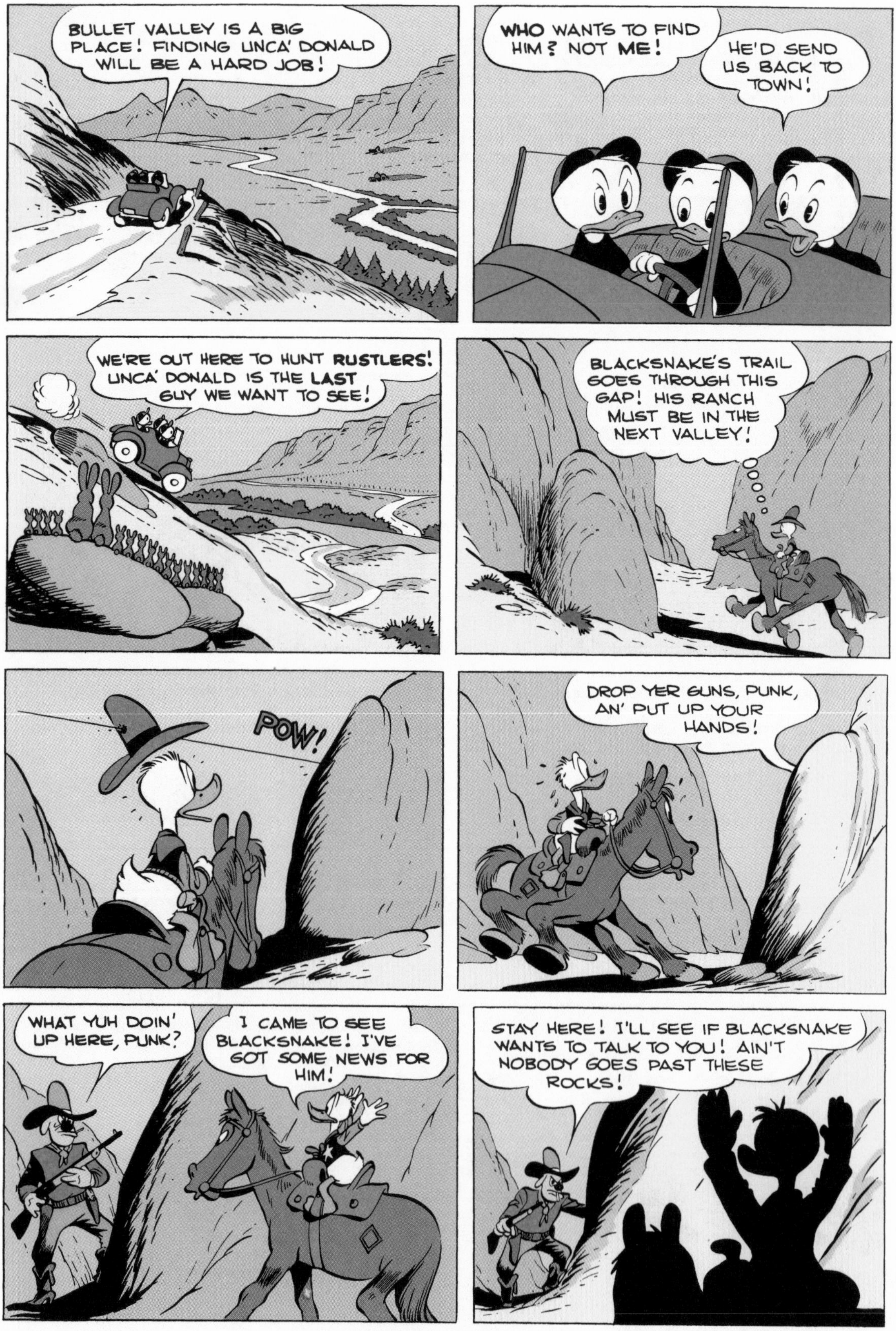
BULLET VALLEY IS A BIG PLACE! FINDING UNCA' DONALD WILL BE A HARD JOB!
WHO WANTS TO FIND HIM? NOT ME!
HE'D SEND US BACK TO TOWN!
WE'RE OUT HERE TO HUNT RUSTLERS! UNCA' DONALD IS THE LAST GUY WE WANT TO SEE!
BLACKSNAKE'S TRAIL GOES THROUGH THIS GAP! HIS RANCH MUST BE IN THE NEXT VALLEY!
POW!
DROP YER GUNS, PUNK, AN' PUT UP YOUR HANDS!
WHAT YUH DOIN' UP HERE, PUNK?
I CAME TO SEE BLACKSNAKE! I'VE GOT SOME NEWS FOR HIM!
STAY HERE! I'LL SEE IF BLACKSNAKE WANTS TO TALK TO YOU! AIN'T NOBODY GOES PAST THESE ROCKS!

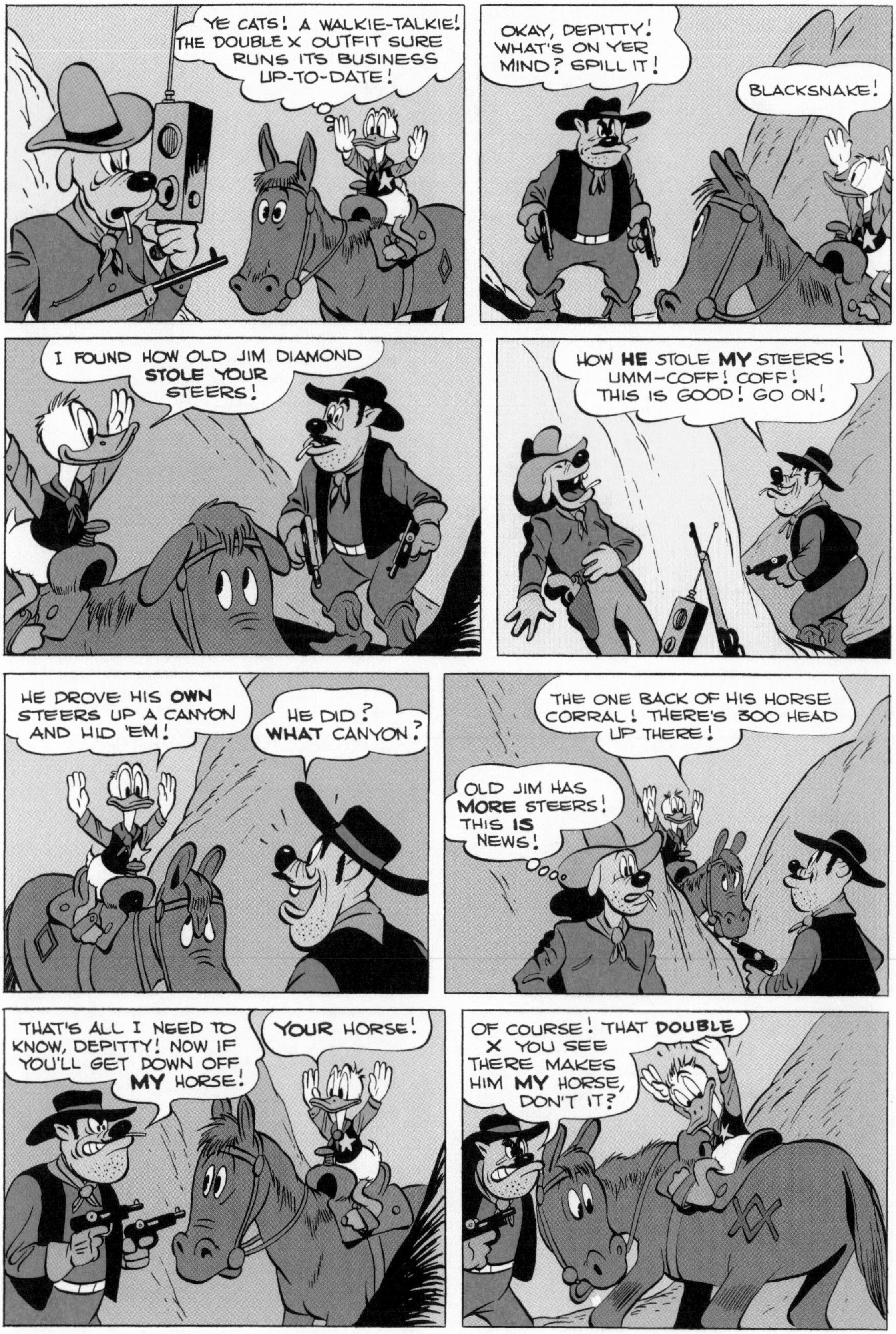
YE CATS! A WALKIE-TALKIE! THE DOUBLE X OUTFIT SURE RUNS ITS BUSINESS UP-TO-DATE!
OKAY, DEPITTY! WHAT'S ON YER MIND? SPILL IT!
BLACKSNAKE!
I FOUND HOW OLD JIM DIAMOND **STOLE YOUR** STEERS!
HOW **HE** STOLE **MY** STEERS! UMM-COFF! COFF! THIS IS GOOD! GO ON!
HE DROVE HIS **OWN** STEERS UP A CANYON AND HID 'EM!
HE DID? **WHAT** CANYON?
THE ONE BACK OF HIS HORSE CORRAL! THERE'S 300 HEAD UP THERE!
OLD JIM HAS **MORE** STEERS! THIS **IS** NEWS!
THAT'S ALL I NEED TO KNOW, DEPITTY! NOW IF YOU'LL GET DOWN OFF **MY** HORSE!
YOUR HORSE!
OF COURSE! THAT **DOUBLE X** YOU SEE THERE MAKES HIM **MY** HORSE, DON'T IT?

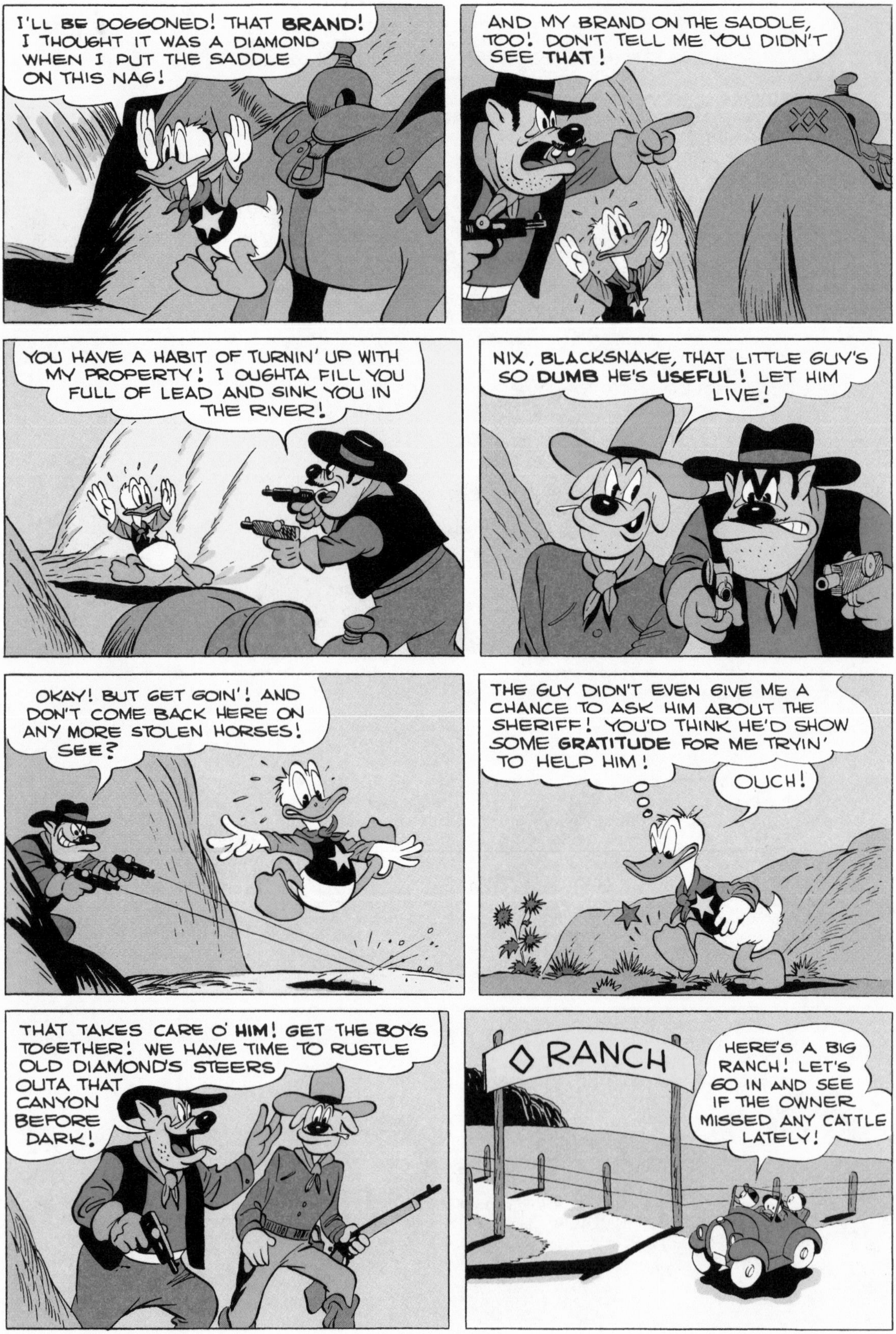
I'LL BE DOGGONED! THAT BRAND! I THOUGHT IT WAS A DIAMOND WHEN I PUT THE SADDLE ON THIS NAG!
AND MY BRAND ON THE SADDLE, TOO! DON'T TELL ME YOU DIDN'T SEE THAT!
YOU HAVE A HABIT OF TURNIN' UP WITH MY PROPERTY! I OUGHTA FILL YOU FULL OF LEAD AND SINK YOU IN THE RIVER!
NIX, BLACKSNAKE, THAT LITTLE GUY'S SO DUMB HE'S USEFUL! LET HIM LIVE!
OKAY! BUT GET GOIN'! AND DON'T COME BACK HERE ON ANY MORE STOLEN HORSES! SEE?
THE GUY DIDN'T EVEN GIVE ME A CHANCE TO ASK HIM ABOUT THE SHERIFF! YOU'D THINK HE'D SHOW SOME GRATITUDE FOR ME TRYIN' TO HELP HIM!
OUCH!
THAT TAKES CARE O' HIM! GET THE BOYS TOGETHER! WE HAVE TIME TO RUSTLE OLD DIAMOND'S STEERS OUTA THAT CANYON BEFORE DARK!
◊ RANCH
HERE'S A BIG RANCH! LET'S GO IN AND SEE IF THE OWNER MISSED ANY CATTLE LATELY!

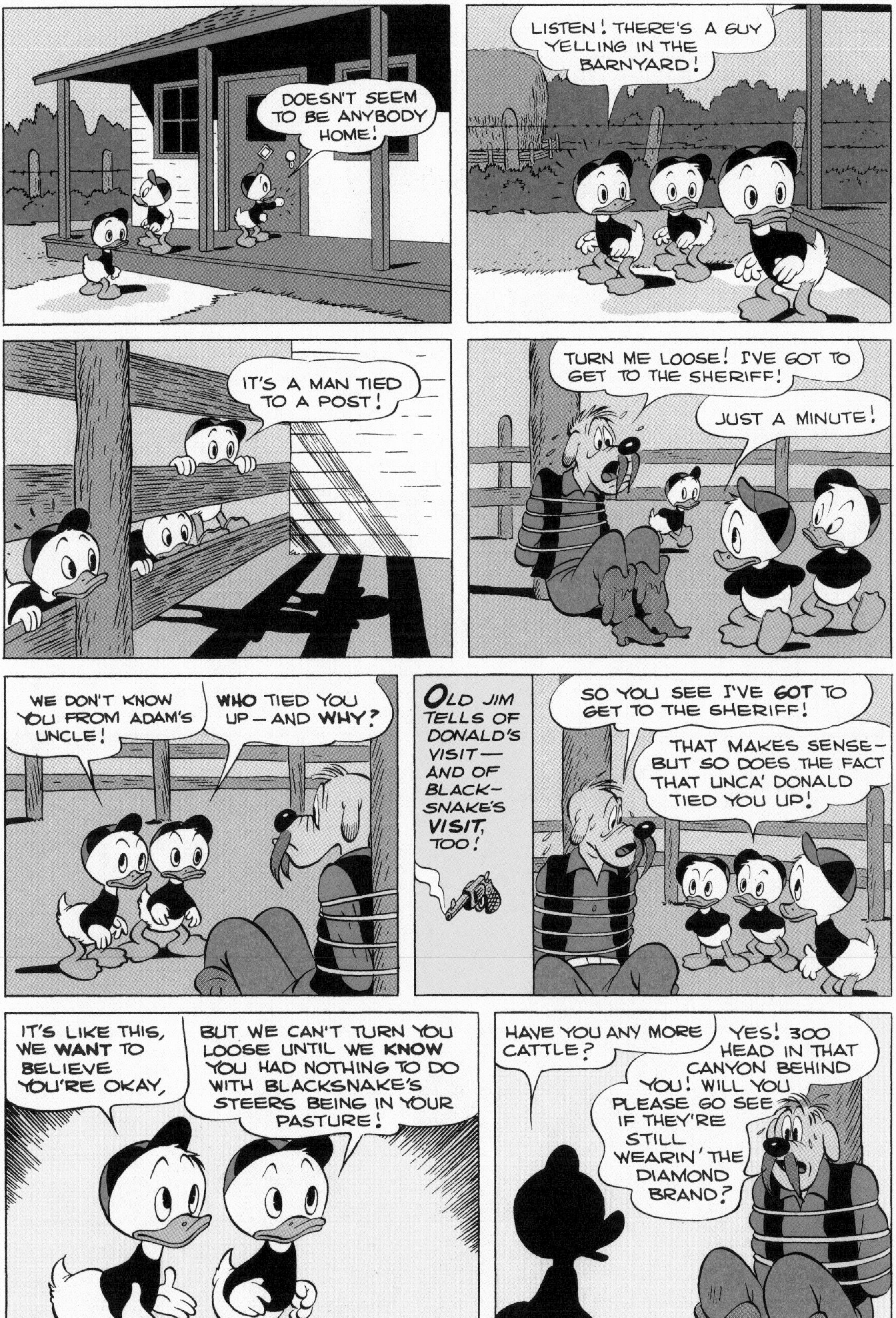
DOESN'T SEEM TO BE ANYBODY HOME!
LISTEN! THERE'S A GUY YELLING IN THE BARNYARD!
IT'S A MAN TIED TO A POST!
TURN ME LOOSE! I'VE GOT TO GET TO THE SHERIFF!
JUST A MINUTE!
WE DON'T KNOW YOU FROM ADAM'S UNCLE!
WHO TIED YOU UP—AND **WHY**?
OLD JIM TELLS OF DONALD'S VISIT—AND OF BLACK-SNAKE'S **VISIT**, TOO!
SO YOU SEE I'VE **GOT** TO GET TO THE SHERIFF!
THAT MAKES SENSE—BUT SO DOES THE FACT THAT UNCA' DONALD TIED YOU UP!
IT'S LIKE THIS, WE **WANT** TO BELIEVE YOU'RE OKAY,
BUT WE CAN'T TURN YOU LOOSE UNTIL WE **KNOW** YOU HAD NOTHING TO DO WITH BLACKSNAKE'S STEERS BEING IN YOUR PASTURE!
HAVE YOU ANY MORE CATTLE?
YES! 300 HEAD IN THAT CANYON BEHIND YOU! WILL YOU PLEASE GO SEE IF THEY'RE STILL WEARIN' THE DIAMOND BRAND?

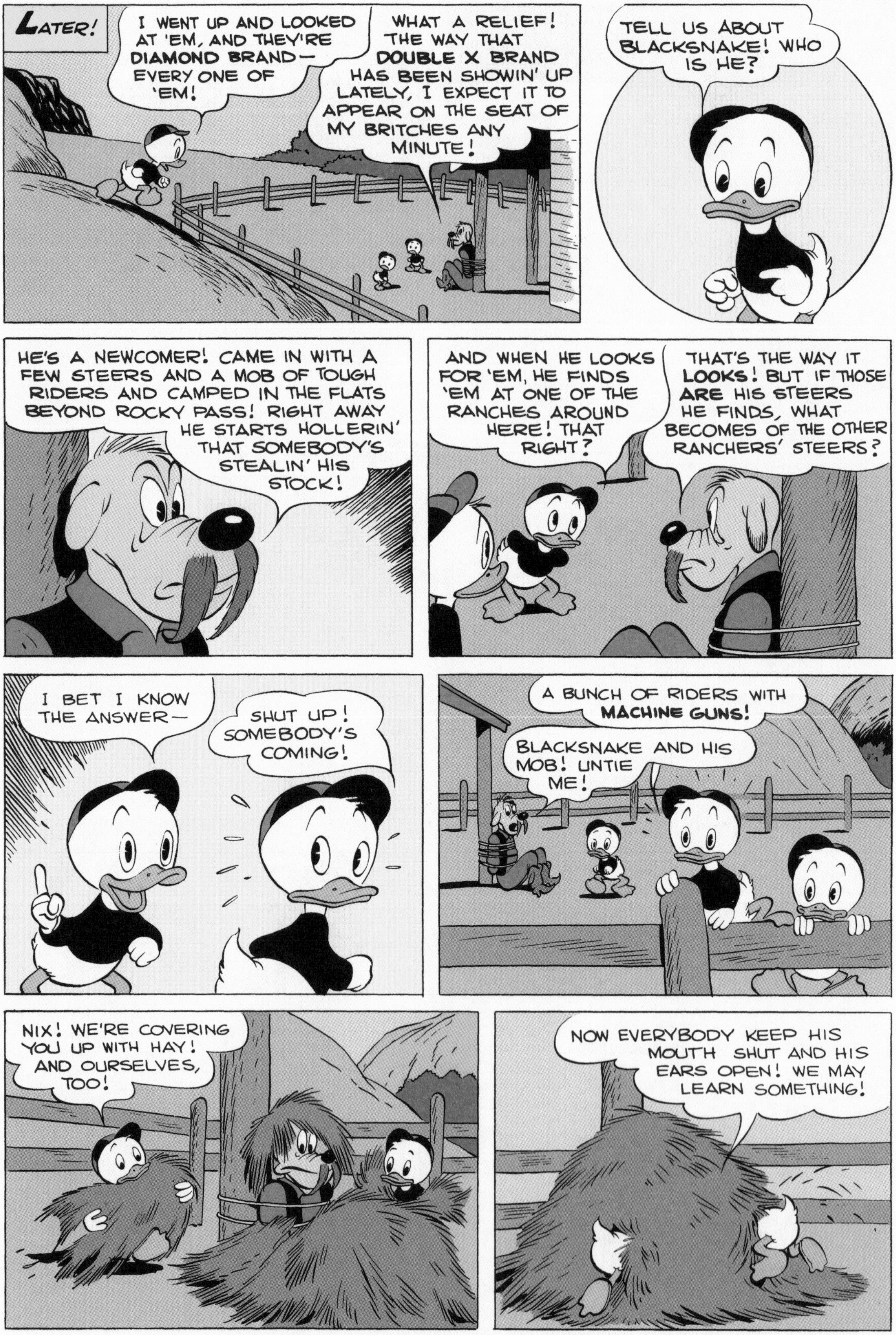
LATER!
I WENT UP AND LOOKED AT 'EM, AND THEY'RE DIAMOND BRAND— EVERY ONE OF 'EM!
WHAT A RELIEF! THE WAY THAT DOUBLE X BRAND HAS BEEN SHOWIN' UP LATELY, I EXPECT IT TO APPEAR ON THE SEAT OF MY BRITCHES ANY MINUTE!
TELL US ABOUT BLACKSNAKE! WHO IS HE?
HE'S A NEWCOMER! CAME IN WITH A FEW STEERS AND A MOB OF TOUGH RIDERS AND CAMPED IN THE FLATS BEYOND ROCKY PASS! RIGHT AWAY HE STARTS HOLLERIN' THAT SOMEBODY'S STEALIN' HIS STOCK!
AND WHEN HE LOOKS FOR 'EM, HE FINDS 'EM AT ONE OF THE RANCHES AROUND HERE! THAT RIGHT?
THAT'S THE WAY IT LOOKS! BUT IF THOSE ARE HIS STEERS HE FINDS, WHAT BECOMES OF THE OTHER RANCHERS' STEERS?
I BET I KNOW THE ANSWER—
SHUT UP! SOMEBODY'S COMING!
A BUNCH OF RIDERS WITH MACHINE GUNS!
BLACKSNAKE AND HIS MOB! UNTIE ME!
NIX! WE'RE COVERING YOU UP WITH HAY! AND OURSELVES, TOO!
NOW EVERYBODY KEEP HIS MOUTH SHUT AND HIS EARS OPEN! WE MAY LEARN SOMETHING!

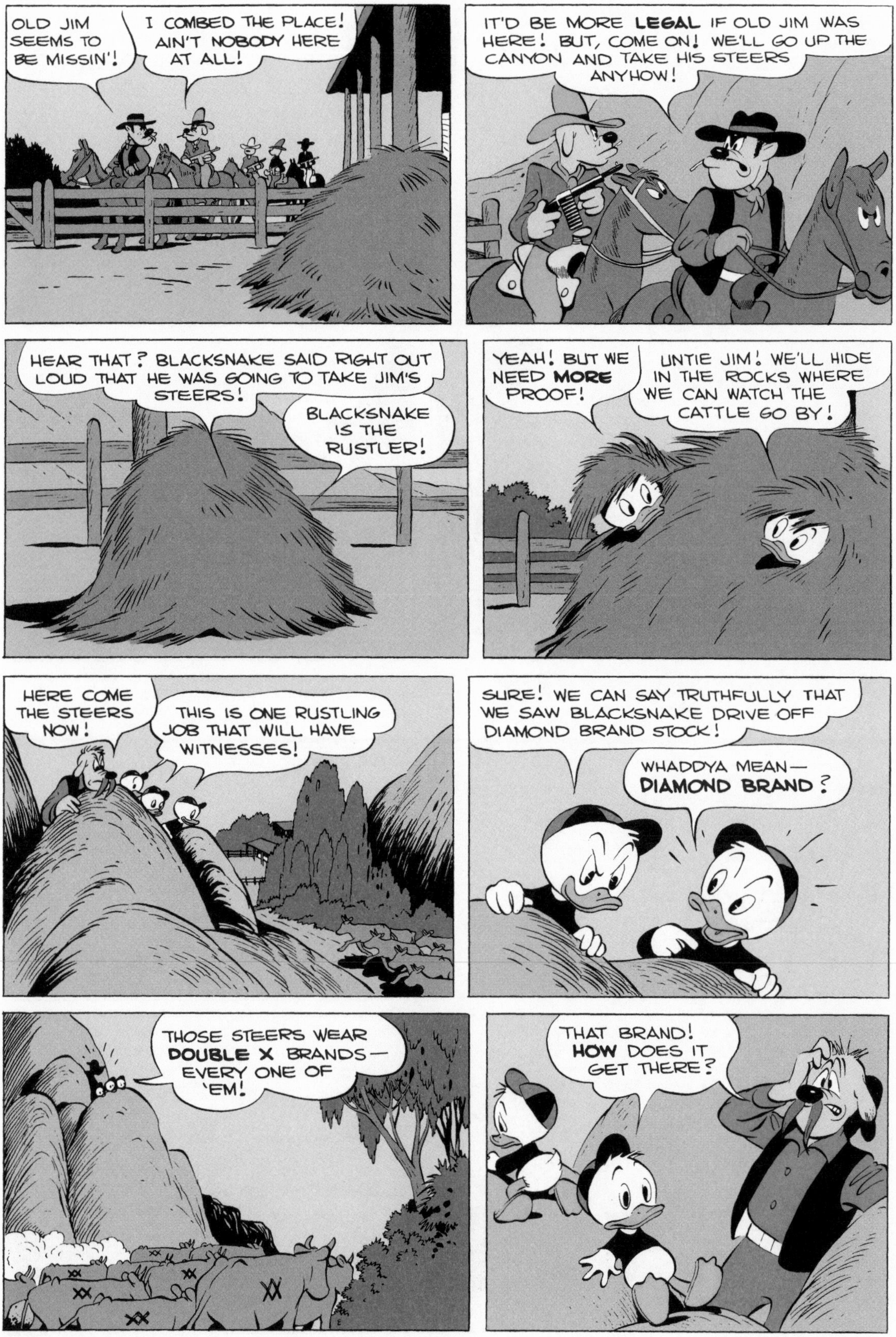

OLD JIM SEEMS TO BE MISSIN'!
I COMBED THE PLACE! AIN'T NOBODY HERE AT ALL!
IT'D BE MORE LEGAL IF OLD JIM WAS HERE! BUT, COME ON! WE'LL GO UP THE CANYON AND TAKE HIS STEERS ANYHOW!
HEAR THAT? BLACKSNAKE SAID RIGHT OUT LOUD THAT HE WAS GOING TO TAKE JIM'S STEERS!
BLACKSNAKE IS THE RUSTLER!
YEAH! BUT WE NEED MORE PROOF!
UNTIE JIM! WE'LL HIDE IN THE ROCKS WHERE WE CAN WATCH THE CATTLE GO BY!
HERE COME THE STEERS NOW!
THIS IS ONE RUSTLING JOB THAT WILL HAVE WITNESSES!
SURE! WE CAN SAY TRUTHFULLY THAT WE SAW BLACKSNAKE DRIVE OFF DIAMOND BRAND STOCK!
WHADDYA MEAN— DIAMOND BRAND?
THOSE STEERS WEAR DOUBLE X BRANDS— EVERY ONE OF 'EM!
THAT BRAND! HOW DOES IT GET THERE?

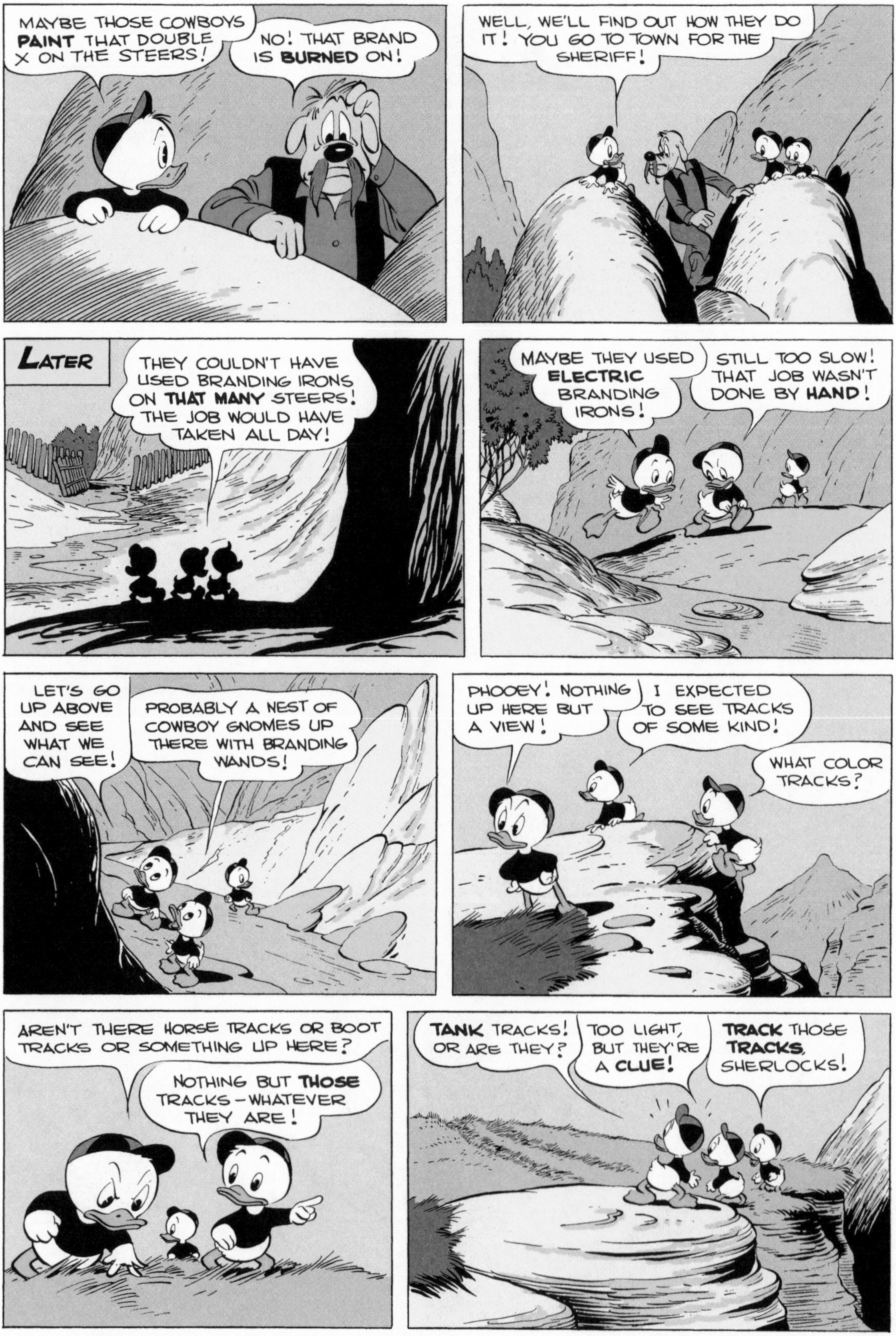
MAYBE THOSE COWBOYS PAINT THAT DOUBLE X ON THE STEERS!
NO! THAT BRAND IS BURNED ON!
WELL, WE'LL FIND OUT HOW THEY DO IT! YOU GO TO TOWN FOR THE SHERIFF!
LATER
THEY COULDN'T HAVE USED BRANDING IRONS ON THAT MANY STEERS! THE JOB WOULD HAVE TAKEN ALL DAY!
MAYBE THEY USED ELECTRIC BRANDING IRONS!
STILL TOO SLOW! THAT JOB WASN'T DONE BY HAND!
LET'S GO UP ABOVE AND SEE WHAT WE CAN SEE!
PROBABLY A NEST OF COWBOY GNOMES UP THERE WITH BRANDING WANDS!
PHOOEY! NOTHING UP HERE BUT A VIEW!
I EXPECTED TO SEE TRACKS OF SOME KIND!
WHAT COLOR TRACKS?
AREN'T THERE HORSE TRACKS OR BOOT TRACKS OR SOMETHING UP HERE?
NOTHING BUT THOSE TRACKS—WHATEVER THEY ARE!
TANK TRACKS! OR ARE THEY?
TOO LIGHT, BUT THEY'RE A CLUE!
TRACK THOSE TRACKS, SHERLOCKS!

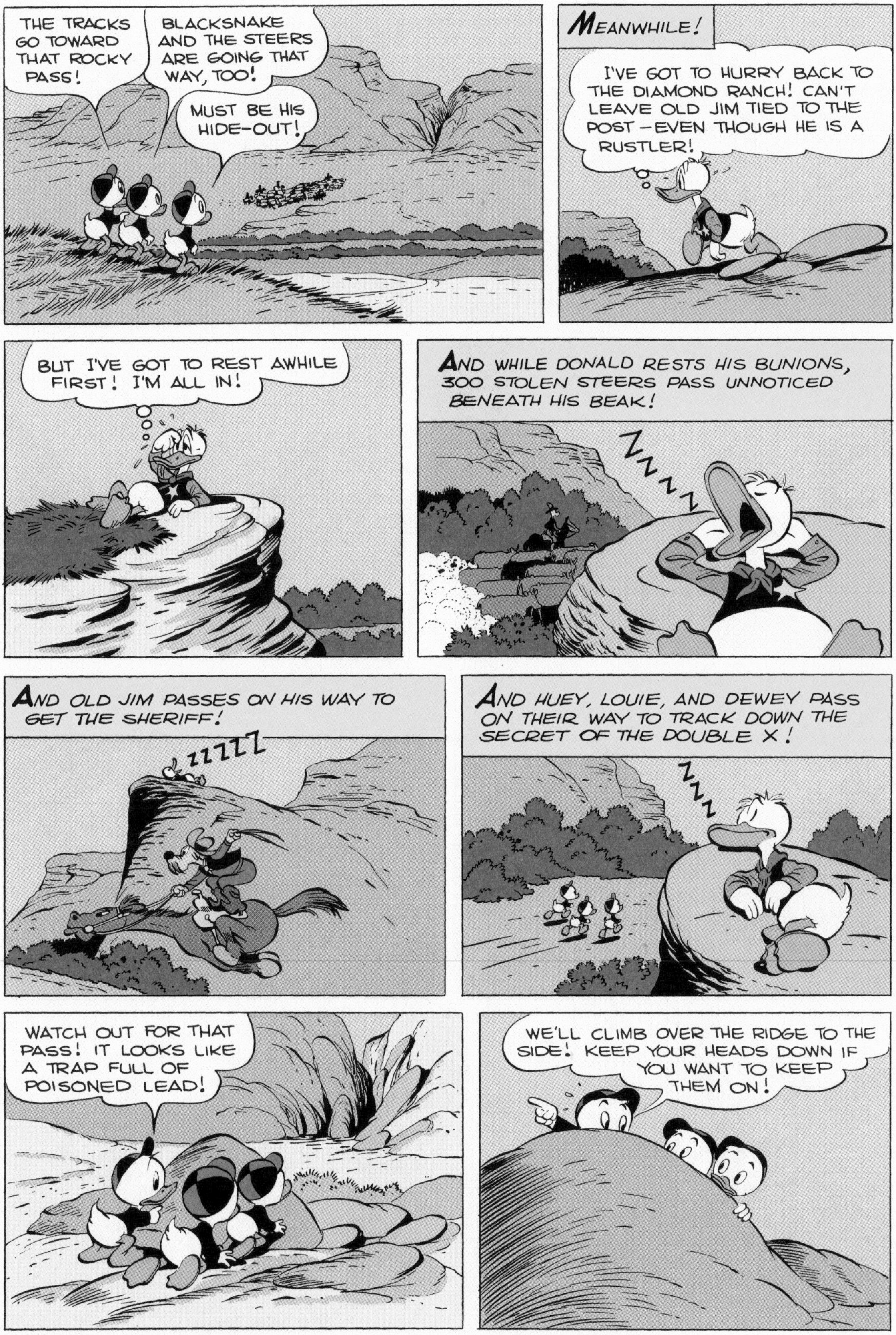
THE TRACKS GO TOWARD THAT ROCKY PASS!
BLACKSNAKE AND THE STEERS ARE GOING THAT WAY, TOO!
MUST BE HIS HIDE-OUT!
MEANWHILE!
I'VE GOT TO HURRY BACK TO THE DIAMOND RANCH! CAN'T LEAVE OLD JIM TIED TO THE POST—EVEN THOUGH HE IS A RUSTLER!
BUT I'VE GOT TO REST AWHILE FIRST! I'M ALL IN!
AND WHILE DONALD RESTS HIS BUNIONS, 300 STOLEN STEERS PASS UNNOTICED BENEATH HIS BEAK!
ZZZZ
AND OLD JIM PASSES ON HIS WAY TO GET THE SHERIFF!
ZZZZZ
AND HUEY, LOUIE, AND DEWEY PASS ON THEIR WAY TO TRACK DOWN THE SECRET OF THE DOUBLE X!
ZZZ
WATCH OUT FOR THAT PASS! IT LOOKS LIKE A TRAP FULL OF POISONED LEAD!
WE'LL CLIMB OVER THE RIDGE TO THE SIDE! KEEP YOUR HEADS DOWN IF YOU WANT TO KEEP THEM ON!

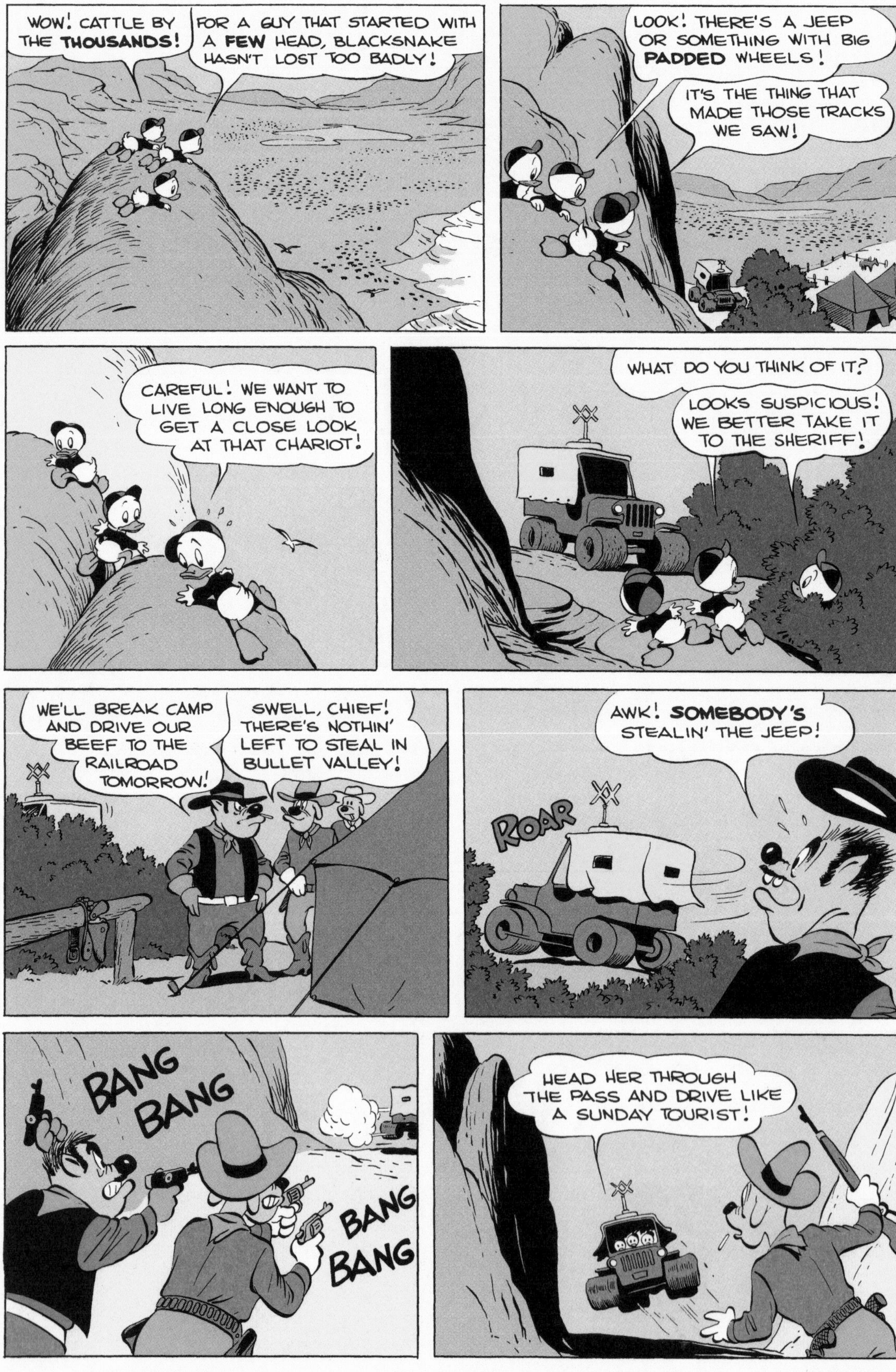

WOW! CATTLE BY THE **THOUSANDS**!
FOR A GUY THAT STARTED WITH A **FEW** HEAD, BLACKSNAKE HASN'T LOST TOO BADLY!
LOOK! THERE'S A JEEP OR SOMETHING WITH BIG **PADDED** WHEELS!
IT'S THE THING THAT MADE THOSE TRACKS WE SAW!
CAREFUL! WE WANT TO LIVE LONG ENOUGH TO GET A CLOSE LOOK AT THAT CHARIOT!
WHAT DO YOU THINK OF IT?
LOOKS SUSPICIOUS! WE BETTER TAKE IT TO THE SHERIFF!
WE'LL BREAK CAMP AND DRIVE OUR BEEF TO THE RAILROAD TOMORROW!
SWELL, CHIEF! THERE'S NOTHIN' LEFT TO STEAL IN BULLET VALLEY!
AWK! **SOMEBODY'S** STEALIN' THE JEEP!
ROAR
BANG BANG
BANG BANG
HEAD HER THROUGH THE PASS AND DRIVE LIKE A SUNDAY TOURIST!

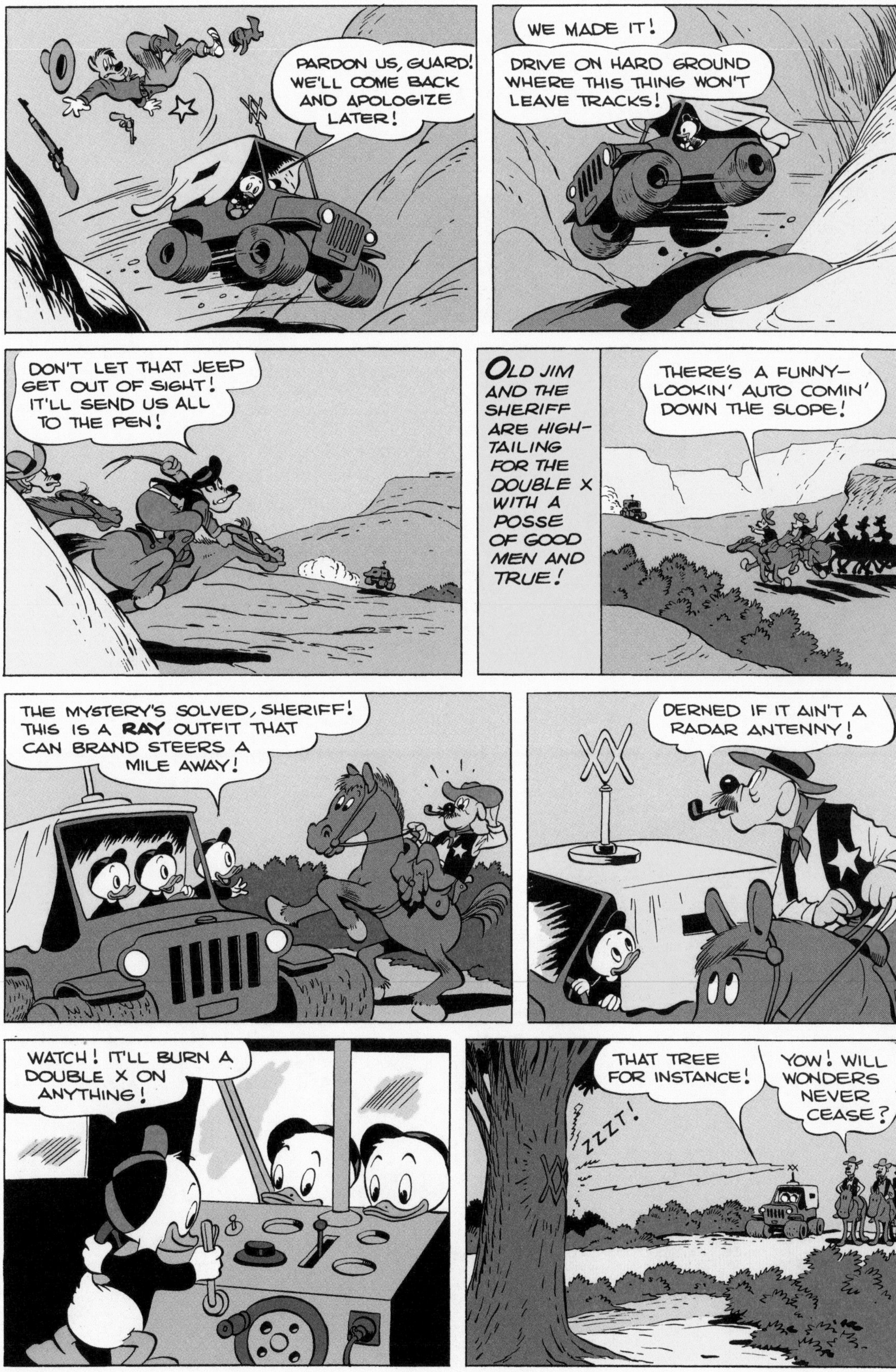

PARDON US, GUARD! WE'LL COME BACK AND APOLOGIZE LATER!
WE MADE IT!
DRIVE ON HARD GROUND WHERE THIS THING WON'T LEAVE TRACKS!
DON'T LET THAT JEEP GET OUT OF SIGHT! IT'LL SEND US ALL TO THE PEN!
OLD JIM AND THE SHERIFF ARE HIGH-TAILING FOR THE DOUBLE X WITH A POSSE OF GOOD MEN AND TRUE!
THERE'S A FUNNY-LOOKIN' AUTO COMIN' DOWN THE SLOPE!
THE MYSTERY'S SOLVED, SHERIFF! THIS IS A RAY OUTFIT THAT CAN BRAND STEERS A MILE AWAY!
DERNED IF IT AIN'T A RADAR ANTENNY!
WATCH! IT'LL BURN A DOUBLE X ON ANYTHING!
THAT TREE FOR INSTANCE!
YOW! WILL WONDERS NEVER CEASE?
ZZZT!

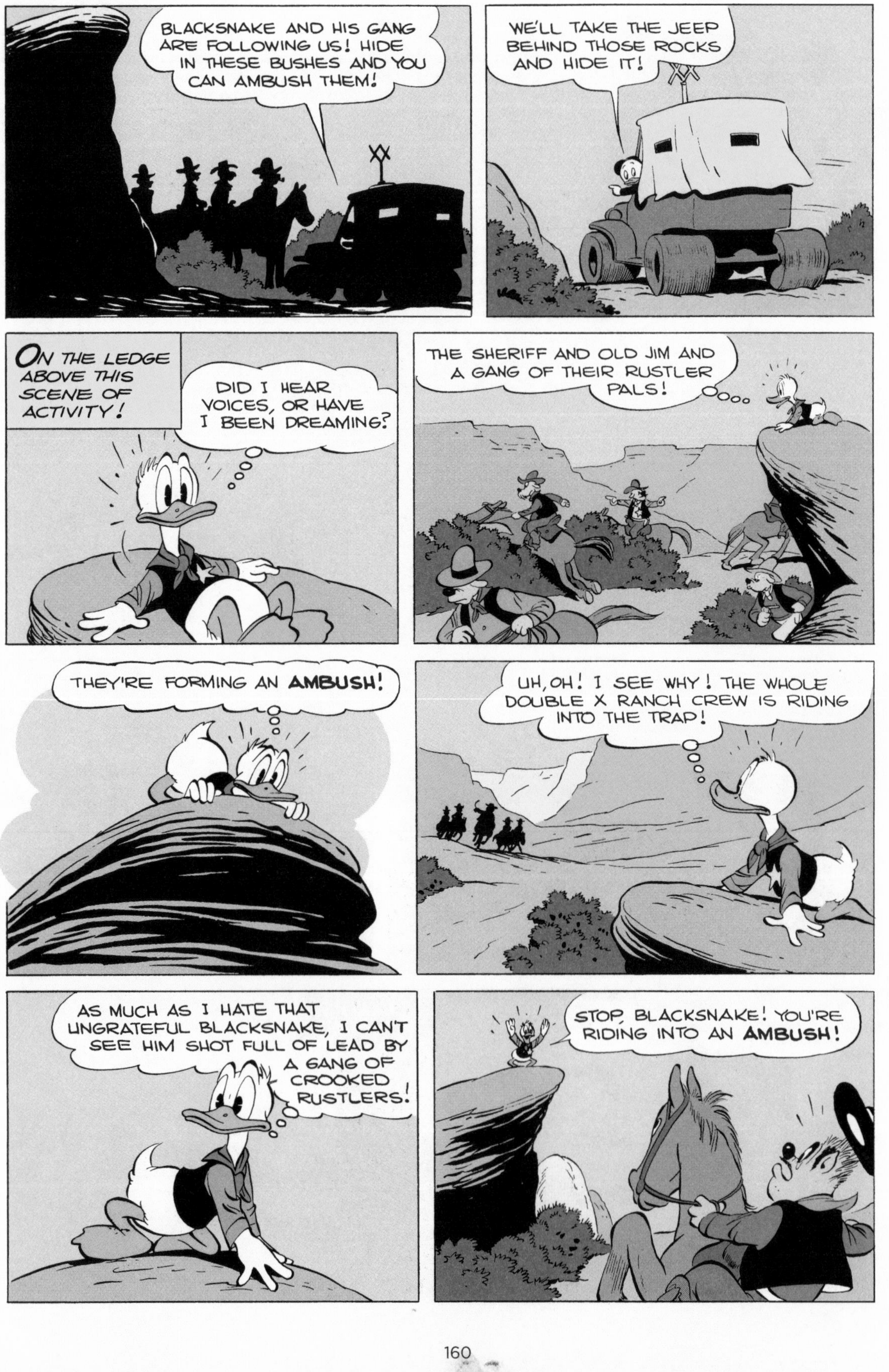
BLACKSNAKE AND HIS GANG ARE FOLLOWING US! HIDE IN THESE BUSHES AND YOU CAN AMBUSH THEM!
WE'LL TAKE THE JEEP BEHIND THOSE ROCKS AND HIDE IT!
ON THE LEDGE ABOVE THIS SCENE OF ACTIVITY!
DID I HEAR VOICES, OR HAVE I BEEN DREAMING?
THE SHERIFF AND OLD JIM AND A GANG OF THEIR RUSTLER PALS!
THEY'RE FORMING AN AMBUSH!
UH, OH! I SEE WHY! THE WHOLE DOUBLE X RANCH CREW IS RIDING INTO THE TRAP!
AS MUCH AS I HATE THAT UNGRATEFUL BLACKSNAKE, I CAN'T SEE HIM SHOT FULL OF LEAD BY A GANG OF CROOKED RUSTLERS!
STOP, BLACKSNAKE! YOU'RE RIDING INTO AN AMBUSH!

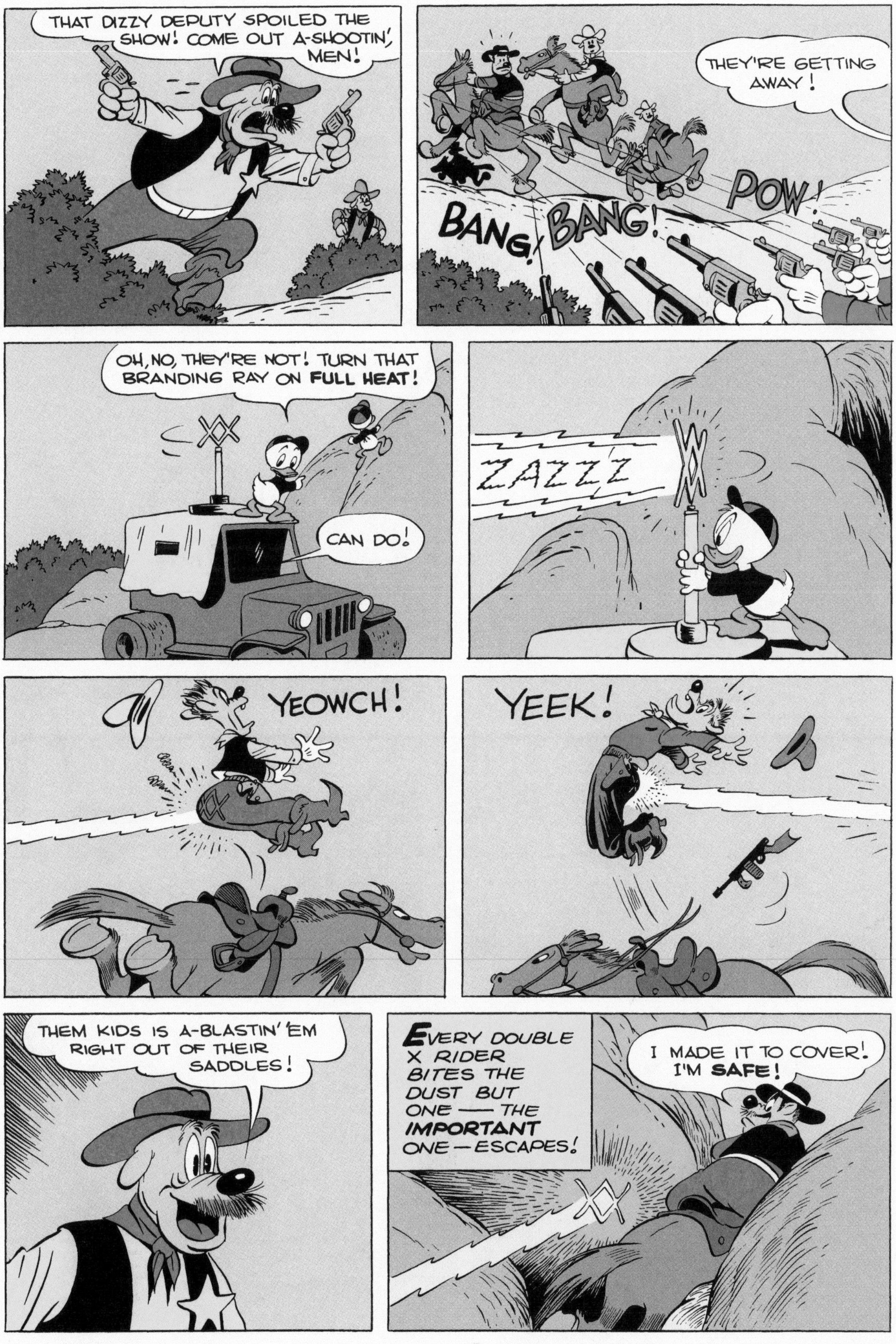

THAT DIZZY DEPUTY SPOILED THE SHOW! COME OUT A-SHOOTIN', MEN!
THEY'RE GETTING AWAY!
BANG!
BANG!
POW!
OH, NO, THEY'RE NOT! TURN THAT BRANDING RAY ON **FULL HEAT!**
CAN DO!
ZAZZZ
YEOWCH!
YEEK!
THEM KIDS IS A-BLASTIN' 'EM RIGHT OUT OF THEIR SADDLES!
EVERY DOUBLE X RIDER BITES THE DUST BUT ONE — THE **IMPORTANT** ONE — ESCAPES!
I MADE IT TO COVER! I'M **SAFE!**

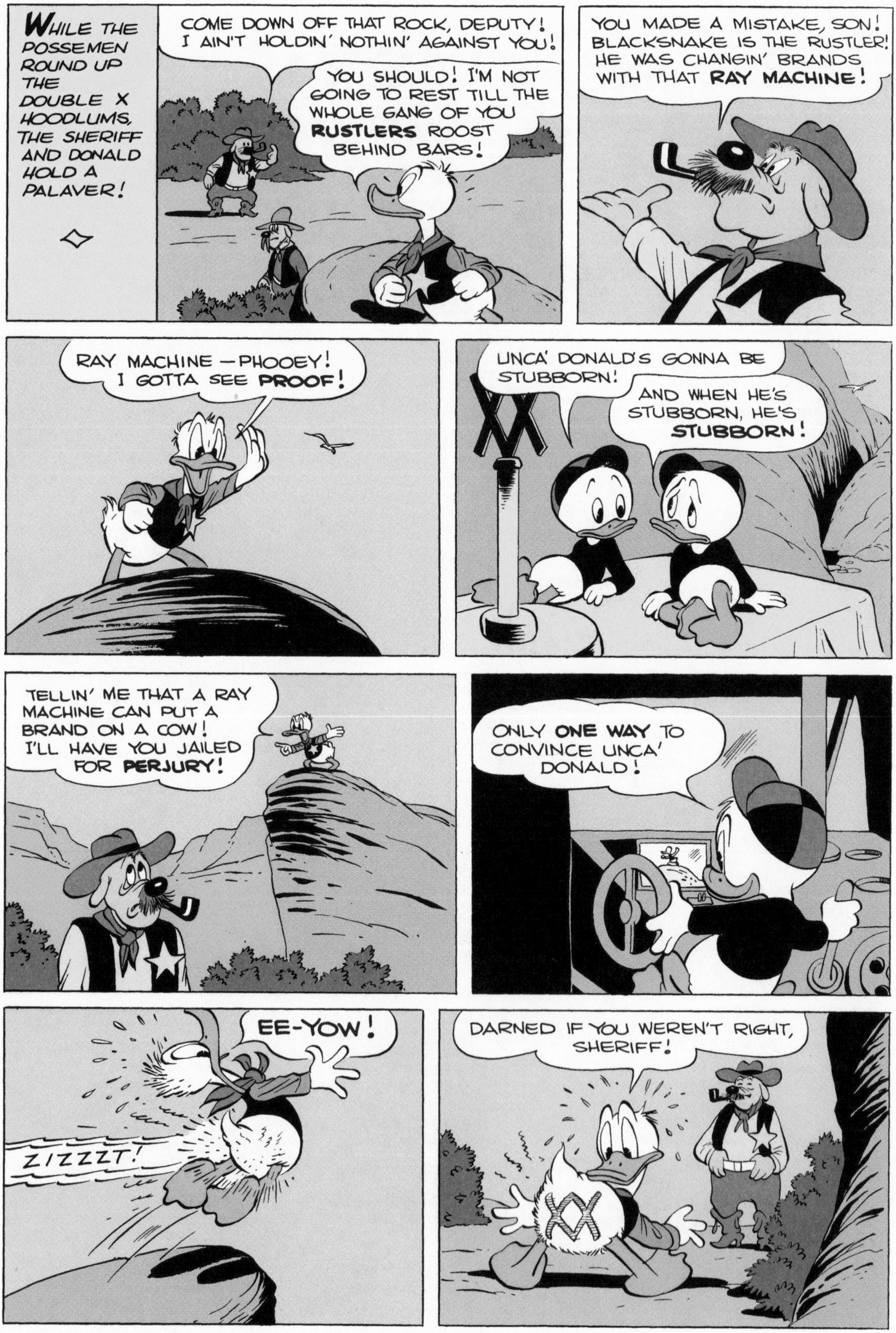
WHILE THE POSSEMEN ROUND UP THE DOUBLE X HOODLUMS, THE SHERIFF AND DONALD HOLD A PALAVER!
COME DOWN OFF THAT ROCK, DEPUTY! I AIN'T HOLDIN' NOTHIN' AGAINST YOU!
YOU SHOULD! I'M NOT GOING TO REST TILL THE WHOLE GANG OF YOU **RUSTLERS** ROOST BEHIND BARS!
YOU MADE A MISTAKE, SON! BLACKSNAKE IS THE RUSTLER! HE WAS CHANGIN' BRANDS WITH THAT **RAY MACHINE**!
RAY MACHINE—PHOOEY! I GOTTA SEE **PROOF**!
UNCA' DONALD'S GONNA BE STUBBORN!
AND WHEN HE'S STUBBORN, HE'S **STUBBORN**!
TELLIN' ME THAT A RAY MACHINE CAN PUT A BRAND ON A COW! I'LL HAVE YOU JAILED FOR **PERJURY**!
ONLY **ONE WAY** TO CONVINCE UNCA' DONALD!
EE-YOW!
ZIZZZT!
DARNED IF YOU WEREN'T RIGHT, SHERIFF!

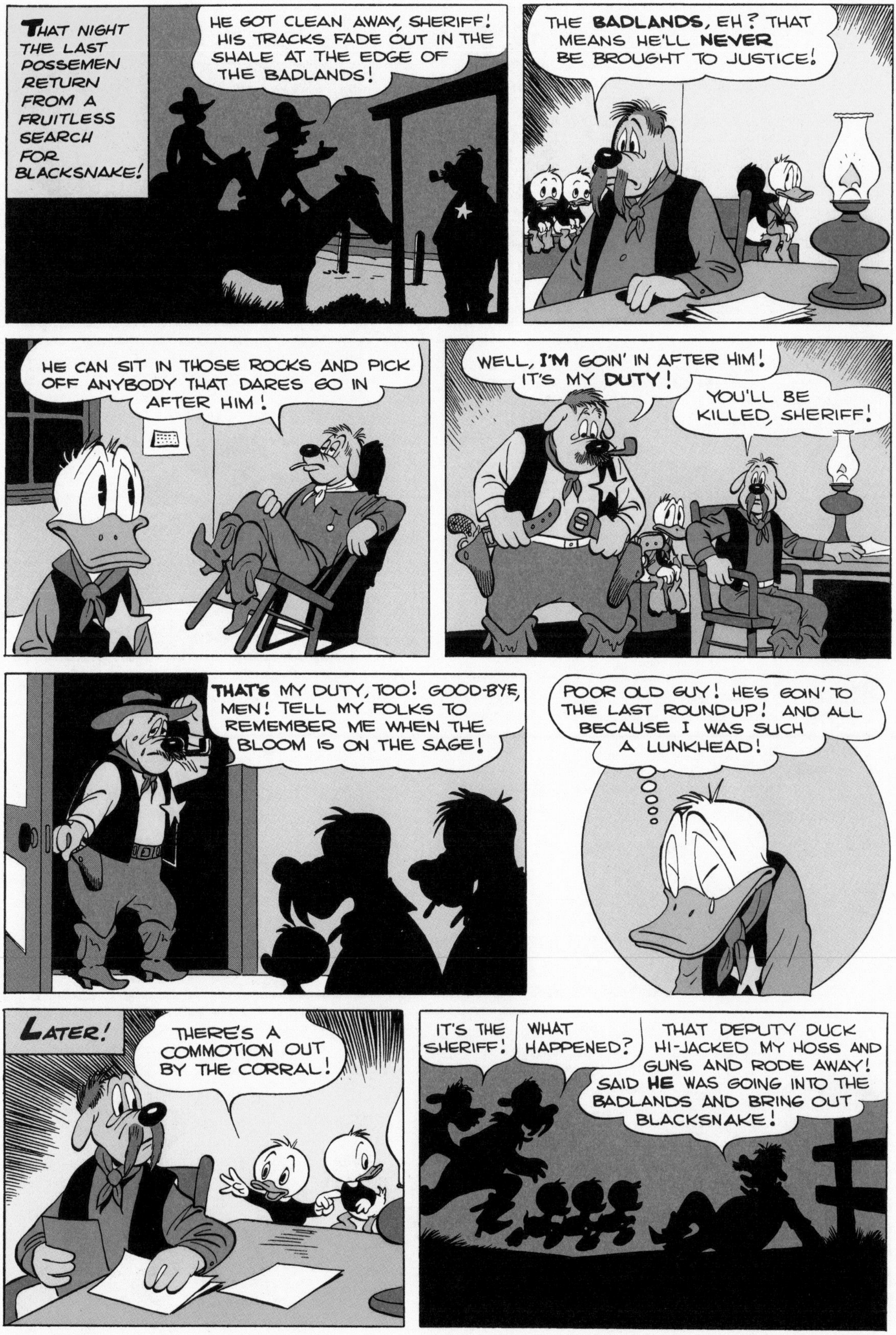
THAT NIGHT THE LAST POSSEMEN RETURN FROM A FRUITLESS SEARCH FOR BLACKSNAKE!
HE GOT CLEAN AWAY, SHERIFF! HIS TRACKS FADE OUT IN THE SHALE AT THE EDGE OF THE BADLANDS!
THE BADLANDS, EH? THAT MEANS HE'LL NEVER BE BROUGHT TO JUSTICE!
HE CAN SIT IN THOSE ROCKS AND PICK OFF ANYBODY THAT DARES GO IN AFTER HIM!
WELL, I'M GOIN' IN AFTER HIM! IT'S MY DUTY!
YOU'LL BE KILLED, SHERIFF!
THAT'S MY DUTY, TOO! GOOD-BYE, MEN! TELL MY FOLKS TO REMEMBER ME WHEN THE BLOOM IS ON THE SAGE!
POOR OLD GUY! HE'S GOIN' TO THE LAST ROUNDUP! AND ALL BECAUSE I WAS SUCH A LUNKHEAD!
LATER!
THERE'S A COMMOTION OUT BY THE CORRAL!
IT'S THE SHERIFF!
WHAT HAPPENED?
THAT DEPUTY DUCK HI-JACKED MY HOSS AND GUNS AND RODE AWAY! SAID HE WAS GOING INTO THE BADLANDS AND BRING OUT BLACKSNAKE!

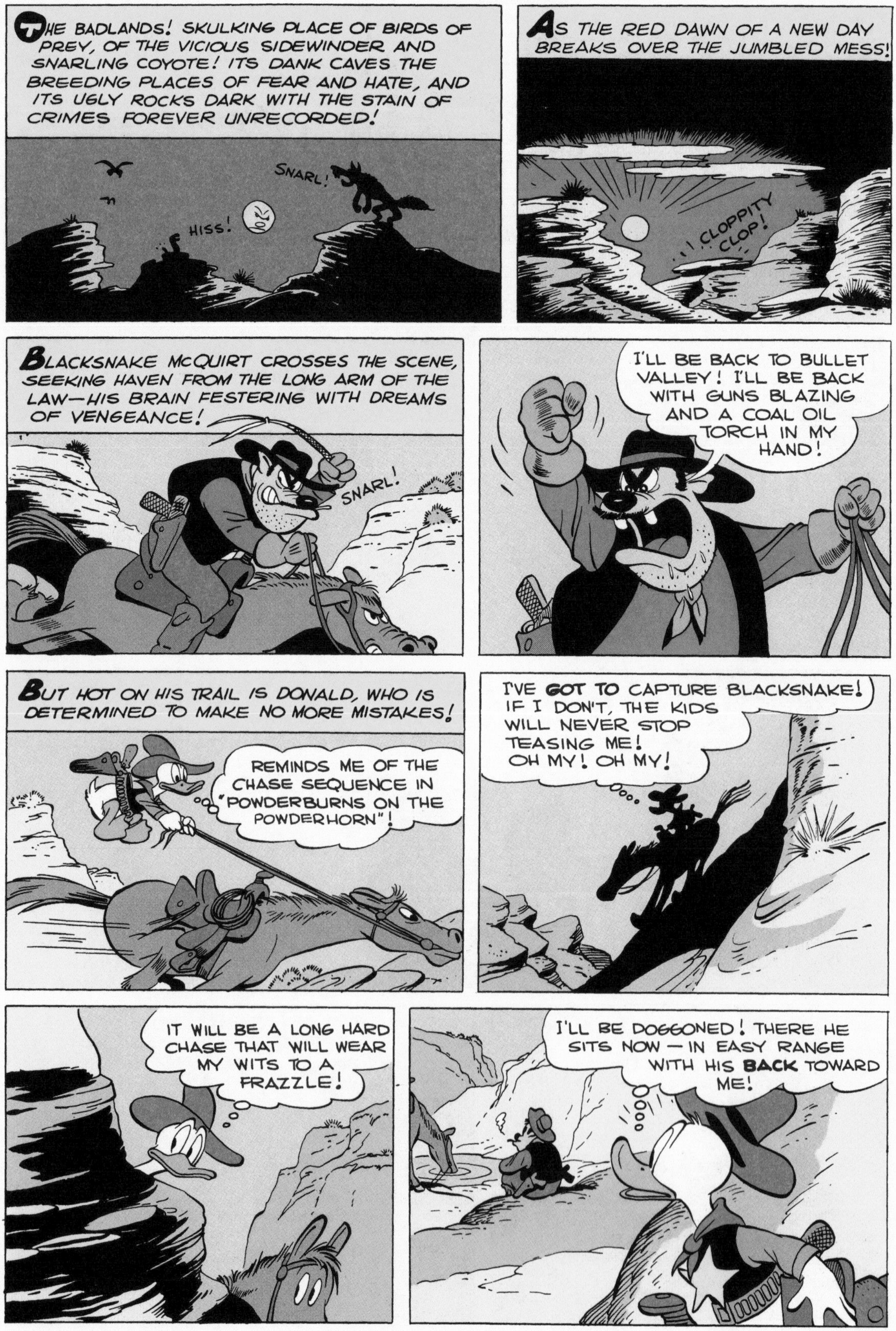
THE BADLANDS! SKULKING PLACE OF BIRDS OF PREY, OF THE VICIOUS SIDEWINDER AND SNARLING COYOTE! ITS DANK CAVES THE BREEDING PLACES OF FEAR AND HATE, AND ITS UGLY ROCKS DARK WITH THE STAIN OF CRIMES FOREVER UNRECORDED!
SNARL!
HISS!
AS THE RED DAWN OF A NEW DAY BREAKS OVER THE JUMBLED MESS!
CLOPPITY CLOP!
BLACKSNAKE McQUIRT CROSSES THE SCENE, SEEKING HAVEN FROM THE LONG ARM OF THE LAW—HIS BRAIN FESTERING WITH DREAMS OF VENGEANCE!
SNARL!
I'LL BE BACK TO BULLET VALLEY! I'LL BE BACK WITH GUNS BLAZING AND A COAL OIL TORCH IN MY HAND!
BUT HOT ON HIS TRAIL IS DONALD, WHO IS DETERMINED TO MAKE NO MORE MISTAKES!
REMINDS ME OF THE CHASE SEQUENCE IN "POWDERBURNS ON THE POWDERHORN"!
I'VE GOT TO CAPTURE BLACKSNAKE! IF I DON'T, THE KIDS WILL NEVER STOP TEASING ME! OH MY! OH MY!
IT WILL BE A LONG HARD CHASE THAT WILL WEAR MY WITS TO A FRAZZLE!
I'LL BE DOGGONED! THERE HE SITS NOW — IN EASY RANGE WITH HIS BACK TOWARD ME!

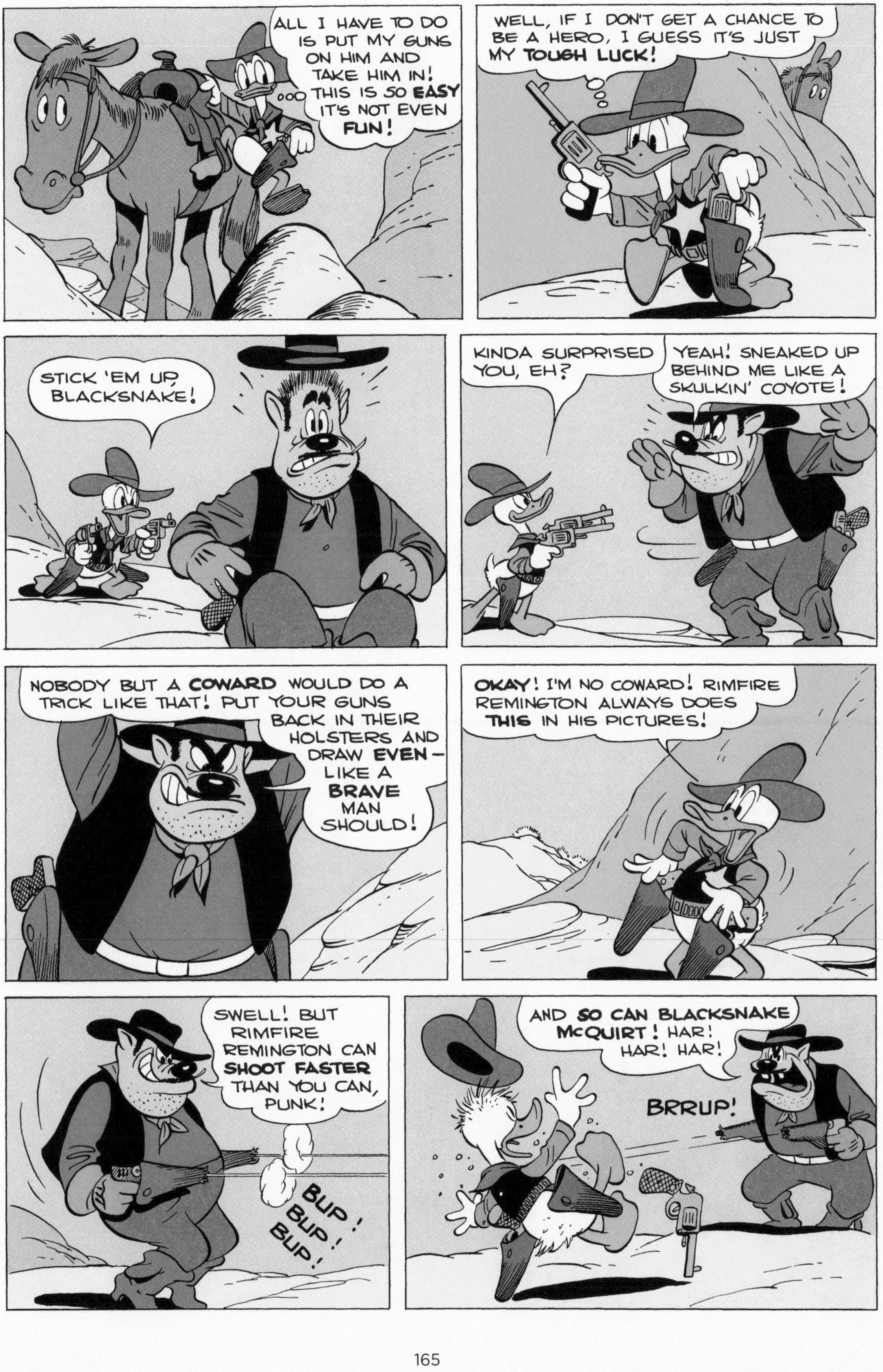

ALL I HAVE TO DO IS PUT MY GUNS ON HIM AND TAKE HIM IN! THIS IS SO EASY IT'S NOT EVEN FUN!
WELL, IF I DON'T GET A CHANCE TO BE A HERO, I GUESS IT'S JUST MY TOUGH LUCK!
STICK 'EM UP, BLACKSNAKE!
KINDA SURPRISED YOU, EH?
YEAH! SNEAKED UP BEHIND ME LIKE A SKULKIN' COYOTE!
NOBODY BUT A COWARD WOULD DO A TRICK LIKE THAT! PUT YOUR GUNS BACK IN THEIR HOLSTERS AND DRAW EVEN — LIKE A BRAVE MAN SHOULD!
OKAY! I'M NO COWARD! RIMFIRE REMINGTON ALWAYS DOES THIS IN HIS PICTURES!
SWELL! BUT RIMFIRE REMINGTON CAN SHOOT FASTER THAN YOU CAN, PUNK!
BLIP! BLIP! BLIP!
AND SO CAN BLACKSNAKE McQUIRT! HAR! HAR! HAR!
BRRUP!

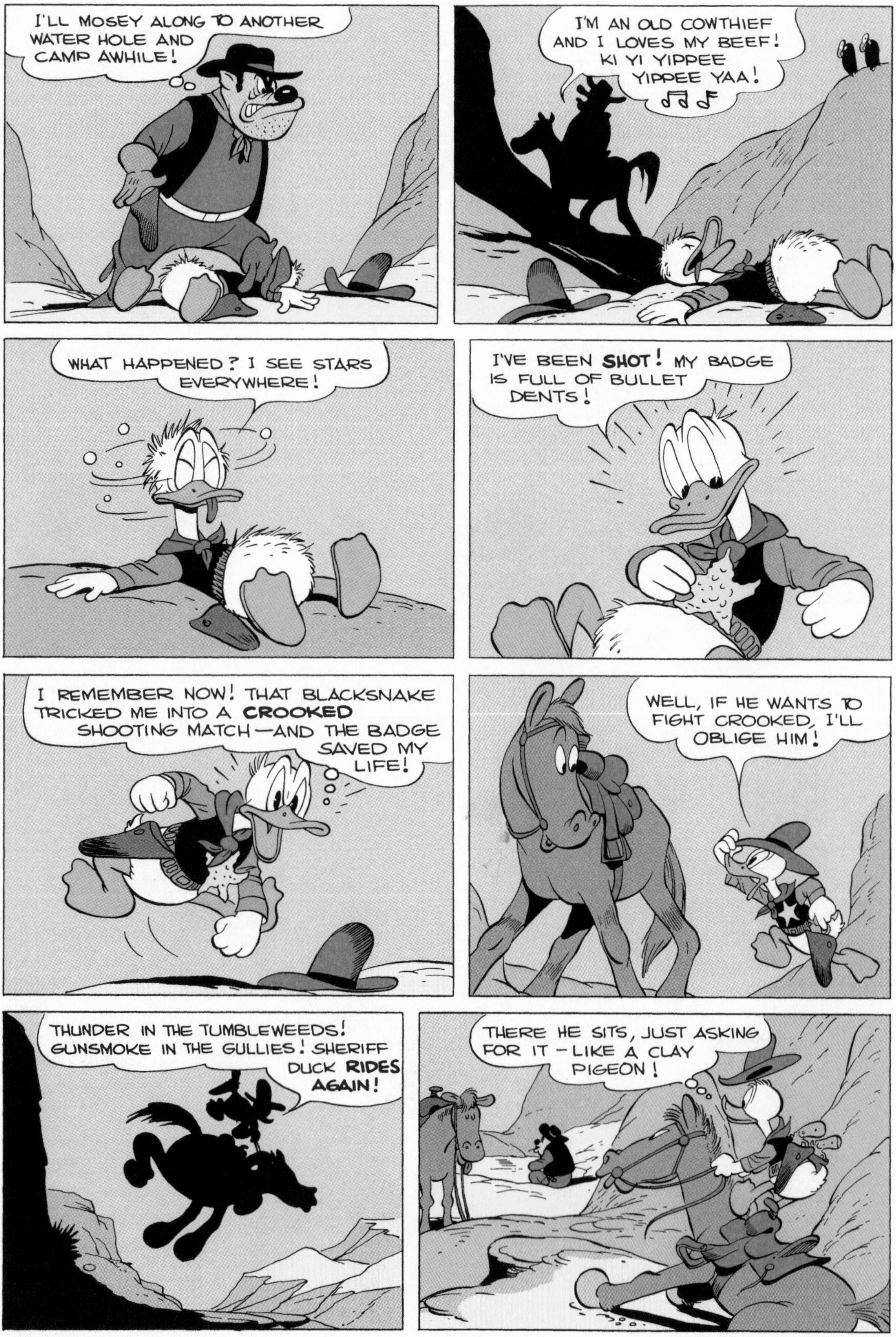
I'LL MOSEY ALONG TO ANOTHER WATER HOLE AND CAMP AWHILE!
I'M AN OLD COWTHIEF AND I LOVES MY BEEF! KI YI YIPPEE YIPPEE YAA!
WHAT HAPPENED? I SEE STARS EVERYWHERE!
I'VE BEEN **SHOT**! MY BADGE IS FULL OF BULLET DENTS!
I REMEMBER NOW! THAT BLACKSNAKE TRICKED ME INTO A **CROOKED** SHOOTING MATCH—AND THE BADGE SAVED MY LIFE!
WELL, IF HE WANTS TO FIGHT CROOKED, I'LL OBLIGE HIM!
THUNDER IN THE TUMBLEWEEDS! GUNSMOKE IN THE GULLIES! SHERIFF DUCK **RIDES AGAIN**!
THERE HE SITS, JUST ASKING FOR IT—LIKE A CLAY PIGEON!

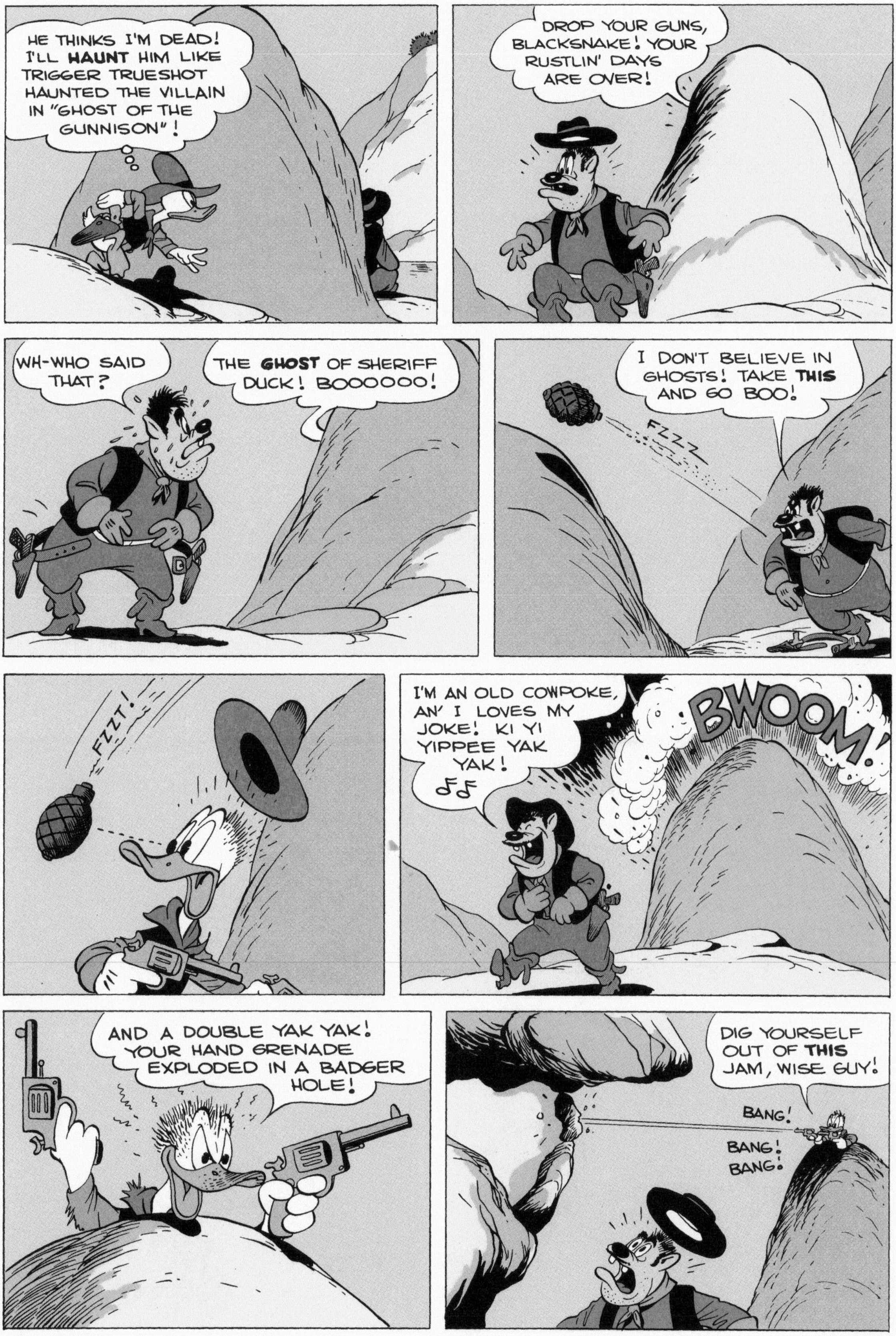
HE THINKS I'M DEAD! I'LL HAUNT HIM LIKE TRIGGER TRUESHOT HAUNTED THE VILLAIN IN "GHOST OF THE GUNNISON"!
DROP YOUR GUNS, BLACKSNAKE! YOUR RUSTLIN' DAYS ARE OVER!
WH-WHO SAID THAT?
THE GHOST OF SHERIFF DUCK! BOOOOOO!
I DON'T BELIEVE IN GHOSTS! TAKE THIS AND GO BOO!
FZZZ
FZZT!
I'M AN OLD COWPOKE, AN' I LOVES MY JOKE! KI YI YIPPEE YAK YAK!
BWOOM!
AND A DOUBLE YAK YAK! YOUR HAND GRENADE EXPLODED IN A BADGER HOLE!
DIG YOURSELF OUT OF THIS JAM, WISE GUY!
BANG!
BANG!
BANG!

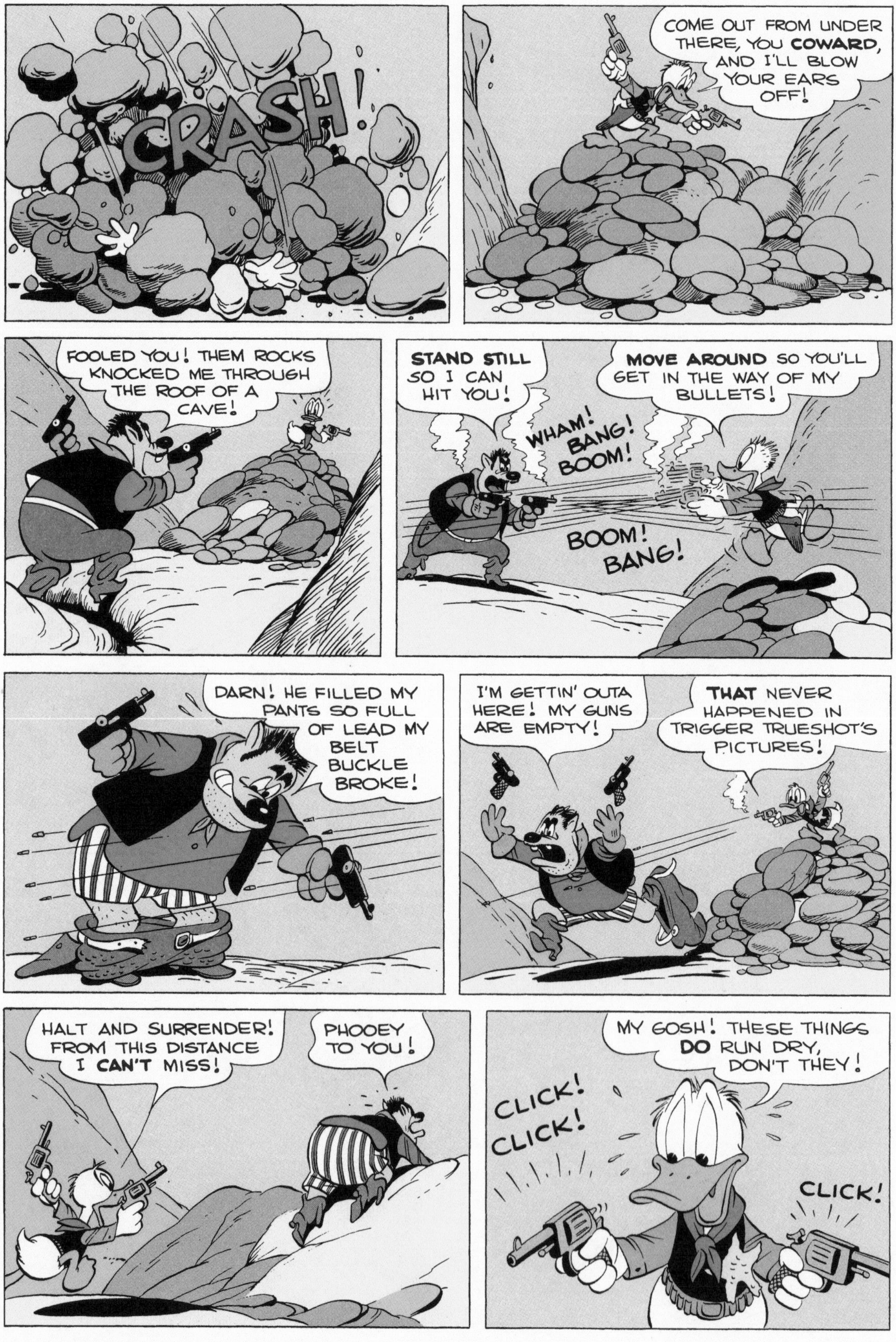
CRASH!
COME OUT FROM UNDER THERE, YOU **COWARD**, AND I'LL BLOW YOUR EARS OFF!
FOOLED YOU! THEM ROCKS KNOCKED ME THROUGH THE ROOF OF A CAVE!
STAND STILL SO I CAN HIT YOU!
MOVE AROUND SO YOU'LL GET IN THE WAY OF MY BULLETS!
WHAM! BANG! BOOM!
BOOM! BANG!
DARN! HE FILLED MY PANTS SO FULL OF LEAD MY BELT BUCKLE BROKE!
I'M GETTIN' OUTA HERE! MY GUNS ARE EMPTY!
THAT NEVER HAPPENED IN TRIGGER TRUESHOT'S PICTURES!
HALT AND SURRENDER! FROM THIS DISTANCE I **CAN'T** MISS!
PHOOEY TO YOU!
MY GOSH! THESE THINGS **DO** RUN DRY, DON'T THEY!
CLICK! CLICK!
CLICK!

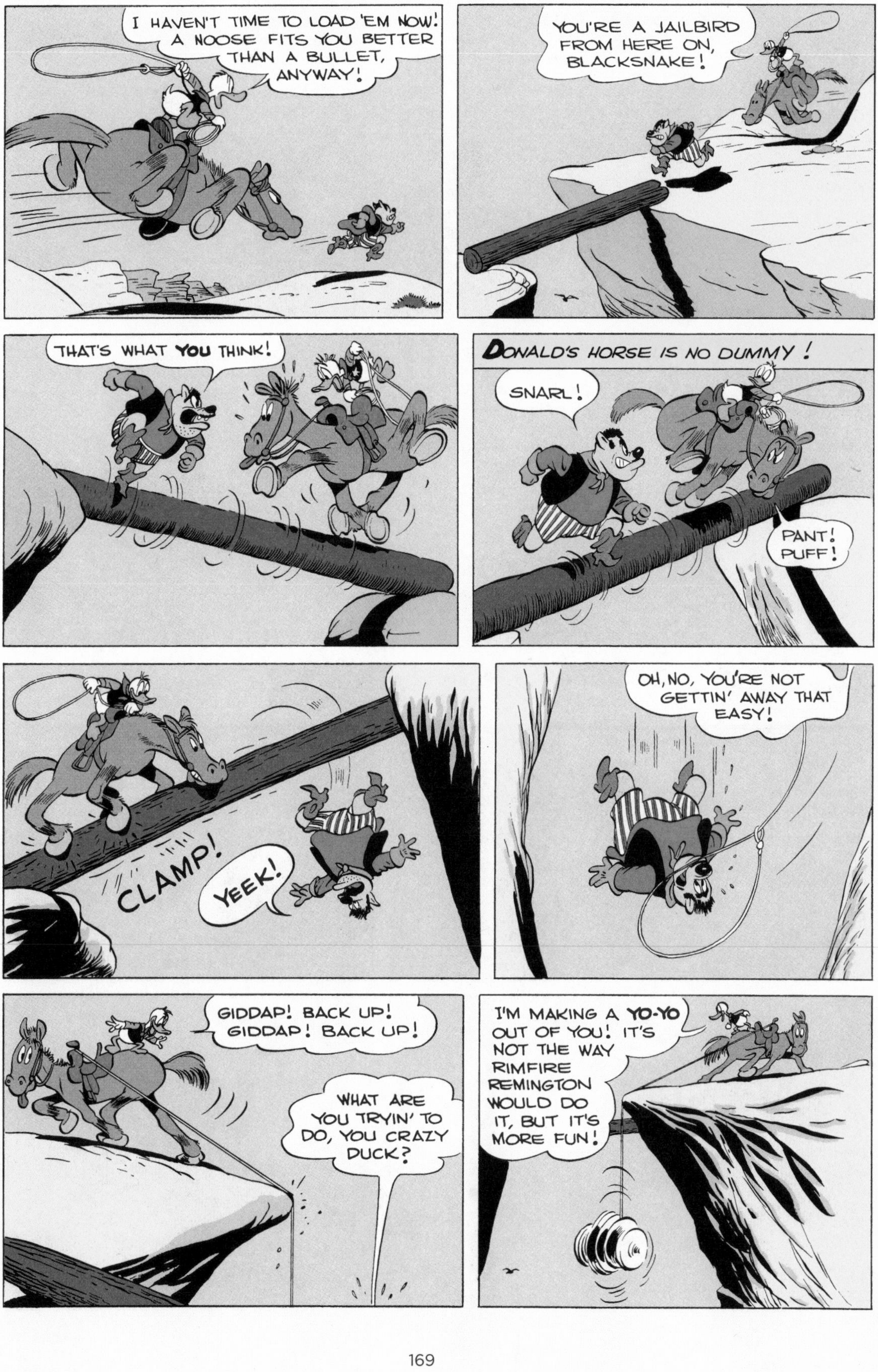
I HAVEN'T TIME TO LOAD 'EM NOW! A NOOSE FITS YOU BETTER THAN A BULLET, ANYWAY!
YOU'RE A JAILBIRD FROM HERE ON, BLACKSNAKE!
THAT'S WHAT YOU THINK!
DONALD'S HORSE IS NO DUMMY!
SNARL!
PANT! PUFF!
CLAMP!
YEEK!
OH, NO, YOU'RE NOT GETTIN' AWAY THAT EASY!
GIDDAP! BACK UP! GIDDAP! BACK UP!
WHAT ARE YOU TRYIN' TO DO, YOU CRAZY DUCK?
I'M MAKING A YO-YO OUT OF YOU! IT'S NOT THE WAY RIMFIRE REMINGTON WOULD DO IT, BUT IT'S MORE FUN!

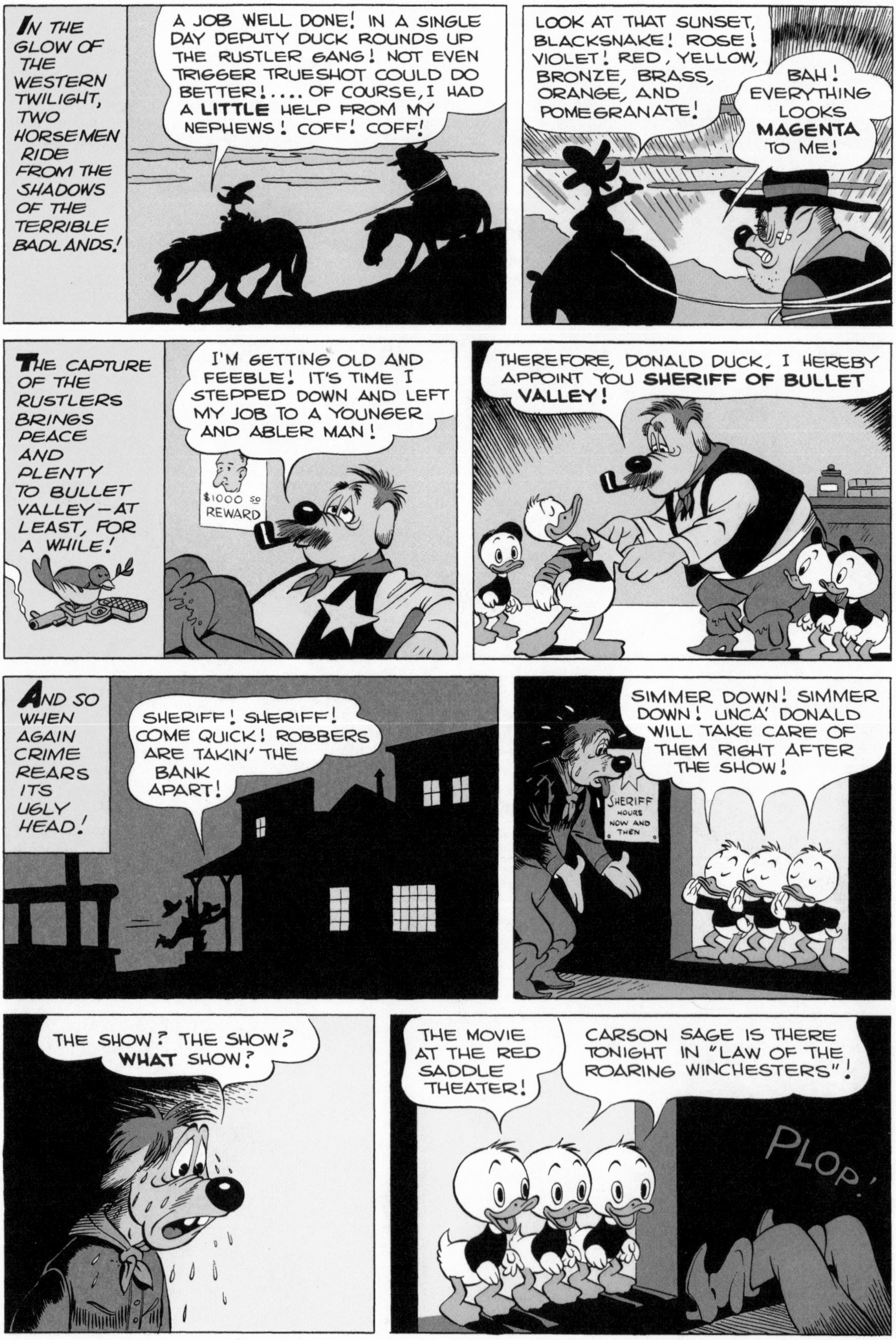
IN THE GLOW OF THE WESTERN TWILIGHT, TWO HORSEMEN RIDE FROM THE SHADOWS OF THE TERRIBLE BADLANDS!
A JOB WELL DONE! IN A SINGLE DAY DEPUTY DUCK ROUNDS UP THE RUSTLER GANG! NOT EVEN TRIGGER TRUESHOT COULD DO BETTER!.... OF COURSE, I HAD A LITTLE HELP FROM MY NEPHEWS! COFF! COFF!
LOOK AT THAT SUNSET, BLACKSNAKE! ROSE! VIOLET! RED, YELLOW, BRONZE, BRASS, ORANGE, AND POMEGRANATE!
BAH! EVERYTHING LOOKS MAGENTA TO ME!
THE CAPTURE OF THE RUSTLERS BRINGS PEACE AND PLENTY TO BULLET VALLEY—AT LEAST, FOR A WHILE!
I'M GETTING OLD AND FEEBLE! IT'S TIME I STEPPED DOWN AND LEFT MY JOB TO A YOUNGER AND ABLER MAN!
$1000 50 REWARD
THEREFORE, DONALD DUCK, I HEREBY APPOINT YOU SHERIFF OF BULLET VALLEY!
AND SO WHEN AGAIN CRIME REARS ITS UGLY HEAD!
SHERIFF! SHERIFF! COME QUICK! ROBBERS ARE TAKIN' THE BANK APART!
SHERIFF HOURS NOW AND THEN
SIMMER DOWN! SIMMER DOWN! UNCA' DONALD WILL TAKE CARE OF THEM RIGHT AFTER THE SHOW!
THE SHOW? THE SHOW? WHAT SHOW?
THE MOVIE AT THE RED SADDLE THEATER!
CARSON SAGE IS THERE TONIGHT IN "LAW OF THE ROARING WINCHESTERS"!
PLOP!

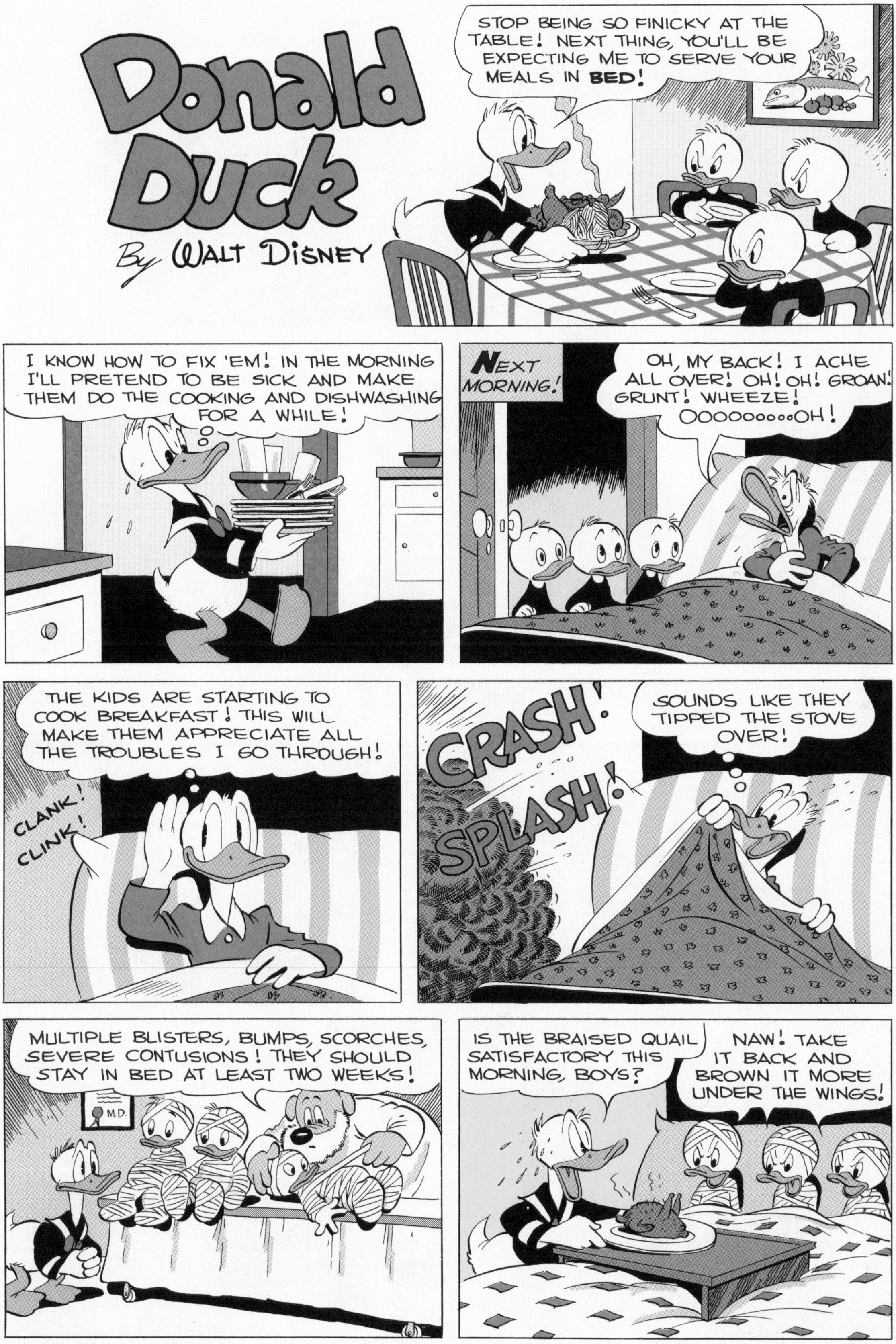
Donald Duck
By Walt Disney
STOP BEING SO FINICKY AT THE TABLE! NEXT THING, YOU'LL BE EXPECTING ME TO SERVE YOUR MEALS IN **BED**!
I KNOW HOW TO FIX 'EM! IN THE MORNING I'LL PRETEND TO BE SICK AND MAKE THEM DO THE COOKING AND DISHWASHING FOR A WHILE!
NEXT MORNING!
OH, MY BACK! I ACHE ALL OVER! OH! OH! GROAN! GRUNT! WHEEZE! OOOOOOOOOOH!
THE KIDS ARE STARTING TO COOK BREAKFAST! THIS WILL MAKE THEM APPRECIATE ALL THE TROUBLES I GO THROUGH!
CLANK! CLINK!
CRASH!
SPLASH!
SOUNDS LIKE THEY TIPPED THE STOVE OVER!
MULTIPLE BLISTERS, BUMPS, SCORCHES, SEVERE CONTUSIONS! THEY SHOULD STAY IN BED AT LEAST TWO WEEKS!
M.D.
IS THE BRAISED QUAIL SATISFACTORY THIS MORNING, BOYS?
NAW! TAKE IT BACK AND BROWN IT MORE UNDER THE WINGS!

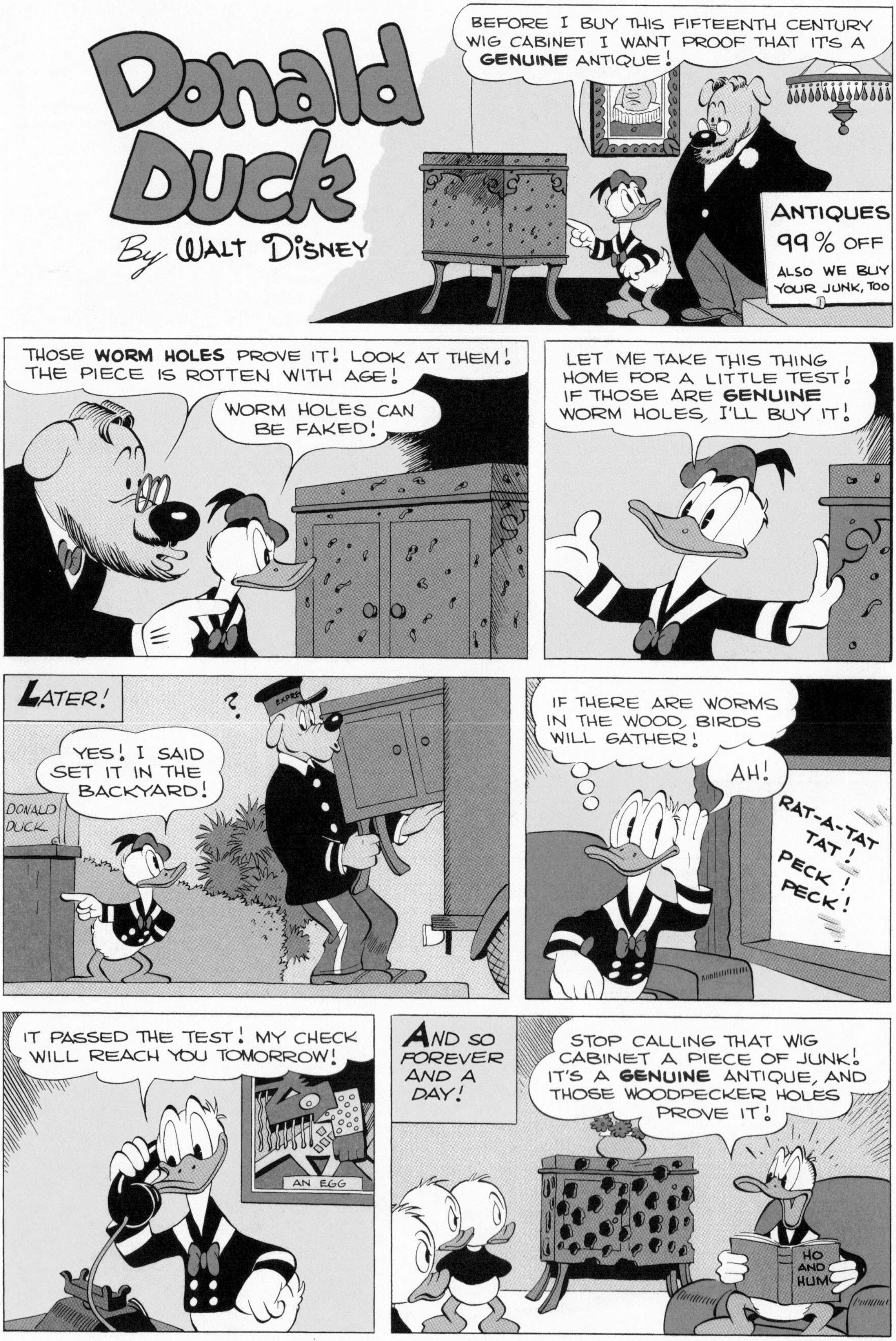
Donald Duck
By Walt Disney
BEFORE I BUY THIS FIFTEENTH CENTURY WIG CABINET I WANT PROOF THAT IT'S A GENUINE ANTIQUE!
ANTIQUES 99% OFF ALSO WE BUY YOUR JUNK, TOO
THOSE WORM HOLES PROVE IT! LOOK AT THEM! THE PIECE IS ROTTEN WITH AGE!
WORM HOLES CAN BE FAKED!
LET ME TAKE THIS THING HOME FOR A LITTLE TEST! IF THOSE ARE GENUINE WORM HOLES, I'LL BUY IT!
LATER!
YES! I SAID SET IT IN THE BACKYARD!
DONALD DUCK
IF THERE ARE WORMS IN THE WOOD, BIRDS WILL GATHER!
AH!
RAT-A-TAT TAT! PECK! PECK!
IT PASSED THE TEST! MY CHECK WILL REACH YOU TOMORROW!
AN EGG
AND SO FOREVER AND A DAY!
STOP CALLING THAT WIG CABINET A PIECE OF JUNK! IT'S A GENUINE ANTIQUE, AND THOSE WOODPECKER HOLES PROVE IT!
HO AND HUM

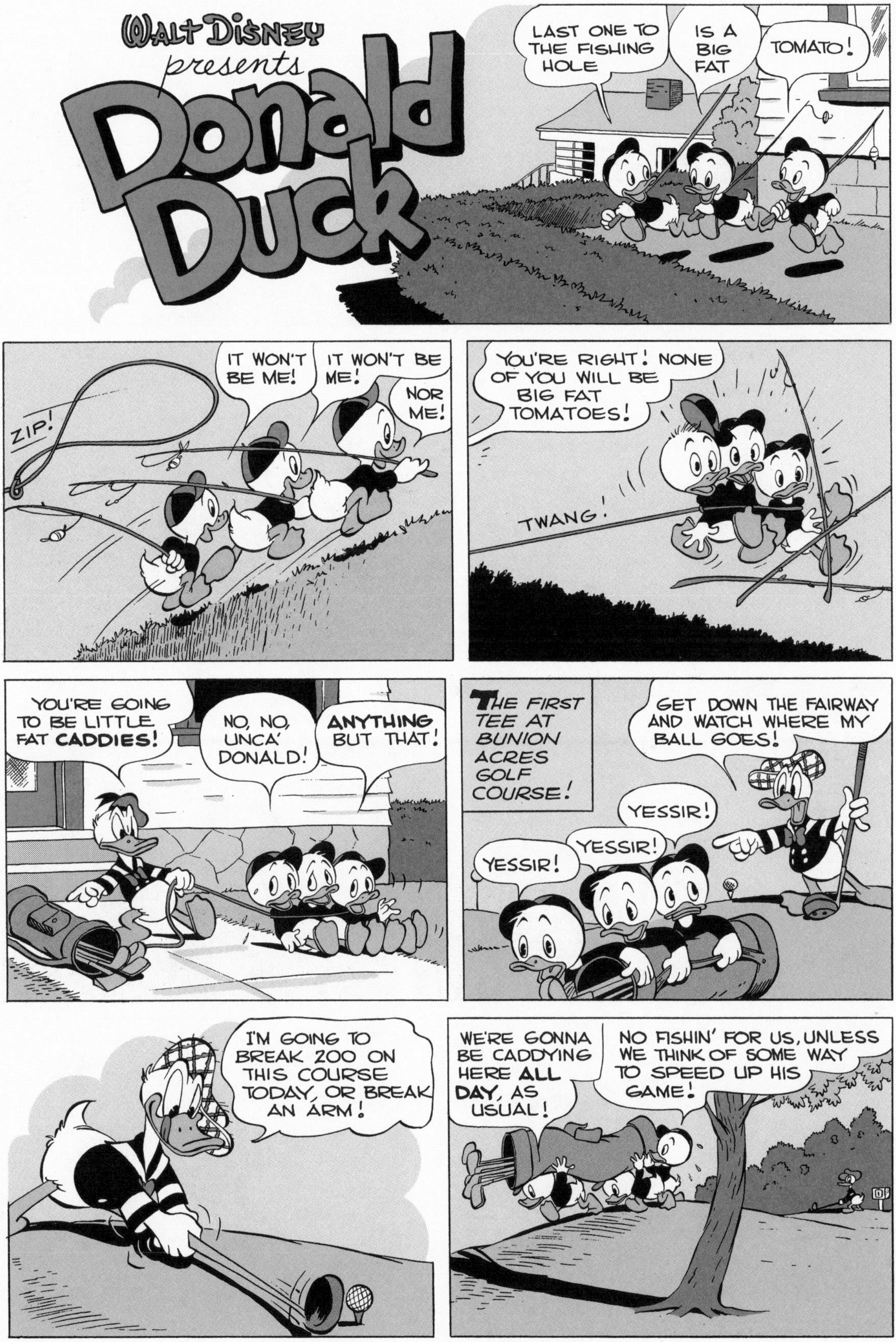
WALT DISNEY
presents
Donald Duck
LAST ONE TO THE FISHING HOLE
IS A BIG FAT
TOMATO!
ZIP!
IT WON'T BE ME!
IT WON'T BE ME!
NOR ME!
YOU'RE RIGHT! NONE OF YOU WILL BE BIG FAT TOMATOES!
TWANG!
YOU'RE GOING TO BE LITTLE FAT CADDIES!
NO, NO, UNCA' DONALD!
ANYTHING BUT THAT!
THE FIRST TEE AT BUNION ACRES GOLF COURSE!
GET DOWN THE FAIRWAY AND WATCH WHERE MY BALL GOES!
YESSIR!
YESSIR!
YESSIR!
I'M GOING TO BREAK 200 ON THIS COURSE TODAY, OR BREAK AN ARM!
WE'RE GONNA BE CADDYING HERE ALL DAY, AS USUAL!
NO FISHIN' FOR US, UNLESS WE THINK OF SOME WAY TO SPEED UP HIS GAME!

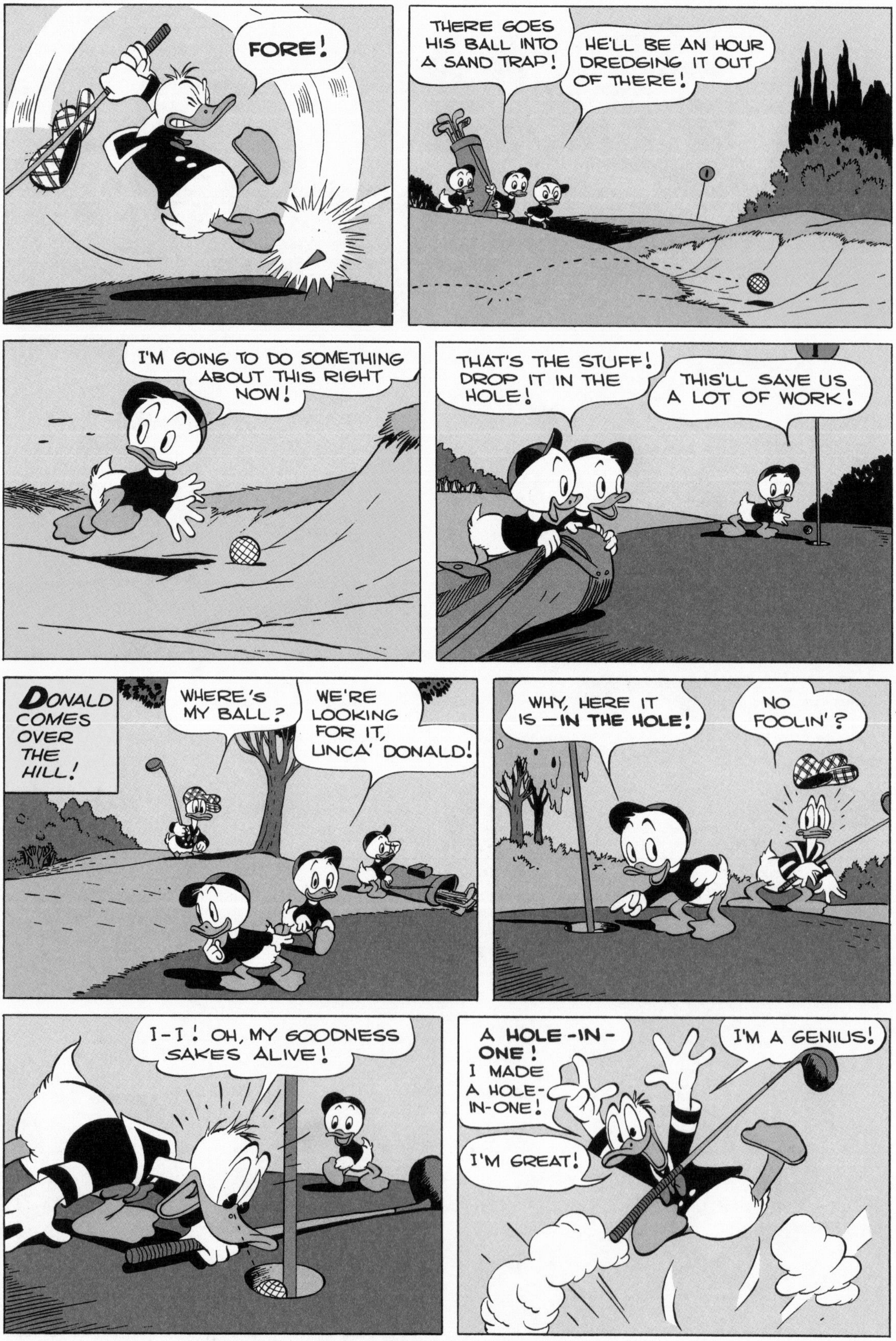
FORE!
THERE GOES HIS BALL INTO A SAND TRAP!
HE'LL BE AN HOUR DREDGING IT OUT OF THERE!
I'M GOING TO DO SOMETHING ABOUT THIS RIGHT NOW!
THAT'S THE STUFF! DROP IT IN THE HOLE!
THIS'LL SAVE US A LOT OF WORK!
DONALD COMES OVER THE HILL!
WHERE'S MY BALL?
WE'RE LOOKING FOR IT, UNCA' DONALD!
WHY, HERE IT IS—IN THE HOLE!
NO FOOLIN'?
I-I! OH, MY GOODNESS SAKES ALIVE!
A HOLE-IN-ONE! I MADE A HOLE-IN-ONE!
I'M A GENIUS!
I'M GREAT!

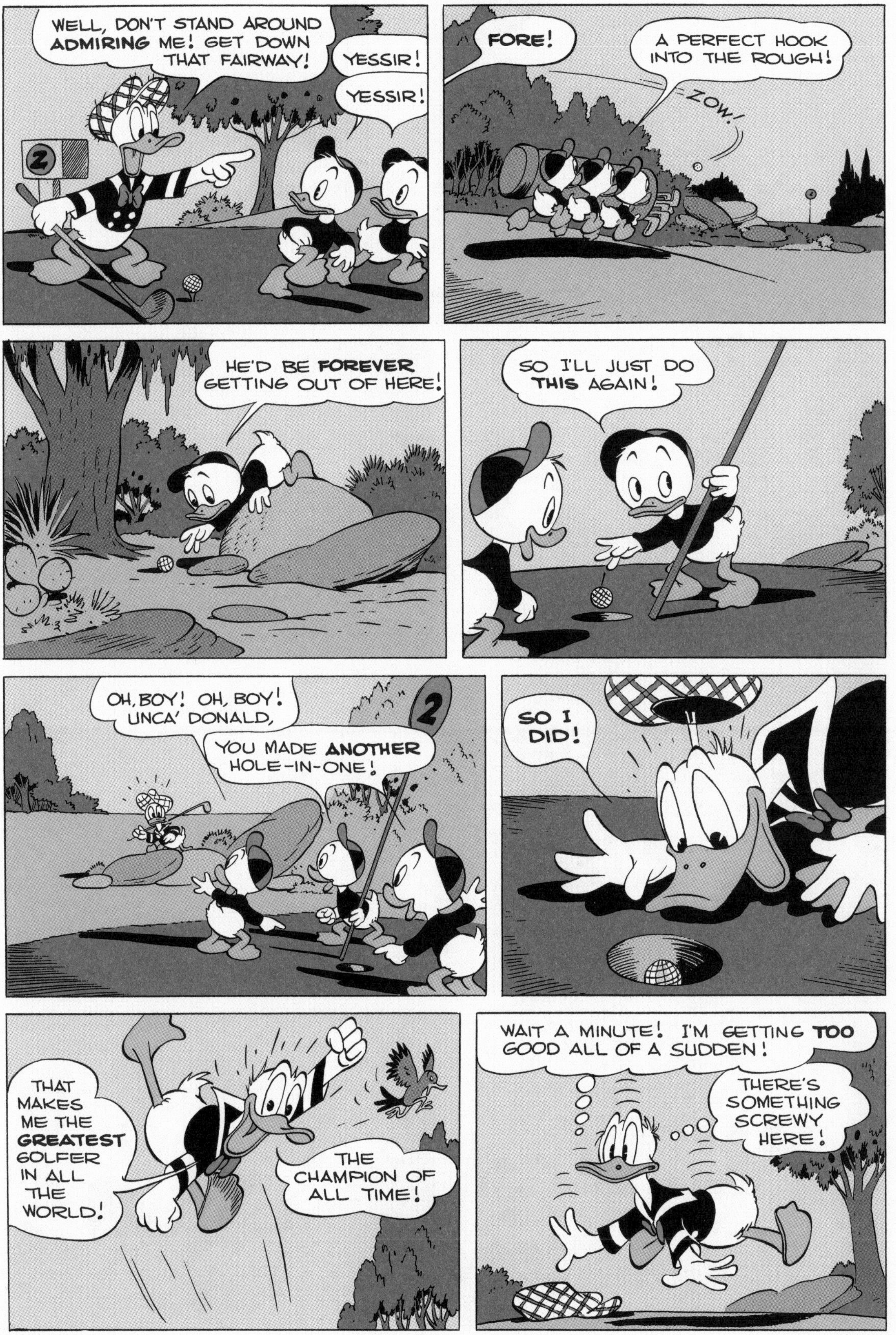
WELL, DON'T STAND AROUND ADMIRING ME! GET DOWN THAT FAIRWAY!
YESSIR!
YESSIR!
FORE!
A PERFECT HOOK INTO THE ROUGH!
ZOW!
HE'D BE FOREVER GETTING OUT OF HERE!
SO I'LL JUST DO THIS AGAIN!
OH, BOY! OH, BOY! UNCA' DONALD,
YOU MADE ANOTHER HOLE-IN-ONE!
SO I DID!
THAT MAKES ME THE GREATEST GOLFER IN ALL THE WORLD!
THE CHAMPION OF ALL TIME!
WAIT A MINUTE! I'M GETTING TOO GOOD ALL OF A SUDDEN!
THERE'S SOMETHING SCREWY HERE!

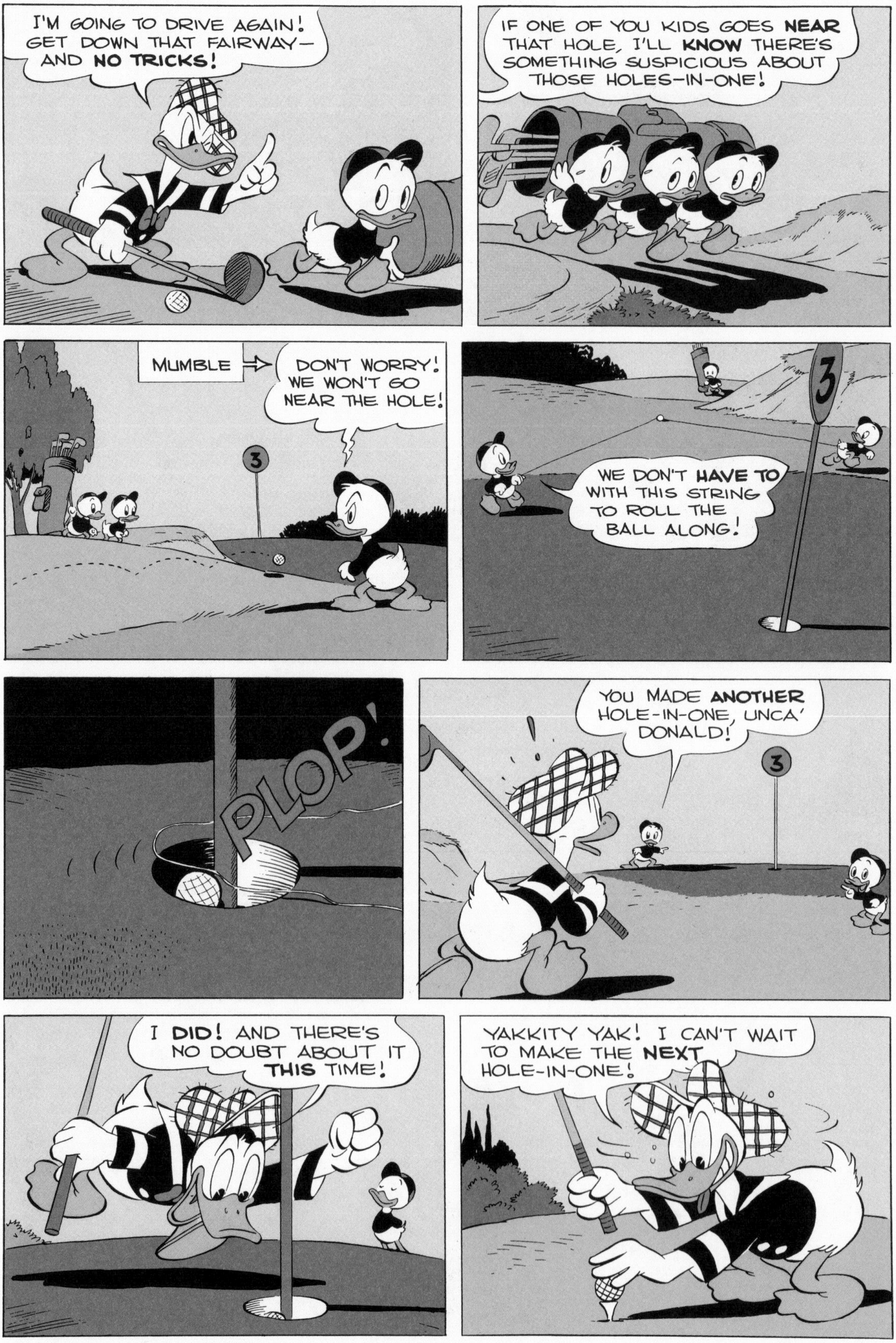
I'M GOING TO DRIVE AGAIN! GET DOWN THAT FAIRWAY— AND NO TRICKS!
IF ONE OF YOU KIDS GOES NEAR THAT HOLE, I'LL KNOW THERE'S SOMETHING SUSPICIOUS ABOUT THOSE HOLES-IN-ONE!
MUMBLE
DON'T WORRY! WE WON'T GO NEAR THE HOLE!
3
3
WE DON'T HAVE TO WITH THIS STRING TO ROLL THE BALL ALONG!
PLOP!
!
YOU MADE ANOTHER HOLE-IN-ONE, UNCA' DONALD!
3
I DID! AND THERE'S NO DOUBT ABOUT IT THIS TIME!
YAKKITY YAK! I CAN'T WAIT TO MAKE THE NEXT HOLE-IN-ONE!

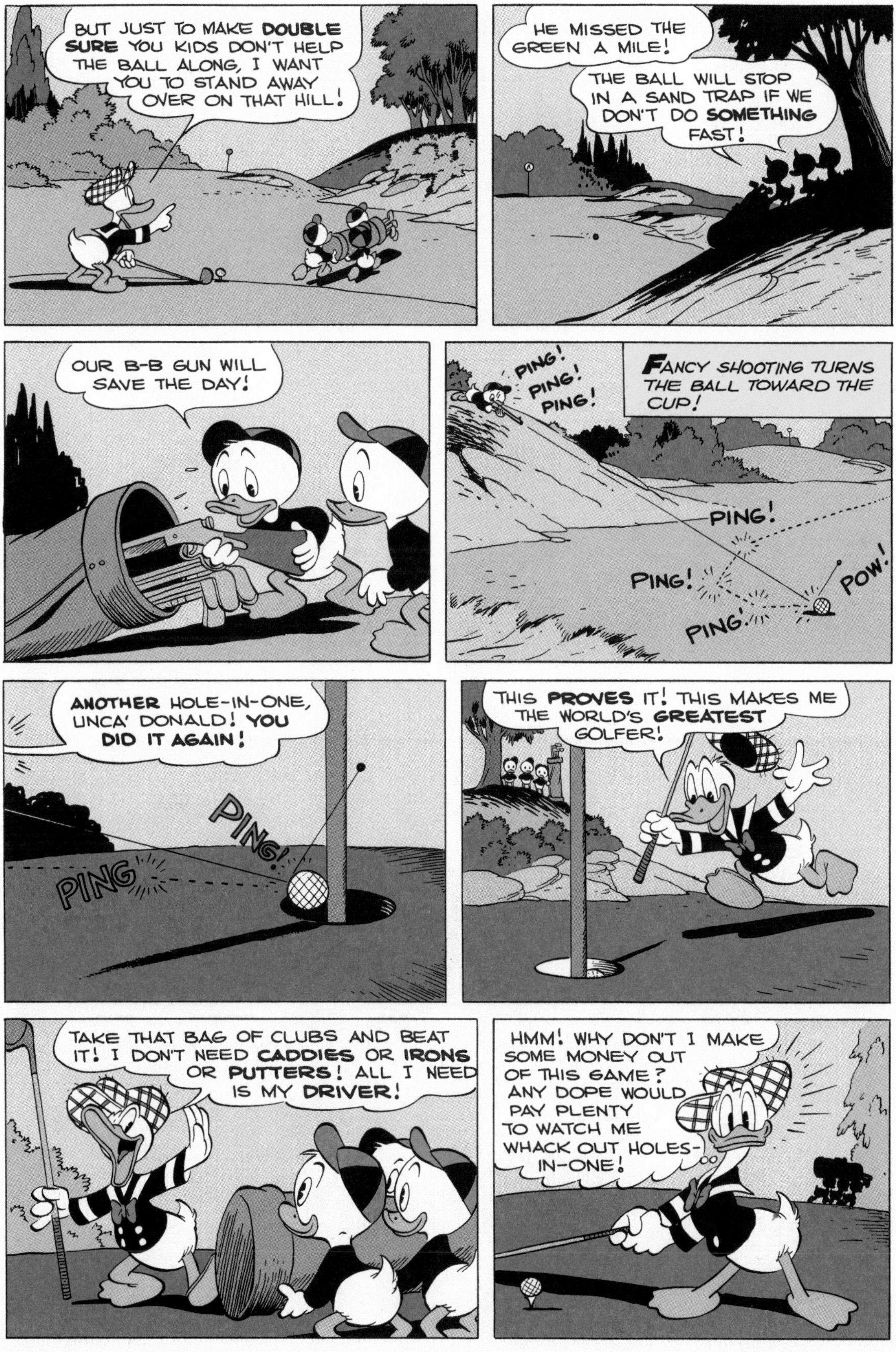
BUT JUST TO MAKE **DOUBLE SURE** YOU KIDS DON'T HELP THE BALL ALONG, I WANT YOU TO STAND AWAY OVER ON THAT HILL!
HE MISSED THE GREEN A MILE!
THE BALL WILL STOP IN A SAND TRAP IF WE DON'T DO **SOMETHING** FAST!
OUR B-B GUN WILL SAVE THE DAY!
PING! PING! PING!
FANCY SHOOTING TURNS THE BALL TOWARD THE CUP!
PING!
PING!
PING!
POW!
ANOTHER HOLE-IN-ONE, UNCA' DONALD! **YOU DID IT AGAIN!**
PING!
PING
THIS **PROVES** IT! THIS MAKES ME THE WORLD'S **GREATEST** GOLFER!
TAKE THAT BAG OF CLUBS AND BEAT IT! I DON'T NEED **CADDIES** OR **IRONS** OR **PUTTERS**! ALL I NEED IS MY **DRIVER**!
HMM! WHY DON'T I MAKE SOME MONEY OUT OF THIS GAME? ANY DOPE WOULD PAY PLENTY TO WATCH ME WHACK OUT HOLES-IN-ONE!

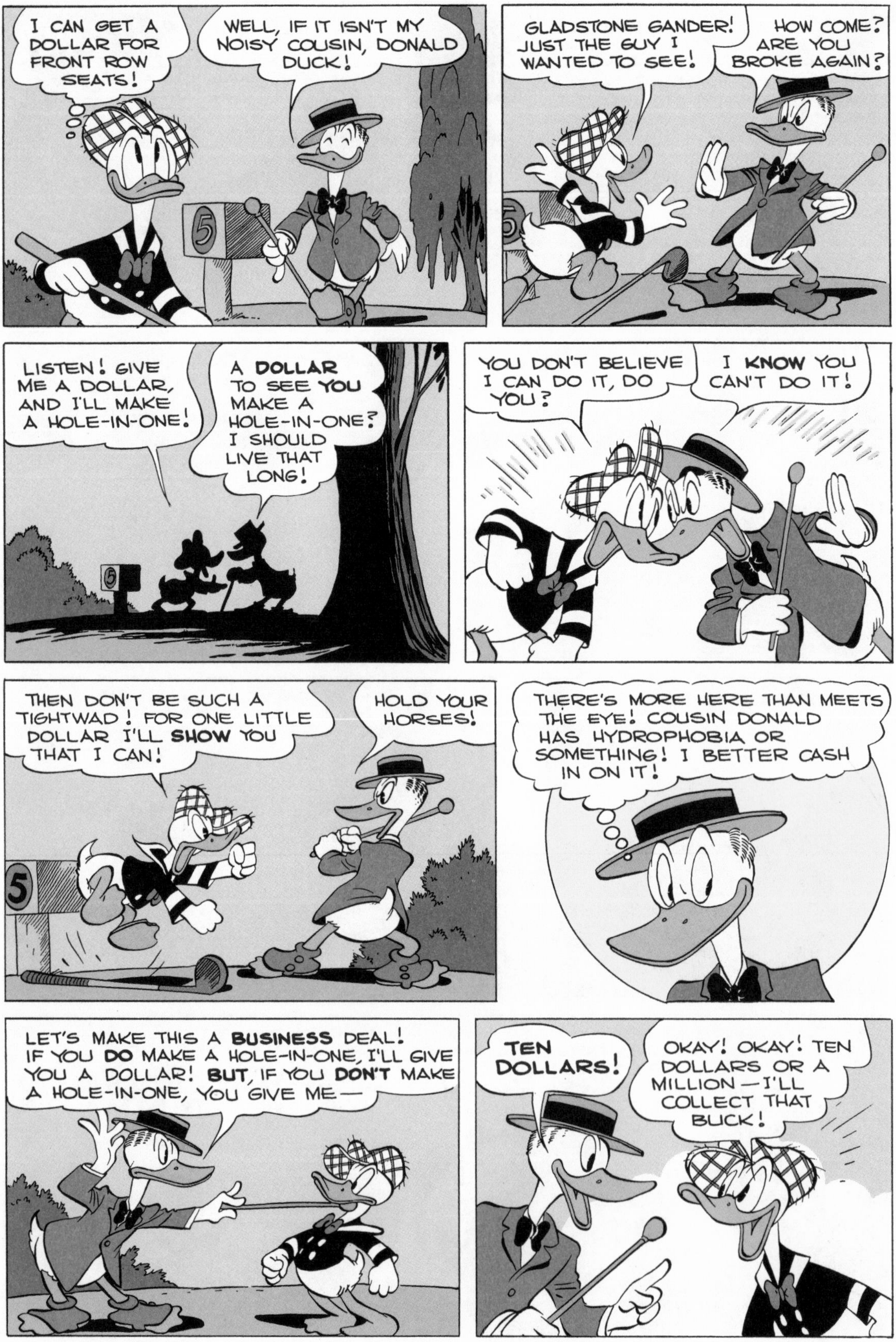
I CAN GET A DOLLAR FOR FRONT ROW SEATS!
WELL, IF IT ISN'T MY NOISY COUSIN, DONALD DUCK!
GLADSTONE GANDER! JUST THE GUY I WANTED TO SEE!
HOW COME? ARE YOU BROKE AGAIN?
LISTEN! GIVE ME A DOLLAR, AND I'LL MAKE A HOLE-IN-ONE!
A **DOLLAR** TO SEE **YOU** MAKE A HOLE-IN-ONE? I SHOULD LIVE THAT LONG!
YOU DON'T BELIEVE I CAN DO IT, DO YOU?
I **KNOW** YOU CAN'T DO IT!
THEN DON'T BE SUCH A TIGHTWAD! FOR ONE LITTLE DOLLAR I'LL **SHOW** YOU THAT I CAN!
HOLD YOUR HORSES!
THERE'S MORE HERE THAN MEETS THE EYE! COUSIN DONALD HAS HYDROPHOBIA OR SOMETHING! I BETTER CASH IN ON IT!
LET'S MAKE THIS A **BUSINESS** DEAL! IF YOU **DO** MAKE A HOLE-IN-ONE, I'LL GIVE YOU A DOLLAR! **BUT**, IF YOU **DON'T** MAKE A HOLE-IN-ONE, YOU GIVE ME—
TEN DOLLARS!
OKAY! OKAY! TEN DOLLARS OR A MILLION—I'LL COLLECT THAT BUCK!

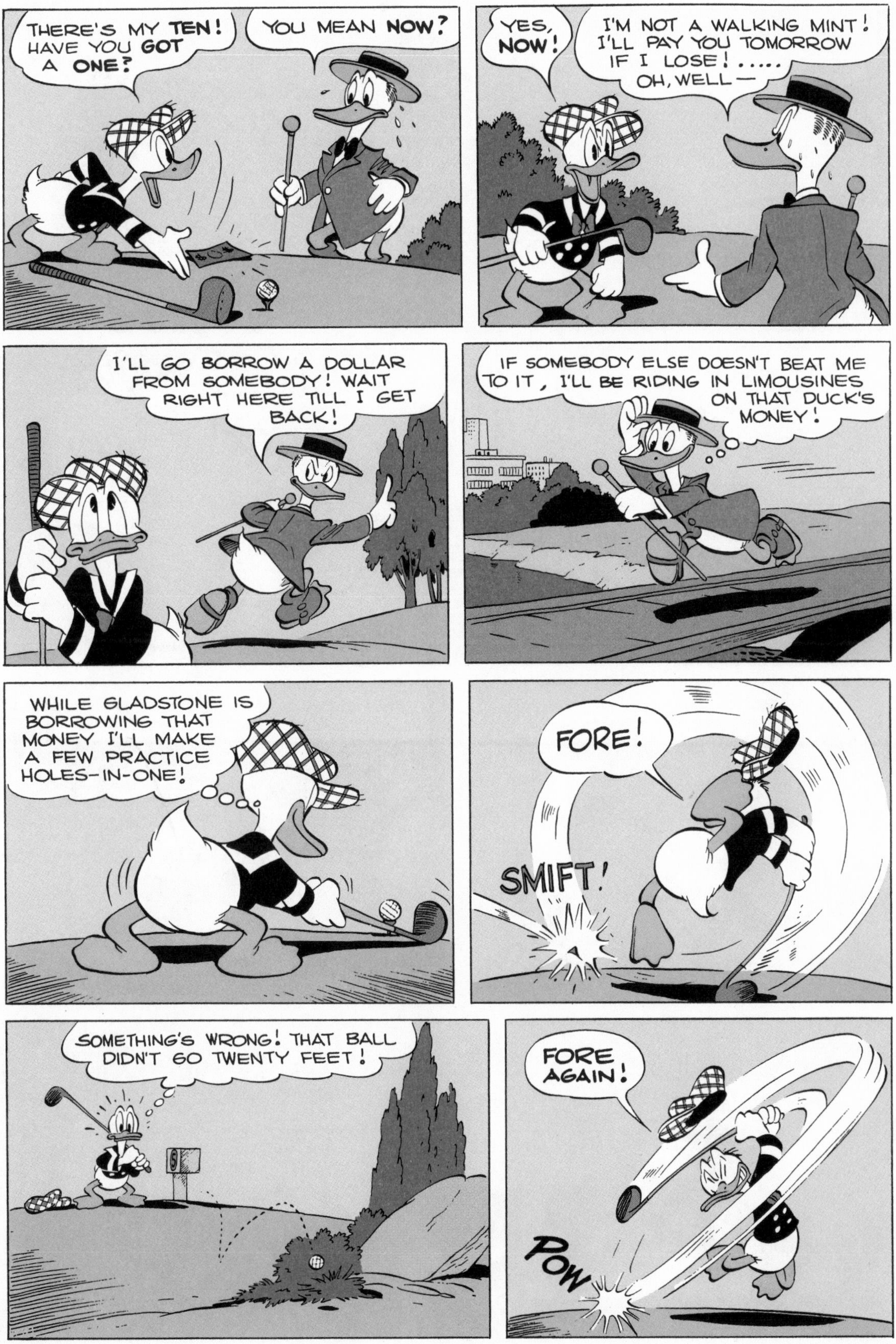
THERE'S MY TEN! HAVE YOU GOT A ONE?
YOU MEAN NOW?
YES, NOW!
I'M NOT A WALKING MINT! I'LL PAY YOU TOMORROW IF I LOSE! ..... OH, WELL—
I'LL GO BORROW A DOLLAR FROM SOMEBODY! WAIT RIGHT HERE TILL I GET BACK!
IF SOMEBODY ELSE DOESN'T BEAT ME TO IT, I'LL BE RIDING IN LIMOUSINES ON THAT DUCK'S MONEY!
WHILE GLADSTONE IS BORROWING THAT MONEY I'LL MAKE A FEW PRACTICE HOLES-IN-ONE!
FORE!
SMIFT!
SOMETHING'S WRONG! THAT BALL DIDN'T GO TWENTY FEET!
FORE AGAIN!
POW

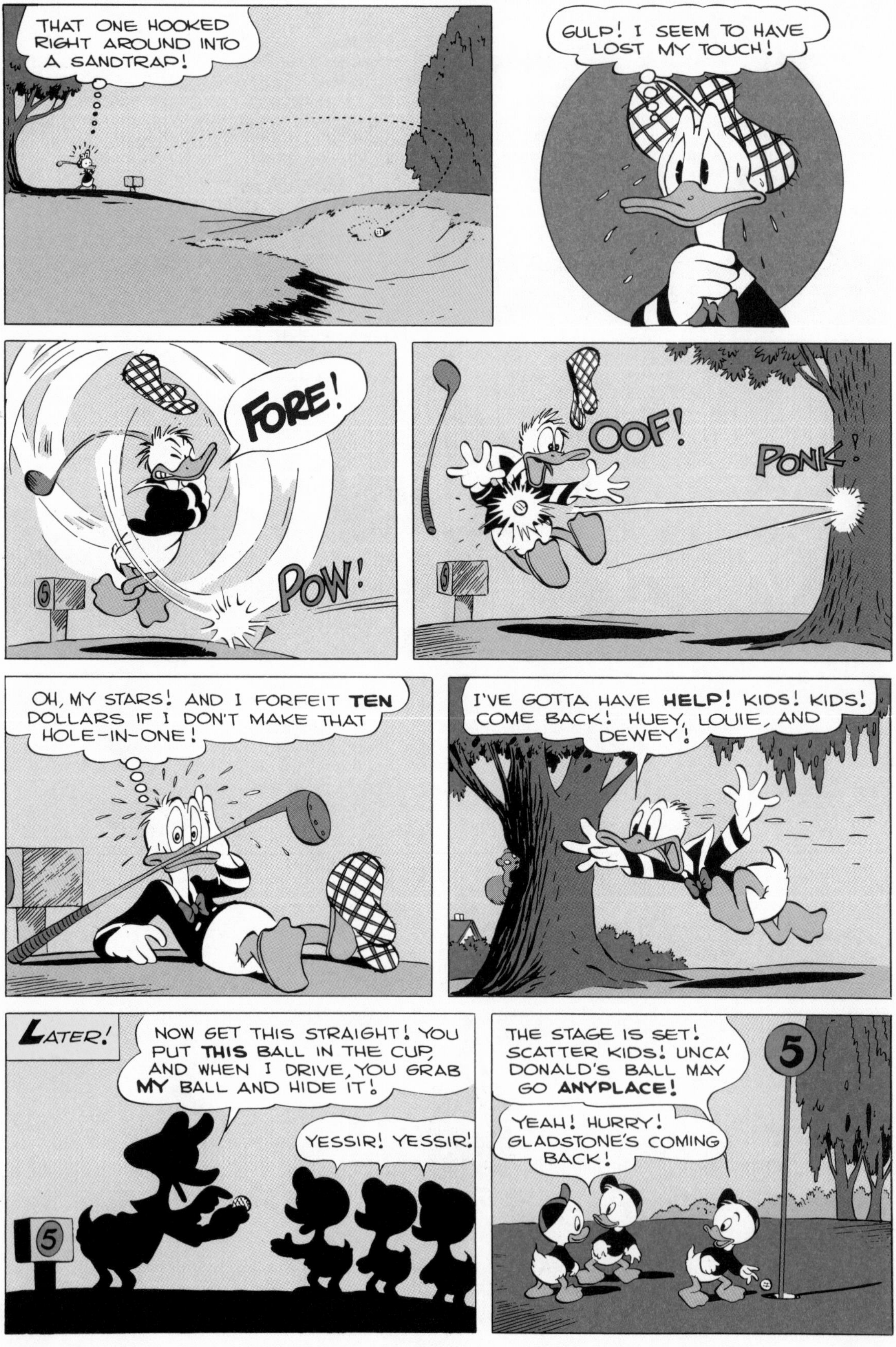

THAT ONE HOOKED RIGHT AROUND INTO A SANDTRAP!
GULP! I SEEM TO HAVE LOST MY TOUCH!
FORE!
POW!
5
OOF!
PONK!
5
OH, MY STARS! AND I FORFEIT TEN DOLLARS IF I DON'T MAKE THAT HOLE-IN-ONE!
I'VE GOTTA HAVE HELP! KIDS! KIDS! COME BACK! HUEY, LOUIE, AND DEWEY!
LATER!
NOW GET THIS STRAIGHT! YOU PUT THIS BALL IN THE CUP, AND WHEN I DRIVE, YOU GRAB MY BALL AND HIDE IT!
YESSIR! YESSIR!
5
THE STAGE IS SET! SCATTER KIDS! UNCA' DONALD'S BALL MAY GO ANYPLACE!
YEAH! HURRY! GLADSTONE'S COMING BACK!
5

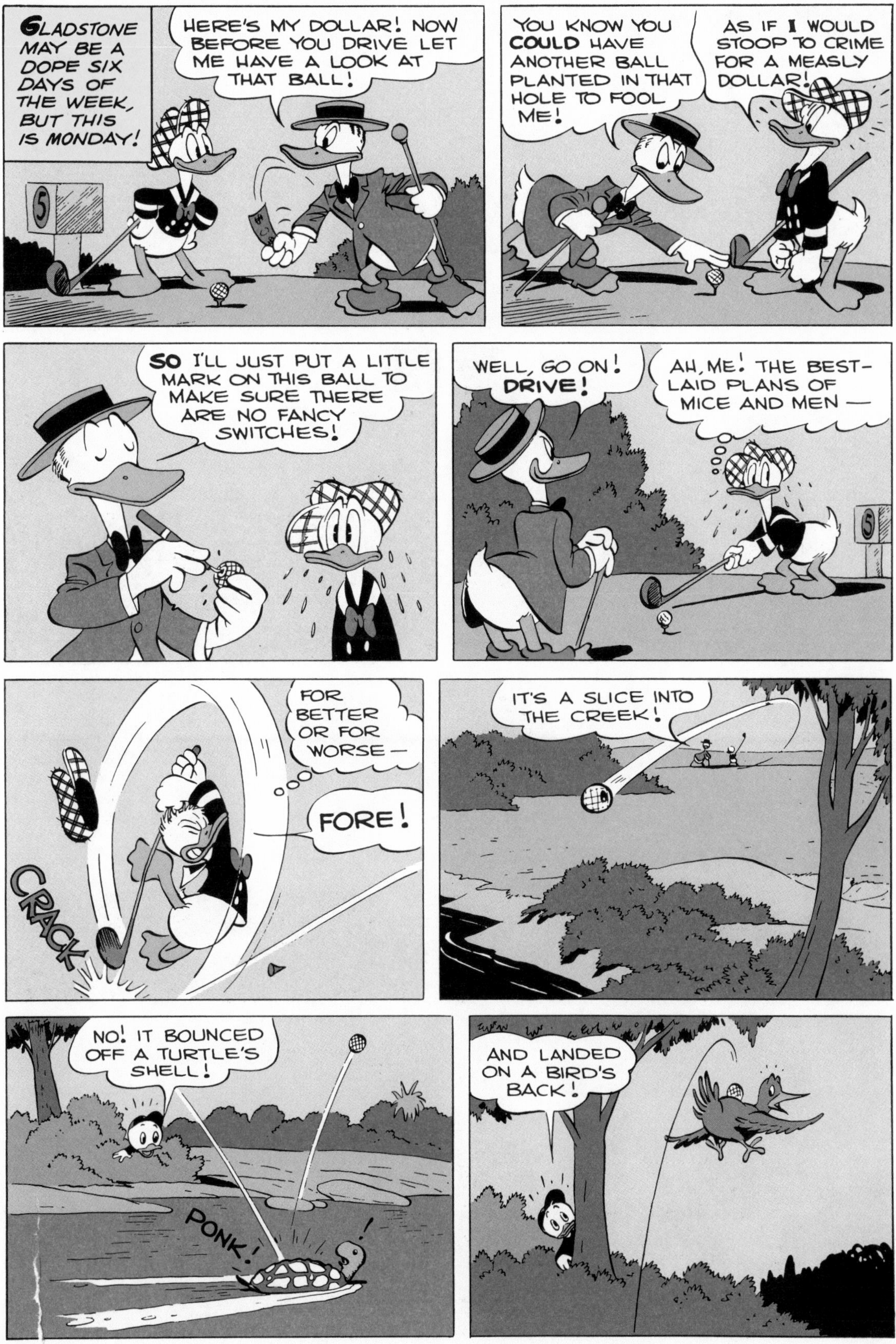
GLADSTONE MAY BE A DOPE SIX DAYS OF THE WEEK, BUT THIS IS MONDAY!
HERE'S MY DOLLAR! NOW BEFORE YOU DRIVE LET ME HAVE A LOOK AT THAT BALL!
YOU KNOW YOU COULD HAVE ANOTHER BALL PLANTED IN THAT HOLE TO FOOL ME!
AS IF I WOULD STOOP TO CRIME FOR A MEASLY DOLLAR!
SO I'LL JUST PUT A LITTLE MARK ON THIS BALL TO MAKE SURE THERE ARE NO FANCY SWITCHES!
WELL, GO ON! DRIVE!
AH, ME! THE BEST-LAID PLANS OF MICE AND MEN —
FOR BETTER OR FOR WORSE —
FORE!
CRACK
IT'S A SLICE INTO THE CREEK!
NO! IT BOUNCED OFF A TURTLE'S SHELL!
PONK!
AND LANDED ON A BIRD'S BACK!

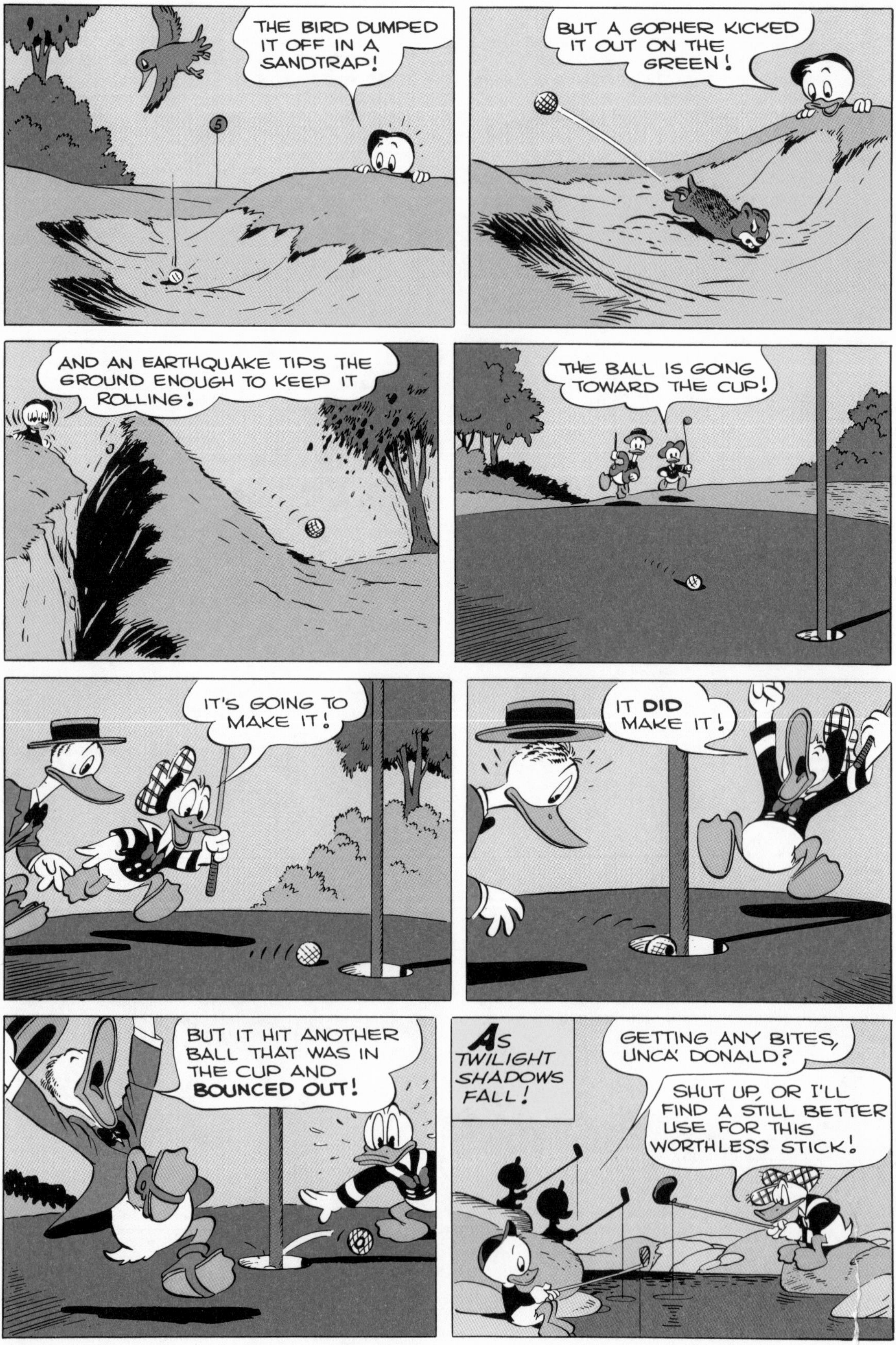
THE BIRD DUMPED IT OFF IN A SANDTRAP!
BUT A GOPHER KICKED IT OUT ON THE GREEN!
AND AN EARTHQUAKE TIPS THE GROUND ENOUGH TO KEEP IT ROLLING!
THE BALL IS GOING TOWARD THE CUP!
IT'S GOING TO MAKE IT!
IT **DID** MAKE IT!
BUT IT HIT ANOTHER BALL THAT WAS IN THE CUP AND **BOUNCED OUT**!
AS TWILIGHT SHADOWS FALL!
GETTING ANY BITES, UNCA' DONALD?
SHUT UP, OR I'LL FIND A STILL BETTER USE FOR THIS WORTHLESS STICK!

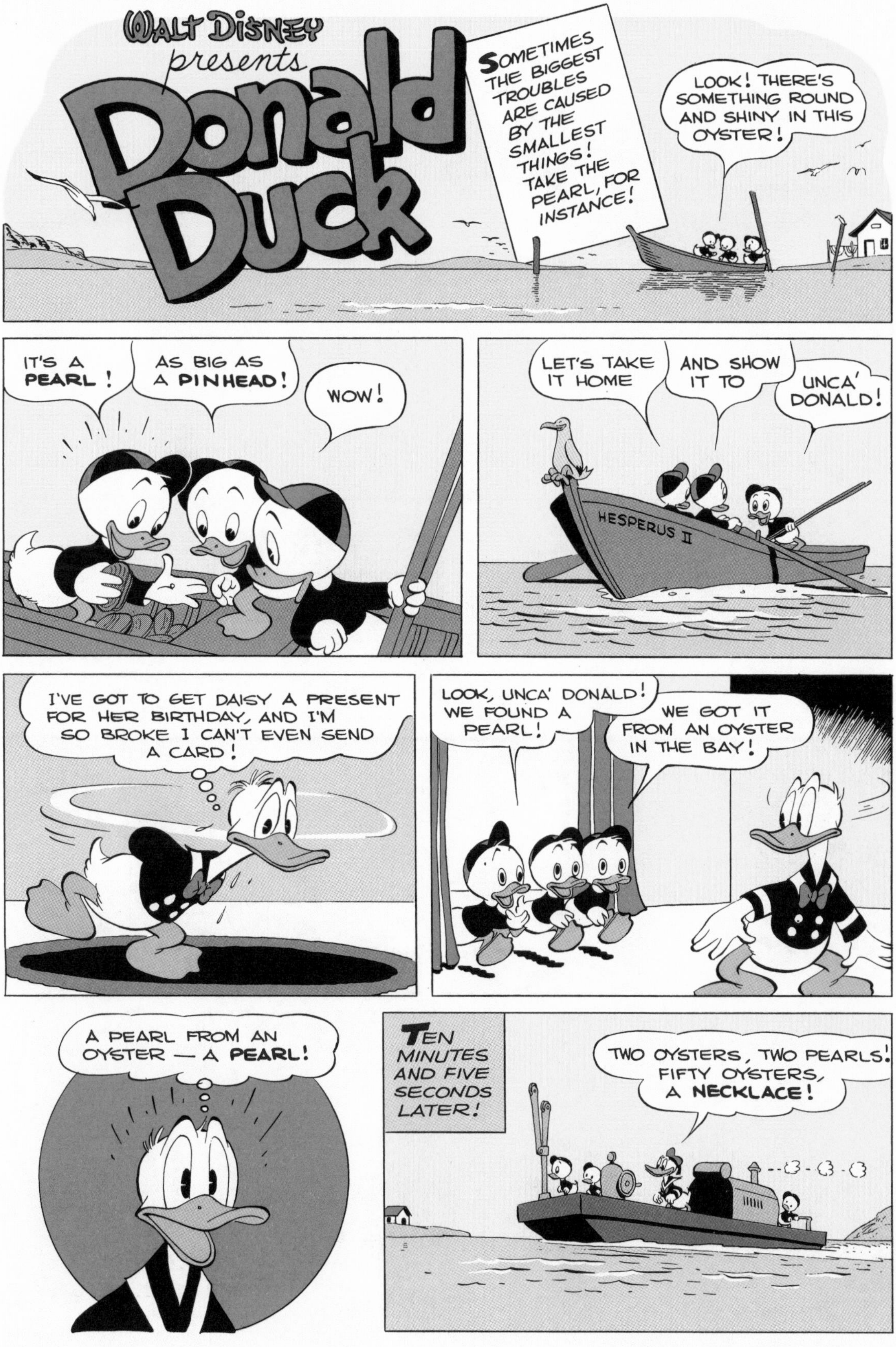
WALT DISNEY presents
Donald Duck
SOMETIMES THE BIGGEST TROUBLES ARE CAUSED BY THE SMALLEST THINGS! TAKE THE PEARL, FOR INSTANCE!
LOOK! THERE'S SOMETHING ROUND AND SHINY IN THIS OYSTER!
IT'S A PEARL!
AS BIG AS A PINHEAD!
WOW!
LET'S TAKE IT HOME
AND SHOW IT TO
UNCA' DONALD!
HESPERUS II
I'VE GOT TO GET DAISY A PRESENT FOR HER BIRTHDAY, AND I'M SO BROKE I CAN'T EVEN SEND A CARD!
LOOK, UNCA' DONALD! WE FOUND A PEARL!
WE GOT IT FROM AN OYSTER IN THE BAY!
A PEARL FROM AN OYSTER — A PEARL!
TEN MINUTES AND FIVE SECONDS LATER!
TWO OYSTERS, TWO PEARLS! FIFTY OYSTERS, A NECKLACE!

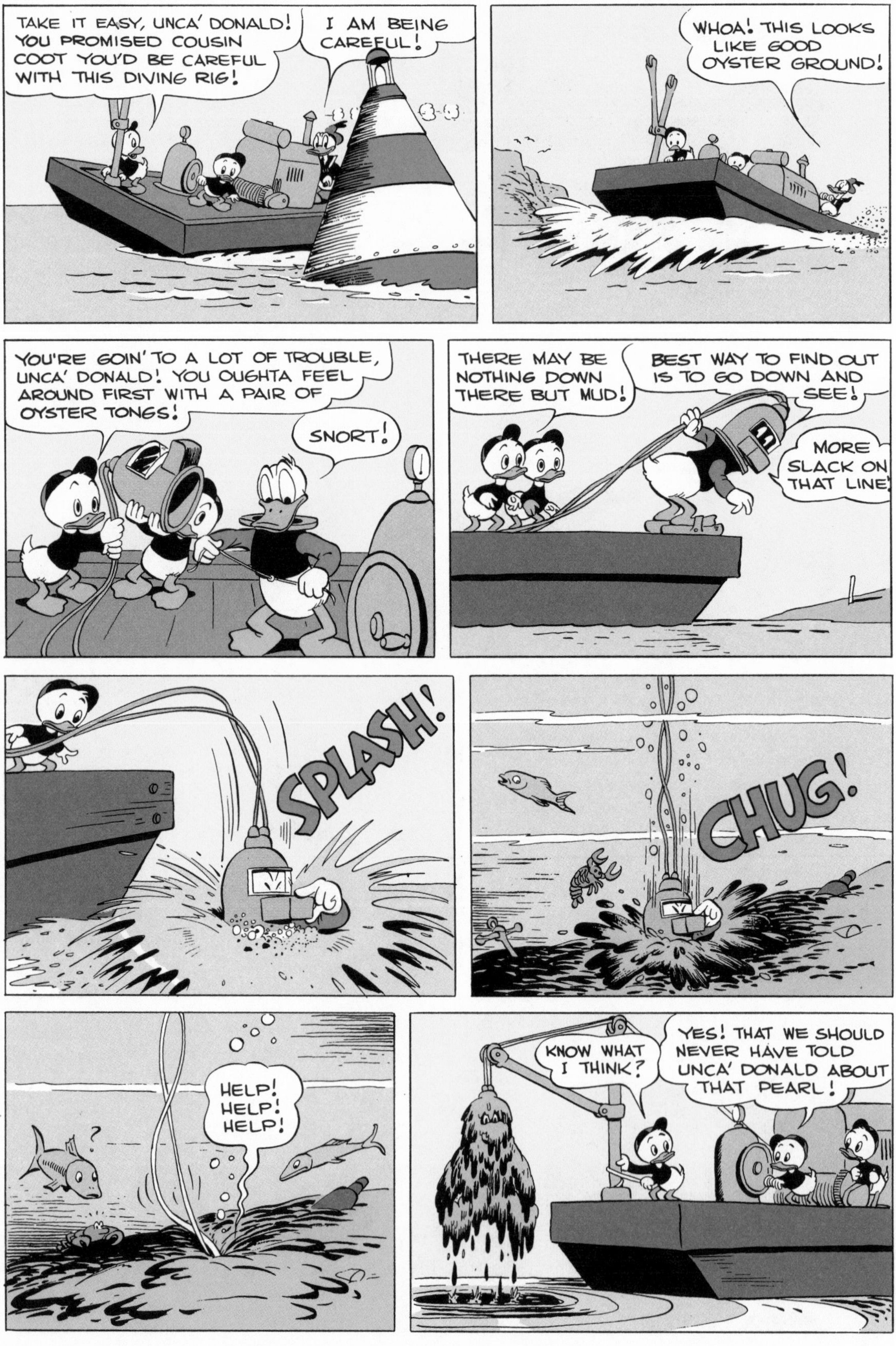
TAKE IT EASY, UNCA' DONALD! YOU PROMISED COUSIN COOT YOU'D BE CAREFUL WITH THIS DIVING RIG!
I AM BEING CAREFUL!
WHOA! THIS LOOKS LIKE GOOD OYSTER GROUND!
YOU'RE GOIN' TO A LOT OF TROUBLE, UNCA' DONALD! YOU OUGHTA FEEL AROUND FIRST WITH A PAIR OF OYSTER TONGS!
SNORT!
THERE MAY BE NOTHING DOWN THERE BUT MUD!
BEST WAY TO FIND OUT IS TO GO DOWN AND SEE!
MORE SLACK ON THAT LINE!
SPLASH!
CHUG!
HELP! HELP! HELP!
?
KNOW WHAT I THINK?
YES! THAT WE SHOULD NEVER HAVE TOLD UNCA' DONALD ABOUT THAT PEARL!

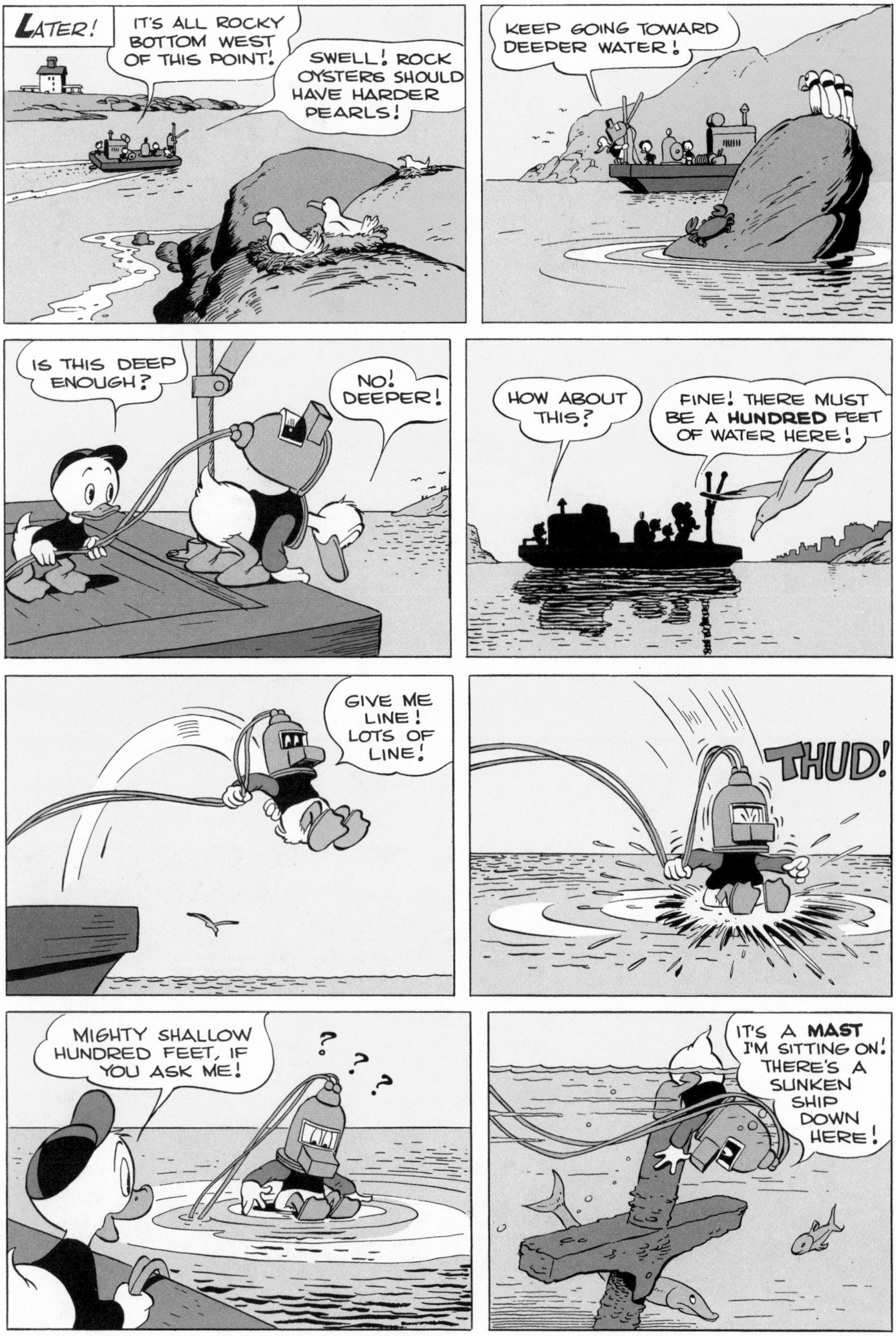
LATER!
IT'S ALL ROCKY BOTTOM WEST OF THIS POINT!
SWELL! ROCK OYSTERS SHOULD HAVE HARDER PEARLS!
KEEP GOING TOWARD DEEPER WATER!
IS THIS DEEP ENOUGH?
NO! DEEPER!
HOW ABOUT THIS?
FINE! THERE MUST BE A **HUNDRED** FEET OF WATER HERE!
GIVE ME LINE! LOTS OF LINE!
THUD!
MIGHTY SHALLOW HUNDRED FEET, IF YOU ASK ME!
? ? ?
IT'S A **MAST** I'M SITTING ON! THERE'S A SUNKEN SHIP DOWN HERE!

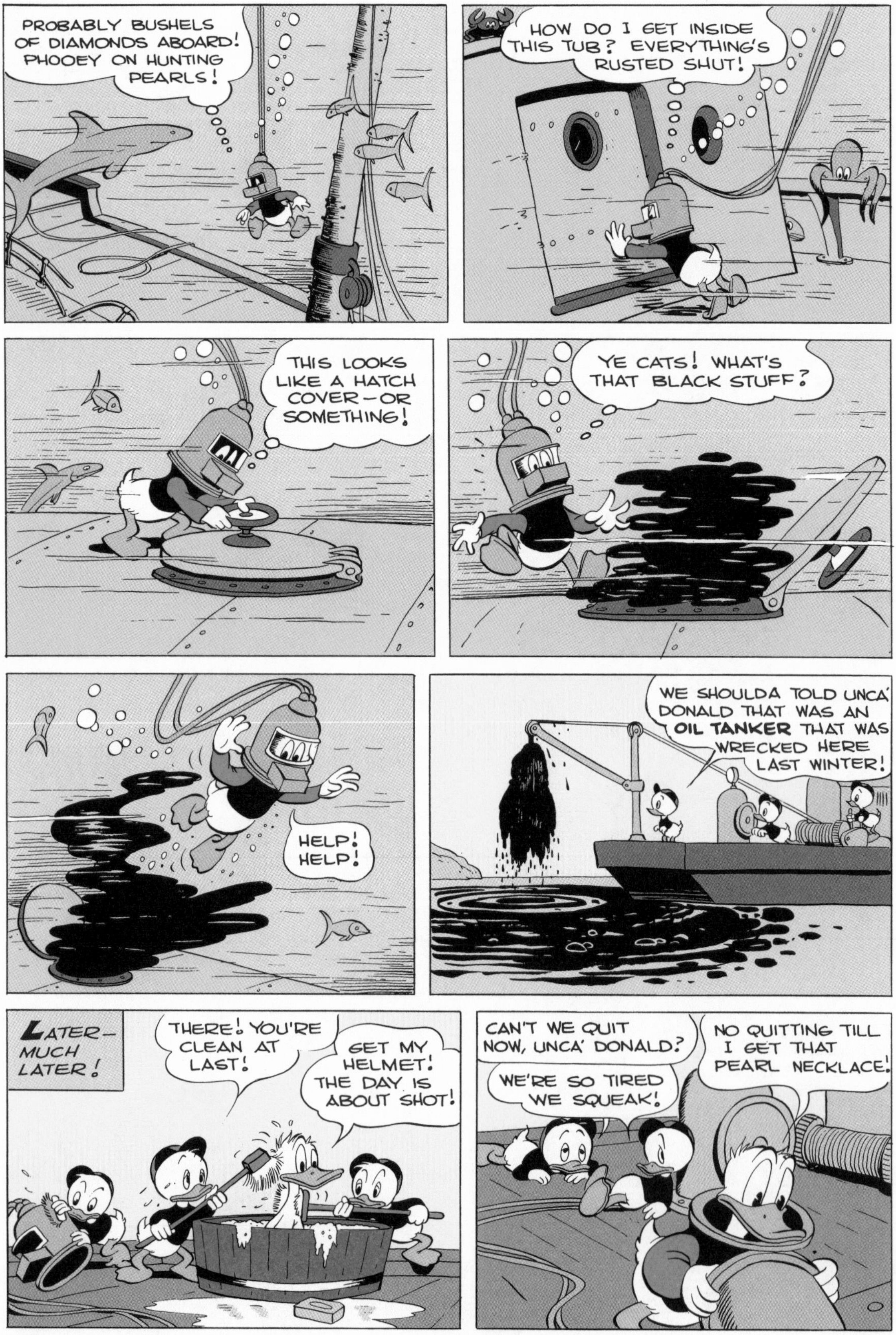
PROBABLY BUSHELS OF DIAMONDS ABOARD! PHOOEY ON HUNTING PEARLS!
HOW DO I GET INSIDE THIS TUB? EVERYTHING'S RUSTED SHUT!
THIS LOOKS LIKE A HATCH COVER—OR SOMETHING!
YE CATS! WHAT'S THAT BLACK STUFF?
HELP! HELP!
WE SHOULDA TOLD UNCA' DONALD THAT WAS AN **OIL TANKER** THAT WAS WRECKED HERE LAST WINTER!
LATER—MUCH LATER!
THERE! YOU'RE CLEAN AT LAST!
GET MY HELMET! THE DAY IS ABOUT SHOT!
CAN'T WE QUIT NOW, UNCA' DONALD?
WE'RE SO TIRED WE SQUEAK!
NO QUITTING TILL I GET THAT PEARL NECKLACE!

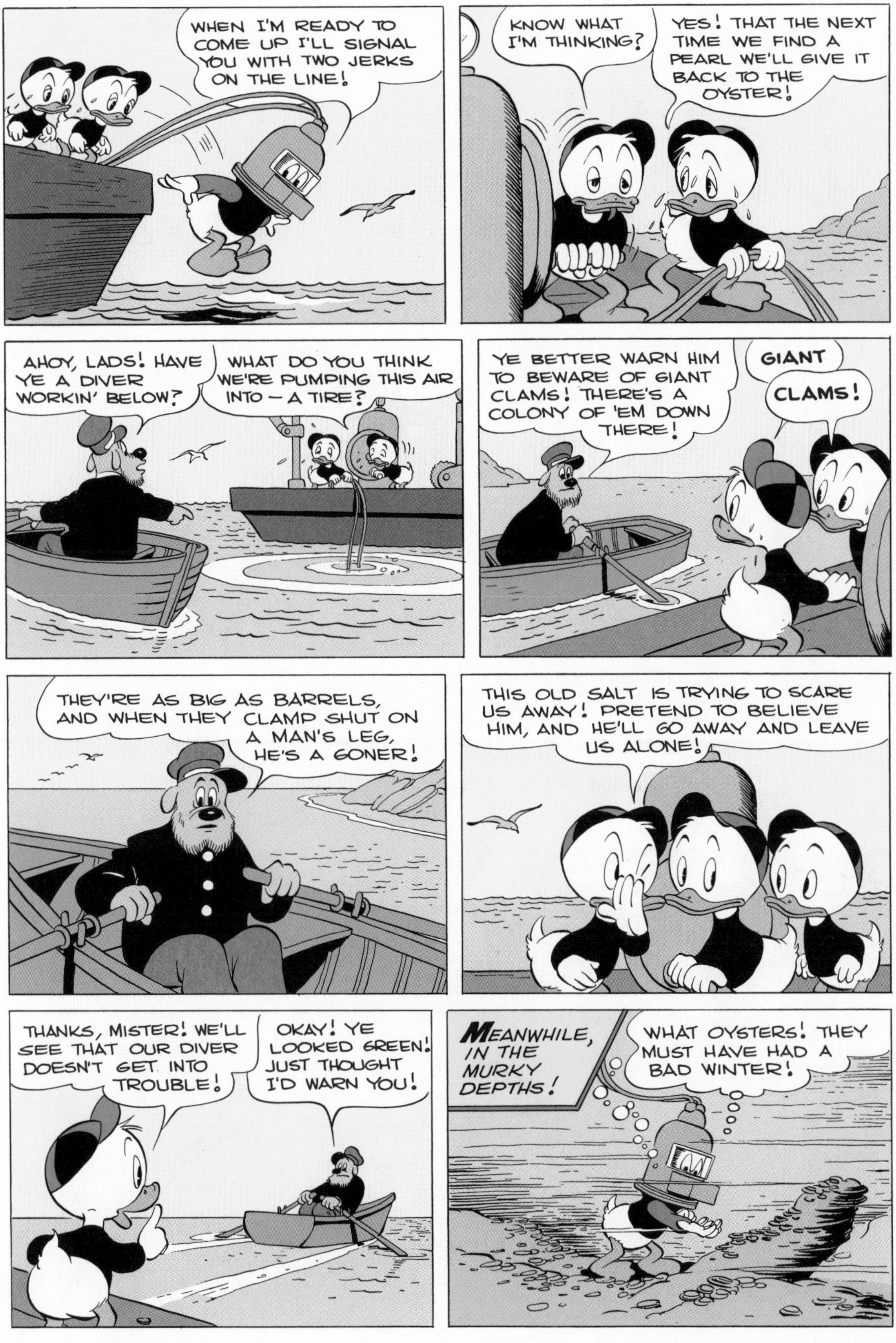

WHEN I'M READY TO COME UP I'LL SIGNAL YOU WITH TWO JERKS ON THE LINE!
KNOW WHAT I'M THINKING?
YES! THAT THE NEXT TIME WE FIND A PEARL WE'LL GIVE IT BACK TO THE OYSTER!
AHOY, LADS! HAVE YE A DIVER WORKIN' BELOW?
WHAT DO YOU THINK WE'RE PUMPING THIS AIR INTO — A TIRE?
YE BETTER WARN HIM TO BEWARE OF GIANT CLAMS! THERE'S A COLONY OF 'EM DOWN THERE!
GIANT
CLAMS!
THEY'RE AS BIG AS BARRELS, AND WHEN THEY CLAMP SHUT ON A MAN'S LEG, HE'S A GONER!
THIS OLD SALT IS TRYING TO SCARE US AWAY! PRETEND TO BELIEVE HIM, AND HE'LL GO AWAY AND LEAVE US ALONE!
THANKS, MISTER! WE'LL SEE THAT OUR DIVER DOESN'T GET INTO TROUBLE!
OKAY! YE LOOKED GREEN! JUST THOUGHT I'D WARN YOU!
MEANWHILE, IN THE MURKY DEPTHS!
WHAT OYSTERS! THEY MUST HAVE HAD A BAD WINTER!

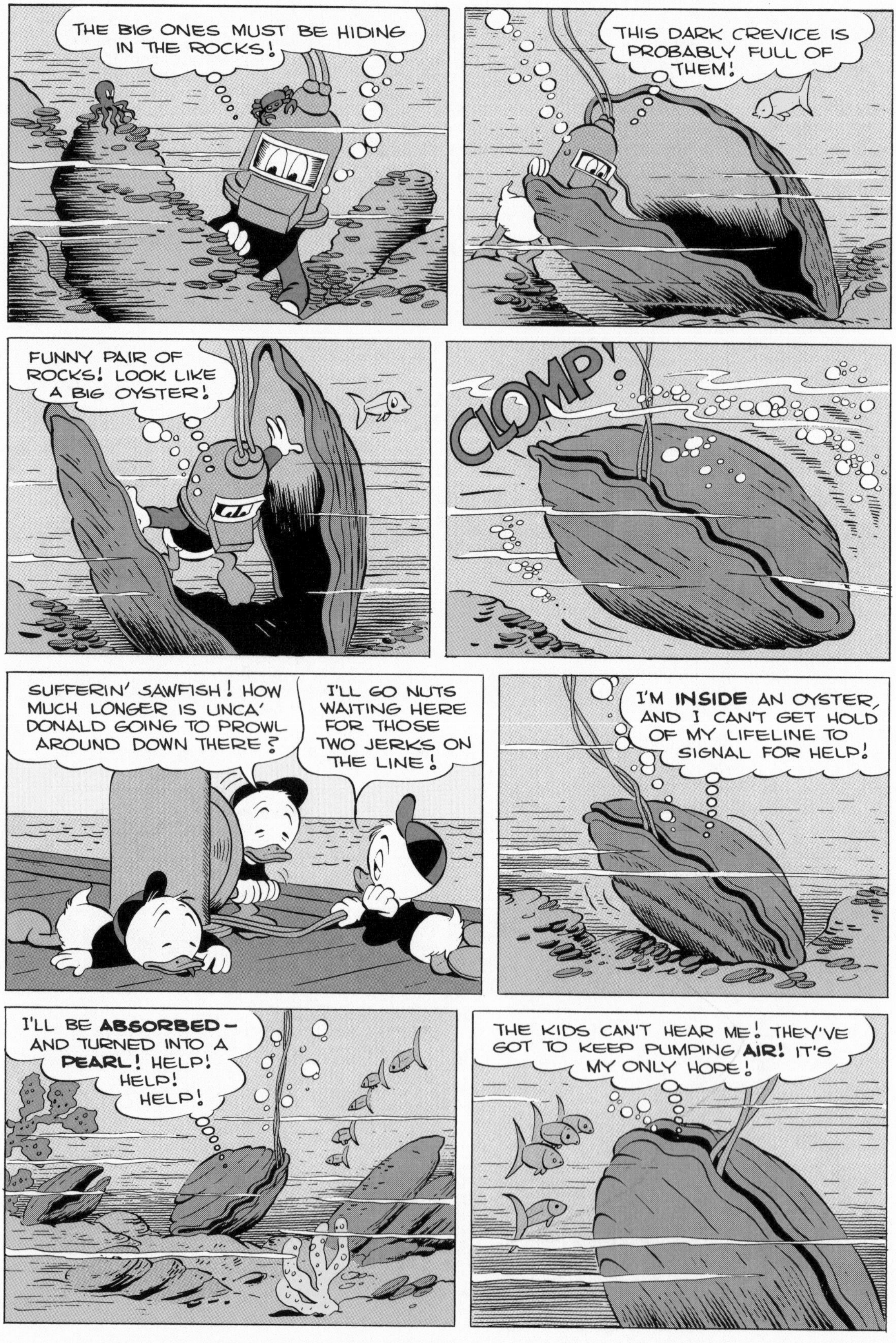
THE BIG ONES MUST BE HIDING IN THE ROCKS!
THIS DARK CREVICE IS PROBABLY FULL OF THEM!
FUNNY PAIR OF ROCKS! LOOK LIKE A BIG OYSTER!
CLOMP!
SUFFERIN' SAWFISH! HOW MUCH LONGER IS UNCA' DONALD GOING TO PROWL AROUND DOWN THERE?
I'LL GO NUTS WAITING HERE FOR THOSE TWO JERKS ON THE LINE!
I'M INSIDE AN OYSTER, AND I CAN'T GET HOLD OF MY LIFELINE TO SIGNAL FOR HELP!
I'LL BE ABSORBED— AND TURNED INTO A PEARL! HELP! HELP! HELP!
THE KIDS CAN'T HEAR ME! THEY'VE GOT TO KEEP PUMPING AIR! IT'S MY ONLY HOPE!

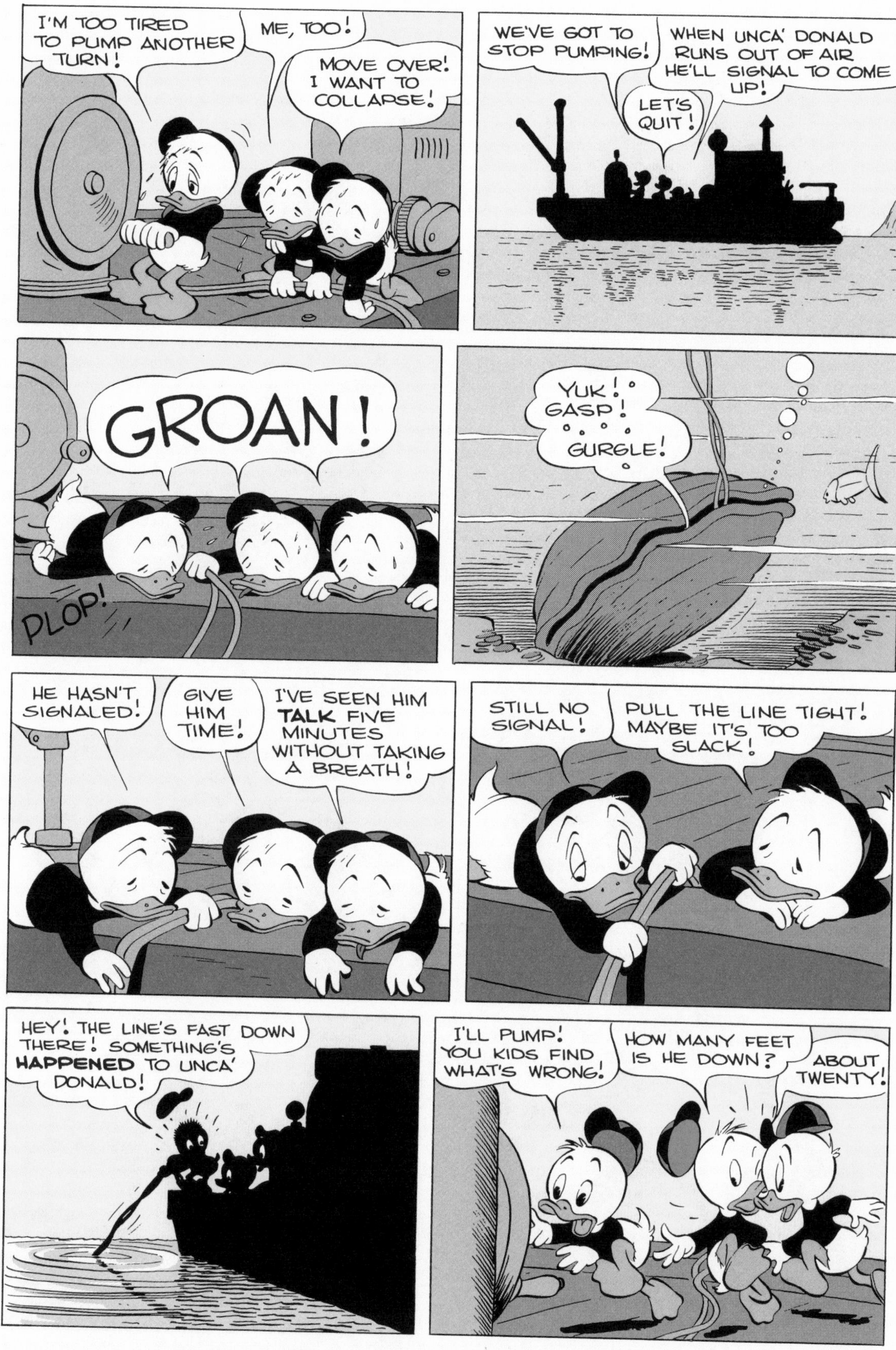
I'M TOO TIRED TO PUMP ANOTHER TURN!
ME, TOO!
MOVE OVER! I WANT TO COLLAPSE!
WE'VE GOT TO STOP PUMPING!
LET'S QUIT!
WHEN UNCA' DONALD RUNS OUT OF AIR HE'LL SIGNAL TO COME UP!
GROAN!
PLOP!
YUK! GASP! GURGLE!
HE HASN'T SIGNALED!
GIVE HIM TIME!
I'VE SEEN HIM TALK FIVE MINUTES WITHOUT TAKING A BREATH!
STILL NO SIGNAL!
PULL THE LINE TIGHT! MAYBE IT'S TOO SLACK!
HEY! THE LINE'S FAST DOWN THERE! SOMETHING'S HAPPENED TO UNCA' DONALD!
I'LL PUMP! YOU KIDS FIND WHAT'S WRONG!
HOW MANY FEET IS HE DOWN?
ABOUT TWENTY!

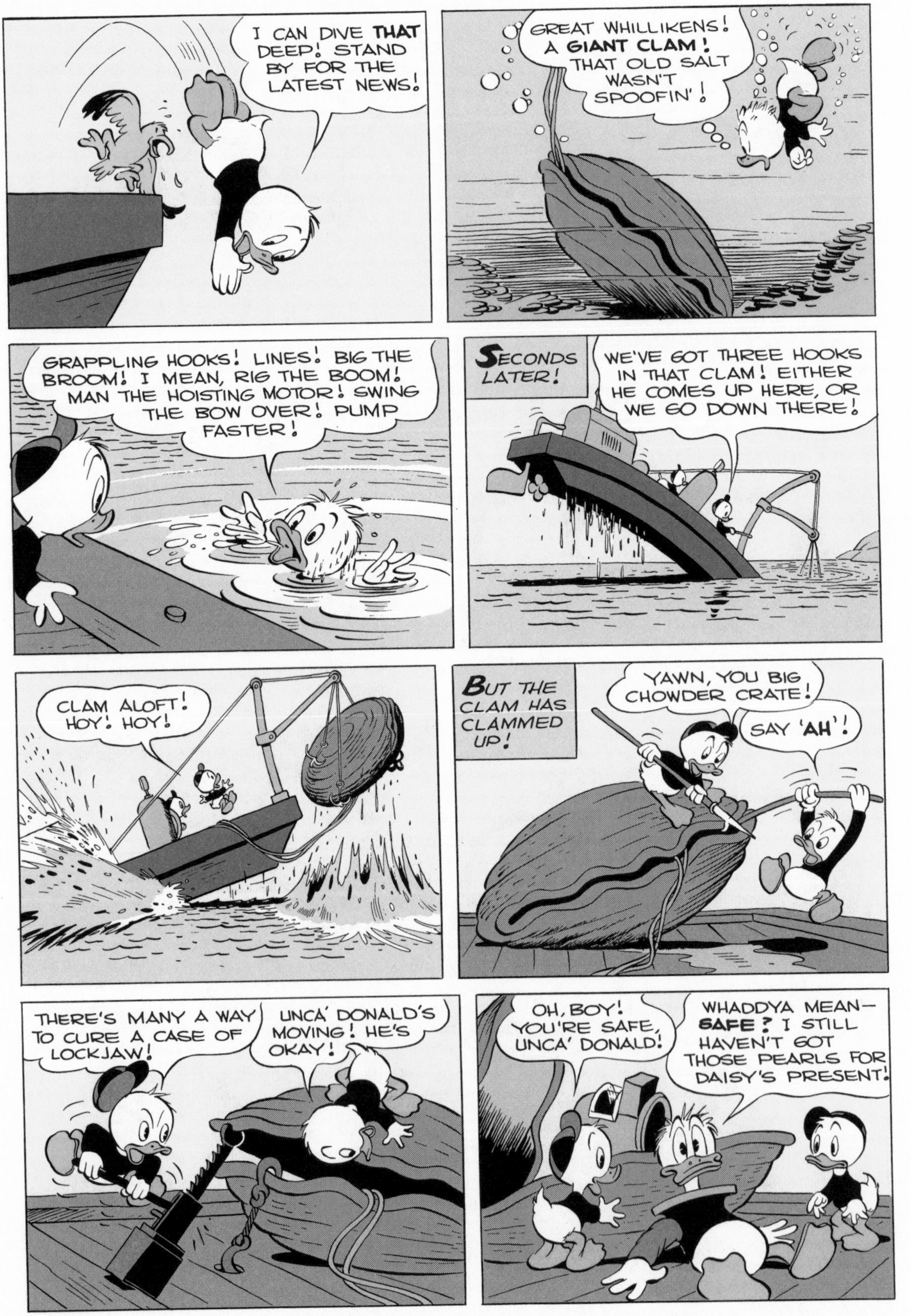
I CAN DIVE THAT DEEP! STAND BY FOR THE LATEST NEWS!
GREAT WHILLIKENS! A GIANT CLAM! THAT OLD SALT WASN'T SPOOFIN'!
GRAPPLING HOOKS! LINES! BIG THE BROOM! I MEAN, RIG THE BOOM! MAN THE HOISTING MOTOR! SWING THE BOW OVER! PUMP FASTER!
SECONDS LATER!
WE'VE GOT THREE HOOKS IN THAT CLAM! EITHER HE COMES UP HERE, OR WE GO DOWN THERE!
CLAM ALOFT! HOY! HOY!
BUT THE CLAM HAS CLAMMED UP!
YAWN, YOU BIG CHOWDER CRATE!
SAY 'AH'!
THERE'S MANY A WAY TO CURE A CASE OF LOCKJAW!
UNCA' DONALD'S MOVING! HE'S OKAY!
OH, BOY! YOU'RE SAFE, UNCA' DONALD!
WHADDYA MEAN— SAFE? I STILL HAVEN'T GOT THOSE PEARLS FOR DAISY'S PRESENT!

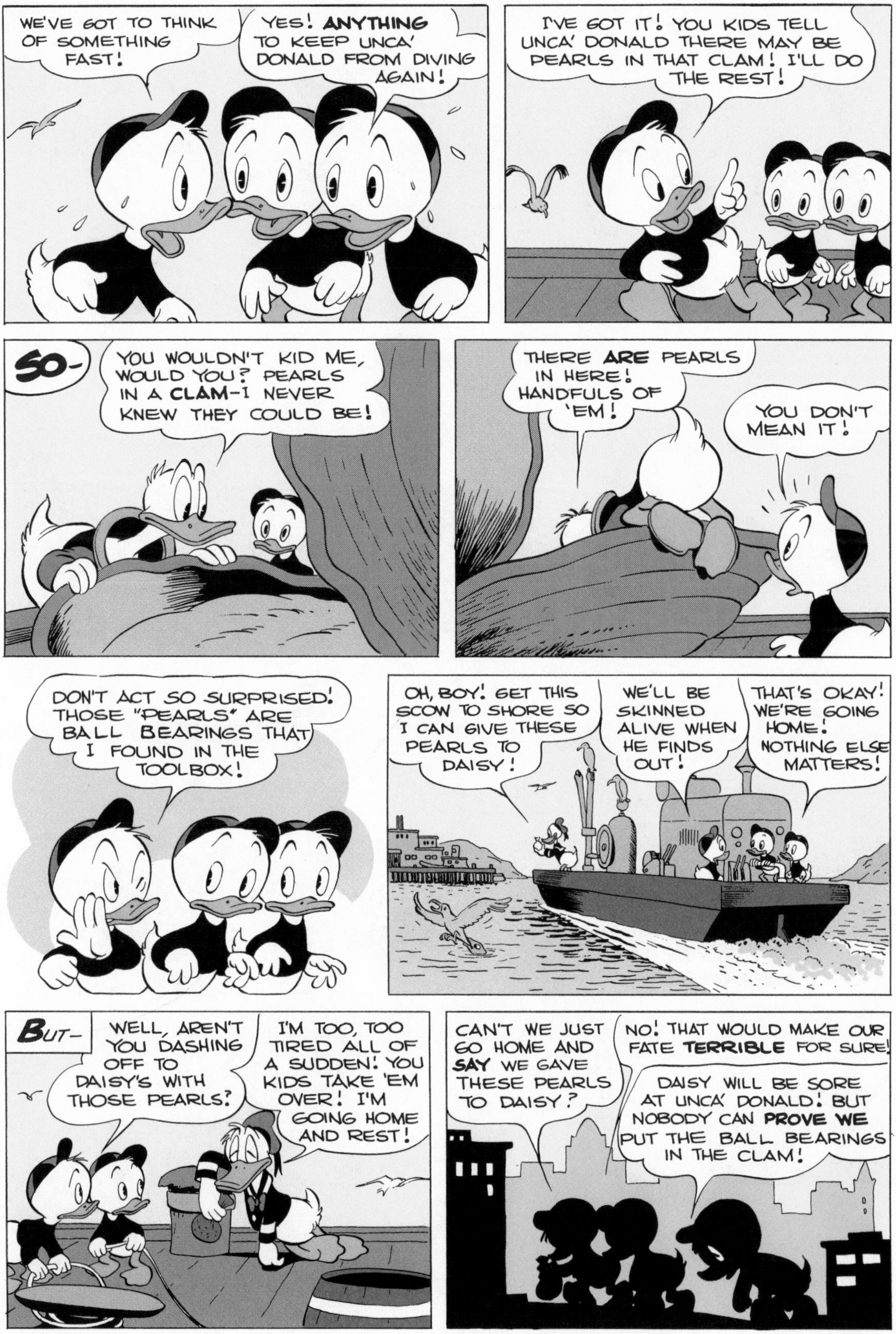
WE'VE GOT TO THINK OF SOMETHING FAST!
YES! ANYTHING TO KEEP UNCA' DONALD FROM DIVING AGAIN!
I'VE GOT IT! YOU KIDS TELL UNCA' DONALD THERE MAY BE PEARLS IN THAT CLAM! I'LL DO THE REST!
SO-
YOU WOULDN'T KID ME, WOULD YOU? PEARLS IN A CLAM-I NEVER KNEW THEY COULD BE!
THERE ARE PEARLS IN HERE! HANDFULS OF 'EM!
YOU DON'T MEAN IT!
DON'T ACT SO SURPRISED! THOSE "PEARLS" ARE BALL BEARINGS THAT I FOUND IN THE TOOLBOX!
OH, BOY! GET THIS SCOW TO SHORE SO I CAN GIVE THESE PEARLS TO DAISY!
WE'LL BE SKINNED ALIVE WHEN HE FINDS OUT!
THAT'S OKAY! WE'RE GOING HOME! NOTHING ELSE MATTERS!
BUT-
WELL, AREN'T YOU DASHING OFF TO DAISY'S WITH THOSE PEARLS?
I'M TOO, TOO TIRED ALL OF A SUDDEN! YOU KIDS TAKE 'EM OVER! I'M GOING HOME AND REST!
CAN'T WE JUST GO HOME AND SAY WE GAVE THESE PEARLS TO DAISY?
NO! THAT WOULD MAKE OUR FATE TERRIBLE FOR SURE!
DAISY WILL BE SORE AT UNCA' DONALD! BUT NOBODY CAN PROVE WE PUT THE BALL BEARINGS IN THE CLAM!

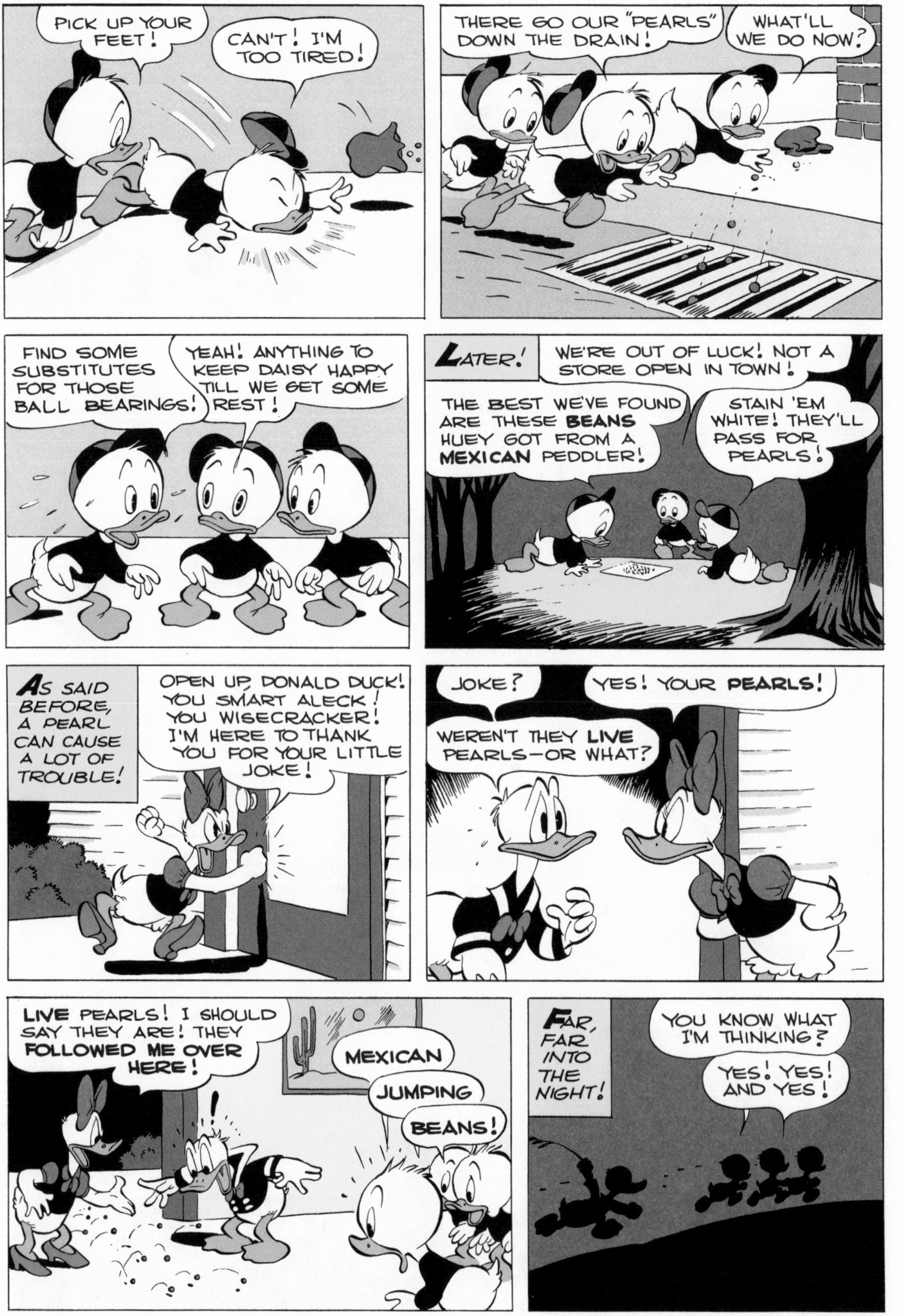
PICK UP YOUR FEET!
CAN'T! I'M TOO TIRED!
THERE GO OUR "PEARLS" DOWN THE DRAIN!
WHAT'LL WE DO NOW?
FIND SOME SUBSTITUTES FOR THOSE BALL BEARINGS!
YEAH! ANYTHING TO KEEP DAISY HAPPY TILL WE GET SOME REST!
LATER!
WE'RE OUT OF LUCK! NOT A STORE OPEN IN TOWN!
THE BEST WE'VE FOUND ARE THESE **BEANS** HUEY GOT FROM A **MEXICAN** PEDDLER!
STAIN 'EM WHITE! THEY'LL PASS FOR PEARLS!
AS SAID BEFORE, A PEARL CAN CAUSE A LOT OF TROUBLE!
OPEN UP, DONALD DUCK! YOU SMART ALECK! YOU WISECRACKER! I'M HERE TO THANK YOU FOR YOUR LITTLE JOKE!
JOKE?
YES! YOUR **PEARLS**!
WEREN'T THEY **LIVE** PEARLS—OR WHAT?
LIVE PEARLS! I SHOULD SAY THEY ARE! THEY **FOLLOWED ME OVER HERE**!
MEXICAN
JUMPING
BEANS!
FAR, FAR INTO THE NIGHT!
YOU KNOW WHAT I'M THINKING?
YES! YES! AND YES!

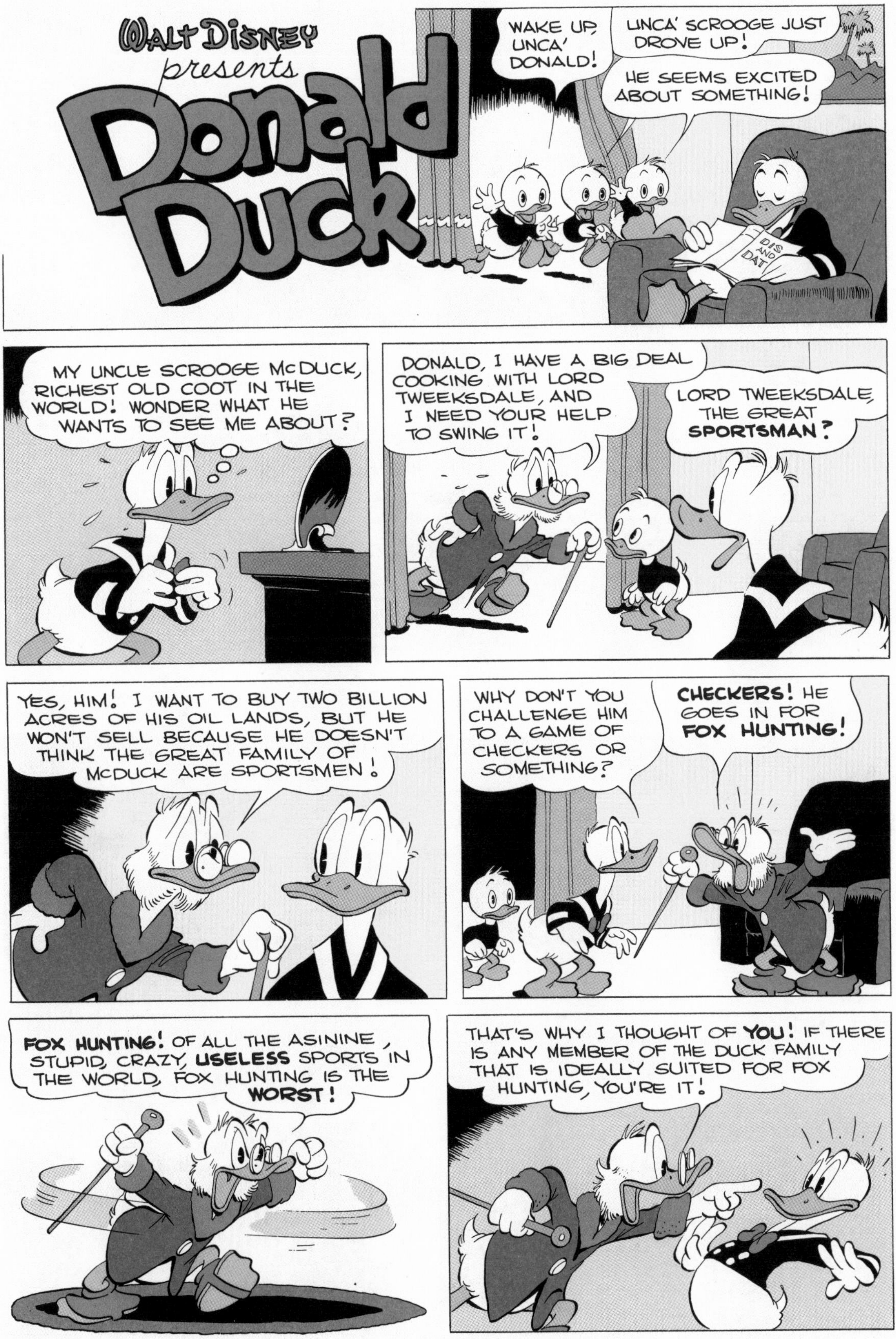
WALT DISNEY presents
Donald Duck
WAKE UP, UNCA' DONALD!
UNCA' SCROOGE JUST DROVE UP!
HE SEEMS EXCITED ABOUT SOMETHING!
DIS AND DAT
MY UNCLE SCROOGE McDUCK, RICHEST OLD COOT IN THE WORLD! WONDER WHAT HE WANTS TO SEE ME ABOUT?
DONALD, I HAVE A BIG DEAL COOKING WITH LORD TWEEKSDALE, AND I NEED YOUR HELP TO SWING IT!
LORD TWEEKSDALE, THE GREAT **SPORTSMAN**?
YES, HIM! I WANT TO BUY TWO BILLION ACRES OF HIS OIL LANDS, BUT HE WON'T SELL BECAUSE HE DOESN'T THINK THE GREAT FAMILY OF McDUCK ARE SPORTSMEN!
WHY DON'T YOU CHALLENGE HIM TO A GAME OF CHECKERS OR SOMETHING?
CHECKERS! HE GOES IN FOR **FOX HUNTING**!
FOX HUNTING! OF ALL THE ASININE, STUPID, CRAZY, **USELESS** SPORTS IN THE WORLD, FOX HUNTING IS THE **WORST**!
THAT'S WHY I THOUGHT OF **YOU**! IF THERE IS ANY MEMBER OF THE DUCK FAMILY THAT IS IDEALLY SUITED FOR FOX HUNTING, YOU'RE IT!

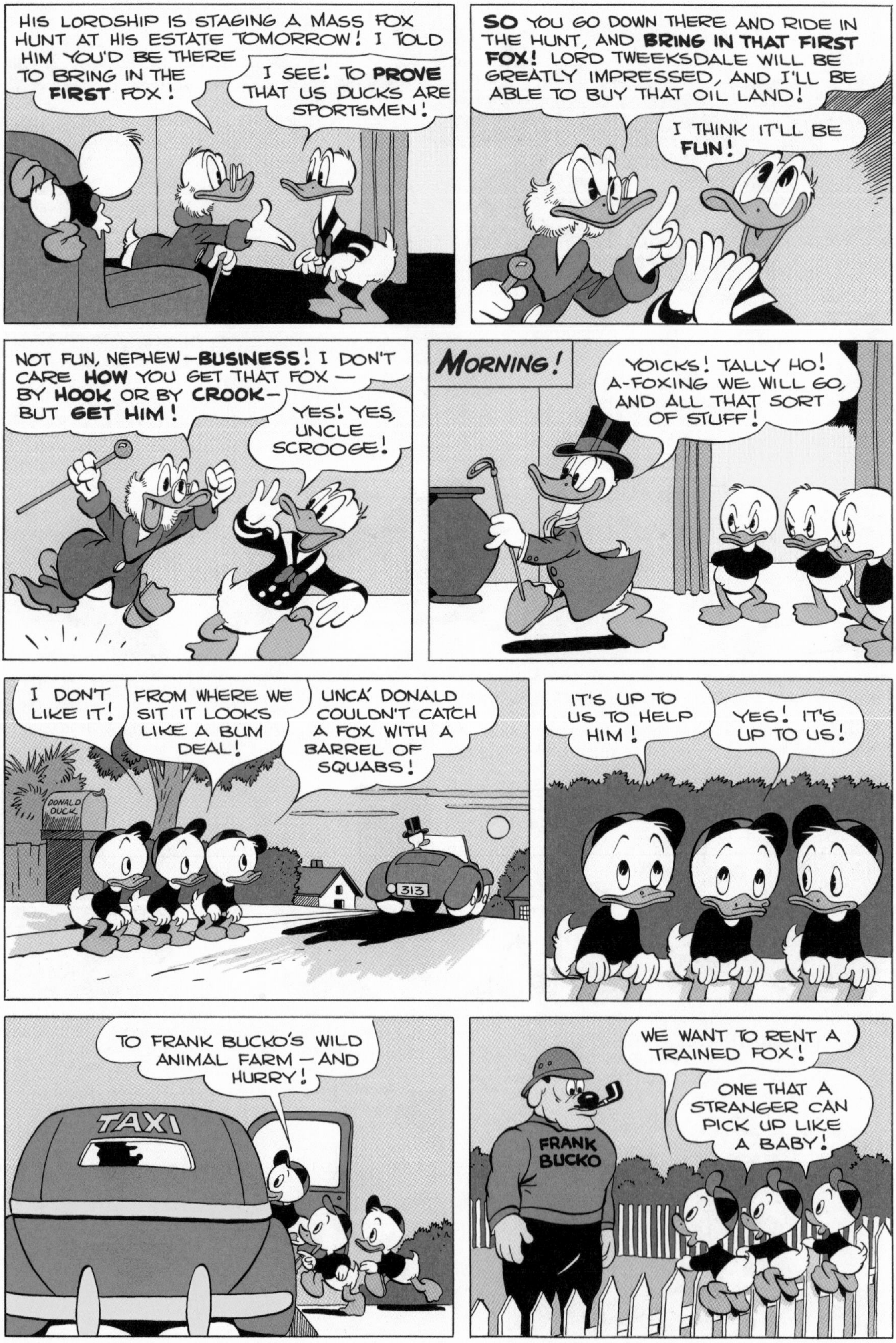
HIS LORDSHIP IS STAGING A MASS FOX HUNT AT HIS ESTATE TOMORROW! I TOLD HIM YOU'D BE THERE TO BRING IN THE **FIRST** FOX!
I SEE! TO **PROVE** THAT US DUCKS ARE SPORTSMEN!
SO YOU GO DOWN THERE AND RIDE IN THE HUNT, AND **BRING IN THAT FIRST FOX!** LORD TWEEKSDALE WILL BE GREATLY IMPRESSED, AND I'LL BE ABLE TO BUY THAT OIL LAND!
I THINK IT'LL BE **FUN**!
NOT FUN, NEPHEW—**BUSINESS**! I DON'T CARE **HOW** YOU GET THAT FOX—BY **HOOK** OR BY **CROOK**—BUT **GET HIM**!
YES! YES, UNCLE SCROOGE!
MORNING!
YOICKS! TALLY HO! A-FOXING WE WILL GO, AND ALL THAT SORT OF STUFF!
I DON'T LIKE IT!
FROM WHERE WE SIT IT LOOKS LIKE A BUM DEAL!
UNCA' DONALD COULDN'T CATCH A FOX WITH A BARREL OF SQUABS!
DONALD DUCK
313
IT'S UP TO US TO HELP HIM!
YES! IT'S UP TO US!
TO FRANK BUCKO'S WILD ANIMAL FARM—AND HURRY!
TAXI
WE WANT TO RENT A TRAINED FOX!
ONE THAT A STRANGER CAN PICK UP LIKE A BABY!
FRANK BUCKO

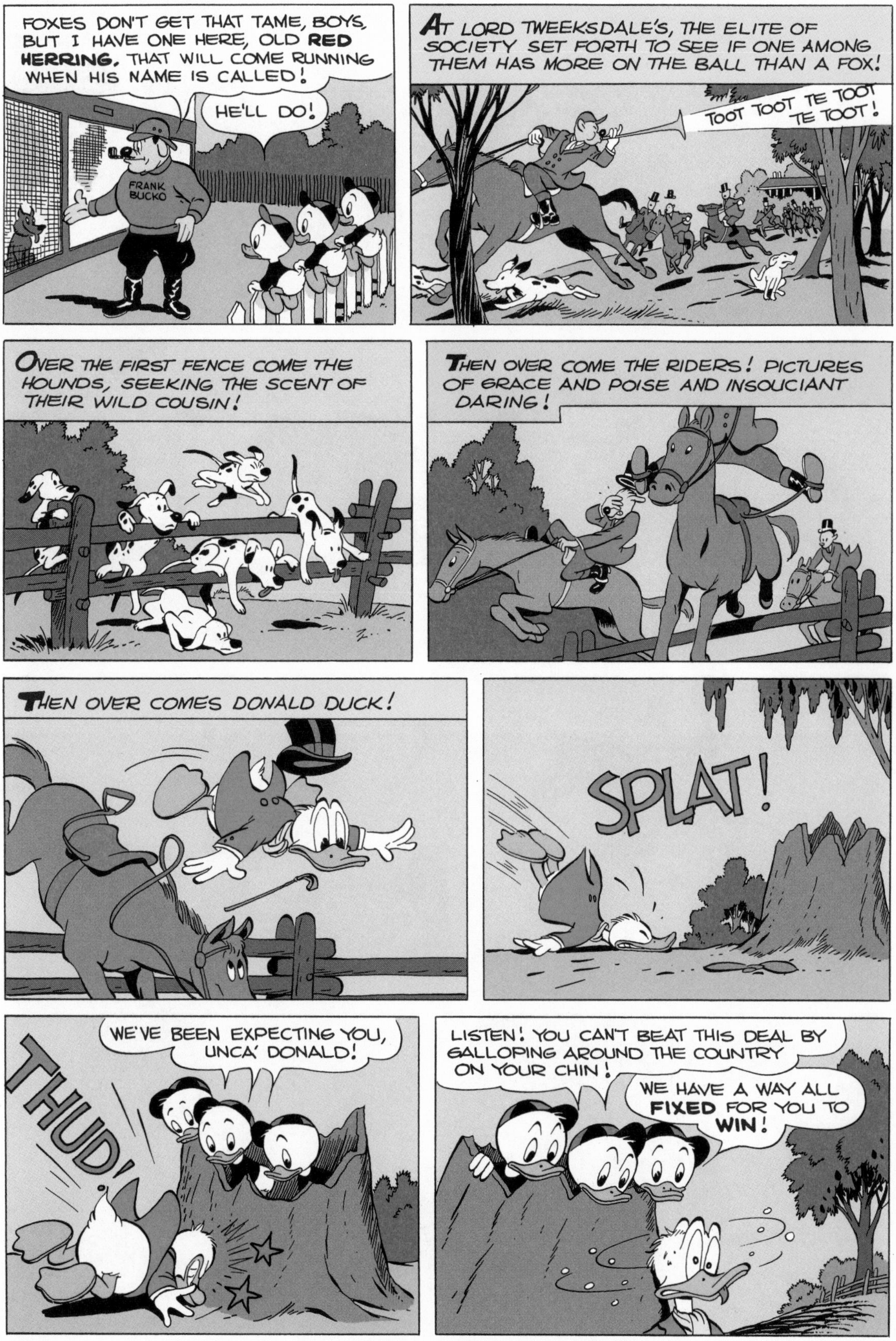
FOXES DON'T GET THAT TAME, BOYS, BUT I HAVE ONE HERE, OLD RED HERRING, THAT WILL COME RUNNING WHEN HIS NAME IS CALLED!
HE'LL DO!
FRANK BUCKO
AT LORD TWEEKSDALE'S, THE ELITE OF SOCIETY SET FORTH TO SEE IF ONE AMONG THEM HAS MORE ON THE BALL THAN A FOX!
TOOT TOOT TE TOOT TE TOOT!
OVER THE FIRST FENCE COME THE HOUNDS, SEEKING THE SCENT OF THEIR WILD COUSIN!
THEN OVER COME THE RIDERS! PICTURES OF GRACE AND POISE AND INSOUCIANT DARING!
THEN OVER COMES DONALD DUCK!
SPLAT!
THUD!
WE'VE BEEN EXPECTING YOU, UNCA' DONALD!
LISTEN! YOU CAN'T BEAT THIS DEAL BY GALLOPING AROUND THE COUNTRY ON YOUR CHIN!
WE HAVE A WAY ALL FIXED FOR YOU TO WIN!

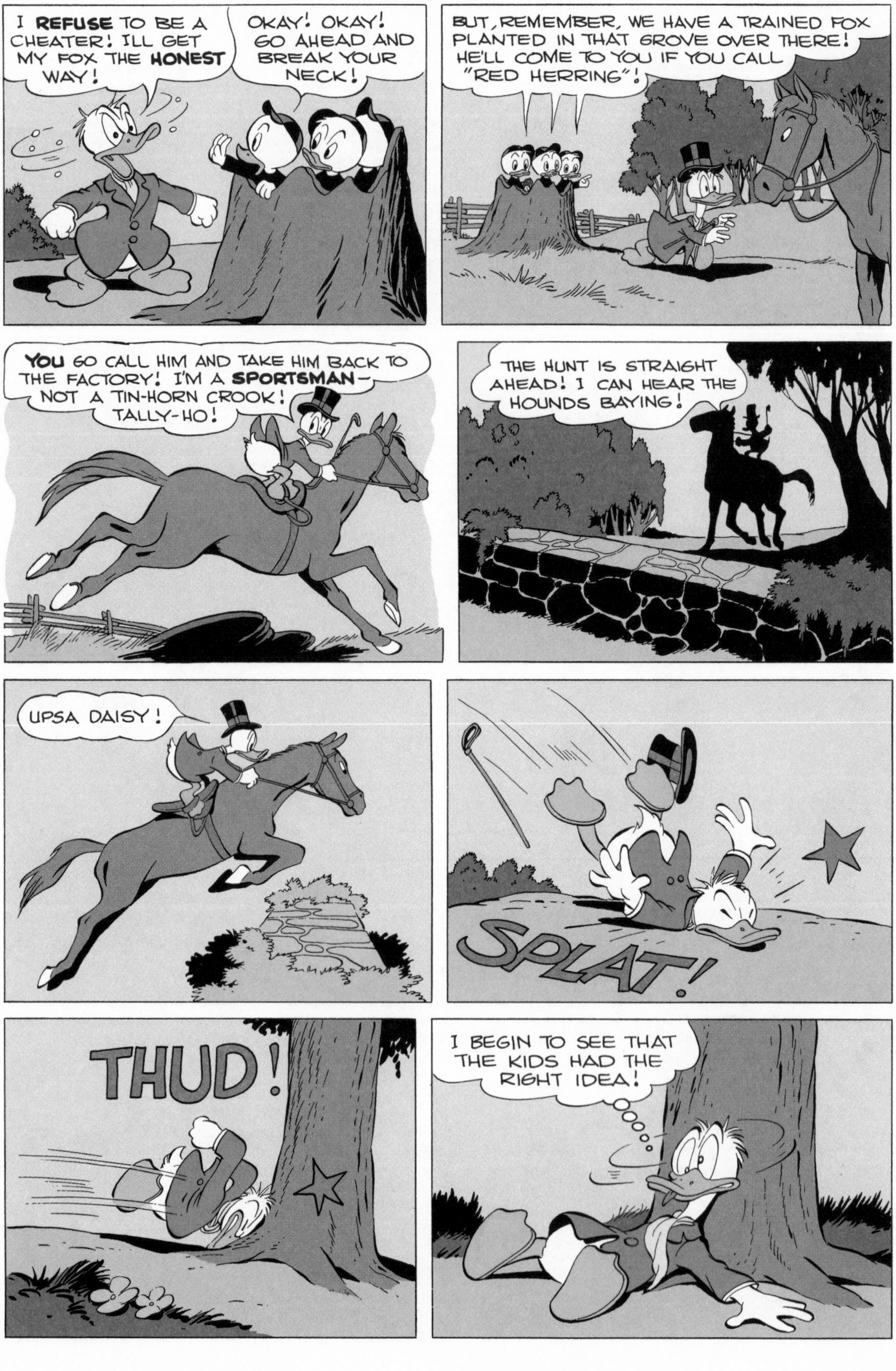

I REFUSE TO BE A CHEATER! I'LL GET MY FOX THE HONEST WAY!
OKAY! OKAY! GO AHEAD AND BREAK YOUR NECK!
BUT, REMEMBER, WE HAVE A TRAINED FOX PLANTED IN THAT GROVE OVER THERE! HE'LL COME TO YOU IF YOU CALL "RED HERRING"!
YOU GO CALL HIM AND TAKE HIM BACK TO THE FACTORY! I'M A SPORTSMAN— NOT A TIN-HORN CROOK! TALLY-HO!
THE HUNT IS STRAIGHT AHEAD! I CAN HEAR THE HOUNDS BAYING!
UPSA DAISY!
SPLAT!
THUD!
I BEGIN TO SEE THAT THE KIDS HAD THE RIGHT IDEA!

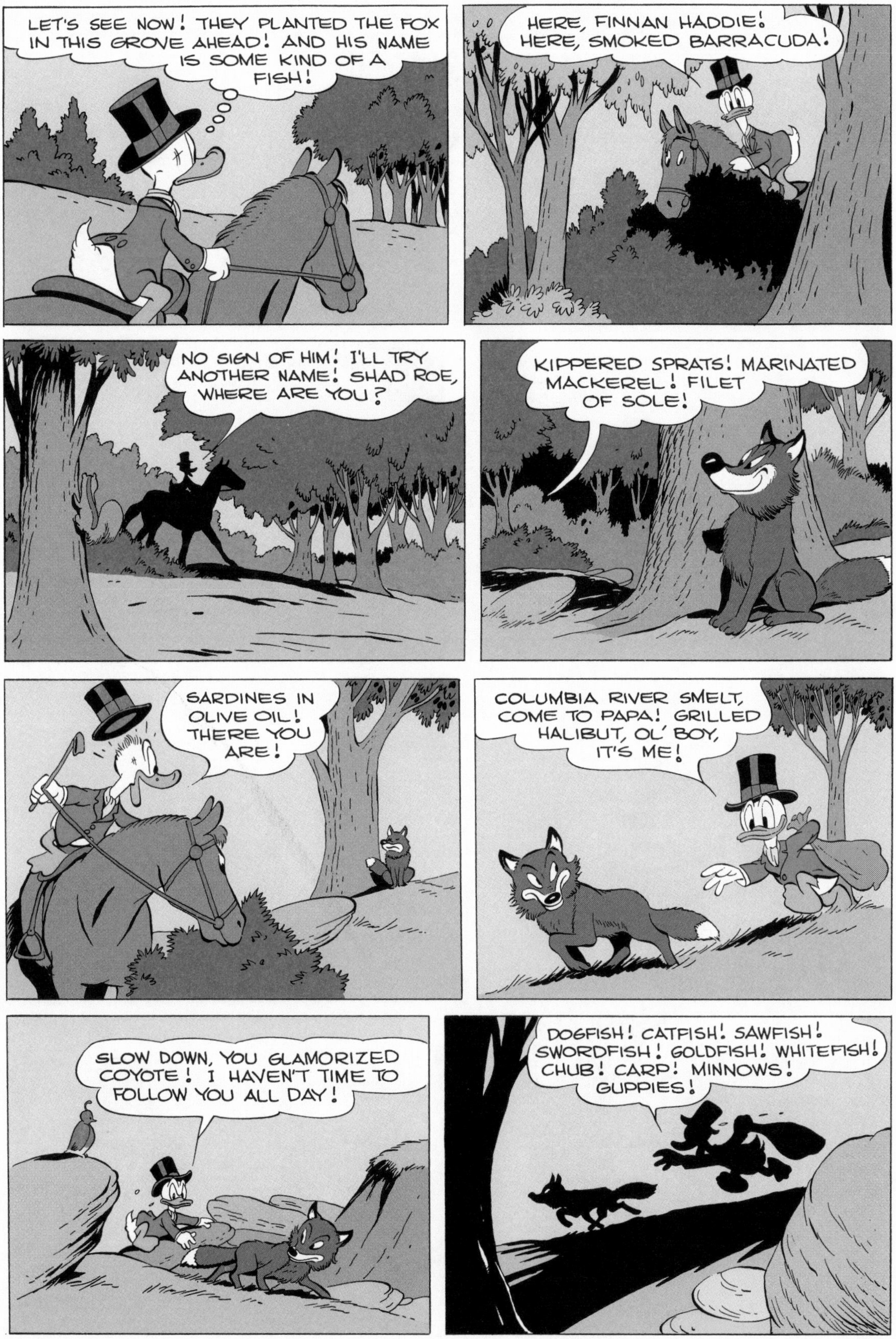
LET'S SEE NOW! THEY PLANTED THE FOX IN THIS GROVE AHEAD! AND HIS NAME IS SOME KIND OF A FISH!
HERE, FINNAN HADDIE! HERE, SMOKED BARRACUDA!
NO SIGN OF HIM! I'LL TRY ANOTHER NAME! SHAD ROE, WHERE ARE YOU?
KIPPERED SPRATS! MARINATED MACKEREL! FILET OF SOLE!
SARDINES IN OLIVE OIL! THERE YOU ARE!
COLUMBIA RIVER SMELT, COME TO PAPA! GRILLED HALIBUT, OL' BOY, IT'S ME!
SLOW DOWN, YOU GLAMORIZED COYOTE! I HAVEN'T TIME TO FOLLOW YOU ALL DAY!
DOGFISH! CATFISH! SAWFISH! SWORDFISH! GOLDFISH! WHITEFISH! CHUB! CARP! MINNOWS! GUPPIES!

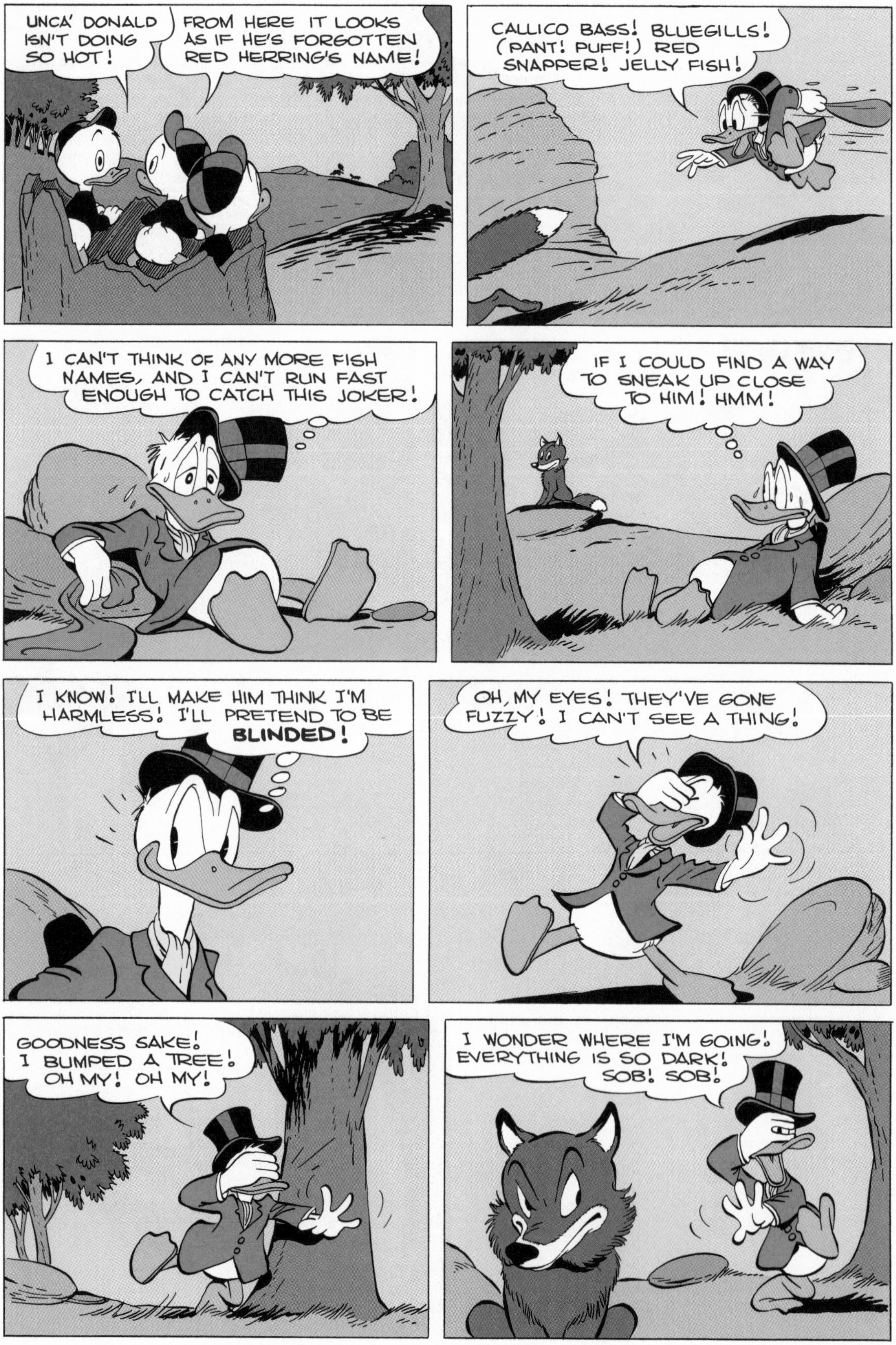
UNCA' DONALD ISN'T DOING SO HOT!
FROM HERE IT LOOKS AS IF HE'S FORGOTTEN RED HERRING'S NAME!
CALLICO BASS! BLUEGILLS! (PANT! PUFF!) RED SNAPPER! JELLY FISH!
I CAN'T THINK OF ANY MORE FISH NAMES, AND I CAN'T RUN FAST ENOUGH TO CATCH THIS JOKER!
IF I COULD FIND A WAY TO SNEAK UP CLOSE TO HIM! HMM!
I KNOW! I'LL MAKE HIM THINK I'M HARMLESS! I'LL PRETEND TO BE **BLINDED**!
OH, MY EYES! THEY'VE GONE FUZZY! I CAN'T SEE A THING!
GOODNESS SAKE! I BUMPED A TREE! OH MY! OH MY!
I WONDER WHERE I'M GOING! EVERYTHING IS SO DARK! SOB! SOB!

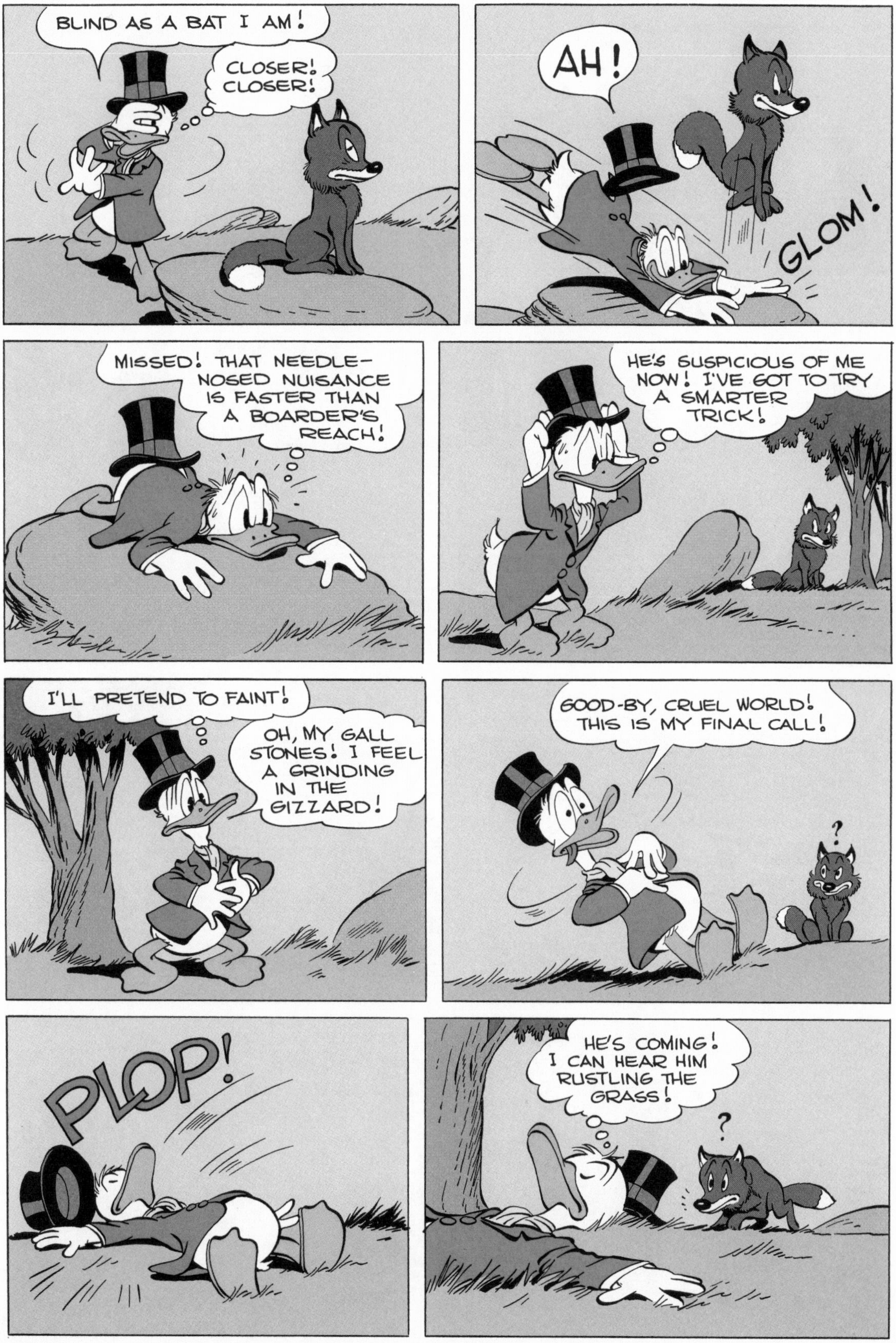

BLIND AS A BAT I AM!
CLOSER! CLOSER!
AH!
GLOM!
MISSED! THAT NEEDLE-NOSED NUISANCE IS FASTER THAN A BOARDER'S REACH!
HE'S SUSPICIOUS OF ME NOW! I'VE GOT TO TRY A SMARTER TRICK!
I'LL PRETEND TO FAINT!
OH, MY GALL STONES! I FEEL A GRINDING IN THE GIZZARD!
GOOD-BY, CRUEL WORLD! THIS IS MY FINAL CALL!
?
PLOP!
HE'S COMING! I CAN HEAR HIM RUSTLING THE GRASS!
?

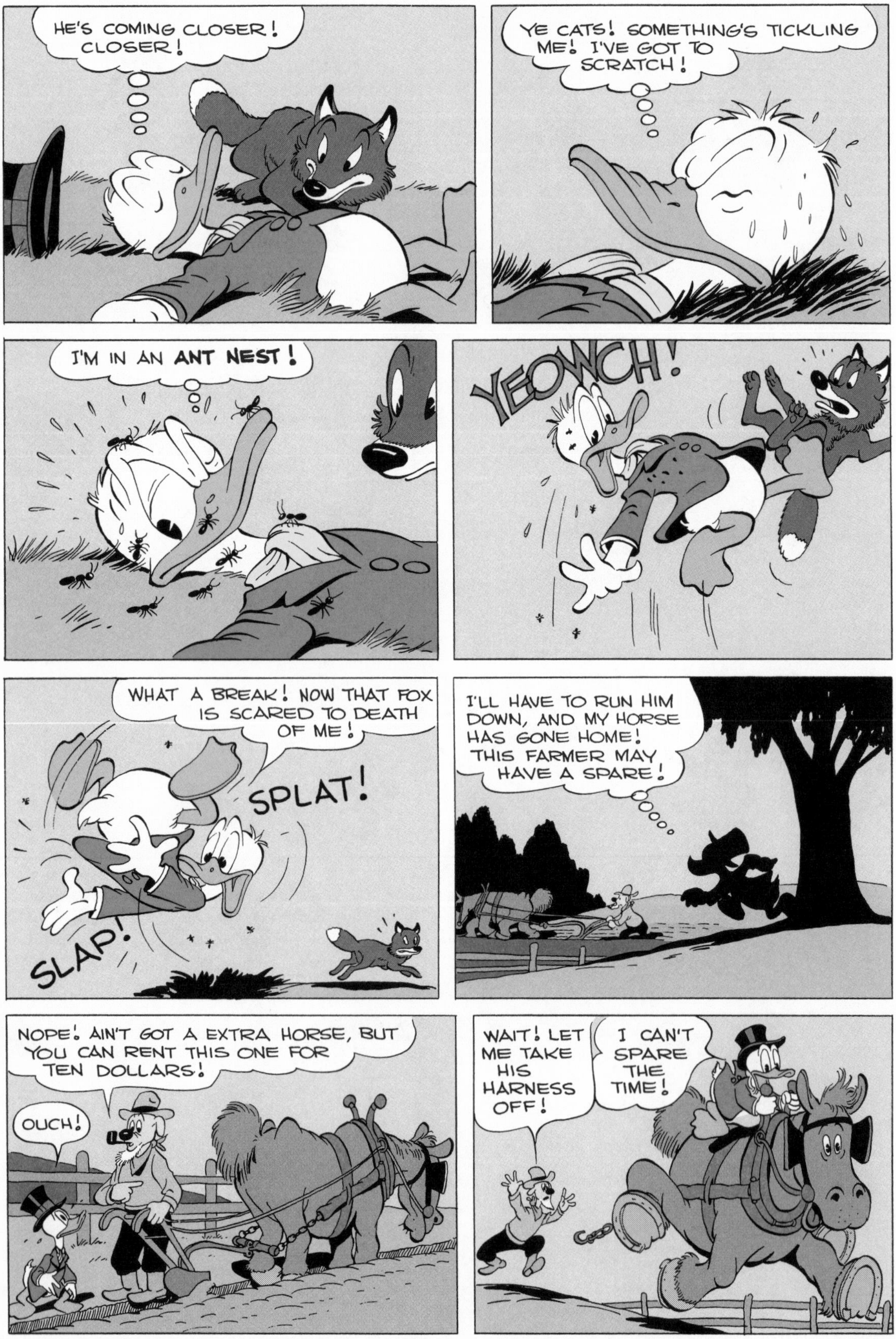
HE'S COMING CLOSER! CLOSER!
YE CATS! SOMETHING'S TICKLING ME! I'VE GOT TO SCRATCH!
I'M IN AN **ANT NEST**!
YEOWCH!
WHAT A BREAK! NOW THAT FOX IS SCARED TO DEATH OF ME!
SPLAT!
SLAP!
I'LL HAVE TO RUN HIM DOWN, AND MY HORSE HAS GONE HOME! THIS FARMER MAY HAVE A SPARE!
NOPE! AIN'T GOT A EXTRA HORSE, BUT YOU CAN RENT THIS ONE FOR TEN DOLLARS!
OUCH!
WAIT! LET ME TAKE HIS HARNESS OFF!
I CAN'T SPARE THE TIME!

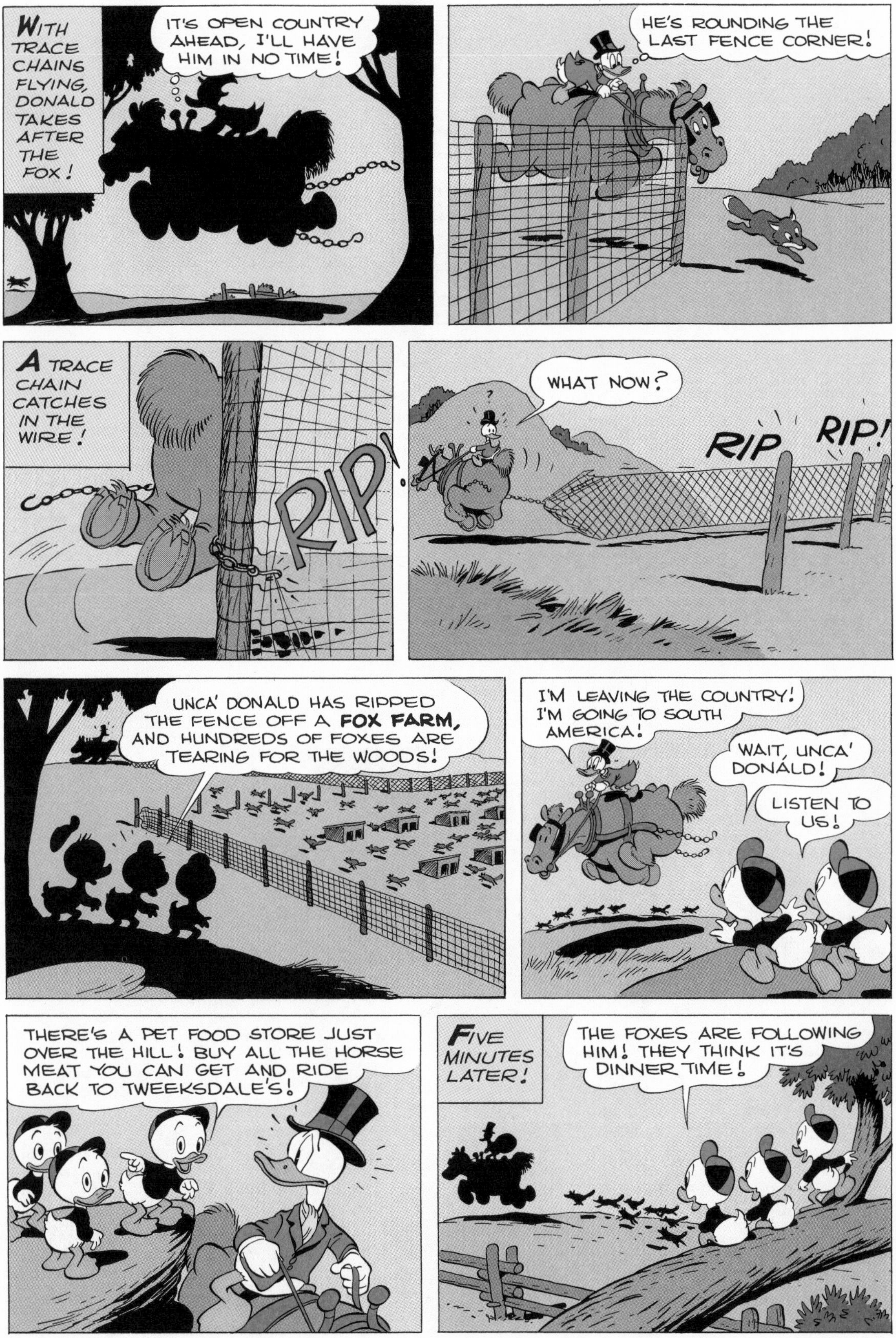
WITH TRACE CHAINS FLYING, DONALD TAKES AFTER THE FOX!
IT'S OPEN COUNTRY AHEAD, I'LL HAVE HIM IN NO TIME!
HE'S ROUNDING THE LAST FENCE CORNER!
A TRACE CHAIN CATCHES IN THE WIRE!
RIP!
WHAT NOW?
RIP
RIP!
UNCA' DONALD HAS RIPPED THE FENCE OFF A FOX FARM, AND HUNDREDS OF FOXES ARE TEARING FOR THE WOODS!
I'M LEAVING THE COUNTRY! I'M GOING TO SOUTH AMERICA!
WAIT, UNCA' DONALD!
LISTEN TO US!
THERE'S A PET FOOD STORE JUST OVER THE HILL! BUY ALL THE HORSE MEAT YOU CAN GET AND RIDE BACK TO TWEEKSDALE'S!
FIVE MINUTES LATER!
THE FOXES ARE FOLLOWING HIM! THEY THINK IT'S DINNER TIME!

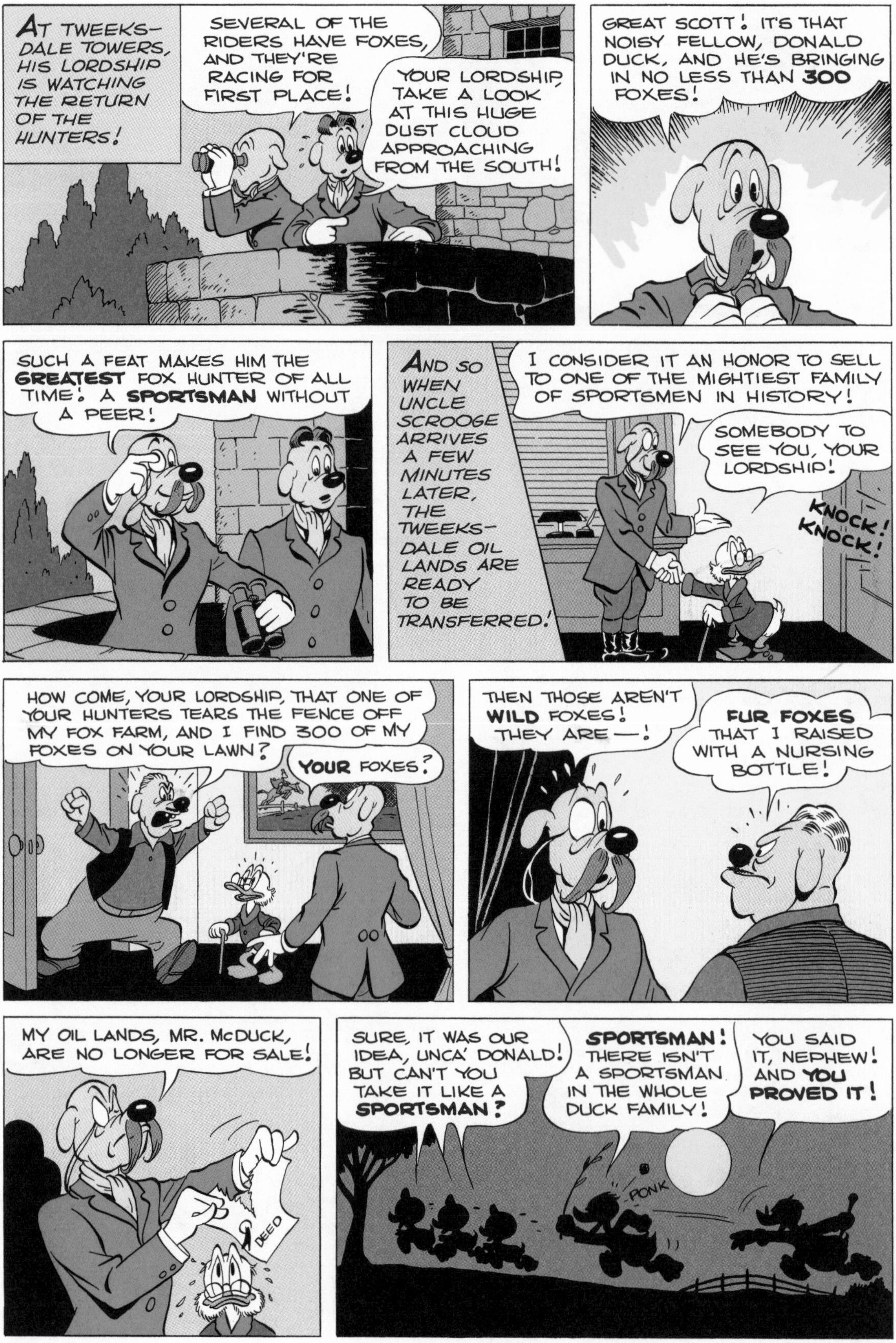

AT TWEEKS-DALE TOWERS, HIS LORDSHIP IS WATCHING THE RETURN OF THE HUNTERS!
SEVERAL OF THE RIDERS HAVE FOXES, AND THEY'RE RACING FOR FIRST PLACE!
YOUR LORDSHIP, TAKE A LOOK AT THIS HUGE DUST CLOUD APPROACHING FROM THE SOUTH!
GREAT SCOTT! IT'S THAT NOISY FELLOW, DONALD DUCK, AND HE'S BRINGING IN NO LESS THAN 300 FOXES!
SUCH A FEAT MAKES HIM THE GREATEST FOX HUNTER OF ALL TIME! A SPORTSMAN WITHOUT A PEER!
AND SO WHEN UNCLE SCROOGE ARRIVES A FEW MINUTES LATER, THE TWEEKS-DALE OIL LANDS ARE READY TO BE TRANSFERRED!
I CONSIDER IT AN HONOR TO SELL TO ONE OF THE MIGHTIEST FAMILY OF SPORTSMEN IN HISTORY!
SOMEBODY TO SEE YOU, YOUR LORDSHIP!
KNOCK! KNOCK!
HOW COME, YOUR LORDSHIP, THAT ONE OF YOUR HUNTERS TEARS THE FENCE OFF MY FOX FARM, AND I FIND 300 OF MY FOXES ON YOUR LAWN?
YOUR FOXES?
THEN THOSE AREN'T WILD FOXES! THEY ARE—!
FUR FOXES THAT I RAISED WITH A NURSING BOTTLE!
MY OIL LANDS, MR. McDUCK, ARE NO LONGER FOR SALE!
DEED
SURE, IT WAS OUR IDEA, UNCA' DONALD! BUT CAN'T YOU TAKE IT LIKE A SPORTSMAN?
SPORTSMAN! THERE ISN'T A SPORTSMAN IN THE WHOLE DUCK FAMILY!
PONK
YOU SAID IT, NEPHEW! AND YOU PROVED IT!

Story Notes

THE OLD CASTLE'S SECRET *p. 1*

In "The Old Castle's Secret," Carl Barks fortifies his still-new creation, Uncle Scrooge, fleshing him out for future stardom by broadening his range and enriching his personality.

Scrooge had been seen only once before, when he was introduced in "Christmas on Bear Mountain" (included in a different volume in this series). There, as a flinty miser, he was much beholden to his namesake, Ebenezer Scrooge, from Charles Dickens's "A Christmas Carol."

Here, as full partner, Scrooge reprises his role as instigator (even though Donald has proven perfectly capable of getting into wild adventures by himself). This refines a model for so many classic tales to come, utilizing Scrooge as the fast-track facilitator for whisking the Duck clan to every corner of the globe — and beyond, in some cases — with perils to match.

Yet Barks was always diligently mindful of the tender sensibilities of his youngest readers. The opening pages of "The Old Castle's Secret" are a purposeful yet note-perfect prologue for the machinations to follow. A cozy, domestic familiarity contrasts sharply with the exoticism of the Scottish estate.

Once within the castle, another revealing contrast is made between its claustrophobic confines and the invigorating stints in the out-of-doors. Nowhere is this more evident than when the nephews burst from the oppressive stone corridors into the fresh, sunlit air of the battlements. United, yet trapped on the parapet, the family will face its direst dilemma even as the widened horizons prove inspiring (and lovely as well, thanks to vistas tailor-made for a sympathetic colorist).

One of the challenges Barks set for himself in "The Old Castle's Secret" was to create a ghost story that would be spooky without traumatizing the susceptible.

He succeeds through several means. First, he establishes early on that the ghost is invisible, thereby dampening the anxiety of any potential graphic horror. Accordingly, Scottie's ominous remark, "He may be standing behind you right now!" is unsettling without being terrifying. The castle's "ghost" conducts the majority of his business while remaining unseen. This includes, as forewarned, most of the comedic violence — all that conking, bonking, and booting.

The shadow skeleton, however striking, is initially glimpsed in retreat, passively withdrawing with his prize. This form, appearing unexpectedly, selectively, and to terrific dramatic and visual effect, resorts

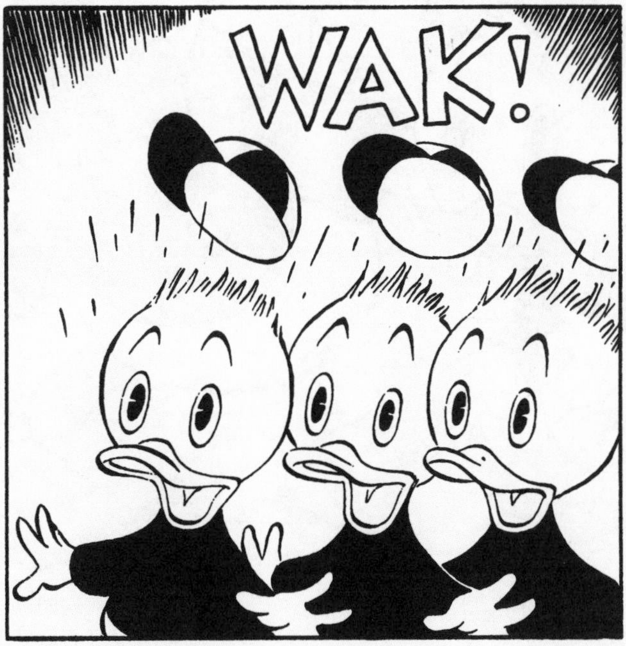
WAK!

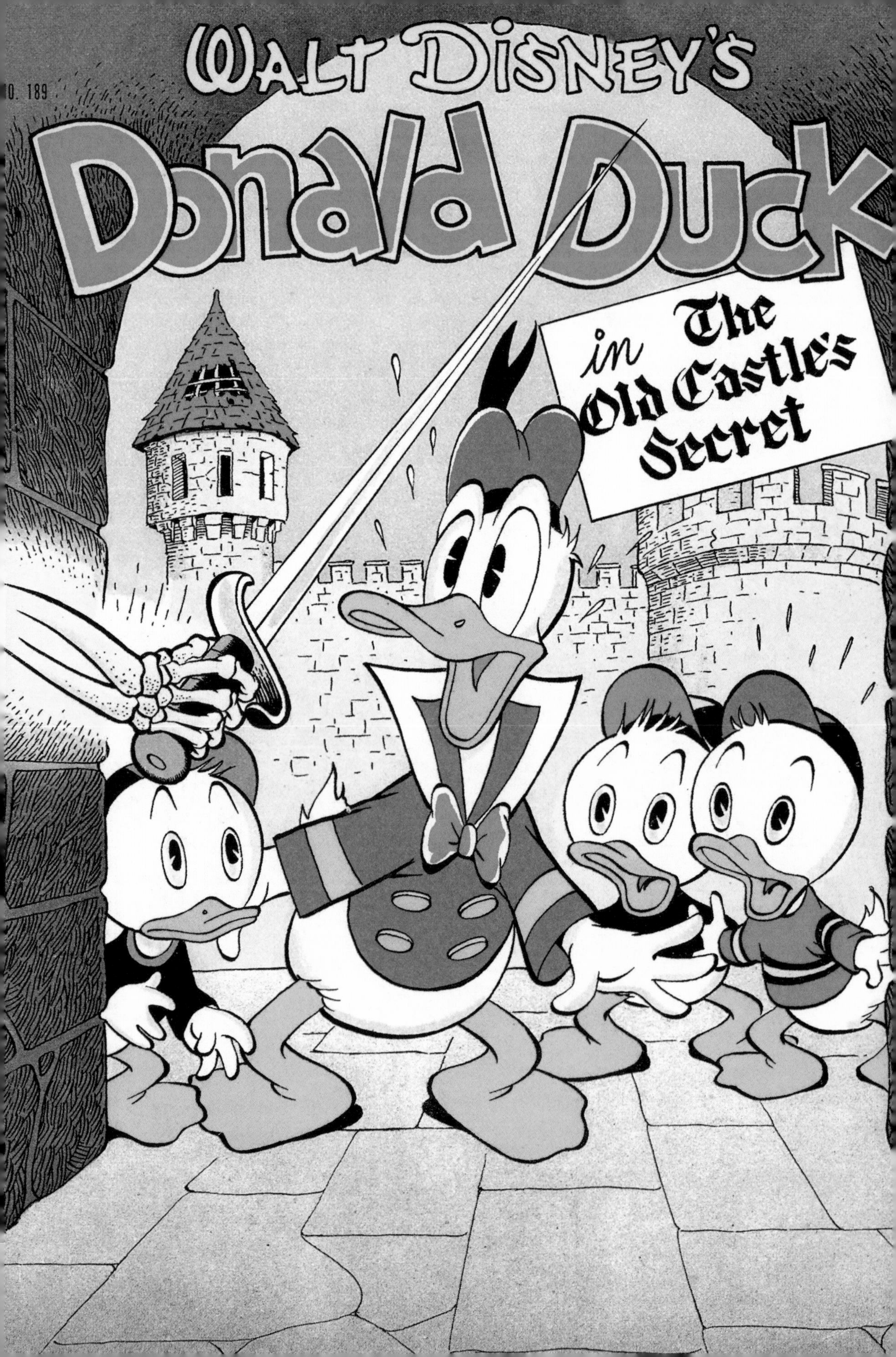

NO. 189
WALT DISNEY'S
Donald Duck
in The Old Castle's Secret

to menace only as the climax ratchets up to highest gear.

But even more crucial to conveying anxiety without inducing it, Barks takes pains to demonstrate to readers, regardless of their own level of empathy or steeliness of nerve, that the Ducks are themselves really scared during the story, particularly the elders. Why, they're sweating bullets and passing out from fright even before they leave the safety of Scrooge's mansion! Such demonstrations of fear serve to make later acts of courage and heroism seem all the more brave.

As the plot gains momentum, the narrative adopts more of the structure and trappings of a mystery. Things get suspicious. Coincidences invite scrutiny, especially on the part of nephews Huey, Dewey, and Louie. Nuggets of new information become clues. As a straightforward detective story, though, it's less of a whodunit (there being only one lone viable suspect) than a howdunit — how to account for the ghost in both its invisible and skeletal guises.

(Barks uses the same technique of postponing an explanation in "Sheriff of Bullet Valley" (p. 139). There, the reader knows the villain, but the puzzle of how his brand is emblazoned on others' livestock lingers throughout the story.)

Outside the castle's walls, mortal derring-do, ingenuity, and enterprise gain the upper hand, insuring that any notion of a supernatural entity will be forced into the clear light of day and the muck of the moor.

— RICH KREINER

WINTERTIME WAGER *p. 35*

Gladstone Gander, appearing here for the first time, is one of Carl Barks's great character inventions. As Donald's foil, he contends not only for whatever riches our hero happens to be chasing, but also for the heart of Daisy. On a more profound level, though, he challenges Donald's fundamental belief in a just world.

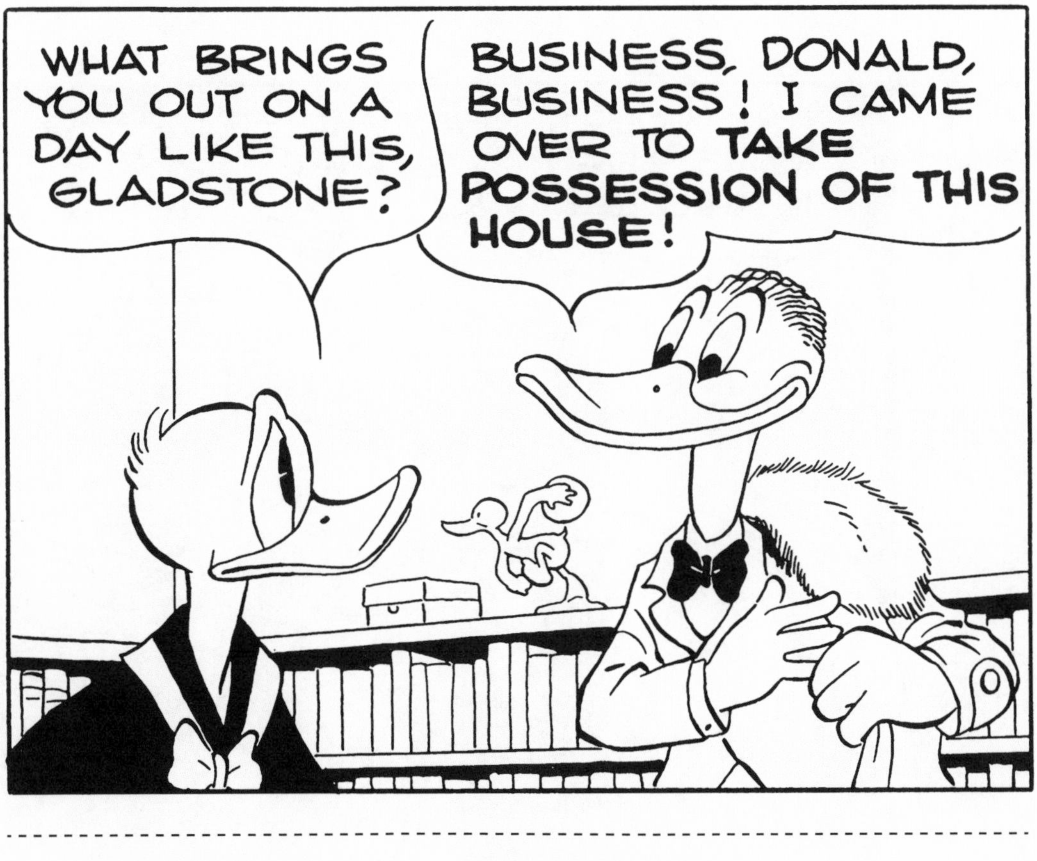
WHAT BRINGS YOU OUT ON A DAY LIKE THIS, GLADSTONE?
BUSINESS, DONALD, BUSINESS! I CAME OVER TO TAKE POSSESSION OF THIS HOUSE!

Essentially, Gladstone serves as a reminder that we are not privileged in this world, even if we convince ourselves otherwise.

The stroke of genius in this regard came with Gladstone's incredible, at times reality-bending, luck. That trait was still to come in this first story, but the insufferable smugness, the foppy nonchalance, and the questionable morality are all in place. He may not yet be the luckiest guy in the world, but he still represents real menace — the threat to the Duck family of losing their house on Christmas Day and having to "sleep in the park" provides the kind of troubling edge Barks would handle to great effect.

Donald's summertime bragging under the influence of what older readers will immediately recognize as lemonade in name only almost lands him in the coldest waters recorded in Duckburg history. He narrowly escapes through hilariously delineated bodily contortion, but essentially fails at saving his family: "Swim, or get out of my house!" commands Gladstone.

Daisy's arrival visually echoes Gladstone's earlier one, signaling a balancing of the scales. We are then treated to an equally inspired sequence with a perspiring Gladstone vainly battling to hold his lemonade, his face bloating with engorgement: "Drink ... or get out of my house!" commands Donald.

It ends with Donald and Gladstone, all a-bluster once more, accepting absurd new challenges from one another.

Having teased the moralizing contours of a fable throughout, Barks subverts expectations, delivering instead a symmetrically impeccable piece of high comedy on human failing.

— MATTHIAS WIVEL

WATCHING THE WATCHMAN *p. 45*

"Watching the Watchman" is full of *pain*. The first two pages establish the story's premise — Donald takes a job that requires him to stay up all night. Then we see how various characters suffer because of Donald's career choice. First are the nephews, who lie in their bed, eyes lined with fatigue, unable to sleep because Donald is blowing up the attic and playing the radio too loud.

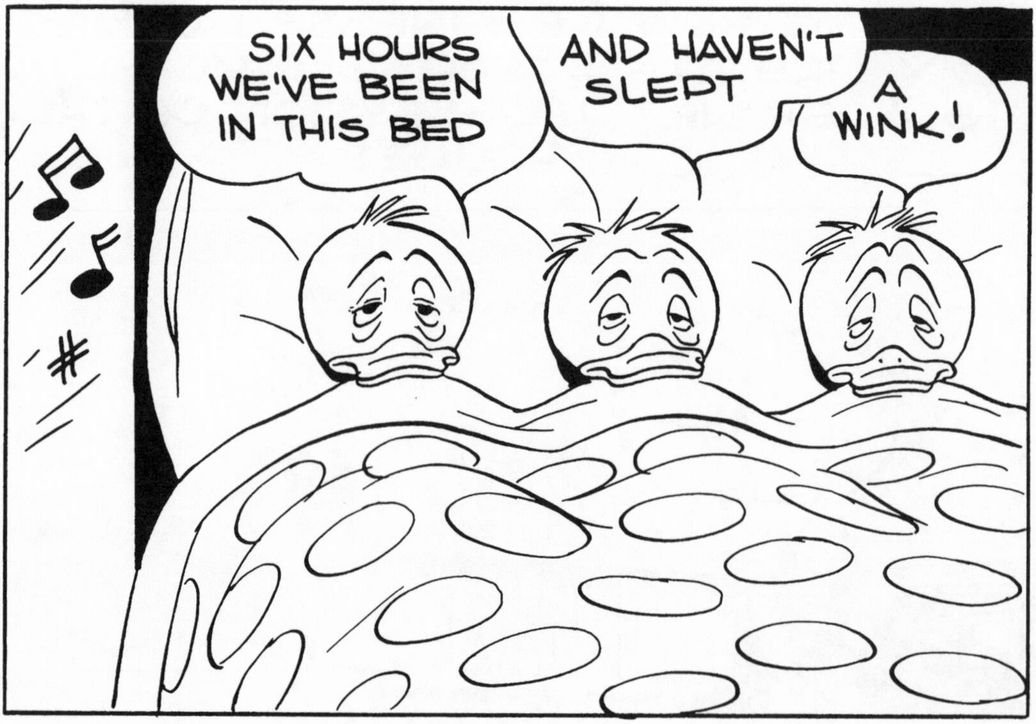
SIX HOURS WE'VE BEEN IN THIS BED
AND HAVEN'T SLEPT
A WINK!

Huey, Dewey, and Louie get their revenge, though, when they follow Donald to the dock and subject him to tortures (tuba music, tacks, an electrical shock), which still fail to keep him awake. Story page 8 (p. 52), with its images of Dewey firing tacks at Donald's behind, and Donald's anguished cries of "Yowch" "Yipe" and "Yow," is the *ne plus ultra* of the story's hilarious and disquieting emphasis on violence.

The irony, of course, is that the nephews didn't need to hurt Donald at all. "Watching the Watchman" begins with Donald dreaming of a nice, soft, cushy job, and when he's allowed to continue his dreaming at the night watchman post, he's able to stop Scarpuss and his thieves from stealing the silk.

Interestingly, the confrontation between Donald and Scarpuss's men is a minor incident. The thieves only appear in four panels (one in silhouette), and here Barks resists the ubiquitous tendency to end pop culture stories with violent confrontation. (There's been enough violence already.)

Rather, Donald's somnambulist shootout makes thematic points — that Donald should have fallen asleep earlier and that our jobs should be a natural extension of our dream-selves and our deepest desires. As Talking Heads sing in "Found a Job" (1978), "If your work isn't what you love, then something isn't right." There's nothing Donald loves more than sleep.

It's tempting to see parallels between "Watching the Watchman" and Barks's own life. Here's a small connection: as a child, Barks was fascinated by the cowboys that he met in Midland, Oregon, while in "Watching the Watchman," Donald is successful as a night watchman because he dreams of cowboys.

Here's a more speculative connection: Donald uses sleep to escape the pricks and shocks of a painful reality, while Barks overcame serious adversity — childhood poverty, hearing problems, failed marriages — by dreaming up a Duck world that provided him with an escape from real-life problems. Sometimes cartoonists live inside their heads because living outside their heads is intolerable.

And just as Donald's dreams get him a "big reward," so too did Barks's dreams lift him out of anonymity and into a better place.
— CRAIG FISCHER

WIRED *p. 55*

It is hard not to confront the obvious flaw in Donald's reasoning. "They want messenger boys at the Coastal telegraph office! ... Messenger boys get *big tips* when they deliver telegrams to rich people! Watch me make a fortune!"

True, Andrew Carnegie had begun his career as a telegraph messenger boy, and, as a result, a popular notion existed in the late 19th century that the job could set a boy on (as Edward S. Ellis's book from the period put it) "The Straight Road to Success."

Before telephones began to spread across the country at the end of that century, the bike-riding telegraph messenger boy was the quickest, most efficient means of getting urgent messages to their destinations. For that brief period between the invention of the telegraph and the invention of the telephone, the telegraph messenger boy rode on the cutting edge of technology.

By 1948, however, the telegraph company messenger boy was already a relic of a bygone era, and Depression-era innovations such as singing telegrams (in "Wired," expertly performed by Huey, Dewey, and Louie) had done little to revive the industry. By mid-century, the telegraph messenger boy had lost his ubiquitous place in American culture.

Of course, Donald's self-delusion goes further here, as the connection to Carnegie reminds us. Like his fellow billionaire, Donald's Uncle Scrooge had emigrated in the 19th century from Scotland to make his fortune. But unlike Carnegie, who would go on to become one of the most dedicated philanthropists in the first decades of the 20th century, Scrooge is the least likely Duck on the face of the planet to give anyone a "big tip." The millionaires Donald encounters in his brief stint as a messenger boy only confirm the lessons he should have already learned about the very rich from his uncle.

Meanwhile, the boys have a very different experience. For one thing, they are clearly better suited to the job, being, after all, *boys*. Telegraph companies, at their zenith, were the major employer of children in the United States. That brought the industry increasingly into the spotlight of reform in the early decades of the 20th century.

One concern of child welfare advocates was that the job brought children into contact

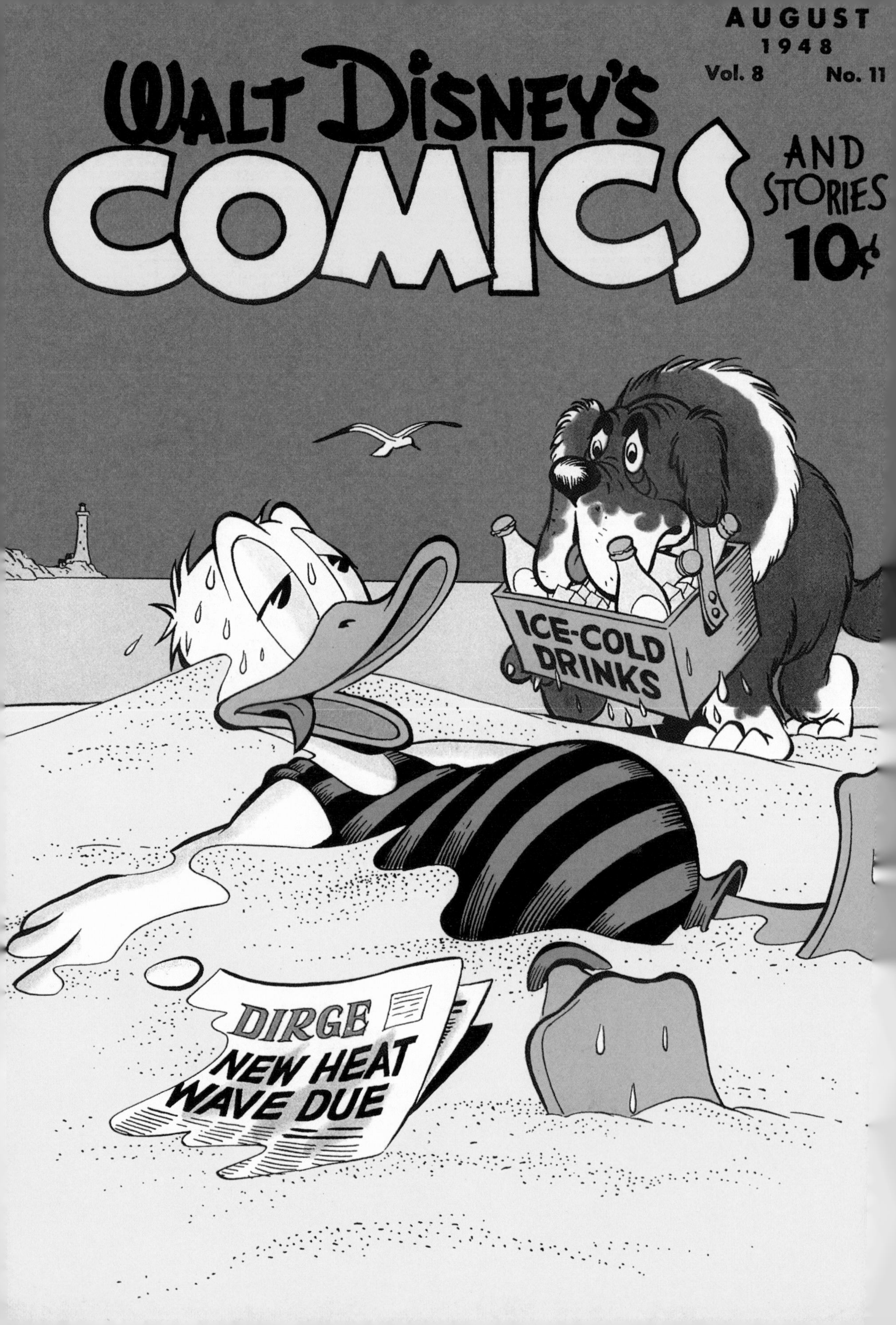
AUGUST
1948
Vol. 8 No. 11
WALT DISNEY'S
COMICS
AND STORIES
10¢
ICE-COLD DRINKS
DIRGE
NEW HEAT WAVE DUE

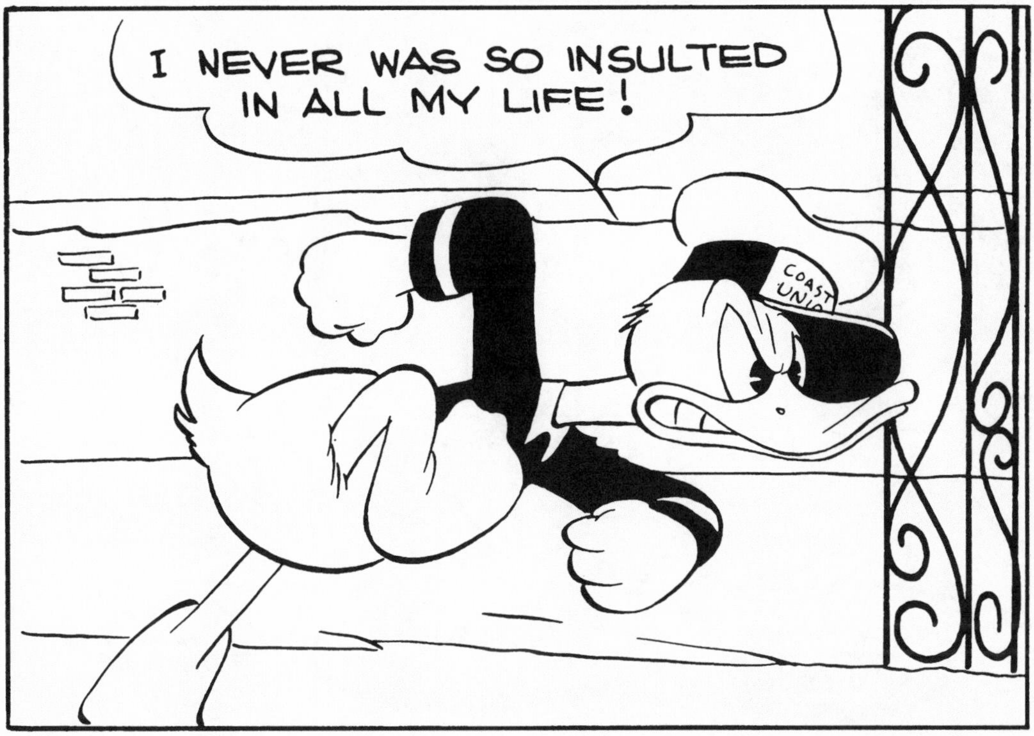
I NEVER WAS SO INSULTED IN ALL MY LIFE!
COAST UNIO

with unsavory characters and sinful behavior, especially as their calls carried them into bad neighborhoods or dens of vice. Indeed, these children found themselves often very much on the front lines of the changing city of the early 20th century.

Sure enough, while Donald is delivering letters to Millionaire Row, the boys are sent off on a fool's errand to Dreary Street, in the "poor section of town." But while the neighborhood is truly dreary and depressed, the boys, unlike Donald, experience the reward — both financial and spiritual — of bringing hope and connection to the reclusive Angina Arthritis. Here in the furthest reaches of the city, where the residents are so disconnected from modernity they have neither sidewalks nor even house numbers, the telegram still works its magic.

— JARED GARDNER

GOING APE *p. 65*

Although his 1948 artwork might look simple compared to that of his best-known adventures from the following decade, Barks by this time is already a master of the 10-pager and his action sequences are irresistible.

In "Going Ape," Donald organizes a jungle-themed garden party for Duckburg's high society and wants his nephews to dress up as monkeys, much to their dismay. The three young rascals, as ever, prove to be smarter than their uncle — they thwart his attempt to hypnotize them via a pair of menacing spectacles, then turn the tables and hypnotize *him!*

The monkey-minded Donald causes much more trouble than anticipated. For a moment it looks as if the nephews regain control of the situation, but soon it all backfires. In a reversal of the usual pattern, it's now the nephews (and Daisy) who make complete fools of themselves and it's up to Donald to attempt to patch things up.

But it has all gone too far already. Donald's posh and wealthy guests are in for a nasty surprise when the nephews raid the party table and treat them just like real monkeys would.

All these reversals of fortune, plus the inevitable epilogue of self-exile to the South

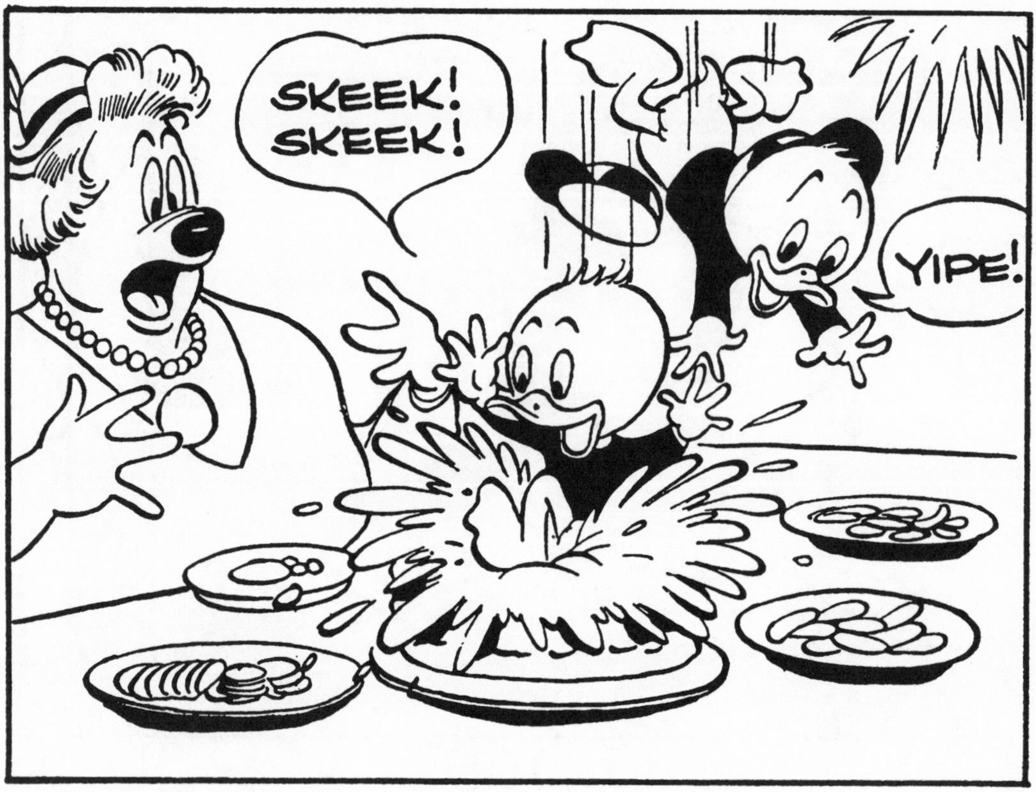
SKEEK! SKEEK!
YIPE!

Pole, fit into 10 perfectly balanced pages that never miss a beat. It's real Barks cartooning here, in both the rhythm and timing of the gags and in the visual dynamics. Look at that great sequence of Donald and Daisy whirling in the trees — it's pure cartoon action!

Barks here is not far from the cinematic panels of Milt Gross and other comics *auteurs* from the 1930s who, like the Duck Man, also started in animation. Indeed, the works of such luminaries as E.C. Segar, Rube Goldberg, Milt Gross, and Carl Barks are tremendously innovative for their time and, taken together, constitute a fertile universe that, decades later, became a source of inspiration for underground comics.

— FRANCESCO STAJANO and LEONARDO GORI

DARKEST AFRICA *p. 75*

In "Voodoo Hoodoo" (*Walt Disney's Donald Duck: "Lost in the Andes,"* Fantagraphics, 2011), a story partly set in Africa, Carl Barks draws two small directional signs near the edge of a single panel. The sign labeled "Lightest Africa" points away from the jungle, and the other, marked "Darkest Africa," directs travelers into the "mysterious" bush. As Barks knew, novelists, filmmakers, and illustrators had repeatedly characterized Africa as the "Dark Continent," a place swarming with shadowy savages, where the light of civilization had yet to shine.

In "Darkest Africa," Barks parodies adventure narratives in which explorers leave their home countries in search of African treasure. Donald and his nephews depart Duckburg to go on safari, seeking the world's rarest butterfly and hoping to outwit a collector who has rankled Donald's immense pride and sparked his competitive nature.

Although "Darkest Africa" first appeared in 1948, it recalls an earlier genre of European colonial adventure — the travel narratives of 19th-century naturalists who journeyed abroad in pursuit of unusual flora and fauna. Barks turns Africa into a comic battleground on which explorers vie for an insect trophy.

The names of the "dog face" competitors evoke Africa's colonial history, specifically the influence of Great Britain and the Netherlands, two European countries that once ruled numerous African colonies. The nattily attired British lepidopterist Sir Gnatbugg-Mothley sends the Ducks as his proxies to defeat a gruff collector with the Scottish-sounding name of Argus McFiendy, who briefly masquerades as Dutch scientist Professor Van Tulip.

Barks, who didn't travel overseas until he was 93, found ideas for plots and exotic settings in popular culture. He was a life-long subscriber to *National Geographic*, an American magazine celebrated for lavish pictorial features that introduced readers to unusual people and places.

The cartoonist was likely inspired by adventure movies such as *Perils of the Jungle* (1927) and *Tarzan's Secret Treasure* (1941), in which explorers traverse Africa's rivers and jungles, encountering dark natives and ferocious beasts. Barks also looked to newspaper adventure comics — his Whambesi River alludes to a fictional African tribe in Lee Falk's *The Phantom* named The Wambesi. "Darkest Africa," then, is a fantasy assembled from other fantasies.

Twenty-first-century readers might be troubled by aspects of Barks's African fantasy. Though Huey, Dewey, and Louie will one day become ardent environmentalists as members of the Boy Scouts-inspired Junior Woodchucks, they and their uncle poison a crocodile and gut

another, shoot a monkey with a slingshot, and cause a massive elephant stampede, one of Barks's most horrifying images.

Some readers have objected to the story's division of Africans into two categories: the "good native" who helps the white man, and the "evil savage" who threatens his enterprise. While both types are caricatures, Barks's savage cannibals are the more disconcerting, with their sinister expressions, cartoonishly exaggerated faces, and necklaces of human teeth. They speak an odd mix of mock-African and mock-Native American dialect, such as "Yigli oofti gefigli gloop" and "... if you no tell us by moonrise, we *eatum!*"

It would be a big mistake, however, to assume that Barks condones all of the story's aggression. The cartoonist prided himself on creating complicated protagonists, especially sympathetic characters who do mean things.

Barks felt that, since humans ultimately act out of self-interest, his human-like Ducks should do the same. Asked about his world-view, he answered concisely, "Everybody's robbin' everybody else, but it's something you expect" — and "Darkest Africa" depicts a lot of "robbin'."

Barks often acknowledged the harm his characters caused themselves and others. Speaking through Donald, the cartoonist comments on the absurd situation the Ducks and collectors have created. Just after he causes the elephant stampede, Donald ruefully exclaims, "All that for a butterfly!"

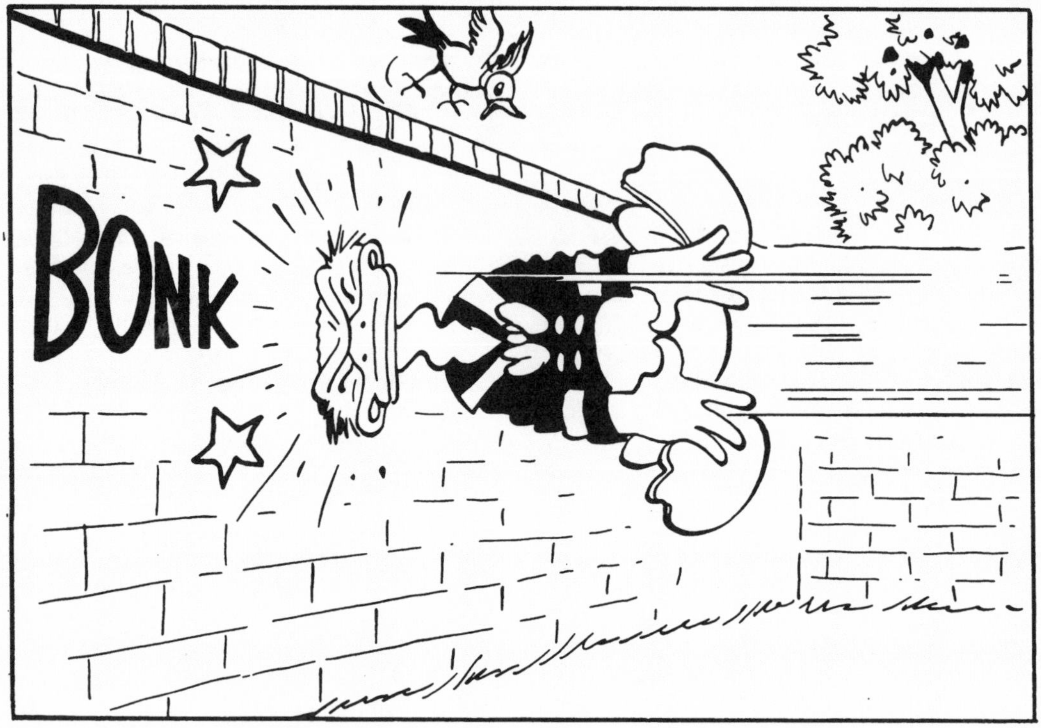
BONK

Many colonialist adventure tales end with treasure-laden explorers returning home. At first, it seems as if "Darkest Africa" will follow this path, with an *Almostus Exctinctus* firmly in Donald's possession. But in a strange reversal, the world's rarest butterfly suddenly, almost magically, becomes plentiful — and therefore undesirable. Nature wins, converting the exotic into the mundane, leaving all of the characters disillusioned.

A Barksian comedy about the futility of greed, "Darkest Africa" offers a lesson in disenchantment perfectly captured in the final panel: the defeated nephews walk away from the reader, throwing to the ground an empty container — a treasure chest without treasure.

Of the story's unhappy ending, Barks might say, in echo of Donald's comment, "All that for nothing, except a few laughs."

The original 1948 version of "Darkest Africa" has never been reprinted in English — until now. All mechanical copies of the artwork were lost, making reproduction a practical impossibility.

In 1982, Disney's Dutch publisher had artists Daan Jippes and Dick Vlottes redraw the story. Their artwork was then altered after editors in America requested that the Africans' stereotypical features and dialogue be changed. This altered faux-Barks version was the basis for all American reprints between then and now.

For this edition, Fantagraphics first went back to the original 1948 *March of Comics* version and then located a 1950s Italian printing of the story. With the help of those two sources, and a lot of painstaking work, the company's fabled technical wizardry has at last given us "Darkest Africa" restored to Barks's original vision.

— KEN PARILLE

SPOIL THE ROD *p. 99*

Carl Barks uses popular misunderstandings of Dr. Benjamin Spock's *The Common Sense Book of Baby and Child Care* (1946), which discouraged corporal punishment, as a springboard for the plot of "Spoil the Rod."

The absence of common sense in raising children gives Barks the opportunity to exaggerate his drawing of Donald's facial expressions and bodily postures — ranging from despair to a broad smile of recognition, from frustration to near-explosive anger, from suffering and defeat to self-satisfied grinning, from depression and sobbing to cuckoo-headedness, and many more, often with a mixture of two or more gestures as only Barks can do.

Pulpheart Clabberhead, a smug, self-righteous, narrow-minded professor, is the agent behind the misery Donald goes through in the story. The name Barks gives this character is appropriate. The pedant has too much clabber (gooey sour milk) and pulp (a soft, shapeless mass) and not enough heart (compassion) and head (common sense).

Clabberhead manages to convert Donald from his reflexive impulse to use a switch for corporal punishment ("... I'll tan your hides pink!") to being utterly permissive and imposing no rules.

The kids see that Donald has come so completely under Pulpheart's sway that Donald will buy them equipment for the kind of adult occupations they've chosen. They exploit Donald's lack of common sense and his promise that he will never use a switch on them again by escalating their demands to the point of tyranny, thus punishing Donald for his irrational authoritarianism at the beginning of the story.

After Donald's head-smashing brain-clearing, he is able to think like "a sensible person" and test Pulpheart's theories.

When the professor becomes a victim of his own philosophy, the switch switches hands, and the final image visually bookends Donald chasing the nephews at the beginning of the story, as Clabberhead comes to recognize that there must be rules, after all.

— DONALD AULT

ROCKET RACE TO THE MOON *p. 109*

"Rocket Race to the Moon" takes Carl Barks into Floyd Gottfredson territory, pitting Donald against a Pegleg Pete-like villain. The numerous marginal gags in the scientists' workshop also recall the specialties of other cartoonists, and Donald's duel with the moon-man echoes Mickey Mouse's run-in with a pail and a mop in the Sorcerer's Apprentice sequence from *Fantasia*.

When this story first appeared in 1948, the farthest a rocket had ever reached was

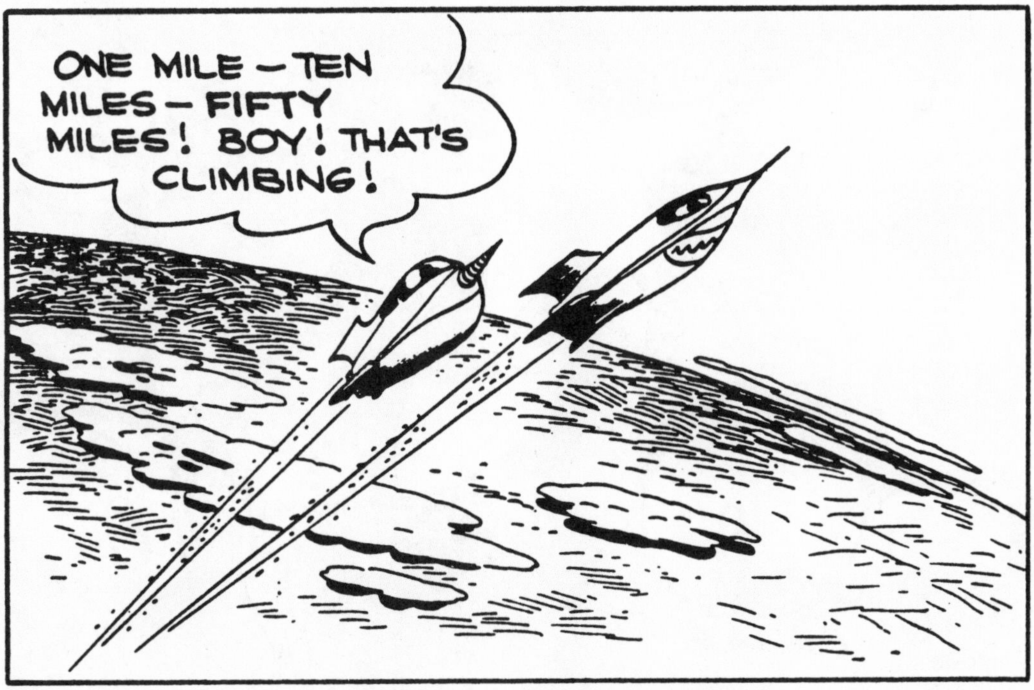
ONE MILE — TEN MILES — FIFTY MILES! BOY! THAT'S CLIMBING!

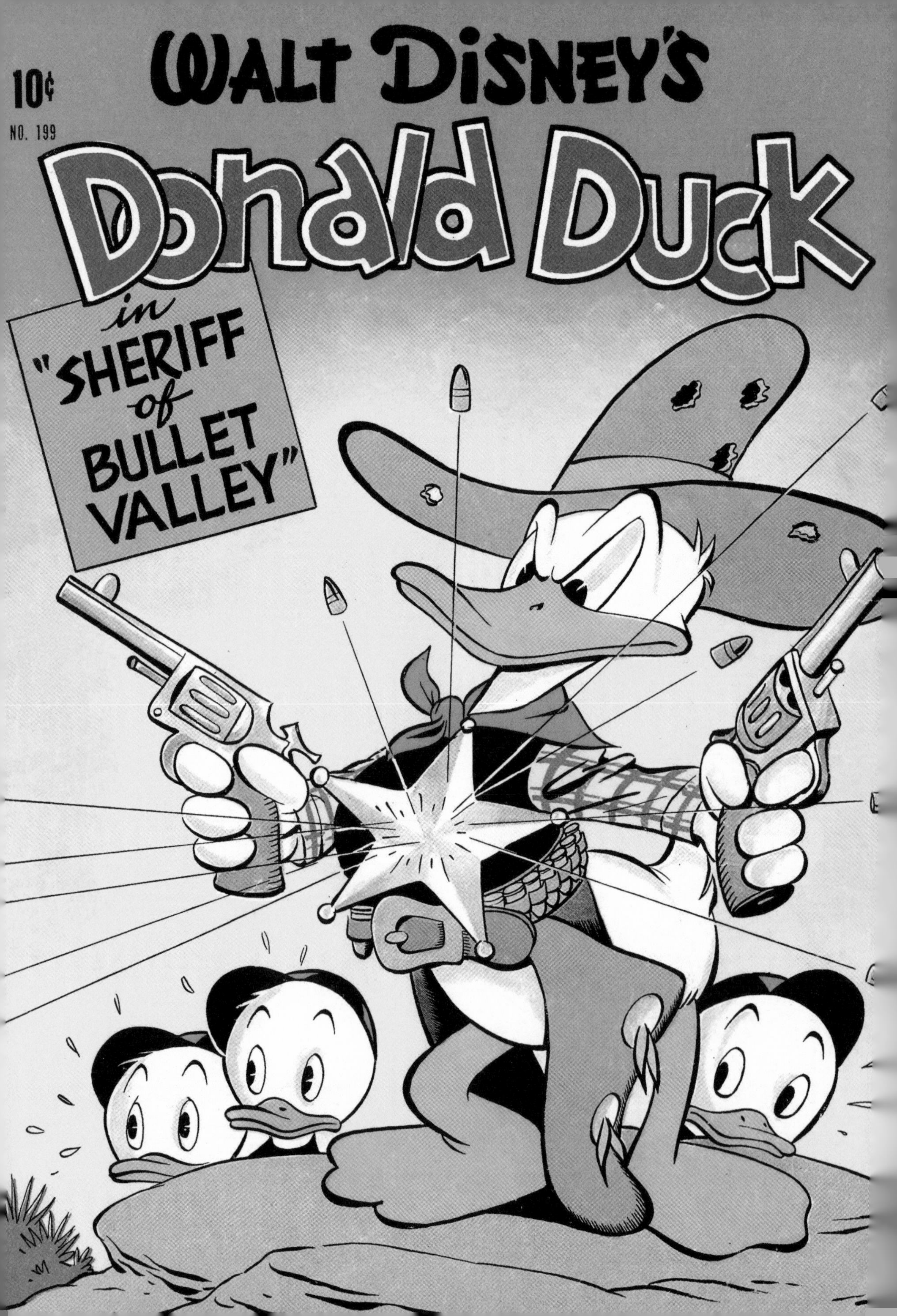
10¢
NO. 199
WALT DISNEY'S
Donald Duck
in
"SHERIFF of BULLET VALLEY"

from Nazi-occupied France to London, and the American space program was only at the stage of de-Nazifying German rocket scientists (a process which consisted of saying, "You never really were a Nazi, were you, Heinz?").

Science fiction had typically depicted the first moon flight as the product of shade tree mechanics working on their own, like the Professors Cosmic and Gamma. This was largely because rocket science in the 1930s was more a hobby than an institutional or national effort.

One of the most celebrated science fiction stories of the 1950s was Tom Godwin's "The Cold Equations," published in 1954, in which a young woman stows away on a medical rescue mission to a space colony, like Huey, Dewey, and Louie do here. Because Godwin's rescue mission carries just enough fuel to carry medical supplies and the pilot to their destination, the stowaway must take a one-way trip out the airlock.

Science fiction readers, who set great store by who comes up with an idea first, were dismayed when EC Comics fans pointed out that the jettison-the-stowaway method of fuel conservation had previously been used by Al Feldstein in "A Weighty Decision," illustrated by Wallace Wood, in 1952.

In Barks's 1948 "Rocket Race to the Moon," we see the question brought up even earlier, which just goes to show that this is one of the things people who thought seriously about space travel thought about.

What made Godwin's story a sensation was its unmerciful adherence to the rigid solution to those cold equations, where a more chivalrous science fiction writer would have cooked up a *deus ex machina* to save the girl. For Carl Barks, the indifference of the scientists to the safety of their sentient supercargo is a given.

— R. FIORE

Earlier, in "Watching the Watchman" (p. 45), Donald had succumbed to sleep while on his night watchman shift, but in "Donald of the Coast Patrol" he is wide awake, and his inability to look beyond appearances — in sharp contrast to his nephews — is so ingrained that it becomes both hilarious and irritating at the same time.

Carl Barks's art is enriched by the presence of two beautiful female spies: a brunette and a blonde, later identified as "Madames X and XX." Here, Barks makes implicit reference to another Madame XX — the gorgeous spy Barks and Jack Hannah created for an unproduced Donald Duck short in 1942.

Barks's original Madame XX was a peroxide blonde Duck version of actress Veronica Lake. In "Donald of the Coast Patrol," Madames X and XX are human except for their dog noses. The pair anticipates yet another master spy: the fully human Madame Triple-X, whom Barks would visualize in "Dangerous Disguise" (1951, in a later volume in this series).

Barks would later offer a revised version of the "Donald of the Coast Patrol" scenario with "Borderline Hero" (1957, in a later volume), moving the setting to the wilderness of Pizen Thorn Flat, where Donald is a border patrol agent. Barks would alter gags and supporting characters for "Borderline Hero," but kept the "Donald of the Coast Patrol" spirit intact. In both stories, it is the nephews who deliver the smugglers to justice, although it is Donald who takes the credit — and gets a promotion.

Shakespeare's Hamlet did not appreciate "the spurns that patient merit of th' unworthy takes," but Donald's nephews don't mind helping their gullible uncle keep his job — even if they seem to resent the arrogance he shows at the very end of "Donald of the Coast Patrol."

— ALBERTO BECCATINI

DONALD OF THE COAST PATROL p. 119

"Who's guarding the guardian?" is the question readers will likely ask themselves while reading "Donald of the Coast Patrol," a story in which Donald appears to be particularly gullible.

"Donald of the Coast Patrol" is basically a story of fakes — fakes that Donald just can't manage to recognize: a fake hot dog stand owner, a fake walrus (in California-like Calisota!), and a fake "girl in distress." All of them fool our hero.

GLADSTONE RETURNS p. 129

This story is the second to feature Gladstone Gander, Donald's new rival, who was created by Carl Barks in "Wintertime Wager" (p. 35). Many of the attributes we will later associate with Gladstone — especially his maddening good fortune — have not yet been developed in this early story.

Instead, Gladstone serves here as another version of Donald, but amplified — more arrogant, more stubborn, more hot-tempered.

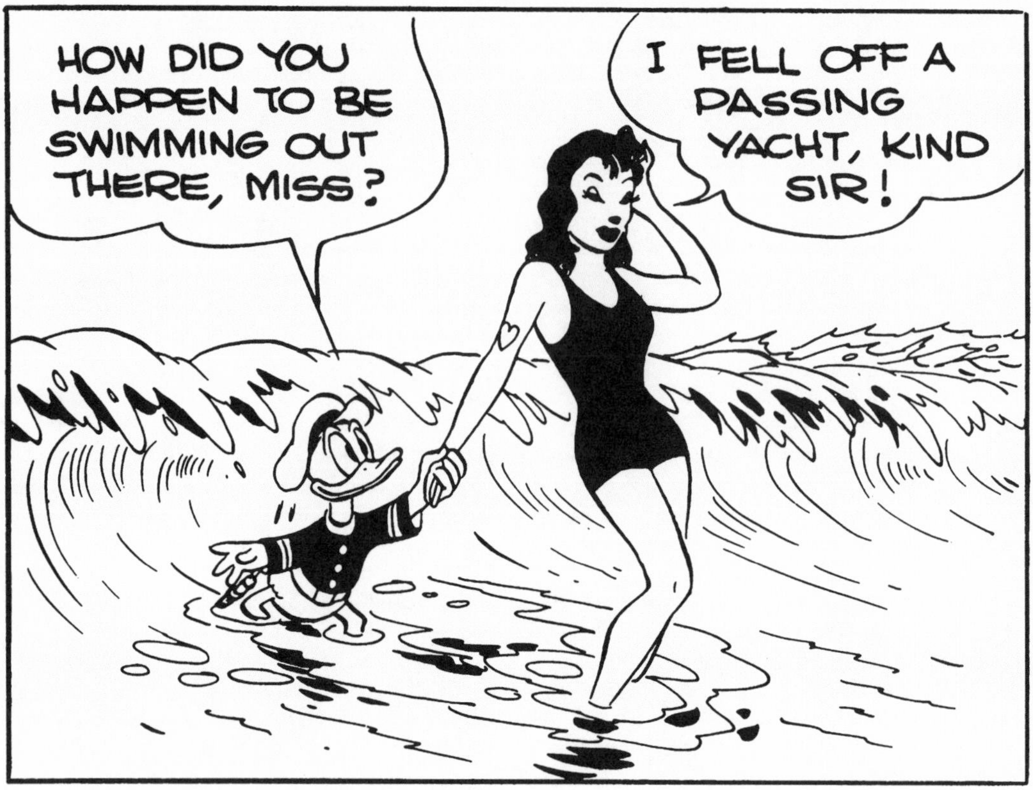
HOW DID YOU HAPPEN TO BE SWIMMING OUT THERE, MISS?
I FELL OFF A PASSING YACHT, KIND SIR!

The amplification, it turns out, makes all the difference, reminding the reader (and Barks himself, who would grow to dislike Gladstone) how thin is the line between sympathetic and hateful when it comes to Duckburg's most famous resident.

As with many of Barks's stories, the underlying message here of the rewards of hard work, saving, and charity is underscored by the boys who have been working hard around town to save their nest egg. They are not saving for any particular purchase, but merely for the satisfaction of having "our bank full." Unlike Uncle Scrooge, for whom money replicates itself as if by magic, the boys must earn their money through the sweat of their brow and their own ingenuity.

Meanwhile, Donald and Gladstone have been one-upping each other with increasingly hyperbolic boasts about their imaginary wealth, boasts that are called out when Daisy comes in search of funds to support her club. Having failed to actually earn or save the money they brag about, Gladstone and Donald head off in search of a quick buck (or five) and arrive at the usual conclusions as to how one might get rich quick.

Donald's attempts to rob his nephews' bank are thwarted by the fact that the boys know him far too well. They have constructed an elaborate series of dummies and traps to keep him from their hard-earned savings.

Donald responds by taking a more indirect approach and his turn as a con man at first seems more promising, but ultimately it proves to be too convoluted and he gets fouled up in the trappings of his own plan. Gladstone, of course, is there to reap the rewards from the victims so masterfully set up by Donald's masquerade as a gypsy fortune teller.

The boys, however briefly, are punished for falling for the "fortune teller's" promise of unimaginable returns from the investment of $5. Their savings were safe from Donald until they became infected by that particular mania reserved for investors who believe that five dollars can be magically transformed into a "great fortune."

Of course, the boys have spent their lifetimes studying Donald, and so they soon

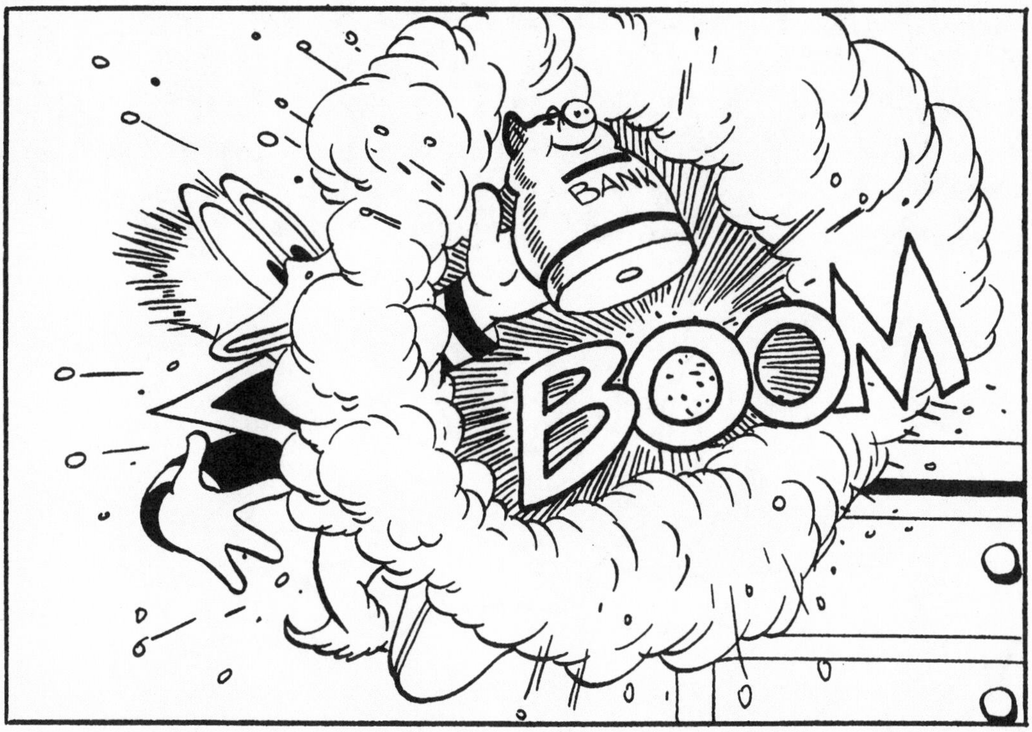
BANK
BOOM

recover both their moral bearings and their fortune by pulling a con on Gladstone: the promise of "pearl seeds" that can grow vast oceans of wealth in old oyster shells.

Any doubts as to the ultimate moral message of the story are clarified when the nephews donate their recovered savings to Daisy for her club — a gesture that spells out how they are different not only from Gladstone and Donald, but from Scrooge as well (for whom such an act would be unimaginable). The boys may be selling "pearl seeds," but Barks also wants us to know that they are truly sowing pearls before swine.

— JARED GARDNER

SHERIFF OF BULLET VALLEY *p. 139*

Carl Barks's fictions were remarkably malleable, sliding seamlessly between genres and narrative registers without losing their sense of reality. In this case, he created his ultimate Western by merging past and present, slapstick and heroism. The genre was a favorite of his and one he returned to several times throughout his career, no doubt fueled by memories of working as a cowpoke in his younger days. He clearly saw the possibilities offered by a contemporary setting, crafting a story about the lost frontier and its myth.

The Ducks appear to be traveling back in time as they drive into Bullet Valley, and in a sense they are — the old ways clearly still rule there. But Donald and the kids are preceded by a more nefarious incursion of modernity in the form of rustlers remote-branding cattle with a heat ray mounted on a jeep and enforcing their racket with submachine guns.

Himself a modern man, Donald believes he knows "*all* the angles" from his avid consumption of Western movies, a presumption immediately subverted, as Geoffrey Blum has observed, by the visual juxtaposition of a bowlegged cowboy leering at him at the bottom of the first page.

This subversion supplies much of the humor, and eventually the drama, of the story. It is immediately apparent how the myths perpetuated by modern Western fiction are unsuitable to the reality of policing the valley, especially for somebody as naïve as Donald. That his cluelessness is merely part of the narrative game, however, is indicated by the

SEPTEMBER
1948
Vol. 8 No. 12

No. 96

WALT DISNEY'S COMICS AND STORIES

10¢

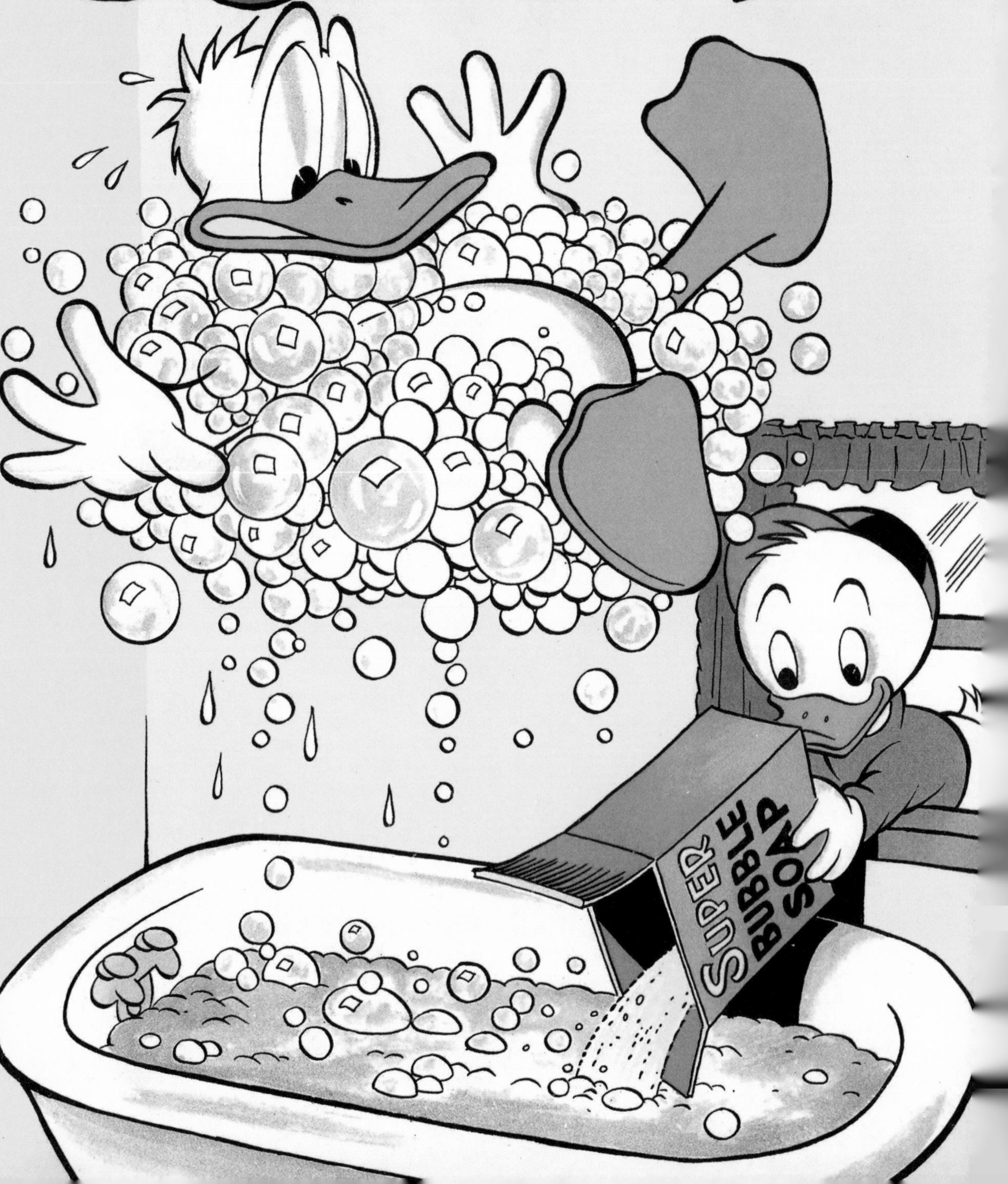
SUPER
BUBBLE
SOAP

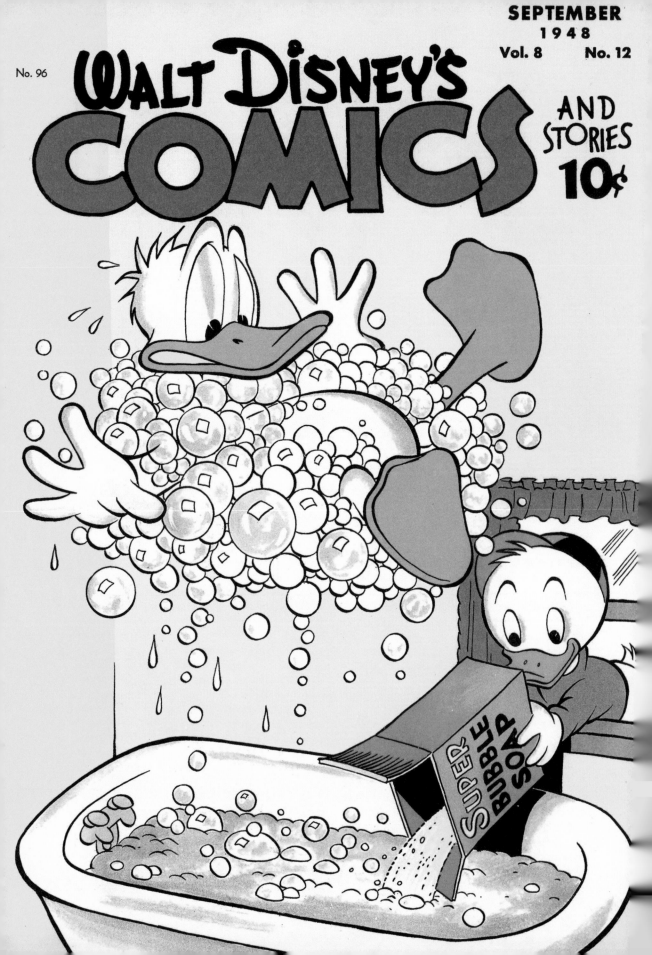

fact that Barks has him wink at the reader straight away, noting, "We're a long way from Hollywood here, boys!"

As Donald rides off on his oversize horse, the ominous words of the townsfolk are echoed by the placement of a coroner's sign behind him. His lofty thoughts of heroism are defused visually by the line of the mountainside plunging onto the bowed heads of the resourceful kids he should not be leaving behind. The portion of sign to his right that we can read says "LAST CH —"

Unsurprisingly, it takes the modern thinking of the kids to foil the rustlers, but at the end of the day, Donald still has to chase the villain, Blacksnake McQuirt, into the badlands to achieve what amounts to a Hollywood showdown, with all aces finally drawn by the hero. Primed by the Western clichés stacked up in the first half of the story, this dramatic shift in tone feels entirely natural.

In a Disney context, this heroic register was usually the domain of Mickey Mouse, and indeed the story seems to have originated in an unfinished animated short featuring the Mouse called "Northwest Mounted" on which Barks worked in his early days at Disney. McQuirt is a dead ringer for Mickey's nemesis, Black Pete. He is also one of the nastiest specimens in Barks's rogue's gallery — he actually *shoots* Donald and coldly leaves him to the vultures. Helping win the day, Donald's resourceful horse is a close cousin to Mickey's brave steed, Tanglefoot.

Like John Wayne, Donald enters the narrative by walking through a door, a savior from another era. Unlike his Hollywood analogue, however, he never leaves, staying instead to watch Western movies as order once again unravels. Although celebrating the moral values at the core of the myth, Barks, the cautious humanist, is fully aware that the story did not end with the West being won.

— MATTHIAS WIVEL

- -

LINKS HIJINKS *p. 173*

- -

Among the diversified, far-reaching, and elaborately constructed 10-page stories in this volume, "Links Hijinks" benefits from a certain concision of focus.

Once the nephews have been corralled as caddies, the action unfolds in a single setting, that of the golf course. The narrative arc is a smooth escalation of inventiveness. Modest conniving grows more elaborate before a wider conspiracy is thwarted by a succession of flabbergasting occurrences.

As morality play it's also relatively straightforward — utilitarian pranks fan Donald's vanity. Then, following a sobering bout of self-realization, a more venal plan is hatched before the miraculous trumps all petty human designs, decisively severing mortal plotting from outcome (although, it should be noted, still in accord with Gladstone's fabulous luck).

None of which quite conveys the antic energy and exuberance that Barks infuses into his tale. Expressive faces, as usual, sparkle, but protean postures upstage, starting with those of Donald himself. He spends an inordinate amount of time airborne, aloft in excitement or exertion.

For Western Publishing, Barks created character model sheets — a diagrammatic series of instructive Duck drawings to be circulated among other comic book artists as guides. They included relevant asides and cautions, such as "Get springiness in walk. The animation type waddle looks stiff in single drawings."

Several of the dynamic poses here are reminiscent of cartoon Donald captured at full tilt, itself no easy task. As static images, these exaggerations need to convince while doing without the fluidity of animated motion. They must hold up, frozen and in isolation, to the more leisurely, concerted gazing possible with comics. It's a testament to Barks's skill and painstakingness that these pretzelated contortions pass the eye test. They simply *look* right.

And even that's not the whole of it. Yes, the climactic instants of vigorous action are vividly dramatized. But each also suggests to the mind's eye a natural progression that includes the unseen, the moments just prior, and an immediate aftermath.

In that way, every picture possesses a real, if entirely subliminal, animation of its own.

— RICH KREINER

- -

PEARLS OF WISDOM *p. 183*

- -

In many ways, this story subverts the character dynamics of most of Barks's 10-pagers. In the typical Barks plot, Donald dreams up

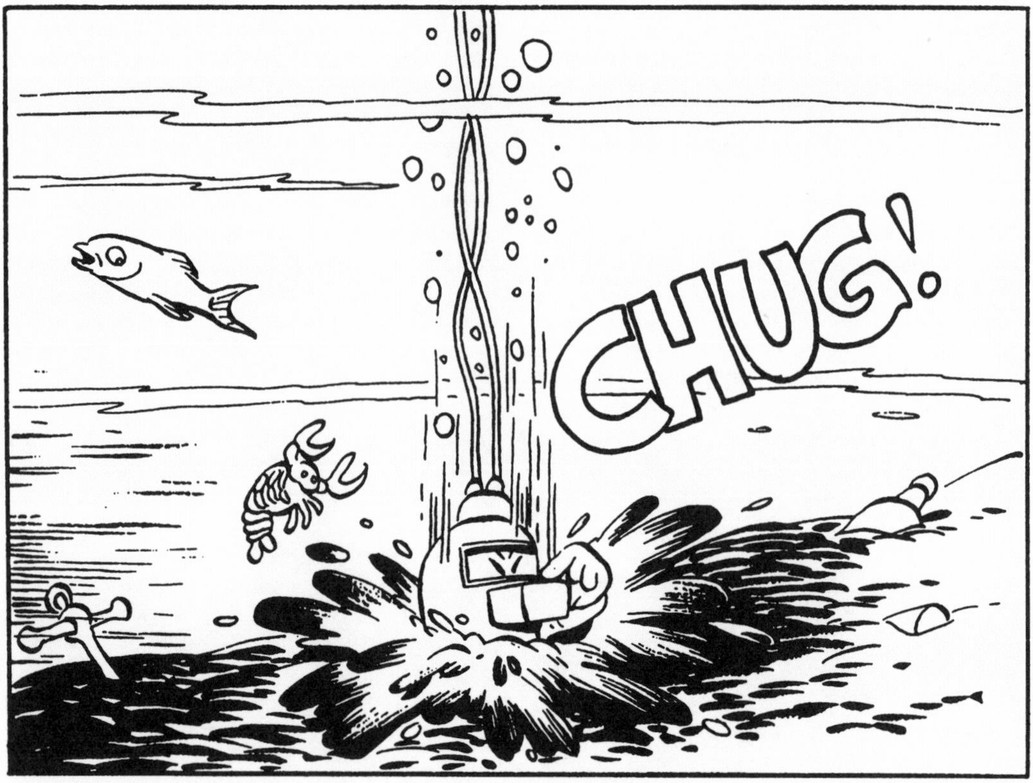
CHUG!

some half-baked scheme, and Huey, Dewey, and Louie then try to protect Donald from the dangerous consequences of his plan.

"Pearls of Wisdom," however, is structured around the nephews' lapses in judgment rather than Donald's. At the bottom of page 2 (p. 184), Huey, Dewey, and Louie acknowledge that they "should never have told Unca' Donald about that pearl!" They should have known better than to dangle that temptation in front of him — and on page 4 (p. 186), their failure to warn Donald about the sunken oil tanker leads to a low-scale environmental accident.

The nephews' mistakes escalate in the second half of the story. They laugh off the old sailor's warning, which puts the scuba-diving Donald at mortal risk; they fool Donald into believing that the giant clam is full of pearls; and they prolong the deception by delivering Mexican jumping beans to Daisy, which gets Donald in trouble with his girl.

One scene repeated in "Pearls of Wisdom" features a nephew saying "Know what I think?" or "Know what I'm thinking?" and the story's conclusion brings back this mantra ("You know what I'm thinking?"). And what, exactly, are Huey, Dewey, and Louie thinking in that silhouetted final panel? Probably that they've messed up yet again.

Another repeated element is jumping. In his scuba helmet, Donald first leaps into soft underwater mud, and then onto the top of a submerged mast. (The sixth panel on page 3 (p. 185), showing Donald landing on the mast with a loud *Thud!*, is some kind of cruel masterpiece — Barks draws Donald's head and limbs vigorously shaking from the impact, and the lines of force emanating from Donald's bottom are dark and powerful.)

And then, of course, the Mexican jumping beans are introduced on the final page, perhaps to remind us of all the jumping earlier in the story.

Yet despite all the athleticism in "Pearls of Wisdom," my favorite moment in the story occurs in the second panel of page 3 (p. 185), where Barks draws in the foreground a rock inhabited by a row of birds and a lone crab, all of whom serve as a mute audience for the pearl-diving exertions of Donald and the boys.

The birds and crab remind me that the quiet details of Barks's art are just as important as the adventure elements.

— CRAIG FISCHER

FOXY RELATIONS *p. 193*

"Foxy Relations" showcases Carl Barks's unfailingly expressive, animated, and genial drawings, from the story's pratfalls and hammy feigns, to Donald rounding the turn and heading for home atop that plug of a plowhorse.

But this story also calls attention to Barks's use of verbal humor. It can be throwaway, such as the title of Donald's book atop the first page, or more concerted, as in that same page's bottom tier: in the penultimate panel, Scrooge cites "the asinine, stupid, crazy, *useless*" and "the *worst*" in one context, then, without missing a beat, emphatically fingers Donald in the following frame, effectively tarring him with the same broad brush.

More elaborate is the caption-heavy quartet of panels on page 3. There, the "elite of society" — plus our hero — begin the chase. With their hounds barely bounding over the fence, the riders, "pictures of grace and poise and insouciant daring," are depicted as anything but.

The stage thus set, Donald re-enters as huntsman in hot pursuit, poised gracefully in all his unintended daring at the height of his in-flight arc.

Then there's that extended litany of names Donald cobbles together in an effort to attract his semi-domesticated quarry. At its lumpiest, it tumbles forth like a polysyllabic grab bag as beholden to foodstuff as it is to fish. Read aloud, it's a peculiar mouthful that trips awkwardly, farcically, off the tongue.

Finally, Uncle Scrooge makes his first appearance in these 10-page tales that Barks created for *Walt Disney's Comics and Stories.*

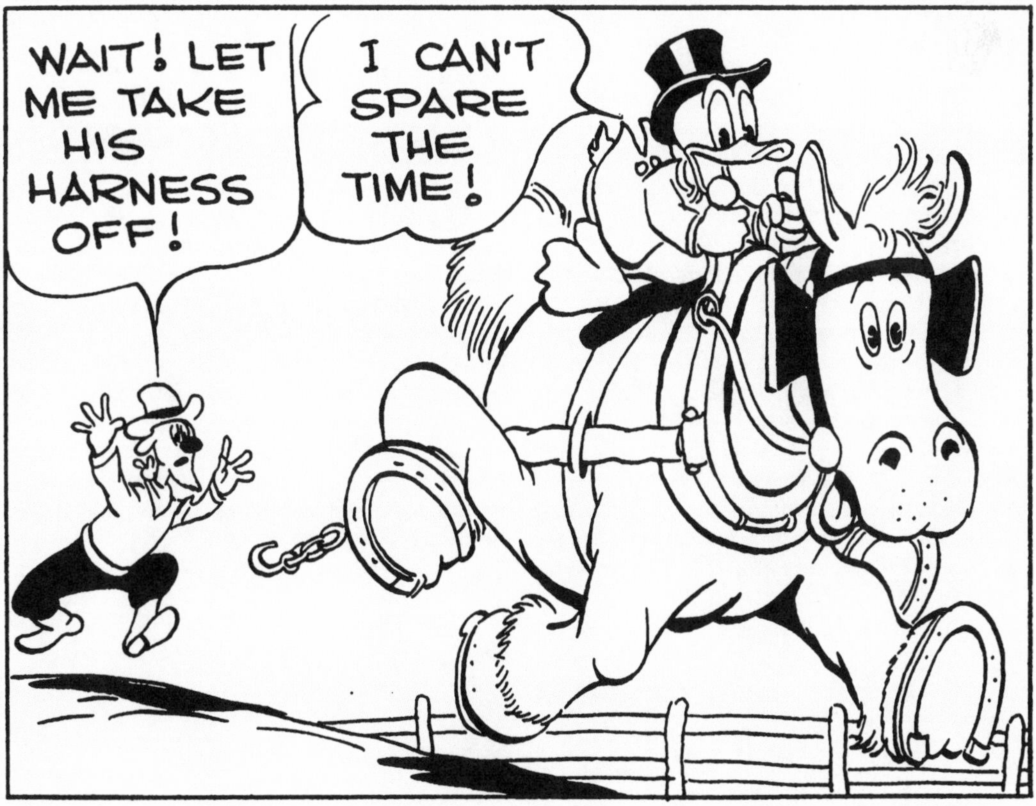
WAIT! LET ME TAKE HIS HARNESS OFF!
I CAN'T SPARE THE TIME!

Some 12 years later, Barks would reprise several of these plot elements for "Yoicks! The Fox!" in Scrooge's own title (1960, in a later volume in this series), where the old tycoon takes up the sportsman's reins himself — and replaces Donald's spectacular concussive collisions with aggravated saddle sores.

— RICH KREINER

THE DONALD DUCK ONE-PAGERS

Luck is a major subject in Carl Barks's work — likely because its very existence challenges the classic American ideology — that with hard work, one can accomplish almost anything.

Americans are hardly fatalists, yet empirical evidence shows that good and bad luck often play a very important role in life. Is it possible to reconcile the arrows of fate with the gospel of individual effort? The question seemed to appeal to Barks's cynical nature.

A more practical reason for Barks to focus on luck might have been that Disney fans expected it. In the animated shorts and Al Taliaferro's newspaper strips, Donald was seen as an unlucky Duck from the beginning, all the better to provoke his famous temper. By 1948, most of the one-pagers reprinted in this book could deal with bad luck, and readers would consider it business as usual.

In "Bean Taken" (p. 97), Donald tries to guess the number of beans in a jar. His nephews offer 10¢ for the right guess. Donald buys a jar of the same size to help him calculate the number of beans, but he gets outsmarted — there aren't *just* beans in the nephews' jar, but a big rock, too!

On the one hand, Donald ends up an unlucky loser. On the other hand, his failure is due not just to fate, but also to a lack of individual effort. Donald lazily assumed the nephews' contest was on the level. He didn't stop to consider their bent for mischief. Donald can't win when it comes to his nephews — by the late 1940s they are no longer the brats they were in Taliaferro's strip, but they are still far from the serious Junior Woodchucks of later years.

"Best Laid Plans" (p. 171) hits Donald with a similar mix of bad luck and personal failings. Donald pretends to be sick in order to make the nephews cook for him — but in his selfishness, he forgets their lack of experience. The nephews hurt themselves in the kitchen, and Donald ends up having to cook for them again.

Of course, not all upsets are due to Donald's most obvious failings — laziness and greed. Often his worst sin is simply to challenge Lady Luck — whom Barks at times portrayed, *à la* classical mythology, as a deity. According to ancient Greeks, the most terrible sin for a mortal being was that of *hubris* — issuing a challenge to the Gods. In "Horseshoe Luck" (p. 34), Donald finds a ten-dollar bill and a horseshoe. Defying fate, he tosses away the horseshoe, refusing to believe in its power. The nephews find it and toss it back, unwittingly conking Donald on the head — so Donald winds up with a doctor bill for ten dollars.

In "Bird Watching" (p. 33), Donald is so overconfident in his ornithological knowledge that he unknowingly insults several old ladies, incurring their wrath.

In "The Genuine Article" (p. 172), his reckless solution to verifying the age of an antique essentially destroys it.

In "Sorry to be Safe" (p. 98), Donald demands the nephews play baseball far from town to avoid breaking any windows. He is all but daring Lady Luck to attack him back — which happens when the kids' baseball hits a gunpowder stock.

Donald is unlucky, true, insofar as an awful lot of bad things happen to him. But according to Barks, Donald's bad luck is generally deserved and, therefore, not entirely due to fate. Donald gambles without caution, he indulges in overconfidence, he challenges Lady Luck — and he loses.

— STEFANO PRIARONE

Carl Barks

LIFE AMONG THE DUCKS

by DONALD AULT

ABOVE: *Carl Barks at the 1982 San Diego Comic-Con. Photo by Alan Light.*

"I was a real misfit," Carl Barks said, thinking back over an early life of hard labor — as a farmer, a logger, a mule-skinner, a rivet heater, and a printing press feeder — before he was hired as a full-time cartoonist for an obscure risqué magazine in 1931.

Barks was born in 1901 and (mostly) raised in Merrill, Oregon. He had always wanted to be a cartoonist but everything that happened to him in his early years seemed to stand in his way. He suffered a significant hearing loss after a bout with the measles. His mother died. He had to leave school after the eighth grade. His

father suffered a mental breakdown. His older brother was whisked off to World War I.

His first marriage, in 1921, was to a woman who was unsympathetic to his dreams and who ultimately bore two children "by accident," as Barks phrased it. The two divorced in 1930.

In 1931, he pulled up stakes from Merrill and headed to Minnesota, leaving his mother-in-law, whom he trusted more than his wife, in charge of his children.

Arriving in Minneapolis, he went to work for the *Calgary Eye-Opener*, that risqué magazine. He thought he would finally be drawing cartoons full time but the editor and most of the staff were alcoholics, so Barks ended up running the whole show.

In 1935 he took "a great gamble" and, on the strength of some cartoons he'd submitted in response to an advertisement from the Disney Studio, he moved to California and entered an animation trial period. He was soon promoted to "story man" in Disney's Donald Duck animation unit, where he made significant contributions to 36 Donald cartoon shorts between 1936 and 1942, including helping to create Huey, Dewey, and Louie for "Donald's Nephews" in 1938. Ultimately, though, he grew dissatisfied. The production of animated cartoons "by committee," as he described it, stifled his imagination.

For that and other reasons, in 1942 he left Disney to run a chicken farm. But when he was offered a chance by Western Publishing to write and illustrate a new series of Donald Duck comic book stories, he jumped at it. The comic book format suited him and the quality of his work persuaded the editors to grant him a freedom and autonomy he'd never known and that few others were ever granted. He would go on to write and draw more than 6,000 pages in over 500 stories and uncounted hundreds of covers between 1942 and 1966 for Western's Dell and Gold Key imprints.

Barks had almost no formal art training. He had taught himself how to draw by imitating his early favorite artists — Winsor McCay (*Little Nemo*), Frederick Opper (*Happy Hooligan*), Elzie Segar (*Popeye*), and Floyd Gottfredson (*Mickey Mouse*).

He taught himself how to write well by going back to the grammar books he had shunned in school, making up jingles and rhymes, and inventing other linguistic exercises to get a natural feel for the rhythm and dialogue of sequential narrative.

Barks married again in 1938 but that union ended disastrously in divorce in 1951. In 1954, Barks married Margaret Wynnfred Williams, known as Garé, who soon began assisting him by lettering and inking backgrounds on his comic book work. They remained happily together until her death in 1993.

He did his work in the California desert and often mailed his stories into the office. He worked his stories over and over "backward and forward." Barks was not a vain man but he had confidence in his talent. He knew what

hard work was, and he knew that he'd put his best efforts into every story he produced.

On those occasions when he did go into Western's offices he would "just dare anybody to see if they could improve on it." His confidence was justified. His work was largely responsible for some of the best-selling comic books in the world — *Walt Disney's Comics and Stories* and *Uncle Scrooge*.

Because Western's policy was to keep their writers and artists anonymous, readers never knew the name of the "good duck artist" — but they could spot the superiority of his work. When fans determined to solve the mystery of his anonymity finally tracked him down (not unlike an adventure Huey, Dewey, and Louie might embark upon), Barks was quite happy to correspond and otherwise communicate with his legion of aficionados.

Given all the obstacles of his early years and the dark days that haunted him off and on for the rest of his life, it's remarkable that he laughed so easily and loved to make others laugh.

In the process of expanding Donald Duck's character far beyond the hot-tempered Donald of animation, Barks created a moveable locale (Duckburg) and a cast of dynamic characters: Scrooge McDuck, the Beagle Boys, Gladstone Gander, Gyro Gearloose, the Junior Woodchucks. And there were hundreds of others who made only one memorable appearance in the engaging, imaginative, and unpredictable comedy-adventures that he wrote and drew from scratch for nearly a quarter of a century.

Among many other honors, Carl Barks was one of the three initial inductees into the Will Eisner Comic Awards Hall of Fame for comic book creators in 1987. (The other two were Jack Kirby and Will Eisner.) In 1991, Barks became the only Disney comic book artist to be recognized as a "Disney Legend," a special award created by Disney "to acknowledge and honor the many individuals whose imagination, talents, and dreams have created the Disney magic."

As Roy Disney said on Barks's passing in 2000 at age 99, "He challenged our imaginations and took us on some of the greatest adventures we have ever known. His prolific comic book creations entertained many generations of devoted fans and influenced countless artists over the years…. His timeless tales will stand as a legacy to his originality and brilliant artistic vision."

Biographies

Donald Ault is Professor of English at the University of Florida; founder and editor of *ImageTexT: Interdisciplinary Comics Studies*; author of two books on William Blake (*Visionary Physics* and *Narrative Unbound*); editor of *Carl Barks: Conversations*; and executive producer of *The Duck Man: An Interview with Carl Barks* (video).

Alberto Beccatini was born in Florence, Italy. He has taught high school English since 1983. Since 1978, he has written essays for Italian and U.S. publications about comics, specializing in Disney characters and American comics generally. Since 1992 he has been a freelance writer and consultant for The Walt Disney Company-Italy, contributing to such series as *Zio Paperone, Maestri Disney, Tesori Disney, Disney Anni d'Oro, La Grande Dinastia dei Paperi*, and *Gli Anni d'Oro di Topolino*.

R. Fiore, he explains, makes his way in life working Square John jobs, when they let him, not far from Historic Duckburg. This marginal existence has even from time to time led onto the grounds of the Walt Disney Company, which is an interesting place. In his spare time he's been writing about comic strips and animation longer than you've been alive, my child.

Craig Fischer is Associate Professor of English at Appalachian State University. His "Monsters Eat Critics" column, about comics' multifarious genres, runs at *The Comics Journal* website (tcj.com).

Jared Gardner studies and teaches comics at the Ohio State University, home of the Billy Ireland Cartoon Library & Museum. He is the author of three books, including *Projections: Comics and the History of 21st-Century Storytelling* (Stanford University Press, 2011). He is a contributing writer to *The Comics Journal*.

Leonardo Gori is a comics scholar and collector, especially of syndicated newspaper strips of the '30s and Italian Disney authors.

He wrote, with Frank Stajano and others, many books on Italian "fumetti" and American comics in Italy. He has also written thrillers, which have been translated into Spanish, Portuguese, and Korean.

Rich Kreiner is a longtime writer for *The Comics Journal* and a longtime reader of Carl Barks. He lives with wife and cat in Maine.

Ken Parille is the author of *The Daniel Clowes Reader* (Fantagraphics, 2013) and has published essays on Louisa May Alcott and boyhood, the mother-son relationship in antebellum America, TV bandleader Lawrence Welk, and, of course, comics. His writing has appeared in *The Nathaniel Hawthorne Review, The Journal of Popular Culture, The Boston Review, The Believer,* and *The Comics Journal.* He teaches literature at East Carolina University.

Stefano Priarone was born in Northwestern Italy about the time when a retired Carl Barks was storyboarding his last Junior Woodchucks stories. He writes about popular culture in many Italian newspapers and magazines, was a contributor to the Italian complete Carl Barks collection, and wrote his thesis in economics about Uncle Scrooge as an entrepreneur (for which he blames his aunt, who read him Barks Scrooge stories when he was 3 years old).

Francesco ("Frank") Stajano began reading Disney comics in preschool and never grew out of it — the walls of his house are covered in bookshelves and many of them hold comics. He has written on Disney comics, particularly with Leonardo Gori, and had the privilege of visiting Carl Barks at his home in Oregon in 1998. In real life he is an associate professor at the University of Cambridge in England.

Matthias Wivel is an art historian specializing in Italian Renaissance art. He has been active as a comics critic, editor, and activist for a decade-and-a-half.

Where did these duck stories first appear?

EDITOR'S NOTE: "The Complete Carl Barks Disney Library" collects Donald Duck and Uncle Scrooge stories originally published in the traditional American four-color comic book format. Barks's first Duck story appeared in October 1942. The volumes in this project are numbered chronologically but are being released in a different order. This is volume 6.

Stories within a volume may or may not follow the exact original publication sequence of the original comic books. We may take the liberty of re-arranging the sequence of the stories within a volume for editorial or presentation purposes.

The original comic books were published under the "Dell" logo and some appeared in the so-called "Four Color" series — a name that appeared nowhere inside the comic book itself, but is generally agreed upon by histori-ans to refer to the series of "one-shot" comic books published by Dell that have sequential numbering. The *Four Color* issues are also sometimes referred to as "One Shots."

Most of the stories in this volume were originally published without a title. Some stories were retroactively assigned a title when they were reprinted in later years. Some stories were given titles by Barks in correspondence or interviews. (Sometimes Barks referred to the same story with different titles.) Some stories were never given an official title but have been informally assigned one by fans and indexers. For the untitled stories in this volume, we have used the title that seems most appropriate. The unofficial titles appear below with an asterisk enclosed in parentheses (*).

The following is the order in which the stories in this volume were originally published.

- -

Walt Disney's Comics and Stories #88
(January 1948)
Wintertime Wager (*)
Walt Disney's Comics and Stories #89
(February 1948)
Watching the Watchman (*)
Walt Disney's Comics and Stories #90
(March 1948)
Wired (*)
Walt Disney's Comics and Stories #91
(April 1948)
Going Ape (*)
March of Comics #20 (1948)
Darkest Africa
Walt Disney's Comics and Stories #92
(May 1948)
Spoil the Rod (*)
Four Color #189 (June 1948)
Cover
Bird Watching (*)
The Old Castle's Secret
Horseshoe Luck (*)
Bean Taken (*)
Walt Disney's Comics and Stories #93
(June 1948)
Rocket Race to the Moon (*)

Walt Disney's Comics and Stories #94
(July 1948)
Donald of the Coast Patrol (*)
Walt Disney's Comics and Stories #95
(August 1948)
Cover
Gladstone Returns (*)
Four Color #199 (October 1948)
Cover
Sorry to Be Safe (*)
Sheriff of Bullet Valley
Best Laid Plans (*)
The Genuine Article (*)
Walt Disney's Comics and Stories #96
(September 1948)
Cover
Links Hijinks (*)
Walt Disney's Comics and Stories #97
(October 1948)
Pearls of Wisdom (*)
Walt Disney's Comics and Stories #98
(November 1948)
Foxy Relations (*)